In this major study the theme of 'church and society' provides a means of examining the condition of the Byzantine Empire at an important period of its history, up to and well beyond the fall of Constantinople in 1204.

Of all the Byzantine dynasties, the Comneni came closest to realising the Caesaro-papist ideal. However, Comnenian control over the Orthodox church was both deceptive and damaging: deceptive because the church's institutional strength increased, and with it its hold over lay society, damaging because the church's leadership was demoralised by subservience to imperial authority. The church found itself with the strength but not the will to assert itself against an imperial establishment that was in rapid decline by 1180; and neither side was in a position to provide Byzantine society with a sense of purpose. This lack of direction lay at the heart of the malaise that afflicted Byzantium at the time of the fourth crusade. The impasse was resolved after 1204, when in exile the Orthodox church took the lead in reconstructing Byzantine society.

'... an admirably comprehensive picture. [Angold's] canvas is broad, and so is his brush; he is the master of the vigorous stroke which blurs the line between evidence and interpretation ... this is not just a book for medievalists but essential reading for all who want to know why the Orthodox church survived the demise of the Byzantine empire, and is still with us.'
Paul Magdalino, *The Anglo-Hellenic Review*

'In this fine work Michael Angold puts forward a major revision of our understanding of the relation of Church and society in the Byzantine empire under the Comneni ... Angold's book is a major achievement: it draws together a mass of scholarship and has an even-handedness that is based on a sure knowledge of the sources.'
Andrew Louth, *Journal of Theological Studies*

MICHAEL ANGOLD is Professor of History, University of Edinburgh.

CHURCH AND SOCIETY IN BYZANTIUM UNDER THE COMNENI, 1081–1261

CHURCH AND SOCIETY IN BYZANTIUM UNDER THE COMNENI, 1081–1261

MICHAEL ANGOLD

University of Edinburgh

CAMBRIDGE UNIVERSITY PRESS

PUBLISHED BY THE PRESS SYNDICATE OF THE UNIVERSITY OF CAMBRIDGE
The Pitt Building, Trumpington Street, Cambridge, United Kingdom

CAMBRIDGE UNIVERSITY PRESS
The Edinburgh Building, Cambridge CB2 2RU, UK
40 West 20th Street, New York, NY 10011-4211, USA
10 Stamford Road, Oakleigh, VIC 3166, Australia
Ruiz de Alarcón 13, 28014 Madrid, Spain
Dock House, The Waterfront, Cape Town 8001, South Africa

http://www.cambridge.org

First published 1995
First paperback edition 2000

Printed in the United Kingdom at the University Press, Cambridge

A catalogue record for this book is available from the British Library

Library of Congress Cataloguing in Publication data
Angold, Michael.
Church and society in Byzantium under the Comneni, 1081–1261
Michael Angold.
p. cm.
Includes bibliographical references.
ISBN 0 521 26432 4
1. Church history – Byzantine Empire – Middle Ages, 600–1500.
2. Orthodox Eastern Church – History. 3. Caesaropapism – History.
4. Byzantine Empire – History – 1081–1453. I. Title.
BX300.A54 1995
274.95′04 – dc20 94-12146 CIP

ISBN 0 521 26432 4 hardback
ISBN 0 521 26986 5 paperback

EBF

CONTENTS

A NOTE ON TRANSLITERATION

I have come to favour far more than in the past a Latin transliteration of Byzantine proper names: so Comnenus, not Komnenos. For technical terms I have normally employed a Greek transliteration: *paroikos* and not *paroecus.* I have normally accompanied technical terms with an explanatory phrase or equivalent English term. I have been happy, for instance, to gloss *adelphaton* as corrody. I have with difficulty resisted the temptation to render *paroikos* – rather an ugly, certainly an unfamiliar, word – by the more homely serf. I know that in legal terms they are not exact equivalents. But they are reasonable approximations. In the context of Byzantine studies a note on transliteration inevitably takes on an ideological colouring. In my case, a preference for a Latin form of transliteration and, wherever reasonably possible, for the use of equivalents rather than unfamiliar technical terms points to a belief that the study of Byzantium should form an integral part of medieval studies and should not attempt to isolate itself as a separate discipline. Far more unites the two than divides them, even if ecclesiastical history sometimes tells a different story.

ABBREVIATIONS

Acropolites	George Acropolites, *Opera*, ed. A. Heisenberg and P. Wirth (Stuttgart, 1978), 2 vols.
Anna Comnena	Anna Comnena, *Alexiad*, ed. B. Leib (Paris, 1937–1945; repr. 1967), 3 vols. English translation by E.R.A. Sewter (London, 1969)
Apokaukos I	N.A. Bees and E. Bee-Seferle, 'Unedierte Schriftstücke aus der Kanzlei des Johannes Apokaukos des Metropoliten von Naupaktos (in Aetolien)', *BNJ*, 21(1976), 57–160
Apokaukos II	S. Petridès, 'Jean Apokaukos, lettres et autres documents inédits', *IRAIK* 14(1909), 69–100
B	*Byzantion*
BCH	*Bulletin de correspondance hellénique*
Beck, *Kirche*	H.-G. Beck, *Kirche und theologische Literatur im byzantinischen Reich* (Munich, 1959)
BF	*Byzantinische Forschungen*
Blemmydes	Nicephorus Blemmydes, *Autobiographia sive curriculum vitae*, ed. J.A. Munitiz (Corpus Christianorum, *Series Graeca* 13) (Louvain, 1984). English translation by J.A. Munitiz (Louvain, 1988)
BMGS	*Byzantine and Modern Greek Studies*
BNJ	*Byzantinisch-neugriechische Jahrbücher*
BS	*Byzantinoslavica*
BZ	*Byzantinische Zeitschrift*
Chomatianos	J.B. Pitra, *Analecta sacra et classica spicilegio Solesmensi parata*, VII(VI) (Rome, 1891; repr. Farnborough, 1967)
Cinnamus	John Cinnamus, *Epitome rerum ab Ioanne et Manuele Comnenis gestarum*, ed. A.

	Meineke (Bonn, 1836). English translation by C.M. Brand (New York, 1976)
Cyril Phileotes	Nicholas Kataskepenos, *La vie de Saint Cyrille le Philéote, moine byzantin († 1110)*, ed. E. Sargologos (Subsidia Hagiographica 39) (Brussels, 1964)
Darrouzès, *Ecclésiologie*	J. Darrouzès, *Documents inédits d'ecclésiologie byzantine* (Paris, 1966)
Darrouzès, *Notitiae*	J. Darrouzès, *Notitiae episcoptatuum Ecclesiae constantinopolitanae. Texte critique, introduction et notes* (Géographie ecclésiastique de l'Empire byzantin) 1 (Paris, 1981)
Darrouzès, *OFFIKIA*	J. Darrouzès, *Recherches sur les* ΟΦΦΙΚΙΑ *de l' église byzantine* (Archives de l'Orient chrétien 10) (Paris, 1970)
Docheiariou	*Actes de Docheiariou*, ed. N. Oikonomidès (Archives de l'Athos 13) (Paris, 1984)
Dölger, *Reg.*	F. Dölger, *Regesten der Kaiserurkunden des oströmischen Reiches* (Corpus der griechischen Urkunden des Mittelalters und der neueren Zeit. Reihe A, Abt. 1) (Munich and Berlin, 1924–65),5 vols.
DOP	*Dumbarton Oaks Papers*
EB	*Etudes byzantines*
ΕΕΒΣ	ΕΠΕΤΕΡΙΣ ΕΤΑΙΡΕΙΑΣ ΒΥΖΑΝΤΙΝΩΝ ΣΠΟΥΔΩΝ
EO	*Echos d'Orient*
Eustathius I	Eustathius of Thessalonica, *Opuscula*, ed. T.L.F. Tafel (Frankfurt am Main, 1832; repr. Amsterdam, 1964)
Eustathius II	Eustathius of Thessalonica, *The Capture of Thessaloniki*, transl. J.R. Melville Jones (Byzantina Australiensia 8) (Canberra, 1988)
FM	*Fontes Minores*
Germanos II	S.N. Lagopates, *ΓΕΡΜΑΝΟΣ Ο Β'*, ΠΑΤΡΙΑΡΧΗΣ ΚΩΝΣΤΑΝΤΙΝΟΥΠΟΛΕΩΣ-ΝΙΚΑΙΑΣ, 1222–1240. *ΒΙΟΣ*, ΣΥΓΓΡΑΜΜΑΤΑ, ΟΜΙΛΙΑΙ ΚΑΙ

	ΕΠΙΣΤΟΛΑΙ ΤΟ ΠΡΩΤΟΝ ΕΚΔΙΔΟΜΕΝΑΙ (Tripolis, 1913)
Grumel	V. Grumel, *Les regestes des actes du patriarcat de Constantinople, I: Les actes des patriarches, fasc. ii et iii: Les regestes de 715 à 1206* (Paris, 1947; revised ed. 1989)
IRAIK	*Izvestija russkago arkheologicheskago instituta v Konstantinopole*
Iviron	*Actes d'Iviron*, II, ed. L. Lefort *et al.* (Archives de l'Athos 16) (Paris, 1990)
Janin I	R. Janin, *La géographie ecclésiastique de l' Empire byzantin, I: Le siège de Constantinople et le patriarcat oecuménique, III: Les églises et les monastères* (Paris, 1969)
Janin II	R. Janin, *Les églises et les monastères des grands centres byzantins* (Paris, 1975)
JöB	*Jahrbuch der Österreichischen Byzantinistik*
Kazhdan/Epstein	A.P. Kazhdan and A.W. Epstein, *Change in Byzantine Culture in the Eleventh and Twelfth Centuries* (Berkeley, 1985)
Kazhdan/Franklin	A. Kazhdan and S. Franklin, *Studies on Byzantine Literature of the Eleventh and Twelfth Centuries* (Cambridge, 1984)
Kekavmenos	*Cecaumeni Strategicon et incerti Scriptoris De Officiis regiis Libellus*, ed. B. Wassiliewsky and V. Jernstedt (St Petersburg, 1896; repr. Amsterdam, 1965); *Sovety i rasskazy Kekavmena*, ed G.G. Litavrin (Moscow, 1972)
Kosmosoteira	L. Petit, 'Typikon du monastère de la Kosmosotira près d'Aenos (1152)', *IRAIK* 13(1908), 17–77
Laurent	V. Laurent, *Les regestes des actes du patriarcat de Constantinople*, I, fasc. 4: *Les regestes de 1208 à 1309* (Paris, 1971)
Laurent, *Corpus*	V. Laurent, *Le corpus des sceaux de l'Empire byzantin*, V, 1–2, *L'église* (Paris, 1963–5)
Lavra	*Actes de Lavra*, I–II, ed. P. Lermerle *et al.* (Archives de L'Athos 6, 8) (Paris, 1970, 1977)
Leontios of Jerusalem	*The Life of Leontios Patriarch of Jerusalem*, in Makarios Chrysokephalos, ΛΟΓΟΙ

	ΠΑΝΗΓΥΡΙΚΟΙ ΑΔ' (Vienna, 1794), 380–434; ed. and transl. D. Tsougarakis (Leiden, 1993)
Meletios the Younger	V. Vasilievskij, 'Nikolaja episkopa Mefonskogo i Feodora Prodroma pisatelej XII stoletija zhitija Meletija Novogo', *Pravoslavnij Palestinskij Sbornik* 6(1886), 1–69
Mesarites I-III	A. Heisenberg, 'Neue Quellen zur Geschichte des lateinischen Kaisertums und der Kirchenunion. I. Der Epitaphios des Nikolaos Mesarites auf seinen Bruder Johannes; II. Die Unionsverhandlungen vom 30. August 1206; III. Der Bericht des Nikolaos Mesarites über die politischen und kirchlichen Ereignisse des Jahres 1214', *Sitzungsberichte der bayerischen Akademie der Wissenschaften*, philos.-philol. und hist. Klasse, 1922, Abh.5; 1923, Abh. 2–3 (Munich, 1923) (= A. Heisenberg, *Quellen und Studien zur spätbyzantinischen Geschichte* (London, 1973), no.II)
Michael Choniates	Michael Choniates, ΤΑ ΣΩΖΟΜΕΝΑ, ed. Sp.P. Lampros (Athens, 1879–80; repr. Groningen, 1968), 2 vols.
Michael Glykas	Michael Glykas, ΕΙΣ ΤΑΣ ΑΠΟΡΙΑΣ ΤΗΣ ΘΕΙΑΣ ΓΡΑΦΗΣ ΚΕΦΑΛΑΙΑ, ed. S. Eustratiades (Athens, 1906; Alexandria, 1912), 2 vols.
Michael Italikos	Michael Italikos, *Lettres et discours*, ed. P. Gautier (Archives de l'Orient chrétien 14) (Paris, 1972)
Migne, *PG*	J.P. Migne, *Patrologiae cursus completus. Series graeco-latina* (Paris, 1857–66)
Migne, *PL*	J.P. Migne, *Patrologiae cursus completus. Series latina* (Paris, 1844–55)
Miklosich & Müller	F. Miklosich and J. Müller, *Acta et diplomata graeca medii aevi sacra et profana* (Vienna, 1860–90), 6 vols.
Nicetas Choniates	Nicetas Choniates, *Χρονικὴ διήγησις*, ed. J.-L. van Dieten (Berlin and New York, 1975). English translation by H. Magoulias (Detroit, 1984)

Nicol I	D.M. Nicol, *The Despotate of Epiros* (Oxford, 1957)
Nicol II	D.M. Nicol, *The Despotate of Epiros 1267–1479. A Contribution to the History of Greece in the Middle Ages* (Cambridge, 1984)
Noctes	*Noctes Petropolitanae*, ed. A. Papadopoulos-Kerameus (St Petersburg, 1913;repr. Leipzig, 1976)
Notre Dame de Pitié	L. Petit, 'Le monastère de Notre Dame de Pitié en Macédoine', *IRAIK* 6(1900), 1–153
OCP	*Orientalia Christiana Periodica*
Patmos I-II	ΒΥΖΑΝΤΙΝΑ ΕΓΓΡΑΦΑ ΤΗΣ ΜΟΝΗΣ ΠΑΤΜΟΥ (Athens, 1980), 2 vols., I: ΑΥΤΟΚΡΑΤΟΡΙΚΑ, ed. E. Vranouse; II: ΔΗΜΩΣΙΩΝ ΛΕΙΤΟΥΡΓΩΝ, ed. M. Nystazopoulou-Pelekidou
Prodromos	*Poèmes prodromiques en grec vulgaire*, ed. D.-C. Hesseling and H. Pernot (Amsterdam, 1910; repr. Wiesbaden, 1968)
Psellus (ed.Kurtz/Drexl)	*Michael Psellus Scripta minora*, ed. E. Kurtz and F. Drexl (Milan, 1936–41), 2 vols.
REB	*Revue des études byzantines*
Rhalles & Potles	G.A. Rhalles and M. Potles, ΣΥΝΤΑΓΜΑ ΤΩΝ ΘΕΙΩΝ ΚΑΙ ΙΕΡΩΝ ΚΑΝΟΝΩΝ (Athens, 1852–9), 6 vols.
Sathas, *MB*	K.N. Sathas, ΜΕΣΑΙΩΝΙΚΗ ΒΙΒΛΙΟΘΗΚΗ (*Bibliotheca graeca medii aevi*) (Venice and Paris, 1872–94), 7 vols.
Theophylact I-II	Theophylact of Ohrid, *Opera*, ed. P. Gautier, I: *Discours, traités, poésies*; II: *Lettres* (Thessalonica, 1980–6)
Theotokos Skoteine	S. Eustratiades, 'Ἡ ἐν Φιλαδελφίᾳ μονὴ τῆς Κοτεινῆς', ΕΛΛΗΝΙΚΑ 3 (1930), 317–30
TM	*Travaux et Mémoires*
Tornikès	Georges et Dèmètrios Tornikès, *Lettres et discours*, ed. J. Darrouzès (Paris, 1970)
Tzetzes I	John Tzetzes, *Epistulae*, ed. P.A.M. Leone (Leipzig, 1972)
Tzetzes II	John Tzetzes, *Historiae*, ed. P.A.M. Leone (Leipzig, 1968)
Varzos	K. Varzos, Η ΓΕΝΕΑΛΟΓΙΑ ΤΩΝ ΚΟΜΝΗΝΩΝ (Thessalonica, 1984), 2 vols.
VV	*Vizantiniskij Vremmenik*

Zepos	I. and P. Zepos, *Ius graecoromanum* (Athens, 1931; repr. Aalen, 1962), 6 vols.
Zhishman, *Eherecht*	H. Zhishman, *Das Eherecht der orientalischen Kirche* (Vienna, 1864)

Byzantine historians in the Bonn corpus are identified by '(ed. Bonn)' without further details.

INTRODUCTION

AS I understood it, this book was originally conceived as part of a series on Byzantine church and society. The inspiration was the success of Donald Nicol's Birkbeck Lectures for 1977. These appeared in print two years later under the title *Church and Society in the Last Centuries of Byzantium.*[1] But the title is rather misleading. As the author explains in his preface, his book was intended as an exploration of the Byzantine identity, as 'a series of reflexions on the Byzantine character'.[2] It was not his objective to examine the relations of church and society. He outlined the difficulties that this would have presented. They lie in a blind spot the Byzantines had for the idea of society. Just as they had no word for 'Christendom' so they had no word for society. They thought in terms of Empire and Oecumene. They assumed an identity of purpose of church and empire. These in their turn subsumed a Christian society, which consequently lacked any clear definition. It is a very real problem that Professor Nicol has outlined with his customary precision.[3] It explains why relatively little attention has been paid to the problem of church and society in modern Byzantine historiography. It is easy enough to examine the relationship of church and state, but this is not the same as church and society. Byzantinists have long been aware of the need for a proper investigation of the relations between church and society. But they have come up against a major barrier. This takes the form of identifying orthodoxy and society. Orthodoxy is presented as the ideal, the motive force, and the cement of Byzantine society. The assumption is that the orthodox liturgy was the central fact of Byzantine life; that the orthodox church could count on the automatic devotion of the bulk of Byzantine society at all levels, from the emperor to the peasant and the urban proletariat. But this is to subscribe to a Byzantine myth.

[1] See my review in *Journal of Hellenic Studies* 102(1982), 297–8.

[2] D.M. Nicol, *Church and Society in the Last Centuries of Byzantium* (Cambridge, 1979), viii.

[3] Ibid., 2–6.

I

H.-G. Beck is the only major modern Byzantine historian to have consistently disputed such assumptions. He has devoted a series of articles to the clarification of different aspects of the relationship of Byzantine church and society. His findings lie at the heart of his *Das byzantinische Jahrtausend* (Munich, 1978), which has not been as influential as it deserves to have been.[4] Perhaps he is too much of an iconoclast. He has little time for Byzantine monasticism. Mount Athos is dismissed 'as almost a Nature Park, or better still a National Park'. His key concept is 'Political Orthodoxy'. This provided the ideological foundation of a totalitarian regime which was identified with a divinely ordained order. For its articulation and enforcement it required the existence of an imperial elite and of an ecclesiastical hierarchy, who were its major beneficiaries and defenders. The 'guardians of orthodoxy' preached the ideal of a harmonious existence under the aegis of the emperor, but this was something of a fiction: there are many instances of friction between the imperial establishment and the ecclesiastical hierarchy. 'Political Orthodoxy' was not quite as solid as it seemed. If there was little open dissent, there was a degree of alienation from the imperial regime and a certain indifference to the hierarchical church in matters of worship and belief. Beck reminds us of the streak of nonconformity which ran through the religious life of the Byzantines.

It emerged in a preference for private devotions. This was complemented, as J.P. Thomas has shown, by private control over churches and monasteries. At all levels the church was permeated by private interests. Thomas emphasises an important fact: that Byzantine society had its own stake in the orthodox church.[5] Despite itself, orthodoxy was therefore forced to respond to the needs of society. This was not simply a matter of providing the necessary rituals to solemnise the critical moments of any life: birth, marriage, and death. It also involved accepting questionable myths and customs that had little to do with orthodoxy, but much to do with the rhythms of life.

The works of H.-G. Beck and J.P. Thomas allow us to put the history of the Byzantine church under the Comneni into a general context. But they do not quite compensate for the lack of detailed studies of the Byzantine church in the period that runs from the triumph of orthodoxy in 843 to the mid-eleventh century. This deficiency can be explained in part by the poverty of the sources. By way of contrast, the Comnenian era is generously supplied. Pride of place should go to the

[4] See my review in *Journal of Hellenic Studies* 101(1981), 228–9.

[5] J.P. Thomas, *Private Religious Foundations in the Byzantine Empire* (Dumbarton Oaks Studies 24) (Washington DC, 1987).

commentaries of Theodore Balsamon on the canons of the church.[6] His method required the citing of official documents, imperial and ecclesiastical. The result is that we not only have many official documents, but also a discussion of the problems of the day to which they applied. This gives Balsamon's commentaries an immediacy denied to most canon law. The twelfth century was a golden age of Byzantine canon law. This has been underlined by the invaluable work of Professor Dieter Simon and the Max Planck Institut at Frankfurt in discovering and editing new legal texts from the period.[7] Next in importance, given the prevalence of heresy under the Comneni, comes the *synodikon* of Orthodoxy. This was originally a statement of orthodoxy issued in 843 on the occasion of the liquidation of iconoclasm. Under the Comneni this was expanded to include the heresy trials of the era.[8] The *synodikon* is supplemented by Zigabenos's *Dogmatike Panoplia*[9] and by Nicetas Choniates's *Treasury of Orthodoxy*,[10] which contain further accounts and documents of the trials for heresy under the Comneni. The realities of monastic life are exposed in the *typika* or rules granted to monasteries usually by their founders. These survive in comparatively large numbers from the middle of the eleventh century. They are the foundation of Alexander Kazhdan's fundamental study of Byzantine monasticism in its relationship with secular society. He sees Byzantine monasteries reflecting or reduplicating in their organisation features of secular society.[11] These *typika* normally contain a certain amount of autobiographical material about the founder. They therefore compensate for the comparative lack of saints' lives.

The Comnenian period is very rich in all kinds of rhetorical and literary materials. The most important for our purposes are collections of the works and letters of a series of bishops: Theophylact of Ohrid,[12] Michael Italikos,[13] George Tornikes,[14] Eustathius of Thessalonica,[15] and Michael Choniates.[16] Much can be extracted from their works and letters about conditions in their sees, but they are not their working papers nor a record of their judicial and administrative work, of the kind that one might expect to find in a Latin episcopal register.

6 Rhalles & M. Potles, II–III.
7 Their work has been the foundation of the periodical *FM*.
8 J. Gouillard, 'Le synodikon de l'orthodoxie: édition et commentaire', *TM*, 2(1967), 1–298.
9 Migne, *PG*, 130.
10 Ibid., 139–40.
11 A.P. Kazhdan, 'Vizantiskij monastir XI-XII vv. kak sotsial'naja gruppa', *VV* I-II. 31(1971), 48–70.
12 Theophylact
13 Michael Italikos.
14 Tornikès.
15 Eustathius I. P. Wirth is preparing a new edition of Eustathius's works.
16 Michael Choniates.

The nearest approximation to this is to be found in the papers of John Apokaukos[17] and the judgements and legal advice of Demetrius Chomatianos.[18] These bishops were active during the period of exile after 1204. They provide the most detailed source of information for the day to day work of a Byzantine bishop. They were Comnenian bishops in the sense that they received their training and education before 1204. Their dossiers illuminate, like no other sources, the realities of the Comnenian episcopate. It was largely on their account that I chose 1261 as the closing date for this study, when 1204 seems so much more obvious a place to end an account of the Comnenian church. But there are other advantages to the choice of 1261: during the period of exile the meaning and direction of change occurring over the Comnenian era become far clearer than they had been in 1204. The period of exile provides a good vantage point from which to survey the developments of the previous century.

II

L. Oeconomos provided for his day a good and interesting general assessment of the Comnenian church in his *La Vie réligieuse dans l'Empire byzantin au temps des Comnènes et des Anges* (Paris, 1918). Even better was J.M. Hussey's *Church and Learning in the Byzantine Empire 867–1185* (London, 1937), which still remains of fundamental importance. But there is a need for a new synthesis. This is a tribute to the massive labours of the Assumptionist Fathers Paul Gautier and Jean Darrouzès, both now sadly dead. It is largely thanks to their dedicated work that there are so many new texts and editions of texts for the Comnenian period, the bulk of which relate to the church. It seems an appropriate moment to take stock, always remembering our debt to them. The first steps have already been taken by A.P. Kazhdan and A.W. Epstein. Their *Change in Byzantine Culture in the Eleventh and Twelfth Centuries* (Berkeley, 1985) is an important work of synthesis and interpretation.[19] They do not dispute the centrality of orthodoxy to Byzantine culture, but their main contention is that over the eleventh and twelfth centuries Byzantine culture was becoming increasingly secular and rational in orientation, in a word humanist!

This might not be the word to apply to the Cypriot saint Neophytos, but both he and his contemporaries understood that his claims to sainthood rested on his writings rather than on any miracles. He has recently been the subject of an exemplary study by Catia Galatariotou:

[17] John Apokaukos's works are scattered in a number of publications. A complete list can be found in K. Lampropoulos, *ΙΩΑΝΝΗΣ ΑΠΟΚΑΥΚΟΣ* (Athens, 1988), 90–161.

[18] Chomatianos. G. Prinzing is preparing a new edition.

[19] See my review in *BZ* 80(1987), 398–400.

The Making of a Saint. The Life, Times, and Sanctification of Neophytos the Recluse (Cambridge, 1991).[20] It breaks new ground in many ways. Her treatment of the relationship between Neophytos and local Cypriot society is fundamental to any examination of the Comnenian church; to be set alongside Paul Magdalino's study of 'The Byzantine holy man in the twelfth century'.[21] Unfortunately, his book *The Empire of Manuel I Komnenos* 1143–1180 (Cambridge, 1993) appeared after I had finished writing.[22] I have tried to incorporate where I could some of his ideas or to indicate where I disagree with him. His chapter entitled 'The guardians of orthodoxy' contains the best account I have come across of the realities of what H.-G. Beck described as 'Political Orthodoxy'.

I owe a debt of gratitude to Ruth Macrides as a guide to the complexities of canon law.[23] I should also mention Alan Harvey's *Economic Expansion in the Byzantine Empire, 900–1200* (Cambridge, 1989).[24] His scrupulous sifting of difficult evidence has put the study of the Byzantine agrarian economy under the Comneni on a much more secure footing. Because so much of his material is monastic in origin, agrarian history becomes in his hands almost a discourse on the relationship of monasticism and society! Finally, I owe much to B. Katsaros's excellent monograph on John Kastamonites, which has added a new dimension to our understanding of the Byzantine church at the turn of the twelfth century.[25]

III

In this book I set out to investigate the relationship of church and society during a specific era of Byzantine history –that of the Comneni and their immediate successors. It has not been my intention to write a history of the orthodox church during this period. There will therefore be some areas of ecclesiastical history which I have ignored because they seemed to have little relevance for lay society. As I have already suggested, the study of Byzantine church and society has received relatively little attention. It presents a great many difficulties, not least because of the blind spot that the Byzantines had over the concept of society. By way of compensation, twelfth-century Byzantine writers

[20] See my review in *English Historical Review* (to appear).

[21] P. Magdalino, 'The Byzantine holy man in the twelfth century', in *The Byzantine Saint*, ed. S. Hackel (London, 1981), 51–66 (= P. Magdalino, *Tradition and Transformation in Medieval Byzantium* (Aldershot, 1991), VII).

[22] See my review in *English Historical Review* (to appear).

[23] E.g. R. Macrides, '*Nomos* and *kanon* on paper and in court', in *Church and People in Byzantium*, ed. R. Morris (Birmingham, 1990), 61–85.

[24] See my review in *Times Literary Supplement*, 17–23, August 1990.

[25] B. Katsaros, ΙΩΑΝΝΗΣ ΚΑΣΤΑΜΟΝΙΤΗΣ (ΒΥΖΑΝΤΙΝΑ ΚΕΙΜΕΝΑ ΚΑΙ ΜΕΛΕΤΑΙ, 22) (Thessalonica, 1988).

paid more attention than earlier generations to the problems of society. This took various forms: there were discussions on the meaning of aristocracy; the appearance of a middle class was noted. There were denunciations of the activities of the Constantinopolitan mob; there were calls for the church to instil a respect for authority and hierarchy .

There was in other words an awareness of social change, however obscurely it might have been felt and understood by contemporaries. This in itself is a cause of difficulties. Byzantine institutions, ideology, attitudes, beliefs, and patterns of behaviour were laid down in late antiquity and were highly resistant to change. The Byzantines preferred to ignore the subtle transformations that distanced them from their roots in late antiquity, but change was something more than this. From the outset Byzantium was built on a mass of contradictions: classical culture vied with Christianity; a Roman state competed with a Greek church; a secular life style existed alongside the ascetic ideal. Out of these discordant elements Justinian was able to create a synthesis, which managed to resolve differences and to hold contraries in a creative balance. This broke down under the pressures associated with the rise of Islam and culminated in the iconoclast crisis. It was followed by the so-called 'Macedonian Renaissance' which, in fact, produced a new synthesis. It was to provide the underlying stability necessary for Byzantine recovery. This began to unravel once again in the eleventh century. There are no simple explanations for the 'Eleventh-century Crisis'. But a feature was an emphasis on the autonomy of the individual. This was a challenge to imperial authority, upon which the effectiveness of the Byzantine synthesis rested. Political Orthodoxy came under scrutiny, just as it had in the iconoclast period. The Comnenian period would see the establishment under imperial auspices of another synthesis. It looked back to the solutions of the Macedonian and Justinianic eras. It seemed to have preserved the essentials of imperial authority over the church. However, this was a veneer. The balance of power was shifting decisively towards the church, as it came to assume greater responsibility for the direction of society.

Such an interpretation may at first sight appear perverse. In many ways, the Byzantine church was far less formidable under the Comneni than it had been in the mid-eleventh century. It seemed to lose much of its independence of action. This was deceptive. If the church became more amenable to imperial control, in other ways its hold over society was more firmly based. The argument of this book revolves around the growing control exercised by the Byzantine church over society. In a sense it was preparation for Ottoman rule. The final fall of Byzantium seems to have been the less traumatic for the identification of church and society. But this sense of a common interest was not always present at Byzantium. There were suspicions on both sides. Church services may have divided rather than united. The public celebration of the liturgy was an occasion for demonstrating the superiority of the clergy rather than the harmony of a Christian society. Many of the laity preferred instead the intimacies of a private chapel or a family monastery, which lent themselves to private devotions. There was also a strong secular streak to Byzantine culture. This all worked against any identification of church and society. What then changed? It is not my contention that it was a matter of sentiment alone. It was much more concrete than this. It had to do with the work of the ecclesiastical courts, with episcopal rights to tax and the building up of monastic estates.

Until the eleventh century the church exercised little control over Byzantine society. This was the business of the imperial administration. This state of affairs would be questioned by a series of patriarchs of Constantinople in the course of the eleventh century. It contributed to the growing weakness of imperial authority. This challenge was taken up by Alexius I Comnenus (1081–1118). His church settlement was central to his restoration of imperial authority and to the creation of a new synthesis. It is proof of his greatness as a ruler. His reputation has suffered in recent years because of the adulation of his daughter, which was justified by and large. Alexius Comnenus reasserted the role of the emperor as the guardian of orthodoxy and as the regulator of the ecclesiastical administration. He was the *epistemonarkhes*, or disciplinarian, of the church, before the term was coined. In order to impose his authority on the church, he stole many of his patriarch's best ideas. He took up the fight against heresy; he defended monasteries against the perils of lay patronage in the shape of *kharistike*. He put himself at the head of a movement for monastic renewal. This proved the inspiration for a new wave of lay piety, of which the emperor and his family were soon the exemplars. He guaranteed the institutional freedom of the church against respect for imperial power; subservience even. The church emerged from Alexius's reign politically weaker, but institutionally stronger.

It meant that his son and, even more blatantly, his grandson, Manuel I Comnenus, were able to exploit their political control over the church for imperial advantage. This was mostly done in the interests of their foreign policy which necessitated moving closer to the papacy. Manuel even succeeded in imposing dogma on the orthodox church that reflected western rather than Byzantine theology. It produced a wave of indignation which Manuel was able to handle. The degree of imperial control was nevertheless demoralising. Nothing makes this clearer than the approval accorded to Andronicus I Comnenus's usurpation by most of the church hierarchy. The political subservience of the church contributed significantly to the malaise that characterised Constantinople on the eve of the fourth crusade.

This state of affairs stemmed ultimately from Alexius's church settlement. Its weak point was what originally recommended it: the reliance of the church on imperial authority. The stronger the church was institutionally the greater the reliance on imperial authority. This applied not only to the patriarch, but also to the bishops. If they were to impose their authority in their sees they needed imperial support. This too has been taken as further evidence of the political weakness of the church. It is true that under the Comneni bishops are often to be found at loggerheads with their flocks. This contrasts with an earlier period when a much easier relationship seems to have existed, even if one tinged with mutual indifference. But bishops were becoming increasingly aware of their pastoral responsibilities. This paradoxically led to deteriorating relations with local interests, for their efforts were more often than not regarded as an attempt to impose episcopal authority over local society. In a sense this was correct. But the ensuing friction should be interpreted as evidence, not of episcopal impotence, but rather of the more active role that bishops were assuming. Beginning in the eleventh century they had acquired certain material advantages. They were stronger financially thanks to tax exemptions for their clergy and for the estates of their church. Their courts attracted an increasing volume of business. Whatever their difficulties, the bishop became a more powerful force in local society in the course of the twelfth century.

Under the Comneni the church became far less liberal in its attitudes. It condemned some of the pastimes and interests of the Comnenian court. Paradoxically, this has led to a tendency to exaggerate the secular orientation of Comnenian culture. Manuel I Comnenus may have been notorious in ecclesiastical circles for his obsession with astrology, but on his deathbed the patriarch forced him to disavow this interest. These harsher attitudes are reflected by the canon lawyer Theodore Balsamon. He condemned the aristocracy and their taste for pornography.[26]

His commentaries provided the Byzantine church with an effective canon law, which began to challenge the primacy of the civil law. The church now possessed a legal instrument that made the supervision of society that much more effective. It inspired in church leaders a more pragmatic and legalistic outlook, which emphasised ecclesiastical rights. Balsamon's main achievement was to alter the balance between canon and civil law. He enriched the former by annexing much of the

[26] Rhalles & Potles II, 546.

latter.[27] Canon law was able to cater for society's wider needs, in a way that it had not done in the past. It meant that the ecclesiastical courts acquired more scope. Balsamon reflected a much tougher stance on the part of the church. He denied Latins access to communion in orthodox churches. He condemned popular customs.

In the past, the church had been prepared to tolerate popular customs. It now stamped them out[28] or lumped them with heresy. There had always been a nonconformist tinge to much of lay piety. In the face of ecclesiastical disapproval it now increasingly spilled over into dualist heresy. This was a problem under the Comneni in a way it had never been earlier. Official paranoia almost certainly exaggerated its danger and extent, but it was no figment of a deluded imagination; it was no social construct. Again the presence of popular heresy might be taken as evidence of the weakening hold of the church over society. The very reverse. It was part of the church's efforts to tighten its grip on society. The suppression of popular heresy was in the end the work of the church. This was a pointer to the changing balance of power between church and emperor. The initial attack on dualist heresy had been an imperial initiative. But after the death of Alexius I Comnenus in 1118 the campaign against heresy was increasingly left to bishops and patriarchs.

The fight against popular heresy reflected an increased awareness of the church's pastoral responsibilities. A sense of social duty also seems to lie behind the initiatives taken by the church in the field of marriage law. This was to have unlooked-for consequences, as more and more marriage litigation went before the ecclesiastical courts. This brought in its train an increasing number of civil suits. This stemmed from the fact that so much wealth, landed and otherwise, was tied up in marriage. It was also connected with the church's pastoral role as the protector of women and orphans. Women seem to have gravitated to the ecclesiastical courts. If they were accorded little public recognition, they were often influential within the family and marriage. Widows and heiresses might control considerable property. Women were susceptible to the power of the church, which had learnt to create and play upon their feelings of guilt. It also knew how to assuage these by offering consolation and absolution in the form of sacraments and penance. But this was a pattern of life that was part of Christianity itself. Why was it only under the Comneni that women became a more significant factor? The church was not consciously cultivating a female constituency in order to drum up business for the ecclesiastical courts!

[27] Cf. B. Stolte, 'Civil law in canon law', in *TO BYZANTIO* KATA TON *12o AIΩNA*, ed. N. Oikonomidès (Athens, 1991), 543–54.

[28] Rhalles & Potles II, 458–9.

It seems to have been a combination of two developments. The first was a slight improvement in the status of women. This was acknowledged by greater respect for their spiritual contribution to a Christian society. There was a call for more nunneries. These would allow women to fulfil their spiritual potential, which, it was now conceded, was equal to that of men. This coincided with the grudging recognition on the part of Alexius I Comnenus that marriage was primarily the concern of the church and not of the state. By and large, the status of women depended on marriage, which offered some legal protection to person and property. It now became natural to look to the ecclesiastical courts when these were threatened. The church's influence over society depended very much on the leverage it had with women.

The power of the hierarchical church over society may have grown considerably, but there seems to have been little affection for it. This was reserved for the monastic church. Spiritual counsellors were usually monks. The monastery served both as a family shrine and a last resting place. It was not uncommon to retire to a monastery or nunnery as the proper preparation for death. The links of monastery and society may have grown closer, but the Comnenian era was not a great period of monastic spirituality. This had been doused by Comnenian patronage of monastic reform and by their suspicion of unconventional forms of spirituality, which extended to the monasteries of Mount Athos. Between them Eustathius of Thessalonica and Prodromos have succeeded in undermining the reputation of monastic life under the Comneni. They have created the impression of communities motivated only by material concerns.[29] A blanket condemnation is unfair, as the example of Patmos clearly shows. The monks of Patmos may have been alive to material advantages, but these they regarded as a necessary evil that allowed the pursuit of spiritual goals. In general, monastic estates were much better managed than they had been previously and, more to the point, managed by the communities themselves. There was far less need for a lay patron to save the monks from their own inefficiency. Effective management on the part of the community gave substance to the ideal of monastic independence. This was a major change that took place over the course of the twelfth century. There are no signs that it diminished the moral purpose of Byzantine monasticism. When Constantinople fell to the Latins in 1204 it was representatives of its monasteries who appeared as defenders of orthodoxy. It was a pointer to the future.

The fall of Constantinople was a cataclysmic event. It fixed the

[29] M. J. Angold, 'Monastic satire and the Evergetine monastic tradition in the twelfth century', in *The Theotokos Evergetis and Eleventh-Century Monasticism*, ed. M. Mullett and A. Kirby (Belfast Byzantine Texts and the Translations, 6.1 (Belfast, 1994), 86–102.

direction of change, which before 1204 still remained obscure and erratic. In exile Byzantine government and society was rebuilt, but relying heavily on the strengths that the church had acquired over the previous century. Orthodoxy guaranteed imperial authority, rather than vice versa. Orthodoxy, rather than imperial authority, ensured some degree of unity to the Byzantine lands. The threat to orthodoxy in the shape of the Latins united Byzantine society behind the church and diminished the distrust and indifference the laity had often displayed in the past towards the hierarchical church. But the grip of the church over Byzantine society only became fully apparent after the return of the capital to Constantinople in 1261. Michael VIII Palaeologus's attempt to effect the union of churches was frustrated by the opposition of all sections of society. It was not only a matter of defending orthodoxy. Michael Palaeologus's opponents rightly saw that his unionist policies were intended as a way of reasserting imperial authority over Byzantine church and society.

The Byzantine laity identified itself with the struggle against the union of churches. Victory came in 1285 when the new Emperor Andronicus II Palaeologos publicly renounced his father's unionist policies. This reflected the changing balance between church, society, and imperial authority, amounting, at long last, to a measure of identification of orthodoxy and society. In the past, the Byzantine laity had been happy to use the church for its own convenience. This was evident in lay infiltration of the church, whether in the shape of private chapels and family monasteries or of private confessors and devotions. It helped to shape that peculiarly Byzantine combination of deep piety and secular enthusiasms, in the sense that it allowed members of the laity to determine the degree of separation they each wished to maintain between religion and secular life. As the church assumed a more active pastoral role, so it became less inclined to tolerate such latitude; whence paradoxically comes the modern impression of the Comnenian court as peculiarly secular in its outlook and tastes. It was much more that these aroused more comment than in a previous era.

Pastoral responsibilities were no longer optional, but central to the life of the church. These were complemented by the development of canon law which provided the church with an instrument that allowed it to operate more effectively in society. This extension of the church's range of operations was at first the cause of resentment on the part of the laity. However, this subsided with the change of perspective brought about by the struggle against the Latins. The immediate reaction was emotional. It intensified the significance of orthodoxy. But underlying this was the realisation of how central the church was to the functioning of society. The loss of Constantinople underlined that it was the orthodox church, rather than 'Political

Orthodoxy', which defined the Byzantine identity. In the course of the thirteenth century we at last see coming true the claims already being advanced on behalf of the orthodox church in the new iconographies of the eleventh century. These, as Father Christopher Walter has shown, depict Christ, no longer in the guise of the universal emperor, but as the universal patriarch.[30]

[30] C. Walter, *Art and Ritual of the Byzantine Church* (London, 1982), 214–21.

INTRODUCTION TO PAPERBACK EDITION

No changes have been made to the original edition apart from some corrections of very minor printing errors. I feel that I need only draw the reader's attention to relevant work produced since the original edition went to the printers in 1994. In the introduction I lamented the absence of any authoritative work on the Byzantine church for the period that runs from the Triumph of Orthodoxy in 843 to the Schism of 1054. This gap, at least for monasticism, has now been filled in exemplary fashion by Rosemary Morris, whose *Monks and laymen in Byzantium 843–1118* was published by the Cambridge University Press shortly after my book came out. It has since become required reading. Margaret Mullett's long-awaited study on *Theophylact of Ochrid* duly appeared in 1997. It locates the archbishop more precisely in his own times thanks to the pioneering use – in the field of Byzantine studies – of network theory, an approach which could be applied with profit to other Comnenian bishops. Two collaborative volumes have recently appeared under Margaret Mullett's auspices: one on *Alexios I Komnenos* with relevant articles by P. Magdalino, P. Armstrong, D. Smythe, and C. Galatariotou; the other on *Work and Worship at the Theotokos Evergetis.* Of particular relevance are articles by K. Corrigan and D. Krausmüller. The history of dualist heresy under the Comneni has now been made much more accessible thanks to Janet and Bernard Hamilton. Their *Christian Dualist Heresies* contains translations into English of the most important Greek texts, but the value of the volume is much increased by the inclusion of a translation of Hugh Eteriano's *Adversus Patherenos.* This is the first time that the whole text has been made available. Its importance lies less in any new information on the Bogomils; more in the light it sheds on the unionist policies of Manuel I Comnenus – Eteriano's master. The tract was designed to find in dualism a common enemy that would unite 'the Holy Church of God, both Greek and Latin'. Finally, Alice-Mary Talbot has produced a translation into English of the *Life* of St Theodora of Arta. Full bibliographical details of all these works and others can be found at the end on p. 587 under *Additional Bibliography.*

MICHAEL ANGOLD
Edinburgh, April 2000

PART I

THE ELEVENTH CENTURY

1

CONFLICT AND DEBATE

THE Byzantines scarcely thought in terms of church and society. For them society was a Christian society defined by membership of the orthodox faith and by citizenship of a Christian Empire presided over by the Byzantine emperor and divinely instituted by God. They were much more exercised by the relationship of the orthodox faith to the Byzantine emperor. The classic definition was laid out in the preamble to Justinian's Novel VI. It begins: 'Among the greatest gifts of God bestowed by the kindness of Heaven are the priesthood and the imperial dignity. Of these, the former serves things divine; the latter rules human affairs and cares for them.' It goes on to elaborate a doctrine of harmony existing between the two, 'which furnishes whatsoever is needful for the human race'. But it could only be maintained if the emperor took due care of the orthodox faith and respected the dignity of the priesthood. Ironically, it was a doctrine which allowed the emperor the initiative in relations with the church without guaranteeing the desired harmony. Relations between the emperor and the church were often anything but harmonious. Soon influential churchmen would be proposing that the church and the faith lay outside the emperor's direct authority. The patriarch Photius set out to vindicate the autonomy of the church in his introduction to the *Epanagoge*, a law code that he was responsible for drawing up. He presents church and state as independent powers, presided over by a patriarch and an emperor, who are of equal status. This was exceedingly contentious and the law code never received imperial approval. Officially, Justinian's doctrine of harmony remained in force with its emphasis on the subordination of the church to the state. This did not mean that it was not questioned. It points to a contradiction there always was at the heart of the relationship of church and state in Byzantium.

The Byzantines may never have formulated any detailed theory of church and society, but this does not mean that the relationship was unimportant; still less, that it is not worth investigating. Contemporaries do not always have a very clear understanding of the structures within which they operate. They will be struck by the obvious. In Byzantium nothing could have been more obvious than the orthodox church and the imperial office. Power inhered in them and was exercised through the elites that were attached to each. The practical purpose underlying Byzantine theories of church and state was the division of control over society between the two elites. Such an interpretation receives support from the Byzantine view of their society. It was seen to be divided into two groups: the powerful and the poor. The theory was that the former had a responsibility to protect the latter. This division lay at the heart of the tenth-century agrarian legislation of the Macedonian emperors, in the sense that imperial intervention was justified on the grounds that the powerful were failing in their duties to the poor. The legislation at first defines the powerful as those who have the influence to bring pressure to bear on others. This was too broad and was replaced by a more precise definition. The powerful were identified as those who held office or position in either the imperial government or in the ecclesiastical hierarchy. It is clear that the pressure they could exert on others derived in normal circumstances from their official positions. The powerful were none other than the members of the imperial and ecclesiastical elites.

By the eleventh century those holding a commission from the emperor or a position in the imperial government were beginning to sign themselves, 'Slaves of the most holy and mighty emperor and autocrat.' It was a recognition of something that was taken for granted: that the emperor's servants had surrendered themselves totally to his power. Bishops and other prelates did not see themselves as having the same kind of relationship to the patriarch, but they were servants of their church and their faith. It was all part of an absolutist theory and system of government, where members of the elite were in that capacity divorced from society. This state of affairs was mitigated by a number of considerations. Members of the elite were also members of society, in the sense that they existed as private individuals as well as public figures. They were heads of families, whose tentacles might spread far and wide through society. Even eunuchs who were esteemed for their devotion to the imperial office had family connections which they were often eager to promote. Within the elite there were cliques who cultivated the interest of the group rather than of the state. In other words, the Byzantine imperial establishment was permeated by private interests.

This was even more the case with the church.[1] All kinds of churches passed into private ownership, including 'Catholic churches', as parish churches were called. At a local level much of the ecclesiastical organisation depended upon private initiative. Monasteries were naturally

[1] Thomas, *Private Religious Foundations, passim.*

prominent. Many of these came under private control. The official church was very much the bishop and his administration doing their best to supervise the monasteries and private churches that came within his jurisdiction. In those areas of the Empire where bishoprics were thick on the ground a reasonable balance was preserved between episcopal and private interests. Naturally enough lay patrons of churches and monasteries were often drawn from the political establishment.

Private interest in Byzantine society was catered for and largely protected by two main institutions: the family and the monastery. As A.P. Kazhdan has shown many of the features of monastic life replicated family structures.[2] It was part of the way that the monastery moulded itself to the contours of Byzantine society. The enduring strength of the monastery and the monastic order stemmed, if only in part, from their social function, which was endlessly flexible. Their charitable role hardly needs mentioning. It is so obvious. Monasteries supported alms-houses and hospitals. At a more mundane level they saw to the upkeep of bridges; they had baths and bakeries attached to them. They provided a safe haven in old age and a last resting place, with the consolation of prayers of remembrance and intercession. For the powerful they served as family shrines and centres of aristocratic influence. Some monasteries were famed for their libraries and *scriptoria*, though generally speaking they never became important centres of education.[3]

Though they catered to the needs of Byzantine society, monasteries were ideally centres of spiritual activity. At different times monastic leaders would claim that the monks formed a spiritual elite. They were capable of challenging established authority, if the orthodox faith appeared to be under threat. This was the case during iconoclasm and again over the union of churches with Rome. The claim that monks formed a spiritual elite was accepted, if with some reservations. This gave monasticism a degree of autonomy which prevented it from being swallowed up by lay society. This was in the case of individual monasteries a real danger. There are plenty of examples of monasteries being treated as though they were private property. The monastery's spiritual role gave it a bargaining counter. Various interests, private and public, lay and ecclesiastical, were attracted to monasteries, not only for financial reasons or for the amenities they provided, but also for the spiritual power that was seen to inhere in them. They became a focus around which public and private interests could interact. In other words,

[2] Kazhdan, 'Vizantijskij monastyr' XI-XII vv'.

[3] See A.-M. Talbot, 'The Byzantine family and the monastery', *DOP* 44 (1990), 119–29.

monasteries mediated between the imperial and ecclesiastical establishments and society at large. It was a process far more intricate than was allowed for by Byzantine theorising about the ideal relationship between church and state. It is best apprehended through the various debates and conflicts which surrounded the life of the orthodox church.

There is a paradox that lies at the heart of Byzantium. It was a polity that 'for a thousand years', to use Lewis Mumford's words, 'made a virtue of arrested development'.[4] It was backward looking and cultivated an air of immutability – fossilisation even. It was also exceedingly contentious. The lack of harmony showed itself in many ways: the coups and the counter-coups and the constant plotting and politicking. Just as characteristic were the theological debates and controversies and the disagreements that set the orthodox church against other churches. These can all be seen as part of a process of adjustment, whereby Byzantium came to terms with its circumstances. The eleventh century was no exception. It was a time when we can detect major changes in the shape of Byzantine society. If we were to look back to the turn of the ninth century, we would have found a society that was relatively uncomplicated. Power was concentrated at Constantinople in the hands of the bureaucracy. Government was to an extent a career open to talents, though the bulk of civil servants probably came from families long associated in government in one way or another. Outside the court and bureaucracy society in the capital was by and large unorganised. Some trades, but mostly professions, were organised into official gilds, but they will only have included a tiny proportion of the working population of the capital. Out in the provinces urban life had not recovered from the collapse of the *polis* in the course of late antiquity. It was still largely a peasant society organised around village communities. It was a society that could be controlled reasonably easily from Constantinople. This state of affairs was soon to be undermined by the growth of great landowning families. In Anatolia they came to monopolise control of the theme organisation and then began to challenge the power of the emperor. The culmination was their struggle with the Emperor Basil II at the turn of the tenth century. The emperor was victorious. The measures that he took to repress the power of the great families effectively bottled up changes. His successors were left to cope with the consequences.

Basil II was able to restrict economic growth. Significant sums of money were taken out of circulation and stored as imperial treasure. The Empire was kept on a war footing. After his death these restraints were relaxed. There was a growth of local trade which centred on Constantinople, but which spread out into the provinces. There are

4 L. Mumford, *The City in History* (London, 1961), 241.

distinct signs of more vigorous economic life in provincial centres. This seems to have been most marked around the Aegean, but may have been Empire-wide. Byzantium became a richer and more complex society. It became correspondingly more difficult to govern. The people and gilds of Constantinople assumed a more active political role. The imperial government was wary of confrontation. It preferred to go with the tide. New wealth demanded recognition. Status still went very largely with position at court and in the administration. Titles and ranks were doled out in profusion. There was a growing demand for education, which was also a mark of social status. It was a prerequisite for a successful career in the civil service. In the tenth century the number of schools and pupils at Constantinople seems to have been rather limited – one is of course dealing in impressions – but estimates have been made, which place the number of pupils then receiving a higher education at Constantinople as low as 200 to 300.[5] In the eleventh century everything points to a considerable growth in numbers both of schools and of pupils. This was fuelled by a greater demand for civil servants as the state apparatus expanded, in part to meet the administrative demands created by a more complex society. It was also in response to the pressure for jobs from those with the proper qualifications for entry into the civil service. The government machinery became bloated by the demands of a system of patronage, where power increasingly depended upon the ability to place relatives and protégés. The effect of all this was to expand the imperial establishment, but at the cost of its coherence as it became increasingly infiltrated by private interests. Government became less an instrument of imperial authority; more the province of different interest groups.

Change and the orthodox church

Social flux also touched the church, if to a lesser degree than it did the imperial government. Christopher of Mitylene gives vent in a poem to the contempt felt by a highly educated civil servant for the aspirations of the *nouveaux riches*. It deals with tradesmen, craftsmen, and merchants, who become priests and deacons. They were quite unable to conduct church services in a seemly manner, because of the habit they had of introducing into the liturgy phrases appropriate to their former callings. Instead of intoning 'Come let us adore him' a sailor-turned-priest would begin 'Come let us set sail.' When serving the communion a former innkeeper would extol the virtues of the communion wine, as though still serving behind the bar. 'This wine

5 C. Mango, *Byzantium. The World of New Rome* (London, 1980), 147.

is sweet, quite exceptionally so', he would say rather than inviting the communicant to approach.[6] Behind the invective we detect the pressures there were for entry into the church. Ecclesiastical office gave status and respectability, even if the remuneration was far less than that offered by a sinecure at the imperial court.

As an institution the church was able to come to terms with the changes that were occurring rather better than the imperial establishment was able to. This was in the first instance thanks to the work of the Patriarch Alexius the Studite (1025–43). He strengthened the juridical and financial basis of the church. Among his concerns was the legal status of the clergy. He forbad monks and clergy – and this was to include the clergy of the imperial churches and the monks of imperial foundations – to seek justice in the secular courts. He also regulated the *kanonikon*, a clerical tax paid to the bishop. Each priest was expected to pay his bishop one *nomisma* annually. More lucrative was the payment of one *nomisma* by a reader and three *nomismata* by a deacon or a priest to the bishop on the occasion of their ordination. This must have gone some way to strengthening episcopal finances. There are one or two examples which suggest that in the mid-eleventh century there were some extremely wealthy bishops.

The monasteries presented a different kind of a problem. From the turn of the tenth century they started to be administered under a form of lay patronage known as *kharistike*. Its origins are still not entirely clear, but they appear to be connected in one way or another with legislation introduced by Nicephorus Phocas (963–9). It was designed to limit the amount of land in monastic possession.[7] There was a decisive growth of *kharistike* in the later part of Basil II's reign. The emperor's role in this is not absolutely clear. There is only the suspicion that he used it as a way of rewarding the new families that he brought to prominence. The Patriarch Alexius the Studite was not the first patriarch to be alarmed by its prevalence, but he was the first to try to regulate the practice. His solution was the registration of all transfers of monastic property and rights of patronage in the patriarchal registry, known as the *chartophylakeion*. His measure actually went further than this. He hoped that through the registration of monastic properties at a local level in the episcopal archives it would be possible to strengthen episcopal control over the monasteries, as envisaged at the council of Chalcedon (451). Monasteries were seen as a source of revenue for

6 E. Kurtz, ed., *Die Gedichte des Christophoros Mitylenaios* (Leipzig, 1903), no.63

7 H. Ahrweiler, 'Charisticariat et autres formes d'attribution de fondations pieuses aux Xe-XIe siècles', *Zbornik radova vizantinoloshkog Instituta* 10(1967),1–27, but see now Thomas, *Private Religious Foundations*, 149–66, who argues that the *kharistike* was a product of the repeal of Nicephorus Phocas's legislation under Basil II.

bishops. Alexius the Studite expected prosperous suffragans to help out their metropolitan bishop, if he was in financial difficulties. He advised that they could do this most easily by passing on to their superior any monasteries that had come into their possession.

Alexius the Studite did not confine himself to institutional concerns alone. He discerned that there was a problem of heresy. There were the Jacobites, Syrian Monophysites, who constituted a good proportion of the population of the Euphrates provinces. The centre of their church was the city of Melitene. Alexius reversed the relatively tolerant religious attitude to minorities that existed under Basil II and insisted that the Jacobites conform to orthodox practice and teaching. He also reopened the attack upon the monastic community originally formed in the mid-tenth century around Eleutherios of Paphlagonia, but now centred in southern Anatolia. His followers kept his body on open display in the church; they also venerated images of their leader.

This is reminiscent of the cult of Symeon Eulabes promoted at the turn of the tenth century by his disciple, the mystic Symeon the New Theologian. Images of the holy man had a large part to play. Symeon the New Theologian used them as a way of proclaiming the sanctity of his spiritual father. This brought down on him patriarchal censure. But the use of images of the founder was not the only offending feature of the community that grew up around the cult of Eleutherios of Paphlagonia. Also included were women. Apparently each monk needed two women to look after his needs.

A similar community existed in the theme of Opsikion in north-western Anatolia. It was founded by a certain Tzourillas. He repudiated his wife, but then appointed her abbess and himself abbot of the community. Under Alexius the Studite Euthymios, a monk of the Peribleptos monastery in Constantinople, was sent to investigate. The members of this cult are called Phoundagiagitai, or Bogomils – the first time that this term is applied in a Byzantine context. The relationship of this sect to the Bulgarian Bogomils remains problematical. The name of the founder has a plausibly Bulgarian ring to it. This does not rule out the possibility that these heretical groups were spontaneous movements that had their roots in monastic or lay piety; nor the possibility that the official church found them disturbing and chose to identify them with the Bulgarian sect as a means of discrediting them. It is clear that by the early eleventh century there were many nonconformist communities in Asia Minor that were passing outside the control of the established church. Alexius the Studite may be given credit for identifying and confronting the problem, but it was not going to disappear.

Alexius the Studite left behind a comparatively large body of writings, mostly of a judicial, canonical, and administrative character, but he is not a figure who emerges very clearly from the sources. He seems to have been on good terms with the Emperor Romanos III Argyros (1028–34), who made an annual gift of £80 of gold to the church of St Sophia. His relations with the next Emperor Michael IV (1034–41) are likely to have been strained, for there was an attempt by a clique of metropolitans to unseat Alexius and replace him by John the Orphanotrophos, the emperor's brother and chief minister. It failed, but the patriarch must have had his suspicions about the degree to which the emperor was implicated. Michael IV was succeeded by his nephew and namesake Michael V, who is best known for his coup against the Empress Zoe, his adopted mother. He also planned to depose the Patriarch Alexius, to which end he had him lured away from Constantinople. News that the empress had been sent into exile brought the patriarch back to the capital. He became the centre of the growing opposition to the emperor. He gave his sanction to the uprising against Michael V – popularly known as the Caulker – by declaring him unfit to serve as emperor. It was tantamount to deposing a reigning emperor and approving the action of the people who had already formally thrown off their allegiance to the emperor with the cry 'Dig up the Caulker's bones.'[8] Byzantine constitutional theory dimly recognised that an unworthy emperor could be deposed through popular action. This was now reinforced by patriarchal sanctions. Michael V was deposed and the Empress Zoe brought back to the capital. Alexius was at the centre of events. He had acted to restore proper order to the body politic.

It was a precedent rich with possibilities. The new Emperor Constantine IX Monomachos (1042–55) understood that the patriarch would have to be placated. He made it possible through a generous donation for the mass to be celebrated every day in the patriarchal church of St Sophia, whereas previously it had only been possible to celebrate mass on the great feast days and on Saturdays and Sundays.

Alexius died in 1043. His successor was to be Michael Cerularius.[9] This was a political appointment on the part of the emperor. The new patriarch was an old ally from a distinguished Constantinopolitan family. His political ambitions had come to grief some years earlier, when he had been convicted of plotting against the Emperor Michael IV. He had reluctantly become a monk. At first, he served

[8] H.-G. Beck, 'Konstantinopel. Zur Sozialgeschichte einer frühmittelalterlichen Hauptsadt', *BZ* 58(1965), 36–7.

[9] See F. Tinnefeld, 'Michael I. Kerullarios, Patriarch von Konstantinopel (1043–1058)', *JÖB* 39(1989), 95–127; M. J. Angold, 'Imperial renewal and orthodox reaction: Byzantium in the eleventh century' in *New Constantines. The Rhythm of Imperial Renewal in Byzantium, 4th-13th Centuries*, ed. P. Magdalino (Aldershot, 1994), 231–46.

Constantine Monomachos loyally. He backed him up during the siege of Constantinople in 1047 by the rebel Leo Tornikios. The only hint of friction between the emperor and the patriarch before the events of 1054 was Cerularius's decision in 1049 to close down the Latin churches in Constantinople. Behind this lay the patriarch's dislike of the Lombard Argyros, who had become one of the emperor's trusted lieutenants. All the same, the hostile actions of Cardinal Humbert of Silvia Candida in 1054 took the patriarch by surprise. He had sought over the previous two years to make friendly overtures to the Holy See. The protection offered to the papal delegation by the emperor started to strain the patriarch's patience. It seemed that the emperor was willing to sacrifice orthodoxy and the interests of the orthodox church; and for what? Political advantages in southern Italy that an alliance with Rome might or might not bring! Forbearance was no longer possible once Cardinal Humbert stormed into the church of St Sophia and laid a bull of excommunication on the altar of the cathedral. Cerularius had the perpetrators anathematised and forced the emperor to abandon his support for the papal delegation. He was able to use the Constantinopolitan mob in order to bring pressure to bear on the emperor. The mob could be a formidable political weapon. No contemporary makes clear why it came out in support of the patriarch. Though it may sound a shade idealistic, the Constantinopolitan mob normally acted when it saw orthodoxy or constitutional propriety under threat.

After his victory in 1054 Michael Cerularius was the most powerful figure in Constantinople. This is in marked contrast with the obscurity which surrounds the early part of his patriarchate. A eulogy of the patriarch describes him as the legislator (*nomothetes*) of the Empress Theodora, who succeeded Constantine Monomachos. But they were to fall out. The patriarch was accused rightly or wrongly of objecting to a woman on the throne.[10] Theodora was succeeded by Michael VI Stratiotikos (1056–7). The patriarch brought about his downfall and raised the rebel general Isaac Comnenus to the imperial dignity. The decisive act in this transfer of power was the coronation of the emperor by the patriarch.

In normal circumstances, it was acclamation that made an emperor and coronation was a formality. But in cases of usurpation it was felt that some ecclesiastical sanction was required. It was argued by the twelfth-century canonist Theodore Balsamon that the stain of usurpation could only be wiped away through unction administered by the patriarch during the coronation.[11]

10 Sathas, *MB* v, 357–8.

11 That Cerularius understood the power he wielded through the coronation is suggested by his refusal to crown Theodora's designated successor Michael VI Stratiotikos while there was still breath in her body.

Isaac Comnenus's debt to Michael Cerularius is apparent from the concessions that he was willing to make to the patriarch. In the past, it was usual for the emperor to appoint the chief officers of the patriarchal administration. Their appointment was now handed over to the patriarch. It meant that instead of the patriarchal administration being controlled to an extent by the emperor it could develop as an independent institution. It pointed the way to greater autonomy on the part of the patriarchal church. Given the immense authority that the patriarch now had, it is perhaps not so surprising that he should have clashed with the emperor. One cause was Isaac Comnenus's determination to control donations to monasteries. This the patriarch interpreted as interference in the affairs of the church. There may have been more to it than this. The emperor acted decisively. He had Cerularius bundled out of Constantinople and arraigned on a series of charges ranging from treason to heresy. The case never came to court because Cerularius died on 21 January 1059.

Cerularius was accused among other things of usurping some of the symbols of imperial authority. He seems to have taken to wearing red sandals. On the basis of such accusations it has been usual for historians to present Cerularius as the Byzantine Hildebrand, not merely concerned to claim equal status for the priesthood alongside the imperial office, but anxious to subordinate the secular arm to patriarchal authority. They can point to a connection between Michael Cerularius and the western reform movement of the eleventh century, in the shape of the Donation of Constantine.[12] This most famous forgery of the middle ages was one of the key documents for western reformers, because it purported to give the papacy imperial prerogatives. It meant nothing to the Byzantines until 1054, when Cardinal Humbert brought a Greek version to the Emperor Constantine Monomachos. He also presented a shorter Latin version to Cerularius, who had it translated into Greek. The argument is that Cerularius seized its potential and transferred the imperial prerogatives it accorded to the papacy to the patriarchate of Constantinople. He could justify this on the grounds that the first council of Constantinople and the council of Chalcedon gave the patriarch of Constantinople the same rights and privileges as the pope in Rome. This was the opinion of the twelfth-century canonist Theodore Balsamon, when he came to review the case of Michael Cerularius.

It was in line with the official charges that were drawn up against Cerularius in 1058 to the effect that he had usurped imperial authority and confused the spheres of imperial and patriarchal authority.

[12] E.g. R.J.H. Jenkins 'A cross of Patriarch Michael Cerularius', *DOP* 21 (1967), 236–8.

However, it does not seem likely that Michael Cerularius would have used the Donation of Constantine as the foundation of an extreme statement of patriarchal authority. After the events of 1054 he remained suspicious of papal claims. Though the source is a thirteenth century one, there are good reasons to believe that at the very end of his patriarchate in 1057–8 he called together a council of the orthodox church, to which the patriarch of Antioch, as well as the archbishops of Bulgaria and Cyprus were invited. Its purpose was officially to remove the name of the pope from the diptychs,[13] thus giving official confirmation to a schism. On this interpretation the Donation of Constantine would only have confirmed patriarchal suspicions about papal claims, rather than have been used to support patriarchal claims against imperial authority. On the imperial side knowledge of the Donation of Constantine could be used to discredit the patriarch. His opposition to Isaac Comnenus could be presented as ideologically motivated. The historian Michael Psellus claimed to know the real cause of the quarrel of the patriarch and the emperor: it was the way the patriarch expected the emperor to take second place in the state behind him.[14] But this must be propaganda: Psellus was the Emperor Isaac's chief minister and masterminded the overthrow of Michael Cerularius.

Michael Psellus was put in charge of the prosecution. He accused the patriarch of 'being democratically inclined and disparaging the monarchy'.[15] 'Democratic' was intended as a slur word, but not mindlessly so. Much thought was given to constitutional matters at a time when the succession was often in doubt. There was an idealisation of the Roman past and Augustus's constitutional settlement, which gave a considerable role to the senate and people in the choice and approval of an emperor. The choice of the word 'democratic' branded Cerularius as one who favoured popular participation in the making and unmaking of emperors. It pointed to the popular support he had, which must have disturbed the emperor.

How well founded were the charges against Cerularius? Our chief guide is the *Panoplia*. This is an anti-Latin polemic. In its surviving form it almost certainly dates from around the second council of Lyons (1274)[16], but its editor A. Michel has advanced convincing reasons for attributing the original version to Cerularius. It shows a certain impatience with imperial authority. It claims that patriarchs have the right to reprove and discipline emperors.[17] It is consistent with

13 Grumel, 846.
14 Sathas, *MB* v, 367.
15 U. Criscuolo, *Michele Psello, Epistola a Michele Cerulario* (Naples, 1973), 30.230.
16 Tinnefeld, 'Michael I. Kerullarios', 109–14.
17 A. Michel, *Humbert und Kerullarios. Quellen und Studien zum Schisma des XI. Jahrhunderts* (Paderborn, 1930), 242.5–8, 268.19–35.

the stance taken by Michael Cerularius as the defender of orthodoxy. The events of 1054 alerted him to the danger that the political order designed to protect orthodoxy might fail in its responsibilities. There then followed a succession of disputed successions, where Michael Cerularius acted as the arbiter of the constitutional process. This laid him open to the charge that he aimed at the creation of a hierocracy.

A. Michel believed that it was more a matter of Cerularius seeking to establish a spiritual ascendancy founded on a *plebs sancta*.[18] It is worth pursuing this line of thought, even if at first sight there seems to be little difference between the two concepts. Michel presumably meant that Cerularius was *not* seeking to usurp imperial authority. He belonged rather to the tradition of Theodore of Stoudios and of Photius, who had sought to vindicate the independence of the priesthood and the autonomy of the patriarchal church. It was more a question of the separation of powers. This they regarded as a necessary precondition for the exercise of spiritual supervision over society. But Cerularius was the successor of Alexius the Studite. By acting in concert with the people of Constantinople to secure the deposition of Michael V Alexius added a political element to patriarchal claims. This called in question any neat division of authority. Cerularius equally used an alliance with the people of the city to act in times of crisis as the arbiter of the political process. This could be presented as an attempt to protect orthodoxy and to preserve order, rather than as a direct challenge to imperial authority. The patriarch may well have looked upon the people of Constantinople as a *plebs sancta*. They were the New Israel; they were the citizens of a city guarded by the Mother of God. Constantinople as the New Sion was a popular propaganda theme of the mid-eleventh century. However, the people of Constantinople were also the citizens of the New Rome with claims to a constitutional role in the making and unmaking of emperors. Any understanding between the patriarch and the people of Constantinople would have struck Cerularius's opponents as a dangerous innovation. It inevitably looked as though the patriarch was exploiting the constitutional rights of the people to dominate political life at Byzantium. It undermined any notion of a separation of powers. Cerularius was working, not on the basis of the Donation of Constantine, but in the tradition of Photius. He may not even have been aware of how radically he was developing his ideas.

Like it or not the patriarch was competing with the emperor for the loyalties of the people of Constantinople. This brought to the surface a basic problem in any Christian society, but one which Justinian's doctrine of harmony neatly sidestepped: the degree of control that

[18] Ibid., 192.

the church exercised over society. Justinian's doctrine assumed that society and imperial authority were inseparable; that the church's function was to pray for their mutual well-being; and that the church was therefore subordinated to the needs of the imperial institution and could not be fully independent. But, that was theory. What happened when the church acquired a degree of autonomy and when it became clear that spiritual ascendancy meant interference in the political process? How then would the church relate to society at large? It certainly had a responsibility for its spiritual welfare, but did this not now require more direct intervention in the affairs of society on the part of the church? There was nothing particularly new about this dilemma, but it was posed more starkly in the eleventh century than at any time since the iconoclast controversy.

The orthodox church and the ideal of society

The patriarchs of the time reacted by displaying a new concern over marriage. Marriage was a sacrament. It comes as a surprise to discover that it had largely been regulated by civil law. Marital cases normally went before the civil rather than the ecclesiastical courts. A change occurred under Alexius the Studite and Michael Cerularius. An increasing proportion of marital litigation started coming before the patriarchal court.

This challenged Justinian's theory of harmony, which assumed that marriage, along with other social concerns, was primarily an imperial responsibility. The patriarchs of the eleventh century thought otherwise: marriage had spiritual ramifications. It should therefore be supervised by the church. It was part of the way that the church was assuming greater responsibility for society on the understanding that its problems were as much spiritual as legal.

It was a question that was debated on a more elevated level in a private correspondence between Michael Cerularius and Michael Psellus. At issue were the conflicting roles of the humanist and the mystic, as proponents of differing ideals of a Christian society. Michael Psellus's views are easy enough to piece together. He was the philosopher who by virtue of his secular education and the cultivation of his rational faculty saw himself as the guide of emperors and the moral arbiter of society. He was quite able to square this with sincerely held Christian beliefs, but it was a secular outlook which placed great stress on the notion that the proper study of mankind is man. Cerularius's views are known only from Psellus's refutation. He seems to have opposed to the philosopher the mystic, who equally possessed a special fund of knowledge, but it had not come through any cultivation of the rational faculty, but through spiritual meditation. It was this which should energise and instruct a Christian society.

Michael Cerularius drew his inspiration from the work of the mystic Symeon the New Theologian. His support for the cult of this saint has some mysterious elements to it. It was not just that Symeon had been condemned by the patriarchal synod for his efforts to promote the cult of his spiritual father Symeon Eulabes and had died in obscurity and semi-exile in 1022. Although his mystical teachings were not officially condemned as heretical, they were regarded as subversive of authority. His spiritual executor was Nicetas Stethatos, a monk and future abbot of the monastery of Stoudios. It was thanks to his efforts that Symeon's writings were rescued from obscurity and his remains were translated with due honour in 1052 to Constantinople. He had the support of Michael Cerularius, who secured Symeon's canonisation. What is mysterious is that not long before the patriarch had been at loggerheads with the abbot and monastery of Stoudios and that Nicetas Stethatos was the chief defender of the Studites. The patriarch tried to stop the deacons of the monastery of Stoudios from wearing liturgical belts, which he believed infringed ecclesiastical tradition. He also refused to allow the name of Theodore of Stoudios to be included among those saints who were honoured in the *synodikon* read out on the feast of Orthodoxy. The abbot of Stoudios protested to the Emperor Constantine Monomachos. Cerularius was compelled once again to read out the *synodikon* on the fifth Sunday after Lent, this time including the name of Theodore of Stoudios.[19]

Michael Cerularius's espousal of the cause of Symeon the New Theologian must have produced some kind of understanding with Nicetas Stethatos and the Studites. In the debates with the Latins that occurred in 1053 and 1054 Stethatos supported Michael Cerularius. It is conceivable that the growing tensions there were between the orthodox and Latin churches in Constantinople provided the occasion for a reconciliation between the patriarch and the monasteries of Constantinople. Again one is working very much in the dark when trying to discover what attractions Symeon the New Theologian's teachings could have held for the patriarch. The mystic claimed that power within the church belonged not to those with vested authority, but to those who possessed the gifts of the spirit. The gibes of Michael

[19] Cedrenus (ed. Bonn) II, 55,II.24–34; Michel, *Humbert und Kerullarios*, II, 20. Cf. the passage in the letter of 1054 from Peter, patriarch of Antioch, to Michael Cerularius: 'Why should we expect others to follow us, when our injunctions are not followed at home? Do not get into a frenzy, but in the holiest monastery of Stoudios the deacons continue to wear belts, doing something which does not accord with ecclesiastical tradition. Look, however hard you have tried you have not been able to get rid of this unprecedented custom.' Migne, *PG*, 120. 808–9.

Psellus suggest that the patriarch hoped to compensate with the gifts of the spirit for his lack of a formal education. Perhaps he hoped to give patriarchal authority a stronger spiritual quality by drawing on Symeon's mystical inspiration. This would fit with the idea that was then circulating in monastic circles that the gifts of the spirit were the essential prerequisite for the exercise of authority within the church. As Nicetas Stethatos expressed it, as long as he possessed the gifts of the spirit any monk, deacon, or priest was the equal of a bishop.[20]

It would be dangerous to claim that Nicetas Stethatos was the patriarch's *porte-parole*, but his writings do allow us an insight into some of the influential currents of opinion that were then circulating in monastic circles. The respective roles of clergy and laity in a Christian society was a theme that attracted Stethatos's attention. He was the author of a treatise on the soul and another on paradise. These produced questions from a sophist – as he is slightingly described – called Gregory. Some of his questions were pettifogging. He wanted to know how it was possible for Cherubim to stand in a circle around the throne of the Lord, when Stethatos maintained that angels were circumscribed within the firmament. It was a clever clever question typical of reason being applied to questions of mysticism, but nonetheless dangerous for that, because it denied that mystical thought had any valid rational basis. It only drew a mild rebuke about the way spiritual knowledge was not open to all, but required a long training.[21]

Other questions touched fundamental points of Christian dogma. Gregory claimed that the saints would sit with Christ in paradise, but only in some future age. This was more dangerous and produced a denunciation of laymen meddling in matters that did not concern them. Nicetas supported this with the quite false argument that St Paul had forbidden any laymen to teach in church. He followed this up by citing canon 44 of the council *In Troullo*, which does prohibit laymen from making public pronouncements on matters of dogma. In which case, why did the sophist not remain silent? Why did he not recognise his proper station?[22]

Stethatos's insistence that the laity should know their place is repeated over another matter raised by the sophist. At one point in the liturgy of St John Chrysostom the deacon calls out to the congregation, 'The doors, the doors, let us pay attention.' Gregory interpreted this to mean that all who were present had a right to watch the preparation of the holy offerings. Stethatos was horrified. For the laity to watch the divine mysteries was to upset all sense of propriety and good order. He

20 Nicétas Stéthatos, *Opuscules et Lettres*, ed. J. Darrouzès 338–42.
21 Ibid.
22 Ibid.

insisted that access to the altar was forbidden to the laity: excepting the emperor alone. The sanctuary was the preserve of the priesthood. Gregory claimed that in private chapels it was permissible for the laity to approach the altar. Stethatos had to reprove him once again. It was not permitted to hold services in the privacy of one's own home. He pointed out that it was strictly enjoined that church services were to be held in the local public or parish church.[23] He was quite right. In 1028 the patriarchal synod had forbidden the celebration of various church services in private chapels and the officiating priest was to be dismissed. There was a rider to the effect that with the permission of the bishop the mass might be celebrated in a private chapel, as well as the liturgy for the feast day of the patron saint.[24] This went a long way towards undermining the main provision.

Private chapels had become a common feature of the orthodox church and not just in the houses of the aristocracy.[25] Stethatos was protesting at this development. His emphasis upon a proper order was designed to preserve for the priesthood their privileged position, entirely separate from the laity, as the dispensers of teaching and of the mysteries. He considered that their independence was compromised by a willingness on the part of certain priests to serve in private chapels. Since private churches and chapels were a constant feature of Byzantine religious life[26] Stethatos was criticising one of the chief manifestations of lay piety in the Byzantine Empire. The laity sought a more active role in the liturgy. There was also a desire in some circles for a more private faith, where a confessor was attached to the household and served as a private chaplain. This did not of itself exclude other forms of piety, such as attachment to monasteries. The Emperor Isaac Comnenus and his brother John were brought up in the monastery of Stoudios and it was to Stoudios that the emperor retired when he was forced to abdicate. Stethatos saw lay piety expressed through the liturgy celebrated in private as a challenge to the spiritual elite, which included not only priests but also monks.

We have already seen how he claimed equality with the priesthood for those monks, who were vouchsafed the gifts of the spirit. His inclusion of monks among the spiritual elite should not be considered a contradiction of his sense of hierarchy. It added to the spiritual strength of the church and its claim to form a separate elite. These now rested not merely on the historical fact that the priests and bishops received their power by succession from the Apostles, but also on the intuition

[23] Ibid., 280–91.

[24] Grumel, no.835.

[25] T. Matthews, 'Private liturgy in Byzantine architecture: toward a re-appraisal', *Cahiers archéologiques* 30(1982), 125–38.

[26] Thomas, *Private Religious Foundations, passim.*

of Symeon the New Theologian that there were some men in each generation endowed with such rare spiritual gifts that they stood in the same immediate relationship to Christ as His Apostles, including St Paul, had done. Michael Cerularius's championing of Symeon the New Theologian has wider implications than are at first apparent. It conforms to a new emphasis upon a clerical elite possessing a monopoly of spiritual authority and thus of access, liturgical and intellectual, to the divine. It challenged some of the compromises on which the Byzantine polity was based.

Christian humanism

The letters exchanged between Nicetas Stethatos and the sophist Gregory reveal the tensions existing in the second half of the eleventh century between apologists for an ecclesiastical elite and those favouring a more secular approach. In a sense, the dispute was about the right to teach. It was inevitable that the humanists thought that their training allowed them to pronounce on those elements of Christian belief that were amenable to reason. It is apparent that there were radically different attitudes to the relationship of the individual to the church and the faith. These were already apparent in the correspondence exchanged between Michael Psellus and the Patriarch Michael Cerularius. The latter more or less excluded the laity from active participation in spiritual life. This was reserved for the priesthood and the monastic order and required separation from human society. With this Michael Psellus could not agree. He was adamant that man was a social being. He could only realise his full potential – and this included his understanding of God – within human society. Man was first and foremost a rational being. It was his ability to reason that most distinguished him from the animals: this was a favourite Byzantine commonplace. To seek knowledge of God by the way of ignorance and renunciation was bound to be a barren experience because it went counter to man's nature. In Psellus's opinion all it did was to give rise to quite futile pride in an ability to suffer. Much better that the individual should develop his rational faculties to the best of his ability, because it was reason which offered the likeliest chance of approaching God, even if it was never possible fully to know God. It also gave hope that it might be possible to live a Christian life within society, which was the essential of lay piety.

Michael Psellus became a monk – a most reluctant monk, the victim of political circumstance. It compelled him nonetheless to consider the question of the monastic life from a variety of angles. He held a number of monasteries in *kharistike* and was much sought after as a generous patron. His affections were lavished on the Constantinopolitan monastery of Ta Narsou. He claimed it as his *patris*. He had been born in its neighbourhood and had been educated there as a boy. The monks looked upon him as the founder. He admitted that he was not the true founder, but was a patron of the monastery and presumably exercised founder's rights.[27] It is easy to discern Psellus's views about monasticism in the *Life* of St Auxentios which he wrote for the nuns of Mount Auxentios. It contains a plea for a sane and well-balanced monastic life. Those who have taken up the monastic vocation 'do not merely exist in the body to be guided by irrational forces, so that they are absorbed in fleshly pleasures, nor do they constantly and continually carry out their allotted tasks, because they consist only of disembodied and unadulterated spirit. Rather are they composed of both natures with an obligation to accommodate their bodily needs and spiritual welfare.'[28] Using St Auxentios as his mouthpiece[29] Psellus is able to emphasise the importance of the celebration of the liturgy to monastic life. He lays due stress on church music, as well as on the power of prayer. He has nothing to say even by implication about the mysticism that was fashionable in monastic circles in his day. St Auxentios was not a mystic, but a miracle-worker – one who held the demons at bay. Psellus held to an old-fashioned view that the first task of a man with spiritual powers was to protect Christians against the malice of demons.

As a good Christian Psellus believed in demons. It was a phenomenon which confronted him with the problem of the irrational. He thought that most natural phenomena had a rational explanation. In the case of the famous echo chamber at Nicomedia he dismissed supernatural causes out of hand and explained its properties entirely in terms of the proportions of the room.[30] He was, however, willing to accept the miracle of the Blakhernai, when at a certain hour on a Friday the veil over an icon of the Mother of God was miraculously lifted. He was all the more inclined to believe in it, because it did not always work. If it had, then 'what occurred might be ascribed to natural causes, but the failure of the miraculous was a more precise testimony of the unusual and supernatural character of the phenomenon.'[31] Psellus did not rule out the supernatural and the irrational, but they must be kept in their

[27] P. Gautier, 'Précisions historiques sur le monastère de Ta Narsou', *REB* 34 (1976), 101–10. Cf. P. Joannou, 'Psellus et le monastère Ta Narsou', *BZ* 44(1951), 283–90.

[28] P.P. Joannou, *Démonologie populaire – démonologie critique au XIe siècle. La vie inédite de S. Auxence par M. Psellus* (Wiesbaden 1971), 112–14.

[29] Cf. Kazhdan / Epstein, 223.

[30] J.F. Boissonade, *Psellus De Operatione Daemonum* (Nuremburg, 1838), 58–62.

[31] V. Grumel, 'Le miracle habituel de Notre-Dame des Blachèrnes à Constantinople', *EO* 30(1931), 129–46.

place. This is apparent in his attitude to images. He describes the feelings evoked by an icon of the Mother of God: 'I am describing not what I observed, but what I felt, for She looked as though She had completely changed Her nature, being transformed into a beauty approaching the Divine, quite beyond the sensation offered by sight.'[32] Psellus's stress upon the human dimension was not limited to the use of reason or that which could be apprehended through the senses. He gave due allowance to the workings of human emotion.

His eminently reasonable attitude was shared by other members of the intellectual elite of the eleventh century. It emerges from the poetry of Christopher of Mitylene. He has no difficulty in moving from secular to religious subjects. Christopher could just as easily provide a vivid description of a piece of classical statuary[33] as he could a moving evocation of an icon. Members of his family and his friends meant much to him, but he was equally devoted to a monk Nicetas, who seems to have been his spiritual father.[34] Yet he had nothing but scorn for another monk who was an avid collector of relics. He had already accumulated ten hands of the martyr Procopius, fifteen jaws of St Theodore, up to eight feet of St Nestor, four heads of St George, and no less than five breasts of St Barbara. As Christopher observed, 'faith without discrimination overturns order and nature'[35] which sums up as well as anything the attitudes of the humanists of the eleventh century. They wanted a Christian society, in which they could participate and to which they could contribute their particular wisdom. They did not want the distortions that mysticism produced. Michael Psellus was willing to accept that a holy man might have special powers. He even expressed qualified approval of mystical knowledge, which 'proceeding by the way of unknowing penetrates to God who is beyond nature'[36] but he could not countenance the notion that it was the only foundation of a Christian life. It was intrinsically selfish. It offered little to society at large. It seemed to place a barrier between church and society. It upset the natural order.

Like all educated Byzantines, Psellus was much concerned with order. The threat to order presented by mysticism was paralleled in his mind by the collapsing order of society. He blamed it in the first instance on the Emperor Constantine Monomachos's willingness to ignore social distinctions:

[32] Psellus (ed. Kurtz/Drexl), II, no.194, 221.1–4.
[33] Christopher of Mitylene (ed. Kurtz), no.50, 30.
[34] Ibid, no.27, 15–16;no.43, 26;no.100, 63.
[35] Ibid, no.114, 77.40–1.
[36] Psellus (ed. Kurtz/Drexl), II, 59.12–24.

> There is, of course, in the political world (*demos*) a cursus honorum and rigid rules governing promotion. These he [Constantine Monomachos] reduced to confusion, abolishing the rules. He made nearly all the riff-raff of the market members of the senate. He granted this favour not to just a few, but at a stroke the whole lot were raised to the proudest offices.[37]

There is more than a little exaggeration. It also at first sight contradicts his objection to the way high office had been the preserve of members of the aristocracy, 'not able to belch forth anything except for their family's great name'.[38] That was just it. They did not merit advancement. It was education and merit which guaranteed a proper order in society. Psellus was acting as the guardian of the meritocratic ideal of the Byzantine bureaucracy. This was almost part of his responsibilities as Consul of the Philosophers, the new office created for him by Constantine Monomachos. His main duty was to oversee the schools and the schoolmasters of the capital.

In many ways, he was the schoolmaster writ large. The schoolmaster was essential to the Byzantine bureaucracy, not just because he provided the necessary education for potential civil servants. He also had an obligation to place his pupils in the bureaucracy. He did this by building up a network of contacts. He maintained his ties with his old pupils. One of the strongest bonds among civil servants was having the same schoolteacher, who continued to act as a mentor. It was not unlike the circles of disciples that grew up around famous holy men. Schoolmaster and holy man were not necessarily in competition, but they did represent rather different views of the ideal of a Christian society. Michael Psellus used his influence as Consul of the Philosophers to promote the careers of his pupils. As we have seen, there seems to have been a greater demand for education in the eleventh century than had been the case in the previous century. This was almost certainly to cater for the sons of *nouveaux riches*, for whom education was a passport to respectability. The balance within the elite was tilted towards those with strong humanist leanings. The heroes of a new generation were Michael Psellus and, increasingly, his successor as Consul of the Philosophers, John Italos.

Michael Psellus was a traditionalist, but he liked to pose as the man who had single-handedly revived the study of Platonic philosophy. This gave his political opponents a hostage to fortune. Michael Psellus found his orthodoxy coming under frequent scrutiny. The immediate cause was always likely to be political, but underlying this was the challenge that his humanism seemed to present to the Christian ideal espoused

[37] Michael Psellus, *Chronographie ou histoire d'un siècle de Byzance (976–1077)*, ed. E. Renauld (Paris, 1926–8; repr.1967), 2 vols., I, p.132 .15–21.

[38] Sathas, *MB* IV, 431.

by the Patriarch Michael Cerularius and, later, by the Patriarch John Xiphilinos. Both were champions of the autonomy of the church and the primacy of mysticism. Michael Psellus was forced to make a profession of faith to the Emperor Constantine Monomachos towards the end of his reign. This may have been a device to protect him from the wrath of Michael Cerularius, who was not likely to forget that Psellus had been one of the emperor's main agents in the events of 1054.[39] Psellus always rejected the charge that he had been led astray by Hellenic wisdom. He claimed only to use it as an aid for the elucidation of the Christian faith. He made his position clear in a letter to a monk: 'If I can make a comparison between our God-given wisdom and Hellenic vulgarity, then the former I liken to a pure spring, bubbling up crystal clear from below and gently filling the thirsty soul with liquid; the latter I compare to a cloudy, undrinkable, brackish water, which flows fast and bears away the mind.'[40] He was deeply hurt by the Patriarch John Xiphilinos's charge that he preferred Plato to Christ: 'Plato is mine! I do not know how to bear the weight of this charge. Have I not in the past preferred the holy cross and now the monastic yoke?'[41] It was all the more painful because Xiphilinos had been a school friend; they had been comrades in arms as they carved out careers for themselves under Constantine Monomachos. Xiphilinos had been put in charge of the law school that the emperor had founded. But in the face of political difficulties he had preferred to retire to become a monk on Mount Olympus in Bithynia. So their paths diverged for a time. But Psellus was to be largely responsible for his appointment to the patriarchate of Constantinople in 1064.

Church and state under the Dovkai

Xiphilinos was a disappointment not merely to Psellus, but even more to the Emperor Constantine X Doukas. Their first meeting was not auspicious. The patriarch designate refused to make obeisance to the emperor or even converse with him. When at last he was induced to speak to the emperor, he made it plain that he was only accepting the patriarchal throne reluctantly and that he refused to be constrained by imperial authority.[42] Relations between patriarch and emperor were from the outset cool, but at the end of his life Constantine X Doukas found that he needed the patriarch's good offices to ensure the succession. The dying emperor called upon Xiphilinos to administer an

39 A. Garzya, 'On Michael Psellus' admission of faith', *EEBΣ* 35(1966), 41–6 (=A.Garzya, *Storia e interpretazione di testi bizantini* (London, 1974), no.VI).

40 Psellus (ed. Kurtz/Drexl), II, no.267, p.312.3–14.

41 Sathas, *MB*, V, 444.

42 Ibid, IV, 447–8.

oath to his consort, Eudocia Makremvolitissa. She bound herself not to marry again and to support the Doukas succession. The patriarch undertook to anathematise her should she break this oath. In the event, he would release her from this oath on the grounds that it was in the public interest which took precedence over any private agreements. Gossip had it that the patriarch had been tempted by the empress's apparent interest in a marriage with either his brother or his nephew.

Constitutional episodes of this kind are always exceptional, but the power both to administer oaths and also to offer release from them gave the patriarch a central political role.[43] It emphasised the patriarch's moral authority. The role of the patriarch as the guarantor of the succession through the administration of oaths was to have a future in Byzantine constitutional history.

Xiphilinos worked to strengthen the power of the church. Michael Psellus reported without further details that this was the cause of friction with the Emperor Constantine Doukas.[44] Perhaps he had in mind a case which came before the emperor over clerical precedence. It concerned the rank of *synkellos*. This was an imperial dignity originally granted to one specially favoured ecclesiastic, who was expected to act as a go-between for the emperor and the patriarch. In 1029 the Emperor Romanos Argyros raised three metropolitan bishops to the rank of *synkellos*. After some heated objections they were able to impose their right of precedence over their colleagues irrespective of the ranking of their sees. After this it became more and more common for such appointments to be made, so that by the middle of the eleventh century it was necessary to create the superior rank of *protosynkellos*. Those metropolitan bishops who were not so honoured continued to object to the precedence accorded to their more fortunate colleagues. In 1065 they took their case before the Emperor Constantine Doukas. He ruled that since these were imperial honours they could only bring precedence at the imperial court; they could have no bearing on ecclesiastical ranking.[45] This might well be taken as imperial capitulation in the face of clerical criticism that an emperor had no right to interfere in ecclesiastical matters. In that case, as V. Grumel observed, is it not a little odd that Xiphilinos did not intervene directly with the emperor? There is no sign that the patriarch supported the metropolitans when they took the case before the emperor. The inference is that it suited the patriarch to have a group of metropolitans raised above the others by virtue of an honour accorded by the emperor.[46]

43 N. Oikonomidès, 'Le serment de l'impératrice Eudocie (1067). Un épisode de l'histoire dynastique de Byzance', *REB* 21(1963), 101–28.

44 Sathas *MB* IV, 450.

45 Rhalles & Potles V, 275.29–32.

46 V. Grumel, 'Les métropolites syncelles', *REB* 3(1945), 92–114.

Why this should have been the case has remained a matter largely of speculation, but one which has centred on the role of the patriarchal synod. Its importance grew over the eleventh century.[47] It became the main instrument of patriarchal government. It stands to reason that the patriarch needed a permanent core of metropolitan bishops on whom he could rely. It was also the case that a metropolitan bishop holding rank at court was more likely to be present in Constantinople and able to attend the meetings of the synod more regularly than those not so honoured. From a practical point of view it must have been useful for these metropolitan bishops to have access to the imperial court. It might be supposed that the growing numbers of metropolitan bishops who enjoyed the imperial dignity of *synkellos* or *protosynkellos* represented greater imperial influence in ecclesiastical affairs. In that case, the decision reached by the Emperor Constantine Doukas in favour of those metropolitan bishops who did not enjoy imperial honours is decidedly odd. Far from being a sign of imperial influence over the church the lavish distribution of imperial honours to prelates – as with the inflation of honours generally – is likely to have been an indication that emperors were losing authority. It looks more like an attempt to win patriarchal support at a time when successive emperors were badly in need of the moral backing of the church. The increasing numbers of *synkelloi* and *protosynkelloi* may well represent a growth of patriarchal influence at the imperial court. On this reading, Constantine Doukas's decision was an attempt to end the confusion between imperial and ecclesiastical dignities, which was working to the detriment of imperial authority. This case emphasises the need there was to redefine the respective spheres of authority of emperor and patriarch.

By the late eleventh century the balance of power seemed to favour the church. The imperial regime of Michael VII Doukas established in the aftermath of the defeat at Mantzikert in 1071 made two scarcely precedented appointments. The chief minister was to be John, metropolitan bishop of Side, while Michael, metropolitan bishop of Neokaisareia, was put in charge of the finances of the state and appointed *sakellarios*. The imperial government clearly needed the support of the church to help it through a period of crisis. Once this had passed John of Side was replaced as chief minister by the logothete of the drome, Nikephoritzes. But the power of the church was apparent from the way the clergy were the centre of opposition to Nikephoritzes. The lead was taken by the exiled patriarch of Antioch, Aimilianos, and by the metropolitan

47 P.J. Hajjar, *Le Synode permanent (synodos endemousa) dans l'eglise byzantine des origines au XIe siècle* (Orientalia christiana analecta 164)(Rome 1962), 179–84;H.-G. Beck, 'Kirche und Klerus im staatlichen Leben von Byzanz', *REB* 24(1966), 1–24.

of Ikonion. Their prominence can be explained by the death of John Xiphilinos in 1075 and the succession of Cosmas to the patriarchal throne. He was deliberately chosen by the emperor for his piety and his lack of worldliness.

If this appointment was made in the hope that it would defuse clerical opposition to Michael VII Doukas's regime, it failed. Nicephorus III Botaneiates was brought to power in 1078 largely through the action of the church in Constantinople. Even before the final overthrow of Michael VII Doukas Botaneiates had been acclaimed emperor in the church of St Sophia. There is no clear evidence as to whether or not he made any specific undertakings to his clerical backers. But John of Side was reinstated as chief minister.[48] Perhaps more than any other Byzantine emperor Nicephorus Botaneiates sought to rule as a constitutional monarch. This meant governing with the assent of the senate and the patriarchal synod. To give an example: in December 1079 Botaneiates issued a chrysobull reviving an old law of Theodosius II which prescribed a thirty days' delay before any capital sentence was carried out.[49] Specifically, it limited the emperor's arbitrary power by enacting that the previous emperor's relatives and servants could not be punished or have their property confiscated without due process of law. It also enjoined on the patriarch the duty of reminding the emperor in writing every four months about the existence of those who had been sentenced to exile, so that they would not be forgotten. The historian Michael Attaleiates who was a partisan of Botaneiates provides the detail that this chrysobull was read out before the senate for its approval. It also received the signatures of the patriarch and members of his synod and was deposited in the archives of St Sophia. In the body of the chrysobull the emperor made it plain that he had found it necessary to associate the patriarch and the synod in the framing of the act. It placed great stress on the emperor's humanitarian responsibilities. It was the duty of the patriarch and his synod to ensure that he did not neglect them.[50]

Nicephorus Botaneiates was trying to find a basis for renewed cooperation between church and state by recognising that imperial government needed the moral authority of the patriarch and synod. A further concession was to issue another chrysobull in January 1080. It confirmed certain synodal rulings over marriage originally promulgated under John Xiphilinos in 1066.[51] Why exactly they did not receive imperial approval there and then is not made clear. It might

48 Zonaras III, 725, 3–4 (ed. Bonn).
49 Dölger, *Reg.* 1047.
50 J.Gouillard, 'Un chrysobulle de Nicéphore Botaneiatès à souscription synodale', *B* 29/30(1959–60), 29–41.
51 Grumel, 896.

be supposed that the Emperor Constantine Doukas would have had reservations about the initiatives being taken by the patriarch in marriage law, which in the past was very largely a preserve of the civil law. We have the detail that when a case about marriage came before the patriarchal synod under John Xiphilinos the senators present left as a body.[52] Botaneiates, it would seem, was being deliberately conciliatory. His willingness to confirm ecclesiastical rulings by imperial chrysobull and to associate the patriarch and his synod in the framing of imperial legislation was an attempt to restore the old ideal of cooperation and harmony between emperor and church. It had always been the case that for general application the rulings of the patriarch and synod required imperial confirmation. This had normally worked to the advantage of the emperor. Now Botaneiates enunciated the general principle that it was valuable for the emperor to confirm synodal decisions, because it meant that he was participating in them.[53] In other words, he was prepared to confirm decisions already arrived at by the patriarch and synod. Add to this his willingness to recognise the patriarch's right of moral supervision over his conduct of government and it is easy to see how the balance between church and emperor had shifted markedly towards the former since the death of Basil II.

It was just one sign of the decline of imperial authority that had occurred since the middle of the eleventh century. Other indications were the way public rights were passing on an increasing scale into private hands. This undermined public authority. In the absence of effective public authority it was difficult to control those necessary adjustments and compromises – known to the Byzantines as *oikonomia* –which were vital for political stability. In the course of Byzantine history this process periodically broke down. The reasons varied, but in the eleventh century it seems to have been connected with the growing wealth and complexity of Byzantine society. This brought into the open the lack of harmony that characterised so much of the Byzantine polity. Often it stemmed from the unsatisfactory relationship between church and state. In the eleventh century a series of strong patriarchs sought to dominate the political process and to take control of society through the exercise of moral and spiritual leadership. The church came to exercise a greater degree of supervision over marriage. Still more striking were the efforts made to promote the notion that the clergy and monks were an elite set over lay society. Humanists riposted by idealising man as a social animal. This signalled a disagreement about the nature of a Christian society which turned on the respective roles of reason and inspiration. Who were to be the legislators of society? Humanists

52 Rhalles & Potles v, 53.11–13; Grumel, 897.
53 Rhalles & Potles v, 278; Dölger, *Reg.* 1048.

or mystics? This led on to the fundamental question of where did orthodoxy lie and to a reexamination of basic dogma. Uncertainty at the heart of orthodoxy helped feed a growth of a nonconformity and lay piety. This at times spilt over into heresy and seeped into monasteries.

Alexius I Comnenus seized power in April 1081. The problems he faced were daunting. His immediate task was to confront the enemies of the Empire. Almost as pressing were the divisions within church and society. These would have to be resolved, if Alexius was to have a chance of establishing a firm foundation to his rule. In one sense, he was fortunate. He did not have to face a powerful patriarch of the calibre of Cerularius or Xiphilinos. But the Patriarch Cosmas's lack of grasp created factions within the church that complicated any return to order. He preferred to shelve problems. He failed to give a lead over John Italos, Michael Psellus's successor as Consul of the Philosophers. John Italos had the backing of Michael VII Doukas and was therefore a target of the opposition. He was accused of introducing heretical concepts into his teaching. He tried to preempt his accusers by submitting some of his propositions anonymously to the synod. These were condemned as heretical. Italos next submitted a profession of faith to the patriarch who studiously ignored it. Here was a serious problem waiting for Alexius. Its solution would reveal much about his style of government. Would he continue Michael Doukas's patronage of a humanist, who applied reason to faith?

Of less immediate concern was the condition of the monasteries. They were the focus of a variety of interests. There was a reformist current that went back to the foundation of the monastery of the Theotokos Euergetis, and even before, but this sat uneasily with the growth of lay patronage in the shape of *kharistike*. There were signs of disquiet from the late 1070s about its repercussions on monasteries. Surprisingly they were first expressed by a member of the laity, who held a number of monasteries and even a nunnery in *kharistike*. This was the historian Michael Attaleiates. He recognised the disadvantages of *kharistike* the moment he came to organise his own pious foundation. His intention was that it should preserve his memory. If his family were ousted from control by some *kharistikarios*, there was the danger that his memory would be forgotten. But *kharistike* presented another and even greater threat: the family might lose control of the wealth which Attaleiates had tied up in his foundation. In other words, monasteries were treated as family trusts that had to be protected against interlopers in the shape of *kharistikarioi*. *Kharistike* set in relief the conflicting roles that monasteries had. They were at one and the same time vital to the functioning of the family and society and by definition set apart. Would Alexius be able to balance these contradictory features? The problems facing Alexius at the time of his accession reveal that Byzantium had lost its equilibrium. If it was to be restored Alexius needed to repair the relationships between church, state, and society at large. These had suffered over the previous half century.

PART II

EMPERORS AND PATRIARCHS

2

ALEXIUS I COMNENUS AND THE CHURCH

Introduction

AT the time of his coup Alexius I Comnenus is unlikely to have had any clear ideas about an ecclesiastical policy. His priorities were to establish his family in power, defend the Empire against its external enemies, and to reassert imperial authority. The day to day running of the imperial government he left in the hands of his mother Anna Dalassena, who did not intend to let the imperial prize slip out of her son's grasp. She had once before seen her family deprived of the imperial office when her brother-in-law Isaac I Comnenus was eased off the imperial throne in 1059. Her husband's reluctance to make a bid for power was a humiliation for a young woman who was both able and ambitious. After his death in 1067 Anna Dalassena took the veil.[1] She was deeply pious and became the patron of monks and holy men. She made sure that her son Alexius Comnenus was accompanied on his campaigns by a monk who acted as his confessor and spiritual adviser.[2] This connection added a dimension to the Comnenian regime, which should not be ignored. Alexius could count on support among the monks of the capital, even if he was on bad terms with the official church.

The young Alexius came to prominence under Michael VII Doukas at a time when the church of Constantinople dominated the political scene. His stance emerges from the advice he gave Michael VII Doukas in 1078 when faced with a coup masterminded by leading prelates. He urged the emperor to use force against his opponents, even though he must have known that many were clerics. The emperor failed to heed Alexius's advice. He preferred to abdicate rather than be the cause of unnecessary bloodshed. His action was applauded by the Patriarch Cosmas who ordained him and appointed him bishop of Ephesus. The

[1] Laurent, *Corpus*, v, 2 nos.1460–1.
[2] Anna Comnena I,viii,2: 42–3 (ed. Bonn); I, 32 (ed.Leib).

new Emperor Nicephorus Botaneiates was beholden to the church for his elevation to the imperial office. As we have seen, he was prepared to defer to ecclesiastical authority. Faced with Alexius Comnenus's bid for the throne he accepted the patriarch's advice that, like Michael VII, he should abdicate to prevent further bloodshed. This was a good example of the moral authority that even a meek patriarch, such as Cosmas, could exercise.[3]

Alexius did not owe the throne to the support of the church. Instead, he had to contend with its disapproval. He was taken to task almost at once by the Patriarch Cosmas and the patriarchal synod for the way he had allowed his supporters in the course of his coup to go on the rampage through the streets of Constantinople. He had to agree to submit along with members of his family to penances prescribed by the patriarch. Anna Comnena's description of the joy with which they acquitted their allotted penance does not quite disguise the humiliation it was.[4] Alexius retaliated by forcing the Patriarch Cosmas to resign and replacing him by Eustratios Garidas, who was one of those monks cultivated by Anna Dalassena. His main qualification was that he had foretold Alexius Comnenus's ascent to the imperial throne.[5] In other words, he had been a propagandist for the Comnenian cause. If he did not command much respect in the official church, his appointment suggests that the Comneni had strong support in monastic circles. This counterbalanced hostility to the Comneni on the part of the ecclesiastical hierarchy.

Confiscation of church treasures[6]

Once in power Alexius Comnenus proceeded to the confiscation of ecclesiastical treasures as the only way of financing his war against the Normans. He claimed to have previously consulted certain 'spiritual and pious men'.[7] They assured him, apparently, that, if he approached the matter in the right spirit, his actions would be justified. This could all have been a downright lie, but there were monks and holy men connected to the Comnenian entourage, men such as St Cyril Phileotes, from whom such an answer might have been expected. The utter failure of Alexius's campaign against the Normans in the autumn of 1081 left him open to attack from opposition that was growing to his rule in

[3] Ibid.,II,xii, 5–6: 131–2 (ed. Bonn); I 100–1 (ed. Leib); Michael Attaleiates (ed. Bonn), 303. 2–23; Nicephorus Bryennios, *Histoire*, ed. P. Gautier (Brussels, 1975), 247.11–22

[4] Anna Comnena, III, v, 1–6: 151–5 (ed. Bonn); I, 116–19 (ed. Leib).

[5] Ibid., III, ii, 7: 142–3 (ed. Bonn); I, 109–10 (ed. Leib).

[6] See A.A. Glavinas, *Η ΕΠΙ ΑΛΕΞΙΟΥ ΚΟΜΝΗΝΟΥ (1081–1118) ΠΕΡΙ ΙΕΡΩΝ ΣΚΕΥΩΝ, ΚΕΙΜΗΛΙΩΝ ΚΑΙ ΑΓΙΩΝ ΕΙΚΟΝΩΝ ΕΡΙΣ (1081–95)* (Thessalonica 1972).

[7] Zepos I, 303.

the official church. It was led by Leo, metropolitan of Chalcedon, a man who had both a popular following because of his reputation for piety and contacts in the highest ranks of society. These included Alexius's mother-in-law. She had reason to be suspicious of how honourable his intentions towards her daughter were.[8] Leo demanded that Cosmas should be reinstated.[9] He accused the new patriarch of conniving at the confiscation of church treasures and of even appropriating some for his own benefit. To Leo's way of thinking the patriarch was little better than an iconoclast. Alexius sought to protect the patriarch and defuse opposition by issuing a chrysobull in August 1082: he promised never again to confiscate the treasures of the church and to make amends as soon as times were more propitious.[10]

This did not put an end to Leo's campaign against the patriarch. His supporters put it about that Garidas dabbled in Messalianism. Alexius set up a commission composed of one metropolitan bishop and five officers of the church of St Sophia to investigate the charges inspired by Leo against the patriarch.[11] Although the patriarch was exonerated, he preferred to resign rather than face continuing pressure from Leo of Chalcedon and his supporters. Leo remained unappeased. He contended that Garidas had no right still to be remembered in the prayers of the church and that his name should be expunged from the diptychs. The new Patriarch Nicholas III Grammatikos (1084–1111)[12] and virtually all the metropolitan bishops rejected this demand out of hand. In an act of defiance Leo refused to concelebrate with them. He thus put himself into a state of schism, though he denied that this was so. He became more isolated, while Alexius's hand had been much strengthened by the death of his arch enemy, the Norman Robert Guiscard in 1085. The emperor was able to have Leo condemned in 1087 for making accusations against Garidas, which he was unable or unwilling to substantiate. Leo was sent into exile, but continued his opposition. He had supporters at court. The mother of the empress tried to intervene on his behalf, but Leo insisted that it was futile: 'How will men who have not spared God spare a man? The fact that he [Alexius Comnenus] has written to me that he has great trust in me and that the scandal is the work of evil men makes me laugh.'[13]

8 V. Grumel,'Les documents athonites concernant l'affaire de Léon de Chalcédoine', *Studi e Testi* 123 (1946), 127–30.

9 Ibid.,125–7.

10 Zepos I, 302–4; Dölger, *Reg.* 1085; see V. Grumel, 'L'affaire de Léon de Chalcédoine. Le chrysobulle d'Alexis Ier sur les objets sacrés', *EB* 2(1944), 126–33.

11 I. Sakellion 'Documents inédits tirés de la bibliothèque de Patmos. 1 Décret d'Alexis Comnène portant déposition de Léon, métropolitain de Chalcédoine', *BCH* 2 (1878), 113.

12 J. Darrouzès, 'L'éloge de Nicolas III par Nicolas Mouzalon', *REB* 46(1988),11–17.

13 Grumel, 'Les documents athonites', 127–30.

There was a story circulating that a priest of St Sophia had been vouchsafed the same vision of Leo on three separate occasions. He had seen him officiating in the Constantinopolitan church of St Euphemia wearing a royal robe and with a large golden circlet on his head. Leo was asked whether he was frightened that the emperor might get to hear of this. Not in the slightest came back the reply, because his defence of the things of God put him on a similar footing with the emperor. It was a story that probably originated among Leo's supporters. It portrayed him as a man in the tradition of those patriarchs who used their spiritual and moral authority to advance the power of the church. In changed circumstances, Leo was left to defend these interests against imperial power. It was a story that was amenable to a rather different interpretation by opponents. It left him open to ridicule for dressing up like an emperor and challenging the proper order of a Christian society.[14]

Often the most significant disputes are those that are hardest to resolve. This seems to apply to Leo of Chalcedon's protracted opposition to Alexius Comnenus. Other emperors, Heraclius for example, had confiscated church treasures in times of need without incurring the same censure. Though the controversy was dressed up with all kinds of implausible theological arguments, the underlying issue concerned the relationship of church and emperor. Leo was defending the autonomy of the church against imperial interference under any circumstances. He has recently been described as 'the original stimulus for a mighty reform movement that ultimately transformed traditional attitudes on the proper role of the laity in the administration of ecclesiastical property'.[15] This is a judgement that begs many questions. What mighty reform movement? Leo seems less an 'original stimulus' of some reform movement, much more the tail end of efforts to vindicate the autonomy of the church. He believed that this was a task that fell to the bishops, where the patriarch proved ineffective. This stance left him increasingly isolated. In the end, he was happy to be reconciled with the emperor at the synod of the Blakhernai in 1094. The solemnity and importance of the occasion was apparent from the attendance. Not only was the patriarch of Jerusalem present, but many metropolitan bishops, as well as the archbishop of Cyprus and his suffragans. Almost all the imperial house attended along with the major office holders. The synod produced a compromise over the theology of images which Leo was obliged to accept. Although he was treated with consideration, the outcome was a victory for Alexius Comnenus. It was evident that he had finally stamped his ascendancy over the church.[16]

[14] Ibid., 127.
[15] Thomas, *Private Religious Foundations*, 192.
[16] P.Gautier, 'Le synode des Blachèrnes (fin 1094)', *REB* 29(1971), 213–20.

The Patriarch Nicholas Grammatikos

It is natural to wonder how far Alexius's success was due to the understanding he had built up with the Patriarch Nicholas III Grammatikos. His patriarchate lasted for nearly thirty years – the longest on record in the Byzantine era. It provided the continuity necessary for carrying through what might be termed the Comnenian church settlement. It was to leave the Byzantine church administratively and structurally sounder, but far more clearly under imperial control than it had been for most of the eleventh century. It was a church settlement that seems almost to merit the description 'Caesaropapist'. Given the claims that had been made only slightly earlier for the autonomy of the church, this was an astounding reversal. Nicholas Grammatikos remains an enigmatic figure. He scarcely figures in the pages of the *Alexiad*, but he was not a cipher, eager to do the emperor's bidding. He refused to countenance the emperor's suggestion that he should return the pope's name to the diptychs without first obtaining a statement of faith from him.[17] He held Alexius to his promise enshrined in a chrysobull that he would never lay hands again on the treasures of the church.[18] He obtained at least on paper useful concessions from the emperor in matters of jurisdiction.

Nicholas was well equipped to be patriarch. He had received his education at the school of St Peter, which was one of the best Constantinopolitan schools. It was probably attached to St Sophia. He had then returned to his native city of Antioch in Pisidia, where he administered the church on behalf of the metropolitan bishop. Tiring of administration he tried the monastic life in the wastes of Cappadocia. Turkish raids forced him to seek refuge in the capital where he refounded next to the gate of St Romanos the monastery of Lophadion. He soon acquired a reputation for holiness, so much so that he figures in a miniature in a contemporary manuscript of the *Ladder* of St John, as famed for his chastity.[19] His election to the patriarchal office was contested, so that Alexius Comnenus had recourse to the drawing of lots. Nicholas's nickname Theoprobletos – proposed by God – indicates that the manner of his election contributed to his reputation. He took his pastoral duties very seriously. His replies to questions of canon law put to him by provincial bishops and monasteries were appreciated and show a wealth of common sense. The bishop of Zeitounion in darkest Thessaly was disturbed by the masquerading that took place during wedding festivities. The patriarch advised that

17 Grumel, 954.
18 Sakellion, 'Documents inédits', 128, 5–8.
19 Darrouzès, 'L' éloge de Nicholas III', 11–17.

it was better that priests did not attend, but ended drily: if the bishop succeeded in putting an end to such things, then he would have his own reward.[20] Nicholas tried to ensure that the liturgy and fasts and festivals were properly observed. He was concerned to put an end to irregularities in the conduct of the clergy. For instance, they were demanding payment for the consecrated communion bread. He brought a sense of decorum to the life of the church by driving out of the churches of Constantinople rowdy bands of revellers who had turned services into Bacchic celebrations.[21] These measures were perhaps his main contribution to the restoration of ecclesiastical order after the troubles of previous years. They complemented and in one very important respect – the creation of an order of preachers to combat heresy [22] – anticipated the more dynamic work of the emperor. Whatever doubts the Patriarch Nicholas may have had about Alexius at the beginning of his patriarchate, he came to accept that emperor's claim to be a defender of orthodoxy was not only genuine, but also in the best interests of the church.

The trial of John Italos

The first step that Alexius made in this direction was the trial of John Italos for heresy in 1082. In a sense, it was unfinished business left over from the reign of Michael VII Doukas. John Italos had then been required to provide a confession of faith, but had not been exonerated. There can be little doubt that behind Alexius's actions in the affair was a high degree of political motivation. John Italos was closely involved in Michael Doukas's policy of rapprochement with the Normans – now the major threat to the Empire. He was of southern Italian, if not Norman, parentage. He was also at the centre of a humanist circle drawn from the old civil service families. This fed Alexius's suspicions, for it was from exactly this quarter that he expected the bitterest opposition to his still shaky regime. Very much under the influence of his mother and her devotion to monastic piety Alexius had little or no sympathy with Italos's brand of humanism[23] and identified it as one of the currents of thought that had been undermining orthodoxy. It did not take Alexius long to appropriate as part of his own programme of reform an idea that was as deeply rooted as any in Byzantine political

[20] E. Papagianne and Sp. Troianos, 'Die kanonischen Antworten des Nikolaos III. Grammatikos an den Bischof von Zeitunion', *BZ* 82(1989), 234–50, at 237.64–8; J. Darrouzès, 'Les responses de Nicolas III à l'évêque de Zeitounion', in *ΚΑΘΗΓΗΤΡΙΑ. Essays Presented to Joan Hussey*, ed. J. Chrysostomides (Camberley, 1988), 327–43, at 302–3.

[21] Darrouzès, 'L' éloge de Nicholas III', 48–50.

[22] Ibid., 50–3.

[23] Cf. Anna Comnena v, viii, 3: II 34 (ed.Leib)

thought: that a strict adherence to orthodoxy was essential for a healthy polity.[24] His most brilliant stroke was to time John Italos's condemnation for heresy with the feast of Orthodoxy, which fell each year on the first Sunday of Lent. It celebrated the victory over iconoclasm in 843. Each year on that day the *synodikon* of Orthodoxy was read out. It was a statement of faith anathematising the many heresies that had troubled the church from its earliest days. It culminated in the condemnation of iconoclasm. Down to the beginning of Alexius's reign the document had remained more or less unchanged.[25] Alexius altered this by having new *anathemata* condemning Italos's teachings added to the *synodikon.* As his reign progressed and there were more trials for heresy, so more *anathemata* were added to the *synodikon.*

It may be that originally Alexius exploited the feast of Orthodoxy in a purely opportunistic way, but he discovered that it served the purpose of underlining his claim to be the defender of orthodoxy. The addition of new *anathemata* to the *synodikon* gave new impetus and meaning to orthodoxy, for there had been a danger for some time that it might either become fossilised or lose its coherence. This was very largely because of the increasing estrangement from the papacy. Without papal consent and participation there could be no general council of the church. In the past this body had provided authoritative answers to the various problems exercising the church. The general council provided a mechanism that kept orthodoxy up to date: a most unorthodox thought that would have horrified Byzantines. But, in retrospect, it is easy to identify, as one of the strengths of orthodoxy, the way that it was continually being reshaped within a fairly well-defined framework provided by the teachings of the Fathers of the church and the acts of the general councils. Without recourse to a general council of the church it was necessary to make do with *ad hoc* rulings such as the Tome of Union (920) on the question of a fourth marriage.

Until Alexius Comnenus's reign the *synodikon* of Orthodoxy remained identified with victory over iconoclasm and the early heresies of the church. Alexius's use of the *synodikon* provided something which had been lacking: an authoritative statement of orthodoxy, or rather, since it was in the shape of *anathemata,* of what orthodoxy was not. This fitted well with the apophatic tradition in Byzantine

24 Th. Uspenskij, 'Deloproizvodstvo po Ioanna Itala v eresi', *IRAIK* 2(1897), 33.4 (= J. Gouillard, 'Le procès officiel de Jean l'Italien. Les actes et leurs sous-entendus', *TM* 9(1985), 139.35)

25 Between 1052 and 1082 an *anathema* was added to the *synodikon* of Orthodoxy against Gerontios of Lampe, who claimed to be the Messiah. Nothing is known of the circumstances, but it was a precedent that Alexius would exploit systematically. See Gouillard, 'Le synodikon de l'orthodoxie', 57.

theology, but must have imbued orthodoxy with a more negative outlook.

The attack on John Italos seems to have originated with the emperor's brother, Isaac Comnenus. After a preliminary examination Italos was passed on to the Patriarch Eustratios Garidas for further investigation before synod. Italos was confident that he would be exonerated. He arrived at St Sophia for examination, surrounded by his pupils and furnished with relevant texts. It was commonly supposed that the patriarch himself was favourably disposed to Italos.[26] Before synod could pronounce the emperor or his agents set the mob to work. They broke into the council chamber within the patriarchal church, where the proceedings were being held. They hunted Italos down. He only escaped by hiding on the roof of St Sophia.

The Constantinopolitan mob was a significant factor in the politics of the eleventh century. It had tended to support the patriarchs of Constantinople against the emperor. That Alexius was able to bring the mob on to his side marked a shift not only in the balance of power on the streets of Constantinople, but also in public opinion. How he managed it remains a mystery, because so little is known about the workings of the mob in Constantinople. The experience of the eleventh century suggests that the mob responded most eagerly to calls to protect orthodoxy or dynastic legitimacy. It would seem that at least on the streets of his capital Alexius succeeded in using the Italos affair to win recognition for his stance as the defender of orthodoxy.

Thoroughly intimidated the patriarch handed over the investigation to the emperor. He convened an assembly in the palace. It consisted of a group of bishops, officers of the patriarchal church, and court dignitaries. It carried out a detailed examination of the profession of faith submitted by John Italos, which did not stand up to scrutiny. It was riddled with misunderstandings. Italos was guilty of Arian and Sabellian formulations. The members of the assembly also detected the underlying influence of the Neoplatonic philosophers Iamblichus and Proclus. John Italos was happy to admit his mistakes. He anticipated eventual rehabilitation. Suddenly ten new charges were brought against him. Italos was taken by surprise. There was no proper examination. Italos admitted the truth of nine of them. It seems that these were propositions culled from his writings and lectures that synod had condemned some six years earlier when Italos had submitted them anonymously.[27] They

[26] Anna Comnena v,ix 5–6: 265–6 (ed. Bonn); II 39–40 (ed.Leib); Gouillard 'Le procès officiel de Jean l'Italien', 142–5. Cf. J. Gouillard, 'Une lettre de (Jean) l'Italien au patriarche de Constantinople', *TM* 9(1985), 175–9, for evidence of John Italos lobbying the patriarch's support.

[27] On the trial of John Italos, see Gouillard, 'Le synodikon de l' orthodoxie', 188–202; Gouillard, 'Le procès officiel de Jean l'Italien'. Also P.E. Stephanou, *Jean Italos.*

included such notions as the preexistence and transmigration of souls, and the eternity of matter. He was also accused of applying Hellenic wisdom to Christian dogma. These formulations 'crammed with Hellenic ungodliness' formed the basis for the *anathemata* included in the *synodikon* of Orthodoxy. On the feast of Orthodoxy which fell in 1082 on 13 March Italos was publicly condemned. He abjured his errors, almost certainly from the pulpit of St Sophia. He was then confined to a monastery.[28] But this was not enough.

There was a vindictive strain to the attack on Italos. The tenth of the new charges brought against him was trumped up. He was accused of stoning an icon of our Lord. It fitted neatly with a major theme of the feast of Orthodoxy: the triumph over iconoclasm. Italos strenuously denied this charge. This was in contrast to his stance over the other accusations. Leaving aside the justice of these charges, it is obvious that they were intended to widen the attack on Italos into an attack on his humanist teaching. This in turn implicated his pupils, who became another of the emperor's targets.[29] Like their master they were forbidden to continue teaching.[30] Some came from great civil service families, such as the Soloman, the Iasites, and the Serblias,[31] who were the centre of potential opposition to the Comnenian regime. Others were deacons of St Sophia. It was suspected that Italos's humanist views had infected members of the episcopal bench and the clergy of St Sophia.[32]

In the monastic circles cultivated by the Comneni there was at this time a distrust of the patriarchal clergy. The *Life* of Cyril Phileotes – a holy man chosen by the Comneni to be a spiritual guide – has the story of a hesychast monk of Constantinople who had a vision of devils disguised as deacons of St Sophia.[33] Alexius pressed home his attack against the patriarchal clergy. He ordered the patriarch to investigate John Italos's pupils. Any of the episcopal bench or the patriarchal clergy who persisted in criticising the actions of the emperor in the Italos case were to be placed under *anathema*. On 11 April 1082 the patriarch summoned five deacons of St Sophia who had been pupils

Philosophe et humaniste (Orientalia christiana analecta 134) (Rome 1949), 63–80; L. Clucas, *The Trial of John Italos and the Crisis of Intellectual Values in the Eleventh Century* (Munich 1981); G. Podalsky, *Theologie und Philosophie in Byzanz* (Byzantinisches Archiv 15) (Munich, 1977), 75–7, 114–16.

28 Uspenskij,'Deloproizvodstvo', 38–41 (= Gouillard, 'Le procès officiel de Jean l' Italien', 140–5); Anna Comnena, v,ix, 5–7: 265–6 (ed. Bonn); II, 39–40 (ed. Leib).

29 Uspenskij,'Deloproizvodstvo', 36.7–9 (= Gouillard, 'Le procès offciel de Jean l' Italien', 141.80–2).

30 Ibid., 57–8 (= ibid., 155, 359–66).

31 Anna Comnena, v, ix, 2: 263.6–8 (ed. Bonn); II, 37.19–21 (ed. Leib).

32 Uspenskij, 'Deloproizvodstvo ', 36.13–16 (= Gouillard, 'Le procès officiel de Jean l' Italien ',141.84–7).

33 Cyril Phileotes, 42, 195–206.

of Italos to explain themselves before synod. One by one they insisted that they had never shared their master's beliefs and they were cleared. What is more they were allowed to go on teaching: this despite the earlier imperial ruling which was held only to apply to other unnamed pupils of Italos.[34] One of the five deacons exonerated was Eustratios. He would later be promoted metropolitan bishop of Nicaea and become the emperor's chief religious adviser.

The rehabilitation of the deacons of St Sophia but not of Italos's other pupils had profound implications. Here was a basis for compromise which pointed to future cooperation between Alexius and the clergy of St Sophia. Among other things, it rested on an understanding that the defence and elucidation of the intellectual foundations of orthodoxy was essentially the work of the patriarchal clergy. It was a way of guarding against the indiscriminate and inexpert application of philosophy to theological questions which had characterised Italos's teaching. Christian humanism increasingly became the preserve of the patriarchal clergy and bishops drawn from their number.

The emperor, the clergy of St Sophia and the bishops

Alexius's attack on Italos nevertheless showed how vulnerable the clergy of St Sophia were. Their numbers had almost certainly grown with the more frequent and more lavish services celebrated in St Sophia from Constantine Monomachos's reign onwards.[35] Their role as teachers had also expanded, but their position remained uncertain and was increasingly overshadowed by the metropolitans and bishops who flooded into the capital to escape the Turkish inroads into Asia Minor. These looked to the patriarchal synod as a forum in which to assert themselves. They added to the ferment in the capital with their demand for livings and preferment. Their presence in Constantinople on a permanent basis contributed to the changing character of the synod. It was no longer an assembly called at irregular intervals, but one that was becoming responsible for much of the day to day administration of the church.[36]

The clergy of St Sophia only began to feature that prominently in the affairs of the church under Alexius. The clearing of the five deacons of St Sophia of complicity in the teachings of John Italos prepared the way for an understanding between the emperor and the patriarchal clergy.

34 Uspenskij 'Deloproizvodstvo', 64–6 (= Gouillard, 'Le procès officiel de Jean l'Italien', 159–61).

35 N. Oikonomidès, 'The mosaic panel of Constantine IX and Zoe in St Sophia', *REB* 36(1978), 219–32.

36 Darrouzès, *Ecclésiologie* 208–37; V. Tiftixoglu, 'Gruppenbildungen innerhalb der Konstantinopolitanischen Klerus während der Komnenenzeit', *BZ* 62(1969), 25–31.

This alliance was to be a new factor in ecclesiastical politics. As V. Tiftixoglu has convincingly shown, it helps to explain the apparently effortless ascendancy that Alexius was able to exercise in ecclesiastical affairs. His understanding with the clergy of St Sophia was dictated by a common opposition to the role that the metropolitan bishops were assuming within the church. It seems to have been reached almost over the head of the patriarch, who found himself caught between the claims of his clergy and those of the synod.[37]

The alliance between the emperor and the patriarchal clergy was forged over a case brought before the emperor in 1084 by Nicetas, metropolitan of Ankyra.[38] It concerned a former suffragan bishopric of his church which had been raised to metropolitan status some years before by the Emperor Constantine Doukas and had consequently been removed from the jurisdiction of his see. It was a case that was of some interest to other metropolitans who had suffered likewise. The patriarchal clergy had no desire to see the imperial decision reversed. Appointments were now made in Constantinople and its members could presumably influence the election. The emperor thought that the existing position over the see in question should stand, but sent the case to the patriarch and synod for a final decision. Three times the patriarch assembled the synod and three times it was broken up by the clergy of St Sophia, who feared that the patriarch and synod would side with Nicetas of Ankyra and reverse the decision. The patriarch confessed that many had been urging him to oppose Nicetas's request in the interests of the patriarchal church. Not knowing where to turn he sent the case back to the emperor, but he appended his own opinion of the matter. It was to the effect that he was opposed to the emperor's intervention in the affair, because the suffragan church had been raised to metropolitan status in a manner that had contravened canon law. Expediency, he insisted, ought never to prevail against the canons. The patriarch's stubbornness delayed a settlement of the case until 1087. The emperor then decided with the grudging assent of the patriarch and synod that questions of precedence and promotion within the ecclesiastical hierarchy came within the emperor's competence. What was more, the emperor was no longer bound by canon 12 of the council of Chalcedon. This laid down that a metropolitan bishop should keep the ancient rights that his church had over any suffragan see that had been promoted to metropolitan status. Especially galling for the metropolitan bishops was the rider that election to such sees should lie with the patriarch alone and that metropolitans should have no

37 Tiftixoglu, 'Gruppenbildungen', 58–9.
38 Dölger, *Reg.* 1117.

part in the appointments made to newly promoted sees.[39] Nicetas of Ankyra protested, quoting John of Damascus to the effect that 'it is not the business of emperors to legislate for the church'.[40] It was not just that the emperor was imposing his will upon the church in defiance of the canons. The emperor was now empowered to intervene in cases of disputed elections to newly promoted sees and the final decision was his.

It is clear from Nicetas of Ankyra's writings that more was at issue than just the question of the emperor's control of the organisation of the church. It also involved the place of the metropolitans within the church and their relationship with the patriarch. The metropolitans increasingly identified their interests with those of the patriarchal synod. Attendance on a regular basis meant that they were forced to neglect the welfare of their churches. Absence in the capital meant few opportunities to hold their own synods. To make good this deficiency Nicetas proposed that they should hold their synods, not in their dioceses, but at Constantinople. This would allow them to remain in the capital with an easier conscience and to participate in the work of the patriarchal synod. Nicetas was aware that the character of synod was changing as a result of the alliance that was being created between the emperor and the clergy of St Sophia. Synod was less and less able to voice the concerns of the metropolitan bishops. Nicetas was particularly worried about the dangers to their position produced by the increasing centralisation of the church for administrative purposes. He saw it as favouring an extension of the rights of the patriarchal church at the expense of the metropolitans and the bishops. He was violently critical of what he took to be the patriarchal usurpation of episcopal rights over monasteries. He disputed the patriarch's 'right to usurp whatever monastery through *stauropegia*'.[41] Nicetas was referring to the increasingly common practice of founding or refounding monasteries in the name of the patriarch, with the result that they depended directly on the patriarchal church, while the rights of the local bishop were excluded.

Nicetas suspected that behind these developments lay the example of Rome. He knew, as well as anybody, that the patriarch of Constantinople had been accorded the rights of the pope of Rome, but this should not be used as a pretext for any extension of patriarchal rights. Quite the contrary, in Nicetas's opinion, for the pope was known to respect local synods and did not seek to usurp their functions. He was trying to counter arguments based on the Donation of Constantine that

39 Ibid., 1140; Grumel, 938, 943.
40 Darrouzès, *Ecclésiologie*, 234–44.
41 Ibid., 208–37.

just as the pope enjoyed paramount authority over the church in the West, so should the patriarch in the East.[42]

The Patriarch Nicholas Grammatikos had sympathy with Nicetas's stand against imperial interference and even with his criticism of the growing power of the patriarchate, for it did not necessarily benefit the patriarch himself. He must have been alarmed at the growing power of the officers and clergy of St Sophia, now that they had the backing of the emperor. The patriarch might easily become a cipher in their hands. The canonist Theodore Balsamon would later argue that the day to day running of the church was far too mundane a business for the patriarch. It was much better left in the hands of the officers and clergy of his church, so that the patriarch could fulfil his spiritual and pastoral role. This never quite happened under Nicholas Grammatikos, but his deep devotion to the pastoral side of his responsibilities suggests that it was beginning to. The privileges accorded to Rome would be used by the officers and clergy of St Sophia to buttress their position.

Nicetas of Ankyra's stand was ineffectual. All he could do was to resign his see in protest.[43] Criticism of the emperor continued into the 1090s in the shape of John of Oxeia, the future patriarch of Antioch, but it failed to ignite any concerted action on the part of the episcopal bench. It may even have been welcomed by Alexius as a way of ventilating dissatisfactions. Given the strength of opposition at the beginning of Alexius's reign its failure demands an explanation. It was not only the rift between the bishops and the patriarchal clergy which Alexius was able to exploit. It was much more that the refugee metropolitans and bishops discovered that they were staying in Constantinople on sufferance. They relied heavily on the patriarch and the emperor for their incomes. Perhaps this explains why Leo of Chalcedon was able to defy the emperor: his see possessed the rich church of St Euphemia in Constantinople. This gave him a degree of financial independence. John of Oxeia found himself in a weak position when the monks of the Constantinopolitan monastery of the Theotokos Hodegoi successfully challenged the rights of patronage he thought he possessed, as patriarch of Antioch, over their monastery.[44]

Refugee metropolitans and bishops sought to acquire livings of various kinds. The monasteries of Constantinople and the surrounding region provided some with corrodies; others settled down as monks, a few succeeded in becoming abbot or steward of a monastery. The parish churches of the capital had some positions to offer; more lucrative was the patriarchal church, to which some of the refugees aspired.

42 Ibid., 218–20.

43 Ibid., 260–5.

44 P. Gautier, 'Jean V l'Oxite, patriarche d'Antioche. Notice biographique', *REB* 22(1964) 146–57.

Among those fortunate enough to find a niche in Constantinople there was little desire to abandon the comforts of the capital for the trials and tribulations of their sees. That was their duty, however. Hanging over them was the threat that they might be compelled to return. Using his discretionary powers Alexius intervened, allowing them to keep their Constantinopolitan livings until such times as were propitious for a return to their sees in Asia Minor. They were now very much in the emperor's debt. He did, however, make one significant exception: they were not to hold any position within the patriarchal church. Alexius had no intention of allowing metropolitans and bishops to infiltrate the patriarchal clergy. It is unlikely that the latter would have been very happy if he had allowed this. He may only have been acceding to their wishes.[45] Alexius also sought to divide the refugee Anatolian bishops from their colleagues in the West. He was critical of the latter. Unlike the Anatolian bishops they were not faced with a ravening enemy. Yet they neglected their flocks by preferring to remain in the capital.[46]

The episcopal bench therefore found itself in a false position which the emperor was able to exploit. In addition, its complexion was changing. The old guard appointed before Alexius came to power was dying off. The emperor was able to influence appointments so that they were more to his liking. There was opposition from the metropolitan bishops. The emperor, in his turn, protested that they were using synod to exclude from consideration some of the ecclesiastical elite (*tines ton tes ekklesias logadon*), by whom were undoubtedly meant the well-educated clergy and teachers attached to the patriarchal church.[47] It was the emperor's intention to get members of the patriarchal clergy on to the episcopal bench, the better to control synod. The emperor presented service in the patriarchal church as a stepping stone to the episcopate.[48] In the long term this aim was realised. Increasingly the most prestigious sees went to members of the patriarchal clergy.

Imperial control over the patriarchal administration had been seriously weakened by the damaging concession made by Isaac I Comnenus, whereby appointment to the two chief offices of the patriarchal administration – the Grand Oikonomos and the Grand Skeuophylax – passed out of the hands of the emperor and into those of the patriarch. Alexius compensated for this loss by strengthening the role of the *chartophylax* of the Great Church, which remained an imperial appointment. He intervened to defend the privileges of this office. These had come under attack from the episcopal bench which had

45 Zepos I, 325–6; Dölger, *Reg.* 1172.
46 Zepos I, 360–1; Dölger, *Reg.* 1278.
47 Zepos I, 361; Dölger, *Reg.* 1278.
48 P. Gautier, 'L'édit d'Alexis Ier Comnène sur la reforme du clergé', *REB* 31(1973), 185.105.

the support of the patriarch.[49] The bishops disputed the right claimed by the *chartophylax* to take precedence over them in the ceremonies and processions conducted in the church of St Sophia. Despite a contrary opinion presented by the patriarch, the emperor ruled that the *chartophylax* was in the right because he was acting as the patriarch's deputy.[50] These questions of precedence were very much a matter of custom. Alexius therefore acted in August 1094 to put them on a proper legal basis by regulating them through an imperial directive (*prostagma*).[51] It was based on a legal definition (*orothesia*) supplied by synod. This represented a capitulation to imperial pressure on the part of the bishops. It was agreed that in the past the patriarchal administration was divided into five departments. Four of these - those of the Grand Oikonomos, the Grand Skeuophylax, the Grand Sakellarios, and the *epi tou sakelliou* – had fixed functions and responsibilities. Only the fifth – that of the *chartophylax* – presented problems. Besides his duties as the archivist and registrar of the Great Church, the *chartophylax* also served as the patriarch's deputy – Aaron to the patriarch's Moses. It was now accepted that as the patriarch's mouth, tongue, lips , and hand the *chartophylax* took precedence over all, including bishops and metropolitans. Admittedly, the canons indicated that a mere deacon should never take precedence over a priest, but for once this injunction did not apply, because the *chartophylax* was the patriarch's living image and the honours accorded to the image naturally went to the prototype. The right to appoint to the office of *chartophylax* provided the emperor with a means of exercising indirect control over the patriarchal administration. As the patriarch's deputy, the *chartophylax* supervised the day to day running of the patriarchal church, whence Alexius's special interest in the privileges of the office.

The understanding of Alexius with the patriarchal clergy was strengthened by the consideration he showed them. He singled them out as the chief instrument for the reform of the church which he envisaged in his edict of June 1107.[52] The edict was addressed to the patriarch and synod and the measures envisaged built on work that the patriarch initiated at the beginning of his patriarchate.[53] The invasion which the Norman Bohemond was threatening at exactly that moment is perhaps a less plausible background to the edict than the relatively recent series of heresy trials which had been presided over by the emperor. The most important of these was that directed against Basil the Bogomil and

49 Grumel, 970.

50 Zepos I, 359–60; Dölger. *Reg.* 1278.

51 J. Nicole 'Une ordonnance inédite de l'empereur Alexis Comnène I sur les privilèges du χαρτοφύλαξ', *BZ* 3 (1894), 18–20; Dölger, *Reg.* 1175.

52 Gautier, 'L' édit d' Aléxis Ier Comnène', 179–201; Zepos I, 351–9; Dölger, *Reg.*1236.

53 Darrouzès, 'L' éloge de Nicholas III',48–53.

his followers. The exact date is not recorded, but it started before the death of Alexius's brother, the *sebastokrator* Isaac, *c.* 1102.[54] According to the edict all had been in danger: episcopate, monks, and laity.[55] The emperor's diagnosis pointed to a failure to spread the word of God, because preaching had been neglected. The emperor therefore proposed to create an order of preachers (*diduskaloi*), who were to be attached to the patriarchal church. They were to be recruited in the first instance from the patriarchal clergy. It was made clear that success as a preacher would open up the way to promotion to bishoprics and office in the patriarchal administration. Failure would equally be a bar to promotion. Preachers might also be drawn from monks and even laity, should any fitting candidates present themselves. They could remain deacons, if they so desired, but there were strong inducements in the shape of significantly higher salaries and allowances to become priests. Furthermore, they were to rank in the hierarchy of the Great Church immediately after the officers of St Sophia. This is a measure of the importance that the emperor attached to this order of preachers. Given that this new order originated with the patriarch, Alexius's edict was a means whereby new developments within the church of St Sophia could be brought more closely under imperial supervision.

The task of the new order involved more than merely preaching. They were expected to exercise moral supervision over the neighbourhoods of the capital; they were to make themselves known by pastoral visits. In a sense, they were expected to make good that lack of a proper parish organisation in the capital. They were to raise moral standards by counselling or, in the more notorious cases, by reporting directly to the patriarch.

The success of the emperor's measure is problematical. No order of preachers of the kind envisaged in the edict can be traced. As an *ad hoc* measure Alexius used preachers drawn from the patriarchal church to combat the Bogomil heresy,[56] but this presumably relates to the period before the promulgation of the edict. The preachers or *didaskaloi* who appear in the twelfth century in some numbers appear to have had duties that were more academic than pastoral. Alexius's edict therefore seems to have been intended to meet a particular danger. The propaganda value that Alexius derived from it was another matter. It showed that he took due regard for his responsibilities as the guardian of the church and orthodoxy.

54 D. Papachryssanthou 'Le date de la mort du *sebastokrator* Isaac Comnène', *REB* 21 (1963), 250–5.

55 Gautier 'L' édit d'Alexis Ier Comnène', 183.67.

56 Anna Comnena, XV, ix,5: II, 360,14–17 (ed. Bonn); III, 225–6 (ed. Leib.).

Alexius I Comnenus and episcopal finances

Alexius was far more concerned with what was happening in his capital than he was with the provinces. There his hopes of raising moral standards rested with the bishop. There were few parish priests. Until such times as suitable candidates could be found, the emperor urged the bishops to go out into the highways and byways, preaching and making their pastoral rounds, not avoiding the huts of the poor. After all, it was for their pastoral work that they received the *kanonikon*. This was a tax now paid by both the clergy and the laity to the bishop. The payments made by the clergy to the bishop were in principle for their ordination and were regulated by the Patriarch Alexius the Studite, but nothing was said about the customary offerings made by the laity. It was left to the Emperor Isaac Comnenus to lay down a standard rate at which they were to be offered: a village of thirty households was to give one gold and two silver pieces, one ram, six bushels (*modioi*) of wheat, six measures of wine, six bushels of barley, and thirty hens. Smaller communities would pay proportionately less. The emperor was apparently only giving force to customary practices which were set out in old surveys (*praktika*) and in the master copy of the cadastre which was kept in the capital.[57]

In the confused conditions of the late eleventh century it must have been difficult to enforce such payments. In September 1100 Alexius confirmed the details of his uncle's measure.[58] The emperor's action was a source of some difficulty to the patriarch and synod, because there was nothing in canon law about the payment of *kanonikon* to the bishop by the laity.[59] They finally decided that there was no contradiction between the imperial chrysobull and canon law and were satisfied that it was yet another example of imperial concern for the welfare of the church. They were also able to point to the analogy of the Old Testament practice of offering the first-fruits to the Temple.

It is far from certain that bishops were ever able to extract the *kanonikon* at the rate laid down in the imperial chrysobulls. By the end of the twelfth century it had returned to being a customary payment at whatever the village or the family were willing to give.[60] Alexius was probably making a gesture towards the bishops at a time when difficulties with Leo of Chalcedon were coming to a head, but he did not thereafter entirely neglect the question of the *kanonikon*. About the year 1102 the emperor issued a *prostagma* empowering

57 Zepos I, 275–6; Dölger, *Reg.* 943–4.

58 Zepos I, 311–12; Dölger, *Reg.* 1127; A. Schminck, 'Zur Entwicklung des Eherechts in der Komnenenepoche', in *TO BYZANTIO*, ed. Oikonomidès, 561–2.

59 Rhalles & Potles V, 60–2; Grumel, 942.

60 Rhalles & Potles IV, 492.

Theophylact, archbishop of Ohrid, to collect the *kanonikon*.[61] He was close to Alexius and was very much one of the emperor's new men. Even allowing that Theophylact was likely to have enjoyed particular imperial consideration, Alexius had more than a passing interest in the financial well-being of the bishoprics of the Empire. Towards the end of his reign the metropolitan of Cyzicus drew his attention to the poverty of his see, one that ranked near the top of the episcopal hierarchy.[62] The previous incumbent had alienated the monasteries and monastic properties belonging to the church into the hands of lay patrons. As a result, the church was so poverty stricken that there were insufficient revenues to pay for the lighting of the cathedral church or for the conduct of church services. Alexius passed on this complaint to the patriarch and synod for action. In cases of need, it was decided, a metropolitan had a perfect right to repossess monastic property which had been alienated, along with any demesne properties (*autourgia*) of the church which had been granted away. The synod returned its decision to the emperor for confirmation and his attention. By the end of his reign the coolness that had previously existed between the emperor and the episcopal bench had disappeared. The bishops were convinced that Alexius had the best interests of the church at heart and were reconciled to the ascendancy that he exercised in ecclesiastical affairs.

The reality was that only with the support of the emperor and his agents did the bishops stand a chance of conducting their affairs effectively, let alone putting their finances on a reasonably sound footing. The near chaotic conditions that existed in the provinces for most of the late eleventh century meant that almost everywhere episcopal and metropolitan churches suffered losses of property, which were often considerable. In 1089 the archbishop of Athens appeared before the patriarchal synod complaining about the way his predecessor had surrendered properties belonging to his church into the hands of lay patrons. The synod decided, just as it was to do nearly thirty years later in the case of the church of Cyzicus, that need required the return of such properties. It was assumed that this would be supervised by the local imperial governor.[63]

The archbishop specifically argued for the return to his church of monasteries gifted to powerful laymen and bishops.[64] He cited the ruling of the patriarch Alexius the Studite to the effect that bishops receiving monasteries from their metropolitans should return them,

[61] Theophylact II, no.9, 156–9.

[62] Th. Uspenskij, 'Mnemija i postanovlenija Konstantinopol'skikh pomestnykh soborov', *IRAIK* 5(1900), 15–16; Grumel, 1000.

[63] Uspenskij,'Mnemija', 32–42; Grumel, 952.

[64] Uspenskij,'Mnemija', 39–40.

if the latter were in need.[65] But the ruling had nothing to say about the responsibilities of members of the laity who had received such gifts. Here one begins to touch on the problem of the *kharistike*, which was raised by the archbishop at the beginning of his submission to synod. He wanted to know if tenants guilty of damage to episcopal properties were subject to the rulings that applied to the *kharistikarioi* of monasteries and chapels.[66] The archbishop must have had in mind the spate of imperial and patriarchal rulings on the matter which had been coming out from 1084 onwards.[67] He hoped that they would provide episcopal property with more legal protection. In the event, synod failed to face the problem directly, but was content to indicate the protection that episcopal property already enjoyed.

Kharistike

There survives from the early years of Alexius Comnenus's reign a dossier on the condition of the monasteries. It consists of imperial and patriarchal rulings. Its very existence is proof of how serious a problem lay patronage of monasteries had become. As we have seen, it took the form of *kharistike*. This was the grant to a layman for the term of a single life, or several, of the administration of a monastery and its property. It was made by an appropriate authority, most often by an emperor, a patriarch, or a bishop. It could also be by a private individual or by a community that had rights over a monastery. Proper procedures were established, it will be remembered, by the Patriarch Alexius the Studite: grants of *kharistike* were not to be passed on to a third party; no woman was to be the patron of a monastery nor any man of a nunnery; all transfers of monastic property had to have the consent of the patriarch or of an appropriate bishop and were to be registered in their archives. Cases over *kharistike* were to go before the patriarchal synod and not before a civil court.[68] In the early years of Alexius Comnenus's reign *kharistike* continued to be a patriarchal responsibility. Patriarch Nicholas Grammatikos saw the need for a tightening

65 Grumel, 833.

66 Uspenskij, 'Mnemija', 33–4.

67 J. Darrouzès, 'Dossier sur le charisticariat', in *Polychronion Festschrift. Franz Dölger zum 75. Geburstag*, ed. P. Wirth (Heidelberg, 1966), 150–65.

68 The earliest document preserved in this dossier was an imperial rescript (*lysis*) of 1084 (Darrouzès, 'Dossier', no.3; Grumel, 931; Dölger, *Reg.* 1115) addressed to the Patriarch Eustratios Garidas. It approved the patriarch's request that all surplus property held by monasteries should pass to the patriarchal church. The background to this request must have been a fiscal survey. It would have shown up property for which monasteries, along with other landowners, were paying either no or insufficient tax. This was labelled by the assessors *perisseia* or surplus property and in normal circumstances escheated to the state. (N. Svoronos, 'Les privilèges de l'église à l'époque des Comnènes', *TM* 1(1965), 338–40.) It was now

up of procedures. It had come to his attention that *kharistikarioi* were taking up the patronage (*ephoreia*)[69] of the monasteries granted to them together with the administration of their properties, but were failing to register them. They were deliberately avoiding complying with the regulations laid down by the Patriarch Alexius the Studite. Their intention was to conceal the exact extent of their monasteries' rights, livestock, and seedcorn, the better to profit thereby. In January 1086 the patriarch therefore declared null and void any grants of *kharistike* made by the patriarchal administration unless they were registered in the *sekreton* or bureau of the patriarchal *sakellarios* within six months.[70]

The scale of the problem is apparent from a case that we have already examined. It was brought before the patriarchal synod in 1089 by the archbishop of Athens. We have seen how he outlined the plight of his church. He reported that it had been ruined by overgenerous grants to *kharistikarioi* made by his predecessor. Synod empowered him to drive them out or, if he preferred, to extract compensation for the damage done. He was reminded of the ruling of the Patriarch Alexius the Studite, whereby impoverished metropolitan bishops had a right to demand the return of prosperous monasteries previously under their control[71] .

To this point the patriarch was treating *kharistike* as a routine administrative matter. He relied in the main on the procedures established by Patriarch Alexius the Studite. It was not until 1096 that Nicholas Grammatikos set up a commission composed of deacons and officers of St Sophia to carry out a detailed survey of all the monasteries that came under his jurisdiction. This proved a thankless task because of the obstructionism of the *kharistikarioi.* They refused to allow members of the commission access, citing patriarchal documents which they had in their possession. It was therefore impossible to investigate abuses associated with lay patronage. It was suspected with good reason that in return for large payments *kharistikarioi* established who they liked in the monasteries under their control; that they shifted their monasteries to different sites without due authorisation and that on occasion they simply demolished them. Asked to make amends for damage done, patrons refused to accept that they had any case to answer. The members of the commission therefore turned in December 1096 to the emperor for help. They wanted guidance on specific points: did they

established that in the case of monastic property it was to go to the patriarchal church. It was a ruling that had nothing directly to do with *kharistike*, but it was an important concession, because it recognised that the supervision of monastic property was the responsibility of the patriarchal administration.

69 *Ephoreia* will be discussed below, pp. 333–7.

70 Darrouzès, 'Dossier', nos.2, 5. In 1094 this term was reduced to three months: ibid., no.1.

71 Uspenskij, 'Mnemija', 33–4.

have the right to enter any monastery administered by a lay patron? Could they recover for the benefit of the monastery gifts made to the patron by third parties? Did they have the power to investigate damage done by the patron to the monastery? Finally, were those enactments to apply which obliged the patron to ensure the monks' spiritual and material well-being?[72]

The emperor promptly returned an answer. It confirmed that the patriarch and his agents had the right to enter any monastery where they suspected that there were spiritual failings. Where lay patrons, or for that matter abbots, were guilty of trading in monasteries, they were to be dismissed. They were also to make good any losses incurred by monasteries during their stewardship. In addition, the emperor also considered the right of the patriarch to create corrodies (*adelphata*) in monasteries. He specified that they should be held within a monastery (*esomonitaton*) and should not be in the form of a pension drawn on the monastery (*exomonitaton*). They should only be granted to deserving cases: to refugee bishops or distressed members of the laity.[73] There seems to be some implied criticism of the patriarch, as though he had been abusing a lucrative source of patronage.

The strange thing is that corrodies were not a matter raised by the commission, but the harm they were doing to the fabric of monastic life had been considered by John of Oxeia in his tract against *kharistike*.[74] Were Alexius Comnenus's measures against *kharistike* a response to the criticisms of John of Oxeia? Such a possibility has usually been ruled out, if only because John of Oxeia seemed to include Alexius and his patriarch among those responsible for failing to halt the deteriorating condition of the monasteries.[75] John also dismissed a justification of *kharistike* in a way that was critical of the emperor.

[72] Darrouzès, 'Dossier', no.6.

[73] Zepos I, 346–8; Dölger, *Reg.* 1076.

[74] P. Gautier, 'Réquisitoire du patriarche Jean d'Antioche contre le charisticariat', *REB* 33(1975), 77–132, text 90–131. Gautier dates the tract to between 1085 and 1092 (ibid., 80–6). His *terminus post quem* is an earthquake mentioned in the text which Gautier identifies with an earthquake dated by Michael the Syrian to 1084/5 (ibid., 83 n.16). His *terminus ante quem* is John of Oxeia's departure to Antioch in 1092. However, John also records the devastations wrought by the Turks, Petcheneks, Cumans, and Franks upon the provinces of the Byzantine Empire (ibid., 585–7). The inclusion of the Cumans in this combination of enemies suggests a date after 1087, when they first impinge on Byzantine history (Anna Comnena VII, 1,1–2: I, 330–2 (ed. Bonn); II, 87–8 (ed. Leib)). However, the situation that John of Oxeia was here describing does not seem to be quite so bad as it was to become in the winter of 1090/1, when John delivered his two denunciations of Alexius Comnenus's government. Alexius's position then seemed untenable in the face of an alliance of the Petcheneks and Turks. His effective authority was reduced to little more than Constantinople (P. Gautier, 'Diatribes de Jean l'Oxite contre Alexis Ier Comnène', *REB* 28(1970), 1–55, text 18–55). It therefore seems reasonable to suppose that the tract against the *kharistike* was composed *c.*1087.

[75] Gautier,'Réquisitoire', 127.541–8.

Monasteries, so the justification went, stood in need of a patron to protect themselves against requisitions by the imperial administration. John's riposte was that requisitions were a matter for the emperor's conscience. If there were no requisitions, there would be no need for *kharistikarioi*. John of Oxeia went on to draw an analogy between the emperor and some archon who gets one of his servants to impose a charge on a poor freeman. Then, as if out of pity, the archon orders the peasant to become his serf, so that he will no longer have the threat of requisitions hanging over him.[76] This analogy would have been the more wounding for being apt commentary on the expedients to which Alexius's regime resorted. Finally, the tract against *kharistike* alludes to Alexius's seizure of church treasures at the beginning of his reign.[77] This, it will be remembered, was the starting point of Leo of Chalcedon's campaign against Alexius Comnenus. The possibility has therefore been raised that John of Oxeia's attack on *kharistike* was a continuation of Leo's struggle against the emperor. Both in their different ways, it is argued, were trying to vindicate the independence of the church.[78]

It is an attractive hypothesis, but one that suffers from the fact that there is more or less nothing to connect the two men. Their backgrounds and outlook were different. Leo of Chalcedon was a champion of the hierarchical church's autonomy and freedom from imperial interference. John of Oxeia numbered himself among 'the piteous monks'.[79] His tract against *kharistike* begins as a history of monasticism, if one designed to show the harm lay patronage was doing to the spiritual life of monasteries. He followed this tract with two denunciations of Alexius Comnenus's regime which date from the winter of 1090/1. He presented these as criticism offered out of concern for the emperor's spiritual and moral welfare. He assured the emperor that he was not an enemy. The emperor had never done him any harm. Far from it, he had been his benefactor.[80] John hints that before he became patriarch of Antioch he was one of the emperor's spiritual advisers, expected to tell him the truth.[81] His first denunciation was delivered in the form of a speech before the emperor and his court and was therefore presumably commissioned by the emperor. John made it clear at the outset that he would have many harsh things to say, but that his intention was to provide an explanation for the reverses suffered

76 Ibid., 117.369–76.
77 Ibid., 113.322–24.
78 Thomas, *Private Religious Foundations*, 186–213; J.P. Thomas, 'A Byzantine ecclesiastical reform movement', *Mediaevalia et Humanistica*, n.s.12(1984), 1–16.
79 Gautier 'Réquisitoire', 127.539.
80 Gautier 'Diatribes', 27.30–4.
81 Ibid., 19.27ff.

by Alexius and to offer moral guidance which might help Alexius to survive a critical moment of his reign. He again brought up Alexius's confiscation of ecclesiastical treasures and the treatment meted out to certain bishops,[82] but he was just as incensed by the sufferings inflicted by Alexius's government on society at large.[83] He was critical of the wealth lavished on the emperor's family, whom he blamed for the state's lack of resources. He reproached the emperor for allowing his relatives to 'become the greatest plague on the Empire'.[84]

John was echoing the general dissatisfaction there was at the time with Alexius's oppressive regime,[85] but this does not mean that he should therefore be identified as one of the emperor's opponents. His elevation to the patriarchal throne of Antioch suggests that he was close to the emperor. Antioch was of great importance to Alexius and he needed somebody that he could trust on the patriarchal throne. It was much the same at Ohrid, to which he appointed Theophylact at almost exactly the same time as John of Oxeia received Antioch. If we believe John of Oxeia, then he was a supporter of the Comneni, one of those spiritual advisers by whom Alexius Comnenus and his mother set such store. They were expected to voice unpalatable truths; they were expected to criticise.[86] John of Oxeia's tract on the *kharistike* therefore takes on new meaning in the sense that Alexius Comnenus was likely to take it seriously and to absorb its lessons. The emperor's state of mind at this time is revealed in a letter he sent to the *protos* of Mount Athos. He confessed himself a sinner. It was on his account alone that God allowed the descendants of Hagar to ravage all the way to Damalis opposite Constantinople.[87]

John of Oxeia's strictures against *kharistike* were dismissed out of hand by the canonist Theodore Balsamon. It was his opinion that 'no attention should be paid to the writings of John, late patriarch of Antioch, who was opposed to the grant of monasteries to private individuals and termed such business impiety'.[88] Modern historians have taken their cue from Balsamon and have been reluctant to accord much weight to John of Oxeia's tract against *kharistike*. It has been usual to assume that *kharistike* worked to the mutual advantage of both patron and monastery.[89] This would be very hard to prove one way or

82 Ibid., 33.1–12.

83 Ibid., 31.6–15; 32.16–28.

84 Ibid., 41.17–25.

85 Cf. Zonaras XVIII, 29, 19–28: III 766–7 (ed. Bonn).

86 Cf. Cyril Phileotes, 146–53, 215–35.

87 Ph. Meyer, *Die Haupturkunden für die Geschichte der Athosklöster* (Leipzig, 1894), 177.27–30.

88 Rhalles & Potles II, 614–15.

89 J.M. Hussey, *Church and Learning in the Byzantine Empire (867–1185)* (London, 1937), 158–81; P. Lemerle, 'Un aspect du rôle des monastères à Byzance: les

the other. There are occasional examples of monasteries suffering, as a result of being granted out in *kharistike*. The ancient monastery of St John Prodromos Phoberos was refounded in 1112, because it had been destroyed by *kharistikarioi*.[90] Admittedly rather later, in 1147, a minister of Manuel I Comnenus found the monastery of St Mamas, Symeon the New Theologian's old monastery outside Constantinople, reduced to two monks and on the point of dissolution. It was the victim of the greed of *kharistikarioi*, who had descended upon it, 'like ravening wolves'.[91]

It seems most unlikely that grants of *kharistike* were any more open to abuse under Alexius I Comnenus than they had been previously. However, John of Oxeia deemed them incompatible with the highest standards of monasticism. These required that a monastery be completely free from outside interests. Because of their connections with monastic circles both the emperor and the patriarch were likely to be sympathetic to the arguments set out by John of Oxeia. They did not legislate *kharistike* out of existence. They clamped down on abuses and extended patriarchal responsibility for the supervision of monasteries. Lay patronage, as we shall see, continued, but in different forms. *Kharistike* was scarcely a problem after the early twelfth century.[92]

This episode is instructive for being typical of Alexius Comnenus's church settlement. At first, he left the matter in the hands of the patriarch. He intervened when there was political capital to be made. His rescript of 1096 went rather further than merely offering the patriarch and his administration support. Quite independently, he tackled some of the abuses highlighted by John of Oxeia. His motives were complicated. There was some implied criticism of the patriarch, as we have seen. He was also genuinely attracted by John of Oxeia's ideas on the monastic life. They had the advantage that they did not necessarily go counter to the political and material interests of the emperor. *Kharistike* was an institution associated with the bureaucratic ascendancy that the Comneni had overthrown, rather than the military aristocracy that they brought to power. But even for a bureaucrat *kharistike* might have its drawbacks. We have only to recall Michael Attaleiates's agonising over the possibility that his new foundation might become the prey of *kharistikarioi*. An attack upon *kharistike* therefore allowed Alexius Comnenus to pose as the guardian and defender of the church. Piety

monastères donnés à des laics charisticaires', *Académie des inscriptions et belles-lettres*, Comptes Rendus 1967, 9–28; Thomas, *Private Religious Foundations*, 167–85.

90 *Noctes*, 51.

91 S. Eustratiades, 'Τυπικὸν τῆς ἐν Κωνσταντινουπόλει μονῆς τοῦ Ἁγίου Μεγαλομάρτυρος Μάμαντος', *ΕΛΛΗΝΙΚΑ* 1(1928) 257, 305.

92 Gautier, 'Diatribes', 41.17–25.

and self-interest were mixed in equal measure. Alexius and his family did much to promote the new wave of monastic piety. They were founders or refounders of several monasteries and nunneries. As so often in Byzantine history, such foundations were a way in which a ruling group could impress its stamp upon society. It was all the more successful because the Comneni were able to identify themselves with the currents of monastic reform espoused by John of Oxeia. Alexius may have been building on the work of the Patriarch Nicholas Grammatikos, but he was able to invest it with a moral purpose that increased the emperor's stature.

Comnenian piety and the Comnenian settlement

Without ever forgetting the political advantages to be gained, Alexius was motivated in his dealings with the church and with monasticism, in particular, by a deep piety and an even stronger sense of right order. Anna Comnena has nothing specific to say about her father's championing of the monastic life. She singles out instead his creation of the orphanage of St Peter and St Paul on the Acropolis of Constantinople.[93] This was a famous example of the exercise of imperial philanthropy. Its immediate purpose was to care for the needs of the poor and refugees whose presence on the streets of the capital contributed to the instability of Constantinopolitan society. Alexius's creation of a city within a city for them met this danger. It was one more demonstration of Alexius's desire to restore order to the Byzantine polity. Order is the key to his church settlement. He was concerned to establish clear divisions of authority. The church in Constantinople was to be the responsibility of the patriarchal clergy; bishops and metropolitans were not to interfere in the affairs of the capital, but to return to their sees and concentrate on their needs. Church and state were to keep to their separate spheres. Bishops were not to hold ministerial positions, as had happened before Alexius came to power.[94] The imperial court titles of *synkellos* and *protosynkellos* which had been granted to increasing numbers of metropolitans were now phased out.[95] Alexius reestablished clear guidelines over jurisdiction. Cases involving the clergy were to go before a metropolitan or a bishop, not before a civil court. If one of the parties happened to be a layman, then a joint tribunal would be set up with the proviso that, if the cleric was found guilty, he would be punished by the ecclesiastical authorities; if it was the layman, by the local imperial governor. The principle

93 Anna Comnena, XV,vii,1–9: II, 345–50 (ed. Bonn); III, 213–18 (ed.Leib).
94 Beck, 'Kirche und Klerus', 1–24.
95 Grumel, 'Les métropolites syncelles', 92–114.

was enunciated that all cases involving spiritual matters, including matrimonial disputes, were to be heard before the church courts.[96] The corollary of this was that monks and clerics were forbidden by the patriarchal synod from pleading as barristers in the civil courts, except in those cases where the church was involved.[97]

Alexius's church settlement was presented as though it was simply a return to some preexisting order that had been lost because of slack government and lax faith, but this is the way in which many radical reforms are carried through. How radical, in other words, was Alexius's church settlement? Most striking was the ascendancy that he established over the Byzantine church. Rarely, perhaps never before, did the Byzantine church tolerate so great a degree of imperial intervention and control, as it did under the Comneni. This was made possible by the understanding that Alexius built up with the patriarchal clergy. They became a force within the church. The role of the patriarch, so powerful in the eleventh century, was diminished, as the administrative duties of the office were increasingly taken over by the *chartophylax*. Nicholas Grammatikos set the example of a patriarch who busied himself with pastoral duties and concerned himself with the proper conduct of church services. When he intervened to tighten up discipline among the patriarchal clergy, who were for various reasons absenting themselves, he did so because their absence disrupted the celebration of the liturgy.[98]

However self-effacing the patriarch may have appeared, however biddable the patriarchal clergy may have seemed, however docile the bishops may have become, the church under Alexius Comnenus was in some ways stronger than it had been before his accession. It had been placed on a sounder financial footing. Monastic property, in general, now came under the strict administrative supervision of the patriarchate, where once there had been some danger that it would pass under lay control. There was almost a reversal of roles. The church became more preoccupied with organisation and law. The rapid development of canon law from this time is to be associated with the church's growing administrative responsibilities. The emperor, for his part, saw orthodoxy as his responsibility. He was in many ways guilty of stealing the patriarch's clothes, for at the beginning of his patriarchate Nicholas Grammatikos had seen the suppression of heresy and the promotion of moral reform as the most compelling part of his duties.[99] Deliberately, Alexius deprived his patriarch of the initiative in these fields. The emperor was the guarantor of ecclesiastical order

96 Zepos I, 312; Dölger, *Reg.*1127.
97 Grumel, 999.
98 Ibid., 974.
99 Darrouzès, 'L'éloge de Nicholas III', 48–53.

and the defender of the faith. He had a duty, if need be, to discipline the church. His interest in monasticism allowed him to demonstrate his good intentions through the promotion of currents of monastic reform. This was best done by extending imperial protection to prestigious new foundations.

Alexius was able to take and hold the initiative in relation to the church. One thing that made this possible was that he put himself and his family at the forefront of a new wave of lay piety. As was usual at Byzantium, its inspiration came from the ideal of monastic life and decorum, as applied to family life. According to Anna Comnena, once the Comneni moved in, the imperial palace became more like a monastery.[100] In keeping with the monastic ideal it was a piety that concentrated on the humanity of Christ and the humiliations that he had endured for Man's salvation. Alexius claimed that through him God had intervened to put an end to the laxness and frivolity which had for so long characterised Byzantine life. God had humiliated himself (*etapeinose*) for Mankind. In return, it was the emperor's duty to protect his flock 'for whom He had been made man, suffered in the flesh, poured out His own blood and suffered a shameful death'.[101] These were sentiments that fitted very well with the new currents of monastic piety with their emphasis on the Passion of Christ. They would find pictorial expression in images such as the Lamentation and the 'Man of Sorrows' or *Akra Tapeinosis*.[102] In the end, it was the emperor who was most in tune with the currents of reform that welled up in the eleventh century. This allowed Alexius Comnenus to restore order and to impose his authority over the church. By championing monastic piety he was also able to deflate the claims of the mystic and the humanist to act as the arbiters of society and to return the emperor to centre stage.

The partnership of Alexius and his patriarch Nicholas was a decisive factor in restoring order to church life. Its character suddenly comes to life in a description of the patriarch's death in 1111 left by a contemporary. Alexius wanted the patriarch to admit certain irregularities in his conduct of office. It was alleged that he had placed the Holy Mountain under an interdict and that he was guilty of alienating churches to archontes. The emperor selected a delegation to go on his behalf to confront the dying patriarch, but one of the members protested that they would never receive his blessing, only his curse. It was Alexius's duty to go in person, which he did. He embraced the patriarch and said, 'Holy Father, we all know your saintly character which is why we all

100 Anna Comnena, III, viii,2: I, 163.22–3 (ed. Bonn);I, 125.30–1 (ed. Leib).
101 Gautier, 'L'édit d'Alexis Ier Comnène', 197.294–8.
102 H. Belting, 'An image and its function in the liturgy: the Man of Sorrows in Byzantium', *DOP* 34/5(1980–1), 1–16.

look upon you as if you were the Great Nicholas himself. We pray that soon you will be of his company. I hope to say nothing that will hurt you, but receive me as your son.' He then raised the question of maladministration. Nicholas declared himself innocent of all charges. He ordered his register to be brought and handed to the emperor. It revealed the immense care the patriarch had taken over his pastoral responsibilities. Astonished the emperor asked for his blessing. This the patriarch duly gave: 'May God support you and strengthen you and vouchsafe you a long life. About the church you need have no worries, for I shall speak in its defence.'[103]

This deathbed scene confirms much of what has become apparent about the Patriarch Nicholas: his devotion to his pastoral duties; his dignity and the regard in which he was held; his conviction that he would be held responsible before God for the well-being of the church. Alexius might have brought pressure to bear upon his patriarch to take the blame for incidents that might otherwise reflect badly on the emperor, but Nicholas was equal to it. The need the emperor had of his moral support is more than evident in the way he sought Nicholas's blessing for the succession to the throne of his son and heir John Comnenus.

[103] Meyer, *Die Haupturkunden*, 177–81.

3

CHURCH AND POLITICS UNDER MANUEL I COMNENUS

Introduction

ALEXIUS I Comnenus composed a political testament for his son and successor John II Comnenus (1118–43) – 'a father's prayers brought to perfect fruition'.[1] In it he set out his achievements, warned of the continuing dangers confronting the Empire, and developed a theory of kingship. His ideas were steadfastly traditional. The central notion was of the emperor as the defender of orthodoxy. If he fulfilled his role it would not just ensure the moral and spiritual health of society, it would also be a guarantee of effective imperial authority. Alexius tied the moral stature of an emperor to his responsibilities towards the church. The emperor was not just the defender of the faith, he was also the governor of the church.

An episode occurred at the end of Alexius's reign which revealed the limits of his authority over the church. His religious adviser Eustratios, metropolitan of Nicaea, was accused of making heretical statements about the relationship of the human and divine in Christ. Alexius tried but failed to protect him against his enemies within the church. They had never forgiven him for escaping condemnation along with his master John Italos. They accused Eustratios of proposing that 'Christ reasoned in the manner of Aristotle.'[2] It was a way of insinuating – correctly – that he remained true to his master's dialectical methods.

Alexius had come to rely increasingly heavily on Eustratios's intellect. He provided the theological justification for the emperor's stance over icons in the struggle with Leo of Chalcedon. He was the imperial spokesman in a series of debates with representatives of the Latin and Armenian churches. The last of these took place in 1114 under the

[1] P.Maas, 'Die Musen des Alexios I', *BZ* 22(1913), 352.

[2] P. Joannou, 'Le sort des évêques hérétiques réconciliés. Un discours inédit de Nicétas de Serres contre Eustrate de Nicée', *B* 28(1958), 29.13; P. Joannou, 'Eustrate de Nicée. Trois pièces inédites de son procès (1117)', *REB* 10(1952), 34.22–3; Podalsky, *Theologie und Philosophie*, 116–17.

presidency of the emperor. Eustratios had as his brief the demolition of the monophysite Christology of the Armenian church. He resorted to dialectic rather than authority to argue the orthodox case. In doing so he adopted a position on the relationship of the human and divine in Christ that could be construed as Nestorianism. He stressed the continuing autonomy of the human element in Christ by asserting that it would always adore and serve the divine.[3]

Eustratios's enemies waited three years before attacking him openly. Alexius tried to protect him in much the same way that Michael VII Doukas had sought to protect John Italos: to get him to abjure the heretical statements imputed to him and to present a profession of faith to the patriarch and synod for scrutiny. Synod met on 26 April 1117 under the presidency of the emperor. The Patriarch John Agapetos (1111–34) working under the eye of the emperor argued that Eustratios was truly contrite and should not only remain in communion but should also retain the priesthood and his see of Nicaea.[4] Emperor and patriarch worked hard to lobby support on the episcopal bench. The metropolitan of Corinth voted with the patriarch, but explained that on the previous day he had been approached by both emperor and patriarch.[5] The metropolitan of Sardis had bound himself in writing to do the same.[6] Another supporter of the official line was the metropolitan of Chonai. He had succumbed to pressure, for he had to disavow a written statement he had made to the effect that he refused to concelebrate with Eustratios.[7] But there were dissenters. These included the archbishop of Ankhialos who was the last to cast his vote. He threatened schism, if Eustratios was allowed to remain in communion.[8] His vote against Eustratios meant that synod tied eleven all. The most damaging intervention had been by the bishop of Leontopolis. He demanded that Eustratios and his teachings should be anathematised in the *synodikon* of Orthodoxy.[9] The matter was adjourned to a new meeting of synod.

This time the emperor was not present. In his absence the patriarch called upon Eustratios's enemies to justify their opposition. Their spokesman was Nicetas, metropolitan of Heraclea. He accused Eustratios of being the author of a new heresy. As such, he was beyond reconciliation with the church. Nicetas's arguments carried the day. Eustratios was condemned as a heretic and anathematised

[3] P. Joannou, 'Der Nominalismus und die menschliche Psychologie Christi. Das *Semeioma* gegen Eustratios von Nikaia (1117)', *BZ* 47(1954), 368–78.

[4] Joannou, 'Eustrate de Nicée', 27–9.

[5] Ibid., 30.8–16.

[6] Ibid., 29.25–9.

[7] Ibid., 30.30–5.

[8] Ibid., 31.28–34.

[9] Ibid., 31.13–19.

in the *synodikon* of Orthodoxy on two counts. First, he was guilty of subordinating the human element in Christ to the divine, in a way that came close to assimilating Christ to the condition of an angel. His second offence was the application of dialectic to the problem of the human and divine in Christ.[10]

There are hidden depths to this episode. Alexius's health was beginning to fail. He had scarcely a year to live. His last months were disfigured by the succession dispute which arrayed his empress and his daughter Anna Comnena against his son John Comnenus. Was there any connection, other than sheer coincidence, between this struggle and the condemnation of Eustratios? The metropolitan of Nicaea was closer to Anna Comnena than he was to John. He had enjoyed her patronage. In her history she mentions his skills as a dialectician, but passes over his condemnation in silence. In the end, John Comnenus outmanoeuvred his mother and sister, very largely because he had the support of the church. The clergy of St Sophia with the assent of the patriarch acclaimed him emperor.[11] It may therefore have been that the condemnation of Eustratios of Nicaea allowed a group favourable to John Comnenus to assert itself within the church.

The relations of church and emperor thereafter take on a different quality. John Comnenus seems to have had little interest in the church and no trouble with his patriarchs, to judge by the sparsity of documentation. This is in contrast to both his father's and his son's reigns. The canonist Theodore Balsamon preserves the texts of twelve pieces of ecclesiastical legislation issued by Alexius I Comnenus and no less than twenty-four by Manuel I Comnenus, but none by John II Comnenus.[12] Equally, Balsamon has eight acts of the Patriarch Nicholas Grammatikos, but only one – and that under Alexius Comnenus – attributed to John Agapetos.[13] John Comnenus was preoccupied with campaigning and foreign affairs and had little time for the church. In so far as the question of the union of churches was pertinent to the conduct of foreign policy John took an interest in this side of ecclesiastical affairs and organised a number of disputations between Greek and Latin theologians.

The condemnation of Eustratios left the traditionalists in the ascendant within the church. They believed in the power of authority and distrusted the use of reason. They had the support of the Patriarch John Agapetos. He dismissed Neoplatonism. It had no intellectual worth, but

[10] Joannou, 'Le sort des évêques hérétiqes réconcilés', 8–30; Migne, *PG* 140, 136–7; Gouillard, 'Le synodikon de l'orthodoxie', 68–71,206–10.

[11] Zonaras XVIII 29. 3–4: III, 763.6–10 (ed. Bonn).

[12] G.P. Stevens, *De Theodoro Balsamone* (Rome, 1969), 298–301.

[13] Ibid. 304–5.

was pure wizardry.[14] He encouraged the view that the prime purpose of education was moral improvement.[15] Appropriately he composed a long series of sermons on the lessons for Sunday.[16] His support of education took a thoroughly practical form: he bought up private collections and encouraged the copying and distribution of manuscripts. He effectively created a patriarchal library.[17] His successor Leo Styppes (1134–43) presided over the posthumous condemnation of Constantine Chrysomallos as a Bogomil. John Comnenus left the matter in the hands of the patriarch, not something that his father was likely to have done. The victory over Eustratios allowed the church to regain the initiative over the suppression of heresy and the defence of orthodoxy.[18]

The tone of John Comnenus's court was set by his Empress Eirene – the Hungarian Princess Piroska. She inspired the foundation of the Pantokrator Monastery at Constantinople and was venerated as a saint after her death.[19] The calm of John Comnenus's reign was a little deceptive. Underneath the surface there were tensions, most obviously in the competition there was for promotion and preferment in the church of St Sophia. Take the career of Michael Italikos. In 1137 he was chosen by John Comnenus to accompany a Byzantine delegation to Rome.[20] This seems to have opened up a successful career in the patriarchal church, where in 1142 he became *didaskalos* of the Gospels.[21] But very soon he was seeking imperial support against his enemies within the church.[22] One of these was Nicephorus Basilakes, a deacon of St Sophia and a future *didaskalos*, who was a competitor for imperial favour.[23] Italikos complained to one of his correspondents that Basilakes enjoyed imperial favour, while he did not.[24] Competition among the patriarchal clergy is also apparent in a case that came before synod on 19 November 1145.[25] It was over promotion within the vestry or *skeuophylakion*. Ignorant of a previous patriarchal ruling the new

[14] K.A. Manaphes, 'Θεόδωρου τοῦ Πρόδρομου Λόγος εἰς τὸν Πατριάρχην Κωνσταντινούπολεως Ἰωάννην XI τὸν Ἀγαπητόν', *EEBΣ* 41(1974), 236.221–2.

[15] Ibid., 227.20–6.

[16] Michael Italikos, 220 n. 3; Beck, *Kirche*, 631.

[17] Manaphes, 'Θεόδωρου', 240–1. See P. Magdalino *The Empire Manuel of I Komnenos 1143–1180* (Cambridge, 1993), 275–6, 323–5.

[18] See Magdalino, *Manuel I Komnenos*, 276.

[19] Cinnamus, 9–10; *Synaxarium Ecclesiae Constantinopolitanae* (ed. H. Delehaye) (Propylaeum ad Sanctorum Novembris) (Brussels, 1902), 887–90.

[20] Michael Italikos, no.23, 173–5.

[21] Ibid., no.10, 116–28

[22] Ibid., no.43, 239–70.

[23] Nicephorus Basilakes, *Gli encomi per l'imperatore e per il patriarcha*, ed. R. Maisano (Naples, 1977), 89–125.

[24] Michael Italikos, no.19, 160–3.

[25] E. Papagianne and Sp. Troianos, 'Die Besetzung der Ämter im Grossskeuophylakeion der Grossen Kirche in 12. Jahrhundert. Ein Synodalakt vom 19. November 1145', *FM* 6(1984), 87–97; Grumel, 1019.

patriarch had allowed existing office holders to appoint replacements to succeed them. According to the old ruling these offices were to be duly filled from a waiting list. This was to apply in future not just to salaried posts, but also to supernumerary positions. The patriarch admitted his fault, annulled the previous appointments, and drew up a new list of candidates for promotion. The original protest was made not by those who had been overlooked, but by their powerful relatives. Positions in the patriarchal administration, salaried or not, were coveted. The details of the case reveal that the patriarchal clergy was recruited not only from the relatives of bishops and clergy, but also from the sons of bureaucrats.

The accession of Manuel Comnenus

This case illustrates the pressures that had been building up within the patriarchal clergy. They were to be aggravated by the circumstances of Manuel I Comnenus's accession, which ushered in one of the stormier periods of Byzantine church history. The accommodation with the church reached by Alexius Comnenus and maintained by his son no longer seemed to operate. It was the church that suffered. While there were only three patriarchs from 1084 to 1143, there were no less than six between 1143 and 1157: of these one was only too thankful to retire, another was removed for consorting with a heretic, another was forced to abdicate, yet another was accused after his death of heresy. The patriarchate of Luke Chrysoberges (1157–69) was respectably long, but it was troubled by two bitter dogmatic controversies and efforts to force the patriarch to abdicate. Only under the Patriarch Michael Ankhialos' (1170–8) was there a return to calm and stability in ecclesiastical affairs.

What had gone wrong? Manuel Comnenus is usually held responsible. He is supposed to have meddled needlessly in the affairs of the church, but this may only be another way of saying that he failed to stamp his authority on the church. The circumstances of his accession told against him. The death of his father found Manuel 500 miles from Constantinople – in camp in Cilicia with the bulk of the army. He was duly proclaimed emperor, as had been his father's wish, but his claim to the imperial throne was by no means unassailable. He had an elder brother, the *sebastokrator* Isaac, who might have expected to succeed to the throne. What is more he was in Constantinople and had his supporters. Control of the capital was vital. A key factor was the support of the church, but the situation was complicated by the recent death of the patriarch. It was the clergy of St Sophia who for the moment counted. Manuel bought their compliance with an imperial chrysobull which granted them a supplement to their revenues of 200 silver pieces a month.[26] Manuel reached Constantinople on 27 June 1143.[27] His coronation was a necessity. This meant that he had first to fill the patriarchal office. His choice fell on Michael Kourkouas, the abbot of the monastery of Oxeia, who succeeded in July 1143. Still there were delays to the coronation. On 1 September the new patriarch threatened to resign.[28] Exactly why is not clear. The coronation finally took place on 28 November 1143. Manuel not only placed a gift of a *kentenarion* of gold on the altar of St Sophia during the ceremony, but also made an annual grant of two *kentenaria* of gold to the patriarchal clergy.[29] Again it looks very much as though Manuel had to buy the support of the clergy of St Sophia.

In March 1146 the Patriarch Michael Kourkouas was allowed to resign and to return to the monastery of Oxeia. His short reign was full of incident. At the very beginning he was faced with the trial of a holy man called Niphon. It was bound to be difficult because the man had been an intimate of the late emperor and still had powerful supporters. On 1 October, even before Manuel's coronation, Niphon was confined incommunicado in the monastery of the Peribleptos.[30] On 22 February 1144 he was condemned by the patriarch and synod for supporting two Cappadocian bishops who had recently been condemned as Bogomils.[31] The emperor and his supporters took a close interest in these trials. He was represented by two of the most senior members of the house of Comnenus, the Grand Droungarios Constantine Comnenus and the archbishop of Bulgaria Adrian Comnenus[32] together with the *protoasekretis* Leo Hikanatos, among the most influential civil servants of the time. Suspicions about a political dimension to these trials are strengthened by the choice of Cosmas Atticus, a deacon of St Sophia, to succeed Michael Kourkouas as patriarch. Cosmas was renowned for his charitable work among the poor of Constantinople, but he was also a friend and supporter of Niphon.[33] Even more surprising were the connections he was known to have had with the emperor's elder brother and potential rival, the *sebastokrator* Isaac Comnenus.

[26] Nicetas Choniates, 49.31–49; Dolger, *Reg.* 1330. See P. Magdalino, 'Isaac *sebastokrator* (III), John Axouch and a case of mistaken identity', *BMGS* 11(1987), 207–14 (= Magdalino, *Tradition and Transformation no.*XII), who gives reasons for believing that the Grand Domestic John Axouch's support for Manuel I Comnenus was not as unqualified as Choniates would have us believe.

[27] P. Schreiner, *Die byzantinischen Kleinchroniken (Chronika Byzantina breviora)* (Vienna, 1976–8), 3 vols., I, 58 n.3.

[28] Michael Italikos, 53–6.

[29] Cinnamus, 33.3–14.

[30] Grumel, 1013.

[31] Grumel, 1015.

[32] Varzos I, nos.27–8; L. Stiernon, 'Notes de titulature et de prosopographie byzantines. Adrien (Jean) et Constantin Comnène, sébastes', *REB* 21(1963), 179–98.

[33] Nicetas Choniates, 79–81; Cinnamus, 64–5.

The timing of the attack on Niphon therefore strongly suggests that it was intended initially to discredit Isaac Comnenus. Equally, can it be mere coincidence that the resignation of Michael Kourkouas and the choice of Cosmas Atticus to succeed him occurred at exactly the same time that a reconciliation between the Emperor Manuel Comnenus and his brother was effected?

Cosmas's patriarchate got off to a bad start when he queried the advice given to him about fasting between Easter and Pentecost by the *chartophylax* of St Sophia.[34] The clergy of St Sophia were divided in their support for the new patriarch. This left him open to a whispering campaign begun against him by certain bishops. The patriarch was unwise enough to bring a charge of heresy against Leo Hikanatos.[35] Such an action against a man close to the emperor lent support to rumours that he was plotting on behalf of the *sebastokrator* Isaac. The patriarch's blatant association with Niphon made him an easy target. On 26 February 1147 he was brought before the imperial tribunal and interrogated by the emperor about his association with a known heretic. Cosmas insisted that Niphon was no heretic. The bishops pointed out that he had been convicted as a heretic by the synod. The imperial tribunal therefore found Cosmas guilty and declared him deposed. Cosmas refused to accept the authority of the tribunal which had condemned him, excommunicated some of those close to the Emperor Manuel, and turned upon his empress, cursing her womb. There was some sympathy for the fallen patriarch. The historian Cinnamus, who belonged to the emperor's entourage, could only say that Cosmas was a good man at heart, but rather naive.[36]

Cosmas must still have had support because there was talk that he might be rehabilitated. His opponents among the clergy of St Sophia concocted a plot to prevent this happening. It was designed to convict Cosmas of impiety towards icons and thus furnish proof that he shared in Niphon's alleged Bogomil beliefs. On the feast of Orthodoxy a few days after the patriarch's dismissal from office they smeared images with honey, but accused Cosmas of smearing them with dung. Their plot was discovered. The ringleader was called before the patriarchal synod and condemned. His intemperate language reveals the passion with which disputes were carried on within the patriarchal church. He referred to the synod as 'a dosshouse of the unhallowed', while 'the palace was full of those fighting against God'.[37] Despite his conviction he was spirited away by an influential member of the patriarchal clergy, whose name is given as Bagoas. It was against the latter that

34 Grumel, 1024.
35 P. Wirth, *Eustathiana* (Amsterdam, 1980), 94–9.
36 Cinnamus, 66.7–9.
37 Nicephorus Basilakes, *Orationes et epistolae*, ed. A. Garzya (Leipzig, 1984), 97.6–18.

at the very end of his career Nicephorus Basilakes, by now a disgraced *didaskalos*, drew up an indictment.[38]

The opening years of Manuel Comnenus's reign saw the patriarchal throne becoming a political shuttlecock. This enhanced the influence of the patriarchal clergy, but also intensified the divisions that already existed within the church of St Sophia. They were made still worse by the vacancy which followed the dismissal of Cosmas Atticus as patriarch. This invited lobbying and faction. It took nine months until December 1147 before another patriarch could be found. There were special circumstances. The task of shepherding the second crusade through the Byzantine Empire cannot have left the emperor much time for ecclesiastical affairs. But he was to make the strangest of choices. Nicholas Mouzalon must at the most conservative estimate have been nearly eighty. Forty years, perhaps fifty years previously, he had been appointed archbishop of Cyprus, but he resigned the see

[38] Garzya, *Storia*, no.XI, 64, 287–9 There is no doubt that it was the last of his works included in the edition he made of his speeches and that it was written after he had been sent into exile. A. Garzya, the editor of the text, has therefore concluded that the Cosmas referred to in the text is just a disguise for Nicephorus Basilakes himself. This would seem to tally with his choice of false names, Hierotheos and Bagoas, for his opponents. However, the description of Cosmas that emerges from the tract just does not fit Nicephorus Basilakes, who claimed that 'I used to love him as a father and to respect him as a pastor' (Nicephorus Basilakes, *Orationes et epistolae*, ed. Garzya 94.26–9). He accused Bagoas of having 'turned the appearance of impiety against the head of bishops, against the pastor and the father revered by all' (ibid., 108–9). The man thus referred to can only be a patriarch. There seems every reason to accept that, if Nicephorus Basilakes called this man Cosmas, he was indeed the Patriarch Cosmas Atticus. We can rule out that other patriarch who was condemned under Manuel Comnenus – the patriarch elect of Antioch Soterichos Panteugenos – because he never exercised any patriarchal, or, for that matter, any episcopal, authority. 'Pastor' was therefore scarcely applicable to him. He was merely a deacon of St Sophia. While Cosmas is known to have had a saintly disposition, this was not true of Soterichos. The occasion of the feast of Orthodoxy also points to the Patriarch Cosmas and away from Soterichos. While the latter was condemned soon after 12 May 1157 (Grumel, 1041) – the feast of Orthodoxy would not come round for another nine months – Cosmas was condemned on 26 February 1147, only a week or two before the feast of Orthodoxy. In his case, lack of respect for images would have been relevant, because of his association with Niphon, who had been convicted of supporting the iconoclast activities of the heretical Cappadocian bishops (Grumel, 1012). Soterichos was condemned on quite different grounds. But why should Nicephorus Basilakes have waited ten years before composing his speech against Bagoas? The most probable explanation is that the latter played a central role in his downfall and in order to get his revenge Basilakes decided to rake up an incident from the past which might be highly embarrassing to his opponent. There is a strong possibility that Bagoas should be identified with that deacon of St Sophia called Basil, who was for long Basilakes's bitter enemy (Cinnamus, 176–8). This seems preferable to the recent identification of Bagoas with Soterichos Panteugenos: P. Magdalino, 'The *Bagoas* of Nikephoros Basilakes: a normal reaction?', in *Of Strangers and Foreigners (Late Antiquity – Middle Ages)*, ed. L. Mayali and M.M. Mart (Berkeley 1993), 47–63.

in 1111 and had since been living as a monk outside Constantinople.[39] Mouzalon was reluctant to accept the patriarchal throne, but bowed before imperial pressure.[40] Whether it was the emperor's intention or not, once in office Mouzalon set about bringing order to the patriarchal church: 'finding that each member was agitating on his own behalf and all alike were opposed to one another and were not interested in promoting peace and quiet'.[41] He soon came under criticism from a number of bishops who objected to the way he had resigned the see of Cyprus. They argued that along with his episcopal dignity he had also shed the priesthood and was therefore ineligible for promotion to the patriarchal dignity.[42] Mouzalon was not without his supporters, even on the episcopal bench. In his defence Nicholas, bishop of Methone, who was to become one of the Emperor Manuel's principal religious advisers, stressed the eternal quality of the priestly dignity, meaning that a bishop might resign his office, but did not thereby cease to be a priest.

Support for the patriarch among the clergy of St Sophia was organised by Nicephorus Basilakes, at this time among the most influential members of the clergy of St Sophia. In a speech he outlined the patriarch's exemplary life. He reminded the patriarch's opponents that they were going contrary to the wishes of the emperor, whose choice he was. Equally, he indicated to the emperor that since Mouzalon was his choice he had an obligation to defend him against his detractors.[43] The emperor nevertheless gave into the pressure from the bishops. Mouzalon was forced to resign and was succeeded by Theodotos, abbot of the Constantinopolitan monastery of the Anastasis, who had a reputation as an ascetic.[44] His reign lasted for two and a half years from 1151 to his death in 1154 and was followed by a six-month vacancy. It was complicated by the refusal of the patriarchal clergy to contribute to his funeral expenses on the grounds that he was a heretic. The instigator of this *damnatio memoriae* was Soterichos Panteugenos, who was still a deacon of St Sophia. He noticed that during the patriarch's last illness the dying man's hand was going black. Research among the tombs of the Bogomils convinced him that this betrayed the patriarch's Bogomil affiliations. He had noted that blackened hands were almost universal among the Bogomil corpses he had inspected! An officer of the patriarchal administration, the *hypomnematographos* George Tornikes, came out in defence of the dead patriarch. He sought support

39 Darrouzès, 'L'éloge de Nicholas III', 7–11.
40 Basilakes, *Gli encomi*, 143, 211–13.
41 Ibid., 146–7, 303–8.
42 Darrouzès, *Ecclésiologie* 310–31.
43 Basilakes, *Gli encomi*, 143–4.
44 Cinnamus, 83–4.

for his stand from George, the archbishop of Athens, who came from the once-powerful family of Bourtzes and had influential relatives in the imperial administration.[45] For his pains Tornikes found himself charged by Soterichos with Bogomil leanings.

Theological controversies[46]

The rivalries within the church of St Sophia flared up in a different form during the patriarchate of Constantine Khliarenos (1154–7). The deacon Basil was promoted to the position of *didaskalos* and given the chair of the Gospels. He began to denigrate not only his predecessor in that position who now held the joint posts of *maistor* of the rhetors and *protekdikos*, but also his old enemy Nicephorus Basilakes, who held the chair of the epistles. They in their turn took exception to his interpretation of the passage in the liturgy of St John Chrysostom, which starts 'Thou art He who offers and is offered and receives.' They accused him of stating that 'the one and only Son of God is both the victim and the recipient of the sacrifice at the same time as the Father'. This seemed to be dividing the human from the divine within Christ too radically and was construed as Nestorianism. Basil found himself under suspension. His opponents had the support of Eustathius, the metropolitan of Dyrrakhion, and of Soterichos Panteugenos. George Tornikes, who had recently become metropolitan of Ephesus, came out against his old detractor Soterichos and his coterie. When a synod was called on 26 January 1156[47] to consider the matter, George Tornikes spoke first in support of Basil's position. A compromise formula was eventually agreed according to which the Word made flesh offered a double sacrifice to the Holy Trinity. For one reason or another Basilakes and Soterichos Panteugenos were not present at the synod and refused to accept the formula arrived at. Soterichos's objections were presented in the form of a Platonic dialogue. He insisted that the sacrifice was made to the Father alone, which laid him open to the charge of exaggerating the divinity of the Father at the expense of that of the Son, after the manner of Arius. Soterichos protested his orthodoxy and demanded that his doctrine be properly examined. At this point, the emperor who had been away on campaign intervened. He called a council in the palace of the Blakhernai on 12 May 1157 and assumed the presidency. Soterichos was forced to abjure his contentions. He was anathematised and never took up the patriarchate of Antioch to which

[45] Tornikès, no.7, 204–19.
[46] See Podalsky, *Theologie und Philosophie*, 118–21; Magdalino, *Manuel I Komnenos*, 279–90.
[47] Grumel, 1038.

he had meanwhile been elected.[48] Basilakes escaped with a censure, but, it seems, was later condemned.[49] The synod was not quite the end of the matter, for George Tornikes composed another tract against the teachings of Soterichos and Basilakes, dated 18 May 1157.[50] Perhaps he intended to make sure that there would be no rehabilitation of his opponents. Their condemnation was a victory for Tornikes, not only because of the personal enmities that existed between them, but also because he had upheld the power of tradition and authority in the face of the more sophisticated approach of his opponents. He contended that they deliberately sought out illogicalities in the dogma of the church, while failing to appreciate the dangers that this approach concealed. They were not clarifying dogma, but turning questions of faith into an intellectual game. Tornikes failed to underline that these dogmatic disputes were also the product of rivalries among different factions within the patriarchal clergy.[51]

The condemnation of Soterichos Panteugenos and his supporters did not bring peace to the church, as the emperor must have hoped. The patriarchate of Luke Chrysoberges was troubled by the most serious theological controversy of Manuel Comnenus's reign. It revolved around the meaning of John 14.28: 'For my Father is greater than I.'[52] A Byzantine diplomat, Demetrius of Lampe, back from the West, drew the attention of the emperor to an interpretation of the verse which he had come across while he was in the West: that Christ was both inferior and equal to God the Father.[53] He considered it was nonsensical. The emperor, for his part, thought it made a great deal of sense, for in so far as Christ was a man he was inferior to the Father, but as God was His equal. Unabashed Demetrius put together a tract defending his point of view and presented it to the emperor, who made it clear that he had no intention of shifting his position on the matter. Demetrius had backers at the imperial court. He also had strong support from both bishops and members of the church of St Sophia. The stance of the patriarch was ambivalent. Cinnamus claims that the patriarch was on the emperor's side from the start, but since he was only able to muster the support of six of the deacons of St Sophia, he dared not express his views openly.[54] The historian is spelling out the weakness of the patriarch's position:

[48] Gouillard, 'Le synodikon de l'orthodoxie', 210–15.
[49] Garzya, *Storia* no.X.
[50] Tornikès, no. 31. 180–5. Cf. no.28, 175–7.
[51] Gouillard, 'Le synodikon de l' Orthodoxie', 216–26.
[52] See J.M. Hussey, *The Orthodox Church in the Byzantine Empire* (Oxford, 1986), 152–3.
[53] Cinnamus, 251–7; P. Classen, 'Das Konzil von Konstantinopel 1166 und die Lateiner', *BZ* 48(1955), 339–68.
[54] Cinnamus (Bonn), 253–4. For the names of Demetrius's supporters, see Varzos II, 294 n. 4.

Luke Chrysoberges may have had no wish to offend the emperor, but his freedom of action was circumscribed by his clergy.

Unable to count on the patriarch, and aware of the opposition there was within the church of St Sophia to his views, the Emperor Manuel set about trying to win his opponents over one by one. The deacons of St Sophia, for their part, made a pact to the effect that neither separately nor in groups would they visit the emperor. They knew his powers of persuasion and had seen too many going over to his side. They assured each other that 'if not now, later, after his death, he will surely be subjected to *anathema*'.[55] To raise the possibility of anathematising an emperor, even posthumously, constituted a derogation of imperial authority. A religious controversy was assuming political dimensions. The deacons met in their own houses to plan their campaign against the emperor and were in touch with certain powerful figures at court. The affair coincided with the escape in 1164 of Manuel Comnenus's most dangerous opponent, his cousin Andronicus Comnenus. The emperor learnt about the pact made against him by the deacons of St Sophia from one of Demetrius's supporters, Euthymios, metropolitan bishop of Neai Patrai. He had been summoned to the palace to discuss the theological question. He gave into pressure from the emperor and revealed all. Manuel rarely lost his temper, but he now railed against the bishop, threatening to throw him off a precipice. The emperor was affronted by the imputations being made against his orthodoxy,[56] but he must have realised what a dangerous position they placed him in.

To defend himself and to bring the matter out into the open the emperor called a council, which met on 2 March 1166 under his presidency. It was packed with members of the house of Comnenus. Manuel's opponents accused him of dividing Christ's essential unity which comprised both human and divine elements. To justify himself the emperor forced through the council the formula: 'By Christ was to be understood His created and concrete nature, according to which He suffered, as others.' There was still opposition. To quell it he drew up an imperial edict, known as the *Ekthesis*, which imposed adherence to the ruling of the council of 1166 on pain of severe punishment: a bishop was to be dismissed from office, as was any official; an ordinary could expect to be sent into exile. To add still further force to the edict it was inscribed on stone and set up in the narthex of the church of St Sophia, which had been the centre of the opposition to the emperor. Having failed to cow the emperor the clergy of St Sophia directed its criticisms against the patriarch who was thought to have a poor grasp

55 Cinnamus, 254.6–8.
56 Cinnamus, 254–5.

of affairs. They concocted new charges against him and demanded his resignation. The emperor felt strong enough to intervene to protect the patriarch. This contrasts with his behaviour in the past, when he had given in rather tamely to any opposition to the patriarch coming from within the church.

There can be no doubt about the seriousness of the crisis that Manuel Comnenus surmounted in 1166. He had been more or less cut off from the church and his orthodoxy had been called into question. He had also aroused considerable disquiet by his apparent willingness to recognise papal primacy in order to further his western-orientated foreign policy. One of his main advisers during the controversy was the Pisan theologian Hugh Eteriano. The prominence of a Latin in imperial counsels was the cause of some resentment. During the dispute Latins were 'pointed out in the streets of the capital as objects of hatred and detestation'.[57] The dispute crystallised anti-Latin sentiment in Constantinople. The emperor tried to defuse this by pardoning his cousin Andronicus Comnenus, the leader of anti-Latin opinion, but he remained unappeased.

How deep the opposition went is evident from the number of prelates who had to make their peace with the emperor and the patriarch once the dispute was over. They included the Grand Skeuophylax John Pantechnes[58] as well as the deacon and *kanistrisios* of St Sophia[59] and a string of metropolitans: Myra, Larissa, Rhodes, Adrianople, Neai Patrai, Thebes, and Maronea.[60] The emperor's success in cowing opposition is evident in the case of George, metropolitan of Nicaea. He was condemned by the patriarchal synod for his continuing opposition to the dogma imposed by the emperor,[61] but he threw himself on the emperor's mercy. He was then pardoned by the synod, which thought that he had shown himself properly contrite and took the emperor's advice to show leniency.[62] As late as 1168 the deacon Basil Pediadites, who was then *maistor* of St Paul's, was convicted by the synod of composing verses lampooning the dogma imposed by the emperor.[63] After Luke Chrysoberges's death in 1169 the controversy flared up briefly once again, when Constantine, the metropolitan of Corfu, accused the dead patriarch of heresy for having accepted a dogma imposed by the emperor. He was condemned, but failed to repent.[64] Soon afterwards the abbot of a monastery near Constantinople was similarly

57 A. Dondaine, 'Hugues Ethérien et le concile de Constantinople de 1166', *Historisches Jahrbuch*, 77(1958), 481.
58 Grumel, 1063.
59 Dondaine, 'Hugues Ethérien', 481–2.
60 Grumel, 1054.
61 Ibid., 1066.
62 Ibid., 1073.
63 Ibid., 1077.
64 Ibid., 1109.

condemned for his continuing opposition to the interpretation of the council of 1166.[65] The emperor's determination to impose his will in the matter is evident. He followed what had now become standard practice: the official ruling of the council of 1166 and the *anathemas* against those who refused to accept it were registered in the *synodikon* of Orthodoxy. More tellingly, these were also included in the confession of faith that a newly consecrated bishop was expected to make.[66] In addition, metropolitan bishops were to ensure that their suffragans signed a copy of the imperial *Ekthesis*, as proof of their adherence to the official dogma. The scale of Manuel's success is underlined by the failure of that other *Ekthesis* of 638, which left the Empire hopelessly divided for nearly half a century.

Manuel Comnenus: concessions to the church

The emperor's victory was a watershed in his relations with the church. Thereafter he set his stamp firmly on the church. Manuel himself realised exactly how important this episode was. Some years later he was carefully questioned about it by the historian John Cinnamus. The emperor remembered that during one of the debates of 1166 news was brought to him that his empress had been delivered of a still-born child, the son and heir that he longed for. He betrayed nothing of this until the end of the session, when he fell at the feet of the bishops and revealed the news. He asked that they intercede with God on his behalf, but he tied this request to his action in the dispute: if his stand was not orthodox, then let him never be vouchsafed an heir. He was staking the fortunes of his dynasty on the soundness of his faith. The birth of a son in 1169 vindicated the emperor's orthodoxy.[67]

There is a striking contrast between the supreme confidence with which Manuel reigned after 1166 and the tentative character of his dealings with the church earlier in his reign. Part of the trouble had then been that Manuel had no very clear idea of the image of kingship that he wished to present, that is, beyond being a new Digenes Akrites or flaunting himself as a new God of Love.[68] In other words, he saw himself as a warrior king, delighting in his prowess in war, hunting, and the pursuit of women. He was subscribing to an aristocratic rather than an imperial ideal.[69] It was not an image that allowed much scope for the development of a coherent policy towards the church. We may

[65] Ibid., 1110.
[66] Ibid., 1060–1.
[67] Cinnamus, 256–7.
[68] Prodromos, no. III, lines 164–6, 400; P. Magdalino, 'Eros the king and the king of *Amours*: some observations on *Hysmine and Hysminias*', *DOP*, 46(1992) 197–204.
[69] Kazhdan/Epstein, 110–16.

sometimes wonder how essential in concrete terms the support of the church was for the exercise of imperial authority at Byzantium, but the conventional wisdom of the time was that it was vital. This was held particularly to be the case where the legitimacy of the ruler was in any way being challenged or if the ruler was engaged in some critical struggle with a foreign enemy. We have already seen the weaknesses there were in Manuel Comnenus's claim to the Byzantine throne. Once established in power he was faced first with the passage of the second crusade and then with a long struggle with the Normans of Sicily. Any direct threat to the Empire passed once Manuel had recovered Corfu from the Normans in 1149, but peace was not finally made until 1158.

During this opening period of his reign he made unprecedented concessions to the church. In February 1144 he exempted priests from the payment of taxes and the performance of services to the state.[70] A chrysobull of 1146 ensured that the monasteries of Constantinople and the surrounding region would not suffer any losses of property to the state, just because their title deeds were not in order.[71] This concession was then extended to the estates of the patriarchal church and to those of bishops and metropolitans in February 1148, at the height of the struggle with the Normans.[72] This was followed by another chrysobull dated August 1153, where the rights and privileges of the church of St Sophia were set out in greater detail. By it the emperor also surrendered to the patriarchal church property it had in its possession that properly belonged to the fisc.[73] In 1158 he made a similar concession to the monasteries of Constantinople and its environs.[74]

There were some limits to imperial generosity. The estates of St Sophia together with those of the monasteries of Constantinople were to be carefully surveyed by the imperial administration. The resulting surveys were to be deposited in the appropriate *sekreta* as a permanent record. The exemptions granted in the imperial chrysobulls were to apply only to those properties listed in the surveys. Similarly, those priests exempted from the payment of taxation to the state had to be registered by the imperial administration.[75] Manuel also issued a series of chrysobulls for individual bishoprics granting exemptions from taxation, but at the same time having their properties and estates inventoried. As a result, the estates of the church became for fiscal purposes a quite distinct category of exempt and privileged property.[76]

70 Zepos I, 366; Dölger, *Reg.* 1334.
71 Zepos I, 367; Dölger, *Reg.* 1347.
72 Zepos I, 376–8; Dölger, *Reg.* 1372.
73 Zepos I, 378–81; Dölger, *Reg.* 1390.
74 Zepos I, 381–5; Dölger, *Reg.* 1419.
75 Zepos I, 366 n. 6; Dölger, *Reg.*1337. Cf. Grumel, 1081–2.
76 Svoronos, 'Privilèges', 325–91.

To that extent the emperor was prepared to accept the autonomy of the church. Since imperial agents showed a marked reluctance to implement in full the concessions made to the church, it is unlikely that pressure for the fiscal independence of the church came from within the imperial administration. It is much more likely that Manuel was bowing to ecclesiastical opinion.

Manuel Comnenus could have expected that his generosity would bring him the support of the church. What it did not do was to bring stability to the church. We have already reviewed the tumult that existed, with patriarch following patriarch amid charge and counter-charge. Father Darrouzès has argued that the frequent change of patriarch over the early part of Manuel's reign should not be attributed to any dogmatic differences within the church, but resulted from imperial interference in its affairs.[77] A propos of the condemnation of Soterichos Panteugenos in 1157 the historian Nicetas Choniates noted that Manuel loved to lecture on matters of dogma.[78] Manuel came to pride himself on his abilities as a theologian. This is often adduced as another reason for his interference in the affairs of the church and as another cause of its disturbed condition.

But how far can Manuel be held responsible for the disarray within the church in the early part of his reign? There is a letter addressed to the emperor from the littérateur John Tzetzes which sheds a rather different light on the emperor's actions.[79] It concerned a whispering campaign against the patriarch of the day, whom Tzetzes described as 'the holiest of men, whose greatest fault was his unsurpassable goodness, his inability to wield the patriarchal rod effectively'. This is a description that applies best to the Patriarch Cosmas Atticus.

Tzetzes was a struggling schoolmaster. His interest in church affairs may at first sight seem a little odd, but it was almost certainly a sign of the control now exercised by the patriarchal church over the organisation of education in the capital. Tzetzes outlined the different motives, all base, that lay behind opposition to the patriarch. One person had not been given the monastery he had hoped for; another was unhappy about his lack of promotion to office in the patriarchal administration; yet another had not got the church property that he coveted. There were those who were dissatisfied with the supervision of affairs (*synedriasis*) by the *chartophylax*; others dreamt of becoming patriarch themselves. Tzetzes begged the emperor not to allow himself to be swayed by such a mixture of envy and self-interest.

[77] Tornikès, 7–20.
[78] Nicetas Choniates, 210.72–84.
[79] Tzetzes I no.44, 65–7.

He reminded him of the responsibilities an emperor had towards the patriarch. There were also constitutional proprieties to bear in mind: an emperor did not appoint a patriarch on the basis of some absolute authority vested in the imperial office (*autonomia basilike*), but had to take into account the considered opinion of the senate and the synod. Tzetzes made a final plea to the emperor to intervene on the patriarch's behalf. It was couched in terms of an appeal to family honour. He thought that while 'it was difficult to persuade the Comneni to overturn the good, it was easy to persuade them to correct what was wrong'.

Tzetzes recognised the aristocratic style of government that Manuel affected at this stage of his reign. We can see that it undermined his grandfather's church settlement and allowed free play to factions within the church. Tzetzes was clear that the cause of much of the trouble within the church lay in the ambitions and resentments of individual members of the patriarchal clergy. Some of them built up followings composed of their former pupils and used them to agitate against imperial decisions, which had been made with their apparent approval. Reading between the lines it is apparent that Tzetzes thought that in the early part of his reign the emperor was out of his depth when it came to ecclesiastical politics.

The clergy of St Sophia

Tzetzes's remarks confirm suspicions that Manuel's clumsy interventions early in his reign fed rivalries, often of a personal nature, within the patriarchal church and allowed them to get out of hand. Since almost all the important sees were filled with former members of the patriarchal clergy, these squabbles threatened to divide the whole church. The metropolitans and the bishops maintained their contacts with the patriarchal church, whose members canvassed their support in their quarrels. The historian John Cinnamus singles out the deacons of St Sophia as a distinct and powerful group within the patriarchal clergy. He refers to them as the 'Levites'.[80] They were not very popular in imperial circles to judge by a story told by Nicetas Choniates. When the patriarchal synod first condemned the views of Soterichos Panteugenos and his supporters in January 1156, the emperor was away from the capital in winter quarters at Pelagonia. At the moment of their condemnation, we are told, there was a crack of thunder. A 'Thunderbook' was at once consulted to find out 'What the Thunder

[80] Cinnamus, 176.14–15; 252.18. The clergy of St Sophia occasionally added the epithet 'Levite' to their seals.

said'. It told of 'the overthrow of the wise men'. This was cause for satisfaction in the imperial camp, for they were immediately identified as the deacons of St Sophia.[81] They were not a very large group. Their numbers were limited to sixty salaried positions. There were also an unspecified number of supernumerary positions.[82] Travellers give as the overall numbers of the patriarchal clergy, from 500 to 700 salaried positions and 1,500 supernumerary. These figures can only be an approximation; they are certainly not impossibly high. The deacons of St Sophia therefore formed rather a small group, even within the patriarchal clergy.

There was intense competition within the patriarchal church to succeed. There were not enough salaried positions to go around. Men were forced to take supernumerary positions in the hope of eventual promotion to a salaried post. As we saw over promotion within the patriarchal *skeuophylakion*,[83] recruits came from a variety of social backgrounds. This helped to sharpen rivalries. There were families that had a tradition of ecclesiastical service. A surprisingly large proportion of the deacons and office holders of the patriarchal administration were the nephews or protégés of bishops, who had in their turn often been deacons of St Sophia. Typical of these was George Tornikes, who became metropolitan bishop of Ephesus, after a distinguished career in the patriarchal church. He was descended on his mother's side from the family of Theophylact, archbishop of Bulgaria. In the early 1160s he was writing from Ephesus to the archbishop of Athens about his cousin Euthymios. He hoped that he would succeed him in his position at St Sophia, 'so that there should be a scion of our family in the [Great] Church to carry on the tradition after us'.[84] But not, by any means, all members of the patriarchal administration came from this kind of traditional background. Nicephorus Basilakes came from a family that in the past had a high military reputation. His maternal uncle enjoyed an influential position in the imperial administration. Nicephorus intended to follow in his footsteps and began his career as an imperial notary, but then decided that the patriarchal church offered a better outlet for his intellectual abilities.[85] Perhaps this background will explain why he seems such an isolated, ambitious, and combative figure within the patriarchal church.

Because ability and education counted, occasionally men of decidedly

[81] Nicetas Choniates, 211.3–14.
[82] E.Sp. Papagianne, *ΤΑ ΟΙΚΟΝΟΜΙΚΑ ΤΟΥ ΕΓΓΑΜΟΥ ΚΛΗΡΟΥ ΣΤΟ ΒΥΖΑΝΤΙΟ* (Athens, 1986), 85–6.
[83] Papagianne and Troianos, 'Die Besetzung der Ämter', 88–90; Grumel, 1019.
[84] Tornikès, no.5, 115.15–17.
[85] Garzya, *Storia*, no.VIII.

humble origins were able to break into the patriarchal administration. Such a man was Basilakes's opponent, whom he nicknames Bagoas. The distaste he felt for the man has something to do with their very different social origins. Bagoas's father was one of the poor. He worked as a fisherman and finally settled in one of the ports at the mouth of the river Don. Even worse from Basilakes's point of view he married a Scythian woman. Their offspring Bagoas was sent back to Constantinople and entrusted to the safekeeping of a maternal uncle. Though poor he was able to send his nephew to a teacher. He was an apt pupil, but to complete his education he depended on the friendship of an older boy. Basilakes assumed that Bagoas became his catamite. His education over he started to hang around churches and monasteries, pretending to be very devout. It was through some monks that report of him reached the imperial palace. This opened the way into the patriarchal church and he became a deacon of St Sophia.[86] There is no reason to suppose that his career was anything but exceptional, but Basilakes's denunciation reveals the bitterness and rivalries that existed among the deacons of St Sophia.

Why should these rivalries have had so disruptive an effect on the church? The deacons formed the elite of the patriarchal clergy. They not only provided the chief officers of the patriarchal administration, but also many of the most influential bishops and metropolitans. Also drawn from their number were the three *didaskaloi* of St Sophia. They formed a hierarchy. At the top came the *didaskalos* of the Gospels, also known as the oecumenical *didaskalos*. Below him was the *didaskalos* of the Apostles followed by the *didaskalos* of the Psalter.[87] These *didaskaloi* only came into prominence in the twelfth century. Promotion to the position of *didaskalos* was highly prized, if only because it often led on to higher things. The *didaskaloi* emerged as the ringleaders of factions within St Sophia. They were a new factor in the politics of the patriarchal church and contributed to the disturbed state of the church under Manuel Comnenus. Contemporaries assumed that the position of *didaskalos* was created as part of the measures taken by Alexius Comnenus in 1107 for the reform of the clergy.[88] This has caused problems, not least because the office of *didaskalos* may already have been in existence.[89] There is now an explanation: Alexius seems to have been taking some of the credit for measures already initiated by the Patriarch Nicholas Grammatikos. It is reasonable to suppose that the office of *didaskalos* went back to an earlier initiative by the

86 Nicephorus Basilakes, *Orationes et epitulae*, ed. A. Garzya, 99–101.
87 Darrouzès, *OFFIKIA*, 66–79; Magdalino, *Manuel I Komnenos*, 325–30.
88 Darrouzès, *OFFIKIA*, 550; Podalsky, *Theologie und Philosophie*, 54–7.
89 A Eustathius who was deacon and *didaskalos* was present at the council of the Blakhernai in 1094.

patriarch, but this was forgotten in the publicity attaching to Alexius's Novel of 1107.

A more serious objection to tracing the office of *didaskalos* back to this novel is that it has nothing to say about the creation of a specific office of *didaskalos*. What it envisaged was more the organisation of a group of *didaskaloi* or preachers attached to St Sophia. They were to receive a fixed salary in order to encourage them to 'pass on to the people orthodox doctrine and a virtuous way of life'.[90] They were to act as a moral police force of the capital. The trouble is that they are tantalisingly hard to find. No seals have survived. They could scarcely have constituted an order. It seems rather that preaching was regarded as an additional task incumbent on the clergy of St Sophia,[91] for which there was special remuneration. One of Alexius's aims was to improve the standard of preaching. The establishment of a hierarchy of posts devoted to the exposition of the scriptures would have been quite in keeping with the intentions of Alexius's novel of 1107.

Their titles – *didaskalos* of the Gospels, of the Apostles, of the Psalter –suggest that originally their duties were specifically ecclesiastical. Their induction into office by the patriarch had a sacramental character. It consisted of blessing and anointing.[92] Their works survive in copious quantities. They include, as might be expected, sermons and expositions of the scriptures. They were also expected to provide inaugural lectures on promotion to office. But an increasingly important part of their duties came to be delivering *encomia* of patriarchs and emperors on set occasions of the year. They became part of the official publicity machine. Their functions related more and more to the calendar of the official year. Their rhetorical and ceremonial duties were a natural development, in the sense that an *encomium* was a secular sermon. Their professional interest in the scriptures honed theological skills which might be utilised for teaching purposes or in disputations with representatives of other churches.

In 1136 the German bishop, Anselm of Havelberg, came to Constantinople on a diplomatic mission. Included in his programme was a debate in which he was called upon to defend the Latin position on the procession of the Holy Spirit and the azymes. His opponent was Nicetas, metropolitan bishop of Nicomedia. Anselm described him as

[90] Gautier, 'L'édit d'Alexis Ier Comnène', 191.221–2. A *didaskalos ton ethnon* and a *didaskalos tes gyras* are attested later in the twelfth century, though their specific functions are not known. They may have preserved the original purpose of the post of *didaskalos*.

[91] Gautier, 'L'édit d'Alexis Ier Comnène', 193.225–7 apparat.

[92] Michel Italikos, 118–19.

> chief among the twelve *didaskaloi*, who organise studies in both the liberal arts and the holy scriptures, as is the custom among the learned Greeks. They are superior to all in matters of doctrine and superintend the work of other learned men. To them are referred all difficult questions. Their solutions are thenceforward held as established doctrine and are enshrined in writing.[93]

Taken at face value this suggests a quite different role and organisation of the *didaskaloi*. They would seem to have formed a college of twelve rather than a hierarchy of three and to have been not mere preachers and publicists, but responsible for the organisation of both secular and religious education. Anselm's information cannot be dismissed out of hand. He knew Constantinople well, visiting it on two occasions. Even so, Anselm is most likely to have been the victim of Byzantine mythmaking. There was the well-known but quite legendary story of how the iconoclast emperor Leo III had burnt twelve *didaskaloi* to death. It would have been the most natural thing in the world to compare with these the group of theologians assembled to dispute with Anselm of Havelberg.[94]

Leaving aside for the moment the question of whether they constituted a patriarchal academy or not, there is no doubt that the church played an essential role in the organisation of education at Constantinople. Schools – even elementary schools[95] – were often attached to churches. By the twelfth century the most important grammar schools of the capital[96] – those at the churches of the Theotokos of the Chalkoprateia, the Forty Martyrs, of St Theodore of Sphorakios, of the Theotokos of the Diakonissa, and of Sts Peter and Paul of the Orphanotropheion – came under the supervision of the patriarchal church.

The emperor still retained a strong interest in the schools of the capital. At the turn of the twelfth century the pupils of the school of the Forty Martyrs were examined in the presence of the emperor.[97] In some cases appointment to teaching posts remained in the emperor's gift, but the headmasters and their assistants were increasingly – perhaps exclusively – drawn from or attached to the patriarchal clergy.

93 Migne, PL, 188, c. 1141.

94 M.J. Angold, *The Byzantine Empire 1025–1204. A Political History* (London, 1984) 239.

95 E.g. that attached to the church of All Saints: Nicholas Mesarites, 'Description of the church of the Holy Apostles at Constantinople', ed. G. Downey, in *Transactions of the American Philosophical Society*, n.s. 47 (1975), 865–7; G. Downey, 'The church of All Saints (church of St. Theophano) near the church of the Holy Apostles at Constantinople', *DOP* 9–10 (1955–6), 301–5.

96 By grammar school I mean schools teaching the *enkyklios paideia*.

97 C.N. Constantinides, *Higher Education in Byzantium in 13th–Early 14th Centuries* (Levkosia, 1982), 54 n. 23.

Grammar school education was effectively annexed to the patriarchal church. This produced administrative problems which were met by the creation first of the office of *maistor* of the rhetors and then that of *maistor* of the philosophers.[98] They were deacons of St Sophia, but the appointment was made by the emperor. The *maistor* of the rhetors, in the same way as the *didaskaloi*, came to have a ceremonial function with an obligation to deliver an *encomium* of the emperor at set times of the year. There is nothing to suggest that the creation, or revival, of these new positions entailed any reorganisation of the curriculum and system of teaching in the grammar schools of Constantinople, but they were instruments of an important change in the organisation of education in the capital. It now came under the supervision of the patriarchal church.

The creation of the *didaskaloi* and the *maistores* was designed to meet different problems: the former were instituted to raise the standard of preaching by the clergy of St Sophia; the latter to supervise the grammar schools that were now attached to the patriarchal church. Both quickly acquired ceremonial responsibilities. By the end of the twelfth century they had come to form a single hierarchy. In the inaugural lecture that Constantine Stilbes gave as *didaskalos* of the Apostles he describes his *cursus honorum* as consisting of five ranks: 'the two outside and the three inside'.[99] This has been taken reasonably enough to refer to the two positions of *maistor* and the three posts of *didaskalos*. But under Manuel Comnenus a *didaskalos* of the Gospels was able to combine this position with that of *maistor* of the rhetors.[100] This suggests that the functions of the two types of offices were then still quite distinct and they were not yet welded into a single hierarchy. There survives the inaugural lecture that the *didaskalos* in question gave as *didaskalos* of the Gospels. In it he outlines his career. He began teaching at a school attached to a church of the Theotokos, probably the Chalkoprateia, and then moved to another school attached to a church dedicated to Christ, perhaps the Chalkites. Thereafter he was promoted to be *didaskalos*

98 The *maistor* of the rhetors is attested under Manuel I Comnenus *c.* 1150. The office of *maistor* of the philosophers only appears *c.* 1200, but it may be a variant on that of the consul of the philosphers revived by Manuel I Comnenus *c.* 1165. Macrides, '*Nomos* and *kanon*', 70 n. 46 cites a letter supposedly written by Michael Psellus to a metropolitan of Thessalonica, formerly *maistor* of the rhetors (P. Gautier, 'Quelques lettres de Psellos inédites ou déjà éditées', *REB* 44(1986), 162–4 (no.18). P. Magdalino also points out to me that Theophylact of Bulgaria held this position in 1087, in which case this position was most likely revived in the mid-twelfth century, as occurred with that of consul of the philosophers.

99 R. Browning, 'The patriarchal school at Constantinople in the twelfth century', *B* 33 (1963), 26.

100 C. Mango and J. Parker, 'A twelfth-century description of St Sophia', *DOP* 14(1960), 233–45, at 233–4. Cf. J. Darrouzès, 'Notice sur Grégoire Antiochos', *REB* 20(1962), 66, for another example.

first of the Psalter and then of the Apostles, before at last attaining his present position at the top of the hierarchy of *didaskaloi*.[101] He stresses that his time as a teacher prepared him for his later work of spiritual edification, which fell to him as a *didaskalos*.

It used to be assumed that teaching must have formed the basic responsibility of the *didaskaloi*, if only because of the name. It was argued that they formed the apex of a hierarchy of teachers or professors at a patriarchal academy that emerged in the twelfth century.[102] This has been firmly rejected by Father Darrouzès. There was no patriarchal academy and the *didaskaloi* were preachers and publicists rather than teachers.[103] This judgement has been condemned as too literal-minded by U. Criscuolo. He does not think that there is any reason to expect contemporaries to provide specific information 'about an institution that they knew well'.[104] He argues for the existence of a patriarchal academy and for teaching, rather than a preaching or publicity, as the prime role of the *didaskaloi*.

The terms of this debate are somewhat artificial, as will appear from any examination of higher education at Byzantium. It was not organised, like elementary and secondary education, through schools and the same is true of the study of theology. It was mostly done by independent study with informal contacts with teachers and other interested parties. As has recently been stressed, the accent was increasingly on debate and disputation as methods of instruction.[105] Occasionally, an emperor might give a more formal structure to higher education by endowing one or more professorial chairs. It is therefore unrealistic to think in terms of a patriarchal school responsible for higher education, but this does not rule out the possibility that the three *didaskaloi* held the equivalent of professorial chairs with a responsibility for the teaching of theology. There is only a thin dividing line between spiritual edification and instruction in theology. As we have seen, *didaskaloi* had often been teachers at an earlier stage of their career and continued to have pupils, if in an informal capacity.

The most vivid impression of higher education at Constantinople at the turn of the twelfth century is provided in the course of Nicholas Mesarites's famous description of the church of the Holy Apostles.

101 J. Lefort, 'Prooimion de Michel neveu de l'archevêque de Thessalonique, didascale de l'évangile', *TM* 4(1970) 387.63–77.

102 R. Browning, 'The patriarchal school at Constantinople in the twelfth century', *B* 32 (1962), 167–80.

103 Darrouzès, *OFFIKIA*, 66–79.

104 U. Criscuolo, 'Chiesa ed insegnamento a Bisanzio nel XII secolo: sul problema della cosidetta "Accademia Patriarcale"', *Siculorum Gymnasium*, n.s. 28 (1975), 373–90, at 380. His line of argument is followed by Katsaros, *ΙΩΑΝΝΗΣ ΚΑΣΤΑΜΟΝΙΤΗΣ*, 163–209.

105 Kazhdan/Epstein, 123–9.

Coming out of the church his curiosity was aroused by the activities going on in the forecourt of the church. It was full of people engaged in earnest discussion and debate. All manner of topics were discussed: among the medical students conception, the nature of sight, the mechanism of sensation; the theory of numbers among those interested in mathematics. There seems to have been no formal teaching, except to the extent that the debates were organised: the participants left the decision in the hands of the patriarch. This may only have been because the patriarch of the day John Kamateros (1198–1206) had a reputation as a scholar.[106]

It is the kind of scene that Demetrius Chomatianos describes with such longing, when he recalls life at Constantinople at the turn of the twelfth century to a fellow student of his and now a fellow exile:

> [Do you remember] when the light of the city of Constantine still gleamed and the great and revered temple of the Holy Wisdom still shone forth, how we frequented the companies of philosophers and gatherings of rhetors and listened to their discourse, but we did more than sit at the feet of the *didaskaloi*: we learnt for ourselves, each of us expounding from one or other of the disciplines some fundamental truth or point of dogma.[107]

Neither this reminiscence nor Mesarites's description have anything to do with a patriarchal academy, unless one thinks of it as akin to a debating society which came under patriarchal auspices. The term the Byzantines used for such gatherings in the twelfth century was *theatron*.[108] It was the arena in which most Byzantine intellectual life took place, whether in the ninth century or the thirteenth. It was here in debates of varying degrees of formality that the *didaskaloi* were expected to shine.[109] They would have been surrounded by their cliques of supporters and former pupils. Some of the strongest ties among the Byzantine elite, whether of the imperial or the patriarchal administration, were formed in the course of an education. Because, in practice, the post of *didaskalos* was the culmination of a career that started with teaching in the schools, the *didaskaloi* had an opportunity of building up followings among potential members of the patriarchal clergy.

It is not therefore surprising that the *didaskaloi* often appear among

106 R. Browning, 'An unpublished address of Nicephorus Chrysoberges to Patriarch John X Kamateros of 1202', *Byzantine Studies/Etudes Byzantines* 5(1978), 37–68, at 51–8.

107 A. I. Papadopoulos-Kerameus, 'Συμβολὴ εἰς τὴν ἱστορίαν τῆς ἀρχιεπισκοπῆς 'Αχρίδος', in *Sbornik statej posvjashchemykh pochitateljami V. I. Lemanskomu*, 1 (St Petersburg 1904), 248.2–7.

108 See M. Mullett, 'Aristocracy and patronage in the literary circles of Comnenian Constantinople', in M. J. Angold, ed., *The Byzantine Aristocracy IX to XIII Centuries* (Oxford, BAR, 1984), 173–201; Magdalino, *Manuel I Komnenos*, 336–56.

109 Cf. Tornikès, 229.16–21.

the ringleaders of factions within the Great Church. They were expected, among other things, to celebrate the deeds of emperors and patriarchs in speeches made on special occasions during the year. They were able to use the pulpit in order to advance their own careers and causes. Nicephorus Basilakes who was *didaskalos* of the Gospels provides an illuminating vignette. Once he was raised to this position his rhetorical skills were the cause of envy and of the hostility of others, but this only spurred him on to greater efforts, 'so that the crowds swarmed to him, like flies around milk, and surged about his pulpit. The patriarch (*politarkhes tes ekklesias*) grew angry, like some Kritias or Hippias seeing the Athenians flocking around various of the orators, fearful of an attack.' Basilakes was not intimidated, but prolonged his discourse, which annoyed the patriarch still more, because he could not give his servants orders to prepare his supper. He quoted St Paul's words at the patriarch: 'But watch thou in all things' (II Timothy, 4,5). He was lecturing the patriarch, if not threatening him. The patriarch considered that he was being sarcastic. He reproved Basilakes by presenting him with an elementary commentary on the Epistles of St Paul. It contained pleasing conventionalities of the kind the patriarch had hoped to hear.[110]

Despite the elements of hyperbole and self-congratulation that are at work here, the meaning behind Basilakes's words is transparent: the rhetorical skills of a *didaskalos* gave him a power that even a patriarch would do well to respect. Another *didaskalos* of the Gospels gave an inaugural lecture that was cool to the point of insolence in its estimate of the patriarch, who was present.[111] Michael Italikos - yet another *didaskalos* of the Gospels - was ironically dismissive of the commentaries compiled by a patriarch on the lessons for Sunday.[112]

As we have argued, the *didaskaloi* did not owe their prominence to a specific responsibility to teach theology. Their duties were rather to preach and publicise. It is difficult to imagine that they would not have used the opportunities they had to pronounce on the theological disputes of the day. They had the means to articulate differences over questions of dogma. We have already seen how such differences that had been simmering for decades burst out into the open in 1156–7, with George Tornikes supporting a traditional approach and with his opponents Nicephorus Basilakes and Soterichos Panteugenos favouring

110 Garzya, 'Il *Prologo* di Niceforo Basilace', in *Storia*, no.XI, ll.175–217. Ibid, no.XII, pp.67–8, has rejected R. Browning's (in 'The patriarchal school', 183) opinion that *politarkhes tes ekklesias* refers to the patriarch of the day. He prefers instead the *oikoumenikos didaskalos* who was the senior *didaskalos*. But he is distorting the meaning of the phrase, in order to support a particular view of the role of the *didaskalos*. Patriarch remains the only convincing meaning.

111 Lefort, 'Prooimion de Michel', 391.121–142.

112 Michel Italikos, no.36.

the application of philosophical methods. This difference of approach to theology had been a potential source of division within the church from at least the middle of the eleventh century and was always threatening to get out of hand. The importance of the issues should not be minimised, for over the twelfth century there was a reassessment of many of the basic dogmas of orthodoxy. This was not conducted in any orderly fashion. It was more a question of providing the setting and the materials out of which careers could be fashioned. Intellectual eminence now counted in the search for preferment and the espousal of a set of arguments might either be the gateway to office or provide hostages to fortune.

Intellectual eminence had not previously counted for very much within the patriarchal church. The scholars and theologians who in the past graced the Byzantine church – patriarchs, such as Nicephorus I, Photius, and Nicholas Mystikos – were usually laymen who had been drafted in rather than promoted from the ranks of the patriarchal clergy. Why were things different under the Comneni? Why were intellectuals attracted to a career in the patriarchal church? Obviously important was the responsibility for education in the capital which St Sophia acquired from the turn of the eleventh century. This was, however, symptomatic of something more profound: the initiative assumed by the deacons of St Sophia in theological debate. They were the self-appointed 'guardians of orthodoxy'. They believed that they had a duty to elucidate orthodoxy. The historian John Cinnamus was shocked by a layman, such as Demetrius of Lampe, presuming to initiate theological debate. A layman had no business, in Cinnamus's opinion, trespassing on the preserve of 'the *didaskaloi* and the officers of the patriarchal administration'.[113]

[113] Cinnamus, 251.15–17: τοῖς διδασκάλοις καὶ τῶν ἱερέων ἐφειμένων τοῖς προὔχουσιν. Cf. Magdalino, *Manuel I Komnenos*, 316–412: chapter 5 'The guardians of Orthodoxy' for a brilliant treatment of this theme. He applies the epithet guardians of Orthodoxy to a much broader social group than the patriarchal clergy. He identifies them with Byzantine intellectuals in general. There was certainly a lack of discrimination on the part of the educated Byzantine in the choice of a career. He might just as easily enter imperial service as the church. Theology was not even in the twelfth century a monopoly of the patriarchal church. Manuel Comnenus had his theologians who were often laymen, but their field of expertise was mainly connected with the debates with the Latin and Armenian churches. These were a special responsibility of the emperor, almost an extension of diplomacy. But the essential point made by John Cinnamus is that theological debate under the Comneni was very largely conducted within the patriarchal church. This was the consequence of Alexius Comnenus's measures against John Italos. He wanted to guard against the indiscriminate debate of theological questions which characterised Italos's career. To do so he made possible an enhanced role for the deacons of St Sophia. They were expected to apply their learning in a responsible way to matters of theology. As we have seen, lack of effective control meant it was a recipe for disorder within the patriarchal church.

The emperor as epistemonarkhes *of the church*[114]

Manuel must bear some of the blame for the turmoil in the patriarchal church. Without the emperor's active support patriarchs found it difficult to discipline the deacons of St Sophia. Manuel neglected the alliance between the emperor and the patriarchal church, which had been at the heart of his grandfather's church settlement. Alexius I Comnenus saw to it that responsibility for good order within the church lay with the emperor. The details of the administrative structure and of responsibilities within the patriarchal church were enshrined in imperial legislation. As we have seen, Alexius acted as the *epistemonarkhes* or disciplinarian of the church, even if the term was not in current usage. It was exactly this function that Manuel failed to fulfil in the early part of his reign. For which reason his grandfather's church settlement ceased to work.

There was a marked change, as we have seen, in Manuel Comnenus's style of government from 1166 onwards. He ceased to act the playboy and *wunderkind* and took his imperial responsibilities towards the church more seriously. He evolved a coherent image of kingship along traditional lines which had been missing in the early part of his reign. It is first given clear expression in the high-flown titulature he adopted in the preamble to his *Ekthesis* of April 1166. It was deliberately reminiscent of that employed by the Emperor Justinian with its series of triumphal epithets. He also claimed in the preamble to be 'the heir of the crown of Constantine the Great and in his spirit holding sway over all his rightful possessions, even if some have broken away from our Empire'.[115] Manuel deliberately looked back to the early Byzantine Empire for inspiration because it fitted among other things with the needs of his foreign policy. This had the effect of stressing imperial grandeur at the expense of dynastic responsibilities or aristocratic diversions. Manuel sought to set himself above Byzantine society and increasingly distanced himself from the imperial clan, which had been the cause of so many difficulties. It was not possible to present so traditional an image of imperial authority without also defining the role of the emperor in ecclesiastical affairs. The near chaos which had characterised the church for twenty years or more made this imperative.

1166 was the year in which Manuel first referred in his legislation to his role as the *epistemonarkhes* or disciplinarian of the church.[116] Thereafter he took his responsibilities very seriously and tightened his grip over the church. Previously, his life had been a scandal:

114 See Magdalino, *Manuel I Komnenos*, 434–70.

115 Zepos I, 410–11.

116 Ibid., 409.6–7. It had been used earlier in 1146 and 1157, but in ecclesiastical documents, not in imperial ones: see Magdalino, *Manuel I Komnenos*, 277, 280–1.

he kept one of his nieces as his official mistress. He did much to set the pleasure-loving tone of his court, where hagiography and theological tracts gave way to mildly scandalous romances as the preferred reading or listening of its members. The taste of his court at this time was blatantly secular. From 1166 onwards Manuel presented a very different face to the world. In 1169 he had the stone of the Unction of Christ brought to the capital from Ephesus.[117] He met it at the port of the Boukoleon at the foot of the Great Palace of the Emperors and carried it on his shoulders to the imperial chapel of our Lady of the Pharos. He had the following inscription engraved on the stone:

> Our Lord Emperor Manuel reenacts the resolve of the disciple as he bears on his shoulders that stone upon which the Lord's body was placed and prepared for burial in a winding sheet. He lifts it up announcing in advance his own burial, that in death he may be buried together with the crucified one and may arise together with our buried Lord.[118]

Here Manuel was presenting the emperor in the guise of a disciple of our Lord. In the preamble to the *Ekthesis* there is a decidedly Petrine flavour to his exposition of the nature of imperial authority.[119] The promulgation of the *Ekthesis* was the culmination of the emperor's intervention in the 'My Father is greater than I' controversy and provides a good example of his exercise of his new role as *epistemonarkhes* of the church. He acted to restore order within the church. This went beyond calling and presiding over church councils which considered and gave judgement on some matter of dogma or ecclesiastical discipline. The emperor himself proposed interpretations of dogma which would then be enshrined in imperial legislation. Increased imperial legislation on the workings of the church almost inevitably revived the question of the sacerdotal character of kingship, which had lain dormant at Byzantium since the iconoclast controversy. G. Dagron has noted how easily contemporary discussions of an emperor's rights as *epistemonarkhes* spill over into an examination of the sacerdotal character of his office. It was left to the canonist Theodore Balsamon to confront the problem. His solution was to place renewed stress on the sacerdotal responsibilities and privileges of an emperor, which he likened to those of a bishop.[120] In this way, he was able to provide another layer of justification for imperial initiatives in ecclesiastical affairs. His success is evident from the surprising weakness of opposition to imperial intervention within the church. Many ecclesiastics

[117] Cinnamus, 277–8. See Magdalino, *Manuel I Komnenos*, 178.
[118] C. Mango, 'Notes on Byzantine Monuments', *DOP* 23/4(1969–70), 272–5.
[119] Zepos I, 411.6–10.
[120] G. Dagron, 'Le caractère sacerdotal de la royauté d'après les commentaires canoniques du XIIe siècle', in *TO BYZANTIO*, ed. Oikonomidès, 165–78.

welcomed the emperor's self-appointed role as disciplinarian of the church. Alexius Comnenus's church settlement only worked if the emperor acted to regulate the affairs of the church.

Theodore Balsamon

This was most clearly the case with St Sophia, where the privileges and duties of the officers of the patriarchal administration were set out in imperial chrysobulls. The *chartophylax* of St Sophia was particularly indebted to imperial support. Theodore Balsamon – its best-known titleholder – regarded Alexius Comnenus's chrysobull in favour of his office as its title deeds.[121] As a young deacon he was commissioned by the Emperor Manuel and the Patriarch Michael Ankhialos' to revise the *Nomocanon* in fourteen chapters. His primary task was to indicate those parts of Justinian's legislation contained in the *Nomocanon*, which still remained in force.[122] His work became increasingly ambitious and was not finished until the 1190s, when he was titular patriarch of Antioch. He extended the scope of his work to include not only the *Nomocanon*, but also the canons of the Fathers of the church, such as St Basil of Caesarea, and the canons of the church councils. What made his work so important was his concern to show how the various canons were applied in his own day. He cited a great deal of imperial legislation and patriarchal decisions relevant to the different passages and problems of canon law that he was discussing. He relied heavily on them for the solutions that he came to. One of the central problems he tackled was that of the relationship of *nomos* to *kanon*; of civil to canon law. He has been accused by H.-G. Beck of failing to give any very clear answers to this question.[123]

Balsamon might almost be said to convict himself of this charge, for at one point he exclaims, 'But I am still in doubt. In so far as it is an ecclesiastical problem I subscribe to the view that *kanon* ought to prevail; in so far as the Basilics were revised after the compiling of the *Nomocanon* and the promulgation (*apolysis*) of this canon, I subscribe to the other opinion.'[124] Despite this his position was usually quite clear. He preferred the most recent statement on any matter. This meant, for example, that Leo VI's legislation might take precedence over the rulings of the Quinisext council.[125] Balsamon plundered the

121 Rhalles & Potles IV, 538–9.

122 Macrides, '*Nomos* and *kanon*', 293–7.

123 H.-G. Beck, *Nomos, Kanon und Staatsraison in Byzanz* (Vienna, 1981), 17–20. Cf. Macrides, '*Nomos* and *kanon*', 82–5, who attributes Balsamon's indecisive treatment of imperial authority to 'Byzantine rhetoric'.

124 Rhalles & Potles II, 699.

125 Ibid., 372, 439.

Basilics wherever canon law proved an insufficient guide. He was asked once what penalties should be imposed on corrupt ecclesiastical judges. His solution was to follow the provisions of the Basilics for civil judges.[126] But, if there was a conflict between canon and civil law, the former was to be preferred to the latter. Both, however, were regulated by the emperor, who as *epistemonarkhes* of the church could impose his will and offer his own solution to any problem. He assumed that such imperial intervention would of necessity receive the approval of the patriarch and synod, because the emperor's authority was divinely inspired. Even so, Balsamon insisted that a patriarchal decision made in synod was not subject to review. There could be no appeal against it to the emperor. The contradiction here is only apparent. In Balsamon's scheme of things, there was a distinction to be made between the office and the person of the patriarch. A patriarch's personal failings were therefore another matter. These required imperial correction. Balsamon declared that 'because it is a legal principle that no one shall suffer injury from another, if the patriarch himself commits sacrilege, is guilty of heterodoxy or errs in any other way, he shall be subject to the judgement of the emperor, the *epistemonarkhes* of the church'.[127] Balsamon tried to strike a balance between orthodoxy and imperial authority, but the powers he accorded to the emperor as the *epistemonarkhes* of the church are scarcely distinguishable from Caesaropapism.

Balsamon argued that the emperor was not necessarily bound by canon law. When it came to the promotion of bishops or even of the patriarch he could set aside the canons and proceed without a preliminary vote. The emperor also had the power to appoint a cleric to a secular office, though this went counter to canon law. He justified this by reference to Chalcedon, canon 4, which allowed bishops discretion over such appointments: 'If a bishop can do this, how much more so can an emperor who is not obliged to follow the canons.'[128] Professor Simon concludes from this passage that Balsamon derived imperial rights in ecclesiastical affairs 'not from the position of a ruler who is placed above canon law, but attached them to a right of appointment through canon law': in other words, even if the emperor was not bound by canon law, he worked through it.[129] Surely it would be nearer the mark to say that Balsamon was trying to minimise the

[126] Ibid., 339.
[127] Ibid., III, 150.
[128] Ibid., 344–51.
[129] D.Simon, '*Princeps legibus solutus.* Die Stellung des byzantinischen Kaisers zum Gesetz', in *Gedachtnisschrift für Wolfgang Kunkel*, ed. D. Norr and D. Simon (Frankfurt am Main, 1984), 449–92, at 475–7.

conflict between canon law and the emperor's absolute authority.[130] To do this, he cited the somewhat shaky analogy with episcopal authority. Balsamon was the first canonist who had to come to terms with the notion of the emperor as the *epistemonarkhes* of the church. It crystallised ideas about imperial authority which can quite properly be described as Caesaropapist. It was a view to which Balsamon subscribed, but to justify it legally required considerable ingenuity and circumspection. Otherwise he might find himself accused of heresy, like the Patriarch Luke Chrysoberges, for accepting dogma imposed by the emperor. Balsamon's uncertainties and lack of clarity therefore reflect the difficulties of his task: his conviction was that the church's best interests were served by imperial supervision, but this flew in the face of a tradition of canon law which emphasised ecclesiastical independence.[131]

Manuel I Comnenus and the law

Balsamon's attitude to imperial authority was symptomatic of the Emperor Manuel's changed priorities. He began to be concerned about the moral state of the Empire. He sought to improve the administration of justice. He reorganised the main law court of the capital with the aim of speeding up the due process of law.[132] The emperor was horrified by the number of murders being committed. In this the Byzantines compared most unfavourably with the barbarians, 'who did not have holy law or the threat of frightful punishment in the future to deter them from doing harm to one another'.[133]

Manuel's solution was to tighten up the law of asylum. This he blamed for the deplorable state of affairs.[134] The law then current on asylum was the work of Constantine Porphyrogenitus (945–59), who had extended the right of asylum from those guilty only of manslaughter to murderers. It laid down that after appropriate penance murderers were to become monks and to spend the rest of their lives in monasteries. By the twelfth century the privilege of asylum was being abused, nowhere more blatantly than at St Sophia. Murderers were known to flee to its protection and obtain the required pardon and absolution. They then returned to their homelands to commit more murders. Local officials connived at this by allowing murderers to slip away to the safety of St Sophia. They were henceforth enjoined to send

130 Cf. Macrides, '*Nomos* and *Kanon*', 82–3.

131 Cf. ibid., 77.

132 R.J.Macrides, 'Justice under Manuel I Komnenos: four novels on court business and murder', *FM* 6(1984), 156–204.

133 Zepos I, 405.33–5.

134 Ibid., 403–8; Dölger, *Reg.* 1467: April 1166.

murderers to the capital, but to hand them over either to the emperor or to the eparch of the city for imprisonment. Murderers who managed to escape to St Sophia were to perform penance in the prescribed way, but were then to be sent to the emperor or to the eparch. It still remained possible for a murderer to receive the monastic tonsure, but the emperor insisted that he must be truly contrite. The presence within a monastery of impenitent murderers made life for the rest of the community intolerable. Finally, the patriarch received instructions to make a much more careful enquiry about murderers seeking asylum in his church, because their confessions were more often than not false. A suitable precaution would be to write to the bishop and clergy of the see where the murder took place, as well as the governor of the theme, in order to inform himself more exactly about the matter.[135]

As Ruth Macrides has noted, this novel of Manuel Comnenus on asylum is implicitly critical of the role of the church in an area where civil and canon law overlapped. The difficulty was how to distinguish manslaughter from murder. It was a problem that attracted the attention of Theodore Balsamon. It was not a simple matter of cases of manslaughter going before the ecclesiastical courts and those of murder before the civil courts. Civil law accepted that self-defence was a justification for killing, whereas canon law following St Basil considered that whatever the circumstances the taking of human life always amounted to murder. Balsamon tried to resolve the discrepancy implicit here between *nomos* and *kanon* by pointing out that the purpose of the civil law was to punish, whereas the intention of canon law was through the application of penances to effect spiritual healing.[136] This opinion was given specifically apropos of killing in self-defence, but its implications were considerable. Balsamon saw the prescriptions of civil and canon law as complementary rather than opposed: the one punished; the other healed.[137] This applied even in cases of murder, for Balsamon followed St Basil's contention that the taking of human life was a challenge to God, and therefore a sin, and thus came within the ambit of canon law. This justified murderers seeking the asylum of the church. Balsamon's formulation equally justified their eventual consignment to the emperor and the civil authorities.

At St Sophia cases of asylum went before a special court, called the *ekdikeion*, which was presided over by the *protekdikos*.[138] This office became increasingly important over the twelfth century, which suggests that the church of St Sophia was in one way or another

135 R.J. Macrides, 'Killing, asylum, and the law in Byzantium', *Speculum* 63(1988) 509–14.
136 Rhalles & Potles IV, 490–1.
137 Cf. Macrides, '*Nomos* and *kanon*', 82–3.
138 Darrouzès, *OFFIKIA*, 323–32; Laurent, *Corpus* I, 86–98; III, 25–31.

processing a growing volume of cases involving manslaughter and murder.[139] But the right of asylum was not to be abused. The emperor had a duty to intervene in his capacity as disciplinarian of the church. Manuel Comnenus sought to redress the balance in favour of the civil courts. Far from necessarily contributing to the well-being of society an extension of ecclesiastical jurisdiction seemed in this case rather to encourage lawlessness. The emperor's legislation was a demonstration of what Balsamon perceived as the complementary character of civil and canon law.

Marriage was another sphere where imperial and ecclesiastical competences overlapped. Alexius I Comnenus may have conceded that marriage along with other spiritual matters belonged to the jurisdiction of the church,[140] but practice, at least in the capital, was different. Marriage litigation continued to come before the civil courts. It was not in the imperial interest to abdicate responsibility for marriage to the church. Too much political weight attached to marriage. Alexius Comnenus reestablished the important principle that by virtue of his discretionary powers (*oikonomia*) the emperor had a right to make dispensations from the age of consent.[141] His grandson took an equally active interest in matrimonial questions. His justification was rather different from that of his grandfather. It was not simply a question of using the discretionary powers vested in the imperial office. He was also acting in his capacity as *epistemonarkhes* or disciplinarian of the church. This gave him, among other things, a moral duty to supervise marriage.

But in the field of marriage his moral duty often conflicted with political expediency. Marriage alliances were a delicate issue for an emperor and the impediments to marriage might be an inconvenience or an unexpected boon. The prohibited degrees were, as always, a problem in a closely knit aristocratic society. Increasingly the seventh degree of consanguinity was being ignored as an impediment to marriage. A loophole had been provided by the ruling of the Patriarch Alexius the Studite (1025–43) to the effect that such marriages might be valid, if there was a genuine ignorance of the relationship. It became the practice simply to claim ignorance. In April 1166 the archbishop of

139 R.J. Macrides notes (in 'Killing, asylum, and the law', 516–17) the striking lack of documentation for cases of killing and asylum in the twelfth century. She suggests by way of explanation that the registers of the *ekdikeion* did not survive in contrast to those of the patriarchal synod, which provide the bulk of our documentation for the Byzantine patriarchate in the twelfth century. Note the comparatively large number of seals surviving from the twelfth century for *protekdikoi* and *ekdikoi* (see Laurent, *Corpus*).

140 Zepos I, 312.24–6.

141 Ibid., 323.6–9.

Athens raised this question before synod.[142] It decided that ignorance was not a sufficient excuse. Such marriages were to be dissolved; those who had given their consent were to be put under penance and the priests who had officiated were to be defrocked. This decision was immediately taken to the emperor for his approval.[143] Exercising his disciplinary power (*epistemonarkhikon dikaion*) Manuel confirmed the decision. He admitted that he had a special interest in the matter:

> Many marriages often occur among the imperial family and other nobility and rank, as well as among those figures who have come to settle in the Queen of Cities from foreign lands ruled over by kings and princes. Because these marriages should never be celebrated without imperial consent, it is right and proper that our imperial majesty should be apprised of the decisions reached by synod over such a pressing problem. Otherwise, some such illegal union might perhaps occur by oversight and in contravention of the sacred canons and civil regulations.[144]

This the emperor concluded would not be good for the prestige of Constantinople which had a duty to set an example.

Was Manuel Comnenus apologising for the lax way he had exercised his control over the marriages of the aristocracy and indicating that in future he was willing to be guided by the church? Or did he have some ulterior diplomatic purpose? Was there some marriage alliance that turned out to be inconvenient? This is what K.G. Pitsakes suspects. He notes that Nicholas Hagiotheodorites, the archbishop of Athens, raised the matter before synod and that it was his brother Michael Hagiotheodorites, the logothete of the drome, who drafted the imperial confirmation of synod's ruling on the matter of the prohibited degrees.[145] But in this instance it is only a suspicion that it was a put up job.[146] It caused no upheaval in the church. The patriarch and synod politely thanked the emperor for his confirmation. They expressed

142 Ibid. 408–10; Dölger, *Reg.* 1468: April 1166.

143 Ibid.

144 Ibid. 409.21–9.

145 K.G. Pitsakes, '"Παίζοντες εἰς 'αλλοτρίους βίους"', in *Η ΚΑΘΗΜΕΡΙΝΗ ΖΩΗ ΣΤΟ ΒΥΖΑΝΤΙΟ*, ed. Chr. Maltezou (Athens, 1989), 226 and n.29.

146 It is possible that Manuel was using this ruling of 1166 to dissolve the betrothal of his daughter Maria to Bela of Hungary, for in 1166 he was proposing that his daughter should marry the young king of Sicily William II, even though she was still formally betrothed to Bela (J.S.F. Parker, 'The attempted Byzantine alliance with the Sicilian Norman Kingdom, 1166–67', *Papers of the British School at Rome* 24(1955), 86–93). The relationship of Bela and Maria is problematical, but was conceivably of the seventh degree of consanguinity. There is some dispute as to which king of Hungary was the father of Manuel I Comnenus's mother Eirene/Piroska: Ladislas or Coloman (F. Makk, *The Arpads and the Comneni* (Budapest 1989), 127). In the latter case it would be the seventh degree. On Comnenian marriage policy cf. Magdalino, *Manuel I Komnenos*, 201–17, who rejects the notion that Manuel Comnenus's marriage legislation envisaged specific cases.

appreciation about the way he was fulfilling his role as *epistemonarkhes* of the church of Christ with which he had been entrusted by God.[147]

This contrasts with the storm produced by Manuel's subsequent intervention which aimed at setting aside the Tome of Sisinnios. Theodore Balsamon expressed uncharacteristic disapproval of the emperor's actions in this case, insisting that they were 'arbitrary and therefore will not effect anything good'.[148] Coming from an apologist of the emperor as disciplinarian of the church these are strong words. Balsamon makes it plain that the emperor was abusing his authority for some political advantage. This time Manuel was all for relaxing the impediments to marriage. It began with a case that came before the imperial tribunal in 1172 involving the marriage of a man to his first wife's second cousin. The emperor allowed the marriage, even though it was barred under the Tome of Sisinnios. Manuel Comnenus argued for a lenient interpretation of the rules governing marriages between those related by marriage and queried the equation made by the Tome of relationship by marriage with relationship by blood, in other words of affinity with consanguinity. The patriarch of the day was Michael Ankhialos'. He protested at the emperor's action. Manuel admitted his ignorance of the laws, but cited in his defence his knowledge of the customs and procedures of other lands. He put special emphasis on his familiarity with Latin practice. Does this mean that one of the parties to the marriage was a westerner? The patriarch rather tartly reminded the emperor that the Latins were responsible for the schism that separated the two churches. Synod was not willing in this case to countenance the emperor's relaxation of the Tome of Sisinnios, but tactfully referred the case back to the imperial tribunal.[149] Manuel apparently relented and issued a *prostagma* or order prohibiting any such marriage.[150] However, it was never registered in the appropriate bureaux and therefore did not have the force of law.

This was an unsatisfactory state of affairs and led to a bishop seeking an authoritative ruling from synod on the matter. The bishop was critical of the Tome of Sisinnios. He pointed to the inconsistencies that it had introduced into the prohibited degrees, for it meant that for all practical purposes relationship by marriage was treated as equivalent to relationship by blood.[151] Synod considered the matter in June 1175. It agreed that the Tome had not always been observed. It even admitted that there was no basis in either civil or canon law

147 D. Simon, 'Ein Synodalakt aus dem Jahre 1166', *FM* 1(1976), 123–5.
148 Rhalles & Potles I, 291.
149 J. Darrouzès, 'Questions de droit matrimonial', 122–37.
150 Zepos I, 425.
151 Darrouzès, 'Questions de droit matrimonial', 136–51; A. Schmink, 'Kritik am Tomos des Sisinnios', *FM* 2(1977) 231–7, 245–8.

for equating affinity with consanguinity, but claimed that it could not be repealed as it had received imperial approval. If the emperor now proposed to rescind imperial confirmation, then that was a different matter.[152] The metropolitan bishop of Amaseia had been a dissenting voice and had defended the Tome against the scepticism displayed by synod, but he too now withdrew his objections to the emperor's actions.[153] Manuel then went ahead with legislation to modify the Tome.[154] Manuel was tactful enough not to repeal the Tome nor to rescind the original imperial confirmation. His novel simply allowed marriages in the seventh degree of affinity as long as appropriate penance was performed. Balsamon's indignation over Manuel's abuse of power is slightly misleading. The incident is more in keeping with the cooperation that characterised the relations of emperor and patriarch from 1166 onwards. This was founded on the broad acceptance by the church of the emperor's disciplinary powers. This might in turn require acquiescence to the imperial will. It was a clear demonstration of Manuel's ascendancy over the church, but that was the price to be paid for a modicum of stability.

Other churches and faiths

The choice of Michael Ankhialos' as patriarch to succeed Luke Chrysoberges in 1170 was symptomatic of Manuel's changed relationship with the church. The new patriarch started his career as a deacon of St Sophia. It was probably in the crucial year of 1166 that Manuel Comnenus revived the post of Consul of the Philosophers for him. In that capacity his task was to assert official control over the study of philosophy, which was to concentrate on the works of Aristotle. Nothing was said about the more dangerous Plato. The intention was to clamp down on theological speculation which a study of Plato was supposed to encourage. It not only endangered the accepted dogma of the orthodox church, but also opened up rancorous disputes within the patriarchal church. Coming after a series of heresy trials Manuel Comnenus's revival of the office of the Consul of the Philosophers aimed at damping down the intellectual ferment within the patriarchal clergy.[155] The comparative lack of doctrinal disputes at the end of Manuel's reign is striking and the *didaskaloi* were less prominent. Taken together they

152 Grumel 1129–30; Darrouzès, 'Questions de droit matrimonial', 150–5; Schmink, 'Kritik am Tomos des Sisinnios', 238–9, 249–52.

153 Darrouzès, 'Questions de droit matrimonial', 154–7; Schmink 'Kritik am Tomos des Sisinnios', 239–40, 253–4

154 Zepos I 424–5; Dölger, *Reg.* 1341: June 1175. Cf. Schminck, 'Kritik am Tomos des Sisinnios', 215–54.

155 R.Browning, *Studies on Byzantine History, Literature and Education* (London, 1977), no.IV.

suggest that Michael Ankhialos' had more success in damping down the intellectual ferment within the patriarchal church than did Manuel Comnenus's previous adviser on religious affairs, Nicholas, bishop of Methone. Nicholas composed a tract denouncing the influence in intellectual circles of Neoplatonism. Despite the emperor's support he seems an isolated figure and retired to his bishopric where he died *c.*1165. Part of his importance is that he broached many of the themes that came into prominence in the later part of Manuel's reign. He urged Manuel to restore the unity of the church universal.[156]

Nicholas was an outsider, where the patriarchal church was concerned. By contrast, Michael Ankhialos' worked from the inside. He could be expected to cooperate with the emperor. Manuel needed somebody he could trust at the head of the church, for by the 1160s the unity of Christendom was central to his foreign policy. He sought an accommodation with the papacy, an understanding with the Armenian church, and a more tolerant attitude towards converts from Islam. On all these issues Manuel was able to impose his wishes on the church. There were those who considered that the emperor was diluting orthodoxy for political ends, but there was no concerted opposition. He had little trouble from the church over negotiations with the Armenians. He left it to the patriarch and synod to lay down the exact terms they found acceptable as a basis for a union of churches.[157] These were then enshrined in a tome drawn up by the emperor. The results of these negotiations with the Armenians were inconclusive.

In terms of practice the differences between the orthodox church and the Armenian church were not dissimilar from those that separated the orthodox church and the Latins, but in each case the stumbling block was different. In the case of the Armenians it was the dogma of the incarnation. This was not a problem dividing the Byzantine and Latin churches. It was much more a matter of the pretensions of the papacy to the primacy of the universal church. The claims of the papacy to a *plenitudo potestatis* constituted a 'scandal' that was a stumbling block in the path of church union.[158] Many Byzantine churchmen must

156 See A.D. Angelou, *Nicholas of Methone: Refutation of Proclus'* Elements of Theology (Corpus Philosophorum Medii Aevi – Philosophi Byzantini 1) (Athens and Leiden, 1984), ix-xxiii, liii-lxiv; G. Podalsky, 'Nikolaos von Methone und die Proklosrenaissance in Byzanz 11/12 Jahrhundert', *OCP* 42(1976), 509–23; A.Angelou, 'Nicholas of Methone: the life and works of a twelfth-century bishop', in *Byzantium and the Classical Tradition*, ed. M. Mullett and R. Scott (Birmingham, 1981), 143–8; Magdalino, *Manuel I Komnenos*, 332–3, 460–2.

157 Grumel, 1123–4, 1132.

158 D.M. Nicol, 'The papal scandal', *Studies in Church History*, 13(1976), 141–68 (= D.M. Nicol, *Studies in Late Byzantine History and Prosopography* (London, 1986), no.II); J. Spiteris, *La critica bizantina del primato romano nel secolo XII* (Orientalia Christiana Analecta 208)(Rome, 1979), *passim*; Magdalino, *Manuel I Komnenos*, 83–95.

therefore have watched Manuel's diplomatic manoeuvrings in the West with alarm. On two different occasions the emperor indicated his readiness to accept papal primacy in return for recognition by Rome of his claim to be the sole 'Roman' emperor. This must have looked very like a willingness to barter away orthodoxy for uncertain political advantage.

There exists a dialogue purporting to be between Manuel and the Patriarch Michael Ankhialos' on this very theme. If genuine, it would shed a very different light on the relations of the emperor and the patriarch. In it the patriarch rejected the emperor's proposal that the Byzantine church should recognise papal primacy. This was to include not only the return of the pope's names to the diptychs, but also acceptance of Rome as a final court of appeal for the church of Constantinople. The patriarch emerged victorious from the debate. A tome was issued breaking all ties with the church of Rome, though it abstained from putting it under *anathema*.[159] As it stands, this dialogue is a propaganda piece, of a kind quite common under the Comneni. Father Darrouzès has rejected the possibility that it could have circulated under Manuel Comnenus and preferred to connect it with the debates over the Union of Lyons of 1274.[160] The dialogue certainly contains views that are rather different from those expressed by Michael Ankhialos' in his correspondence with Pope Alexander III, which is to be dated to 1173.[161] The pope wrote to express his delight at the news brought back from Constantinople by the papal emissary. It seemed that the patriarch was seeking reunion with the Mother Church of Rome. The patriarch's reply was polite but guarded. He agreed that nobody desired reunion of the churches more fervently than he did. He recognised St Peter and St Paul as upholders of the unity of the church and congratulated the pope for his fidelity to this ideal, but it could only become a reality if the ancient ecclesiastical order was respected.[162] He went on to remind the pope that to achieve what was pleasing to God it was necessary to work with humility and to avoid pretension.[163] The pope urged the patriarch to keep the emperor abreast of developments.[164] The patriarch thought this unnecessary,

159 V. Laurent and J. Darrouzès, *Dossier grec de l'union de Lyon (1273–1277)* (Archives de l'Orient chrétien 16)(Paris, 1976), 45–52 – Text: 346–75; Grumel, 1121–2. The mention of friars (*phrerioi*) in the title (p. 347) certainly points to a thirteenth-century date for the piece as we have it.

160 Darrouzès, 'Les documents byzantines sur la primauté romaine', *REB* 23(1965), 79–82. Cf. Spiteris, *La critica bizantina*, 203–10

161 G. Hofmann, 'Papst und Patriarch unter Kaiser Manuel I. Komnenos. Ein Briefwechsel', *EEBS* 23 (1953), 74–82.

162 Ibid., 79.70–3.

163 Ibid., 79.73–5.

164 Ibid., 76–7.

because the emperor had been working for reunion many a long year.[165] This exchange of letters suggests that Michael Ankhialos' was willing to go some way to accommodate the wishes of the emperor on the question of the reunion of churches. But elsewhere, as we have seen, the patriarch was capable of delivering a harsh judgement on the Latins.[166]

This provides support for Paul Magdalino's suspicion that the Dialogue may indeed reflect ideas current at the end of Manuel Comnenus's reign. It contains one particular passage that fits far better with the reign of Manuel Comnenus than it does with that of Michael VIII Palaeologus. The Dialogue attributes the following sentiment to the patriarch: 'Let the Muslim be my master in outward things rather than the Latin dominate me in matters of the spirit, for, if I am subject to the Muslim, at least, he will not force me to share his faith. But, if I have to be under Frankish rule and united with the Roman church, I may have to separate myself from God.'[167] Islam was scarcely a problem for the Byzantine church under Michael Palaeologus, whereas it was a matter of some concern to Manuel Comnenus. He initiated a debate within the church as to whether or not converts from Islam should be dealt with more leniently.

Admittedly, the Byzantines had very little experience of Frankish rule, in contrast to what was to happen in the thirteenth century. There was, however, an exception: the crusader states. Towards the end of Manuel Comnenus's reign relations between the orthodox and Latin churches of Jerusalem deteriorated. Leontios, the orthodox patriarch of Jerusalem, made a secret visit to his see in 1176 and was apprehended and imprisoned by the Frankish authorities. This contrasted with the invitation he received from Saladin to take up residence at Damascus. This he declined, but only because the Emperor Manuel had already ordered his return to Constantinople.[168] The experiences of Leontios fit rather well with the sentiments of the Dialogue. They reflect the undercurrents of opposition that continued to exist within the Byzantine church to Manuel's policy of an accord with the papacy. That is not to say that Michael Ankhialos' necessarily disapproved of imperial policy, but it suited opponents of entente with the papacy to pretend that he did. The Dialogue may well have been one of those anonymous pamphlets produced at the end of Manuel Comnenus's

165 Ibid., 80.86–90.

166 See above p. 107; Magdalino, *Manuel I Komnenos*, 291–2.; M.J. Angold, 'Greeks and Latins after 1204: the perspective of exile', in *Latins and Greeks in the Eastern Mediterranean after 1204*, ed. B. Arbel, B. Hamilton, and D. Jacoby (London, 1989), 64–6.

167 Laurent and Darrouzès, *Dossier*, 367.6–8.

168 See R. Rose, 'The *Vita* of St Leontios and its account of his visit to Palestine during the crusader period', *Proche-Orient Chrétien* 35 (1985), 238–57.

reign, about which a pro-unionist writer of the late thirteenth century complained so bitterly.[169]

Islam was a problem in the reign of Manuel Comnenus because of his Anatolian ambitions. The emperor had a responsibility to the Christian communities under Seljuq rule. He tried to ensure that bishops and metropolitans appointed for the Anatolian sees did not remain in Constantinople but took up residence in their sees.[170] The Christian communities in Anatolia needed the protection of the Seljuq sultan. Manuel tried to procure this by bringing the sultan more securely within the Byzantine orbit. This culminated in 1161 with a spectacular state visit to Constantinople by the Seljuq Sultan Kilidj Arslan. There was to have been a procession by the emperor and the sultan to the church of St Sophia, but this had to be called off because the Patriarch Luke Chrysoberges refused to allow an infidel within the portals of the Great Church.[171]

He was also unsympathetic to any relaxation of the terms on which converts from Islam were to be received into the orthodox church. In the mixed communities of Anatolia apostasy to Islam and conversion or reconversion to Christianity were constant problems for the ecclesiastical authorities, made none the easier by the blurring that already existed between Christianity and Islam.[172] It was, apparently, the custom for Muslims in Seljuq Anatolia to have their children baptised by orthodox priests. This was supposed by the Byzantines to prevent their possession by demons and their smelling like dogs. Some converts from Islam came before Luke Chrysoberges and the synod, wondering whether such a baptism sufficed. It was decided not, even in those cases where their mothers had been Christian.[173] The emperor took a different stance. He had been alerted to the difficulties surrounding conversion to Christianity by a vizier of the Seljuq sultan. His name was Iktiyar ad-Din Hasan ibn Gabras. He came from a branch of the Byzantine family of Gabras which had taken service with the Seljuq sultan and had apostatised to Islam.[174] He suggested that the emperor might like to remove the *anathema* which any convert from Islam to Christianity had to pronounce against the God of Muhammad. It was this which had prevented his conversion to Christianity.[175]

169 Laurent and Darrouzès, *Dossier* 49. George Metochites is the pro-unionist writer in question (p. 165).

170 Dölger, *Reg.*1334.

171 Cinnamus, 206.12–22.

172 See F.W. Hasluck, *Christianity and Islam under the Sultans* (Oxford, 1929), 2 vols., II, 363–83.

173 Grumel, 1088.

174 C. Cahen, 'Une famille byzantine au service des Seldjouqides d'Asie Mineure', in *Polychronion*, ed. Wirth 145–9; A. Bryer, 'A Byzantine family: the Gabrades, *c.*979–*c.*1653', *University of Birmingham Historical Journal* 12(1970), 164–87, at 181.

175 Nicetas Choniates, 213, apparat 54.

Manuel took his point and assumed that there were many at the Seljuq court who might be tempted to convert to Christianity, if the terms were less stringent. He therefore proposed a new formula for abjuration from Islam, in which the anathema against the God of Muhammad was dropped, the assumption being that Christians and Muslims worshipped a common God. When the emperor put this to the patriarch and synod, it brought forth a violent protest from Eustathius, the metropolitan of Thessalonica. A compromise was reached, whereby an *anathema* against Muhammad and his teachings was substituted for that against Muhammad and his God.[176] Manuel reckoned that he had outwitted the synod and got his own way.

Church and society

Manuel's ascendancy over the church was demonstrated in March 1171 when he imposed an oath of loyalty to the emperor upon the higher clergy.[177] It was in the form of an imperial *tomos* and was presented to the patriarch and synod for approval. It proposed an exalted notion of imperial authority. Lèse-majesté was analogous to apostasy:

> In the same way that anybody denying belief in God is expelled from the community of the orthodox, so, whoever renounces his loyalty to the imperial office and acts treacherously and falsely towards it, is deemed by us to be unworthy of the name of Christian, seeing that he who wears the crown and diadem of Empire is the anointed of the Lord.

In future those who were promoted to patriarchal and episcopal office were to take an oath of loyalty to the emperor at the same time as they made their profession of faith. Otherwise they would not be worthy of promotion.[178] The purpose behind administering this oath was to guarantee the succession of Manuel's young son and heir apparent Alexius Comnenus. To that extent it was a recognition of the moral authority vested in the patriarch and the synod, but implicit was the subordination of the church to the emperor. Opposition to him was tantamount to apostasy.

In the last years of his reign Manuel Comnenus was notably less generous to the church than he had been earlier on. The monasteries came under attack. Unlike his forebears Manuel was not a patron of monasteries. At one stage he had plans for a monastery at Kataskepe on the Bosphorus dedicated to St Michael. It was to have been a model

176 Ibid., 213–20.
177 Grumel, 1120.
178 A. Pavlov, 'Sinodal'nyj akt' Konstantinopol'skago patriarkha Mikhaila Ankhiala 1171 goda', *VV* 2(1895), 383–93, at 389.1–11.

monastery, but the scheme was never carried through.[179] Instead, the emperor became increasingly critical of the amount of landed property in monastic hands. The wealth of the monasteries could only be justified in his opinion if it was used to benefit society. 'Otherwise it would be better for the monks to die the most miserable death from famine than to possess a disproportionate share of wealth.'[180] This sentiment was enshrined in an imperial *prostagma* of June 1176 which removed much of the protection that monastic property enjoyed under the chrysobull of 1158. It was seen as a revival of the anti-monastic legislation of Nicephorus Phocas which forbad new monastic foundations and the acquisition of further landed property by the monasteries.[181]

Professor Svoronos[182] has argued that Manuel's anti-monastic measures were forced upon him because of financial difficulties and increasing competition for land from other sections of society, with secular landowners and *pronoia*-holders to the fore. There can be little doubt that such practical considerations played a part, but his lack of enthusiasm for monasticism may also be connected with the style of kingship he was evolving from the middle of his reign. He sought both to set himself above church and society and to escape from the stranglehold of dynastic responsibilities. If he had been a patron of monasteries and monks, he would have been acting much like any other member of the Byzantine aristocracy. He was increasingly concerned to impose order on church and lay society, which for administrative and fiscal purposes were to be carefully separated. For instance, gifts of imperial property to members of the senate or to the army were not to be alienated to the church or monasteries.[183] The church, for its part, was to be set apart from secular society, distinguished by special privileges for persons and property. As we saw above, priests were exempted from the payment of taxation to the state in 1144, but their numbers were to be carefully registered and those not on the register were denied these fiscal concessions.[184] In 1166 the patriarch and synod considered the equity of this measure. They put the problem to the emperor. In their opinion the priesthood enjoyed exemption from taxation out of imperial recognition of priestly status. For priests to pay taxes to the state meant that they were being treated as members of the laity.[185] The emperor was apparently willing to accept this interpretation which was based on the separation of the priesthood from lay society. It was a recognition

179 Nicetas Choniates, 206–7.
180 Eustathius I, 231.
181 Nicetas Choniates, 206.85–91; Zepos I, 425; Dölger, *Reg.* 1553.
182 Svoronos, 'Privilèges', 379–82.
183 Dölger, *Reg.* 1333, 1398.
184 Ibid. 1335–6.
185 Zepos I, 366 n.6; Grumel, 1081–2.

of the autonomy enjoyed by the church with the rider that the arbiter and the guarantor of this autonomy was the emperor in his capacity as *epistemonarkhes* of the church.

The Patriarch Luke Chrysoberges equally strove to maintain the separation of church and lay society. Members of the clergy were often found following secular callings. This was strictly against canon law, but little attention was usually paid to such infringements. One of Luke Chrysoberges's first acts as patriarch[186] was to forbid the clergy to engage in secular activities. One of the victims of this prohibition was the distinguished canon lawyer Alexius Aristenos who had occupied a series of the highest positions in both the imperial and patriarchal administrations.[187] The promiscuity of secular and clerical pursuits was a problem that Chrysoberges kept coming back to. His stance was taken to its logical conclusion by his successor Michael Ankhialos'. He decided that the prohibitions against members of the clergy engaging in secular activities should apply to readers – the lowliest clerical grade.[188] Manuel Comnenus for his part legislated to prevent members of the clergy occupying changers' stalls and acting as bankers.[189]

The church obtained the administrative and fiscal autonomy which had been one of its long-term aims, but the price was the recognition of the emperor's supervisory role. The failure of the young Manuel Comnenus to exercise this role in the early part of his reign produced division and dissension within the church and revealed how dependent the church was upon imperial sanction for the maintenance of order. This reliance on imperial authority would then be enshrined by Theodore Balsamon in Byzantine canon law. This had fateful consequences: it left the church subservient to imperial authority. The church would be caught up in the political upheavals that followed the death of Manuel Comnenus in 1180. The church failed to provide any worthwhile initiatives. Its passivity contributed to the turmoil of the time.

186 Grumel, 1048.
187 Tornikès, 53–7.
188 Grumel, 1119.
189 Zepos I, 416–17; Dölger, *Reg.* 1384.

4

THE FAILURE OF THE COMNENIAN CHURCH SETTLEMENT

The succession crisis

CONTEMPORARIES were unanimous in their high regard for the moral qualities of the Patriarch Theodosius Boradiotes (1179–83). In the closing months of Manuel Comnenus's reign he stood up to the emperor and indicated his unease about his proposal that the anathema against Muhammad and his God should be dropped from the formula of abjuration from Islam. The resulting compromise might be said to have vindicated the patriarch's stand. He was able to get the dying emperor to renounce his notorious interest in astrology and pay more attention to the concrete problems surrounding the succession of his young son Alexius Comnenus. It is not clear that Manuel appointed him as guardian for his son and heir, but the patriarch's moral authority counted during his minority. As Manuel lay dying, he appointed his Empress Maria as regent for their son Alexius.

The patriarch was soon disillusioned by the empress. He was alarmed at the way she was handing over the government of the Empire to her lover, the *protosebastos* Alexius Comnenus. This was all the more ominous because the young emperor had yet to be crowned. The patriarch was sympathetic to the opposition to the empress's regime that was growing up around Maria Comnena, the Emperor Manuel's daughter, and her husband the Caesar John (of the house of Montferrat). He received them with open arms when in February 1181 they fled to St Sophia for asylum.[1] When agents came from the imperial palace to drag them out, the patriarch interceded on their behalf. His relations with the empress became so bad that he dared not proceed to the imperial palace on Easter Sunday, when it was the custom for patriarch and emperor to exchange the kiss of peace. He put off the ceremony until the following Friday. This gave the *protosebastos* his chance. He had the patriarch confined in the monastery of Christ Pantepoptes. He called an assembly

[1] Eustathius I, cap. 16, p.272; II, 22–25.

of bishops hostile to the patriarch reinforced by members of the senate hoping to persuade this body to vote for the dismissal of the patriarch. But this it failed to do, because there were no convincing charges that could be laid against the patriarch.[2]

With the patriarch out of the way Maria Comnena and her supporters turned St Sophia into an armed camp. Their action divided the church. The majority of metropolitans and bishops opposed her, but she had the enthusiastic support of many, if not all, of the clergy of the capital.[3] When the supporters of Maria Comnena came to blows in the Augoustaion with the empress's troops, they were urged on by a priest holding aloft an icon of Christ, by another with a cross, and by yet another with a sacred banner. They called it a holy war, their justification being the treatment of the patriarch by the empress's regime. By 2 May 1181 the patriarch was back in St Sophia. Clad in his patriarchal robes and holding a bible he went out into the forecourt of St Sophia. A battle was raging outside, but he was determined that no combatant should break into the precincts of the Great Church. By nightfall he had sent his personal servant to the palace and had managed to engineer a truce. It therefore seems that he had been released from confinement either on 2 May or a few days before.

His release is described in detail by Nicetas Choniates.[4] Members of the patriarchal administration and those few bishops who remained loyal to the patriarch together with 'the whole demos of the city' went to the monastery of the Pantepoptes and escorted him in triumph back to St Sophia. His opponents among the bishops and metropolitans dared not show their faces on the streets of Constantinople. Theodosius was able to negotiate a safeconduct for Maria Comnena and her husband. Peace was restored to the city and Theodosius effected a reconciliation with the bishops and metropolitans who had been opposed to him.[5]. It was a triumph for the patriarch. The strength of his position soon became apparent. In July 1181 the young Alexius Comnenus issued a

[2] Ibid. I, cap.18, p.276; II, 25; Nicetas Choniates, 241–2.

[3] Eustathius I, cap.19, p.278; II, 25–7.

[4] Nicetas Choniates, 241–3.

[5] Eustathius I, cap. 23; II, 29. There is a discrepancy between the accounts given by Eustathius and Choniates.The former was writing more or less contemporaneously, but at the time was away from the capital in his see of Thessalonica. Nicetas was at Constantinople when the events took place, but wrote his account many years later. Eustathius places the patriarch's dismissal and confinement soon after the first Sunday after Easter (12 April 1181) and in the context of Maria Comnena's search for asylum at St Sophia. According to this account the patriarch's seclusion in the Pantepoptes monastery lasted roughly a month, which accords with his presence in St Sophia on 2 May. Nicetas, on the other hand, places the patriarch's condemnation after the battle between the imperial troops and the supporters of Maria Comnena on this date, in other words at the moment that Eustathius suggests he was being released. I have resisted the temptation to conflate the two accounts and suggest that the patriarch was condemned on two separate occasions. I have accepted

rescript (*lysis*) rescinding his father's restrictive legislation on monastic estates.[6]

Theodosius's success in restoring peace to the capital ensured that he was for a time the arbiter of events in the capital. His influence was apparent to Andronicus Comnenus, the late emperor's cousin, who was plotting the overthrow of the empress's regime from his base in Paphlagonia. He wrote to the patriarch, assuring him of his loyalty to the young emperor.[7] His cultivation of the good-will of the patriarch paid off, for it was Theodosius who handed the city of Constantinople over to him in May 1182. Andronicus immediately disabused the patriarch of any hopes that he might have had of a share in government. Theodosius was informed that the Emperor Manuel had left Andronicus as the young emperor's sole guardian and had entrusted the government of the Empire to him. He was therefore under no obligation to associate any colleague with him in the regency, not even his holiness. The patriarch accepted the situation, but was determined to protect the interests of the young emperor. Otherwise, as he remarked, the boy might as well be numbered among the dead with Andronicus in charge of the government. This exchange comes from Nicetas Choniates's history and may well be *ben trovato*, designed to protect the patriarch's reputation and to indicate future developments.[8]

Be that as it may, the patriarch was able to ensure that on 16 May 1182, a few days after Andronicus had taken possession of Constantinople, the young emperor was at last crowned. Andronicus carried him into St Sophia on his shoulders and behaved as though he was his devoted supporter. The empress-mother was still in the palace. She was a barrier to Andronicus's ambitions because it was stated very clearly in the oath that all officers of the crown and prelates had taken to Manuel Comnenus in 1171 that until Alexius Comnenus attained his majority at the age of sixteen she was to be regent. Andronicus embarked on a campaign against the woman. He encouraged the mob to shout uncomplimentary things about her. The main obstacle was the patriarch who did not want her expelled from the palace. Andronicus threatened to turn the rabble with their demagogues (*kynognomones*) on him unless he did what he was told.

Eustathius's dating because he is the more specific about the circumstances and date of the patriarch's dismissal. This incident also attracted the attention of Michael the Syrian (*La Chronique de Michel le Syrien*, transl. J.B. Chabot (Paris, 1899–1910), 4 vols., III, 381–2).

6 Zepos I, 427–8; Dölger, *Reg.* 1550.

7 Nicetas Choniates, 228.43–52.

8 Ibid., 252–4.

The patriarch gave in very tamely. Then in September 1183 he relinquished the patriarchal office and retired to his monastery on the island of Terebinthos in the sea of Marmora. What occasioned his abdication was Andronicus's demand that the church approve the marriage he was arranging between his bastard daughter and Manuel Comnenus's bastard son Alexius. It is true that since the fathers were first cousins, the prospective couple were only second cousins, a relationship within the prohibited degrees, but dispensation was not unknown. The mothers were the complicating factor: the mother of Manuel's bastard was one of the emperor's many nieces; the mother of Andronicus's was one of his cousins, but also a niece of Manuel. The tangle of incestuous relationships placed the marriage scandalously within the prohibited degrees. The argument that because they were bastards the relations created by affinity did not count was specious. Theodosius tried to oppose the marriage, but he found himself pretty much isolated; only Leontios, the exiled patriarch of Jerusalem, was willing to support his opposition to the marriage.[9] He was outmanoeuvred by Andronicus who persuaded the archbishop of Bulgaria to officiate at the wedding in the place of the reluctant patriarch. Theodosius retired defeated. To succeed him Andronicus appointed Basil Kamateros, who came from a great court family. He had previously bound himself in writing only to do those things that Andronicus wished, even if contrary to canon law. His first act was to legitimise the marriage.[10]

There was a marked contrast between the confidence and moral fortitude displayed by Theodosius before Andronicus's coup of May 1182 and his rather tame abdication over a relatively unimportant matter. His position had become weaker. Whether his moral authority had been compromised in Byzantine eyes by the terrible slaughter of Latins which occurred just before Andronicus's entry into Constantinople can only be a matter of conjecture. What is certain is that he was deprived of that popular support on which he had counted in his opposition to the empress's regime. This now belonged to Andronicus who made clever use of mob leaders. Nor did Theodosius have much backing from the church. The *Life* of St Leontios, patriarch of Jerusalem, provides an insight into the self-serving attitudes that prevailed among the higher clergy. Leontios was formerly abbot of the monastery of St John the Theologian on the island of Patmos. The *oikonomos* or steward of the monastery approached Leontios and asked him to end his opposition to the marriage of the imperial bastards. Otherwise Andronicus was not

9 Leontios of Jerusalem, 427; ed. Tsougarakis. 142–3. Cf. W. Hecht. 'Der *Bios* des Patriarchen Leontius von Jerusalem als Quelle zur Geschichte Andronikos' I. Komnenos', *BZ* 61 (1968), 40–3.

10 Grumel, 1162.

likely to exempt the monastery of Patmos from the payment of customs duties for one of its ships, which is what the monastery was angling for. Leontios refused to budge even for the sake of his old monastery, but he was a saint![11]

Theodosius was in any case unpopular with the episcopal bench. Almost all the metropolitans and bishops had deserted him in his previous trial of strength with the empress's regime. It was partly that the habit of obedience to the wishes of the imperial government had become engrained in the closing stages of Manuel Comnenus's reign. It may also be that the episcopal bench was suspicious of a patriarch, such as Theodosius, who was willing to intervene so openly on the political stage. His prestige might be such that it would allow him to impose his will on the synod.

Without the full support of the synod the Patriarch Theodosius was in no position to protect the young emperor Alexius from the ambitions of his guardian Andronicus Comnenus. Within weeks of Theodosius's abdication the young emperor was eliminated. Andronicus then required the new patriarch and his synod to absolve both him and his accomplices from the oath they had taken to Manuel Comnenus that they would safeguard the life of his young son. It was perhaps not just their habitual subservience that made them comply with the new emperor's wishes. They demanded and got in return from the emperor an undertaking that henceforth the patriarch and synod would sit in council with the emperor.[12] Nicetas Choniates who provides this detail never makes plain its significance. Presumably, by cooperating with Andronicus the new patriarch Basil Kamateros hoped to extract significant concessions that had been denied to Theodosius. It looks as though he was seeking recognition by the emperor of the constitutional right of the patriarch and synod to participate in government along with the senate. If so, it would have been harking back to the arrangement that had been sanctioned by the Emperor Nicephorus Botaneiates (1078–81).

Andronicus outmanoeuvred the patriarch. Once he had been absolved of his oath, he simply rescinded the concession he had made to the patriarch and synod. Discredited Basil Kamateros and the bishops remained on the sidelines during the bloody unfolding of Andronicus's reign. Such opposition to the tyrant as there was within the church came from individuals, such as Leontios of Jerusalem and George Disypatos, a reader of St Sophia, who had the courage to denounce Andronicus for the cruelty of his regime.[13]

[11] Leontios of Jerusalem, 428; ed. Tsougarakis, 142–5.
[12] Nicetas Choniates, 276–7.
[13] Ibid., 312–13.

Isaac II Angelos and the church

Andronicus was overthrown in September 1185 by a spontaneous uprising in the capital. The mob brought Isaac Angelus to power. The Patriarch Basil Kamateros was hopelessly compromised. Under pressure from the mob he crowned Isaac emperor. Just as in the past he had done the tyrant's bidding, so now he fell in with the new emperor's desires. He gave his approval to an imperial act rescinding all Andronicus's legislation; he forbad the marriage of Bela, king of Hungary, to Theodora, Manuel Comnenus's only surviving sister. Such a marriage would have been politically embarrassing for the new emperor because Theodora had as good a claim as anyone on dynastic grounds to the Byzantine throne.[14] The patriarch hurried to give his assent to the new emperor's decision to allow a politically expedient marriage to go ahead between his sister and John Cantacuzenus, even though it was within the prohibited degrees.[15] Having served his purpose Basil Kamateros was dismissed from office by the emperor in February 1186. The first act of his successor was to have him condemned by synod for authorising the marriage of Andronicus's bastard daughter to Manuel Comnenus's bastard son.[16]

Isaac Angelus owed his elevation to the imperial dignity to luck, as much as anything, but once on the throne he determined to rule in the grand style of his uncle Manuel Comnenus. It was the style rather than the substance that counted. Playing the disciplinarian – the *epistemonarkhes* – of the church, in the manner of his uncle, was central to the image he wished to project. He hoped that ascendancy over the church would provide an effective basis for the exercise of imperial authority. After the humiliations and uncertainties of the last two patriarchates there was a section within the church that was only too happy to welcome a return to the conditions existing at the end of Manuel's reign. Theodore Balsamon, the former *chartophylax* of St Sophia, was just finishing his commentaries on the canons with their insistence on the emperor's disciplinary role within the church. Balsamon looked to imperial authority as a guarantee of the privileges of his office and of the position of the patriarchal clergy. He was now titular patriarch of Antioch and had the ear of the emperor who consulted him on occasion. Indicative of Balsamon's influence with the new emperor was the regard he paid to the officers and clergy of St Sophia. It was because it was unpleasing to the *chartophylax* of the Great Church that Isaac Angelus outlawed the practice of bishops

14 Grumel, 1166; G. Moravcsik, 'Pour une alliance byzantino-hongroise', *B* 8(1933), 555–68 (= G. Moravcsik, *Studia Byzantina* (Amsterdam, 1967), 309–12).

15 Grumel, 1167.

16 A. Papadopoulos-Kerameus, 'ΚΕΡΚΥΡΑΙΚΑ', *VV* 13(1906), 346–7; Grumel, 1168.

continuing to live with their wives, or so he claimed.[17] When it came to legislating about episcopal elections he gave almost equal weight to the ancient custom of St Sophia as he did to the canons.[18] The emperor's reliance on the clergy of St Sophia sometimes embarrassed them. Asked to express his opinion before synod, the Grand Skeuophylax, the future Patriarch George Xiphilinos, replied, 'It is not at all for us to give an opinion on such great matters, but to follow the lead of synod.' Perhaps he protested too much, for he and his colleagues nevertheless provided the emperor with the opinion that he was looking for.[19] This concerned the dismissal of Dositheos from the throne of Constantinople, which was the central episode of Isaac's reign, at least where his dealings with the church were concerned.

Isaac replaced Basil Kamateros as patriarch with Nicetas Mountanes, who was the Grand Sakellarios of St Sophia. He dismissed him abruptly in February 1189 on the grounds that he was old and incompetent. He claimed that there was nobody to be found among the clergy of Constantinople who was worthy of the patriarchate. He therefore consulted Theodore Balsamon, now patriarch of Antioch, as to whether it might not be possible, despite the prohibition of the canons, to transfer somebody from another patriarchal throne to that of Constantinople. The emperor, apparently, let it be understood that he had Balsamon in mind as the next patriarch of Constantinople. The great canonist hastily contrived a tract to justify such a transfer. It was presented to synod in the form of a tome for approval.[20] Having prepared the ground in this way Isaac then imposed the titular patriarch of Jerusalem Dositheos on the patriarchal throne of Constantinople. This man was very close to the emperor. He was of Venetian descent, but had been a monk of Stoudios. He was Isaac's spiritual director. He had encouraged him to secure the throne and inspired his dreams of imperial grandeur – the recovery of Palestine and driving the Turks back beyond the Euphrates.[21] The synod was outraged by Isaac's appointment of Dositheos who was forced to resign after a reign of nine days. The emperor found himself a new patriarch, apparently recommended to him by the Mother of God in a dream. In the end, such powerful support counted for little beside the emperor's desire to have his mentor on the patriarchal throne. He induced the new patriarch to abdicate.[22] The emperor then restored Dositheos, using force to cower any opposition

[17] Zepos I, 434, 15–16; Dolger, *Reg.* 1573.
[18] Zepos I, 434, 15–16; Dolger, *Reg.* 1572.
[19] A. Papadopoulos-Kerameus, *ΑΝΑΛΕΚΤΑ ΙΕΡΟΣΟΛΥΜΙΤΙΚΗΣ ΣΤΑΧΥΛΟΓΙΑΣ* (St Petersburg, 1891–8; repr. Brussels, 1963), 5 vols., II 365–7.
[20] V. Grumel, 'Le *Peri Metatheseon* et le patriarche de Constantinople Dosithée', *EB* 1(1943), 239–49; Nicetas Choniates, 406–8.
[21] Nicetas Choniates, 405, 432–3.
[22] Grumel, 1176.

there might be to the move. Dositheos was hated perhaps unfairly, as a man who coveted the patriarchal throne (*philothronos*). Though resolutely anti-Latin, his Venetian parentage also counted against him.[23]

Despite the resentment engendered in all walks of life by his imposition of Dositheos on the patriarchal throne, Isaac was able to maintain him in office for some two years. These were the years 1189–90 when Isaac faced the greatest trial of his reign: the passage through his lands of the German contingent of the third crusade under the Emperor Frederick I Barbarossa. Loyal to his understanding with Saladin he planned to oppose the German crusaders.[24] He had the support of the Patriarch Dositheos, who was seen, at least by the crusaders, as the heart of the Byzantine opposition to their passage. They believed that he preached against them, calling them dogs and assuring convicted murderers that they would be able to wipe away their guilt by killing crusaders. When peace was made in November 1189, Frederick Barbarossa insisted that the treaty should be signed by the patriarch, as a guarantee that he would cease to foment opposition to the crusaders. The patriarch's compliance with this demand was delayed until February 1190.[25] Dositheos's anti-Latin stance does not seem to have endeared him to the bishops. Once the crisis was over pressure built up again within the church for his removal. There was a demand that he return to the patriarchate of Jerusalem. The emperor wanted to protect him and on 3 September 1191 called an assembly in the palace of St Zacharias, which, in the tradition of Manuel Comnenus, he packed with relatives, ministers, and servants. Bishops, patriarchal officers, even deacons of St Sophia were hauled before it to give their opinion as to the fate of the patriarch. They were in favour of his return to Jerusalem. Dositheos had had enough. He preferred on 10 September 1191 to resign both patriarchates. He wished all well, except those who had impugned his orthodoxy.[26] He was succeeded by the Grand Skeuophylax George Xiphilinos. This was not quite the end of the affair. When on 13 September the patriarch-designate came to receive the priestly unction, some of the bishops expressed doubts as to whether the assembly of 3 September was empowered to examine the patriarch. There was the danger that they might refuse to recognise the promotion of the new patriarch and that therefore schism might ensue. This was averted when in the presence of the officers and deacons of St Sophia sixteen metropolitans and bishops declared themselves willing to accept the emperor's new promotion to the patriarchal throne and to

23 J. Darrouzès, 'Notes inédites de transferts épiscopaux', *REB* 40(1982), 159.42.
24 C.M. Brand, 'The Byzantines and Saladin, 1185–1192: opponents of the third crusade', *Speculum* 37(1962), 167–81.
25 Grumel, 1177.
26 Ibid., 1178.

concelebrate with him.[27] One can only suppose that the new patriarch used the backing of his former colleagues, the officers of the patriarchal administration, to overawe opposition from the episcopal bench.

The choice of George Xiphilinos as patriarch was a skilful one on the emperor's part, even if his support for the emperor seemed to waver. He was likely to have been acceptable to the episcopal bench because, as we have seen, he made the most judicious reply when asked for his opinion by the emperor about Dositheos's resignation, to the effect that he was inclined to follow the lead of the bishops in the matter. He added that in his opinion all should be done to avoid a scandal within the church. He stood, in other words, for conciliation. He had also been an officer of St Sophia and was therefore more likely to be loyal to the emperor in his longstanding battle with a section of the episcopate over control of synod and appointments to vacant sees.

The emperor needed support for his ally on the episcopal bench: the metropolitan bishop of Cyzicus. This bishop had in September 1187 formally requested that the emperor, in his capacity as disciplinarian of the church, should investigate the rigging of elections by a clique of bishops.[28] As such, the emperor had, in the words of the metropolitan, a 'responsibility to put right anything that was done contrary to the canons'.[29] Specifically, elections were taking place without all the bishops and metropolitans present in the capital being expressly informed that a vote in synod was about to take place. The metropolitan bishop of Cyzicus's opponents led by the metropolitan bishop of Ephesus countered that he had been summoned to the previous meeting of the synod, when elections had taken place. They reminded him that he had excused himself on the grounds that he was too ill to attend and therefore unwilling to express his preferences.

The metropolitan of Cyzicus retorted that the invitation had not been in writing and was therefore not valid. He was backed up by his colleague of Caesarea, who claimed never to have been summoned to synod since the day of his election. He had not even been summoned to the present meeting before the emperor and his appearance in the palace was quite accidental. On the basis of these exchanges the emperor declared all recent elections to vacant sees to be null and void and ordered new elections. In future, all bishops and metropolitans present in the capital were to be formally summoned in writing to take part in the elections of new metropolitans. It must have been to embarrass the emperor's opponents on the episcopal bench that ten days later on 20 September 1187 the metropolitan bishop of Cyzicus brought another

[27] Papadopoulos-Kerameus, *ΑΝΑΛΕΚΤΑ*, II, 370–1.
[28] Zepos I, 434.15–16; Dolger, *Reg.* 1572.
[29] Zepos I, 430.19–22; Dolger, *Reg.* 1572.

question of ecclesiastical discipline before the emperor: why was it that bishops and metropolitan bishops were ignoring the canonical injunction about bishops putting away their wives, once elected to their sees?[30]

There was another way open to the emperor to ensure a more amenable synod. This was to create new metropolitan sees. There had been few creations since early in the reign of Alexius I Comnenus. By 1189 Isaac had set up five, possibly six, new metropolitan sees. It is now clear that Isaac did not carry through, as was once thought, any general reorganisation of the ecclesiastical hierarchy.[31] Since three of his new creations, Hypaipa, Pyrgion, and Nyssa, and possibly a fourth Arkadioupolis, were suffragans of the metropolitan of Ephesus,[32] Isaac's motive would seem to be to weaken the hold that his opponents, led by this prelate, had over synod. His promotions provoked criticism. His opponents among the bishops contended that his promotions were merely honorific in line with canon 12 of the council of Chalcedon. The implication of this was that the new metropolitans would continue to be installed in office by their former metropolitans. The emperor refused to countenance this and in 1193 declared that his promotions must be elected by the synod at Constantinople, just like any other metropolitans.[33] But by now Isaac was making concessions to the metropolitans. In April 1192 he reissued the decrees of John II Comnenus and Manuel Comnenus protecting their estates from the depredations of imperial administrators and fiscal agents. The penalties were increased: restitution was now to be double the value of the property taken with a quadruple fine to the state, while the culprits were to be excommunicated, for their crime was deemed an insult to the emperor.[34] The Patriarch George Xiphilinos also had to make concessions to the metropolitans. In November 1191 he agreed to a marked reduction of the rights that the patriarch exercised over the dependencies of stauropegial or patriarchal monasteries. These were to remain under the control of the local bishop. Two months later, he had to concede that this applied retrospectively.[35]

In Isaac's dealings with the church the resignation of Dositheos was a turning point. No longer was there talk of the emperor's disciplinary powers over the church.[36] It meant that Isaac had failed to establish

[30] Zepos I, 435–6; Dolger, *Reg.* 1573.

[31] Darrouzès, *Notitiae* 134–5; J. Darrouzès, 'Un décret d'Isaac II Angelos', *REB* 40(1982), 135.

[32] P. Culerrier, 'Les évêchés suffragants d'Ephèse aux 5e-13e siècles', *REB* 45(1987), 139–64.

[33] Dolger, *Reg.* 1614.

[34] J. Darrouzès, 'Un décret d' Isaac II Angelos', 150.

[35] Grumel, 1179–80.

[36] Ibid., 1178.

the desired ascendancy over the church. His treatment of the church in the early part of his reign was extremely high handed, whether it was removing the worthy Patriarch Nicetas II, promoting suffragan sees to metropolitan status, or imposing Dositheos on the church by force. The failure of Isaac's attempt to oppose the passage of the third crusade destroyed the emperor's credibility, because it exposed as fantasies his plans for a restoration of imperial authority. He was forced on the defensive.

The eve of the fourth crusade

Isaac Angelus was overthrown in April 1195 by his brother Alexius. The coup occurred out of town in Thrace. It remained for Alexius's supporters to secure the capital. Nicetas Choniates was contemptuous of the role of the clergy of St Sophia and the patriarch who was inclined to oppose the usurpation. One of the doorkeepers bribed with a few coins ascended the *ambo* and began to acclaim Alexius as emperor without waiting for the patriarch's assent. The patriarch tamely submitted to this infringement of his authority.[37] As a sop to potential opposition within the church the new emperor returned the see of Argos raised by Isaac to metropolitan honours to its original episcopal status.[38]

Alexius's solution to the management of the church was to put its affairs in the hands of his favourite and chief minister Constantine Mesopotamites. The better to deal with the church Mesopotamites was promoted to the rank of deacon and the Patriarch George Xiphilinos had to issue a tome allowing him to carry out both secular and ecclesiastical functions. As if this was not enough Mesopotamites was then promoted to the metropolitan see of Thessalonica.[39] There was soon agitation that Mesopotamites be removed both from the post of *epi tou kanikleiou* or keeper of the imperial inkstand and from the see of Thessalonica. A case for his dismissal from the latter was brought before the synod. The charges were not considered sufficient to warrant his dismissal. The Patriarch George Xiphilinos then had new charges added; this time serious enough for his dismissal.[40]

After this Alexius withdrew to the safety of the Blakhernai palace and allowed his city and the church to look after themselves. This produced a curious incident. A successful Byzantine banker Kalomodios was seized by the tax inspectors. The business people of Constantinople responded by marching on St Sophia and threatening to tear the

37 Nicetas Choniates, 456.75–82.

38 J. Darrouzès, 'Notes inédites de transferts épiscopaux', *REB* 40(1982), 159.9–12.

39 Nicetas Choniates, 489–90; Grumel, 1185.

40 Nicetas Choniates, 491–2; Grumel, 1187.

patriarch from his altar, unless he interceded with the emperor on behalf of Kalomodios. The patriarch calmed the protestors and rescued the banker from the clutches of the imperial agents.[41] This incident combined both a lack of respect for the person of the patriarch and a recognition that he had the power to intercede with the emperor to right acts of apparent tyranny. This may only have been because the patriarch was more open to popular pressure than the emperor safe in the fastness of the Blakhernai palace.

It was at least proof that St Sophia remained the hub of the city. People streamed into the forecourt, now known as the *protekdikeion*, with petitions on a variety of matters which they presented to the *protekdikos* and his tribunal. This office grew in importance over the twelfth century. The Patriarch George Xiphilinos admitted its holder into the top tier of the office holders of St Sophia, the so called *exokatakoiloi*, which to that point had consisted of the *oikonomos*, the *sakellarios*, the *skeuophylax*, the *chartophylax*, and the *epi tou sakelliou*.[42] The claims of the *protekdikos* had irritated Theodore Balsamon who saw them as a direct challenge to the privileges of his own office of *chartophylax*. He did not dispute the *protekdikos*'s traditional responsibilities for those seeking asylum and redress of grievances, but contested his claims to jurisdiction over the clergy of St Sophia and the churches of the capital. He rejected out of hand the possibility that the *protekdikos* might have the right to condemn a party that failed to appear before the court of the *ekdikeion* after three summons. At stake was the right to discipline the clergy. Balsamon contended that it belonged to the *chartophylax* by virtue of his position as the patriarch's deputy. His stance underlines the departmental rivalries within the patriarchal church.

Balsamon was exaggerating the powers of his office. The patriarch preferred the claims of the *protekdikos*.[43] This function gave the patriarchal church a vital role in the life of the capital. It meant that for the redress of grievances people looked to St Sophia. But this increased the pressures on the patriarchate, as the Kalomodios incident showed. It revealed a lack of respect for the patriarch, as though he could be constrained by a show of force.

The church was also to be divided by a new dogmatic controversy, which Isaac Angelus had held in check. Emperors preferred to clamp down on discussion of contentious points of theology. In this Andronicus Comnenus was typical. One day Euthymios Malakes, the metropolitan bishop of Neai Patrai, and the historian John Cinnamus began discussing in his presence issues raised by the 'Father is greater

41 Nicetas Choniates, 523–4.

42 Grumel, 1190.

43 Rhalles & Potles IV, 530–32; Darrouzès, *OFFIKIA*, 86–98, 343–4; Beck, *Kirche*, 115, 119–20.

than I' controversy. The emperor at once told them to desist or he would throw them into the river Rhyndakos, which happened to be close by.[44] The controversy that was once more going to divide the church concerned the eucharist. Were the communion elements corruptible or incorruptible, mutable or immutable? It was normally assumed that the prayer of consecration turned them into the body and blood of Christ and that they were therefore incorruptible. This assumption was to be questioned by Michael Glykas, also known as Sikidites, who had been a secretary of Manuel Comnenus.[45] He was blinded in 1159 on the orders of the emperor after being found guilty on a charge of necromancy. Disgraced he became a monk and turned to theology. He was struck by the way the priest broke the bread when administering communion. He could not see how this tallied with the notion that the communion elements were incorruptible. He was even more forcibly struck by one detail of the institution of the communion service at the Last Supper: Christ presided over it as a man. He therefore argued that the communion elements were the body and blood of the incarnate Christ. The communion was a sacrifice of the living Christ. To his way of thinking the communion elements remained corruptible until they were sacrificed; that is to say, consumed by the communicant, when they were miraculously transformed, in the same way as the Risen Christ. Thus transformed they helped to reinforce man's immortal soul and brought salvation a little closer. It was an approach to the mystery of the eucharist that emphasised its reality.[46]

Glykas's ideas circulated in monastic circles and attracted little outside attention. It was only when they were championed by John Kastamonites at the end of the twelfth century that they were taken seriously and were to divide the church. By that time Michael Glykas was most probably dead. John Kastamonites came from one of those bureaucratic families that were prominent at the end of the twelfth century. It was even allied to the Angelus dynasty.[47] He began his career as a secretary to the future Patriarch Basil Kamateros, who promoted him first to the position of *didaskalos* of the Apostles and then to that of *didaskalos* of the Gospels.[48] Kastamonites's career must have suffered a set back with the dismissal of Basil Kamateros, but by 1191 he had been appointed to Chalcedon, that most coveted of sees.

He used his position to promote Michael Glykas's views on the eucharist and seems to have had the tacit support of the Patriarch

[44] Nicetas Choniates, 331.93ff.

[45] See Magdalino, *Manuel I Komnenos*, 370–82.

[46] Michael Glykas, II, 133–5, 348–79. Cf. Mahlon H. Smith III, *And Taking Bread* ... (Paris 1978), 119–35.

[47] Katsaros, *ΙΩΑΝΝΗΣ ΚΑΣΤΑΜΟΝΙΤΗΣ* 121–62.

[48] Ibid., 82–7.

George Xiphilinos. His opponents in synod sought the help of agitators off the streets – a significant detail.[49] Isaac Angelus intervened to silence debate.[50] It was renewed after Alexius III Angelus ascended the throne and provided the background to John Kamateros's accession to the patriarchal throne in August 1198. He had already made an enemy of the historian Nicetas Choniates, who then held the position of Grand Logothete and was a man to be reckoned with. Nicetas explains the circumstances. He and John Kamateros were invited with others to celebrate the feast of St George in April 1197 at the house of a common acquaintance. The guests settled down to enjoy the concert of choral music that their host had organised for the festival. John Kamateros spoilt the occasion. He insisted on inflicting his opinions about the eucharistic elements on the company. There were protests led by Nicetas Choniates that these had nothing to do with the celebration of the feast. John Kamateros took umbrage and numbered Nicetas and others among his opponents. He composed a tract directed against them though he did not name names. Attributed to them was a belief that it was wrong to break or bite the communion bread. It had to be swallowed whole to be efficacious. This was a crude parody of Michael Glykas's teachings about the eucharist. Nicetas Choniates was livid. It was not only a false accusation. It was a dangerous imputation against his orthodoxy, which might have political implications. John Kamateros was then *chartophylax* of the patriarchal church. He was using the controversy over the eucharist as a way of presenting his claims to succeed to the patriarchal throne, or so Nicetas Choniates believed. The old patriarch was ailing and authorised Kamateros to give the Lenten address for 1198 in his place. As it happened, Kamateros was too ill to deliver it, but he leaked its contents in advance. Again John Kamateros took the opportunity to impute opinions to Nicetas Choniates and his friends. Nicetas Choniates struck back. His accusations against Kamateros have a strong political tinge to them. They were designed to question his fitness for high office. He was offending against the canon of the sixth council that forbad altering the dogma of the church. He was guilty of perverting the understanding of the emperor and disregarding the proclamation of the patriarch. He was already usurping the powers of the patriarch. The attack failed and Kamateros duly became patriarch.[51]

If Nicetas Choniates is to be believed the new patriarch was an

49 Ibid., 254 n. 50.

50 Ibid., 280.

51 F. Grabler, *Kaisertaten und Menschenschichsale* (Byzantinische Geschichtesschreiber XI) (Graz, 1966), no.8, 123–48. To judge by Nicetas Choniates's invective Kamateros was a bitter enemy. This is in contrast to his *History*, where his treatment of Kamateros is entirely neutral.

enthusiastic supporter of the ideas of Michael Glykas. He was supposed to have dismissed the communion elements as corruptible, without life or spirit, in a word dead. Nicetas has him insisting that a communicant did not receive the whole Christ, but only a part. This is a crude travesty of Glykas's teachings, but what else should we expect from an invective! Kamateros informed Choniates, even before he became patriarch, that he intended to impose his views on the church.[52] They were more moderate than Nicetas Choniates allowed. The patriarch emphasised that the mystery is always a mystery and hoped naively that this would be a sufficient basis for compromise.[53] He backed up this approach 'with complex arguments and dialectical methods'.[54] He gave a Lenten address that set out his views on the controversy, but failed to do justice to those of his opponents. Worse than this, he imputed to them ideas that they had never entertained.[55] He removed opponents from episcopal office.There were meetings of synod packed with the patriarch's supporters. Kamateros used his connections at court to obtain the backing of ministers.[56] The church was in a turmoil. It is impossible to catch all the undercurrents, but the patriarch appears to have cowed the opposition. He was in a position to impose his views on synod. It met in 1200 and censured – probably posthumously – Myron Sikidites (alias Michael Glykas) as a heresiarch. It forbad further discussion of his writings. But there was no direct condemnation; only a reiteration of two of the *anathemas* added to the *synodikon* of Orthodoxy on the occasion of the condemnation of Soterichos Panteugenos in 1157. The first condemned those who interpreted Christ's words 'Do this in memory of me' figuratively. In other words, they understood the eucharist to be little more than a memorial. The second took issue with those who believed that the reconciliation of Christ's humanity and divinity was a continuing process beginning with the incarnation and completed at the crucifixion.[57]

The patriarch was thus able to dispose of Michael Glykas's ideas about the eucharist without directly engaging with them. They were erroneous in so far as they did not agree with the *synodikon* of Orthodoxy. The renewal of the *anathemas* added in 1157 may have been directed as much against the patriarch's opponents as the supporters of Michael Glykas, who were not condemned.

Synod's decision then went before the emperor for confirmation.

52 Ibid., 129.

53 Nicetas Choniates, 514.46–7.

54 Ibid., 514.47–9; J.L. Van Dieten, *Zur Überlieferung und Veröffentlichung der* Panoplia Dogmatike *des Niketas Choniates* (Amsterdam, 1970), 61.4–5.

55 Nicetas Choniates, 514.50–6.

56 Van Dieten, *Uberlieferung*, 61.1–16.

57 Grumel, 1195; Gouillard, 'Le synodikon de l'orthodoxie', 72–5.

John Kastamonites was not invited to the ceremony, but he burst in at the moment when the imperial secretary was reading out what purported to be the decision of synod from a tablet. He snatched it out of the secretary's hands so that he could confirm that the text was genuine. He objected to an addition equating 'the mystery of the resurrection with the whole economy of Christ'. This had been added in the interests of compromise to balance Kastamonites's stand on the eucharist, but it made a nonsense of Kastamonites's views which required the inclusion of the incarnation in Christ's economy: the point being that Christ instituted communion as a man, before and not after His resurrection. Kastamonites was allowed to defend his position before the emperor. He questioned the validity of a document prepared in advance, even down to the signatures. He had the support of the chief minister, the *epi tou kanikleiou* Theodore Eirenikos.[58] Kastamonites's intervention may explain why the condemnation of Sikidites was not included in the *synodikon* of Orthodoxy. Kastamonites was not even censured and he retained the see of Chalcedon.

It was an unsatisfactory conclusion. The controversy over the communion elements continued to the fall of the city in 1204 and even beyond. As so often, a compromise failed to do justice to an important matter of dogma. The church remained divided. This emphasised the emperor's impotence and inability to bring order to the church. He was unable or unwilling to exercise his epistemonarchic authority over the church. The outcome also undermined the Patriarch John Kamateros's position. He found himself caught between two factions. He never again exercised effective leadership. The controversy must also have contributed to the Byzantine establishment's curious lethargy in the face of approaching crisis. Civil service families – some ancient, such as the Tornikes, the Kamateros, Chrysoberges; others, such as the Choniates, relative newcomers – monopolised high office in both church and state. It should have been a recipe for effective government, but turned out not to be. In part, this must have been a result of the bitter personal divisions engendered by the controversy over the eucharistic elements.

The city of Constantinople was allowed to run more or less out of control. The mob dominated the streets and squares of the capital. The slightest incident now earned their displeasure: for instance, a demonstration ensued when too long a discourse in honour of St Gregory of Nazianzus curtailed the celebration of the feast of St Xenophon, a saint with a popular following in Constantinople.[59] There was scant respect

58 Katsaros, *ΙΩΑΝΝΗΣ ΚΑΣΤΑΜΟΝΙΤΗΣ*, 98–115, 251–7. On Theodore Eirenikos: Nicetas Choniates, 492–3.

59 A.Papadopoulos-Kerameus, 'Ἐπιγράμματα Ἰωάννου τοῦ Ἀπόκαυκου', *ΑΘΗΝΑ* 15 (1903), no. 8, p.470.

for either emperor or patriarch. The stages of this breakdown of law and order are fairly clear. The start was the death of Manuel Comnenus with all the political uncertainties and weaknesses that ensued. The Patriarch Theodosius relied on popular support in his stand against the Empress Maria's regime. Andronicus Comnenus followed his example, raising up gangleaders to positions of political power in order to gain power and eventually the imperial throne. When he failed them he was overthrown and the mob brought Isaac Angelus to power. The new emperor sought to escape their clutches by building on hostility to the West and posing as disciplinarian of the church. It was hoped that control of the church would provide a firm basis for imperial authority. Isaac failed in part because he was not able to manage the church. His brother Alexius III Angelus more or less opted out.

This political and social failure provides one of the major themes of Nicetas Choniates's history. As Alexander Kazhdan puts it, 'the central theme of Choniates' Chronicle is the societal disease that progressively infected the Empire's population, from the mob of Constantinople to the emperor in the Great Palace'.[60] At least, superficially the situation bore a resemblance to the failure of Byzantine political life in the 1070s, from which Alexius Comnenus had rescued Byzantium, restoring social and political order. This prompts a series of questions. What was the nature of this 'societal disease'? Was it endemic to Byzantine society, breaking out at various intervals? Given that cooperation with and ultimately ascendancy over the church was central to Alexius Comnenus's settlement, what role did the church play both in ensuring social order and in its breakdown?

The 'societal disease' afflicting Byzantium was a combination of a failure to live up to one's responsibilities and of an unwillingness to respect one's place in society. Nicetas was struck by the lack of deference shown by the people of Constantinople to their betters and even to their rulers: 'It was like an evil engrained in them. Whom they single out today as their lawful leader (*archon*), next year they will tear to pieces as a criminal'.[61] He attributed their volatility to their lack of any sense of a common interest. This was intensified because Constantinople was a melting pot with a great number of different ethnic groups and as great a variety of trades. The result, Nicetas concluded, was as many different ways of thinking.[62] The society of the capital was probably rather less cohesive than it had been, say in the early eleventh century, for the reasons given by Nicetas. The proportion of foreigners and provincials was higher and the gild system

[60] Kazhdan/Epstein, 229.
[61] Nicetas Choniates, 234.87–8.
[62] Ibid., 283–4.

no longer acted in quite the way it had as a means of social control. Even so, Nicetas was pointing to more or less permanent features of Constantinopolitan society. Its people were always unruly, but it was only periodically that they ran out of control. These occasions almost always coincided with periods of political weakness at the centre.

How did the church contribute to this? Was it more prone to factionalism? Was it enough for friction to develop between the church and the emperor for the resulting differences to be exploited by the people of Constantinople? Did such friction weaken the effectiveness of imperial authority because it deprived it of its moral foundations? This is to assume that the Byzantine church exercised some kind of social control: that it could predispose society towards respect for the established order or arouse it against any emperor with whom it was at odds. No doubt it would be possible to cull from the full range of Byzantine history examples to support both propositions. The evidence of the iconoclast dispute or of the struggle over the union of churches in the last phase of Byzantine history suggests that the monks had a decisive role in moulding public opinion against imperial policies, rather than the official hierarchy of the church, but in the twelfth century monks scarcely feature as a political factor. Only one serious attempt was made in the period to use the church as an instrument of social control. This was Alexius Comnenus's establishment of an order of preachers. The intention was that they should supervise the neighbourhoods of the capital, but this proved abortive. There were other reasons, however, why the hold of the church on the capital at parish level was declining. Towards the end of the century Balsamon noted that there were so few clergy in Constantinople that they had to serve in two sometimes three different churches.[63] The trouble was that St Sophia and one or two other churches, such as the Holy Apostles and the Blakhernai, attracted far more than their fair share of the clergy, because of their prestige and the rewards they had to offer.

The church scarcely acted in any obvious way as an instrument of social control. It was something of a confidence trick. An emperor who had the support of the church could pose more convincingly as the guardian of orthodoxy and was therefore in a better position to dominate society, than one without these advantages. The emperor could display his care for orthodoxy by heresy trials. Those directed against the Bogomils were likely to have been particularly effective in cowing the people of Constantinople. They sowed distrust of neighbours – how could you tell who was not a Bogomil? – and suspicion of pious monks. The heresy trials of the mid-twelfth century were of benefit to Manuel Comnenus and allowed him to impose his

[63] Rhalles & Potles II, 620.

will on the patriarchal clergy, but this may have been at the expense of its morale. With rare exceptions the patriarchs and the officers of St Sophia of the late twelfth century failed to give moral and intellectual leadership to church and society. The church may seldom have acted as an agent of social control, but it had social responsibilities. It dictated some of the rhythms of life. Through the *protekdikos* the patriarchal church responded to the need for redress of grievances in the capital. Increasingly, it seems as though the patriarch and his clergy wished that their moral and political responsibilities would go away, so that they could concentrate on other things: running the church and its estates or pursuing personal vendettas. They would have preferred to escape the hubbub that surrounded most of the churches of the city and retire to the peace and quiet of the church of the Holy Apostles with its school in a colonnaded *peribolos* outside. 'For the rest of the churches of God lie, so to speak, in the middle of confusion, and the ministers of God are jostled by the mob and cannot sing their hymns with freedom, but this [church of the Holy Apostles] is free and untroubled by all such things.'[64]

This passage comes from the description of the church of the Holy Apostles by Nicholas Mesarites, who by 1200 held the office of *epi ton kriseon* in the patriarchal administration. It expresses a desire to escape from the popular pressures there were on the clergy of the capital. Such escapism was in keeping with an abdication of responsibility and a lack of leadership. These failings on the part of the patriarch and his clergy contributed to the dismal condition of the Byzantine Empire at the turn of the twelfth century. A clear example of this failure of the church to provide a lead to society can be seen over the Latin question. There was anti-Latin sentiment in Constantinople to be detected in all walks of life. Individual priests and monks were involved in anti-Latin disturbances. With the exception of the Patriarch Dositheos the official church showed little interest in directing or exploiting it. Dositheos's disgrace soon after the passage of the third crusade typified the lack of interest in the question among the patriarchal clergy. It was left to members of the orthodox clergy exiled from the Holy Land, such as Leontios, patriarch of Jerusalem, to provide some kind of a lead.

The Comnenian church settlement did not exactly break down. It reached an impasse. There was to be no return to the conditions existing before Alexius Comnenus came to power. For one thing, the church then counted as a political force. Nicephorus Botaneiates's accession was openly engineered by a party within the church at Constantinople. Patriarchs, such as Michael Cerularius and John Xiphilinos, intervened as arbiters of the political situation. With the exception of

64 Nicholas Mesarites, 'Description of the church', ed. Downey, 862–3

the Patriarch Theodosius's stand against the regime of the Empress Maria the patriarchs of the last decades of the twelfth century did not interfere in politics. They preferred to remain aloof. After the experiences of Andronicus Comnenus's tyranny there was suspicion of imperial intervention in ecclesiastical affairs, which explains the failure of Isaac Angelus to reassert imperial ascendancy over the church in the manner of Manuel Comnenus.

Nicetas Choniates interpreted Alexius III Angelus's failures against the Bulgarians as evidence of divine indifference. This was made all the worse because neither prelates nor monks appeared to notice the withdrawal of God's favour from the Byzantines. They made no effort to counteract divine displeasure through preaching or through using their influence with the emperor.[65] Their indifference masked a failure of nerve, which, the following anecdote reveals, reached as far as the Patriarch John Kamateros. In July 1200 John Comnenus, nicknamed the Fat, tried to seize power. With a few supporters he broke into St Sophia where he was acclaimed emperor. Rather than offer any resistance, the patriarch locked himself in a broom-cupboard. Perhaps it was the sensible thing to do, since the coup was soon put down by the reigning Emperor Alexius III Angelus. But it was not the action of a man with any confidence in the power and majesty of his office.[66]

Nicetas Choniates denounced John Kamateros for allowing a group among the episcopate to plunder the church. They were 'more rapacious than customs officers'.[67] Their activities meant that access to the emperors was denied; that respect for the clergy and the patriarchal office had disappeared.[68] There is a degree of exaggeration in these charges, but they help to explain the lack of effective leadership and the sense of drift that existed at the time of the fourth crusade. During the crisis of 1203–4 the Patriarch John Kamateros displayed a signal lack of conviction. He raised no voice in protest – he seemed rather to have given his blessing – when in 1203 the newly restored Emperor Isaac Angelus ordered the churches of the capital to be stripped of their treasures. These were then handed over in gratitude to the soldiers of the fourth crusade! Nicetas Choniates tried to protest, but was ejected from the meeting.[69] He concluded bitterly: 'If one wishes to consider the matter dispassionately, it will doubtless emerge that the harm caused by the clergy was worse than that done by the

65 Nicetas Choniates, 472–3.

66 A. Heisenberg, *Nikolaos Mesarites. Die Palästrevolution des Johannes Komnenos*, (Würzburg, 1907) 23.21–2.

67 Van Dieten, *Uberlieferung*, 62.18.

68 Ibid., 63.1–4.

69 Ibid., 63.17–19.

lay authority.'[70] Choniates meant that elements within the church had pursued their own interests and quarrels without regard for the common interest. The emperors had connived at this state of affairs. In Choniates's biting words, 'they had been taught to fawn, like Maltese spaniels'.[71]

[70] Ibid., 63.21–3.
[71] Ibid., 63.11–12.

PART III

THE BISHOP AND LOCAL SOCIETY

5

THE FRAMEWORK

CHURCH and Empire experienced many vicissitudes, but the pattern of bishoprics and metropolitan sees at the end of the eleventh century was, at least on paper, much as it had been in late antiquity. Over the centuries new metropolitan sees and archbishoprics were created, but this rarely made a great deal of difference to the existing pattern because it was only slowly, if at all, that they acquired suffragan bishoprics. There was never any drastic overhaul of the ecclesiastical organisation of the kind that occurred in provincial administration with the establishment of the themes. City life declined from the end of the sixth century, until the bishop and his church were often all that was left of the civic tradition associated with the *polis*. The ancient Didyma, known to the Byzantines as Hieron, dwindled to a fortified church and a small fortress.[1] Much the same is true of Sardis and other prosperous Anatolian cities of late antiquity. A few managed to retain their urban character through the early middle ages, but, to take the case of Ephesus, the circuit of the walls was much reduced and the cathedral was halved in size. These are clear indications of decline.[2]

What happened in smaller centres is a matter of guesswork, but even in late antiquity some Anatolian bishoprics never amounted to very much. This is how Gregory of Nazianzus described his church of Sasima: 'There is a post station on the middle of the main road of Cappadocia, where it divides into three branches: a waterless, dismal, not altogether free, frightfully abominable, poky little village; nothing but dust and noise and carriages, wails, groans, tax-collectors, torments, and fetters; a population of strangers and vagabonds. This was my Church of Sasima.'[3] In the twelfth century it was still a suffragan bishopric of Tyana. It was likely to have been just as dismal, but even

1 L. Robert, 'Sur Didymes à l'époque byzantine', *Hellenica* 11/12(1960), 490–505.

2 See M.J. Angold, 'The shaping of the medieval Byzantine "city"', *BF* 10(1985), 1–10.

3 Migne, *PG*, 37 1059–60, quoted by M. Hendy, *Studies in the Byzantine Monetary Economy, c.300–1450* (Cambridge 1985), 99.

more of a backwater, since it was no longer a staging post for imperial couriers. Although on the surface the ecclesiastical organisation in Anatolia seemed to have changed very little, this was deceptive. In the sixth century it was largely urban in character. Christianity was still in the process of spreading into the countryside. But with the decline of city life episcopal organisation became more clearly orientated to the needs of the countryside. If the location of bishoprics had scarcely changed, their character often had. In many instances, the old cathedral city survived as a village, more or less, and catered for a rural population rather than for city dwellers.

There were greater changes in the ecclesiastical organisation of the church in the European provinces. The history was different. Anatolia held out in the face of the Arab invasions, while in Europe most of the countryside was occupied by Slavs and others. Only a few cities managed to survive. When the Greek lands were recovered from the Slavs an effort was made to ensure that the old organisation was restored: most of the former metropolitan sees were restored but new suffragan bishoprics were often created, either for new centres where the local population had taken refuge, or for the Slav tribes which had settled. Did this mean that the ecclesiastical organisation in the European provinces was less archaic and better adapted to the needs of the population than that in Anatolia and therefore rather more effective? It is an obvious assumption to make, but it is not necessarily correct. Anatolia may have become less urbanised, but there were no great shifts of population. The existing pattern of bishoprics was adapted easily enough to the new conditions.[4]

For the distribution of bishoprics in the Comnenian era we have to rely on the *Notitiae Episcopatuum*. Michael Hendy has warned about 'their unreliable, and indeed positively deceptive, nature' and the need to check them against other evidence.[5] This is often hard to find. These *notitiae* were semi-official lists. Their compilers were often content to reproduce earlier *notitiae*. They can therefore only provide a rough and ready guide to episcopal organisation at any given time.[6] There are six *notitiae* dating from the mid-eleventh to the mid-thirteenth century.[7] With one exception (no.14) their compilers and editors made determined efforts to bring them up to date or at least add notes indicating recent changes to the episcopal hierarchy. These *notitiae* show fifty-three metropolitan sees boasting a significant number of

4 This is the conclusion of Culerrier ('Les évêchés suffragants d'Ephèse', 149) for the suffragan bishoprics of Ephesus. See, more generally, Hendy, *Byzantine Monetary Economy*, 68–145, maps 15, 20–3.

5 Hendy, *Byzantine Monetary Economy*, 76.

6 Darrouzès, *Notitiae*, esp. 171.

7 Ibid., nos.10–15.

suffragans.[8] Of these metropolitan sees thirty one were within the political frontiers of the Byzantine Empire under the Comneni. They include a series of hard cases, such as Side, Myra, Seleucia, and Hierapolis, where imperial control veered on the nominal. Between them these thirty-one metropolitan sees had 399 suffragans. There were considerable variations in the number of suffragan bishoprics a metropolitan see had. For historical reasons south-western Anatolia boasted the greatest density. Ephesus had thirty-eight; Sardis twenty-five, Stavropolis or Aphrodisias twenty-six or twenty-seven, Laodicea twenty-one, and Myra thirty-five. But the last two places were so exposed to Turkish attacks in the twelfth century that it is difficult to believe that their ecclesiastical organisation existed except on paper. In Europe the number of suffragan bishoprics was more restricted. Thessalonica only had twelve, Corinth eight, Patras seven, Naupaktos six, Philippopolis ten. Larissa was something of an exception with eighteen and Thracian Heraclea had sixteen. The church of Bulgaria's position was anomalous in that it enjoyed autocephalous status. It had twenty-three or perhaps as many as twenty-five suffragans.

These lists reveal little that is unexpected. The greatest density of bishoprics was around Constantinople in Thrace and Bithynia and in western Asia Minor. These were areas where the church had a history that went back to Apostolic times. There was a desire, if possible, to keep things as they had always been. These areas also happened to be the core of the Byzantine Empire with the largest concentrations of population. What the *notitiae* rarely show are the additions and subtractions among the suffragan bishops. Let us take the example of Smyrna: its growing importance and prosperity is reflected in the addition of five suffragan bishoprics. They were sited in market towns, such as Nymphaion, Sosandra, Monoikos, Psithyra, and Petra, all within easy reach of Smyrna.[9] Ephesus equally saw the creation of eight new suffragan bishoprics from the eleventh century, though this may have compensated for the disappearance of others.[10]

The Byzantine church responded to changes in population and prosperity by creating bishoprics for quite modest settlements, sometimes scarcely more than villages. This may explain why it was that, unlike the West, Byzantium never developed any formal parish organisation.

8 There were, in addition, another thirty or so metropolitan sees, but they were new promotions and with a single exception possessed no suffragans. That exception was the metropolitan church of Thebes, which by the late twelfth century had acquired five suffragan bishoprics: Darrouzès, *Notitiae*, no.13, 751–6.

9 H. Ahrweiler, 'L'histoire et la géographie de la région de Smyrne', *TM* 1(1965), 75–91.

10 Culerrier, 'Les évêchés suffragants d'Ephèse', 161–4.

Byzantine bishoprics were often the size of large western parishes. In some ways they are reminiscent of Anglo-Saxon 'minsters'.

The *notitiae* are better at charting promotions to metropolitan and archiepiscopal status. The most prolific creator of new metropolitan sees was Isaac II Angelus. His motivation, it would appear, was political: to embarrass an ecclesiastical opponent – the metropolitan bishop of Ephesus. Promotions were more usually a recognition of the growing importance of a particular city. This is explicitly stated rather later in the case of the promotion of Monemvasia to metropolitan status.[11] It therefore comes as no surprise that the church of Lakedaimonia received metropolitan status in 1082/3 and the church of Attaleia in the following year; or the church of Corfu by 1094 or, for that matter, Mesembria by 1140 or Philadelphia by 1191. These were all cities that were prospering at the time. Similarly, a series of Anatolian towns came into prominence after 1204 under the Nicaean Empire and their churches were awarded metropolitan status.[12]

The creation of new metropolitan sees was the cause of concern within the church. There was resentment at the promotion to metropolitan status of Basilaion – an obscure suffragan of Ankyra. Though the work of Constantine X Doukas, it was left to Alexius Comnenus to face the indignation of the episcopal bench. It was agreed in 1087 that in future a proper check would be kept on such promotions.[13] Father Darrouzès believed that this put an end to the nigh indiscriminate elevation of bishoprics to metropolitan status.[14] The view prevailed that these new promotions should disturb existing arrangements as little as possible. Failing this the old metropolitan church should receive compensation, in the shape of a new suffragan. This happened when the new metropolitan see of Lakedaimonia was carved out of the diocese of Patras. A new bishopric was created at Amykleion, a few miles to the south of Lakedaimonia, and subordinated to Patras.[15] Theodore Balsamon was adamant that newly promoted metropolitan bishops only enjoyed honorific status: they did not have the right to any suffragans and in matters of jurisdiction remained subordinate to their old metropolitans.[16] The newly created metropolitan see of Thebes was exceptional in that it soon acquired suffragan bishoprics. This was the work of a mid-twelfth-century metropolitan bishop, John Kaloktenes,

[11] H.A. Kalligas, *Byzantine Monemvasia* (Monemvasia, 1990), 213–14.

[12] Prousa, Pontic Heraclea, Achyraous, Kallioupolis, Antioch on the Maiander: see Darrouzès, *Notitiae*, 122–3, 130–2.

[13] Dölger, *Reg.* 1140; Darrouzès, *Ecclésiologie*, 176–207.

[14] Darrouzès, *Notitiae*, 124.

[15] A. Bon, *Le Péloponnèse byzantin jusqu'en 1204* (Paris 1951), 110.

[16] Rhalles & Potles II, 247–8. Cf. H. Saradi, 'Imperial jurisdiction over ecclesiastical provinces: the ranking of new cities as seats of bishops or metropolitans', in *TO BYZANTIO*, ed. N. Oikonomidès, 149–63.

who had a reputation for sanctity. He was flouting the rules. The matter was therefore referred after his death to the patriarchal synod, which reluctantly approved his actions. Properly, the bench grumbled, he ought first to have obtained synod's permission.[17]

This is an example of how changes, if frowned on, could occur in the episcopal organisation of the church. In good Byzantine fashion the church recognised the force of exceptional circumstances. Because of the Turkish occupation the metropolitan bishop of Neokaisareia was allowed to transfer his see to the safety of Oinaion on the Black Sea coast and his colleague of Antioch in Pisidia to that of Sozopolis, which remained a Byzantine outpost on the Anatolian plateau. But needless change was to be avoided. The bishop of Derkos in Thrace requested that his see be transferred to the market town of Philea because it was more populous. Synod turned this down as unreasonable. Strictly speaking, it was not even permissible for a bishop to move his cathedral to another church within the same town.[18]

The *notitiae* were guides to the hierarchical ranking of sees. This had little or nothing to do with their respective wealth. Incidental information suggests that to the middle of the eleventh century at least some metropolitan bishops disposed of considerable wealth. For instance, in the early 1040s a metropolitan of Thessalonica was able to amass the huge sum of thirty-three *kentenaria* of gold. But when the emperor of the day - Michael IV - asked for a loan he claimed only to be able to lay his hands on thirty pounds of gold. Michael Hendy believes that this sum represents something like the reserve that a wealthy metropolitan bishop could be expected to have in ready cash.[19] The metropolitan church of Reggio di Calabria is also known to have been extremely wealthy in the mid-eleventh century. It owned, among other things, extensive plantations of mulberry trees.[20] But there were warning signs. While addressing the problem of *kharistike* the Patriarch Alexius the Studite (1025–43) came face to face with another problem - impoverished metropolitan churches. By way of a solution he suggested that prosperous suffragans should gift monasteries to their metropolitan bishops.

Episcopal revenues suffered as a result of a decree of the Patriarch Sisinnios (995–1000). It forbad bishops to impose additional charges on the churches under them. More significant was the ban it contained on levying a tax called *kanonikon* from the monasteries under their jurisdiction. Bishops found to have appropriated monastic properties

17 Rhalles & Potles III, 247; Grumel, 1145.

18 Rhalles & Potles II, 147–8, 613; III, 486–7.

19 Hendy, *Byzantine Monetary Economy*, 240.

20 A. Guillou, 'Production and profits in the Byzantine province of Italy (10th–11th centuries): an expanding economy', *DOP* 28(1974), 89–109.

were to be suspended until they had returned them and made good any damage.[21] Episcopal revenues came from a variety of sources but a significant proportion of a bishop's income came from the monasteries under his jurisdiction. This was now curtailed.

Bishops had benefited from the rapid growth of monastic estates from the mid-ninth century onwards, but from the early eleventh century they seem to have been the principal promoters and victims of *kharistike*. In the wake of the Patriarch Sisinnios's ruling, it made sense, at least in the short term, for a bishop to grant monasteries to lay patrons. In the long term it could mean impoverishment, as happened to the church of Cyzicus. The culprit, in this case, was a previous metropolitan bishop who had alienated monasteries belonging to the church; 'and now the *kharistikarioi* draw from them not a little in the way of revenues, from olive groves and so on'. The state of this church was referred, it will be remembered, to Alexius I Comnenus who passed the matter on to synod. It ordered the *kharistikarioi* to return to the church of Cyzicus the monasteries they held. It also restored demesne land that had been alienated. This decision in favour of the church of Cyzicus was reenacted twice more in the course of the twelfth century. This indicates the difficulties churches had in recovering their properties.[22] In similar fashion the church of Athens suffered because of the incompetence of one of its archbishops. Again, synod decreed the restitution of properties, including monasteries held by *kharistikarioi*.[23] This measure may or may not have had immediate effect, but in the course of the twelfth century the fortunes of the church of Athens were restored by a series of able archbishops, culminating in Michael Choniates.

There are other indications that in the eleventh century bishops were experiencing financial difficulties. The Emperor Isaac Comnenus (1057–9) felt the need to put episcopal incomes on a regular basis. The *kanonikon* paid by the laity was fixed according to the size of the village and consisted of a payment in cash and of contributions in kind.[24] Isaac also fixed a tariff of fees for ordination. Alexius Comnenus reiterated his uncle's regulations about *kanonikon* and ordination fees and confirmed Constantine Monomachos's scale of marriage dues payable to the ordinary. He also added a new, if modest, source of revenue: a share in judicial fines.[25] The bishops complained to synod that the emperor had failed to regulate the *kanonikon* owed by the clergy. It was decided

[21] Sp. Troianos, 'Ein Synodalakt des Sisinios zu den bischoflichen Einkünften', *FM* 3(1979), 211–20; Grumel, 808.

[22] Uspenskij, 'Mnenija 15–29; Grumel, 1000–1.

[23] Ibid., 32–41; Grumel, 952.

[24] Zepos I, 275–6; Dölger, *Reg.* 943–4.

[25] Zepos I, 311–12; Dölger, *Reg.* 1127.

that the old rate of one *nomisma* or its equivalent in kind should be paid by each priest to the bishop.[26] Alexius Comnenus considered that the *kanonikon* provided bishops with the financial basis to carry out the responsibilities of their office.[27] He may have been oversanguine, but it was a start.

By Manuel I Comnenus's reign there are distinct signs of improvement in episcopal finances. His chrysobull of 1148 confirmed the title deeds to episcopal estates, supplied them where they were missing, and granted them immune status.[28] These blanket provisions were complemented by the issue of chrysobulls to individual sees. One that survives is for the obscure Thessalian bishopric of Stagoi or Kalambaka, later famous for its proximity to the monasteries of Meteora. The chrysobull dates from 1163. There is no way of assessing exactly how wealthy the church of Stagoi was, but it was among the most important local landowners. Its bishops were sufficiently prosperous around, or a little before, the middle of the twelfth century to rebuild the cathedral.[29]

A chrysobull has not survived for the church of Athens, but Innocent III's bull issued in 1209 for this church, now in Latin hands, was surely based on some Byzantine original. The same is likely to be true of the survey in Greek carried out some fifty years later of the estates of the Latin bishopric of Kephallenia. Both churches were rich landowners.[30] This evidence relates to Greece, but not all Greek bishoprics prospered in the twelfth century. The church of Naupaktos surrendered much of its landed property to the state under Alexius I Comnenus in return for exemption from taxation. Whatever the benefits of this deal, by the late twelfth century Naupaktos was suffering from pirate attacks and its church was reduced to poverty. It lost its properties and the dependent peasants that cultivated them. The clergy which had earlier numbered a hundred was reduced to ten.[31] This seems only to have been a temporary setback, since John Apokaukos was able to restore its prosperity in the course of the early thirteenth century.

Estate management was the key to success. It was, as we shall see, a major care and responsibility for any bishop. The success

26 Rhalles & Potles v, 60–2; Grumel 942. See E. Hermann, 'Das bischofliche Abgabenwesen im Patriarchat von Konstantinopel vom XI. bis zur Mitte des XIX. Jahrhunderts', *OCP* 5(1939), 437–44; Papagianne, *TA OIKONOMIKA*, 78–99.

27 Gautier, 'L'édit d'Aléxis Ier Comnène', 199.338–9.

28 Zepos I, 376–8; Dölger, *Reg.* 1372.

29 C. Astruc, 'Un document inédit de 1163 sur l'évêché théssalien de Stagi, Paris Suppl. gr. 1371', *BCH* 83(1959), 206–46; E. Vranouse, 'Τὸ ἀρχαιότερο σωζόμενο 'έγγραφο γιὰ τὴ θεσσαλικὴν 'επισκοπὴ Σταγῶν', *ΣΥΜΜΕΙΚΤΑ* 7(1987), 19–32.

30 Migne, *PL*, 215 1559–62; Miklosich & Müller v, 16–67.

31 *Noctes*, no.2, 251.6–25; V. Vasiljevskij, 'Epirotica saeculi *XIII*, iz perepiski Joanna Navpaktsago', *VV* 3(1896), no.29, 296–7.

of a bishop could at one level be measured by the wealth of his see. It was a major consideration, when accepting appointment to a see. George Tornikes was offered Corinth (*c.* 1155), but turned it down in favour of the church of Ephesus because it seemed likely to offer greater rewards.[32] Eustathius was appointed towards the end of Manuel Comnenus's reign to the metropolitan throne of Myra, but before his ordination could take place he was transferred by imperial decree to Thessalonica.[33] There were distinct financial advantages in this transfer, since the see of Myra cannot have been much of a prospect. It was more or less isolated by Turkish tribesmen who were settled in large numbers in the mountains of Lycia.[34]

In their different ways George Tornikes and Eustathius were typical of those appointed under the Comneni to prestigious metropolitan sees. They both served in the patriarchal administration and had distinguished teaching careers. Eustathius seems to have come from quite a humble background and had some difficulty at first in making headway in the patriarchal church. He was the protégé of Nicholas Kataphloron who held the position of *maistor* of the rhetors, a post to which Eustathius eventually succeeded in the mid-1160s.[35] We have already touched on George Tornikes's rather grand connections: related on his mother's side to Theophylact of Ohrid and a member of Anna Comnena's circle.

Patriarchal service was the accepted path to ecclesiastical preferment. It was not exactly a career open to talents, but it was possible for people from a range of social backgrounds to prosper, as long as they had the necessary education and ability. All the metropolitan bishops of the twelfth century about whom we are even reasonably well informed started their careers in the patriarchal administration. Recruitment to the episcopal bench is an area of Byzantine history that has been neglected. This may be because bishops' surnames are scarcely ever given. They rarely appear on episcopal seals. And the surnames that do appear are sometimes so obscure that they are no guide to a bishop's background. One bishop of Pontic Heraclea came from the Kopantites family, as we learn from his seal, but this family is otherwise unrecorded.[36] But more often than not the surnames on episcopal seals are distinguished: a Melissenos was bishop of Abydos; a Makrembolites bishop of Methymna.[37] Another episcopal

32 Tornikès, 25–32.
33 Chomatianos, 631; Dölger, *Reg.* 1518.
34 P. Wittek, *Das Fürstentum Mentesche* (Istanbul 1934), 1–3.
35 Kazhdan/Franklin, 115–23.
36 Laurent, *Corpus* v, no.816. They do not appear in Kazhdan's list of the top 257 Byzantine families: A.P. Kazhdan, *Sotsial'nyj sostav gospodstvujushchego klassa Vizantii XI-XII vv.* (Moscow, 1974), 116–22.
37 Laurent, *Corpus* v, nos. 1796, 1798.

seal that survives from the twelfth century belonged to Constantine Manasses, bishop of Panion.[38] This is not likely to be the littérateur and diplomat Constantine Manasses,[39] nor the man of the same name who became metropolitan bishop of Naupaktos. The latter was the uncle of John Apokaukos, who succeeded to the same see at the turn of the twelfth century. Were they related in any way to that Constantine Apokaukos who was metropolitan bishop of Dyrrakhion at roughly the same time?[40]

It may not be possible to make any firm identifications, but these examples demonstrate that under the Comneni episcopal honours ran in some families. They might be great families, such as the Tornikes. An even better example are the Chrysoberges. At the end of the eleventh century a Chrysoberges was metropolitan bishop of – yet again – Naupaktos.[41] This family provided a patriarch of Constantinople at the end of the tenth century, a patriarch of Antioch in the mid-eleventh century, another patriarch of Constantinople under Manuel Comnenus, when a Stephen Chrysoberges was successively *chartophylax* and *sakellarios* of St Sophia before becoming metropolitan bishop of Corinth.[42] Just before the fall of Constantinople in 1204 a Nicephorus Chrysoberges was prominent as *maistor* of the rhetors. After the fall he became metropolitan bishop of Sardis.[43]

Members of great families did not have a monopoly of episcopal office. It is just as common to find the nephews and protégés of bishops following in their footsteps, first in the patriarchal church and then in the episcopate. But bishops were not only drawn from those who entered the patriarchal administration. Monasteries were also a source of bishops. Given how many patriarchs of Constantinople had a monastic background, it might even have been anticipated that the majority of bishops were monks. This is a supposition, however, that receives little support from the seal evidence. Comparatively few episcopal seals bear the legend 'monk and bishop'.[44] The monastic contribution was important, but must be kept in proportion. Another source of recruits to the episcopate was the cathedral clergy.

38 Ibid., no.322.
39 See O. Lampsidis, 'Zur Biographie von Konstantinos Manasses und zu seiner *Chronike Synopsis*', *B* 58(1988), 97–111.
40 Laurent, *Corpus* v, no.738.
41 Theophylact II, no.35.
42 Laurent, *Corpus* v no.101; V. Laurent 'Etienne Chrysobergès, archevêque de Corinthe', *REB* 20(1962), 214–18.
43 Browning, 'An unpublished address' (= R. Browning, *History, Language and Literacy in the Byzantine World* (Northampton, 1989), no.IX).
44 Laurent, *Corpus* v, nos. 277, 279, 373, 376, 472, 618, 638, 645, 657, 724, 777, 2016.

Theodore Balsamon on the clergy

There is no disguising how little – in comparison with the Latin church – can be gleaned about the basic facts of ecclesiastical organisation in the Byzantine Empire. Theodore Balsamon, for so long *chartophylax* of St Sophia, could have enlightened us. The records of his office would have contained all manner of precise information as to the numbers and the remuneration of the clergy of Constantinople. There would have been lists of bishops and registers of ecclesiastical property and incomes; even copies of the privileges granted to individual sees. We should be grateful for small mercies: at least, Balsamon used some of the information from the archives of St Sophia in the preparation of his commentaries on the canons. As we have seen, the young Balsamon was jointly commissioned in the 1170s by the emperor and the patriarch to provide a new commentary on the *Nomocanon* in XIV titles, the basic handbook of canon law. He then went on to supply commentaries to a range of texts: the canons of the Apostles, the canons of St Basil of Caesarea, and the acts of the councils of the church. His purpose was to weed out inconsistencies and contradictions. A major task was to reconcile civil and canon law. As a result, the ecclesiastical courts were able to use civil law more freely than in the past. This widened the scope of ecclesiastical justice. Balsamon's great achievement was to bring canon law up to date. His solutions took into account not only civil law in the shape of the Basilics, but also recent imperial legislation and synodal decisions. His work was the culmination of a revision of canon law going back to the eleventh century. Balsamon displayed a concrete grasp of the problems of his day, unlike his predecessors Alexius Aristenos and John Zonaras. Their commentaries rarely provide more than a general explanation of the contents of individual canons, enlivened in Zonaras's case by a tendency to moralise.

Balsamon's commentaries have the great merit of providing a guide to what an influential churchman saw as the problems of his time. The ones that he keeps coming back to are: ecclesiastical jurisdiction and discipline; the clergy as an order in society; monks and monasteries; lay piety, and marriage and morals. Balsamon presents these as living issues, providing their historical background, and the arguments which surrounded them; the official position taken, and his own views. These are often confused. He was all too aware of the gap that existed between the ideal and the reality of the clergy's role in Byzantine society. He was also realistic enough to allow that there would always be discrepancies. His discussions provide an insight into the day to day problems confronting a bishop in the twelfth century. Many were matters of ecclesiastical discipline: the reception of priests and monks from other dioceses;[45] ordinations of priests and suffragan bishops;[46] attendance at local and patriarchal synods;[47] the appointment of episcopal officers.[48]

A bishop also had responsibilities for the monasteries of his diocese. Canon 8 of the council of Chalcedon placed all monasteries under the authority of the local bishop.[49] This was the cause of friction. Bishops always had difficulty in maintaining control over the monasteries of their dioceses. At its most mundane bishops went to some lengths to ensure that they rather than the abbot ordained readers for a monastery.[50] A much more serious infringement of episcopal authority was the way that the hearing of confessions was becoming a monastic preserve. Properly, it belonged to the bishop.[51] We have already seen how the alienation of monasteries to the laity could impair episcopal finances. This became less of a problem in the twelfth century. Balsamon reveals that episcopal control over monasteries was now coming under challenge from a different direction: the patriarchate of Constantinople. This provoked a reaction on the part of the bishops. Balsamon did not sympathise with the episcopal claim to dispose of monastic property. In his opinion a bishop had no rights of property over the monasteries in his diocese; only rights of supervision. He had a duty to investigate spiritual failings and supervise monastic administrators. He had the right to institute the abbot into his office. In return his name was commemorated in the prayers of the community.[52]

At this point Balsamon fails to mention another right that a bishop possessed: the authorisation of any newly founded monastic community within his diocese. The act of foundation of a monastery required the bishop's prayer or *stauropegion*, as it was called, presumably because at the same time he implanted his cross. Among other things it symbolised that the new foundation came under his authority. By Balsamon's time it was becoming increasingly common for the act of foundation to come under patriarchal auspices or *stauropegion*. Balsamon records the agitation there was on the part of the bishops against the spread of this practice. They demanded its justification on the basis of canon law. Balsamon refused to comply on the grounds that the patriarchal church had met all their objections. He claimed that it was 'a long-standing unwritten custom, which from time immemorial up until the present took precedence over the canons'. He had to admit that it was not an argument that carried much conviction. He therefore

45 Rhalles & Potles II, 589–90, 661–2; III, 503–4.
46 Ibid. II, 275–6; III, 424–5, 439–4; Grumel, 1118.
47 Rhalles & Potles II, 325–6; III, 357.
48 Ibid. II 591–2; III, 383–6.
49 Ibid. II, 236.
50 Ibid., 616–19.
51 Ibid. II, 236; III, 311–12, 314–15.
52 Ibid. II, 310.

fell back on a different line of argument. He suggested that canon law does not give a specific diocese to a bishop, but only recognises the five patriarchates. Since each patriarch had rights of discipline and ordination over the dioceses subject to him, he ought also to enjoy the right of *stauropegion* at the founding of a monastery and effectively enjoy the powers normally vested in the ordinary.[53] On this matter Balsamon is unabashedly acting as the apologist of the extension of patriarchal authority. His arguments are so specious that they are hard to take seriously, but they illuminate one of the pressures that bishops worked under: competition from the patriarchs of Constantinople.

Another cause of difficulties was jurisdiction. It was inseparable from the problem of where the bishop and clergy stood in relation to Byzantine society. Balsamon's presentation of the respective competences of the ecclesiastical and civil courts rests on a theory of church and society. Ideally, the bishop and clergy formed a spiritual elite above, but not entirely separate from, lay society. They were responsible for its moral and spiritual well-being. This meant that a range of judicial business should properly belong to the ecclesiastical courts. But it was difficult to define: in a Christian society almost all crimes and misdemeanours have a moral and spiritual dimension. Marriage, for example, is both a contract and a sacrament. At Byzantium marriage litigation went before both the civil and ecclesiastical courts, more or less indiscriminately. Balsamon did not challenge this state of affairs. He merely drew attention to the differences of treatment that litigants could expect under civil and canon law. He took the example of the abduction of a bride. Civil law was much harsher. It prescribed capital punishment where force was used and mutilation where it was absent. The church only imposed three years' excommunication. If the woman had given her consent, then the church was still more lenient. It was content with whatever penance the local bishop deemed appropriate.[54]

Balsamon considered penance the proper penalty under canon law for a whole range of moral offences. These he defined very broadly. They included manslaughter, because the taking of human life was an offence against God. It was therefore best treated through penance. Balsamon contended that 'ecclesiastical penalties are not punishment, but a benison and a form of healing'.[55] The use of penance gave ecclesiastical justice a distinctive character. It may well have made it more attractive to the laity, but this is unlikely to have been Balsamon's purpose. He did not see canon law as a competitor to civil law.

53 Ibid., 40–2.
54 Ibid. IV, 171–2, 183, 187.
55 Ibid., 490.

Ideally, they were complementary. In practice, Balsamon underlined that a wide range of crimes and misdemeanours might go before the ecclesiastical courts, because of their spiritual implications. This had, in a sense, always been true, but the development of canon law created a greater awareness of the possibilities. More to the point Balsamon provided an instrument that facilitated the application of canon law.

There was the potential for an extension of the competence of the ecclesiastical courts. But this was not of immediate concern to Balsamon. He was more interested in ensuring that in matters of law the clergy formed a separate estate. As such, they should have been exclusively justiciable before the ecclesiastical courts. In practice, this was far from being the case. Under canon law a cleric was to be stripped of his orders for citing a fellow member of the clergy before a civil court on a criminal charge or moving a case from an ecclesiastical to a civil court. But in Balsamon's day, for reasons that escaped him, this penalty had fallen into abeyance. Ecclesiastical and civil courts were used promiscuously without regard to the status of litigants, so that it was not unknown for members of the clergy to bring bishops before a civil court. Balsamon cited the recent case of Meletios, abbot of the Constantinopolitan monastery of Pantepoptes. He had been brought before synod. This was not to his liking, so he obtained an imperial order that allowed him to transfer the hearing to a secular court. The Patriarch Luke Chrysoberges found this insulting, but there was nothing he could do. The civil judges assured him that with imperial authority anything was possible. Balsamon disapproved of the situation. He thought that bishops should only appear before the civil courts on personal matters; not where it touched the church. He was, however, willing to countenance lay assessors being added on imperial orders to synod for specific cases.[56]

For some time patriarchs had been grappling with a related problem which blurred the competences of the civil and ecclesiastical courts. In 1115 the Patriarch John Agapetos forbad members of the clergy to act as barristers in secular courts, unless it concerned ecclesiastical business: a rider which must have weakened the general intention.[57] Some years later we find the Patriarch Luke Chrysoberges having to prohibit a deacon from pleading before the imperial tribunal. He had to climb down in the face of the specious argument that the canons only concerned the appointment of a barrister; not the act of pleading![58] This was a minor setback. The effort continued to deny secular employment to the clergy. The prevailing opinion was that the clergy should abstain

[56] Ibid. III, 333–40.
[57] Ibid., 349; Grumel 999.
[58] Rhalles & Potles I, 159–60; Grumel, 1099–100.

from the more disreputable professions, such as poncing or managing an inn. Luke Chrysoberges believed that this did not go far enough. He considered that running perfumeries or bathhouses was just as reprehensible because it involved profit. The inference was that profit sullied the priesthood, but it was more than this. The patriarch also forbad priests and deacons from becoming doctors: it would mean that members of the clergy had to wear secular dress and would have to parade on official occasions with members of the laity. Nor were secular concerns to intrude into the physical space of the church. Time and again patriarchs ordered bankers, bakers, greengrocers, and other traders to depart from the Augoustaion and the precincts of St Sophia. Perfumers and hairdressers were driven from the Great Church itself where they plied their trade.[59]

Luke Chrysoberges was at pains to emphasise the exclusive character of the clergy. This meant establishing clear boundaries between the laity and the clergy. There were those who believed that the most minor order of clergy – that of reader (*anagnostes*) – belonged with the laity rather than the clergy. Cited in support of such an opinion was the custom whereby readers turned in the middle of their duties to the congregation and made obeisance. Luke Chrysoberges banned this practice. Thenceforward readers should only bow to priests and bishops in deference to their priestly orders. 'The people', intoned the patriarch, 'are far removed from the priesthood.'[60] The next patriarch Michael Ankhialos' went on to consider the question of whether readers should be barred from secular professions, along with the rest of the clergy. There were those who argued that this ban should not apply to readers. Their clerical status was open to question because they performed their duties outside the sanctuary. This line of argument did not impress the patriarch. As far as he was concerned, readers were fully members of the clergy: they carried out a sacred duty and had received holy orders from a bishop. The ban on clergy engaging in secular affairs therefore applied to them.[61]

So much concern with the status of readers was symptomatic of a desire to separate the clergy from lay society, which showed itself in various other ways. Theodore Balsamon wished, for example, to exclude as far as possible lay participation in church services. He had come across instances of laymen claiming the status of preacher (*didaskalos*). This, in his opinion, contravened the canons which reserved preaching for the priesthood. Laymen who persisted in claiming the right to preach were to be placed under the ban of

59 Rhalles & Potles II, 481–3.

60 Ibid. III, 342–5.

61 Ibid., 349–50; Grumel, 1119 (= V. Laurent, 'Résponses canoniques inédites du patriarcat byzantin', *EO* 33(1934), 310–11).

the church for forty days.[62] The emperor excepted, no member of the laity was properly allowed to enter the sanctuary of the church. Balsamon could not explain why it was that anybody who so wished could enter the sanctuary of the church of Christ in Khalke. He had tried to prevent the laity entering the sanctuary of the church of the Hodegetria, but had failed in the face of the plea that it was ancient custom.[63] He also noted that the laity sometimes spited the clergy by taking control of the chanting of hymns and psalms. This was expressly forbidden. Balsamon singled out for blame people whom he calls choristers (*khorostatai ton kondakion*). These were laymen who performed both in churches and in the market places. Balsamon relented to the extent of allowing the laity to sing along (*sympsallein*) with the clergy as long as they respected the order of service and did not improvise.[64] In other words, the laity still had a role to play in the staging of church services, but this was now cause for disapproval on the part of the ecclesiastical authorities. It questioned the status of the clergy by challenging their absolute control over the conduct of church services. This was why Balsamon was so disturbed by lay penetration of the sanctuary. The right to enter the sanctuary provided direct access to the holy which properly belonged to the priesthood.

Another danger was the subordination of the clergy to lay interests. Balsamon was suspicious of the proliferation of chapels, where the priest was appointed by the householder and might be little more than a family servant.[65] He was concerned how easily they could evade episcopal supervision and control.[66] It was also possible for ecclesiastical office to become hereditary in particular families. Balsamon admitted that this occurred in the cathedral churches of Athens and Mesembria and elsewhere. The offices stayed in the hands of the same families which retained the profits. If there was no member of the family capable of filling the office – as might happen if there were only daughters in a particular generation – then they hired a priest to carry out the functions. This practice was taken still further at Constantinople in the churches of the Forty Martyrs and the Theotokos Kyrou, where members of the laity drew clerical salaries (*klerikata offikia*).[67]

Balsamon was shocked by the lack of respect the laity often had for the clergy and monks. There were clowns who made fun of monks and the monastic habit. They even gilded their pates in mock imitation of a

62 Rhalles & Potles II, 455–6.
63 Ibid., 486–7.
64 Ibid. III, 184–5.
65 Ibid. II, 372, 589–90.
66 Ibid., 627.
67 Ibid., 380–1.

tonsure.[68] Still worse were members of the clergy who demeaned the dignity of their orders. Balsamon records with horror that on certain festivals it was the custom for members of the clergy to dress up as soldiers or monks, or even wild beasts and indulge in improper gestures in the hope of making their congregation laugh. These were the remnants of an easier relationship between church and lay society that had existed previously. Such impropriety could easily spill over into irreligion. Balsamon records the various popular customs, such as jumping over bonfires on the evening of 23 June, that were outlawed by the Patriarch Michael Ankhialos'. Such things were not just an indictment of the church's failure to fulfil its pastoral responsibilities. Balsamon saw them as a threat. There was the possibility that orthodoxy might be endangered if appropriated by the people. The Patriarch Nicholas Mouzalon ordered a *Life* of St Paraskeve to be burnt. It had been written by a peasant to celebrate the saint who was much honoured in his village. The patriarch found it illiterate and did not think that it did justice to the life of the saint. He therefore commissioned an official life from one of the deacons of St Sophia.[69]

Balsamon's discussions underline the discrepancy between ideal and reality. The ideal espoused by the Comnenian church was the separation of church and secular society; the assumption was that the clergy would constitute a spiritual elite with ultimate responsibility for the welfare of society. Balsamon was not an apologist of bishops, but his commentaries reveal that the implementation of this ideal rested very largely with individual bishops. He preserves a curious detail which reflects the high opinion that bishops had of their place within a Christian society and the high hopes that rested on them. It was apparently the custom in the twelfth century to bury a bishop with a piece of consecrated bread in his mouth. This was to ward off evil spirits and to provide him with nourishment on his journey to heaven.[70] This was almost to number the bishop with the saints. Balsamon also pays attention to the niceties of episcopal dress. This is another sign of a new self-consciousness, which found expression in the art of the time.[71]

Christopher Walter has shown how from the ninth century the decoration of Byzantine churches experienced a process of 'clericalisation'. He sees this as 'symptomatic of the increasing preponderance of the

68 Ibid., 506. The Patriarch Nicholas Grammatikos banned such revelries from the church of St Sophia: Darrouzès, 'L' éloge de Nicholas III', 50.652–71.

69 Rhalles & Potles II, 453. Cf. the learned *Lives* of St Cyril Phileotes and Hosios Meletios written at approximately the same time.

70 Rhalles & Potles II, 496. Cf. R. Browning, 'Theodore Balsamon's commentary on the canons of the council in Troullo as a source on everyday life in twelfth-century Byzantium', in *ΚΑΘΗΜΕΡΙΝΗ ΖΩΗ ΣΤΟ ΒΥΖΑΝΤΙΟ*, ed. Ch. Maltezou (Athens, 1989), 426–7.

71 Walter, *Art and Ritual*, 7ff.

Church in Byzantine society'.[72] Art was used to celebrate the 'wisdom of saintly bishops', which was one of the main defences of orthodoxy. Still more important was the emphasis upon the eucharist. The communion of the Apostles came to dominate the decoration of the middle register of the apse with a depiction of officiating bishops below. The message was clear: Christ is most accessible to mankind through the sacrament of the eucharist, a ceremony presided over by a bishop or a priest. Walter concludes that 'an obvious consequence was the exaltation of those who rendered Christ present by consecrating the bread and the wine'.[73] Art thus proclaimed the central role of the bishop in a Christian society by virtue of his mediating role between Christ and mankind. This required a different concept of Christ. To quote Walter once again: 'He ceases to be present as universal emperor, becoming rather the universal patriarch.'[74]

Walter contends that the decisive moment of change occurred in the eleventh century.[75] This is true in the sense that art reflected ideas that were crystallising at that time. For example, the scene most often used to celebrate episcopal wisdom was that of the 'Three Hierarchs' – St John Chrysostom, St Basil of Caesarea, and St Gregory of Nazianzus. Its popularity was enhanced with the institution in the later eleventh century of a festival in honour of these doctors of the church.[76] The dignity of the episcopal office was an issue in the eleventh century. It was defended with passion in a series of treatises usually attributed to Nicetas, bishop of Ankyra.[77]

Ideas are one thing; their application another. The glorification in art of the eucharist[78] did not mean that the church was advocating that the laity should partake of it more frequently. The very reverse. By the end of the eleventh century there was concern in ecclesiastical circles about the multiple celebration of the mass by a priest on a single day. The Patriarch Nicholas Grammatikos banned the practice. It was turning a mystery into a business venture![79] The patriarch's action seems designed to discourage the laity from taking communion. This would have emphasised its transcendent quality and exalted the status of the

[72] Ibid., 4.
[73] Ibid., 212.
[74] Ibid., 166.
[75] Ibid., 237–49.
[76] Ibid., 111–15. This was the work of John Mauropous, bishop of Euchaita: C.G. Bonis, 'Worship and dogma. John Mauropous, metropolitan of Euchaita (11th century): his canon on the three hierarchs and its dogmatic significance', *BF* 1(1966), 1–23.
[77] Darrouzès, *Ecclésiologie*, 37–53.
[78] G. Babić, 'Les discussions christologiques et le décor des églises byzantines au XIIe siècle. Les évêques officiant devant l'Hetimasie et devant l'Amnos', *Frühmittelalterliche Studien* 2(1968), 368–86.
[79] J. Darrouzès, 'Nicolas d'Andida et les azymes', *REB* 32(1974), 200–3; Darrouzès, 'L'éloge de Nicholas III', 49.636–45 .

priesthood. There was a popular desire for communion, especially at Easter, but the church was suspicious. Theodore Balsamon arrived at a village in Thrace one Easter Sunday. He found the local peasants bringing their priest various offerings in gratitude for the communion they had just received. It was a charming local custom, but Balsamon disapproved and thought that the priest should be dismissed.[80] It is a story that emphasises the gulf separating the hierarchy from the church at large.

Comnenian bishops brought high ideals to the conduct of their office. They took their pastoral responsibilities seriously. But such a high estimate of the episcopal dignity could equally lead to clashes with all kinds of interests. Being a bishop could be a thankless task. There were bishops who preferred to resign their sees rather than continue in the face of local difficulties. One example from the twelfth century was a bishop of Amykleion in the Peloponnese. The rapacity of the local tax collectors wore him down. He resigned and became a monk.[81] Other bishops were exposed to real danger: Leo Charsianites, bishop of Dristra on the Danube, is one example. Out on his pastoral rounds he was seized by local people who lashed him to a stake and beat him senseless.[82]

Bishops were subjected to enormous pressures. They occupied a central role in Byzantine society. They were the essential link between the localities and central authority. They were either ground down or they came to dominate their surroundings. Comnenian bishops had some advantages. They were better educated. A much higher proportion were drawn from the patriarchal clergy. Whatever the politicking that went on in the Great Church, the patriarchal clergy possessed a discernible *esprit de corps*. Once appointed to an often distant see, they maintained contact with their contemporaries through extensive correspondence. They may not have been able to visit Constantinople as often as they would have wished, but they kept themselves informed of what was happening at the imperial court and in the patriarchal church. They made use of their inside knowledge and contacts for the benefit of themselves, their churches, and their communities. This helped to counterbalance the disadvantages under which they laboured. They were outsiders more often than not and initially the object of suspicion and hostility. The challenges and pressures of office can best be followed through the experiences of the bishops themselves. Among these I have included John Apokaukos, bishop of Naupaktos, and Demetrius Chomatianos, archbishop of Ohrid, even though their

[80] Rhalles & Potles II, 355–6.

[81] Ibid. III, 27, 427–8.

[82] Tzetzes I, no.66, 93–6; J. Shepard, 'Tzetzes's letters to Leo at Dristra', *BF* 6(1979), 191–239, at 194, 228–32.

careers fall mainly after 1204. Their writings constitute perhaps the richest source for the life of a Byzantine bishop. Their education and outlook was formed during their early careers at Constantinople before the fall of the city. Their experience as bishops had much in common with that of their predecessors in the twelfth century: Theophylact of Ohrid, Eustathius of Thessalonica, and Michael Choniates, archbishop of Athens.

6

THEOPHYLACT OF OHRID

The church of Bulgaria in the eleventh century

THE archbishops of Athens had their palace on the Acropolis in the Propylaea. Such a grand residence makes it tempting to think of them as somehow resembling the prince-bishops of the western church. But Athens was no Cologne or Milan. It may not have been quite the miserable place that Michael Choniates describes. It may even have been one of the more prosperous Byzantine provincial towns and its church one of the wealthiest sees of the orthodox church, but Byzantine bishops were never territorial magnates like their counterparts in the West. The scale was different, and so was the history. In the West it was the bishop who continued the traditions of Roman government and urban culture after the fall of the Roman Empire. A political role was forced upon the bishop in the West to an extent which rarely happened within the orthodox world.

One exception was the archbishop of Bulgaria with his see at Ohrid. His position was rather different from the general run of metropolitan bishops. The archbishopric of Bulgaria was created in the aftermath of the destruction of the Bulgarian Empire in 1018. Basil II could not countenance the continued existence of a Bulgarian patriarchate, but he was willing to grant the church in Bulgaria autocephalous status. He established the bounds and privileges of the see in a series of documents issued after the submission of the Bulgarians.[1] These measures were a major part of the emperor's pacification of the Bulgarians and and were bound to emphasise the archbishop's political role. Basil II was generous. He restored to the church of Bulgaria a series of bishoprics which had been lost to the patriarchate of Constantinople. He also set out the clergy and dependent peasants that each of the suffragan bishops was entitled to. The grand total for the whole Bulgarian church

[1] H. Gelzer, 'Ungedruckte und wenig bekannte Bistümerverzeichnisse der orientalischen Kirche. II', *BZ* 2(1893), 42–6.

was set at a modest 745 clergy and 715 dependent peasants, but it has to be remembered that these were all exempted from the payment of taxation to the state. It was clearly stated that none of these clerics were to pay the *oikomodion* – the basic tax in Bulgaria – or any surcharges. These were valuable privileges, designed to provide the church of Bulgaria with a sound financial base. The presumption was that some, if not all, of the revenues formerly due to the state would go to the church of Bulgaria. These arrangements do not exclude the possibility that there were other, many other, clergy serving the church of Bulgaria and other peasants settled on its estates.[2] In addition, the archbishop of Bulgaria had the right to levy the ecclesiastical tax of *kanonikon* from his suffragan bishops, as well as from the nomad Vlachs and Vardariots, who were settled within the boundaries of his church. Basil II urged the imperial administration to respect the archbishop of Bulgaria and to seek his advice. Its members were forbidden to interfere in ecclesiastical affairs on pain of incurring the emperor's righteous indignation.

Basil II's settlement of the Bulgarian church was shrewd and far-sighted. If he deprived it of patriarchal status, he allowed it to retain its separate and independent status. He was also tactful enough to appoint a native Bulgarian as the new archbishop of Bulgaria with his seat at Ohrid. These measures were designed to reconcile the bulk of the Bulgarian population to Byzantine rule. The archbishop of Bulgaria therefore had a vital role in the efforts made over the eleventh century to pacify the Balkans. He was effectively the Byzantine viceroy. In 1037 Leo, the *chartophylax* of St Sophia at Constantinople, was appointed to succeed the Bulgarian John as archbishop of Bulgaria. He reigned until 1055. It was a matter of comment at the time that he was the first Byzantine to head the Bulgarian church. He was one of the leading Byzantine churchmen of the mid-eleventh century and played a prominent part in the affairs that led up to the schism of 1054. He left his mark on the city of Ohrid in the shape of the cathedral of St Sophia. It was designed to leave a Byzantine stamp on the church in Bulgaria. After the suppression of the Bulgarian uprising of 1041 it might have been thought to celebrate the final pacification of the Balkans.

Instead, a series of events, including another Bulgarian rebellion, meant that by the time Alexius I Comnenus came to power the Byzantine hold on the Balkans was uncertain. The key to the situation remained the city of Ohrid, not just because it was the seat of the archbishops of Bulgaria. Its position astride the Via Egnatia also meant that it had a vital part to play in the campaigns against the

[2] See N. Oikonomidès, 'Tax exemptions for the secular clergy under Basil II', in *ΚΑΘΗΓΗΤΡΙΑ*, ed. Chrysostomides, 317–26

Normans at the beginning of Alexius's reign. In the winter of 1082 the people of the city surrendered the lower town to the Normans, which can be taken as a token of local disaffection from Byzantine rule. A Byzantine garrison held out, however, in the citadel and the place soon returned under Byzantine control.[3] At some point in the late 1080s the archiepiscopal throne of Bulgaria fell vacant. It was a crucial appointment that Alexius Comnenus now had to make. His choice fell on Theophylact Hephaistos. He was a deacon of St Sophia, but was also *maistor* of the rhetors. Alexius entrusted him with the education of Constantine Doukas, the porphyrogenite son of Michael VII Doukas, but still the heir apparent to the Byzantine throne. In other words, Theophylact was close to the emperor and was an ecclesiastic in whom Alexius had confidence. He was just the man for the daunting responsibilities that awaited any archbishop of Bulgaria at this time.[4]

The events of the later eleventh century had undone the work of pacification of the Balkans. It had to begin all over again. The archbishop of Bulgaria was a key figure, because it was his business to use the church as a means of reconciling the local population to Byzantine rule, which at the time was harsh in the extreme. He was also expected to cooperate with or, at least, give moral support to the imperial administration. These tasks were often difficult to reconcile. To win the hearts and minds of the local people it was often necessary to remonstrate with imperial governors about the harshness of their rule. Theophylact also had a duty to his church. It was this that very largely guided his actions. When he arrived he found it in a poor way. Its estates were at the mercy both of the imperial administration and also of local people. Theophylact must have realised that, unless he could protect ecclesiastical property, he would never be able to assert his presence and would remain an ineffective figure. Assuming that Theophylact's correspondence provides a roughly accurate guide to his activities, then the defence of the rights and properties of his church was among the most urgent of his concerns.

The defence of the estates of the church of Bulgaria

The immediate impression is that the archbishopric of Bulgaria did not dispose of vast landed properties. Theophylact only mentions three of its estates, though there may have been others. Two lay at some distance from Ohrid. One was at Mongila, near Pelagonia. This had

[3] Anna Comnena v,v,1: I, 242.17–20 (ed. Bonn); II, 22.13–16 (ed. Leib).

[4] P. Gautier, 'L'épiscopat de Théophylacte Héphaistos archevêque de Bulgarie', *REB* 21(1963), 159–78; D. Obolensky, *Six Byzantine Portraits* (Oxford, 1988), 34–82. See now M. Mullett, 'Patronage in action: the problems of an 11th-century bishop', in *Church and People*, ed. Morris, 125–47

been an old residence of the archbishops of Bulgaria. Theophylact found it occupied by a military commander, but thanks to the good offices of the Grand Duke John Doukas had obtained its restitution to the church of Bulgaria.[5] The other was the village of Ekklesiai on the Vardar.[6] It was of some importance to Theophylact, perhaps because it was a convenient staging post on the way to Thessalonica where the archbishops of Ohrid kept a house.[7] This village would seem to have been situated somewhere along the middle or lower reaches of the Vardar, since it was connected with Thessalonica[8] and seems to have been administered from Thessalonica.[9] In other words, the village of Ekklesiai would have lain perhaps a hundred miles to the east or south-east of Ohrid. Margaret Mullett has traced the considerable efforts the archbishop made to maintain control over it in the face of the demands of the fisc and the claims of local people. He mobilised his contacts in Constantinople in order to bring pressure to bear on the local governor.[10] She assumes, however, that a dependent peasant (or *paroikos)* of the church of Bulgaria called Lazarus had designs on this village on the Vardar. I think this can be ruled out. Lazarus not only possessed a house in Ohrid. He also relied on the support of the people of Ohrid. It seems out of the question for an inhabitant of Ohrid to have an interest in a village so far away.

It is much more likely that the village in question was one described as 'the village of the church in Ohrid'.[11] This lay just outside the city. It seems to have been the most important estate belonging to the archbishops of Bulgaria. It was a relatively recent acquisition. It had been obtained in exchange for rights that the church of Bulgaria had previously exercised over the nomads of the region. The fisc was unwilling to accept the legality of this transaction.[12]

This village was the cause of one of Theophylact's most difficult encounters with the *kastrenoi*[13] of Ohrid. He wrote to one of his suffragans, sympathising about the difficulties the latter had with crafty *kastrenoi*. He assured him that they could be but babes in arms compared with their Ohrid counterparts.[14] To wrest control of the village

5 Migne, *PG*, 126.521–4, 533–6 = Theophylact II, 186–9, 214–17.

6 Migne, *PG*, 126.432–3, 480–1 = Theophylact II, 232–5,460–3, 468–9, 548–9.

7 Theophylact II, 534–5.

8 Mullett, 'Patronage in action', 125–39, and review in *BS* 52(1991), 157–62.

9 Theophylact II, 534–5. It is tempting to identify it with Asprai Ekklesiai at or near the point where the Via Egnatia crosses the Vardar: Anna Comnena V,V,1: I, 243.5,16 (ed. Bonn); II, 22–3 (ed. Leib).

10 Mullett, 'Patronage in action', 127.

11 Theophylact II, 447.30–1.

12 Migne, *PG* 126.421–5 = Theophylact II, 444–51.

13 This is a term applied to influential local people who lived in the fortress or *kastron*.

14 Migne, *PG*, 126. 336–7 = Theophylact II, 322–5.

outside Ohrid from the archbishop they corrupted one of the church's dependent peasants. This was the *paroikos* Lazarus. He was clearly on the make. He already possessed a house in the city of Ohrid. He started a campaign against Theophylact, seeking out those that had suffered at his hands in one way or another. Lazarus was in this way able to assemble a group of supporters who invaded the village on the pretext that they were citizens of Ohrid who had been deprived of their rights in the village by the archbishop. The campaign then moved to the city. Lazarus persuaded those due to appear on various charges to go around calling on the name of the emperor. This, Theophylact assures us, was done to slander him. The word he used was *dysphemein*, which could also be used to signify defiance of a tyrannous emperor. In this case, it seems to have been a question of getting rid of a tyrant archbishop by invoking the help of the emperor. Lazarus claimed that the archbishop had had him burnt out of house and home. Theophylact was forced to flee from Ohrid and sought refuge at Pelagonia, while Lazarus and some of his fellow villagers travelled to Constantinople in order to lay their case against him before the emperor. Lazarus was sufficiently plausible to convince the emperor of the justice of his case.

Theophylact had also to defend those members of his clergy who had property in the village from the attentions of the fisc. His clergy were supposed to enjoy exemption from the payment of taxes on holdings of up to one *zeugarion* – a standard fiscal unit. Despite this the officials of the fisc were still demanding the whole range of different taxes. Theophylact connected the actions of the fisc with the activities of Lazarus. He closes his letter of protest about this disregard of the clergy's privileged fiscal status with the tidings that Lazarus is still in charge of things.[15] How the affair ended is not known. It illustrates the predicament that faced many prelates: they found themselves caught between the demands of the imperial fisc and the cupidity of local people. It was not unknown for imperial agents and local personalities to make common cause.

How would Theophylact defend the interests of his church against, as he saw it, such an unholy alliance? He was, in the first place, able to make use of his extensive contacts within the imperial family and government. The most powerful figure on whom he could count was the emperor's brother, the Grand Domestic Adrian Comnenus. It cannot only have been the ties of friendship which prompted the spate of letters that he addressed to Adrian Comnenus. As Grand Domestic Adrian had final responsibility for the military administration of the region. Theophylact did not leave matters there. He also wrote to the emperor's new son-in-law Nicephorus Bryennius who had the added advantage

[15] Migne, *PG*, 126. 441–52, 453–60 = Theophylact II, 482–93, 498–505.

of a father who was governor of neighbouring Dyrrachium. To bring further pressure to bear on Bryennius, he kept in touch with the people around him. From about the same time there dates another letter from Theophylact. This one was addressed to George Palaeologus, one of Alexius Comnenus's companions in arms and trusted advisers. In it the archbishop expresses gratitude for his intervention on behalf of the church of Ohrid with the local tax collector. He assures him that the church of Ohrid is now enjoying some respite: the tax collectors' designs on the village outside Ohrid have been thwarted, but without his aid Theophylact would have been devoured by serpents.[16]

Theophylact was also at loggerheads with the *protostrator* Michael Doukas, brother of the Empress Eirene Doukaina.[17] Theophylact got in touch with their mother Maria of Bulgaria, by then a nun, in the hope of making him see sense. Rather conveniently, one of Theophylact's former pupils was now her confidant. He wrote to him urging him to use his influence with her to encourage her to use her influence with her son! How the affair turned out we shall never know for sure, but it looks as though Theophylact got his way, for not long afterwards he was full of praise for the promise shown by the new governor of the Vardariots: he was a son of the 'stout-hearted' *protostrator*.[18] It sounds as though he had found a satisfactory solution to his quarrel with Michael Doukas.

If all else failed, Theophylact had to go to the emperor himself, but not before he had carefully prepared his approach. Those close to the emperor were primed. The emperor's doctor Nicetas was a friend of Theophylact. He was asked to put in a good word with the emperor on his behalf in the Ekklesiai affair. Theophylact was also in touch with the *protoasekretis* – the emperor's chief secretary – Gregory Kamateros. He refers to his powerful position with the emperor and urges him to use his good offices to support the present governor of Ohrid, who receives a glowing testimonial for the way he has purged the city of elements hostile to the interests of the church. It is a plea for more appointments of governors of this calibre.[19] It was essential for Theophylact that he had the support of the imperial governor. He was full of praise for the emperor's son-in-law Nicephorus Bryennius, to whom he addressed a detailed account of the troubles of his church.[20]

Theophylact was far less happy with John Comnenus, the son of the emperor's brother, the *sebastokrator* Isaac. The tone of his letters to this

16 Migne, *PG*, 126. 489 = Theophylact II 568–9.
17 Migne, *PG*, 126. 420–1 = Theophylact II 440–3.
18 Migne, *PG*, 126. 489–97 = Theophylact II 570–9, at 571.16–21.
19 Migne, *PG*, 126. 368–9 = Theophylact II, 368–71.
20 Migne, *PG*, 126. 441–52 = Theophylact II, 482–93 = Nicephorus Bryennius, *Histoire*, ed. Gautier, 320–33.

scion of the imperial house becomes more and more ironic and bitter. He chides him for inconsistency: 'You see how easily the *sigillion* of the *pansebastos* Comnenus is overturned by the same Comnenus.' He still hopes that the *pansebastos* will take the necessary steps to exempt priests from various corvées and to compensate them for dues illegally exacted.[21] The archbishop must have been disappointed, for he is soon telling him bluntly how badly he is administering Ohrid. Under his rule it suffers far more than any other theme.[22] Theophylact noted his failure to protect one of the estates of the church. He told him sarcastically that he might just as well burn down its buildings, but 'Let the Mother of God, to whom the land and the house belong, take care of you.' That was food for thought![23]

The two men became enemies. Theophylact would denounce John Comnenus to the emperor on the grounds that he was preparing a rebellion. John was duke of Dyrrakhion. This was a sensitive posting because it was the centre of Byzantine operations against the Normans of southern Italy, but there was always a suspicion that the governor of Dyrrakhion might be plotting with the Normans. Alexius I took Theophylact's charge very seriously. John was summoned to explain himself to the emperor. It was the cause of a bitter quarrel between the emperor and his brother Isaac, who found the weight of opinion in the emperor's inner circle going against his son. In the interests of family harmony, John was eventually presumed to be innocent and was reinstated.[24] Theophylact was summoned to Constantinople to explain himself. It was a dangerous thing to denounce a prince of the house of Comnenus. The archbishop seems to have got away with a reprimand, even if John Comnenus was able to frustrate his plans to visit his former patron, the ex-Empress Maria of Alania.[25]

The episode therefore ended inconclusively. It was not a victory for Theophylact, more a drawn battle. Margaret Mullett doubts the effectiveness of Theophylact's defence of his church's interests and believes that he was normally at a disadvantage in his dealings with the governors sent out from Constantinople, where power was still

21 Migne, *PG*, 126. 516–17 = Theophylact II, 166–9 (at 167.15–16).

22 Migne, *PG*, 126. 532–3 = Theophylact II, 208–11.

23 Migne, *PG*, 126. 533–6 = Theophylact II, 214–17. Although this letter is addressed to the *sebastos*, son of the *sebastokrator*, i.e. John Comnenus, Gautier has expressed some reservations about its authenticity. This is because there is a reference to the pious family of Doukas (p.215.13), which he thought applied to the addressee. Consequently, the addressee was likely to belong to the house of Doukas, which was hardly the case with John Comnenus. The passage can, however, be understood quite differently. The Doukas had recognised the church of Ohrid's title to the village in question in contrast to the Comneni. In other words, the archbishop was reproaching John Comnenus.

24 Anna Comnena VIII, vii-viii: I, 411–17 (ed. Bonn); II, 147–51 (ed. Leib).

25 Migne, *PG*, 126. 501–5 = Theophylact II, 136–41.

concentrated.[26] It remains an open question, for it is rarely possible to establish the outcome of Theophylact's lobbying. But there is one factor that must be given due weight. Theophylact was operating against a background of the desperate search by the Comnenian regime for money and recruits. There was precious little compassion or respect for the privileges of a church. For Theophylact it could only be a holding action, but the occasional letters of gratitude to his supporters in Constantinople suggest that he had some success.

Theophylact's surviving correspondence ends about the year 1107, but he stayed on in office until after 1125.[27] This discrepancy may possibly be explained by an accident of survival. It is conceivable, however, that it is connected with the greater security that existed in the southern Balkans after Bohemond's capitulation in 1108. At the same time, the reorganisation of the fiscal system made for a less oppressive regime. There would no longer have been the same pressures on Theophylact. There would not have been the same need to keep up assiduous contacts with Constantinople. For most metropolitans, bishops, and archbishops the first years in office were often very difficult – and many went under. However, if they survived, they possessed certain advantages. They were there until they died or retired, while imperial governors came and went. The local community would with time come to coalesce around its pastor for many reasons, not least because he was an effective channel of communication to the centres of power. Imperial governors came to rely upon him and seek his advice about local conditions. In Byzantium – and not only in Byzantium – the effective exercise of authority depended on how well a person was able to manipulate the currents of power descending from the centre in a series of interlocking circuits. A bishop stood at the point where these touched on other circuits of power, those that were generated locally and those produced by the church. It created a complicated interplay which not all prelates could manage and their churches suffered as a result. Theophylact not only understood the system, but knew how to work it to the advantage of his church and himself. Power and the final decision rested ultimately with the emperor and his family. Their decisions were often arbitrary; they were sometimes swayed by a plausible petitioner. But decisions could be reversed. They could also be implemented in many different ways. Their implementation depended upon the emperor's advisers, ministers, bureaucrats, and quite humble provincial officials. A man such as Theophylact was at home in such company. He also knew that the imperial apparatus of government relied upon men such as himself

26 Mullett, 'Patronage in action', 143–7.

27 Gautier, 'L'épiscopat de Théophylacte', 159–78.

for information and for smoothing the path of various agents sent out from Constantinople.

There is a letter to the bishop of Pelagonia, which shows Theophylact at work, juggling the different elements of the provincial scene. He starts by informing his suffragan of important new appointments that had recently been made in the imperial administration of the area. He was concerned about how they would affect some brothers who were especially dear to him. They occupied positions in local government, but they had made enemies. Theophylact asked the bishop to give them all the help he could. This could best be done by supporting the newly arrived imperial commissioner, because the latter's interests were, in the end, Theophylact believed, identical with those both of the bishop and of the brothers.[28]

Diocesan administration

Theophylact had not only to defend the interests of his church, but he had also to impress his authority over his suffragan bishops. He had some twenty-three or perhaps twenty-five suffragan bishops.[29] Though his church had lost a number of the dioceses accorded to it by Basil II, it had gained others and still covered a vast swathe of the western and central Balkans from the Danube to the confines of Thessaly. It was not an easy task to wield effective authority over such a large area. Over the appointment of suffragans he often faced interference and pressure from local governors. He wrote a sharp letter to the duke of Skopia who had suggested a candidate for a vacant bishopric. He was told that it was none of his business. Theophylact was scathing about the recommendation. The man in question did not appear to be known in the church of Bulgaria, while in Constantinopolitan circles he was esteemed neither for his piety nor his learning. Theophylact then lectured the duke on the kind of appointments that had recently been made. Two had proved their worth as officers of the church of Bulgaria, two others had had distinguished teaching careers at Constantinople, another was noted for his monastic vocation. Theophylact was trying to raise the standard of his episcopal bench. He dismissed the duke's intervention as impudence. He was told in no uncertain terms that Theophylact took orders from God and not from men. In any case, only the bishopric of Vidin remained to be filled. Because of its exposed position on the Danubian frontier it needed a man who combined piety with practical ability.[30]

[28] Migne, *PG*, 126. 528 = Theophylact II, 198–201.
[29] Darrouzès, *Notitiae*, 371–2.
[30] Migne, *PG*, 126. 524–5 = Theophylact II, 190–3.

Once appointments were made, there were always those who were happy to stir up trouble by intriguing against Theophylact with his suffragans. Prominent was somebody that Theophylact refers to as a second Senachereim the Assyrian. This may just be a nickname, but it is possible that he came from the Armenian family of Senachereim. Theophylact claimed that the man 'did not consider the Mother of God Herself worthy of worship'. He not only barred the orthodox from attending church. He was also guilty of inciting one of Theophylact's suffragan bishops against him. Theophylact tells us that this bishop was a nasty piece of work, but prompted by Senachereim had turned into a homicidal maniac. Theophylact claimed that he had been lucky to escape with his life. The affair was getting out of hand and Theophylact decided that, dangerous as it might be, he had to go to the emperor and seek his support.[31]

He does not give the name of this bishop with homicidal tendencies, but the bishop who gave him most trouble was the bishop of Triaditsa or Serdica. That they may be one and the same is suggested by Theophylact's remark that the bishop of Triaditsa's behaviour towards him amounted to parricide.[32] They had quarrelled over a monastery. The bishop had driven out the abbot and had refused to countenance Theophylact's intercession on the latter's behalf. Getting no redress through the good offices of the archbishop, the abbot then went to the emperor and obtained imperial letters reinstating him. These the bishop ignored on the grounds that they were clearly forgeries, obtained through Theophylact's influence with the imperial receiver of petitions (*epi ton deeseon*). The bishop also refused to attend the archbishop's synod when summoned and went instead to Constantinople to further his case by slandering Theophylact, or so the archbishop claimed. He was again summoned to present himself before the synod of the Bulgarian church. His excuses for not attending were deemed to be specious and he was placed under an interdict. There was, however, to be a reconciliation. Theophylact undertook to persuade the other bishops present at the synod to lift their ban. The exact terms of the reconciliation are not disclosed, but they probably included dropping the charges that the bishop had brought against one of his fellow suffragans. This episode illustrates some of the realities involved in the exercise of ecclesiastical power in the provinces. The main parties looked to the emperor and Constantinople for a decision and support. The obduracy of the parties appears to be connected with this. There was always the hope that a decision taken in Constantinople could be overturned. The final settlement was made locally through the

31 Migne, *PG*, 126. 396–401 = Theophylact II 406–13.
32 Migne, *PG*, 126. 349–53 = Theophylact II, 342–9, at 343.20–2.

synod. It looks as though Theophylact prevailed, but this was thanks to the support he could muster in his synod.[33]

Management of his synod was a significant element in the control that Theophylact was able to exercise. Its importance can be gauged from the way he insisted that despite being seriously ill he must go ahead and attend synod;[34] from the way too that he put its needs before all the other concerns of his church.[35] Meetings of his synod meant that he kept in personal touch with many, if not all, of his suffragans. Theophylact also travelled through the lands of his church. Perhaps the most exacting journey he contemplated was to Kanina, only some hundred miles as the crow flies south-west of Ohrid, but through difficult country.[36]

Theophylact took his pastoral duties seriously. He complained about the poor state of his health, but this was as nothing beside his responsibilities to his people and his clergy. His presence was needed not just at Ohrid, but at Glabinitsa, Vidin, and Sthlanitza, in other words, throughout his archdiocese.[37] He was devoted to the traditions and the interests of his church. He was not therefore likely to take kindly to possible infringements of its autocephalous rights by the patriarch of Constantinople. This apparently occurred in the case of a monastery. It had been founded in the diocese of Kittaba in Thessaly which, Theophylact insisted, came within the bounds of the church of Ohrid. The founder was a monk, but he had failed to obtain permission for his foundation from the archbishop of Bulgaria. He claimed that this was not necessary because he had the approval of the patriarch of Constantinople. Theophylact proceeded to have the monk excommunicated. The church of Bulgaria was autocephalous. This meant that the patriarch of Constantinople had no rights over it. The monk was therefore guilty of contumacy. Theophylact's action earned him the displeasure of the patriarch. We do not know the outcome of this affair, but it shows Theophylact quick to defend the rights of his church, or, given that Kittaba seems no longer to have been a suffragan bishopric of Ohrid, to extend them.[38] Theophylact may even have claimed for his church the privileges granted by Justinian I to Justiniana Prima. At the very least, the claim can be traced back to Theophylact's time.[39]

33 Migne, *PG*, 126. 337–44, 344–9, 349–53, 429–32 = Theophylact II, 326–35, 336–41, 342–9, 456–9.

34 Migne, *PG*, 126. 469 = Theophylact II, 526–7.

35 Migne, *PG*, 126. 537–40 = Theophylact II, 232–5.

36 Migne, *PG*, 126. 544–5 = Theophylact II, 244–7.

37 Theophylact II 294–5.

38 Migne, *PG*, 126. 416–17 = Theophylact II, 434–7.

39 G. Prinzing, 'Entstehung und Rezeption der Justiniana-Prima-Theorie im Mittelalter', *Byzantinobulgarica* 5 (1978), 269–87.

Theophylact was himself the subject of a complaint on the part of the patriarch. It arose over his chief psalmist in the cathedral of St Sophia at Ohrid. His skill was vital for the staging of services in the cathedral. He had come from a monastery under the patriarch of Constantinople, but he had failed to obtain a discharge from the lay patron of the monastery, nor had he got the abbot of the monastery to inform the *chartophylax* of St Sophia of his departure for Ohrid. Theophylact had tried to obtain his discharge, but had met with nothing but obstructionism from the officials of the *chartophylax*'s office. Theophylact had then to tackle the *chartophylax* of St Sophia directly, requesting the psalter's official transfer to the church of Bulgaria.[40]

Again, the outcome is not known. The nature of the sources is such that we are left only with impressions. It is possible that Theophylact's various actions met with little positive success. On balance, the vigour and skill with which he intervened militate against such an interpretation, as does the high reputation he left to posterity. It is equally possible that his ambitions were restricted, if not to self-interest and the advancement of his family, then to the material and spiritual well-being of his church and flock. Theophylact was a man of affairs: he knew how important economic independence was to the church. He complained that it was becoming necessary to breed horses three times a year if there were to be sufficient numbers and that the church's ploughs needed to bring forth a harvest of gold and its trees bear golden fruit, if it were to prosper. This prospect might be jeopardised if he had to depart to seek the emperor's intervention: the implication being that his presence was necessary for the effective management of his church's estates.[41]

The church and clergy were always his first concern. His interventions with the imperial authorities couched in terms of social justice nearly always turn out to be a defence of the interest of his church, though there is no reason why he should not at times have been concerned about the welfare of the whole of his flock. One of his major preoccupations was with the status of his clergy. He saw this being infringed or undermined in various ways. He objected to the activities of priests in private service. He claimed that their lords used them to intimidate the common people, so that they could profit from their priests and destroy the privileges of the church to their advantage. The authority of the archbishop and the finances of his church obviously suffered from competition from private churches. His clergy could best be protected if their special status was respected. 'Do not allow those

40 Migne, *PG*, 126. 365–8; Theophylact II, 364–7.

41 Migne, *PG*, 126. 400–1; Theophylact II, 412–13.

consecrated to [God] to be included along with the common people', Theophylact warned one governor.[42]

In the first instance, this was a matter of their not being assessed for taxation along with the general population. Basil II had granted the clergy of the church of Bulgaria exemption from *oikomodion* – which in Bulgaria was the principal tax – and from other exactions.[43] Theophylact saw to it that this privilege continued to be respected. He protested to the governor of the time, John Comnenus, that this was not happening in the case of the priests of Pologa and demanded that orders should be immediately sent to put the matter right.[44] The privilege of Basil II for the Bulgarian church also attached to each diocese a number of dependent peasants. But the rights that the individual churches had over these dependent peasants were not respected. Theophylact protested, again to John Comnenus, that the peasants attached to the church of Prespa had been forced to abandon their family homes and to seek refuge in the forests because of the oppressions of the imperial administration. Deprived of their peasants the clergy abandoned the cathedral. Theophylact begged the governor to take pity on the most beautiful of the Bulgarian churches – the cathedral of St Achilles at Prespa – which that most Christian of men Boris, *basileus* of Bulgaria, built as one of the seven cathedral (*katholikai*) churches'.[45]

Theophylact and St Clement

Because occasionally Theophylact refers slightingly to his Bulgarian flock, he has been seen as a proconsular prelate sent to civilise the natives by imposing Byzantine ways and the Greek language: 'Hellenization begins with the introduction of the Greek liturgy' is how one art historian has put it.[46] Theophylact's highly respectful attitude towards the Bulgarian ruler Boris should put us on our guard against such views. A different and more convincing portrait of Theophylact has recently been drawn by Sir Dimitri Obolensky.[47] At the heart of

42 Migne, *PG*, 126. 525; Theophylact II, 195.

43 Oikonomidès, 'Tax exemptions', 320–2.

44 A. Leroy-Molinghen, 'Prolégomènes à une édition critique des "lettres" de Théophylacte de Bulgarie', *B* 13(1938), 255–9, 260–1 = Theophylact II, 166–9, 194–5.

45 Migne, *PG*, 126. 529–32 = Theophylact II, 202–5. I have translated *katholike ekklesia* as cathedral church to suit the context. In other cases parish church is a better translation, though the Byzantine church never evolved a systematic parochial organisation.

46 A.W. Epstein, 'The political content of the paintings of St Sophia at Ohrid', *JÖB* 29(1980), 324.

47 Obolensky, *Six Byzantine Portraits*, 34–82. See I.G. Iliev, 'The manuscript tradition and the authorship of the Long Life of St Clement of Ohrid', *BS* 52(1992), 68–73, for conclusive proof that Theophylact was indeed the author.

it is his convincing attribution of the authorship of the long *Life* of St Clement of Ohrid to Theophylact.[48] He also assigns the *Martyrdom* of the Fifteen Martyrs of Tiberiopolis to Theophylact. Their church at Stroumitsa was rebuilt during his archiepiscopate. The *Martyrdom* contains an enthusiastic account of Boris's conversion to Christianity. As a result, 'the Bulgarian people have become a royal priesthood, a holy nation, a special people'. These could scarcely have been the words of a man who was filled with contempt for the Bulgarians. Far from trying to suppress the traditions of the Bulgarian church, Theophylact sought to appropriate them. Theophylact put a great deal of himself into his portrait of St Clement. This is evident from the emphasis that he places on the saint's educational activities and his improvement of the calibre of the clergy. St Clement strove to eradicate imperfect knowledge of Christianity existing among the rural population. Even his introduction of fruit trees and new crops very likely replicates Theophylact's concerns. Theophylact saw himself taking up the task of evangelisation begun by St Clement. He took great pleasure in the conversion of a group of Armenians settled within the bounds of the church of Bulgaria to orthodoxy.[49]

There was of course an essential difference. St Clement worked in Old Church Slavonic; Theophylact in Greek, but this does not necessarily mean that he was opposed to the continuation of Old Church Slavonic and tried to stamp it out. The very reverse, it seems, since there continued to be a strong Old Church Slavonic literary tradition centred on Ohrid throughout the eleventh and into the twelfth century.[50] However, Old Church Slavonic no longer had a monopoly as a liturgical language within the church of Bulgaria. Services would have been celebrated in the main churches and cathedrals in Greek. Theophylact recruited young Bulgarians, so that he could teach them Greek. The cultural independence of the Bulgarian church may have been compromised. However, Theophylact's undoubted respect for the traditions of his church went some way towards reconciling the Bulgarians to its increasingly Greek character. Appointments to bishoprics were largely Greeks and Theophylact set about training a native clergy who would celebrate the liturgy in Greek. From a political point of view Theophylact played a major role in the pacification of the Balkans by reconciling the native people to Byzantine rule. His success may well have stemmed from the fact that his chief loyalty was increasingly to his church rather than to the imperial government.

48 Obolensky, *Six Byzantine Portraits*, 62ff.

49 Migne, *PG*, 126. 520 = Theophylact II, 178–81.

50 A. Dostal, 'Les relations entre Byzance et les Slaves (en particulier les Bulgares) aux XIe et XIIe siècles du point de vue culturel', *Thirteenth International Congress of Byzantine Studies. Oxford 1966 – Supplementary Papers* (Oxford, 1966), 41–2.

He would have had no difficulty in reconciling this with a devotion to the imperial office, for he saw the emperor as the guarantor of the privileges of his church. His main concern was with strengthening the legal and economic basis of his church and raising the calibre and the status of his clergy. The nature of the sources means that his success must remain problematic, but he left a formidable reputation, both as an archbishop and as an exegete. His powers of judgement were remembered more than a century later by another archbishop of Ohrid, Demetrius Chomatianos, as 'wonderful and worthy of praise for their subtlety and discernment'.[51] A failure would not have made so powerful an impression on later generations.

[51] Chomatianos, 730. Cf. 626–9.

7

MICHAEL ITALIKOS AND GEORGE TORNIKES

THEOPHYLACT'S immediate successors as archbishop of Bulgaria were not very distinguished. One was of Jewish origin and held the post of *didaskalos ton ethnon* before being appointed to the church of Bulgaria. It is to be assumed that this office was connected with evangelisation and it was this that recommended him for the post of archbishop of Bulgaria. At the end of his reign John II Comnenus appointed his cousin Adrian Comnenus to the throne of the Bulgarian church. Adrian was a son of the *sebastokrator* Isaac and therefore a younger brother of that John Comnenus who had given Theophylact such trouble. His early career was very similar to that of his brother. He too was sent out as a provincial governor. He was a distinguished soldier, but in mid-career he abandoned the world to become the monk John. In this capacity he accompanied his cousin, the Emperor John Comnenus, on his Syrian campaigns and in 1138 made a pilgrimage to the Holy Places. He was a trusted figure in the imperial entourage, but also had contacts among the clergy and teachers of St Sophia. Nicephorus Basilakes, who either held or would hold the office of *didaskalos* of the Apostle, delivered a speech, celebrating his return from Syria in 1139.[1] Another *didaskalos* Michael Italikos composed a valediction for him on the eve of his departure for Bulgaria. He envied the Bulgarians their luck that they should have such a pastor and regretted those tranquil hours he had spent in the archbishop's residence at Constantinople. Most of all, he would miss his affable countenance. They were friends, and Italikos relied on his support.[2]

Although it was not unknown for metropolitans and archbishops to be drawn from distinguished Byzantine families, Adrian Comnenus is the only example of a prelate from the imperial house at this time. The Emperor John Comnenus decided that the church of Bulgaria

1 Nicephorus Basilakes, *Encomio di Adriano Comneno*, ed. A. Garzya (Naples, 1965).

2 Michael Italikos, no.34, 211–12. Italikos became *didaskalos* of the Gospels at Christmas 1142.

required a prestigious figure at its helm. In this instance, he could act directly, because the appointment was his. The church of Bulgaria enjoyed autocephalous status, which meant among other things that the archbishop was appointed by the emperor. Adrian held the office until his death some time between 1157 and 1164.[3] He carried out his duties conscientiously, attending synods in Constantinople, hearing cases that came before his court. He left behind a *nomocanon* as testimony to his pastoral work. His sense of the importance of his see is evident: he signed himself officially as archbishop of Justiniana Prima and all Bulgaria.[4]

When Michael Italikos wrote to Adrian Comnenus, regretting his imminent departure for Bulgaria, he little thought that a similar fate awaited him. Soon afterwards he would be appointed metropolitan bishop of Philippopolis. Italikos was more typical of the appointments made at this time to the major sees of the Byzantine church. He had behind him a distinguished teaching career at Constantinople, which culminated in the office of *didaskalos* of the Gospels. At some point, he was selected for an embassy to the West by the Emperor John Comnenus. The assumption is that he went and his protests over the appointment were a matter of form.[5] His presumed diplomatic experience in the West would have stood him in good stead, for the first major test that he had to face as metropolitan of Philippopolis was the passage of the second crusade in the summer of 1147. The German contingent started plundering the suburbs of the town. Michael Italikos was able to persuade the German Emperor Conrad II over a glass of wine to discipline his troops. All his skill was needed to pacify Conrad, when soon afterwards a number of Germans were murdered by the local inhabitants. His success in saving the city was long afterwards remembered in Philippopolis.[6]

For whatever reason, very little survives of Michael Italikos's writings from the period when he was metropolitan bishop of Philippopolis. A little light is shed on his activities at that time by an exchange of letters with a former pupil, the littérateur Theodore Prodromos. In the usual way, Michael Italikos found his new home poor and the local people were not to be trusted. The particular problem was that Philippopolis was a centre of heresy. Paulicians had been settled there since the tenth century; there was also a large Armenian population. Prodromos

[3] Stiernon, 'Notes de titulature', 179–92.

[4] H. Gelzer, *Der Patriarchat von Achrida. Geschichte und Urkunden* (Leipzig, 1902), 8–9.

[5] Michael Italikos, 21–4.

[6] Nicetas Choniates, 62–4. By this I mean that Nicetas saw fit to record this incident in his history. He must have obtained the details when he was posted to Philippopolis in 1189.

assures Italikos that his eloquence and intellectual powers were more than sufficient to deal with the problem. This may have been one of the reasons why Italikos was appointed to this particular see. He also had difficulties with some of his clergy – 'the priests of shame', as Prodromos calls them. To deal with them it was best to rely upon the support of the patriarch, or so Prodromos thought. The ringleader was a certain Kampsorhymes, 'the son of perdition'. Prodromos assured Italikos that there was a Kampsorhymes in the capital, who had been going round the streets, alleys, squares, public buildings, and churches, but had been driven away like a bit of filth. Prodromos had raised his voice against him.

Professor Browning has seen this as a reference to the activities of the monk Niphon, who had been condemned as a Bogomil sympathiser, but had then been released by the Patriarch Cosmas Atticus in 1146.[7] This identification is plausible enough, but there is one inconvenient detail. The real Kampsorhymes's case came before the patriarchal synod under Nicholas Mouzalon (1147–51). He had been excommunicated by Italikos and had sought redress from the patriarchal synod. There were those present who argued that he had no right to take his case to the patriarch, because he should have gone first to his local synod. Kampsorhymes insisted that he had tried to get other metropolitans to intervene on his behalf with Italikos. The patriarchal synod judged that Kampsorhymes had done nothing uncanonical in bringing his case to the patriarch. The assumption is that he was pardoned. This case was heard in the aftermath of the deposition of the Patriarch Cosmas Atticus on the grounds that he had been consorting with the heretic Niphon. It seems unlikely that Kampsorhymes would have escaped condemnation, if his activities had in any way been linked with those of Niphon.

The only firm conclusion we can come to is that Italikos not only had difficulties with members of his clergy, but these were made worse by the failure of the patriarchal synod to give him support.[8] This is the most likely background to his decision to resign his see. He tried to make it a condition that the patriarchal synod would appoint his *oikonomos* in his place. This request was refused on the grounds that a bishop could not bequeath or gift property that he acquired from the revenues of his church after his ordination, still less the episcopal office itself.[9] It was another snub administered by the patriarchal synod. Italikos, it would seem, did not have a happy time as metropolitan bishop of Philippopolis. Unlike Theophylact of Bulgaria he does not

7 R. Browning, 'Unpublished correspondence between Michael Italicus, archbishop of Philippopolis, and Theodore Prodromos', *BB* 1(1962), 287–8, 296 (= Browning, *Studies on Byzantine History*, no. VI).

8 Rhalles & Potles III, 321.

9 Ibid. II, 99.

seem to have been able to impose himself on his clergy, but this can only be an impression. His decision to resign his see can plausibly be taken as an admission of failure. It might possibly have been the result of ill health, but there are plenty of examples of bishops struggling on for years in bad health and positively glorying in their infirmities.

The difficulties and inconveniences facing a bishop when he first arrived in his see are graphically related in George Tornikes's correspondence. He was appointed to the metropolitan see of Ephesus in 1155. He was a younger contemporary of Michael Italikos. He followed a very similar career, holding the teaching posts of *didaskalos* of the Psalter and *didaskalos* of the Gospels, before being appointed to the administrative office of *hypomnematographos*, which placed him among the chief officers of the patriarchal administration.[10] His ascent was swifter than that of Michael Italikos and promotion came at a rather younger age. This may have had something to do with his impressive family connections. As we know, George Tornikes was a member of the circle around Anna Comnena and his mother was a niece of Theophylact of Bulgaria. He was first offered the see of Corinth, which he was tempted to take because it would mean that he was closer to his mother, who still lived in the family home at Thebes. He turned it down, perhaps because it was too poor, but he must also have been impressed by the greater prestige attaching to the see of Ephesus. He sent his cousin Euthymios ahead to prepare his arrival in his new see. He furnished his cousin with various letters of introduction: to the governor of the theme of Thrakesion, of which Ephesus was one of the chief cities, and to the governor's representative at Ephesus itself.[11] He also had another letter of introduction to the metropolitan bishop of neighbouring Smyrna, after Ephesus the most important church of the region.

Such precautions did not lessen the shock of arriving in a provincial city. Though born and brought up at Thebes long years in Constantinople had left him, as so many of his colleagues, with a poor appreciation of the realities of provincial life. He was horrified by the conditions prevailing in Ephesus. His cathedral, the great Justinianic church of St John the Theologian, was in a poor state of repair: the roof was leaking and it was full of birds.[12] The native people were unfriendly. He complained to the metropolitan of Athens that he was 'beset by men who are wilder than the local panthers, craftier than foxes and richer in malice than they are poverty stricken in other things'.[13]

[10] Tornikès, 7–13.
[11] Ibid., nos.19–20.
[12] Ibid., no.23. See C. Foss, *Ephesus after Antiquity: A Late Antique, Byzantine and Turkish City* (Cambridge, 1979), 116–37.
[13] Tornikès, no. 21, 153.8–10.

Tornikes wrote to a series of acquaintances and patrons in Constantinople, describing the plight of his church and seeking their support and good offices. He turned to members of the powerful Kamateros family;[14] to the chief minister of the time Theodore Styppeiotes;[15] to the *nomophylax* Theodore Pantechnes, who in the past advised him against taking the see of Corinth;[16] and finally to Eirene, the daughter of his former patroness Anna Comnena.[17] It was a tactic followed by all bishops who had influence in the capital: to mobilise support in the face of potential difficulties, but these still had to be confronted on the ground. Soon after his arrival at Ephesus George Tornikes set out on the arduous journey to Philadelphia. His purpose was to meet the new duke of Thrakesion, Alexius Kontostephanos – a young aristocrat at the start of his career, who would become one of Manuel Comnenus's most successful marshals. George Tornikes complained about the duke's treatment of the bishop of Palaiopolis, though he failed to go into details.[18] Palaiopolis was one of Ephesus's thirty-six suffragan churches. Ephesus had more suffragan bishops at this time than any other see under the patriarchate of Constantinople. One of the metropolitan's major tasks was to fill his suffragan sees as they fell vacant. This happened with the bishopric of Pyrgion. George Tornikes received a letter from Isaac Comnenus, a great nephew of the Emperor Alexius I Comnenus, but now the monk John, seeking the bishopric for the *ekklesiarkhes* of his monastery. George Tornikes was at first inclined to turn the request down, but thought better of it. It was useful to remain on good terms with members of the imperial family.[19]

Nothing more is heard of George Tornikes after 1156, when he attended a meeting of the patriarchal synod. He was not present at the synod of 1157, which condemned his enemy Soterichos Panteugenos. Only death would have prevented his attendance at such a meeting,[20] for his last piece of writing was a tract directed against the views of Soterichos Panteugenos.[21] It is more than likely that he died worn out by the exertions of his office, for the early years when a bishop was feeling his way were the most difficult. His last letter was to one of his partisans encouraging him in the struggle against Soterichos Panteugenos. It starts with the words, 'Just as I take pleasure in your successes, so I know you will be downhearted by my misfortunes.'

[14] Ibid., nos.15–16.
[15] Ibid., no.17.
[16] Ibid., no.23.
[17] Ibid., no.22.
[18] Ibid., no.27.
[19] Ibid., no.25.
[20] Ibid., no.20.
[21] Ibid., no.31.

Both Italikos and Tornikes had very good connections at the imperial court and in the patriarchal church alike, but these do not disguise the fact that appointment to an important metropolitan see meant heavy responsibilities that could drive the incumbent to an early death or to resignation.

8

EUSTATHIUS OF THESSALONICA

EUSTATHIUS of Thessalonica had more than enough time in his see to prove himself, but by the end of his life he may have had his doubts about the wisdom of accepting his translation from the church of Myra to the church of Thessalonica. Myra was not by the twelfth century the most glamorous of appointments, even if it boasted what had been the major shrine of St Nicholas. Cut off from other Byzantine territory by Turkish shepherds it was the kind of see that bishops were reluctant to visit, let alone take up residence. Though designated metropolitan bishop of Myra in 1174 there is no evidence that Eustathius ever visited this see. His appointment was made at a moment of optimism when the Emperor Manuel Comnenus's plans for the recovery of Anatolia from the Turks seemed to have a good chance of success. When these came to grief at the battle of Myriokephalon in 1176, appointment to the see of Myra became even less attractive. Eustathius must therefore have welcomed his translation to the see of Thessalonica towards the end of Manuel Comnenus's reign.

Still he may have come to regret it, for it was not long before the new archbishop began to realise what an arduous task he had taken on. The city was large, populous, and prosperous, bursting out of its late antique walls. It was the great emporium of the southern Balkans, set in rich farming country. Prelates sent out from Constantinople could not grumble, as they did almost everywhere else, that they had landed up in some provincial backwater. Eustathius complained about many things that were wrong with Thessalonica and its people, but never that life there was dull.

By the time of his appointment to Thessalonica Eustathius was perhaps in his late fifties, if anything, a little older, with a distinguished career in the patriarchal administration behind him. In the late 1160s he was appointed *maistor* of the rhetors in deference to his scholarly reputation. He was perhaps the most impressive Homeric scholar of all times. This gave him immense standing in the capital, while his teaching meant that in the usual Byzantine fashion he was at the centre of a nexus of former pupils, ever anxious to increase the prestige of their teacher, since this redounded on them and their careers. Eustathius took with him to Thessalonica excellent contacts in Constantinople: at court, in the imperial government, and in the patriarchal church. He also had a very high opinion of the role of the teacher as an arbiter of society and a clear idea of the duties and responsibilities of a bishop. He was almost immediately at loggerheads with the people of Thessalonica.[1]

Scarcely a year can have elapsed after his appointment to Thessalonica and Eustathius was appealing to the Emperor Manuel Comnenus for help in difficulties that he was having. The people of Thessalonica were up in arms over some action of their new archbishop. Manuel sent one of his most experienced and trusted agents, the Grand Heteriarch John Doukas, to sort out matters.[2] But Eustathius's relations with his flock remained uneasy. In 1180 he took the opportunity of the feast of St Nicephorus (9 February) to lecture the people of Thessalonica on the evils of ill will.[3]

The fall of Thessalonica 1185

Bishops almost always found their opening years the most difficult. As we have seen, they tended to bring with them from the capital ideas about the right way of doing things. They were also in a sense representatives of Constantinople. The result was, as often as not, conflict and friction with local interests. It was a situation that required presence, tact, and political skills. Eustathius was not tactful, was not one to compromise; was not sufficiently a politician. The difficulties encountered in his early years continued and, if anything, grew worse. His experience was more extreme than that of other Comnenian prelates whose careers we can follow. For example, as archbishop of Philippopolis Michael Italikos had only to negotiate the passage of the second crusade. Eustathius, for his sins, had to endure the siege and sack of his city by the Normans in August 1185.

He has left a vivid account of terrible events.[4] It was delivered first in

[1] On Eustathius, see Kazhdan/Franklin, 115–95; Wirth, *Eustathiana.*

[2] W. Regel, *Fontes rerum byzantinarum* (St Petersburg, 1892–1917; repr. Leipzig, 1932), 2 vols., I, 1, no. ii, 16–24. On John Doukas, see P. Karlin-Hayter, '99. Jean Doukas', *B* 42 (1972), 259–65, who corrects D.I. Polemis, *The Doukai. A Contribution to Byzantine Prosopography* (London, 1968), 127–30. Cf. A.P. Kazhdan, 'John Doukas: an attempt of de-identification', *Le parole e le idee*, 11(1969), 242–7; Tornikès, 43–9.

[3] Eustathius I, 1–7. For dating Kazhdan/Franklin, 124.

[4] The text has been most recently edited by St. Kyriakides. This is reproduced together with an English translation in Eustathius II. There is also a German translation: H.Hunger, *Die Normannen in Thessalonike* (Graz, 1955).

the form of a Lenten sermon to the people of Thessalonica in February 1186, less than six months after the Normans had evacuated the city. The events were fresh in everybody's minds. It was far too close to the events to have any claim to objectivity. It bears many of the marks of an *apologia* for Eustathius's role at the time. He needed to disassociate himself from the regime of Andronicus I Comnenus, which had in the meantime been overthrown. Like many others, Eustathius had at first given it a cautious welcome. He had also been far too close to David Comnenus, the governor of Thessalonica appointed by Andronicus I Comnenus to defend the city against the Normans.[5] David Comnenus would be made the scapegoat for the fall of the city, but everything suggests that until the very last moment Eustathius supported his conduct of the defence of Thessalonica. However, David escaped from the siege, letting himself down by a rope from the walls of the acropolis, while Eustathius stayed behind and shared, at least vicariously, in the sufferings of the people of Thessalonica. His constant complaints about how little he had been getting of the right kind of food suggest he cut a less than heroic figure. He was, however, honest enough to admit that he wanted to flee from the city the moment he knew of the approach of the Normans, but was prevented from doing so by the governor for reasons best known to himself and by moral pressure from his clergy.[6]

Eustathius's reactions to the circumstances of the sack of the city and the imposition of Norman rule are instructive. He was appalled by the disappearance of the old social landmarks. The Greeks were all dressed in the same garb, so that it was impossible to distinguish the clergy from the laity.[7] So lacking was he in a sense of proportion that he placed loss of a dowry on almost the same footing as loss of virginity.[8] He noted the usual accommodations of local people with the occupying forces.[9] Some of his most bitter comments were directed against the Jews and especially the Armenians for the way they profited from and gloried in the disaster that had overtaken the Greeks.[10] He catalogues with a degree of resignation the atrocities committed by the Latins. Dreadful things happen in war, especially when it is God's way of visiting his wrath upon an erring people. Eustathius was concerned about the fate of the church and the clergy. He noted the lack of respect shown by the Latins for the church services of the Greeks.[11] He remonstrated about

5 Eustathius II, 12.11–14.
6 Ibid., 66.31–68.3.
7 Ibid., 124.9–15.
8 Ibid., 138.1–3.
9 Ibid., 138.9–18.
10 Ibid., 124.17–30.
11 Ibid., 126.20–6; 134.17–22.

this to the Norman governor Alduin; he admits, to no avail. Alduin had more success curbing the other excesses of his troops. He was able to provide the citizens of Thessalonica with some measure of protection.[12] He also returned books and church furnishings to Eustathius, who distributed most of them to those around the Norman governor. There is a note of apology at this point in Eustathius's narrative: they had been demanded of him and he could not refuse. This incident nevertheless left him open to the charge of collaboration.[13]

Like others in Thessalonica he had to remain on good terms with the occupying forces. Perhaps, it was all the more urgent for Eustathius because he became responsible for the citizens of Thessalonica before the Norman authorities. His main concern was for his own well-being and for his clergy. He remembered how he was able to wheedle fifty gold pieces out of the Normans and this saved them from the desperate position they were in. Eustathius was somehow able to supplement his meagre rations through the action of the patron of the city, St Demetrius, who fed not only the clergy, but also the rest of the remaining population.[14] He later specifies that this was the work of 'those from the Myrobletes'.[15] He refers almost certainly to the members of the confraternity of the Myrobletes who had distinguished themselves earlier in the defence of the city.[16] This was not the only confraternity in Thessalonica at the time. There was also a confraternity of the Hodegetria.[17] Eustathius does not take any credit for the work of St Demetrius in feeding his people. It might be uncharitable to take this at face value and suggest that Eustathius did very little to help the people of Thessalonica in the aftermath of the sack of the city. He did what he could, no doubt.

The people of Thessalonica do not seem to have felt themselves especially in debt to their metropolitan bishop. Eustathius presented the fall of Thessalonica as punishment for the sins of its people. He charged that the experience, terrible as it was, seemed not to have changed the people of Thessalonica. The old failings of envy, pride, avarice, ingratitude, ill will, were still there.[18] In the aftermath of the conquest of Thessalonica Eustathius was temporarily in charge of the Greek community. But this was only thanks to the Normans. Once they evacuated the city his relations with the people of Thessalonica continued as bad as ever.

[12] Ibid., 126.26–35.
[13] Ibid., 128.1–4.
[14] Ibid., 112.9–23.
[15] Ibid., 124.22–4.
[16] Ibid., 94.25.
[17] Ibid., 142.3–6, where it is referred to as an *adelphotes*.
[18] Ibid., 154–6.

Eustathius and the people of Thessalonica

Eustathius's frustrations were apparent in another Lenten homily he addressed to his flock in 1186.[19] Three things in particular vexed Eustathius. He thought that the people of Salonica had a rather casual attitude to marriage. He found the conduct of divorce cases very trying. The parties egged on by their supporters made a mockery of the archbishop. Worse were the local customs that were quite out of line with canon law. Betrothals were often no more than a cover for concubinage. Eustathius was also shocked by the practice of couples seeking out some simple-minded priest outside the city and going through a form of marriage ceremony which did not conform to canonical regulations; contracts were not even exchanged. Eustathius took to task those he heard had got married in this way. He was told for his pains to mind his own business. He was horrified by the way it was normal for consummation to follow immediately after betrothal.

Eustathius then recalled a specific incident. He had summoned somebody accused of this particular misdemeanour for cross-examination. The man in question resented what was happening and denounced the failings of the clergy. If the governor had not cited him, he would never have deigned to appear before an ecclesiastical court. He gave vent to some mild anti-clericalism to the effect that as far as God was concerned ecclesiastical property and personages were surplus to requirement. Eustathius was deeply offended.[20] Marriage does not surface again as one of the points of issue dividing Eustathius from the people of Thessalonica, but his austere and unsympathetic attitude was not likely to endear him to his flock. Marriage was one of those areas where the church impinged directly on lay society. Ecclesiastical authority had to be exercised with discretion. Tact was not one of Eustathius's strong points.

Another thing that irritated Eustathius about life in Thessalonica was the presence of a prosperous Jewish community. He was not being exactly anti-semitic. His charge was not so much that the Jews prospered because of the toleration extended to them by a Christian society; more that the people of Thessalonica were not charitable to poor Christians in their midst, while their behaviour to one another was quite the reverse of their lenient attitude to the Jews. In their dealings with their fellow Christians they displayed little in the way

19 Ibid., 61–75 It was written after 1185, since there is a reference to the three-month occupation of Thessalonica by barbarians (ibid., 75.52–9, 69). However, Eustathius also complains that he has been preoccupied with the marriage problems of his flock for six years (ibid., 63.95–6). Since he was appointed at the end of Manuel I Comnenus's reign, *c.*1179, this only leaves 1186. See Kazhdan/Franklin, 132.

20 Eustathius I, 64–5.

of tolerance or brotherly love, only suspicion and envy. Eustathius was using the Jews in this instance to mount an attack on the way of life then prevailing in Thessalonica.[21]

But the Jews of Thessalonica could also be used by his enemies as a weapon against him, as we learn from a panic-stricken letter he sent to the patriarch of Constantinople. The facts of the matter were these: under the previous archbishops of Thessalonica the Jewish community had expanded, taking over areas that had long been abandoned by Christians, but they had also moved into tenements still occupied by Christians. These buildings often had shrines containing icons, for which reason the presence of Jews was offensive. It was a matter that had only recently been brought to Eustathius's attention. It was made all the worse because a register was produced, which proved that some of this property belonged to the church of Thessalonica. This was a cause of embarrassment to Eustathius and he needed the advice and support of the patriarch, if he was to extricate himself.[22] He clearly felt that he had put himself into a false position and had given hostages to fortune to his enemies at Thessalonica.

The Jews were of minor importance beside the question of charity and the treatment of the poor. Eustathius placed the poor at the centre of Christian life. It was through them that prayers were mediated to God. He calls them the ushers of God.[23] It was one of the church's most solemn responsibilities to care for the poor. But what did Eustathius find at Thessalonica? The poor were cheated and duped and forced to pay exorbitant rates of interest.[24] The archbishop complained that the church could not carry out its charitable duties because its property had been appropriated by those who disputed the right of the church to own property. He was challenged to explain what need God or his saints had of property, since they neither sowed nor reaped, neither ate nor drank; to explain, too, why it was even necessary to feed the poor. 'We were once poor', he was told, 'but *we* have managed to prosper.'[25]

Eustathius brought with him from Constantinople rather conventional Christian sentiments about charity and social harmony, which were at odds with the bustling, competitive society that he found in Thessalonica. The friction this produced would soon turn into bitter hostility. Eustathius would be hunted down by his enemies. He was lucky to escape unscathed from Thessalonica. Eustathius must bear some, perhaps much, of the blame. He could be a singularly

[21] Ibid., 66.69–92; see A. Sharf, *Byzantine Jewry from Justinian to the Fourth Crusade* (London, 1972), 148.
[22] Eustathius I, 340.
[23] Ibid., 70.61–87.
[24] Ibid., 71–2.
[25] Ibid., 72.20–7.

unpleasant and sarcastic old man. He brought to his episcopal duties the violence of the class-room. He remembered with appreciation and affection his old master who had been in the habit of beating him. How else was it possible to learn![26] Eustathius admitted to slapping one of his priests across the face. He indignantly dismissed the priest's claim that he had been beaten up at Eustathius's orders and that the archbishop's laughing and clapping had shown how much he had enjoyed the spectacle. Eustathius thought that the priest failed to display a properly Christian disposition: he should have turned the other cheek![27] Eustathius more or less condemns himself on the charge against him of using violence. One imagines that the priest did not appreciate his sense of humour. Possessed of such a sense of humour it was easy to make enemies.

It is a pity that Eustathius is reluctant to specify exactly who his enemies were. He dismisses them as no more than 'one or two among the distinguished laity and the nobility; also members of the clergy, who are easily numbered and do not count for much'.[28] The impression is that many of the leaders of Thessalonican society were against him. The only opponent that he mentions by name was one Leo, described rather maliciously by Eustathius as a poor man, who would have died of hunger but for the charity he received from the church.[29] Why he should have been singled out is not made clear. There was surely somebody behind him.[30] The tenor of the passage suggests that formal charges were laid against Eustathius, in which case Leo is likely to have been the plaintiff. Eustathius admits that his conduct was investigated by a panel of bishops. He is presumably referring to the patriarchal synod. He objected intensely to the lack of consideration and courtesy that he was shown.[31]

Eustathius had a more general grievance against the people of Thessalonica. He complained about the way they stayed away from the processions organised to celebrate the new year, a festival that was very dear to his heart.[32] Much to his shame a visitor from Athens emphasised the much greater success his city had in attracting the participation of the people in such festivities. The visitor claimed that

26 Ibid., 103.90–4.
27 Ibid., 68.49–59.
28 Ibid., 160.61–3.
29 Ibid., 164.9–11.
30 Ibid., 164.11–12.
31 Ibid., 164.13–38. The word which I render panel of bishops is ʼαρχιερατεύουσι (l.13). Kazhdan/Franklin, 136, have emended this to ʼαρχιετρατεύουσι, but fail to indicate why. They take this passage to mean that Eustathius's "opponents took control of the archiepiscopal see". I find this difficult to follow. The only panel of bishops able to investigate a metropolitan bishop would be the patriarchal synod or bishops specially delegated by it.
32 Eustathius I, 314–17.

on such occasions 'not a child stayed at home'.[33] It is a detail which underlines how distant Eustathius was from the people of his city. He addressed a sermon to them on the meaning of New Year's Day. He was well aware of its origins in the Roman calends. It was a time for giving presents, of forgiving past wrongs, in a word of celebrating social harmony. Eustathius exhorted the people of Thessalonica to turn over a new leaf and abandon their unsocial ways.[34] He reminded them of one particular benefit that he had brought them. Most of his predecessors made distributions of money to the clergy of the churches of St Sophia, of the Akheiropoietos, and of St Demetrius on the occasion of various festivals. But the *typikon* of St Sophia at Constantinople included two feast days which were not celebrated at Thessalonica: the elevation of the cross and Holy Monday. These Eustathius accordingly introduced into the Thessalonican calendar. He also celebrated New Year's Day and the beginning of spring, when distributions of money were also made. He passed over in silence his expenditure on the decoration of churches at Thessalonica, for which he had been criticised by his clergy. He rebuked them for only being interested in what was spent on them.[35]

The introduction of new festivals with distributions of money was an obvious way for an archbishop to ingratiate himself with his flock, but it failed to endear Eustathius to the people of Thessalonica. In the case of those for the New Year and for the beginning of spring he was almost certainly trying to take over what had been secular festivals and annex them to the church. He failed, however, to enter into the spirit of the occasion and acquired the reputation of one who objected to processions and festivities. He admitted that he considered them pure vanity. People would do better, in his opinion, to think on their own funeral cortège, and to remember that their coffin would be insulted with noses thumbed. He found it hard to understand the mania for such processions, when one was either choked with dust or knee-deep in mire, depending on the season.[36] He was unable to appreciate the central role that religious festivities and processions had in the life of a city.

This lack of empathy was reciprocated by the people of Thessalonica. Soon a caricature of Eustathius was going the rounds of the city. It bore the legend, 'A malicious man, the present bishop of Thessalonica.'[37] What horrified Eustathius was not so much the injustice done to him,

33 P. Wirth, 'Das religiose Leben in Thessalonike unter dem Episkopat des Eustathios im Urteil von Zeitgenossen', *Ostkirchliche Studien* 9(1960), 293–4.

34 Eustathius I, 152.

35 Ibid., 153.

36 Ibid., 110–11.

37 Ibid., 98.42–64.

as the possibility that copies might reach Constantinople and damage his reputation there.[38] He set out to refute the charges. There were good men in the city who would vouch for his excellent intentions and willingness to forgive.[39] To his friends he showed the softer side of his character, not the stern countenance that he reserved for prying citizens.[40] His discourse among his friends was simpler and more direct; he was capable of calling a spade a spade.[41] He was more or less condemning himself out of his own mouth.

There was a world of difference between the private and the public man. Eustathius admits it. His main defence against the charge that he was a malicious old man was that of self-defence and a refusal to tolerate evil. It is clear that he was not able to come to terms with life at Salonica and was impatient with its social niceties. One of the more serious charges against him was that in his bearing he made no distinction between the Thessalonian elite and their inferiors. He claimed that it was scarcely his fault that society was so unstable. One day a citizen was rich and respected and the next living in poverty and a social outcaste.[42] Again, this is a detail that reveals how little he knew or cared about the social life of Thessalonica.

Eustathius could not conceal how little respect there was for him and his church. Only a few days previously, a money changer stormed into the cathedral of St Sophia and dragged out a wretched slave of his who had sought asylum at the altar. Eustathius was appalled at this act of sacrilege and horrified that so many people found the incident amusing, including some of the clergy. This only revealed, in Eustathius's opinion, their continuing attachment to the market place.[43] In other words, the sympathies of, at least, a section of the clergy were not with their metropolitan. Eustathius accused them of remaining attached to the values of a lay society.

There was a coolness between Eustathius and some of his clergy,[44] but this was as nothing beside the rancour that he reserved for the monks of Thessalonica. Much of his diatribe against hypocrisy is directed at monastic duplicity.[45] Eustathius composed a long treatise exhorting the monks of his diocese to mend their ways. The picture he draws of the monastic condition as he found it in Thessalonica is anything but edifying. There was an unabashed search for more

38 Ibid., 98.61–2.
39 Ibid., 105.82–91.
40 Ibid., 106.15–27.
41 Ibid., 106.27–34.
42 Ibid., 109–10.
43 Ibid., 156.43–92.
44 Ibid., 152.72–91.
45 Ibid., 93–7.

and more property.[46] There was blinkered ignorance and contempt for study.[47] Underlying Eustathius's criticism was the mutual hostility which characterised the relations between monks and their local bishop. Eustathius expostulates:

> How can any monk who has been blessed in this mysterious way by them [the bishops and priests], dare to answer back that he is not subject to the presiding bishop and that the latter is less than him? Do they not realise that the Fathers of the church were distinguished by the episcopal office and held that the bishop is the father of fathers?[48]

Eustathius wanted to know why monks so hated their bishops. His answer was that 'they reckon that if there were no bishops, they would be everything in the world and the only people to whom churches would be subject would be to those dressed in black all over'.[49] Eustathius is only expressing in his vitriolic fashion the perennial opposition of episcopal authority and monastic autonomy. He holds up to the monks of Thessalonica as a model of monastic order the monasteries of Constantinople.[50] This is more a reflection of his nostalgia for the capital than an objective assessment of the state of metropolitan monasticism. He describes Constantinople as a paradise.

Eustathius's expulsion from Thessalonica

Eustathius left his heart in Constantinople – a condition that goes some way towards explaining his isolation in Thessalonica. He relied heavily on his household. It included young men sent from Constantinople.[51] He also had a former pupil and later a colleague among the deacons of St Sophia elected as one of his suffragan bishops.[52] The bishop of Serres was a friend, as was his secretary and Eustathius encouraged the bishop to get his secretary to write to him.[53] It was part of the civilities of friendship which meant so much to Eustathius and sustained him through his unhappy years in Thessalonica.[54] Only a selection of his letters has survived.[55] Nearly half – at least twenty, but perhaps as many as twenty-three[56] – were addressed to one man Nicephorus

46 Ibid., 222.31–2.
47 Ibid., 249.24–44.
48 Ibid., 215.86–9, 216.1–2.
49 Ibid., 262.12–15.
50 Ibid., 234.80–97.
51 Ibid., II, 66.25–8.
52 Ibid., I, 340–1.
53 Ibid., 343.
54 See M. E. Mullett, 'Byzantium. A friendly society?', *Past & Present* 118(Feb.1988), 3–24.
55 Eustathius I, 308–61.
56 Viz. ibid., nos. 1–18, 24[25]-5[2], 27[28]-8[2], 34[35].

Comnenus who was dead by 1173.[57] He was a grandson of the Caesar Nicephorus Bryennius and Anna Comnena and a man of some influence at the court of Manuel I Comnenus. He was in a loose sense a patron of Eustathius. After his death Eustathius seems to have relied on John Kamateros who was made receiver of petitions (*epi ton deeseon*) about the time that Eustathius was appointed to Thessalonica. It was a position of some influence close to the reigning emperor. Earlier Eustathius had dedicated his commentary on Dionysius Periegetes to him.[58] He wrote to him from Thessalonica. He wanted to know if the emperor had any plans to visit his western provinces. Eustathius's position was so desperate that he had to see the emperor, even if it meant using a litter to reach him.[59]

The circumstances were those Eustathius enlarged upon in his '*Letter* to the people of Thessalonica'. There he accused them of forcing him to flee the city.[60] But when was this? P. Wirth placed it in 1191, but A. Kazhdan has disputed this dating.[61] He claimed that this letter was written before 1185. His main reason he adduces was the lack of any reference to the Norman sack of the city. In addition, Eustathius described himself in the letter as ὁ ἄρτι ἀρχιερεὺς,[62] which suggested to Kazhdan his relatively recent appointment to the see of Thessalonica. The meaning is, however, ambiguous. It could equally mean no more than the present incumbent. This is likely to be the case, for in the letter Eustathius mentions in passing how the rhythm of the seasons has been disrupted and how he has already treated this theme in a previous discourse.[63] Sure enough it survives. It contains among other things a bitter condemnation of the Latin occupation of Thessalonica.[64] In other words, Eustathius's '*Letter* to the people of Thessalonica' must be dated after 1185. It favours a return to Wirth's original dating for Eustathius's expulsion, but there is other evidence to support this date. In a sermon preached on 25 February 1191 Eustathius expressed his intention of leaving the city. He had to because the 'foolish mob' were bringing a case against him before the emperor or the patriarch. He sought the help of the Emperor Isaac II Angelus who was encamped at Philippopolis. He was there by Easter 1191 when he delivered a speech

57 Varzos II, no.115, 87–97.
58 See Tornikès, 45–6; Polemis, *Doukai*, no.99, 127–30.
59 Eustathius I, no.34[35], p.341.
60 Ibid., 158–65.
61 P. Wirth, 'Die Flucht des Erzbischofs Eustathios aus Thessalonike', *BZ* 53(1960), 83–4; Kazhdan/Franklin, 134–6.
62 Eustathius I, 164.2–3.
63 Ibid., 164.46–50.
64 Ibid., 152–7. For a passing mention of the sack of the city by the Normans, ibid. 157.82–4. I have to thank Paul Magdalino for drawing my attention to these references.

celebrating the emperor's apparently successful Balkan campaign.[65] Eustathius appears not to have returned immediately to Thessalonica. He seems instead to have been sent on a diplomatic mission to Richard Coeur de Lion, then on crusade, presumably to discuss the fate of Cyprus. At least, Alberic de Tre Fontane records the presence in Richard's entourage at Acre in 1191 – it would have to be late in the year – of the bishop of Thessalonica.[66] Eustathius was back at Thessalonica by Lent 1193.[67] But there is a lacuna in his life for much of 1191 and all of 1192. It is reasonable to suggest that this was the period of his exile from Thessalonica.

Eustathius on society[68]

In many ways Eustathius's ideas about society were very conventional. Social harmony was only to be obtained by respecting a hierarchical order established by God and supervised by the emperor. He retained the traditional division between an elite and the rest of society. The elite from the emperor down had a responsibility for the well-being of society, while the ordinary citizen had a duty to obey the elite. Eustathius divides the elite into two hierarchies: political and ecclesiastical. This is all quite unexceptional. The interest comes when he applies theory to the realities of his own day. He recognised that the elite was structured in a more complicated way than his schema at first sight suggested. The political elite was divided into aristocrats and bureaucrats. The former were primarily soldiers and the latter administrators. He approved of the former rather than the latter because they displayed the quality of nobility to a much greater extent than the latter. Nobility carried with it a sense of noblesse oblige. You knew your responsibilities and fulfilled them. You knew how to bear yourself through the vicissitudes of life. Bureaucrats were more likely to put self-interest first. It was possible for an aristocrat to fulfil a bureaucratic function, as was the case with Eustathius's patron and paragon, Nicephorus Comnenus.

Eustathius's views about the elite conformed to those that crystallised at the court of Alexius I Comnenus. By the end of Manuel I's reign they had become thoroughly traditional. The ecclesiastical elite to Eustathius's mind should have consisted of the hierarchy of ecclesiastical offices, but this was complicated by the undeniably important role

65 Ibid., 41–5. See Wirth, 'Die Flucht', 82–5; V. Grumel, 'Sur la fuite et le retour de l'archevêque Eustathe de Thessalonique', *REB* 20(1962), 221–4.

66 Alberic de Tre Fontane, *Chronicon*, ed. G.H. Pertz (Monumenta Germaniae historica, SS 23), (Hanover, 1874), p.86. Cf. V. Laurent, 'La succession épiscopale de la métropole de Thessalonique dans la première moitié du XIIIe siècle', *BZ* 56(1963), 288.

67 Kazhdan/Franklin, 135.

68 Ibid., 140–67.

played by monks and monasticism. We have already seen the competition that existed between the monks and the official hierarchy of the church. Eustathius was determined that monasticism should be brought under the authority of the bishops, as was right and proper. Again, Eustathius was only reflecting the official thinking of the Comnenian court towards the end of Manuel I's reign. The events that followed Manuel I's death showed how far from reality Eustathius's official and conventional schema was. Society was not composed of a monolithic citizen body. There were gradations among the citizens, just as there were among the elite. Eustathius tried to meet this by recognising a middle class, which was separate from the elite, but superior to the general run of citizens, the criteria being very largely wealth. Generally, he was left to bewail the breakdown of the ordered society of his youth. Craftsmen were no longer content to work out of professional pride, but thought in terms of profit.[69] He noted how the society of a city now revolved around fixers, to whom everybody entrusted their business.[70] For Eustathius Andronicus I Comnenus's regime represented, at least in retrospect, a perversion of the Byzantine political order, because the emperor had relied upon these fixers, and worse, gang leaders, first to seize power and then to preserve it.[71] He deliberately ignored the clear division that should exist between the elite and the rest of society.

In Constantinople in the closing years of Manuel I's reign people like Eustathius were more or less cocooned against the realities of change. This was not the case once he reached Thessalonica. Eustathius had to confront a rapidly changing society. It revealed the deficiencies of his views on the ordering of society. The relationship of the political and ecclesiastical elites had not appeared in the comfort of Constantinople to raise any awkward questions. The one was concerned with government; the other with moral and spiritual guidance; the one complemented the other. He found in Thessalonica church property at the mercy of imperial tax collectors and of local people. The support that he had expected from the imperial authorities was not forthcoming. Eustathius was appalled by the social divisions, the lack of harmony, and the poverty that existed in Thessalonica. He saw it as part of his responsibility as a pastor to rectify these conditions. Eustathius took his duties as a preacher very seriously. Moral exhortations to the people of Salonica poured from his pulpit. They had to learn to respect and care for each other. In his opinion, the greatest social problem was the neglect of the needs of the poor. This became a major concern. Eustathius sought to channel charity through his administration. It was

69 Eustathius I, 92–3.
70 Ibid., 92.
71 Eustathius II, 42.20–7.

a practical way of making the bishop the focal point of an urban society. It was his duty to guide it according to Christian principles. This would produce a state of social harmony, so lacking at Thessalonica. Care for the poor was to be the catalyst. So much wishful thinking!

It was an ideal that went back to the Fathers of the early church, notably St Basil of Caesarea. It was an ideal that appealed to bishops because it justified their claim to be the leaders of local society. Local society was less enthusiastic. Eustathius brought with him from Constantinople ideas that were designed to ensure that Thessalonica was amenable to control from the centre. He sets these out in a speech entitled 'On the obedience and submission appropriate to a Christian society.'[72] He starts by recasting sacred history as the creation of a hierarchically organised society. This is the work of teachers and prophets inspired by God – the King of Kings, but also the Universal Teacher.[73] He commands submission to magistrates 'who are His icons and images'.[74] Any insult to their authority challenges God. Those societies that respect this divinely instituted order flourish. Those that fail to, fall into anarchy and lose direction and cohesion.[75] It was a view of society designed to bolster established authority. Eustathius found himself under challenge from those who retorted that 'it was neither [morally] good nor socially beneficial that among men there should be the greater and that there should be others reduced to inferiority and subservience'.[76] Eustathius mocked their demands for equality. Would this not mean that a teacher would be subject to his pupils, a master to his slaves, and a husband to his wife?[77] All sense of a proper order would be lost. Eustathius is likely to have exaggerated, if not misrepresented, his opponents' views. He accuses them of equating friendship with equality, of legalising citizens' rights, and of creating a communal regime.[78] This was, in the first instance, a way of underlining their opposition to the hierarchical authority emanating from Constantinople. But it was also a recognition of something more: the control exercised over city life by Eustathius's opponents. They had either acquired or would soon acquire imperial privileges for Thessalonica.[79] Like other Byzantine cities of the time Thessalonica

72 Ibid. I, 13–29.
73 Ibid., 25.75–9.
74 Ibid., 26.53–4.
75 Ibid., 24.63–91, 25.54–74, 27,54–65.
76 Ibid., 28.59–61.
77 Ibid., 28.64–29.16.
78 Ibid., 28.62–3.
79 In 1204 the Latin Emperor Baldwin of Flanders confirmed the privileges of Thessalonica 'in accordance with the usages and customs granted by the Greek emperors' (Geoffroi de Villehardouin, *La conquête de Constantinople*, ed. E. Faral (Paris, 1961), 2 vols, II, 88–9 (ch. 280)).

was in the process of recovering its legal personality and a measure of autonomy.[80] It was a sign of the growing independence of provincial centres in the late twelfth century and pointed to the weakening of the bonds uniting capital and provinces. It produced a sense of alienation from the imperial government at Constantinople.[81] This made the position of bishops more difficult and, at the same time, more vital. They had to try to bridge the gulf between the capital and provinces. Eustathius was too abrasive to have had much success.

Eustathius in the light of his correspondence

Eustathius had a high conceit of himself as the upholder of a Christian order. It was his duty as a teacher to inculcate respect for authority. In public life he does not emerge as a sympathetic character, but the private man was different. His correspondence may provide a corrective to the unfavourable impression left by his other works.

Only a relatively small proportion of this correspondence – perhaps twenty out of some fifty letters – dates from Eustathius's time at Thessalonica.[82] There are two letters to the patriarch over administrative matters.[83] There are two (perhaps three) letters to Euthymios Malakes, metropolitan of Neai Patrai;[84] one to the bishop of Serres.[85] There is one letter to Michael Autoreianos, who was promoted to the office of *chartophylax* of St Sophia. Eustathius complains that when Michael was merely *protonotarios* they were friends, but now that he has been promoted he has expunged Eustathius from his soul.[86] It may just have been a matter of a busy man neglecting former acquaintances or it may have been something more serious that lay behind Michael Autoreianos's coolness towards Eustathius. Whatever, a bishop must always have valued the support of the *chartophylax* of St Sophia. There are four letters to acquaintances and former pupils.[87] There are four letters to imperial officials. There is one to the *mystikos*,

80 Leo VI (886–912) formally abolished the old city councils.

81 Angold, *The Byzantine Aristocracy*, 243–4.

82 Eustathius I, 335ff. The first letter that can be shown to have been written while Eustathius was at Thessalonica is Letter no.29[30] to two of his former pupils. There follow another nineteen letters written by Eustathius. There is a good chance that the bulk of these were also written from Thessalonica. Eustathius's letters which have been preserved are just a fragment of his correspondence. For example, the letters that we know he wrote from Thessalonica to Michael Choniates, archbishop of Athens, are not included (Michael Choniates, II, no.6, 8–10). One can only assume, but without much confidence, that the sample that has survived is representative of his contacts during the time he was at Thessalonica.

83 Eustathius I, nos.32 [33], 33[34].

84 Ibid., nos.44–6 [45–7].

85 Ibid., no.38[39].

86 Ibid., no.30[31].

87 Ibid., nos.29[30], 35[36], 39–40 [40–1], 43[44].

a member of the emperor's inner circle of advisers and agents, asking him to intervene on behalf of one of his household (*kellion*) who was the victim of injustice.[88]

There is another to Michael Hagiotheodorites, the logothete of the drome, who was one of Manuel's most trusted ministers and incidentally the putative father-in-law of Eustathius's former patron Nicephorus Comnenus. This contains a reference to the recent death of the logothete's brother, Nicholas, who was archbishop of Athens. Eustathius had made a speech over his byre just outside the walls of Thessalonica as his remains were being conveyed to the capital.[89] The purpose of the letter was only partly to offer the logothete of the drome consolations on the death of his brother the archbishop. It was also to persuade him to use his considerable influence with the emperor to get a favourable response to the petition that Eustathius was forwarding along with the letter of consolation.[90] He hoped that the emperor might visit him.[91] This was never to be, but in his various confrontations with the people of Thessalonica he made great play with the support and approval that he had from different emperors.

Eustathius emerges from his correspondence little changed. He never forgot that he was a member of the Constantinopolitan elite. His letters show that he was at ease in their company. Like other bishops, he tried to use his connections in high places to the advantage both of himself and of his church. It is likely that he had more influence both at the imperial court and in patriarchal circles at the beginning of his time as metropolitan. The intervention on his behalf by the Grand Heteriarch John Doukas seems adequate proof of this. But the confused events in the capital following the death of Manuel I Comnenus must have made it difficult for Eustathius to maintain the right sort of contacts and he may well not only have been isolated in Thessalonica but also from the political life of the capital. There may have been a measure of rehabilitation towards the end of his life. His enforced absence from Thessalonica may have been to his advantage. Over the question of whether the *protekdikos* ranked among the major or the minor officers of the patriarchal administration the Patriarch George

88 Ibid., no.37[38].

89 Kazhdan/Franklin, 129–30, argue that because Eustathius refers to Nicholas as his *despotes* and not as his colleague, it must mean that Eustathius was not yet appointed metropolitan of Thessalonica. It may be that he had been so recently appointed that out of respect he did not refer to the deceased as a colleague. But he calls Euthymios Malakes, who was appointed to his see before Eustathius was appointed to his, *despotes*. What makes it certain that Eustathius was already metropolitan of Thessalonica when he wrote to the dead man's brother was that he refers to himself as our ταπεινότης.

90 Eustathius I, no.36[37].

91 Ibid., no.34[35].

Xiphilinos (1191–8) followed Eustathius's opinion: namely that this office should be numbered among the major offices of the patriarchal church. The opponents of this view were led by Theodore Balsamon, the titular patriarch of Antioch.[92] This suggests that Eustathius's opinions still counted for something in the patriarchal synod. It is not impossible that he was in Constantinople when the matter was debated.

The prestige which he enjoyed among his fellow bishops and the affection in which they held him are revealed by the monodies that his death in 1195/6[93] inspired from Michael Choniates, archbishop of Athens,[94] and from Euthymios Malakes, metropolitan of Neai Patrai.[95] Michael Choniates had been one of his pupils, while Malakes had been a contemporary in their student days. Choniates's celebration of Eustathius is rather conventional. It was his abilities as a teacher and as an orator that stood out. Choniates claimed that almost all the bishoprics within the Byzantine Empire were now filled with his pupils: a pardonable exaggeration, no doubt.[96] Very little is said about his achievements as metropolitan of Thessalonica. His bearing during the siege of Thessalonica in 1185 comes in for praise,[97] as does his willingness to stand up against the tax-collector and the local bosses.[98] Michael Choniates delivered his monody at Athens. Euthymios Malakes, on the other hand, delivered his over Eustathius's grave only a few days after his death. Perhaps this helps to account for its greater immediacy and conviction. It was a defence of Eustathius against his detractors. He might have been small and unimpressive, but this was deceptive. Though he never bothered with an armed escort nor surrounded himself with flatterers and hangers-on, he was always proceeded by an aura. He might have been rather sarcastic, but this was part of the art of government. He never had recourse to the rod; his gaze and his turn of phrase were quite enough. Malakes indignantly rebutted the charges repeatedly made against the dead man that he loved wealth and piled up money.[99] His defence comes in the shape of a series of rhetorical questions. These boil down to the assertion that, at the very least, he never did anything illegal! The hidden impression of Eustathius's own works seems to find confirmation. He was a harsh

92 Chomatianos, 654.

93 On the date of his death, see Michael Choniates II, 503; Kazhdan/Franklin, 137; P. Wirth, 'Ein neuer *Terminus ante quem non* fur das Ableben des Erzbischofs Eustathios von Thessalonike', *BZ* 54(1961), 86–7; Laurent, 'La succession épiscopale', 286 and n. 9.

94 Michael Choniates I, 283–306.

95 Migne, *PG*, 136. 756–64.

96 Michael Choniates I, 300.1–3.

97 Ibid., 286.3–10.

98 Ibid., 295–6.

99 Migne, *PG*, 136, 756–64.

old man who knew the value of money. He was very different from the beloved teacher remembered by so many from Constantinople. To his fellow bishops he still seemed a model, because he had remained true to an ideal.

Eustathius was by no means an ineffectual bishop, but his obstinacy earned him the dislike of the majority of his flock. But to his fellow bishops he was a shining light who remained true to the episcopal ideal. After his death his reputation for sanctity grew. It was an acknowledgement of his moral qualities, however prickly they made him. Though never officially recognised as a saint, he was revered as such locally. The drops of moisture that accumulated on his tombstone were appreciated for their healing properties.

Eustathius's qualities become all the clearer after his death. Alexius III Angelus appointed his chief minister Constantine Mesopotamites to succeed to the throne of Thessalonica. It was a scandal. The emperor had already forced the patriarch George Xiphilinos to promote him to the rank of deacon and make him head of the deacons of St Sophia, so that he could control the patriarchal administration. Quite uncanonically, Mesopotamites was to hold both clerical and secular office. He was then promoted to Thessalonica. For a short time Mesopotamites combined the roles of chief minister and metropolitan bishop of Thessalonica. Leaving his brothers behind in Constantinople as his eyes and ears, Mesopotamites made a flying visit to Thessalonica. He hurried back to Constantinople, but his brief absence allowed his enemies at Constantinople to combine against him. Alexius III Angelus disowned him. Synod met to dismiss him from the throne of Thessalonica early in 1198. A new bishop was appointed. He was John Chrysanthos, who was another product of the patriarchal administration. He held the post of *kanistrios*. His reign was short. Mesopotamites was soon reinstated, only to be driven from his see in 1204 by the Latins. He fell into the hands of pirates. Finally, he reached the safety of Nicaea. At least, he had been spared the vengeance meted out to the inhabitants of Thessalonica by their Latin ruler, Boniface of Montferrat. This occurred in the spring of 1205 in the aftermath of the defeat at Adrianople of the Latin Emperor Baldwin of Flanders by the Bulgarians. Boniface imposed punitive fines on some of the citizens and drove them from the city; others he executed. He also hanged some of the common people and members of the clergy. In the light of so melancholy a history it is easy to see why Eustathius was remembered as a saint.[100]

[100] Nicetas Choniates, 489–93, 620.52–66; Laurent, 'La succession épiscopale'.

9

MICHAEL CHONIATES

MICHAEL Choniates was a pupil of Eustathius and, as we have seen, held him in the highest regard. His career was rather different from that of his master. For one thing he held no teaching position in Constantinople. He began his career as secretary to the Patriarch Michael Ankhialos' (1170–8). He was then singled out in 1182, still only in his early forties, by the Patriarch Theodosius Boradiotes (1179–83) for promotion to the important see of Athens. There seems not to have been that struggle for preferment which faced Eustathius at the start of his career. The origins of Michael Choniates and of his younger brother, the historian Nicetas, are nonetheless obscure. As their surname betrays they came from Chonai, a town of western Asia Minor close to the Turkish frontier. They had the backing of the saintly metropolitan of Chonai, also called Nicetas, whose reputation counted for something at the imperial court.[1] Their family may have been important locally, but nothing more. It is therefore likely that the brothers owed their success in the first instance to their undoubted ability rather than to family background. But ability could still bring wealth and social prestige. In Michael's case the best evidence is provided by the impressive library that he brought with him from Constantinople to Athens. His brother Nicetas had more tangible signs of wealth in the property he accumulated at Constantinople. He carved out for himself a career in the imperial administration, which was more lucrative than one in the church. When he married, he married into the Belissariotes family, which was prominent in the imperial administration under the house of Angelus. Michael Choniates benefited from the contacts built up by his brother. There were also other brothers and sisters, though it is not known what marriages they made.

Though of provincial origin the Choniates brothers fitted in to the administrative elite that ran both the church and the imperial administrative machine at Constantinople. They built up a range of professional

[1] Nicetas Choniates, 219–20; Michael Choniates I, 46.17–23, 61.3.

contacts which were still further strengthened by family ties.[2] As a member of this elite Michael Choniates subscribed to a clear set of principles, which its representatives espoused, partly in all sincerity and partly to justify the power they wielded. The basic tenet was traditional: they were the upholders of a just society where the powerful looked after the poor. In addition, it was peculiarly part of a bishop's pastoral duties to see that this ideal was put into practice. Michael Choniates's social ideas were little different from those expounded by Eustathius.

Whereas Eustathius managed to alienate important sections of his flock in his effort to implement his ideals, his pupil Michael Choniates appears to have had greater success both in remaining true to his ideals and in winning the support of local society. This impression is scarcely vitiated by the fact that Choniates's correspondence has survived in a far fuller form than has that of Eustathius. For Eustathius we are largely dependent on works of a high rhetorical content. This is also true, by and large, of Choniates. But rhetoric was supposed to serve practical ends. Both Eustathius and Michael Choniates used their rhetorical skills to cultivate contacts in Constantinople with a view to strengthening their position locally. But Choniates does not seem to have relied as exclusively upon support from Constantinople as Eustathius did, nor do his sermons have that hectoring, hurt quality, which characterises Eustathius's sermons to the people of Thessalonica. Like Eustathius, Choniates was an outsider, but this was true of most of the appointees to the major churches of the Empire under the Comneni whom we know about. This was a handicap, which Eustathius, like many another prelate, never quite overcame.

Michael Choniates and his clergy

By contrast, Michael Choniates succeeded without much apparent difficulty. At the beginning of his episcopate he came into conflict with an important member of his administration. A bishop was always liable to be at loggerheads with the officers of his church. This was a real danger at Athens, where the custom prevailed that sons should follow fathers into the cathedral clergy, even if they did not proceed to holy orders. A bishop newly arrived from Constantinople was bound to be the object of suspicion, a potential threat to old privileges. So it proved with Michael Choniates. He was faced with a demand from the *sakellarios* of the church of Athens that he should be promoted to the office of *skeuophylax*. Michael Choniates refused to countenance

[2] Kazhdan & Franklin, *Studies*, 256–7.

this. The *sakellarios* took this as a slight to his person and an affront to his old age. His career in the church of Athens went back more than thirty years. He, not the new archbishop, knew the customs of the church. Michael Choniates dealt with him very firmly. What right had he to question the decision of his bishop? Choniates then carefully underlined the *sakellarios*'s lack of a proper education. More gently he alluded to the latter's blindness, which was an absolute disqualification for the office of *skeuophylax*. He had already taken on the responsibilities of the office and church plate was beginning to go missing. The man threatened to take his case against Michael Choniates to the patriarchal synod. Choniates pointed out that he would find no support in canon law nor in the practice of the Great Church, where promotions were made on merit. He closed with a quote from the canons of the Apostles to the effect that the deaf and the blind should not become bishops, not because they were in some way polluted, but because their disability might jeopardise the material interests of the church. 'Such considerations deterred us from promoting you to the office of *skeuophylax*, lest the sacred vessels were left unguarded and easy prey for sacrilegious rogues.'[3]

No more was heard of the *sakellarios*. There are no signs that Michael Choniates ever again had any trouble from his clergy. It was an incident that allowed him to assert himself over his cathedral clergy. He was able to stress his superior qualities, which stemmed from his Constantinopolitan education and his distinguished service in the patriarchal administration. The close contacts that he continued to maintain with the patriarch and his administration were carefully underlined.

Michael Choniates had his personal staff on whom he could rely. The most important member was his secretary. First to hold this position was Nicholas Antiocheites.[4] He may have been from a local family. At least, Michael Choniates was in correspondence with an abbot called Esaias Antiocheites. The detail that he was sending the abbot soap and olive oil on a Monemvasiot boat suggests that his monastery was not too far from Athens.[5] Choniates's next secretary was called Thomas. His surname is not given, but his relatively high social standing can be deduced from the courtesy title of *kyr* accorded to him. Michael Choniates also recruited into his entourage various of his nephews who had followed him to Athens. They do not seem to have had regular positions in the church of Athens, but they played an important role in its affairs. Choniates's nepotism even extended to a nephew of the

3 Michael Choniates II, 30–4.
4 Ibid., 36.29.
5 Ibid., 136–7.

Belissariotes brothers who were relatives by marriage. The young man had previously served in the imperial palace. Accompanying Choniates to Athens was presumably expected to widen his experience. As it happened, he was to die shortly after arriving in Athens.[6] In his memory his uncles granted the Athenian monastery of the Holy Confessors – where he was presumably buried – immunity from taxation.[7] It would seem that, like Eustathius and others, Choniates brought an entourage with him. It was a natural thing to do. In this instance, there is nothing to suggest that it was a cause of local resentment. In one respect, Choniates was fortunate. He had contacts with many of the leading families of the Greek cities, who in their turn were well represented in the imperial government and patriarchal administration. His nephews are likely to have married into such families, though this can only be positively shown in a single case.[8]

Choniates built on these contacts by taking charge of the education of boys from local families. They look as though they provided him with a source from which to recruit clergy and ultimately the officers of his church. Again, one has only a single example to go by. This was George Bardanes, the son of one of Choniates's suffragans, the bishop of Karystos. He was educated by Choniates and then entered the church of Athens, where he was first *hypomnematographos* and then *chartophylax*.[9]

Unlike Eustathius who was on the worst possible terms with the monasteries of his diocese, Michael Choniates took time and care to cultivate the abbots of the monasteries of his see as the best way of preserving his episcopal rights over these monasteries. He has left a monody for the archimandrite of the monasteries of Athens. Its theme was the cooperation and harmony that existed between the archbishop and the archimandrite.[10] To judge by his correspondence Choniates was on good terms with the abbots of most of the monasteries of his diocese. In a sense, Michael Choniates was operating from a position of strength because he not only inherited a church that was relatively prosperous, but he was also able to build on the work of his immediate predecessors as archbishop. He boasts in a poem he wrote in gratitude to the Mother of God, the patron of his church, that he extended the estates and wealth of his church. But that was not all: he had increased the clergy under him; he had renovated his cathedral church and restored other churches, and he had reduced the amount

[6] Ibid. I, 199–200.
[7] Ibid. II, 89.14–20.
[8] Ibid. II, 320–3.
[9] G. Stadtmüller, *Michael Choniates, Metropolit von Athen* (Orientalia christiana analecta 208) (Rome, 1934), 199.
[10] Michael Choniates I, 262–70.

of taxation to be paid for them.[11] There was a strong practical streak to Michael Choniates, which is revealed by his request at the beginning of his episcopate that the Patriarch Theodosius send him a handbook of husbandry.

A successful bishop was one who knew how to manage the estates of his church efficiently.[12] Eustathius was also interested in the agricultural potential of the estates of his church. He claimed that on one field he had achieved a yield of nearly twenty to one, which is unbelievably high,[13] but it is unlikely that the church of Thessalonica would have been as dominant an economic force in the life of that city as the church of Athens was in its. The list of the properties and monasteries of the church of Athens drawn up for Innocent III in 1209 provides an approximate idea of the wealth of the church under Michael Choniates and very impressive it is. It had estates (*casalia*) in twenty-five villages around Athens and another block of land around Karystos in southern Euboea. It had mills, gardens, irrigation rights, baths, as well as market rights at Athens and Euripos. There were twenty-one monasteries under the control of the church. The list itemises 200 priests along with 400 *paroikoi* at Athens, another 100 at Thebes, and yet another 100 at Euripos.[14]

A successful metropolitan had also to impose his authority over his suffragans. The main challenge came over the see of Euripos. It started with a series of charges being laid against the bishop of Euripos by Euthymios Malakes, metropolitan of Neai Patrai. This was a serious matter for Michael Choniates, given that Malakes had been a metropolitan since the mid-1160s and was one of the most powerful figures of the patriarchal synod. As a metropolitan see Neai Patrai ranked relatively low with almost no suffragan bishops, but this allowed Malakes the opportunity to concentrate on political activities in Constantinople. He was a dangerous man to cross. He came from a powerful Theban family and his sister had married Demetrius Tornikes, who was logothete of the drome at the time and had special responsibility for Athens.[15] Malakes wrote to Michael Choniates charging that the bishop of Euripos had put churches under interdict and had oppressed his clergy. On one occasion the bishop had some of them paraded around the *agora* as impious miscreants. Still more deplorable was the way the bishop set about mobilising the people,

[11] A. Papadopoulos-Kerameus, ''Αθηναικ'α 'εκ τοῦ ιβ' και ιγ' αἰῶνος', *ΑΡΜΟΝΙΑ*, 3(1902), 284–5.

[12] Michael Choniates II, 34–5.

[13] Kazhdan/Franklin, 162–4.

[14] Migne, *PL*, 116. 1560–1.

[15] On Euthymios Malakes, see Stadtmuller, *Michael Choniates*, 306–12; J. Darrouzès, 'Notes sur Euthyme Tornikès, Euthyme Malakès, et Georges Tornikès', *REB* 23(1965), 148–67, at 155–63.

who went around shouting slogans in his support. Malakes warned Choniates that the bishop intended to come with his supporters to Athens on the occasion of the feast of the Koimesis. He feared that their well-rehearsed heckling would persuade Choniates to absolve him from the condemnation he so justly deserved.[16]

As it turned out, Michael Choniates did not hear the case in Athens, but instead went himself to Euripos because the abbots of the monasteries of Euripos had pleaded old age and infirmity as an excuse for not making the journey to Athens and their testimony was vital. The bishop of Euripos wanted Choniates to effect a reconciliation between himself and Malakes, but there were concessions that he was not prepared to make. He refused to abandon the episcopal right of *anaphora* or commemoration by the monasteries of his diocese, which was at least a token of his authority over them. He was also unwilling to keep company with Malakes when he visited Euripos, for fear that the metropolitan would not allow him to remain in his episcopal residence.[17]

The quarrel between Malakes and the bishop of Euripos begins to become clearer. Malakes had obtained control of a monastery or conceivably monasteries at Euripos – he almost certainly had family property there – and acted as though they came under his jurisdiction and claimed *anaphora* over them. When he visited Euripos, presumably to take ship for Constantinople, he behaved as though the bishop was his suffragan and insisted that he give up the episcopal residence to him. It was a delicate matter because Michael Choniates did not wish to offend Malakes needlessly. He had, however, to support his suffragan against the intrusions of another metropolitan, which were also an infringement of his own metropolitan rights. He tried to do this by means of reconciliation, which called forth an indignant letter from Malakes, who refused to be reconciled.[18] He again bitterly criticised the bishop's use of popular assemblies and the activities of his supporters who interfered with proceedings in the law courts with shouts of 'Holy is our bishop, exceedingly holy!'

Michael Choniates noted the role of popular assemblies in the life of Euripos. He chided them for their unruliness[19] and lectured them on the need for social harmony. It was couched in thoroughly traditional terms. The powerful were not to oppress the poor, while the poor were to respect their betters. Exactly what bearing this had on the quarrel between the bishop of Euripos and Malakes is not made clear. It is impossible to know exactly the nature of the support that the bishop

[16] *Noctes* 7.94–8 = K.G. Mpones, *ΕΥΘΥΜΙΟΥ ΤΟΥ ΜΑΛΑΚΗ ΤΑ ΣΩΖΟΜΕΝΑ* (Athens, 1937), 2 vols., I, 34.72–5.
[17] Michael Choniates II, 26–30.
[18] *Noctes*, 9.98–102 = Mpones, *ΕΥΘΥΜΙΟΥ*, I, 38–43.
[19] Michael Choniates I, 183.10–20.

could call upon. Malakes refers to the bishop's most ardent supporters as *paideutai* who surrounded the bishop and generally terrorised his opponents. The classical meaning of tutor or teacher cannot apply. It is more likely to refer to the young men who were attached to the bishop's household in one way or another. But that is a long way from claiming that there were marked social divisions at Euripos between the powerful and the poor which would explain the clashes there were in the assemblies that were called and still further from claiming that the bishop of Euripos was exploiting these divisions in his quarrel with Malakes. That said, the bishop was capable of mobilising elements of the lay population of Euripos; there were popular assemblies that broke up in disorder; and Michael Choniates related this state of affairs to the division of society into the powerful and the poor. There is a further complicating factor. The episode can be dated to the very end of Andronicus I Comnenus's reign.[20] Malakes later insisted that the bishop of Euripos had been prompted by the 'terrible and most oppressive tyrant',[21] by whom he could only have meant Andronicus. His relations with Andronicus had not been good. The emperor had once threatened to throw him into the river Rhyndakos.[22]

The Euripos incident provided Michael Choniates with problems of some complexity. He dealt with them, as far as it is possible to tell, effectively. He protected the rights of a suffragan against a neighbouring metropolitan without allowing a host of other factors, social and political, to cloud his judgement. Nor did his action lead to a permanent breach with Malakes. At least, on a later occasion Michael Choniates took advantage of Malakes's nigh permanent presence at Constantinople to seek his help over two matters. The first concerned a monastery that came under the church of Athens. The abbot had been driven out by the lay patron, who was administering the monastery himself. Choniates asked Malakes to intervene with the powers at Constantinople to have the old abbot reinstated. Choniates also drew to Malakes's attention an affair in the suffragan see of Diauleia: a monk had been able to use his influence with the emperor to get a canonical appointment to the abbacy of his monastery overturned in his favour.[23]

Spokesman for Athens

Even for quite minor matters it helped greatly to be able to put your case in Constantinople, but Choniates's responsibilities went further than routine diocesan affairs. He was the spokesman for Athens. He made

20 Grumel, 1164.
21 Mponis, *ΕΥΘΥΜΙΟΥ*, I, no.9, 101.9–10.
22 Nicetas Choniates, 331.1–11.
23 Michael Choniates II, 119–20.

speeches of welcome to the imperial governors of the theme of Hellas when they entered Athens. The intention was to make them as well disposed to the city and its church as he could. These speeches were formalities that would impress shrewd and often rapacious governors only because their elegance bespoke a metropolitan education and contacts in high places. In one way, Michael Choniates was lucky to become archbishop of Athens when he did, for it coincided with Andronicus Comnenus's effort to improve provincial administration and to make the collection of taxes less arbitrary and oppressive. Michael tried to capitalise on this by emphasising the miserable conditions existing in Attica. It was already beginning to suffer at the hands of pirates. Aigina which belonged to the church of Athens was becoming – with the cooperation of the local inhabitants – a pirate's lair. This took its toll on what had been a prosperous city. In 1202 the Grand Duke Michael Stryphnos told the archbishop about his first visit to Athens. Then it resembled the Queen of cities, 'and just as the latter reaped all sorts of benefits through cargo ships, so Athens through seaborne trade flourished and was populous'.[24] Its prosperity depended on the sea, whence its vulnerability to pirates.

In the face of growing difficulties Choniates used all his influence at Constantinople on behalf of Athens. He knew that by themselves chrysobulls and tax exemptions meant relatively little. They had to be respected by the agents of the imperial administration. He found that the tax exemption granted to the district of Attica had been applied by the governor only to the advantage of the powerful. He intervened with friends and contacts at Constantinople to ensure that it covered the whole population. Admittedly, we do not know the outcome of his frequent démarches among the bureaucrats and ministers of Constantinople; only that he did the right things, such as having Athens placed under the special care of the logothete of the drome, now Constantine Tornikes, one of the most powerful figures at the imperial court. When this did not produce the expected benefits, we find Choniates writing to Theodore Kastamonites, the emperor's uncle, complaining about the arrangement and requesting his protection.[25]

It is more than likely that Michael Choniates painted a deliberately sombre picture of conditions around Athens in the hope of persuading the imperial administration to take the necessary action. In 1198 he drafted a petition (*hypomnestikon*) for the citizens of Athens to present to the Emperor Alexius III Angelus. It consists by and large of protests against the oppressive character of provincial administration. The people of Athens had had to pay ship-money (*ploimoi*) to three

[24] Ibid., 99.5–7.
[25] Ibid., 69–72.

different authorities; the cost of entertaining the imperial governor and his staff was exorbitant; and this, despite their possession of a chrysobull that barred his entry into the city. They also asked to be excused further fiscal surveys because these were just an excuse for officials to line their pockets. Much more interesting was their criticism of the *mystikos*, whom they refer to as their *dephendarios* or advocate. He had retained moneys collected by the imperial governor which it was his duty to remit to the city of Athens. The duties of the *mystikos* are set out in some detail in a decree of 1192 issued by Isaac II Angelus.[26] Specifically, the *mystikos* had a responsibility to repay sums of money illegally exacted from episcopal estates out of the revenues of a particular theme. In the case of Athens his jurisdiction was extended to include the whole city. It would appear that a privileged status formerly accorded only to the bishop and his church was now enjoyed by the whole city. A plausible explanation is that the city had come to form part of an archiepiscopal immunity. The petition was not exclusively directed against the abuses of the imperial administration. It closes with criticism of the way the *kastrenoi* were acquiring villages and peasant holdings. The *kastrenoi* were the local ascendancy, so called because they occupied the *kastron* or Acropolis of Athens. Their activities threatened the system of *droungoi* – originally military, but now fiscal units – on which the well-being of the area depended. Michael Choniates hardly had to spell out the implications: if matters went much further, it would be impossible for the imperial administration to collect any taxes.[27]

This petition was ostensibly from the city of Athens, but it was the work of the archbishop and it reflected his ideas. He did all he could to ensure that it had a favourable reception at the imperial court. He lobbied his influential contacts in Constantinople. He put the whole matter of the presentation of the petition in the hands of his trusted secretary Thomas, who was a person of some standing. It was a reflection of the preeminence that Michael Choniates now enjoyed within the city of Athens, even to the extent of being able to challenge the local landowning ascendancy.

Whether the petition accomplished anything is hard to say because the situation around Athens was deteriorating rapidly. The chief culprit was Leo Sgouros, a local dynast who had inherited control over the town of Nauplion in the Argolid from his father. In 1202 he seized control of Argos and then laid siege to the Acrocorinth where the

[26] Darrouzès, 'Un décret d'Isaac II Angelos', at 150–2. Cf. P. Magdalino, 'The not-so-secret functions of the *Mystikos*', *REB* 42(1984), 229–40 (= Magdalino, *Tradition and Transformation*, no.XI).

[27] Michael Choniates I, 307–11.

metropolitan of Corinth held out against him. The church seems to have been his main opponent. Leo Sgouros had a decidedly anti-clerical streak . He had the metropolitan bishop of Argos and Nauplion imprisoned,[28] while the metropolitan bishop of Corinth was seized, blinded, and hurled to his death from the cliffs of Nauplion.[29] But when Sgouros advanced on Athens, Michael Choniates organised a successful defence of the Acropolis. Sgouros burnt the lower town and advanced northwards, leaving Choniates still in control of Athens. The conflict between Sgouros and Michael Choniates reveals the opposing forces struggling for control of the Byzantine provinces. The church hierarchy became the defenders of traditional order against local bosses or dynasts, as they were termed.[30] The latter's power depended on the support of the local landowning ascendancy, such as the *kastrenoi* of Athens.

We have already seen Michael Choniates taking up a hostile position where these were concerned, because of the inroads they were making on peasant properties. His efforts were hampered by the lack of support that he got from Constantinople. His bitter denunciation of the authorities at Constantinople for their indifference to conditions in the provinces is a reflection of this. A man such as Sgouros could count on influential voices at court. Michael Choniates complained to the logothete of the drome Constantine Tornikes that Sgouros had the support of the emperor's relatives by marriage.[31] By the eve of the fall of Constantinople in 1204 to the fourth crusade conditions in the Byzantine Empire were confusing. Members of the imperial family were ready to support a rebel against the upholders of established authority. But these were increasingly the bishops and metropolitans, which meant that the nature of established authority in the provinces was changing. It lay at the heart of the difficulties that Eustathius experienced at Thessalonica. In contrast, not just to Eustathius, but also to virtually all other twelfth-century prelates about whom we have adequate information, Michael Choniates was able to assert his ascendancy over his city. Personal qualities were important. He was astute; he built up the wealth of his church and the numbers of his clergy. Whether it was his doing or not, the city of Athens appears to have been annexed to the church for administrative purposes. Michael Choniates was able to act as spokesman for the city, but his authority almost certainly went far wider than this.

28 Ibid. II, 122.22–3:
29 Ibid., 170.21–4; Nicetas Choniates, 638.
30 See Angold, *The Byzantine Aristocracy*, 236–53.
31 Michael Choniates II, 125.3–4.

In exile

How much wider became apparent after Constantinople had fallen to the Latins. He was the man to whom all looked. He made his way to Thessalonica where he debated with a representative of the Latin church, Cardinal Benedict of Sta Susanna. He returned to Greece and stayed at Euripos, before seeking refuge on the island of Keos, which was close enough to Attica for him to supervise the affairs of his diocese. He was urged to depart for Nicaea – the main centre of resistance to the Latin conquest – where the new patriarch Michael Autoreianos was one of his oldest and dearest friends, but he preferred to stay on at Keos, ministering to the needs of his flock.[32] He was able to maintain the fabric of the orthodox church in his diocese, despite the presence of a Latin archbishop in Athens itself. Cases involving the lay patronage of monasteries, clerical offices and incomes were brought before him at Keos.[33] He ordained new priests.[34] He found that the effort involved in administering his see from his place of exile very taxing.[35] He entrusted more and more of the burdens of office to his nephews Michael and Nicetas and to his secretary George Bardanes, whom he promoted to the rank of *chartophylax*.[36] Supplies were a problem. For a time he was able to have produce from the estates of the church of Athens near Karystos forwarded to him at Keos.[37] But increasingly he had to depend upon gifts of food made mostly by abbots of the monasteries around Athens.[38]

As in other cases, where the orthodox church came under Latin rule, monasteries acted as focal points of ecclesiastical organisation. Around Athens most of the monasteries remained in orthodox hands, even if there were those, such as Daphni, that passed to the Latins. Michael Choniates assigned a monastery to George Bardanes and another to his servant, a monk called Peter, in order to provide them with food and lodging.[39] He also wrote to the abbot of the monastery of Hosios Meletios requesting that he take in the *protekdikos* of the church of Athens, who had suffered at the hands of the Latins.[40]

Michael Choniates's letters to the abbots of Hosios Meletios and the Holy Confessors leave the impression that under Latin rule Greek monasteries were having a hard time. The monastery of the Holy

32 Ibid., 149–55.
33 Ibid., 240.
34 Ibid., 237–8, 254.
35 Ibid., 240.
36 Ibid., 237–40, 267–71, 314–17.
37 Ibid., 209–20, 242–4.
38 Ibid., 247–8, 257, 312.
39 Ibid., 311–12.
40 Ibid., 313–14.

Confessors suffered the attentions of pirates. Encouraged by local people they seized the monastery and the abbot was forced to flee, but thanks to divine intervention he had been able to return almost immediately.[41] The abbot of Hosios Meletios contemplated abandoning his monastery out of penury. Michael Choniates urged him to stay on, citing the way he himself had endured twelve years of hardship.[42] Some monasteries were abandoned. The most worrying example was that of St George in the Kerameikos. Michael Choniates tried to compensate for its loss by refounding a dependency it had on the island of Makri.[43] It was not necessarily because of the direct action of the Latins that orthodox monasteries went into decline. The abbot of St George in the Kerameikos was well respected by the Latins.[44] It was more that local people took advantage of the disarray of the orthodox church to seize monastic property.

Most instructive is a letter written by Michael Choniates to the abbot of the monastery of Kaisariani. Here it was the abbot himself who was the culprit. He had appropriated other monasteries. He had failed to honour his agreements with other abbots. Despite all Choniates's protests he remained contumacious. This incident reflected the demoralisation and dislocation that followed in the wake of the Latin conquest.[45] But it was more than this. The Latin occupation and the exile of the archbishop allowed local people to recover or simply usurp monastic and church property. There was always a strongly proprietorial attitude to the church on the part of local society, including abbots and clergy. Episcopal efforts to check such tendencies were a source of friction between a bishop and the local community. We have seen how Michael Choniates tried to circumvent this by cultivating the friendship of the abbots under him, but there must still have been resentments, which came to the surface after 1204. It was apparently believed by many Greeks as well as Latins that Choniates was living very comfortably in exile on the proceeds of a vast treasure that he was supposed to have accumulated before the Latin conquest. Michael Choniates was at pains to scotch this rumour. He painted an amusing picture of living conditions on Keos. The sole amenity was a smoky and draughty bathhouse.[46]

The only treasure that interested Michael Choniates was his beloved library. To judge by his letters his overriding concern in exile was to

[41] Ibid., 254–6.
[42] Ibid., 319–20.
[43] Ibid., 160–2, 237–40.
[44] Ibid., 237–40.
[45] Ibid., 311–12.
[46] Ibid., 235–6.

recover as many of his manuscripts as he could,[47] but he displayed a set of priorities that became a bishop. In order to recover a copy of Euclid and another of Theophylact of Ohrid's commentaries on the Epistles of St Paul – both useful for teaching – he was willing to sacrifice a manuscript of Thucydides, more precious to a bibliomane but not so necessary for a teacher.[48] He recovered the Euclid soon enough,[49] but it was some time before he learnt that his copy of Theophylact's commentaries was in the hands of the bishop of Euripos and he asked that it should be returned.[50] He also recovered a copy of Homer, but some of the folios were missing and he hoped that George Bardanes would be able to find them for him.[51]

He also showed a particular interest in the works of Galen.[52] While in exile he was in correspondence on medical matters with two Athenian doctors.[53] In the twelfth century Athens was well-known for its medical doctors. Michael Choniates's interest in medical matters was not just a matter of hypochondria – a Byzantine addiction – but stemmed from a desire to keep alive different branches of Byzantine learning. Even before 1204 he had considered that the Latins posed a cultural threat.[54] He continued to take an active interest in education during his exile on the island of Keos. He encouraged the abbot of the monastery of the Holy Confessors to send his nephew to Keos, where he would have the company of other pupils. His tutor would be George Bardanes considered by Choniates to be the best teacher in Greece.[55] He thought this a much better arrangement than allowing the abbot to educate his nephew himself. He chided the abbot for the unmethodical way in which he saw to the education of the monks in his charge.[56] Education was one way in which Michael Choniates could keep the torch of orthodoxy alight in the Greek lands.

He did his best to sustain the morale of the orthodox communities in Latin-occupied Greece. He kept in touch with various landowners from notable local families, such as the Makrembolites,[57] the Kalokairos,[58] and the Doxopatres.[59] Inevitably, he maintained contact with as many

47 N.G. Wilson, *Scholars of Byzantium* (London, 1983), 204–6.

48 Michael Choniates II, 241–2.

49 Ibid., 242–4.

50 Ibid., 295–6.

51 Ibid., 220.

52 Ibid., 201–3, 234–7.

53 Ibid., 147–8 (Nicholas Kalodoukes), 201–3 (George Kallistos), 263–7 (Nicholas Kalodoukes).

54 See Wilson, *Scholars of Byzantium*, 204–6

55 Michael Choniates II, 256–7.

56 Ibid., 261–3.

57 Ibid., 249–50 (Demetrius Makrembolites), 292–4 (Demetrius Makrembolites), 301–2 (Demetrius Makrembolites).

58 Ibid., 275 (John Kalokairos).

59 Ibid., 232 .

of the orthodox prelates as he could. The metropolitan of Thebes found refuge on the neighbouring island of Andros,[60] but his closest ties were with Euboea, where Theodore, bishop of Euripos, had done a deal with the Latins and had been allowed to stay in office. He was the only orthodox bishop in this part of Greece who had managed to accomplish this. It was done with the approval of Michael Choniates, who understood the advantages of the arrangement.[61] Many exiles made their home there. The most important group for Michael Choniates centred on Euthymius Tornikes, the son of Demetrius Tornikes, a logothete of the drome. The family, it will be remembered, came originally from Thebes. Euthymius had followed a career in the patriarchal church, where he was a deacon. At some point after the fall of Constantinople he returned to Greece together with two companions, who had also served in the patriarchal church, Manuel Beriboes and Nicholas Pistophilos, who had been a *didaskalos*. Both came from local families.

A surprisingly large proportion of Michael Choniates's correspondence from exile was with this group at Euripos. They had received invitations to go to Nicaea, but preferred not to leave Greece.[62] Michael Choniates initially encouraged them to go to the safety of Asia Minor, where they could worship in freedom, but he saluted their steadfastness in staying on and expressed his gratitude. He supported them in their refusal to abandon their fellow orthodox. It was part of his effort to hold together the orthodox in Latin-occupied Greece, but this became harder and harder to do. The leading archon of Euripos abandoned his estates on Euboea because of Latin harassment and went to Nicaea. Michael Choniates provided him with letters of recommendation to the Nicaean Emperor Theodore I Lascaris, to the Patriarch Michael Autoreianos, and to the metropolitan of Crete, who now held the see of Smyrna.[63]

He sent his beloved George Bardanes to act for him at meetings that were being held at Constantinople in 1214 between representatives of the two churches over the union of churches.[64] Bardanes did not return directly to Greece, but went on to Nicaea where Michael Choniates hoped selflessly that his protégé might find preferment with the Patriarch Manuel I.[65] For whatever reason Bardanes had no luck and returned to Greece. Another sign of the times was that Michael Choniates's nephew, also called Michael, entered the service of the

60 Ibid., 142–7.
61 Ibid., 198, 308–9.
62 Ibid., 157–60, 225–32, 273–4, 306–8.
63 Ibid. 276–7, 277–9, 279–80. Cf Ahrweiler, 'Smyrne', 104.
64 Michael Choniates II, 318–19; Stadtmüller, *Michael Choniates*, 202.
65 Ibid., 336–7.

Burgundian rulers of Thebes.[66] Soon after this *c.* 1216–17 Michael Choniates finally abandoned windy Keos and moved to the monastery of the Prodromos at Mountiniza, better known as Thermopylae. He made an attempt to revisit Athens but stayed only a very short while, because the Latins were on the look-out for him. His new abode put him in much closer touch with Epiros, whose Greek rulers were in striking distance of Attica. By 1219 Neai Patrai, only some twenty miles as the crow flies from Thermopylae, was in their hands. Michael Choniates received an invitation from Theodore Angelus to move to Epiros. This prompted a meeting of orthodox leaders at Euripos, who protested that acceptance would be unfair to Choniates's nephews and to the monastery of the Prodromos. Their fear was that, if Michael Choniates departed for Epiros, they would suffer at the hands of the Latins.[67] Michael Choniates therefore stayed on in the monastery of the Prodromos until death finally overtook him *c.* 1222. Deprived of his protection most of his followers and intimates now preferred the safety of Epiros.

Before his death Choniates had been in regular contact with John Apokaukos, the metropolitan of Naupaktos. They had a go-between in the shape of Euthymius Tornikes. In 1219 Apokaukos recommended him to Theodore Angelus for the vacant see of Neai Patras. He thought it fitting because it had once been occupied by Tornikes's maternal uncle, Euthymius Malakes. Tornikes did not in fact receive the see.[68] Michael Choniates also recommended to John Apokaukos an unnamed student of his, whom he had advised to go to 'your world still preserved free in the grace of Christ'. He trusted that Apokaukos would provide the student with an introduction to the Greek ruler of Epiros, Theodore Angelus.[69] Michael Choniates's nephew Nicetas also went to Epiros and eventually succeeded John Apokaukos, as metropolitan of Naupaktos. George Bardanes too departed for Epiros, where he was to become metropolitan of Corfu. It may have been Bardanes who was responsible for bringing to Epiros Choniates's works, which were preserved in the Epirot monastery of St Nicholas at Mesopotamon.[70] Thus in the shape of his pupils and his works much of Michael Choniates's achievement was passed on to Epiros. For John Apokaukos he was an object of veneration: 'that wonderful man' was how he described him. He exemplified the ideal of the bishop as the upholder of established order and social justice, as the focus and arbiter of local society: never more so than after

66 Ibid., 324–6.
67 Ibid., 326–9.
68 Darrouzès, 'Notes sur Euthyme Tornikès', 152–5.
69 Michael Choniates II, 350–1.
70 Nicol II, 244–5.

1204, even if in the face of the Latin occupation his efforts proved unavailing. If he was never venerated as a saint, his portrait has been preserved in a local church with the legend *panierotatos* – 'All Holiest'.[71]

[71] Walter, *Art and Ritual*, 223 and n. 318.

10

JOHN APOKAUKOS

JOHN Apokaukos was metropolitan of Naupaktos for some thirty years from *c.* 1200 to *c.* 1230. He was a key figure in the history of the orthodox church in Epiros after the fall of Constantinople to the Latins in 1204. Ordained metropolitan before the fall he represented legitimacy, continuity, and a modicum of stability during the 'cosmic cataclysm' that overwhelmed the Byzantine Empire. He is also important for quite another reason. A large part of his correspondence has survived, but in a rather different form to that of other Byzantine bishops. Byzantine epistolography was a deliberately literary pursuit. Letters were composed and edited with an eye to their literary and stylistic merits. Somewhat exceptionally, John Apokaukos's correspondence seems to have undergone rather little in the way of editing either by himself or by some literary executor. It would be quite wrong, however, to deny his letters any literary merit. Recently Paul Magdalino has underlined the vivid way in which his letters portray aspects of everyday life.[1]

We are presented with the raw material from which a selection of letters might have been made. This is entirely appropriate. Apart from a handful of epigrams written before he became metropolitan bishop of Naupaktos,[2] John Apokaukos showed few signs of literary pretensions. Unlike so many of his contemporaries he was not called on to deliver speeches. There are relatively few of his letters that can be described as belletrist in intent. The vast bulk of his surviving letters are to do with the running of his see. They are addressed to other metropolitans, to his suffragans, to the rulers of Epiros and their relatives and officials, in other words to those whose help might be useful. In addition, there survive among his correspondence a fair number of official acts of his administration. It looks rather as though we have before us the remains of a bishop's working papers; and this is a unique survival from Byzantium.

1 P. Magdalino, 'The literary perception of everyday life in Byzantium', *BS* 47(1987), 28–38 (= Magdalino, *Tradition and Transformation*, no. x).
2 Papadopoulos-Kerameus, ''Επιγράμματα'.

But unique survivals present difficulties. A specialist in the western church would at best be only slightly impressed by the riches offered by Apokaukos's correspondence. It does not offer a detailed picture of diocesan administration of the kind you might expect in the West. Such a perspective underlines how much has been lost and how superficial and tentative our understanding of the Byzantine church must be. Nevertheless, it remains difficult to resist the temptation to use Apokaukos's correspondence, *faute de mieux*, as a general guide to the Byzantine church in the provinces.

The countercry will always be that Apokaukos's circumstances were unique: his correspondence only illuminates the church in Epiros after 1204. This, it might be asserted, was an experience utterly different from anything that had gone before, simply because of the destruction of the Byzantine Empire. This line of argument does not convince. There may have been a short period of dislocation that followed the fall of Constantinople in 1204, but life in those provinces that remained under Byzantine control soon resumed its earlier rhythms.

Ecclesiastical politics

In so far as anybody is typical, John Apokaukos seems a fair representative of those chosen for metropolitan sees in the twelfth century.[3] He was a nephew of a previous metropolitan bishop of Naupaktos. He had served his uncle as a secretary and deacon,[4] before returning to Constantinople *c.* 1187, where he was enrolled among the patriarchal notaries. He received due reward for conscientious, if undistinguished, service when he was promoted to the metropolitan see of Naupaktos by the Patriarch John Kamateros about the year 1200. He must have been in his forties. The contacts he had built up at Naupaktos as a young man were presumably among the factors that recommended him.

Naupaktos had been a rich see. The town was surrounded by mulberry groves and produced raw silk, which was processed in workshops belonging to the church. But when John Apokaukos took up residence as metropolitan the position was gloomy. The city suffered from pirate raids and the church was impoverished. The clergy which had been one hundred strong was reduced to less than ten.[5] Naupaktos was still an important metropolitan see. With its suffragan bishoprics of Khimara, Dryinoupolis, Butrinto, Bella, Ioannina, Arta, Vonitza, Astakos, Aetos,[6] its boundaries were coterminous with Epiros – a

[3] On Apokaukos's background see now Lampropoulos, *ΙΩΑΝΝΗΣ ΑΠΟΚΑΥΚΟΣ*, 39ff.
[4] Papadoupoulos-Kerameus, 'ΚΕΡΚΥΡΑΙΚΑ', 351.
[5] *Noctes*, 251.6–25.
[6] Leukas enjoyed autocephalous status before 1204, but was effectively another suffragan diocese of Naupaktos.

potentially rich land but under pressure from the Sicilians and the Venetians. It was exactly this region that Michael Angelus turned into a centre of resistance against the Latin conquest. Naupaktos was exposed to attacks both along the coast from Salona, a Latin outpost to the east, and across the straits from Latin-held Patras. For whatever reason, there was to be no attack from the Latins. It came instead from a different direction. Greek refugees who had taken to piracy first ravaged Patras and then turned their attention to Naupaktos where they burned down the lower town and the mulberry groves. The citizens took to the surrounding hills and the garrison seized this opportunity to plunder the town.[7] As we shall see, John Apokaukos had more trouble from the garrison and the local governor than from the Latins. He lived through difficult times, but the crises he faced were no worse than those confronting a Eustathius, a Michael Choniates, or even a Theophylact or a Michael Italikos.

In a region, such as Epiros, which escaped Latin occupation, little changed. The provincial administrative system remained much as it had been. The main difference was that there could no longer be constant reference to Constantinople. This apart, John Apokaukos's work as metropolitan bishop of Naupaktos is not likely to have been significantly different from what it had been before the fall of Constantinople. The same kind of cases would have been brought to his court. Few of the petitioners were of the highest social status. Where they were, it is likely that before 1204 they would have gone to the courts of the capital rather than to their local metropolitan. Life continued much as before; the major difference being the presence of the ruler of Epiros, Michael Angelus, at Arta. In practice, his authority was not very different from that of a provincial governor before 1204. In any case, his successor, his half-brother, Theodore Angelus, made Thessalonica his capital after its recovery from the Latins in the autumn of 1224.

These rulers of Epiros took a close interest in church affairs. Their first concern was to ensure that the sees in the lands they controlled were filled. In one sense, they were fortunate because both the metropolitan churches of Corfu and of Naupaktos had incumbents appointed before 1204. But by 1210 Michael Angelus had secured possession of Dyrrakhion on the Albanian coast; and two years later Larissa in Thessaly was his. Both these cities were the seats of metropolitan bishops. To fill them he called a synod which met at Arta in 1213 under the presidency of John Apokaukos. Michael Angelus was the moving spirit, but his choices were approved by the synod. The new metropolitan of Dyrrakhion was ordained by his suffragans, but the new metropolitan of Larissa was ordained by the bishop of Leukas,

7 Apokaukos I, no.99, 149–50.

who could lay claim to autocephalous status.[8] These were irregularities which could be overlooked because of the uncertainty of the times.[9] Theodore Angelus acted in much the same way as his half-brother over ecclesiastical appointments. We have the order which he despatched to the metropolitan of Larissa, instructing him to ordain the son of the late bishop of Domokos in his father's place.[10]

How far did John Apokaukos support this control of episcopal appointments by the rulers of Epiros and what was his reaction to the objections raised to this by the orthodox patriarchs resident at Nicaea? It is a question over which there is a fundamental disagreement. D.M. Nicol has argued that Apokaukos was extremely reluctant to approve the actions of the rulers of Epiros, while A. Karpozilos prefers to see Apokaukos as a loyal supporter of the ecclesiastical policies of Theodore Angelus.[11] The test is the appointment of John Kostomoires, alias Mesopotamites, to the metropolitan see of Neai Patrai (*c.* 1222). This Karpozilos claims was the work of John Apokaukos, who was instrumental in getting Theodore Angelus to appoint him to the newly won see. This is based on a misunderstanding. The man recommended by John Apokaukos was not Kostomoires, but Euthymios Tornikes, nephew of the previous incumbent, Euthymios Malakes.[12] Before 1204 Kostomoires had been a deacon of the Great Church and a patriarchal notary.[13] He afterwards turns up in the service of Theodore Angelus. He held the position of logariast or minister of finance.

He was the recipient in this capacity of three letters from John Apokaukos.[14] It is apparent from these letters that he also held the position of logothete bestowed upon him by the patriarch at Nicaea.[15] This gave him some unspecified competence in ecclesiastical affairs. John Apokaukos tried to enlist his support on behalf of a protégé – almost certainly Euthymios Tornikes – who, he thought, was deserving of a bishopric. Apokaukos concludes in the friendliest fashion: 'You see how great my friendship for you is and how ready I am to carry out your commands.'[16] Later letters are in contrast distinctly chilly. Kostomoires obtained the see of Neai Patrai for himself. Apokaukos complained

[8] Vasiljievskij, 'Epirotica saeculi XIII', 270.20–6.

[9] Ibid., 268.8–20. See Nicol I, 79; A. Karpozilos, *The Ecclesiastical Controversy between the Kingdom of Nicaea and the Principality of Epiros (1217–1233)* (Thessalonica, 1973), 52.

[10] *Noctes*, no.29, 291.

[11] Karpozilos, *Ecclesiastical Controversy*, 61; Nicol, *Epiros*, 89–90.

[12] Vasiljievskij, 'Epirotica saeculi XIII', no.2, 243–4.

[13] Ibid., 276.5–6. He was also *didaskalos tes gyras*, a position which is not otherwise attested.

[14] Apokaukos I, nos. 36, 43, 64.

[15] Apokaukos I, no.43, 100–1.1,7,44; no.64, 119–20.13–14. Cf. Vasiljievskij, 'Epirotica saeculi XIII', 276.7–8.

[16] Apokaukos I, no.36, 95–6.36–8.

bitterly about the way Kostomoires had slandered him before Theodore Angelus. He had made some observation about metropolitan bishops who resist emperors![17] Apokaukos dismissed him as an agent of the Nicaean patriarch at the Epirot court.[18] In other words, the appointment of Kostomoires to the metropolitan see of Neai Patrai fits neither Nicol's nor Karpozilos's interpretation. He was imposed by Theodore Angelus, but Apokaukos was not called upon to give his approval. Kostomoires had close connections with the patriarchs at Nicaea, but this was not a bar to his promotion by Theodore Angelus. Apokaukos's stance in the matter was dictated by his failure to get the position for his friend and protégé Euthymios Tornikes.

In contrast, another protégé George Bardanes had been made metropolitan of Corfu in 1219. John Apokaukos originally wanted to appoint him to the bishopric of Vonitza.[19] He then received a letter from Theodore Angelus informing him of the death of Basil Pediadites, the metropolitan of Corfu, and instructing him to assemble his synod at Arta and to proceed to the election of a new metropolitan bishop. Theodore Angelus recommended George Bardanes. Whether this had anything to do with Apokaukos is not made clear. Michael Choniates wrote to Apokaukos urging Bardanes's eminent qualifications.[20] Apokaukos agreed enthusiastically with Choniates's assessment.[21] John Apokaukos duly called his synod together and it promoted George Bardanes to the metropolitan see of Corfu. The essential documents it had before it were the order from Theodore Angelus and the recommendation from Michael Choniates.[22] The synod insisted that in proceeding to the election it was not in any way usurping the rights of the patriarch but was merely reacting to circumstances.[23] The conclusion can only be that John Apokaukos cooperated with Theodore Angelus over filling vacant sees. It was a way of finding preferment for friends and protégés, though Apokaukos might have seen this as raising the standard of the Epirot episcopate. There was inevitably friction with the patriarch at Nicaea.

John Apokaukos's initial taste of Nicaean interference in the affairs of the church in Epiros had put him on his guard. He had been appointed before 1204 by the patriarch John Kamateros to the post of exarch of patriarchal monasteries and rights in his metropolis. Then, quite without warning, a certain Sampson was appointed in his place about the year 1215 by the patriarch at Nicaea. Apokaukos protested

17 Ibid., no.64, 119–20.21.
18 Ibid., no.43, 100–1.33–42.
19 Vasiljievskij, 'Epirotica saeculi XIII', no.5,248–50; no.6,250–2.
20 Ibid., 250–2.
21 Ibid., no.10,255–6.
22 Ibid., no.13, 260–3.
23 Ibid., 261.34–6.

to the patriarch,[24] to his *chartophylax*,[25] and to others who might be of help.[26] He complained that it was not a fit appointment. Before 1204 his replacement had been a mere notary. How much success Apokaukos had is difficult to say. Sampson was dead by 1219.[27] The matter seems to have been shelved.[28]

In 1222 John Apokaukos was called to account for the ordinations of bishops and metropolitans which had occurred in Epiros without reference to the patriarch at Nicaea.[29] Very much on his dignity he gave a long defence of his actions and insisted on the good order that now existed in the church in Epiros.[30] He equally defended the ordination of Demetrius Chomatianos as archbishop of Ohrid. He accused the patriarch of inconsistency, since his predecessors at Nicaea had subsequently approved ordinations made without reference to them. John Apokaukos made a plea that the same spirit of *oikonomia* should apply to the church in Epiros. He assured the patriarch that his authority was upheld in Epiros. Rather than reviling Theodore Angelus for his intervention in ecclesiastical appointments, the patriarch should praise him for the way he had restored the orthodox church in the West.[31]

Apokaukos was in a difficult position. He wholeheartedly supported the unity of the orthodox church under the patriarch, even if the latter was now resident at Nicaea. He was equally devoted to Theodore Angelus, who had acted to protect the church in his dominions. His objection was to the way the patriarch at Nicaea was mounting an attack upon the church in Epiros in the political interests of the emperor at Nicaea. This was to be resisted. The upshot of the quarrel between the patriarch at Nicaea and the church in Epiros over ordinations was a statement drafted by Apokaukos with the support of Theodore Angelus. It professed respect for the rights of the patriarch, but insisted that the organisation of the church in the territories controlled by Theodore Angelus must remain autonomous. The patriarch was being offered a primacy of honour. This was not enough and a state of schism ensued.[32] Apokaukos may have regretted this, but he seems to have been happy to continue to appoint Theodore's nominees to his suffragan sees, retaining, of course, his right to vet their credentials.[33]

24 *Noctes*, 292–3 (= Apokaukos I, no.57, 112–13).
25 Apokaukos I, no.51, 107–8.
26 Ibid., nos.52–3, 108–10.
27 Vasiljievskij, 'Epirotica saeculi XIII', 257.32–3.
28 Ibid., 259.30–1.
29 Ibid., 268–9; Laurent 1230.
30 Vasiljievskij, 'Epirotica saeculi XIII', 270.15–20.
31 Ibid., no.17, 270–8.
32 Ibid., no.26, 288–93.
33 *Noctes*, 25.287–8 (= Apokaukos I, no.84, 141–2).

John Apokaukos recognised that the church needed imperial protection. This did not prevent him from reprimanding the lay power where it was failing in its responsibilities to the church and society. His loyalty and appreciation were not inexhaustible. The breaking point came with the activities of Theodore Angelus's brother Constantine Doukas, who around 1212 was appointed by his brother viceroy of Akarnania and Aitolia.[34] He came into conflict with John Apokaukos over the taxation owed by the church of Naupaktos on its estates. Apokaukos claimed that it was exempt from taxation as a result of a deal struck between a previous bishop and the government of the Emperor Alexius I Comnenus. Constantine refused to accept this plea of immunity from taxation and insisted on a payment of 1,000 *nomismata.* Apokaukos equally refused to pay. A series of charges were fabricated against him. Apokaukos was fairly confident that he would have the support of Theodore Angelus. The ruler had recently – at Easter 1218 – visited Naupaktos and had been entertained by Apokaukos who had made him a special gift of red silk in recognition of his imperial role.[35] Apokaukos also provided a written explanation of the charges that were made against him, but to no avail.[36] Theodore refused to exonerate him. Apokaukos sent him a bitter protest. How was it possible for his church to pay 1,000 *nomismata* when its tax burden had never been more than 180 *nomismata*? He had never seen that much money: neither in the hands of a banker nor in those of a plutocrat! He accused Theodore Angelus of ingratitude. Had he forgotten the gold and silks he had donated to his cause, worth 343 gold pieces or as much as 500, if you included the horses he had taken? Throughout this letter John Apokaukos adopts a very high moral tone. The poor peasants settled on the estates of the church will be the ones to suffer. He protests against Theodore Angelus's actions with the following words:

> My indignation knows no bounds, when I see the poor who are entrusted to the church being punished, plundered, and forced to flee for the sake of gold. If you hearken to my voice and put an end to this calamity, you will have both our gratitude and that of the poor, which is worth a thousand gold coins. If you do not, I pass over in silence my own feelings, but I fear that the Lord of vengeance, Who does not forget the poor, will give His verdict. He will rise up and raise His hand against those that wrong the poor.[37]

These were very harsh words to address to a ruler.

The letter contained no reference to Constantine Doukas's seizure of

34 Varzos II, no.170, 656–64.
35 Apokaukos II, no.xxi, 23.
36 Apokaukos II, no.ix, 10–13 (= *Noctes*, no.3, 254–8)
37 Apokaukos II, no.xiii, 12–18 (= *Noctes*, 257.31 – 258.3)

the episcopal palace at Naupaktos, so this is likely to have occurred after the despatch of the letter. Not only did Constantine occupy the episcopal palace, but he also took over the running of the church and its estates. Apokaukos complained that he had turned the bishop's quarters into a market and a house of common repair. The estates of the church were distributed among his soldiers, some of whom were recruited from ex-monks. The clergy were driven out; some were imprisoned. Constantine Doukas brought in clergy from outside to officiate in the cathedral, including the bishop of Zeitounion in Thessaly who received a sharp rebuke from Apokaukos.[38] 'Our tyrant', as Apokaukos calls him, also took it upon himself to appoint abbots and to interfere in matters of marriage law.

John Apokaukos was confined in a farmstead outside Naupaktos. He decided to flee northwards to the court of Theodore Angelus, where he hoped to put his case.[39] He tried to drum up support among his fellow metropolitans. He claimed the right to be judged by his fellow metropolitans of Corfu, Dyrrakhion, and the archbishop of Bulgaria along with those appointed from Theodore Angelus's court.[40] It was a dramatic gesture, which seems to have worked, for the next thing we know is that there was sweetness and light between the metropolitan and his tyrant. What lay behind this about-turn is never made clear. Circumstances had changed. Theodore Angelus needed John Apokaukos's support in the quarrel over ordinations with the patriarch at Nicaea. It became even more necessary once he had decided after the conquest of Thessalonica in 1224 to assume the imperial dignity. Apokaukos's formal reconciliation with Constantine Doukas took place in the aftermath of Theodore's imperial coronation in 1226/7.[41] Even then, relations between the two men could be tense.[42] This, despite the grant of a chrysobull by Theodore Angelus in which the estates and fiscal privileges of the church of Naupaktos received official confirmation.[43] This was Apokaukos's reward for his voyage to Thessalonica on the occasion of Theodore's coronation. It was appreciated as a gesture of loyalty.

38 Apokaukos II, no. xvii, 21.25–36.

39 The most detailed accounts of Apokaukos's clash with Constantine Doukas are to be found in Papadopoulos-Kerameus, 'Συμβολή', 239–44; Apokaukos I, no.27, 87–8.

40 A. Papadopoulos-Kerameus, 'ΔΥΡΡΑΧΗΝΑ', *BZ* 14(1905), no.3, 573–4.

41 Apokaukos I, no.2, 57–8.

42 *Noctes*, 18, 281–2 (= Apokaukos I, no.77, 137–8), where Apokaukos again found himself excluded from Naupaktos by Constantine Doukas. This has to be after May 1228 because there is a reference to the chrysobull issued by Theodore Angelus on that date.

43 *Noctes*, no.2, 250–4 (= Vasiljievskij, 'Epirotica saeculi XIII', no.29, 296–9).

Defending the church of Naupaktos

It is not clear if Constantine Doukas's seizure of the church of Naupaktos was done with the approval of his brother, who may not have had much control over his actions. But it was certainly done in the pursuit of a common aim – the need to raise money. Friction between the church and the secular authorities seems to have most commonly occurred over taxation, rather than, as was the case in the West, over judicial competence. This points to a fundamental difference between Byzantium and the West at this stage. Autonomy at Byzantium was measured in terms of freedom from taxation rather than in the exercise of rights of justice. Disregard for a church's fiscal privileges was an affront to the autonomy that the church sought. The defence of a church's fiscal privileges could not therefore be couched in purely material terms. They had also to be presented as a necessary part of its spiritual and moral role in a Christian society. John Apokaukos knew as well as any other bishop that without wealth the church would wither away. No list of the properties of the church of Naupaktos has survived so that it is impossible to gain any clear idea of its landed wealth. It certainly possessed estates and villages around Naupaktos. Not only did it have dependent peasants to work its fields, there were also weavers, tailors, and cobblers to staff its workshops and fishermen to provide the clergy with fish. As we have seen, when John Apokaukos took up residence at Naupaktos as bishop, the material state of the church was grim. The clergy had dropped from around the hundred mark to ten or so. John Apokaukos quickly succeeded in restoring the fortunes of his church and increasing the number of clergy. He was even in a position to set about refurbishing his cathedral which had been neglected. He recruited painters to decorate the interior of the church.[44]

Pride suffuses his description of his church and city contained in a letter he wrote to the metropolitan of Thessalonica. Apokaukos began with the episcopal palace which adjoined the cathedral. It was constructed entirely of marble. He went on: the public places, the thoroughfares through the city, and the flights of steps are all paved in marble, so that its citizens go dryshod the whole year round. How fortunate they were in comparison to the people of Thessalonica who spent much of the year caked in mud! They were also lucky enough to have ample supplies of spring water; so much better and so much healthier than the brackish well water at Thessalonica.[45] Since this letter was written when Constantine Doukas's occupation of the city

44 Apokaukos I, no.58, 114–15; no.103, 153, where it is specifically said that the pterygia and the narthexes need decoration.

45 Ibid., no.67, 122–4.

was over, it sounds as though it had no appreciable impact upon the prosperity of Naupaktos. This must have been largely due to the sound guidance of Apokaukos. It must also be a reflection of the wealth of his church, for, as we have seen, this depended not only upon its landed possessions, but also on its workshops. Naupaktos was still a centre of silk production.

This is to assume – not unreasonably – that the church of Naupaktos was a significant element in the local economy and that its well-being brought general benefit to local society. Apokaukos never seems, however, to have acted as the spokesman for his city, in the way Michael Choniates had done at Athens. Even his protests to Theodore Angelus and his officials on behalf of the peasantry were part of an effort to protect the estates of the church. His other interventions with the authorities were either on behalf of his suffragans or of various dignitaries. He pleaded the case of the *kastrophylax* of neighbouring Angelokastron who, he was certain, had been falsely accused. At least, the women who had nursed the man should be allowed to return. He was paralysed and close to death.[46] Apokaukos also provided the abbot of Hosios Loukas who had been driven out by the Latins with a letter of recommendation to Theodore Angelus.[47] There are a great many more examples of this kind that could be cited. Practically speaking, this may well have been the most effective way that Apokaukos could protect and represent local interests.

These interventions with the secular authorities presupposed a modicum of respect for justice and social harmony; their chances of success depended upon the moral authority that a bishop wielded. They were also part of a political process of lobbying, upon which a man such as John Apokaukos depended. If he did favours, he also asked for favours from others. To defend himself against Constantine Doukas he turned for support not only to his fellow bishops, but also to those high in Theodore Angelus's favour. Especially valued and valuable was the good opinion of his consort Maria Petraliphina.[48] This was all part of the preparation necessary for a direct appeal to the ruler himself.[49] Its *leitmotif* was the spiritual and moral assistance that John Apokaukos had rendered Theodore Angelus. As we have seen, it would in due course have its effect. Rulers always found themselves at some time or other in need of spiritual and moral help.

[46] *Noctes*, no.13, 273 (= Apokaukos I, no.69, 128).
[47] *Noctes*, no.22, 285–6 (= Apokaukos I, no.79, 138–9).
[48] Vasiljievskij, 'Epirotica saeculi XIII', no.21, 282; *Noctes*, no.14, 275–6.
[49] *Noctes*, no.8, 263–4 (= Apokaukos I, no.38, 96–7).

The episcopal court

The chief way in which John Apokaukos fulfilled his social and moral responsibilities to society was through his court. Leaving aside for later the purely ecclesiastical business, where he dealt with the problems of his suffragans and other members of the clergy, the range of business that came before Apokaukos's court may not have been that varied, but it touched the most vital aspects of everyday life. The laity brought three main kinds of cases to his court: marriage, property, and homicide. That marriage was the central institution of society; that in one way and another most property in lay hands was tied up in marriage, hardly needs repeating. Equally, it goes without saying that there was a great deal of casual violence both within and between families, resulting often enough in death. All these were types of cases that could have gone before the civil courts. Before 1204 they mostly did at Constantinople. But the signs are that in the provinces the episcopal court had a larger part to play. In early thirteenth-century Epiros – and it is only here that any real evidence has survived – marriage suits came before the episcopal courts, as a matter of course. When John Apokaukos was listing the episcopal duties usurped by Constantine Doukas, he specified the supervision of marriage. As has already been argued, the fall of Constantinople is unlikely to have radically changed judicial practice in the provinces.[50]

The church of Naupaktos had already evolved clear procedures before John Apokaukos's time for dealing with various aspects of marriage. A man suspecting his wife of adultery would go to the church and make known his suspicions. Members of the clergy would then make an investigation. On the basis of their evidence the metropolitan would give his verdict.[51] At Naupaktos, as almost certainly elsewhere, it was the responsibility of the *chartophylax* of the church to check the legality of the marriages that were to be celebrated. The priests could only proceed once they had received sealed approval of the marriage from the *chartophylax*.[52] Apokaukos discovered that his *chartophylax* had been failing in his duty and had allowed the marriage of under-age girls. He relieved him of his duties and gave them instead to another officer of the church.[53] As we know, Apokaukos was concerned about the moral side of marriage. This included protection of the rights and well-being of women. He acted by and large in a humane way: he placed considerable emphasis on the consent to marriage of both parties and recognised incompatibility as grounds for divorce. What

50 Apokaukos I, no.27, 87.90–1.
51 Ibid., II, no.XVI, 20–1.
52 Ibid., I, no.9, 62.1–6.
53 Ibid., no.9, 67–8; no.10, 69.

he would not condone, following the precepts of St Basil of Caesarea, was the subsequent marriage of a woman to her lover.

Marriage was a spiritual union, but it was also a civil contract. It was this double character that meant that marriage cases might go before both the ecclesiastical and the civil courts. In theory, property disputes arising out of marriage should properly have gone to the civil courts, but there are a number of cases of this kind that came before John Apokaukos. It may have been a matter of sheer practicality, but there is also the possibility that the church considered that it had a special responsibility over the dowry as part of the role it had in protecting the rights of women. Through the supervision of marriage the bishop was able to act in the interests of moral order and social justice.

Society was most obviously shaken by acts of violence. It was the duty of the ruler first and foremost to ensure that peace and order reigned. It therefore comes as something of a surprise to find cases of homicide being brought before John Apokaukos. The justification for this lay in the taking of human life. It was seen as much as a sin as an offence against public order. As a sin it was best cleared through penance which could only be prescribed by an ecclesiastical court. John Apokaukos warned government officials against trying to impose other punishments on murderers who had come before his court, 'for the confiscation of a murderer's property cannot wipe away such a sin: only the fulfilment of the church's prescriptions'.[54] Penance was the main sanction that John Apokaukos had at his disposal. It normally consisted of exclusion from the church for a set period of time. The penitent was ordered to wait outside the church each Sunday and throw himself before his fellow citizens, crying, 'Have mercy upon me a sinner'. This must have been a humiliating experience. Its effectiveness is not easy to gauge. It must have depended on the degree of moral authority exercised by the bishop over the local community. There was also an element of collusion. The church offered the penitent protection against officialdom. This was an inducement for murderers to throw themselves on the mercy of the church. At the same time, the church provided a mechanism both for defusing the bitterness and mixed emotions that casual violence was bound to create in any community. To that extent a bishop both contributed to social order and served as a focus for local society.

In a sense, this was the incidental work of an episcopal court. The procedures for dealing with casual violence could be informal in the extreme. Apokaukos describes a visit he made to one of his suffragans, the bishop of Vonitza: 'After divine service we walked together around the cathedral portal and sat down on some marble benches there.

[54] Ibid., no. 18, 79.55–7.

We started chatting about illnesses and superficial troubles and how nowadays each commits whatever evil deed takes his fancy'.

Suddenly there appeared out of nowhere an old man with a bandaged head – a victim of assault and battery. He had come to present his case. A bishop caught in an off-duty moment was his best hope of redress![55]

The clergy

The specific cares of a bishop related to his clergy. One of the pressing tasks that faced John Apokaukos was to increase the size of his clergy. Something of his methods of recruitment emerges from his papers. He was on the look-out for young boys, orphans mostly, whom he could train to be clergy.[56] He also passed on some of his recruits to his suffragans. One of his favourites had been given to him by his mother before he was born, but he parted with him to the bishop of Vonitza, whose brother was the local schoolmaster. Apokaukos entrusted his education to this man and promised payment of the fees. Typically, he recommended beating as an essential educational aid.[57] Apokaukos regarded his charges as his spiritual sons. Such exchanges built up links of a personal kind with his suffragans. There is no doubting the affection that John Apokaukos had for his 'orphans'.[58]

It was not always reciprocated. There are a series of cases where members of the clergy of Naupaktos, trained up by Apokaukos from boyhood, simply abandoned their calling or fled to other churches.[59] Apokaukos suffered the humiliation of having to ask for them back. They came, as he put it, 'under his spiritual lordship'.[60] He explained their defection in personal terms. One had a marriage ruined by magic; another ran off with the wife of a fellow cleric. We can only accept his word for it and resist the temptation to delve deeper into the nature of the proxy father–son relationship that united Apokaukos to his charges.

There were certainly other factors that made for friction between a bishop and his clergy. Some of these emerge from a dispute between the bishop of Dryinoupolis, a suffragan of the church of Naupaktos, and his clergy. It eventually came before John Apokaukos.[61] The clergy

55 Ibid., no.8, 61.10–16.

56 Ibid., no.27, 85.6–8; Papadopoulos-Kerameus, 'Συμβολή', 234.1–12; Papadopoulos-Kerameus, 'ΔΥΡΡΑΧΗΝΑ', 572.13–18.

57 Apokaukos I, nos.100–1, 150–2. Cf. Lampropoulos, *ΙΩΑΝΝΗΣ ΑΠΟΚΑΥΚΟΣ*, 54–5, for further examples.

58 See Magdalino, 'Literary perception', 32–3.

59 Apokaukos I, no.27, 85–6; Papadopoulos-Kerameus, 'Συμβολή', 234–5; Papadopoulos-Kerameus, 'ΔΥΡΡΑΧΗΝΑ', 572–3.

60 Papadopoulos-Kerameus, 'ΔΥΡΡΑΧΗΝΑ', 573.2.

61 A. Papadopoulos-Kerameus, 'Συνοδικὰ γράμματα Ἰωάννου τοῦ Ἀπόκαυκου', *ΒΥΖΑΝΤΙΣ* 1(1909) no.1, 8–9.

claimed that their bishop had imposed dues on them. The bishop agreed that this was indeed the case, but insisted that he had since compensated his clergy. John Apokaukos reconciled the parties. The bishop agreed to respect the rights the clergy possessed over that part of the church's properties laid down in the sealed documents (*sigillia*) of previous bishops.

Another of Apokaukos's suffragans, the bishop of Arta, also had trouble with two members of his clergy. They were brothers who were deacons of the church. They had failed to pay the taxes and the services which they owed to the church as hereditary bondsmen of the church – the word used is *enoikos*. The bishop of Arta therefore excommunicated the two brothers. They did not deny their dependent status, but they maintained that they had been reduced to such penury that it was impossible for them to fulfil their obligations. There had been a terrible flood at Arta and their father's house rented from the bishopric was rendered uninhabitable, while the surrounding orchards and vineyards from which they obtained a livelihood had reverted to marsh. The brothers then countercharged that the bishop had signally failed to provide them with their daily subsistence, which they were owed as members of his clergy.[62] John Apokaukos intervened. He had little sympathy with the bishop's case. He agreed with the brothers that the point at issue was the bishop's failure to provide members of the clergy with their daily bread. He therefore released the two brothers from the sentence of excommunication imposed upon them.[63] The bishop, however, refused to reinstate them.

This case highlights one of the problems of the relationship of a bishop with his clergy. There was a possibility that the clergy would be reduced to the status of dependants of the bishop, little different from the peasantry settled on the episcopal estates. It went further than this: a bishopric might become quasi-hereditary in the hands of a particular family. We have already seen how Theodore Angelus recommended that a son of the recently deceased bishop of Domoko should succeed his father as bishop. His other sons were to receive what the metropolitan bishop considered proper from the revenues of the see of Domoko.[64] Apokaukos, for his part, tried to guard against such irregularities. He insisted upon the bishop's prime responsibility to his clergy. It was his duty to ensure that they were properly fed and housed. To this end it was normal to set aside special holdings (*staseis*) for the clergy, which is what happened at Naupaktos.[65] The condition

62 Ibid., no.9, 23–4.
63 Ibid., no.9, 26–7.
64 *Noctes*, no.29,291 (= Papadopoulos-Kerameus, *ΑΝΑΛΕΚΤΑ*, IV, 118–19).
65 *Noctes*, no.2, 251.27 (= Vasiljievskij, 'Epirotica saeculi XIII', no.29, 297.11); Papadopoulos-Kerameus, 'Συμβολή', 241.14.

of the clergy varied from see to see. At Corfu, as we shall see, they formed a college, which provided them with a measure of autonomy, while at Dryinoupolis the privileges of the clergy were enshrined in the written guarantees issued by the bishop. But whether as a college or as the *familia* of the bishop the clergy formed a distinct group in local society.

The case just discussed involving the bishop of Arta was not a straightforward matter of a difference between a bishop and members of his clergy. It turned into a bitter quarrel between a metropolitan bishop and a suffragan. There was bound to be tension between Apokaukos and the bishop of Arta. Apokaukos found himself spending more and more time in Arta, because it was one of the residences of the 'despots' of Epiros. He had no hesitation in taking over monasteries for his own convenience that properly belonged to his suffragan. For this he would be posthumously condemned by the Patriarch Germanos II.[66] Apokaukos admitted that he was mostly to blame for the quarrel. He had treated the bishop of Arta unjustly.[67] He had built up close ties with members of the clergy of Arta, which strained their loyalties to their bishop. He acknowledged that it was this, rather than the question of the obligations of a bishop to his clergy, that lay behind the differences between the bishop of Arta and the two brothers.

Apokaukos had known them since they were children. They would come to pay him their respects when he was staying in Arta at his residence in the monastery of the Peribleptos. This was the real reason why the bishop had excommunicated them.[68] John Apokaukos treated the bishop as contumacious. He barred him from the church and excommunicated members of the clergy of Arta who supported their bishop.[69] He explained his position to the leading archontes of Arta, who happened to be his godsons. He ordered them to have nothing to do with the bishop on pain of excommunication.[70] He justified his actions to Theodore Angelus, claiming among other things that the bishop aspired to autocephalous status for his church.[71]

Apokaukos also came into conflict with an archbishop of Leukas. Before 1204 this church was directly dependent on the patriarchate of Constantinople. This gave its archbishop a freedom of action which may explain why in 1212 he was called upon to ordain the new metropolitan bishop of Larissa. His successor was of less account. Complaints were laid against him by members of his clergy. He had

66 Rhalles & Potles v, 106–9; Laurent 1283.
67 Vasiljievskij, 'Epirotica saeculi XIII', no.21, 282.25–6 (= *Noctes*, no.16, 278.29–31).
68 Papadopoulos-Kerameus, 'Συνοδικά', no.5, 21.7–9; no.6, 22.6–9.
69 Ibid., 5.21.
70 Ibid., 6.21–2.
71 *Noctes*, no.13, 273–4 (= Apokaukos I, no.69, 128–9).

beaten members of his clergy with his own hands; he had sold off church lands; he had failed to hold services in his cathedral; for a consideration he had overlooked spiritual failings and had connived at incestuous marriages. Apokaukos considered these charges and threatened him with a trial, if he did not mend his ways. He reminded him that his conduct as bishop had already earned him the displeasure of Theodore Angelus. The approval or disapproval of the ruler continued to count within the church.[72]

These clashes with other bishops were isolated incidents. It is safe to say that Apokaukos was on very good terms with most of his suffragans most of the time. He was closer to some than to others. Towards the end of his life he was especially close to the bishop of Ioannina, Theodore Vatatzes, who was a godson of his. He provided him with support and advice in a whole series of different matters, but he did this for most of his suffragans. Despite ill-health he travelled extensively around his metropolitan diocese. The contacts that he maintained with his suffragans both in this way and by letter were the foundation of effective control over his suffragans. He also lobbied on their behalf with the ruler. His suffragans, in their turn, seem constantly to have been consulting him over the everyday business of administering their sees. This provides a glimpse of one of the strengths of the church: a combination of experience, well-tried procedures, and a network of contacts and informants.[73] To be effective it needed somebody with the skill, stamina, and patience of Apokaukos.

It is therefore surprising that the abbots of the monasteries who came under Apokaukos's authority scarcely figure in his correspondence. This is in contrast to the correspondence of Michael Choniates where, especially after 1204, the abbots of the monasteries surrounding Athens feature prominently. It was hardly that John Apokaukos was out of sympathy with the monastic life. Towards the end of his life he expressed a fervent desire to end his days in the monastery of Hosios Loukas, which he calls his spiritual birth place.[74] We saw how he intervened on behalf of the abbot of Hosios Loukas, when driven out by the Latins.[75] Apokaukos was to live out his last days in the monastery of Kozyle, not far from the old city of Nikopolis, from where he could more easily keep in contact with his old friends and suffragans.[76] In his capacity as metropolitan he saw it as his responsibility to supervise monasteries: 'The holy canons have awarded to the bishops

[72] Apokaukos I, no.81, 139–40.

[73] Like the priest and notary whose custom it was to tell Apokaukos all the gossip when he stayed in Arta: Papadopoulos-Kerameus, *ΑΝΑΛΕΚΤΑ*, IV, no.40, 124–5.

[74] Apokaukos I, no.95, 147–8. Cf. Lampropoulos, *ΙΩΑΝΝΗΣ ΑΠΟΚΑΥΚΟΣ*, 88–9.

[75] *Noctes*, no.22, 285–6 (= Apokaukos I, no.79, 138–9).

[76] Nicol I, 221, 223.

the examination and disciplining of monks, the appointment of abbots, and the visitation and government of the holy monasteries, as well as ordaining that they appoint stewards for the monasteries.'[77] If he regarded monasteries as spiritual refuges, cut off from the world, he also treated them as agricultural units, which should be made as productive as possible. It is this side of monastic life which receives most attention in his letters. Usually, it was a matter of handing over abandoned monasteries to lay patrons. These were often closely connected with Apokaukos. The important monastery of Kremastou, not far from Naupaktos, he handed over to Nicholas Gorianites, who was both his godson and duke of Akheloos – the most important government agent locally and a man on whom Apokaukos much relied.[78]

Another monastery went to another godson of Apokaukos, but with the proviso that he must respect the rights of the local bishop.[79] Monasteries provided Apokaukos with a useful form of patronage. He used it wisely. For example, he gave a monastery to the bishop of Gardikion who had been driven out by the Latins.[80] It was a gesture that was gratefully remembered.[81] On another occasion, Apokaukos persuaded his suffragan, the bishop of Vonitza, to hand over a semi-derelict monastery in his diocese to a retired bishop, who had now embraced the monastic estate.[82] Equally, Apokaukos defended his rights to dispose of the monasteries within his see, as he considered proper. He protested vigorously when Theodore Angelus's *protovestiarios* handed over without any consultation a monastery within his diocese to a young monk from Lakedaimonia. It was done, Apokaukos complained, without proper examination or regard for his rights as metropolitan.[83]

Apokaukos and the ideal of order

John Apokaukos was a stickler for his rights. He made great play with his knowledge of the law. He poured scorn on the archimandrite of the monasteries of Ioannina – the most incompetent of incompetents and the dimmest of dimwits – not so much because he coveted the episcopal

77 Apokaukos I, no.6, 62.1–5.

78 Ibid., no.6, 62–4. For Apokaukos's considerable correspondence with Gorianites, see ibid., 189; Lampropoulos, *ΙΩΑΝΝΗΣ ΑΠΟΚΑΥΚΟΣ*, 127–8. For the monastery of Kremastou, see A.D. Paliouras, *Byzantine Aitoloakarnania* (Athens, 1985), 41, 84–94, 187–96; B. Katsaros, 'Μία 'ακόμα μαρτυρία διὰ τὴ βυζαντινὴ μονὴ τοῦ Κρεμαστοῦ', *ΚΛΗΡΟΝΟΜΙΑ*, 12(1980), 367–88'.

79 Apokaukos II, no.v, 6–7.

80 Ibid., I, no.12, 72.174.

81 Ibid., no.35, 94–5.

82 Ibid., no.105, 154–5.

83 Ibid., no.34, 93–4.

throne of Ioannina, more because he had no idea about the canonical procedures to be followed.[84] In a case involving a contumacious monk that came before him he rejected the documents that his opponents produced, on the grounds that they did not conform to canon law. The abbot had barred the monk's return to the monastery on pain of imposing an interdict on the whole community. Such an action was proper where heresy was involved, Apokaukos maintained, but there was no suggestion of such an offence in this instance.[85] M. T. Fögen has recently suggested that Apokaukos's legal expertise was less profound than he made out.[86] She picks over the details of a very complicated case involving the prohibited degrees. Apokaukos's position came in for criticism on strictly legal grounds from his clergy and from local notaries. What Dr Fögen fails to appreciate is this: it was not so much ignorance of the law as political expediency that determined Apokaukos's stand. The parties involved belonged to the ruling house of Angelus. Apokaukos extricated himself by citing a similar case that had been heard by the patriarchal synod before the fall of Constantinople. He had been present! This gave him an authority that confounded his critics. He basked in the reflected glory of the patriarch of the day Basil Kamateros, whom Apokaukos described as 'that wonderful man'. Apokaukos's legal knowledge and forensic skills were such that he could make the law work for him!

Apokaukos liked to think of himself as the upholder of an ideal order – an ideal order enshrined in the city of Constantinople. The loss of the city to the Latins must have intensified his attachment to Constantinople and nostalgia must have clouded the reality of the Constantinople of his youth. He preserved an ideal that was scarcely different from that espoused by a Eustathius. Both Eustathius and Apokaukos would hold up Constantinople as an ideal. However unrealistically Eustathius cited Constantinople as a monastic paradise where the highest standards were preserved.[87] Apokaukos did much the same over nunneries. He received a request to turn the monastery of the Blakhernai at Arta into a nunnery. He complied and justified his action by reference to Constantinople, where before 1204 there were many nunneries. In Epiros, by contrast, there were almost none. Women with a vocation were forced to live in miserable huts outside the precincts of the churches. This was a reflection, Apokaukos contended, of a provincial prejudice that women were spiritually inferior to men. A quite different

[84] Ibid., no.106, 155–6.
[85] Papadopoulos-Kerameus, 'Συνοδικά', no.2, 9–13.
[86] M.T. Fögen, '*Horror iuris.* Byzantinische Rechtsgelehrte disziplinieren ihren Metropoliten', in *Cupido Legum*, ed. L. Burgmann, M.T. Fögen, and A. Schminck (Frankfurt am Main, 1985), 47–71.
[87] Eustathius I, 234–7.

ideal had held sway at Constantinople before 1204: male and female were considered equals and women just as capable of following a spiritual calling as men. Apokaukos may have been a shade unrealistic, but he hoped that in this matter Epiros would be guided by the example of Constantinople.[88] As we have seen, Apokaukos also liked to prove his point by citing cases that had come before the patriarchal synod while he was still at Constantinople. It emphasised his connection with the old order that remained an ideal.

For Apokaukos Constantinople was the paradigm of an ideal order, but it needed a guarantor. In the old days, it had been the emperor at Constantinople. Now it was his successor in exile, whence the deference that on most occasions John Apokaukos displayed to Theodore Angelus. If the ruler was failing in his duty, then it was the church's responsibility to recall him to the high standards of government the church demanded – above all, that he protect the privileges of the church. As we have seen, John Apokaukos took it upon himself to intervene on behalf of those who had suffered injustice at the hands of the ruler.

The state of affairs Apokaukos had to face after 1204 provided peculiar problems for a prelate so steeped in the Comnenian ideal. The quarrel with the patriarch at Nicaea presented him with a case of divided loyalties, which he never fully resolved. In practice, he worked for an Epirot church under the protection of Theodore Angelus. His relations with his fellow metropolitans were extremely cordial. Those with Demetrius Chomatianos, the archbishop of Bulgaria, were complicated by the autocephalous status of the latter's church. But there seems to have been little friction between them. The main institutional framework was provided by the church. The circumstances of exile may have exaggerated this state of affairs, but in its general outlines John Apokaukos's role as metropolitan cannot have been so very different from that exercised by his predecessors of the twelfth century. They were the representatives of an ideal order, which they strove to uphold. It brought them into conflict with local interests, but equally the modicum of order that a bishop was able to offer in so many areas of life was an advantage that most recognised.

88 Papadopoulos-Kerameus, 'Συνοδικὰ', no.3, 14–20.

11

GEORGE BARDANES

OF the Epirot prelates John Apokaukos was perhaps closest to his friend and protégé George Bardanes. He had played an important part in getting him appointed metropolitan of Corfu in 1219. By the time of Apokaukos's retirement *c.* 1230 Bardanes was a considerable figure in the Epirot church, involved in negotiations both with the Latin church and with the patriarchate at Nicaea. John Apokaukos turned to him for help when faced with a tricky case involving the prohibited degrees. The parties were both closely, too closely, related to the ruling house of Angelus for Apokaukos to be confident in his unsupported judgement.[1] Bardanes equally submitted cases to John Apokaukos. One concerned a priest accused of manslaughter, whom the previous metropolitan bishop of Corfu had placed under suspension. John Apokaukos advised a reexamination. Either he was guilty and was to be dismissed the priesthood or he was innocent and deserved no punishment. He was to be cross-examined before the whole 'presbytery' (*epi pantos tou presbyteriou*).[2] What exactly did Apokaukos mean by 'presbytery'? He can only be referring to the college of priests at Corfu which was later known as the 'Sacred Band'.[3] Its existence in the twelfth and thirteenth centuries is known from a chrysobull of January 1246 issued in the name of Michael II Angelus. It had apparently been exempted from all taxation and dues since the time of Manuel I Comnenus. It was composed of thirty-two priests of the city of Corfu. Except where it was a matter of spiritual failings the metropolitan of Corfu had neither authority over them nor right to punish them.[4] This may explain why the clergy of Corfu were able to present cases to John Apokaukos without reference to their metropolitan bishop.[5]

[1] Papadopoulos-Kerameus, 'KERKYRAIKA', no. 8, 342–8.

[2] Ibid., no.1, 335–6.

[3] Nicol, I, 143.

[4] P. Lemerle, 'Trois actes du despote d'Epire Michel II concernant Corfou connus en traduction latine', *ΠΡΟΣΦΟΡΑ ΕΙΣ ΣΤ. Π. ΚΥΡΙΑΚΔΗΝ.* (Thessalonica, 1953), 420 (= P. Lemerle, *Le Monde de Byzance: histoire et institutions* (London, 1978), no.VI).

[5] Apokaukos I, no.20, 81–2.

This was not the only college of priests on the island. There was another for the ten *dekarkhies* into which the island was divided. These priests too were normally exempt from the payment of taxes and dues but they were expected to pay any land tax (*akrostikhon*) on their properties in excess of six *nomismata* – still a considerable sum in the thirteenth century. They numbered thirty-three divided unequally among the *dekarkhies*. Membership of this college was to remain in the families of the priests. The governors of Corfu were expressly forbidden to introduce outsiders.[6]

Membership of these colleges meant membership of an elite on the island.[7] The college of the city of Corfu must have constituted the cathedral clergy. It numbered thirty-two members, which seems an adequate staff for a cathedral, though it is more than likely that there were others excluded from the college. The other college had thirty-three priests, but for an island, as large as Corfu, this seems a niggardly provision. In 1262 on neighbouring Kephallenia, which is of comparable size, there were at least twenty-two orthodox priests settled on the estates of the Latin bishop of the island.[8] They can only have represented a fraction of the orthodox clergy. But they were not freemen. It is therefore more than a possibility that there were other priests serving in Corfu, who did not enjoy the considerable privileges bestowed on the members of the colleges.

But for the reference by John Apokaukos to a 'presbytery' at Corfu the authenticity of the documentation about the colleges of priests at Corfu would have been open to question, since it has only survived in later Latin versions. Were these colleges unique or were they little different from arrangements in other bishoprics? How important was the hereditary element? This was an issue that attracted the attention of the canonist Theodore Balsamon. He noted the situation that existed in the churches of Athens and Mesembria. There the descendants of the cathedral clergy claimed a hereditary right to be enrolled in the clergy, even if they remained members of the laity; in which case, they found others better qualified to carry out the incumbent ecclesiastical duties.[9] This led on to the question of members of the laity holding *klerikata offikia*, which can be loosely rendered as ecclesiastical benefices.[10] Theodore Balsamon may have rejected the idea of hereditary succession to benefices as uncanonical and reminiscent of the practice

6 Lemerle, 'Trois actes', 422.

7 Cf. the historian George Sphrantzes who at the end of his life was enrolled in the college of the thirty-two priests of the city of Corfu: ibid., 425.

8 Miklosich & Müller v, 43–4, 66–7.

9 Rhalles & Potles II, 380–1.

10 Cf. Thomas, *Private Religious Foundations*, 273.

of the Armenian church, but it was clearly a problem in the Byzantine church, as were benefices in lay hands.

These questions have been thoroughly explored by Eleutheria Papagianne.[11] She singles out *klerikato* as a key problem. She identifies its primary meaning as the property that went with clerical office. She is, however, wary of identifying this with benefice in the western sense, because by the twelfth century there was an important difference between Byzantine and western practice. The Byzantine clergy were expected to pay a tax to the bishopric for their property, which meant that they were in a sense the dependants of the bishop. Strictly speaking, Papagianne is correct to insist that benefice is not an accurate translation of *klerikato*. But she herself admits that it may sometimes be used more generally for clerical office. In its wider meaning of the rewards and obligations associated with clerical office, benefice seems an adequate rendering of *klerikato*.

It seems to have been a coinage of the eleventh century and reflects a substantial change in the funding of the cathedral clergy, which in its turn was to complicate the relations between bishop and clergy. In the past, the cathedral clergy had been entitled to a stipend or *diaria*, which was paid out of the episcopal revenues, and which continued to be so.[12] However, starting with grants made to the churches of Bari and Bulgaria under Basil II,[13] bishops began to receive tax exemptions for a set number of clergy. This meant the creation of property exempt from taxation to the state in return for which members of the clergy performed their ecclesiastical duties, but were also expected to pay tax (*telos*) to the bishop.[14] The payment of tax to a superior was increasingly taken as proof of dependent status. A *paroikos* or dependent peasant paid tax to his lord. Consequently, members of the clergy came to be regarded as dependants of the bishop. The term *klerikoparoikoi* was coined for them.

We catch a glimpse of them in a document of 1163 for the bishopric of Stagoi in Thessaly. The bishop was entitled to forty-six *klerikoparoikoi*, though so far only thirty-six had been established in possession of their property by the imperial authorities. They were all settled around the cathedral at Stagoi and held ecclesiastical offices from simple deacon to *protekdikos* and *skeuophylax*. They quite clearly constituted the cathedral clergy, but they were divided up like peasants into different fiscal categories – *zeugaratos*, *boidatos*, and *aktemon* – according to the size of their holdings and they paid tax to the bishop proportionately.[15]

[11] Papagianne, *TA OIKONOMIKA*, 186–216.
[12] Ibid., 57, 61–2, 67, 109–10; Thomas, *Private Religious Foundations*, 114, 118.
[13] Oikonomidès, 'Tax exemptions', 317–26.
[14] Papagianne, *TA OIKONOMIKA*, 190–1.
[15] Vranouse 'Tὸ 'αρχαιότερο', 28–9.

The emergence of *klerikoparoikoi* created an anomaly: there was a discrepancy between the status of a *paroikos* and the dignity of the clergy. It could be the cause of friction between a bishop and members of his clergy. This happened in a case coming before John Apokaukos, which we have already examined. It is worth looking at it again. It concerned two brothers, deacons of the church of Arta, who were put under the ban of the church by their bishop. It will be remembered that he deprived them of their *klerikata* and their property. He also barred them from singing in church. The bishop justified his action by claiming that they had failed to perform their ecclesiastical duties. One of the brothers explained why this was: a flood had inundated the property that they and, before them, their father had held from the bishopric. It had turned gardens and orchards into marshland and made them unproductive. The bishop was unwilling to provide them with alternative property, but still expected them to perform their ecclesiastical duties and pay their dues. He also refused to provide their stipends. The brothers therefore withdrew their services. The case came before Apokaukos. They admitted that they were *klerikoparoikoi*, but they then pointed to the anomalies of their position:

> Was it right for the clergy of any church to be subjected to such oppressive behaviour by their bishop? It meant that they were not accorded the right of changing their abode, but after the manner of serfs (*douloparoikoi*) they were bound against their will to the soil. If the dignity and name of cleric did not free them from servitude, what was the point of taking holy orders, being enrolled in the church and calling themselves members of the clergy?

The bishop of Arta refused to relent and to reinstate them. All Apokaukos could do was to release them from the ban of the church.[16] This underlines the power that a bishop was able to exercise over his clergy by virtue of their fiscal status as *paroikoi* of the bishopric.

The outcome was likely to be different where the clergy acted as a body. This happened with the cathedral clergy of Dryinopolis. We have seen how they took their grievances against their bishop to John Apokaukos. The bishop was forced to admit that he had imposed heavy exactions on his clergy. Under Apokaukos's prompting he agreed to abide in future by the sealed documents (*sigillia*) of his predecessors, which defined the clergy's rights.[17] In this case, the clergy had some protection against the arbitrary power of a bishop. This had grown with the fiscal privileges accorded to bishoprics in increasing numbers from the turn of the tenth century.

As so often in Byzantium fiscal practice had profound legal implications.

[16] Papadopoulos-Kerameus, 'Συνοδικά', nos.5–9. The quote is from ibid., 26.9–16.

[17] Ibid., no.1, 8–9.

Klerikoparoikoi were essentially a fiscal category, but there was a danger that they would be reduced to the condition of episcopal serfs. It produced a need to redefine the respective rights of bishop and clergy. There was a range of solutions. The example of the bishop of Arta shows the power that a bishop could wield over individual members of his clergy, but undertakings of the kind made by the bishops of Dryinopolis to their clergy are likely to have been a more common solution. The colleges at Corfu seem only to be a more extreme variant of this. Their status received official confirmation from Michael II of Epiros, who claimed only to be renewing a grant of the Emperor Manuel I Comnenus.[18]

This may be so much wishful thinking, but Manuel Comnenus was a generous benefactor of the church of Corfu, which was of great strategic importance in his struggle with the Normans of Sicily. His first grant consisted of eighty *paroikoi* and forty clerical households. Then came gifts of sixty *hagiodouloi*, as they were called. These were presumably men and women who served the various churches of the metropolis. This was followed by the grant of twenty-four exempt households in the city and another fifty in the surrounding countryside. Finally, Manuel Comnenus issued a *sigillion* granting the church of Corfu another twenty *paroikoi*. It was emphasised that they were free from the payment of taxation to the state, in the same way that the households of all the other *paroikoi* (including forty-four labourers) settled on the estates of the church of Corfu had been exempted.[19] It is interesting that these grants have nothing to say about land, only about peasants, clergy, and their households. The word used for household is *oikia*, which presumably designated an economic unit. In the case of the clergy it would have been the equivalent of a benefice or *klerikaton*. The grants made by Manuel I Comnenus to the church of Corfu emphasise how the wealth of a church depended on rights accorded to a bishop over peasants and clergy.

It is not possible to establish any exact equivalence between the numbers of households granted by Manuel Comnenus and the numbers of clergy in the two colleges of Corfu, thirty-two and thirty-three respectively. Manuel's original grant included forty clerical households, to which another seventy-four exempt households were added – twenty-four in the city and fifty outside. The probability is that at some point the rights over these households were divided between the clergy and the bishop. It was presumably a private arrangement not unlike that between the bishops of Dryinopolis and their clergy; the

[18] Lemerle, 'Trois actes', 418–21.

[19] A. Martin, 'Inscription grecque de Corcyre de 1228', *Mélanges d' archéologie et d'histoire* 2(1882), 379–89; Miklosich & Müller v, 14–15.

difference being that at Corfu the privileges of the clergy would later receive imperial confirmation.

The bishops of Corfu exploited the tax exemptions they enjoyed to build up the landed property of their church. It was a custom of longstanding at Corfu for the people to go to the metropolitan and request a grant of church land in exchange for double the equivalent of their own land. It may not have been quite so one-sided a deal as at first appears. The lay proprietors presumably enjoyed the tax advantages that went with episcopal property. Whether they also had rights of ownership over this property was not clear. The question was brought to John Apokaukos who thought that they had. Otherwise, it was a distinctly bad bargain.[20] This was an issue that might be expected to produce friction between the metropolitan of Corfu and the people of the island, but it also underlines how intertwined their interests were.

The surviving documentation for the church of Corfu from the twelfth and early thirteenth centuries offers a new perspective on the position of bishops in the Comnenian era. It underlines how deeply the fiscal privileges accorded to bishops affected relations with their clergy and with local leaders. It makes it easier to understand why Comnenian bishops should so often have been at loggerheads with their clergy and with local society. Members of the clergy objected to their reduction to dependent status. Local landowners cast envious eyes on episcopal property. The difficulties produced were resolved in various ways. The creation of colleges of priests seems to have been unique to Corfu. Their privileges afforded them protection against their bishop, but they still had to contend against local landowners. We find John Apokaukos placing one of the leading families of Corfu – the Primmikeriopouloi – under the ban of the church for usurping the rights of the clergy of Corfu.[21]

By and large the arrangements arrived at in Corfu appear to have worked in the sense that Bardanes seems to have had very little trouble from local people. Only one incident suggests that all was not well between Bardanes and his flock. John Apokaukos heard a rumour that there was a young man of Corfu who started recounting the terrible visions vouchsafed him: he claimed to have seen Bardanes being punished for the way he had drunkenly abused God on earth and to have been told that before Bardanes died he would make a distribution of his goods.[22] Ramblings of this kind were one way in which an attack might be mounted on a bishop. The experience of one of Bardanes's colleagues, the bishop of Khimara, shows how covetous local people

20 Papadopoulos-Kerameus 'ΚΕΡΚΥΡΑΙΚΑ', no.9, 348–9.

21 Apokaukos I, no.115, 242–3.

22 Papadopoulos-Kerameus, 'ΚΕΡΚΥΡΑΙΚΑ', no.2, 336–8.

were of episcopal property. The bishop fell into a coma. After five days and nights had passed he was given up for dead. He finally regained consciousness and found that some of the property of his church had been dispersed in gifts to the poor. This was what custom demanded on the death of a bishop, but much more of the church's property had just been seized by the 'common and unruly people'.[23]

Bardanes was a figure of some importance in the ecclesiastical politics of the day. The rulers of Epiros appreciated his abilities. His reward was the chrysobull that Theodore Angelus issued for his church in 1228, confirming its privileges. Bardanes had it inscribed in stone.[24] Government service often called him away from his see. In 1231 and again in 1235 he spent considerable time in Italy on diplomatic business. On his return from his second visit he found Corfu under threat almost certainly from Michael II Angelus, the new ruler of Epiros. Nominally, the island was still under the rule of the latter's uncle, the Despot Manuel Angelus of Thessalonica. Bardanes was put in charge of the defence. He carried out an array of the inhabitants living both inside and outside the town. He made some effort to repair the cisterns in the fortress. He reported that the walls were in a state of readiness and the harbour defences would soon be completed.[25] But it never came to a fight. By December 1236 Corfu had been surrendered to Michael Angelus. The price was a chrysobull confirming the privileges of the Corfiots.[26] No corresponding chrysobull for the church of Corfu has survived. It was specified though that the dependants of the metropolitan bishop of Corfu would enjoy exemption from the payment of customs duties along with the other inhabitants of the island. But there were still troubles to come. The arrival of Michael Angelus's agent was awaited with apprehension. Bardanes mentions some kind of a public meeting which recommended making overtures to Michael Angelus: Bardanes and the leaders both of the town and of those outside were instructed to write to him and urge him to restrain his agent. If not, there was likely to be resistance to his measures. Bardanes insisted that the Corfiots were more audacious than the normal run of people and capable of defying their ruler.[27]

These events show Bardanes in a new but scarcely unexpected light. At a time of crisis, he prepared the city for a siege. In the aftermath he represented the interests of the local inhabitants but in concert

23 Apokaukos I, no.20, 81–2.

24 Martin, 'Inscription grecque'; Miklosich & Müller V, 14–15.

25 J.M. Hoeck & R.J. Loenertz, *Nikolaos-Nektarios von Otranto, Abt von Casole. Beitrage zur Geschichte der ost-westlichen Beziehungen unter Innozenz III. und Friedrich II.* (Studia Patristica et Byzantina, II) (Ettal 1965), no.23, 223–5.

26 Lemerle, 'Trois actes', 414–18.

27 Hoeck and Loenertz, *Nikolaos-Nektarios von Otranto*, no.26, 229–30.

with their archontes. Bardanes was acting as a bishop should: as the leader and the spokesman of the community. Perhaps this was easier for a metropolitan bishop of Corfu than for some others. The existence of the colleges of priests defined his relationship with his clergy, while landowning arrangements gave him a shared interest with the archontic families of the island.

12

DEMETRIUS CHOMATIANOS

DEMETRIUS Chomatianos was a younger contemporary of John Apokaukos, who recalled their student days together at Constantinople.[1] Apokaukos seemed the one destined for the more brilliant future. He entered the patriarchal administration and then received the metropolitan throne of Naupaktos. Chomatianos had to make his career in the autocephalous church of Bulgaria. He served first as the archbishop's *apokrisarios* or representative at Constantinople before being appointed (*c.* 1200) *chartophylax* of the church of Bulgaria. But it was not until 1217 that Theodore Angelus promoted him to the archiepiscopal throne. Theodore's action had the full support of John Apokaukos. Chomatianos's success as archbishop of Bulgaria owed much to Apokaukos's loyalty.

The autocephalous status of the church of Bulgaria was a matter of some importance in the confused political situation that followed the conquest of Constantinople by the Latins in 1204. In the first place, Demetrius Chomatianos found that large areas of his church were controlled by the Serbs and the Bulgarians, who were creating their own ecclesiastical organisations. One of his concerns was to vindicate the traditional rights of his church. If Demetrius Chomatianos never recovered all the suffragan sees lost to the Serbs and Bulgarians, his authority in practice came to extend over the churches within the territories of Theodore Angelus. These included metropolitan churches that lay outside the traditional boundaries of the church of Bulgaria: Naupaktos, Corfu, Larissa, Thessalonica. The patriarch in exile at Nicaea objected to this. Demetrius Chomatianos became the spokesman for the autonomy of the church in the West. In 1227 he crowned and anointed Theodore Angelus emperor at Thessalonica. To complement this new imperial order he sought patriarchal status for his church. These ambitions dissolved with Theodore's defeat and capture by the Bulgarian Tsar John Asen in 1230 and the church in Epiros

[1] Papadopoulos-Kerameus, 'Συμβολή', 248.2–13.

was rapidly brought back under the patriarchate at Nicaea. Demetrius Chomatianos died in 1235. His church still possessed autocephalous status, but this meant less and less, once the Serbian church was consolidated and a Bulgarian patriarchate created in 1235.

Demetrius Chomatianos's legacy was a series of legal works. The most extensive consisted of cases and queries that were brought before his court. There are nearly 150 of them. They are certainly not a register as such. The exact purpose and the date are still unclear. They are arranged very roughly according to subject matter. They start with a series of cases dealing with aspects of marriage. There follow property disputes that arose out of marriage, whether because of a second marriage or simply over the disposition of a dowry. Then come property disputes, usually involving uncertainty about validity of documents or the absence of documents. Next, there is a shift to cases involving the clergy in one way or another. Then it is the turn of the weak, 'since God has ordained the great bishops like you as a refuge for orphans, victims of injustice, and the defenceless'.[2] Thereafter, there is very little clear order: it looks as though a series of cases have been tacked on to the original work. This suggests that there was an attempt to bring the work up to date, by adding new material. This seems to have been done after Chomatianos's death.[3] The Byzantine lawbook it most resembles is the *Peira*, where cases coming before the court of the hippodrome were noted and used to exemplify Byzantine legal practice of the early eleventh century.[4] There is no way of telling whether Demetrius Chomatianos intended something of the sort, but his record of cases provides a very good guide to the practice of his court. It would have been equally useful for his successors or for other bishops. It provides the most detailed evidence of the cases that came before an episcopal court. Its value is impaired because once again it is a unique survival.

The circumstances of the church of Bulgaria and its archbishop were rather different, at least to all appearances, in Chomatianos's time from those existing in the twelfth century under his great predecessor Theophylact of Bulgaria. There was, in the first place, a ruler with imperial claims on the spot. This would mean that Chomatianos came to assume more of a patriarchal role than his predecessors: he was consulted by the ruler and his aristocracy over various problems and his court acted as a court of appeal for a wider area than previously. Demetrius Chomatianos was also by any standards a remarkable occupant of the throne of Bulgaria. There is a temptation to see him

[2] Chomatianos, c.370.

[3] Ibid., c.526.

[4] See N. Oikonomidès, 'The Peira of Eustathios Romaios: an abortive attempt to innovate in Byzantine law', *FM* 7(1986), 169–92.

as another Theophylact, but their writings are so different that it is scarcely possible to make a direct comparison. Theophylact – his successors too for that matter – was a competent administrator, but he was not a lawyer. His consuming interest was Biblical exegesis. He was appointed to the church of Bulgaria because, like many of his successors, he had influential connections. Chomatianos, by contrast, does not seem to have been well connected. He was, first and foremost, a lawyer, who saw the need for clear statements of how the law stood over a number of topics. He also recognised the value of a guide to court practice at a time when the fall of Constantinople to the Latins threatened Byzantium's legal and educational traditions. Although necessity might occasionally lead to innovation, Chomatianos's intentions were conservative: to preserve the law as it had been taught at Constantinople when he was a student. It is possible that in the aftermath of the Latin conquest of Constantinople and the dislocation it brought there was a greater reliance on the ecclesiastical courts in the lands controlled by the rulers of Epiros. But by the time Demetrius Chomatianos became archbishop of Bulgaria the ruler of 'Epiros' had his own tribunal, while the system of local government and courts based on the themes had been restored much as it had been before 1204. The Latin conquest of Constantinople produced a hiatus, rather than any clear break. It meant that Chomatianos's activities as archbishop of Bulgaria were different from those of his predecessors, but not all that different. His predecessors would have dealt with the duke of Bulgaria, whose powers, if not their pretensions, were in practice almost as extensive as those of the 'despots' of Epiros. The volume of cases that came before his court may have been greater than that dealt with by his predecessors, but their range was much the same.

Chomatianos's law court

Perhaps more clearly than any other source Demetrius Chomatianos's writings allow us to plumb the relationship of the secular and ecclesiastical courts at Byzantium. This has been the subject of a study by D. Simon.[5] His most surprising finding is how few were the judgements that Chomatianos gave. In only roughly a third of the cases that came before him did he give judgement and most of these related to marriage suits. It was partly that he would only give judgement if both parties to a lawsuit were present. In the majority of cases he provided an opinion. This was a practice that we have already noted in the twelfth century, when it was often the case that parties went to the patriarchal synod to obtain an opinion, which might later be presented to a different court,

5 D. Simon, 'Byzantinische Provinzialjustiz', *BZ* 79(1986), 310–43.

civil or ecclesiastical. Many of the cases that came before him were brought from other courts. One of the parties might want a decision made in another court confirmed. Alternatively he might want to contest it. In the circumstances of the time recourse to the court of the archbishop of Bulgaria was the best solution. There were also cases that were sent to Demetrius Chomatianos either by the ruler or by a provincial governor. Equally, there were cases that Chomatianos would refer back to the ruler's court. There is very little sign of any serious rivalry between the secular and ecclesiastical courts. There is instead cooperation.

It was based on two considerations. The first is that there was a very rough division of competence. Cases touching upon marriage or involving the clergy or the weak and defenceless normally went to the ecclesiastical court; as did cases which were amenable to ecclesiastical punishments because there was a spiritual dimension to them. The most obvious were those involving manslaughter rather than murder. It has been argued that even so this represented a marked increase of ecclesiastical jurisdiction. In the *Peira* marriage was seen as falling within the competence of the civil courts. Despite Alexius Comnenus's ruling that marriage belonged to the ecclesiastical courts, there is plenty of evidence that throughout the twelfth century marriage suits still came before the civil courts. This should not disguise the fact that the church had steadily been extending its control in this area. The circumstances of the Latin conquest may only have facilitated the completion of a development already far advanced before 1204. Similarly, it has been argued that in cases of manslaughter the church extended its control because it could offer penance instead of the more serious penalties that the civil courts prescribed.[6] Demetrius Chomatianos was well aware that ecclesiastical penalties were much less severe than those of a civil court.[7] Like John Apokaukos he took those subject to penance under the protection of the church and forbad imperial officials to take any action against them.

Professor Simon may be quite correct from a strictly legal point of view, when he argues that Chomatianos was not trying to substitute ecclesiastical penalties for civil ones; that he sought only to complement the work of the civil courts. However, the legal point of view is rarely the most important. Practically speaking, there was much to gain from going to an ecclesiastical court. Normally, it was the litigants who decided where to take their cases. Not only might they expect more humane justice from the ecclesiastical courts. There are also reasons for believing that the ecclesiastical courts had a better

[6] Ibid., 315–16.

[7] Chomatianos, no.27, 119–24.

chance of enforcing their decisions. The first essential was always to get the parties to accept a judgement. This was frequently a matter of reconciling the parties on the basis of a judgement, or even opinion, delivered. The moral authority of an episcopal court was often the best means of achieving this, especially where the crime or the quarrel was seen to have a moral or a spiritual dimension.

If the Byzantines appear a litigious people, it was only because they took their troubles to a court, rather than relying on self-help. Byzantine society was also a literate society which took care to document its activities. At most levels of society there was a respect for official documentation, be it a will, a dowry, or a marriage contract. In one case,[8] which is to be dated to 1220, the following documents were produced: a marriage contract of 1167, a receipt for a dowry of 1168, a judgement made by the duke of Skopia of 1193, and another from a Constantinopolitan law court from the reign of Alexius III Angelus (1195–1203). The petitioner came from an archontic family and possessed a private archive on which he could draw. Lower down the social scale there were fewer such resources, but documents were still respected and constituted the most powerful evidence available. There was always the danger of forgery and Demetrius Chomatianos's court was quite capable of testing the validity of documents produced in evidence. There is no reason to suppose that a civil court was not equally capable of doing this. However, the drawing up of official documents came increasingly within the church's competence. The notarial organisation was annexed to the local episcopal church.[9]

The problems are apparent from another case that came before Demetrius Chomatianos which turned on the validity of a will.[10] One party produced a copy, but without the signatures of witnesses. The other produced the original. The notary responsible for drawing up the original will was contacted to give his opinion about how genuine the documents were. Another case equally turned on the validity of a document, which was challenged for two reasons: it had not been signed by the local *taboullarios* or notary nor had it been confirmed by the then metropolitan bishop of Corfu, where this particular case had originated. Demetrius Chomatianos intervened, like the good lawyer he was, to indicate that there were circumstances when these were not necessary for the validity of a document. It so happened that at the time that the document was drawn up the metropolitan was away on a mission to Rome and the local notary was dead.[11] In another dispute –

[8] Ibid., no.59, 261–8.

[9] Darrouzès, *OFFIKIA*, 120–1, 258–9, 379–85; M.J. Angold, *A Byzantine Government in Exile* (Oxford, 1975), 261–2, 273–4.

[10] Chomatianos, no.31, 135–42.

[11] Ibid., no.36, 153–60.

over property belonging to a wife, who had died – the widower presented their marriage agreement, but backed up by a written statement of its authenticity signed by two bishops.[12] Bishops might also collect evidence. There is a case where the decisive evidence consisted of episcopal affidavits containing the sworn testimony of witnesses.[13]

If documents were lacking, then there was recourse to evidence given on oath. There was a case taken first to the ruler's court which turned on the details of a mother's dowry, but the son could not produce the document. The parties to the disputed property agreed before Theodore Angelus that they would accept the sworn evidence of an old man, who was the paternal uncle of one of the parties. The ruler then sent them to their local governor with instructions that the oath was to be administered by the metropolitan bishop. Once again, the case originated from Corfu. In due course, the business was transacted in the presence of the duke of the island and 'trustworthy people' by the metropolitan in his cathedral. The case would be reopened and would eventually come before Demetrius Chomatianos who approved the procedure.[14] The administration of oaths gave the bishop great power.

At this time, the validity of the ordeal by hot iron began to be debated. This practice seeped into Byzantium from the West in the aftermath of 1204.[15] It had considerable implications for the church, since to be efficacious it had to be approved and administered by the church. Chomatianos was the first to examine the problem within the framework of Byzantine law. He considered that there was a danger that it might supplant or dilute the oath. He insisted on the absolute validity of the oath. It did not need to be supported or supplemented by an ordeal. He gave the following grounds for this opinion: the ordeal was a barbarian custom and not known to Byzantine law, civil or canon.[16]

Over the ordeal Demetrius Chomatianos could pose as the upholder of proper Byzantine procedures, whether it was a matter of the proper administration of the oath or the use of written evidence. In another case, he defended the sanctity of wills. The provisions of a will had been overturned by Bulgarian justice. 'Is there anybody with any nous who would countenance this as having any legality?' Demetrius Chomatianos thundered. He went on: 'Given that the Bulgarians are utter barbarians, incapable of appreciating Roman law, for to the barbarian law consists of personal desire, how could a barbarian implement

12 Ibid., no.102, 433–8.
13 Ibid., no.37, 159–64.
14 Ibid., no.90, 397–402.
15 See M.J. Angold, 'The interaction of Latins and Byzantines during the period of the Latin Empire. The case of the ordeal', *Actes du XVe Congrès international des études byzantines*, IV (Athens, 1980), 1–10.
16 Chomatianos, no.87, 389–92; no.127, 525–8.

legal procedures laid down by our pious laws?'[17] Under Chomatianos's guidance the church came out as the defender of Byzantine traditions against the barbarians. The ecclesiastical courts rejected the use of the ordeal. It was only employed by the secular courts. This must have given an edge to the moral authority enjoyed by the church.

It would have enhanced more practical considerations, such as the large measure of control that the church exercised over the means of proof employed in Byzantine courts, both lay and ecclesiastical. We have seen the role it had in the drawing up of all kinds of documents and in the administration of oaths. Although there are no examples from the cases cited by Demetrius Chomatianos, it was, as a further precaution, possible to have documents registered in the episcopal court. These must all have been factors that would have weighed fairly heavily with litigants, when they came to decide which court to choose. As one petitioner confessed, he was taking his case to Demetrius Chomatianos because his court had a reputation for swift justice (*euthydikia*). Once again it turned on the validity of a document: had an earlier will been overturned by one made on a man's deathbed? How much weight could be placed on testimony that the dying man had expressed no intention of making a new will?[18] It would seem that ecclesiastical courts were coming to have a special competence where the validity and authenticity of documents were concerned. Did this mean that the variety of business coming before them continued to grow? It is a reasonable assumption.

As interesting as the variety of business is the social range of the petitioners and litigants who laid their problems before Demetrius Chomatianos. There are eleven examples of rulers having recourse to Demetrius Chomatianos for advice; twenty of members of the lay aristocracy; twenty-three, if soldiers are included. Twenty-one involved bishops or their officials and twenty-three monks and members of the clergy. Twenty-seven petitioners were farmers or peasants; twenty-three townsmen and craftsmen. Eleven cases were brought by women, though they might be represented by male relatives. It is a broad cross-section of society.

The variety of business, the social range of the litigants, and their reasons for taking their cases before an episcopal court all testify to an attitude of lay society towards the church. It can be summed up as a belief in the church and the church courts as the guardian of a moral and social order. The range of business was largely a matter of cases with a moral and spiritual content, but this applied to a wide variety of cases. The church was seen as having a special responsibility for

[17] Ibid., c.361.
[18] Ibid., no.65, 285–90.

the weak in society. Where the church was breaking new ground was in testing the validity of documents. This seems to lie behind the large number of property disputes that came before Demetrius Chomatianos. Before 1204 such cases were more likely to have gone to the civil courts rather than to the ecclesiastical.

Ecclesiastical property

Property was an area where church and lay society were bound to come into contact. Churches and monasteries often passed into private hands, while bequests to churches and monasteries were a common act of piety. Piety could easily disadvantage a man's heirs. Chomatianos ordered that a bequest to a monastery should be overturned for just this reason and the property should be returned to the donor's son.[19] It was always possible for families to challenge or circumvent bequests to the church. Chomatianos heard a very complicated case, where a woman had left property that was to go to a church, but only after her husband's death. Her intention was to convert the church into a monastery. After her death her husband propositioned the local metropolitan bishop, who agreed that the husband should be allowed to buy back the property in question and thus frustrate his wife's plans. The purchase price presumably went to the metropolitan. The church never received its endowment. Demetrius Chomatianos declared the deal struck between the husband and the metropolitan null and void.[20] In another case a church formed part of a dowry. The wife died and so did the only child of the marriage. The husband restored the church which had suffered at the hands of the Bulgarians. He installed a priest-monk to celebrate the divine liturgy. Then with the consent of the local bishop he turned it into a monastery to preserve the memory of his wife and child. His sister-in-law challenged this on the grounds that the property should have come to her, seeing that there was no surviving issue of the marriage. Demetrius Chomatianos refused to countenance this.[21] In this case Chomatianos did not challenge the validity of a church forming part of a dowry and therefore in lay possession, but on another occasion, where a church was in private hands, he gave it as his opinion that under no circumstances should a church be private property.[22]

There were similar problems with monasteries. Demetrius Chomatianos impressed upon the newly appointed abbot of the monastery of St Demetrius at Glabinitza the need to keep his monks free of worldly

19 Ibid., no.24, 101–4.
20 Ibid., no.101, 429–34.
21 Ibid., no.48, 215–22.
22 Ibid., no.35, 149–52.

entanglements.[23] But abbots were not always to be trusted. There were cases where monasteries had no monks and the abbots allowed the buildings to fall down, while they retired to the nearest town, where they built a comfortable residence and enjoyed the revenues from the monastic estates. Any remonstration on the part of the local bishop was treated with contempt because these abbots considered that they were exempt from episcopal authority. Chomatianos naturally insisted that monasteries were subject to the authority of the local bishop.[24] However hard prelates, such as Demetrius Chomatianos, upheld the rights of bishops over churches and monasteries within their sees, the truth is that it was impossible to eradicate the existence of private churches or the secularisation of monasteries.

Monasteries could be used to challenge the authority of the local bishop, as the following episode shows. Vlach shepherds had built a church at their own expense and the local bishop appointed a priest to officiate, but the village was granted to a monastery, which insisted that the Vlachs should worship in the monastery church. It was there that their weddings and their baptisms took place. They paid nothing in *kanonikon* to the bishop. This was not unique. The bishop who brought the case to Demetrius Chomatianos remembered another incident where a predecessor of his had built a parish church, but the local archon had promptly built another, but directly subject to the patriarch of Constantinople; this was done deliberately to exclude episcopal authority. Demetrius Chomatianos judged that subjection to the patriarch of Constantinople was honorific. It did not rule out the local bishop's authority. He still had a responsibility to supervise the marriages contracted within his diocese. Equally, parishioners had a duty to make their yearly offerings to the bishop.[25] This case reveals the competition there was for control over parish churches between the local bishop, on the one hand, and monasteries and archontes, on the other. The dues paid to the church must have been a major consideration, but it was also a part of the management of their estates by monasteries and lay landowners.

Chomatianos and the clergy

The impression is that Chomatianos paid relatively little attention to the problems facing the church at parish level. This can be explained by a failure on the part of the Byzantine church to evolve any coherent parish organisation. It was a sphere best left to suffragan bishops

[23] Ibid., no.147, 569–72.
[24] Ibid., no.77, 329–34.
[25] Ibid., no.80, 339–50.

who understood local arrangements. We know of only a single case involving a village priest which came before Chomatianos's court. It revolved around a priest who made himself lord (*exarkhon/dynastes*) of a village. He used his power to oppress the villagers and extort property from them.[26] He had clearly exceeded his powers and responsibilities in so flagrant a way that the archbishop had to intervene. This case nevertheless underlines how influential priests could be in village life. They were prominent members of the village court of *oikodespotai* (or heads of households), which supervised the affairs of a village. The village priest may have been one of the enduring strengths of orthodoxy, but his life is almost entirely hidden from us.

If a priest could oppress his flock, priests in their turn might find themselves exploited by their bishop. Demetrius Chomatianos discovered that one of his suffragans, the bishop of Pelagonia, was at odds with the priests of his diocese. It was the custom of the church of Pelagonia – and presumably in other churches too – for the priests to make a contribution in kind at harvest time to the bishop. Servants of the bishop had taken to demanding more and more of the priests. Chomatianos intervened. He regularised these customary payments according to the size of each priest's property.[27] These corresponded to the holdings of the prosperous peasantry.[28]

Chomatianos showed a surprising lack of interest in church life at the parish level, beyond, that is, protecting the clergy from extortionate demands, but without jeopardising the church's revenues. This was not an easy balancing act. Income emerges as the major concern of the instructions which Chomatianos drew up for a newly appointed *protopappas*. They have little to say about spiritual responsibilities; much more about the need to forward the revenues of the church to the local bishop. Chomatianos may have warned the *protopappas* against increasing them unjustly, but equally he was not to allow them to diminish. It was also important to maintain the dignity of his office and to ensure the respect due to it from priests, people, and lay authorities alike.[29]

Chomatianos had several ends in mind. He was acting against fiscal oppression on the part of the church, whether by priests or bishops. He also understood how important it was that ecclesiastical revenues should not be eroded. These concerns connected with a keen regard for the dignity of the priesthood. Chomatianos knew how serious a matter loss of clerical status was. One case he heard concerned a

[26] Ibid., no.94, 409–12.
[27] Ibid., no.148, 571–6.
[28] Priests were divided into *zeugaratoi* and *boidatoi*, in the same way as peasants were for tax purposes.
[29] Ibid., no.149, 575–6 .

deacon who was a member of the cathedral clergy of Ioannina. The man had previously brought a financial suit against a layman, who had cleared himself in a secular court through the ordeal by hot iron, thus laying his opponent open to the charge of false accusation. The deacon was now alarmed that such a charge, if proved, would deprive him of his clerical status. Chomatianos was able to reassure him that the ordeal by hot iron had no legal validity and that therefore he had nothing to worry about.[30] Demetrius Chomatianos was reluctant to defrock. When a priest-monk came before him confessing that he had been guilty both of theft and perjury, he prescribed penance, but left the question of whether he should be defrocked to his synod.[31] He found it even more difficult to deal with sinful monks, because being a monk was the ultimate penance! A bishop consulted him about two of his clergy. One had killed a neighbour with a slingshot, pretending that he was protecting himself against a pack of dogs. The other had helped man the walls of the city and had killed many of the enemy with his arrows. Chomatianos agreed that both had deliberately killed their fellow men and that they should be defrocked.[32] Where it was less clear that killing had been intentional Chomatianos usually defended any clergy involved and tried to protect them against the action of the lay authorities.[33]

Generally speaking, Chomatianos saw the defence of the clergy as part of his responsibilities. The *chartophylax* of the church of Drama was sentenced quite unjustly by the local governor to pay a fine. His refusal to pay led to beatings and finally the compulsory purchase of a vineyard belonging to him. Chomatianos agreed that it had been done under duress and had no legality. Whether the *chartophylax* ever recovered his vineyard is not recorded.[34] Poverty was another form of pressure bearing on members of the clergy. There was an impoverished priest from Berroia who had fallen into the hands of a moneylender. He had borrowed two gold pieces, promising to provide in return ten *modioi* of wheat at the end of three months. As surety he put up the produce of a vineyard belonging to him, but with the additional safeguard that if this did not suffice, the moneylender would be compensated from the remainder of the priest's property. The harvest failed and the priest could not pay back the loan in the way agreed. The moneylender demanded that he should now be owed six gold pieces. This was an impossibility, so the moneylender took the case to the court of the local *praktor* or government agent, who found

30 Ibid., no.87, 389–92.
31 Ibid., no.88, 391–4.
32 Ibid., no.75, 323–6.
33 Ibid., no.76, 325–8.
34 Ibid., no.96, 413–16.

against the priest and clapped him in jail. To get out the priest agreed in writing that the moneylender should have the vineyard. Poverty now condemned him to a wandering life that lasted for seven years. Chomatianos decided that the property had been extorted from the priest and ordered that it should be returned to him.[35] This case reveals that, however hard bishops tried to maintain the dignity of the priesthood, priests faced much the same difficulties as other cultivators of the soil. Like many peasants this priest was anticipating his harvest with unfortunate results.

The clergy were not immune either from life's temptations or hard knocks. A priest would have as much difficulty as anyone else in safeguarding the rights of succession of a young son. From the church of Ohrid came the case of the son of a priest trying to recover his inheritance. The problem was that part of it had purportedly been sold off to pay the taxes due on it. Though the facts of the matter were not absolutely clear, Chomatianos gave it as his opinion that this should not have been done, since the plaintiff had then been under age.[36] Chomatianos felt that a bishop had a special duty to protect the rights of orphans. This sense of responsibility can only have increased when it involved the son of a priest of his church.

Chomatianos's dossier reveals a situation reminiscent in many ways of medieval Russia, where groups known as 'church people' came under the special protection of the church. They included the poor, debtors, even the sons of priests who had failed to follow in their fathers' footsteps.[37] Their status was enshrined in law, which was not the case at Byzantium. But to judge by the cases that came before Chomatianos the church still acquired a special responsibility for these kinds of people.

At Byzantium there may not have been any rigid separation of church and secular society. The clergy may never have acquired hereditary, let alone caste, status, but there were, as we have seen, pressures in this direction. Theodore Balsamon disapproved, but only because it was reminiscent of the custom in the Armenian church.[38] Otherwise he might have been more sympathetic. In practice, the orthodox clergy in Byzantium often formed a distinct group in local society. It is surprising how often one finds the clergy intermarrying, to form what can only be called priestly families.[39] This was particularly the case with the cathedral clergy.[40]

35 Ibid., no.92, 403–8.
36 Ibid., no.73, 319–22.
37 G. Vernadsky, *Kievan Russia* (New Haven, 1948), 151–4.
38 Rhalles & Potles II, 380.
39 Chomatianos, no.98, 417–20.
40 Ibid., no.66, 289–94.

Chomatianos reveals some of the contradictory trends of Byzantine society. He wanted to protect the dignity and the interests of the clergy and to ensure that they formed a distinct group within society. His justification would be that this was necessary if the clergy was to carry out its spiritual and pastoral duties. Chomatianos never forgot the church's social responsibilities. He showed a real concern for the poor and disadvantaged whom he tried to protect through due process of law. But this had much wider repercussions, because the advantages offered by the ecclesiastical courts were not lost on society at large. Chomatianos found himself dealing with a growing volume of judicial business, which had little to do with the church or clergy or even the poor. This might seem to defeat the separation of judicial competence that canon law envisaged, but it brought church and lay society together in a harmonious community of interest. Counterbalancing this was the age-old interpenetration of lay and ecclesiastical property. This continued to produce friction between the church and lay interests.

Conclusion: a profile of a Comnenian bishop

No more than a partial portrait emerges of each of the bishops we have examined. Their dossiers reveal not only a limited range of their experience, but for the most part different aspects of their life and work. Only Theophylact of Bulgaria and Michael Choniates have left dossiers that are in any way comparable. These consist of a mixture of public and private correspondence which illustrate their activities as a pastor. They have much in common. Both strive to protect the interests of their church against the imperial administration and local ambitions. They work in a similar fashion. They exploit their extensive contacts throughout the Byzantine establishment. There are some similarities with the dossiers of Michael Italikos and George Tornikes, which are again made up of public and private correspondence, but with more in the way of official speeches. Unfortunately very little of their correspondence and none of their speeches relate to their time as bishops, possibly because they did not survive very long in office. Eustathius, in contrast, was archbishop of Thessalonica for nearly twenty years, but his correspondence only survives in a fragmentary form. Few of his letters come from his time at Thessalonica. His dossier is *sui generis*: it takes the form of sermons and other treatises. Their great value lies in the way that they are largely directed to his flock and therefore central to his role as bishop of a great city. They illustrate a different side of a bishop's activities. They underline the tensions there were between a bishop and the local community. A quite different impression emerges from Chomatianos's dossier. It consists of his legal works and a selection of cases that came before his court. It is a unique survival and illustrates yet another aspect of a bishop's responsibilities. The only dossier with any claims to completeness is that of John Apokaukos. Much of his correspondence, both official and private, has survived. Also preserved are some of his judicial decisions, so that we have an idea of the work of his court. These dossiers may illuminate different sides of a bishop's work. They may reflect differences of temperament and ability; circumstances and experience. But they also complement one another. There are enough common features uniting our bishops to attempt a profile of a Comnenian bishop, or rather of a certain rather grand Comnenian bishop. They all held metropolitan or autocephalous sees. There are no representatives among them of the more humble sort of bishop. Their experience is more or less irrecoverable for our period.

Our bishops all had a similar kind of background – even George Bardanes. If it were not for the fall of Constantinople in 1204 it is most likely that he would have gone to the capital to make his career, like his master Michael Choniates. Bardanes was the son of a local bishop and had the backing of his metropolitan. Choniates's origins were also provincial. He came from a border town in Anatolia. He too had the support of the metropolitan. In fact, all the bishops, Eustathius excepted, had provincial origins or connections. Tornikes was born in Thebes, even if his family was quite grand. Theophylact came from Euboea. But they went to Constantinople to complete their education. This was the old story of able young men from respectable provincial families being drawn to the capital. High birth was not an essential, though it helped at the beginning of a career. George Tornikes rose rapidly thanks in part to his connections. Equally, John Apokaukos profited from having an uncle who was a bishop. Eustathius alone seems to have come from quite a modest background, but he found a patron, who engineered his entry into the patriarchal administration. Normally this was the most important step, for it opened up the path to high office within the church. Chomatianos was unlucky and had to be content with a position in the church of Bulgaria, which was very much second best. The patriarchal clergy was conscious of forming an elite. Its members belonged to the Byzantine establishment. They built up extensive contacts both within the church and at court and in government, which might serve them in good stead.

The patriarchal administration began to emerge as a force within the church in the late eleventh century. The power it wielded was a new feature of the Comnenian period. Its chief exponent in the twelfth century was Theodore Balsamon. He found in the cardinals of the Roman church a fitting analogy with the officers of the patriarchal church. It was an expression of a sense of *esprit de corps*. Under the

Comneni the patriarchal administration became a nursery of metropolitan bishops. It is notable how many of the major sees of the church of Constantinople went to members of the patriarchal administration. It is likely that the calibre of the episcopal bench improved as a result.

Elites need ideals to justify their assumption of power. Our bishops brought with them from Constantinople a very clear concept of episcopal authority and responsibilities. They saw themselves as the upholders of an ideal order, in which justice prevailed and the poor and disadvantaged were protected. The well-being of society was the responsibility of the bishop. It could be obtained through exhortation, through the use of influence, and through the exercise of a bishop's moral and judicial authority. The ideal was scarcely new. Its roots certainly go back to the Cappadocian Fathers and John Chrysostom in the fourth century, but it was given clearer shape and renewed emphasis in the course of the eleventh century. As Christopher Walter has shown, it is best caught in the art of the time. It celebrates the bishop as a teacher and as a mediator with Christ through the eucharist. The triumphalism of the iconography places the bishop at the very centre of Christian society. The ideal may have been unrealistic, but it certainly inspired. It was nurtured in the comfort and safety of the capital. It had as its corollary the freedom of the church and clergy from secular interference and control. It went counter to the happy mingling of church and lay society that had in the past been one of Byzantium's strengths. The emergence of a new elite is always disruptive. Its imposition in the provinces would always be difficult. The Comnenian bishops challenged too many local interests for the sake of their ideal which demanded that the clergy and church function as a separate element in local society.

In an earlier period the Byzantine bishop may have had an easier time. His role was less ambitious and more restricted. This was in keeping with the limited development of urban life. Before the eleventh century it was a matter of Constantinople and a handful of provincial centres. In such circumstances a bishop need not be rich and powerful to act as the leader of local society. He was regarded as an asset. The local community benefited from his spiritual wisdom, from his organisation of religious life, and from such wealth as his church possessed. The bishop also represented its interests with the imperial administration and was a channel of communication with Constantinople. There are examples of bishops being chased out of their sees. Twice in the ninth century the people of Athens rose up against their archbishop, but these incidents were extremely rare. Mutual toleration was more the order of the day, even if it sometimes turned to indifference.

A Comnenian bishop was less likely to come to such an easy understanding with his flock. Part of his task, after all, was to vindicate the independence of his church. The new ideal did not automatically mean jettisoning the old functions. There was no clear break with the past. The most successful Comnenian bishops knew how to respect the traditions of their church. They continued to act as orchestrators of the local cult. As often as not, it was veneration for a patron saint which gave some cohesion to local society; to set against the competition and envy which were otherwise its dominant characteristics. This was still the case at Thessalonica early in the twelfth century, as we learn from the *Timarion*. The satire begins with a description of the city. The author sketches the famous fair of St Demetrius and then goes on to describe the religious festivities. The feast of St Demetrius was celebrated with three all-night vigils. Two choirs chanted hymns in honour of the patron saint of the city. The presiding figure was the archbishop who was there conducting the ceremony. The high point was the arrival of the governor of the city at the church of St Demetrius. He was acclaimed by the people and then received into the church by the archbishop.[41]

Local susceptibilities must have been pricked at Thessalonica when in 1149 Manuel Comnenus approved the removal to the Pantokrator monastery at Constantinople of the image of St Demetrius which had covered his coffin. The emperor's offer of a new – 'much superior' – icon in its place was not likely to have been appreciated.[42] The incident reveals the lack of sensitivity to local sensibilities in Constantinopolitan circles. It was an attitude of mind which Eustathius took with him to Thessalonica. He paid little attention to the cult of St Demetrius.[43] He preferred instead to introduce festivals and cults that smacked of Constantinople. This was unlikely to endear him to the people of Thessalonica and may help to explain his uneasy relationship with the people of Thessalonica. It only emphasised his role as an agent of Constantinople.

Others were less tactless. Both Theophylact and Chomatianos were exponents of the cult of St Clement, the founder of the church of Ohrid. Theophylact was the author of the major *Life* of St Clement, while Chomatianos produced an *epitome*.[44] At Athens Michael Choniates understood the importance of popular processions and festivities. He also acted as the spokesman of the local community. He received the imperial governors sent out to Greece and made known the needs and

41 [Pseudo-] Lucian, *Timarion*, ed. R. Romano (Naples, 1974), 53–9.

42 Papadopoulos-Kerameus, ΑΝΑΛΕΚΤΑ, IV, 239–42. See Magdalino, *Manuel I Komnenos*, 178–9.

43 Eustathius tried to promote the cult of the obscure Kalytenoi brothers supposedly martyred under Diocletian. Their chapel happened to form part of the archiepiscopal palace: Eustathius I, 30–7.

44 Obolensky, *Six Byzantine Portraits*, 71–7.

discontents of the people of Athens. He even petitioned the emperor in the interests of his flock. He used his network of contacts in the capital on their behalf. Michael Choniates was an exemplary archbishop. He seems to have avoided the friction that characterised Eustathius's relations with his charges. But there were underlying tensions which began to take shape just before the Latin conquest. Choniates had to defend Athens against the dynast of the Argolid Leo Sgouros. He was acting as leader of his community, but it is clear that some of the *kastrenoi* of Athens sympathised with Sgouros.

The *kastrenoi* of Ohrid were the bane of Theophylact's life; and their equivalents at Thessalonica plagued Eustathius. *Kastrenoi* is only a convenient term for the local elite who normally resided in the *kastron* or acropolis of a city. Why should Comnenian bishops have so often been at loggerheads with their *kastrenoi*? This contrasts with the generally good relations which existed earlier between the bishop and the local community. Any tensions there may have been in the ninth century seem to have evaporated once a regular system of provincial administration based on the themes was functioning properly. Imperial authority was exercised through the armies of the themes. This allowed the bishop to dominate urban life, such as it was, from his cathedral. There was a rough division of competence. Before the eleventh century most cathedral cities were at best market towns. But Byzantine provincial society was changing rapidly. Cities began to grow and ceased to be episcopal preserves. The character of local government altered. Imperial authority was channelled through the cities rather than through the armies of the themes, which became less important. One result was increased friction between bishops and imperial governors. Bishops also had to contend with powerful local families, who served in the imperial administration and who often had an interest in the episcopal clergy and estates. Bishops might either find themselves out of their depth or more probably come to terms with the new conditions; support the activities of the local administration and tolerate private interests in the episcopal administration.

They might even connive at the way more and more of the monasteries under their control were passing into private hands. Monasteries were always a contentious issue. It was not simply that they were often richly endowed. It was also that they were the main focuses of Byzantine piety. They concentrated great material and spiritual power. There are plenty of instances of a local magnate or an imperial governor oppressing a bishop and seizing episcopal estates, while at the same time richly endowing a monastery. The bishop was regarded as a public figure who might for one reason or another have to be coerced. The monastery was a private matter. It provided an appropriate medium of Christian piety.

To an extent this interpenetration of church and lay society had always been and continued to be the reality at Byzantium. But it did not conform to the ideal that crystallised in the eleventh century. The bishop's duty was to ensure that his church and clergy were clearly separate from lay society. Only then would the church have the independence of action and moral authority to carry out its mission to teach and minister and to maintain social justice. The ideal inevitably brought the bishops into conflict with local society. The attempt to extricate the church from the trammels of lay society was bound to be disruptive. Families who in one way or another had shared in the wealth of the church would find themselves under scrutiny.

The conflict that seems to characterise the relations of the Comnenian bishop and local administration and society can therefore be explained quite easily. It was partly a matter of the changing scale of urban society. It was also a growing unwillingness on the part of bishops to tolerate the old accommodations. Instead, there was more of an effort to impose episcopal authority on the local scene. This threatened established interests and was resented. This might bring the bishop into conflict with his cathedral clergy, who might have much to lose if their understanding with other local elites was questioned. Equally, the bishop might regard them as a fifth column within the church. The clergy had to learn that they formed an order distinct from lay society and that their first loyalty was to their bishop.

By the turn of the eleventh century any bishop who subscribed to the new ideal was almost certain to clash with local groups. Conflict is a property of change, but is in itself indicative neither of strength nor of weakness, neither of success nor of failure. The fact that a Comnenian bishop might find himself embroiled in petty hostilities cannot be taken as proof of the weakness of his position. It is true, however, that there were bishops and archbishops who were unequal to their task and were forced to resign their sees.[45] One such was Nicholas Mouzalon, later to become patriarch of Constantinople. In 1107 Alexius I Comnenus appointed him to the autocephalous archbishopric of Cyprus. Mouzalon had his misgivings. He was still comparatively young and inexperienced, but the emperor was not to be gainsaid. The church of Cyprus was in its way as important an appointment as that of the archbishopric of Bulgaria. The conquest of Jerusalem in 1099 and the creation of the crusader states turned Cyprus into a province of the greatest strategic importance to the Byzantine Empire. Nicholas

45 E.g. Nicholas, metropolitan of Corfu, who has left some iambic verses apologising to the patriarch and synod for resigning his see: S. P. Lampros, *ΚΕΡΚΥΡΑΙΚΑ ΑΝΕΚΔΟΤΑ* (Athens, 1882), 30–41. He does not specify the difficulties he had, but a later incumbent Basil Pediadites complained in exaggerated terms of the poverty of the see and the malice and ignorance of the Corfiots: ibid., 48–9.

Mouzalon was young and idealistic. He came under the influence of that saintly patriarch Nicholas Grammatikos. He was completely out of his depth. This we learn from the poem he wrote justifying his abdication from the archiepiscopal throne of Cyprus in 1111.[46]

He singles out one of the governors of the island, Eumathios Philokales, as the main cause of his miseries, but he was on bad terms with other governors and their officials.[47] They were at loggerheads over control of the Cypriot church. Mouzalon itemises five such incidents.[48] The first three concerned suffragan bishops. One was involved in tax collection. Mouzalon remonstrated with him. Tax collection was no part of the duties of a bishop. The bishop refused to mend his ways and turned to the governor of the island for protection. Mouzalon could do nothing.[49] Another suffragan was a boon companion of the governor. His way of life was unbecoming: he liked feasting and songs and dancing. He allowed games and festivals to be staged in church. Mouzalon removed him from office pending his appearance before synod. The governor replied by reinstating him.[50] Mouzalon did remove a third suffragan bishop from office by due process of canon law. It made little difference because he continued to occupy his see illegally.[51]

Mouzalon also sought to discipline a monk who had abandoned his vows and entered the service of a tax collector. He went once again to the governor of the island and was told to mind his own business.[52] The final incident concerned the abbot of one of the island's monasteries. Mouzalon had him convicted for some misdemeanour and ejected from the monastery. The ex-abbot immediately went to the chief tax collector for the island, who may well have been the governor, and bribed him to secure his reinstatement. Mouzalon's decision was simply ignored.[53]

These incidents are instructive. They can easily be paralleled from the experience of Theophylact of Bulgaria and other Comnenian archbishops. They were the kind of thing that most archbishops could expect to encounter. They were not normally resigning matters. Like Theophylact Mouzalon also complains about the activities of tax collectors, but they were directed against the peasantry, rather than

[46] S. Doanidou, 'Ἡ παραίτησις Νικόλαου τοῦ Μουζάλωνος 'ἀπὸ τῆς 'ἀρχιεπισκοπῆς Κύπρου. 'Ανέκδοτον 'ἀπολογητικὸν ποίημα', *ΕΛΛΗΝΙΚΑ*, 7(1934), 109–50. On Cyprus under the Comneni see C. Galatariotou, *The Making of a Saint. The Life, Times and Sanctification of Neophytos the Recluse* (Cambridge, 1991), 40–67, 185–204; C. Mango, 'Chypre. Carrefour du monde byzantine', *XVe Congrès international d'études byzantines. Rapports et co-rapports* v,5 (Athens, 1976).

[47] Doannidou, 'Η παραίτησις Νικόλαου', 112–13.

[48] Ibid., 120–9.

[49] Ibid., 120–2.

[50] Ibid., 122–4.

[51] Ibid., 124–6.

[52] Ibid., 126–8.

[53] Ibid., 128–9.

specifically at the estates of the church. He makes a solitary allusion to bishops being harried by tax collectors.[54] His problem was quite the opposite: we know that at least one of his suffragan bishops engaged in tax collecting and others were just as reprehensible. What made Mouzalon's position untenable was the opposition he met within his church. If we read between the lines of his poem, we can see that the archbishop's actions called into question the easy relationship that existed between the imperial administration and the local church. They cooperated to ensure that a province of great strategic value was properly administered. This meant two things: Cypriot dissidence was repressed and the taxes were brought in. The Comnenian regime was highly oppressive. It meant that the clergy might often have to take on roles that belonged to the laity. Bishops and priests acted as tax collectors; deacons received military rank and were enrolled in the galley crews.[55] More innocuously, bishops allowed games and festivals to be celebrated in their church.[56] This we know to have been a feature of the church in the tenth and eleventh centuries. It somehow symbolises the easy relationship of church and lay society. Mouzalon found the practice outrageous. He was only anticipating the patriarchs of the twelfth century who did their best to outlaw such revelries.[57] They were an affront to the dignity of the church.

Mouzalon denounces the governor of Cyprus Eumathios Philokales and his staff in the most lurid fashion. But Philokales was a benefactor of the Cypriot monastery of St John Chrysostom, known as Koutsovendis. He added the chapel of the Holy Trinity and had it decorated. This, he tells us, he did in expiation of his sins, but it is only a surmise that this was an act of contrition for his part in Mouzalon's abdication.[58] There was a spate of ecclesiastical and monastic foundations on the island of Cyprus from the turn of the eleventh century. This was the work not only of imperial governors, such as Philokales, but also of members of the local ascendancy. For example, in 1105/6 the Magistros Nicholas Iskhyrios founded the church of Panagia Phorbiotissa at Asinou and paid for its decoration.[59] Mouzalon was not impressed. He has nothing to say about

54 Ibid., 130.652–3.

55 Ibid., 130.654–6.

56 Ibid., 123.414.

57 Rhalles & Potles II, 449.

58 C. Mango and E.J.W. Hawkins, 'Report on fieldwork in Istanbul and Cyprus, 1962–1963', *DOP* 18(1964), 333–9; A. and J. Stylianou, *The Painted Churches of Cyprus. Treasures of Byzantine Art* (London, 1985), 456–7.

59 Stylianou, *The Painted Churches*, 114–17; D. Winfield, 'Hagios Chrysostomos, Trikomo, Asinou. Byzantine painters at work', in *ΠΡΑΚΤΙΚΑ ΤΟΥ ΠΡΩΤΟΥ ΔΙΕΘΝΟΥΣ ΚΥΠΡΟΛΟΓΙΚΟΥ ΣΥΝΕΔΡΙΟΥ*, II (Levkosia, 1972), 285–91; Galatariotou, *The Making of a Saint*, 173–4; Mango, 'Chypre, carrefour du monde byzantin', 5–8.

the contribution of lay patronage to the well-being of the church in Cyprus.

The new ideas about episcopal responsibilities that Mouzalon brought with him from Constantinople were highly disruptive. The island united against him. Mouzalon closed his poem with a dialogue in which he wrestles with his failure to meet the exacting standards required of an archbishop. He was deserting his flock, abandoning them to the mercies of the tax collector.[60] He was articulating the social responsibilities of a bishop: his duty to protect the poor and disadvantaged from injustice and oppression. His self-pity only emphasises the magnitude of his failure. His fault was to allow himself to be isolated. This was something that his more successful colleagues were able to avoid. This is not to minimise the difficulties Mouzalon faced. Philokales was an uncompromising character. He was a lone wolf (*monolykos*). He had a reputation not only for harsh government but also for misappropriating the wealth of the church.[61]

Even so, Mouzalon's resignation of the throne of Cyprus was a humiliation. It seems to bear out Margaret Mullett's neat dictum about Byzantine bishops 'not exuding a powerful persona'.[62] Certainly not in comparison with their counterparts in the West. That grandee of the western church, Liutprand, bishop of Cremona, as Margaret Mullett reminds us, came across various Greek bishops during his visit to Constantinople in 968 and was not impressed by the state they kept.[63] Byzantine bishops were aware of the power and pretensions of their western counterparts. Leo, bishop of Synada, visited Milan at the end of the tenth century on a diplomatic mission for the Emperor Basil II. He pointedly referred to the archbishop as the archon and bishop of Milan, or 'prince-bishop', which is how the translator renders it.[64] However, the Comnenian bishop was a more powerful figure than his tenth-century predecessor. He was more often than in the past a former member of the patriarchal clergy with an excellent education, a training in law, and a high conceit of episcopal authority and responsibilities. He was imbued with a belief in the autonomy of the church. Eustathius of Thessalonica believed in presenting a grim exterior to the world.

The Comnenian bishops might be accused of trying to assume a more powerful persona. This inevitably brought them into conflict with elements of the imperial administration and local interests. Against

60 Doannidou, 'Ἡ παραίτησις Νικόλαου', 134–7.
61 Cyril Phileotes, 146–53.
62 Mullett, 'Patronage in action', 146.
63 Ibid., 145–6.
64 M.P. Vinson, *The Correspondence of Leo, Metropolitan of Synada and Syncellus* (Dumbarton Oaks Texts 8) (Washington DC, 1985),no.3, 6.14–15.

this, there are signs that the position of the bishop improved over the twelfth century. There was better protection for episcopal estates in the shape of the chrysobulls that emperors of the house of Comnenus issued in increasing numbers to individual sees. Episcopal wealth was most vulnerable during a vacancy. First Manuel Comnenus and then Isaac Angelus issued orders protecting vacant sees from government agents and making them the special responsibility of the *mystikos*.[65] Bishops also seem to have had some success in recovering control over the monasteries of their dioceses. By the end of the twelfth century they were able to challenge the practice of placing monasteries in their dioceses under the authority of the patriarch of Constantinople.[66]

Vital to the bishop's position was the work of his court. Its importance was apparent to Nicholas Mouzalon. He may have been a failure as an archbishop, but he had instilled in him the latest ideas about the role of a bishop. He criticised his suffragans for the way they discouraged plaintiffs, even members of the clergy, from bringing their cases to the episcopal court.[67] This points to a greater emphasis on a bishop's judicial responsibilities. Unfortunately, we only have detailed records of the workings of episcopal courts from the early thirteenth century. By then, they were of central importance to local society. But this must have equally been the case before 1204, for the growing strength of the episcopal court is linked with the development from the late eleventh century of an effective system of canon law. This not only gave episcopal judgements and opinions more weight; it also extended their range. Legal knowledge and training among bishops improved over the twelfth century. The legal expertise of Demetrius Chomatianos was impressive, but so too was that of John Apokaukos, who did not have the same pretensions to be a legal expert as his fellow student. They owed their legal skills to that upsurge of interest in canon law which culminated in the work of Theodore Balsamon. He was set the task of harmonising civil and canon law. One of the consequences of his work was that canon law annexed much of civil law. It meant that the episcopal courts could deal authoritatively with business that had previously tended to go to the civil courts. Balsamon provided a sound legal basis for the extension of episcopal authority. This is something of a paradox. The original impulse behind the development of canon law was to vindicate the separate status of the clergy, but its ultimate effect was to give the church courts a wider competence over lay suits.

Around the middle of the eleventh century new iconographies announced a renewal of episcopal authority. They celebrated the role

65 Magdalino, 'The not-so-secret functions of the *Mystikos*' (= Magdalino, *Tradition and Transformation*, no.XI).
66 Rhalles & Potles V, 101–102; Grumel, 1185.
67 Doannidou, ''Η παραίτησις Νικόλαου', 130.662–5.

of the bishop in the scheme of salvation. They proclaimed an ideal. It was probably a response to the challenge that the episcopal hierarchy faced from monasteries and private interests and increasingly from the patriarchal clergy. The ideal was fragile. It required a stronger institutional base if it was to become a reality. Participation in the patriarchal synod contributed to a sense of episcopal solidarity. This was enhanced from Alexius I Comnenus's reign with the appointment of an increasing number of leading bishops from the patriarchal clergy. It consolidated a sense of belonging to an elite, but it was more than this. Such bishops disposed of greater influence by virtue of the education they had received and the connections they had made in the Great Church. Their authority was underpinned by the concurrent development of canon law. The Comnenian bishop was a force to be reckoned with. The turmoil that he confronted and the opposition he provoked should not be taken as signs of the weakness of his position. They were a necessary part of his assertion of authority.

PART IV

MONASTERIES AND SOCIETY

13

ALEXIUS I COMNENUS AND MONASTICISM

THE monastery was both the focus and the mirror of Byzantine society. It provided not only a means of expressing its ideals, but also a way of meeting many of its needs. There can hardly have been a Byzantine who, at some stage of his or her life, did not come into direct contact with monasticism. A surprisingly high proportion entered the monastic life. Often, this took the form of a deathbed conversion. Just as in the early church it was quite common to delay baptism until death was imminent, so Byzantines often took their monastic vows when close to death. It was a commonplace of the monastic ideal that a monastery hovered between this world and the next. Where better to prepare yourself for death! Entry into the monastic state came most commonly with retirement, bereavement, and the prospect of death, but it might also come at almost any stage in a person's life. Even before they were born, children were vowed by grateful or just pious parents to the monastic life. Although legally tonsure could not take place until the age of twelve, children entered monasteries and nunneries before this. It was often a solution for orphans or for the poor. The monastery was at all stages of life an alternative and a refuge. Another commonplace of hagiography has entering a monastery as a way of escaping marriage or a way out of a marriage that had become unendurable. The monastic life was also a solution for misfits and criminals. Adulteresses were condemned to life in a nunnery as a form of discipline. Criminals, including murderers, were often confined in monasteries. But men and women might equally take monastic vows out of a sense of gratitude for delivery from some crisis. There were always those who entered the monastic life because they glimpsed its superiority to secular life. The Cypriot St Neophytos describes very well the state of mind that predisposed him to embrace the monastic life. From childhood he had been struck by the flux of life. People always seemed so anxious. It might be over the death of a child, but there were those with many children who were weighed down by poverty. He had seen rich men turned into paupers. He took solace from the fact that in the face of death such concerns were of little importance. It was better to confront the inevitable and this could best be done by becoming a monk.[1] The motives for embracing the monastic life were many, ranging from idealism to necessity, from convention to compulsion.

Monastic renewal

These were old established patterns, but it was not so much conservatism as flexibility and flux that were characteristic of Byzantine monasticism. Monasteries were for the most part small and short-lived. This favoured a continuous process of modification. Though there were influential guides to the monastic life there was no single monastic rule. Each new founder of a monastery was at liberty to provide his or her own rule or *typikon*. This meant that within limits Byzantine monasticism attuned itself without much difficulty to changes taking place in Byzantine society. But there were limits: the most important was a strong awareness of a monastic tradition. It was impossible to escape the controlling influence of the classics of Byzantine monasticism: the *Ascetica* of Basil of Caesarea, the *Apophthegmata* of the Egyptian Fathers, *The Spiritual Meadow* of John Moschus, and more recently the writings of Theodore of Stoudios. Though apparently amorphous, even anarchic, Byzantine monasticism possessed a solid core.

This was provided by those centres that were held to have best preserved this monastic tradition. In Constantinople the monastery of St John of Stoudios was a model of the monastic life. It had a continuous history reaching back to its foundation in the middle of the fifth century, but it owed its enduring influence to the work of Theodore of Stoudios. Its rule would be used as a guide for the monastic life throughout the orthodox world. Its position was such that it was able to maintain a considerable degree of independence and could even defy a patriarch, as powerful as Michael Cerularius. Outside the capital, it was not so much individual monasteries that were seen as custodians of monastic standards, as holy mountains. Bithynian Olympus was the most powerful of these to the eleventh century. Its monasteries had an important part to play in the defeat of iconoclasm. There were others, mostly in western Asia Minor, at Kyminas, at Latros, and most recently Galesion, which was the work of St Lazarus. These communities were organised under an archimandrite or *protos*, who was the president of a monastic confederation. They suffered as a result of the Turkish conquest of the Anatolian plateau at the end of the eleventh century and were in decline. This was only temporarily arrested under the

[1] I.P. Tsiknopoulos, *ΚΥΠΡΙΑΚΑ ΤΥΠΙΚΑ* (Nicosia, 1969), 74–5. See Galatariotou, *The Making of a Saint*.

emperors of Nicaea. There were also holy mountains in the European provinces of the Empire. Mount Ganos was in Thrace within easy reach of the shores of the sea of Marmora and Constantinople, but more powerful – and far better documented – was Mount Athos. Though the earliest monastic settlements can be traced back to the early ninth century, the fortune of Mount Athos was made by the Emperor Nicephorus Phocas's patronage of St Athanasius and his foundation of the Lavra. This monastery enjoyed generous imperial patronage and supervision down to the early twelfth century. Emperors felt that they had a special responsibility for the Holy Mountain.

This thread of continuity and coherence was complemented by bursts of monastic revival. These took different forms and were of varying intensity. The inspiration might well be the work of a monastic reformer. St Athanasius's work at Athos was the culmination of one such movement. He introduced to the Holy Mountain the lavriot form of monasticism which he had learnt at Kyminas from his master St Michael Maleinos. The 'common life' remained the heart of his regime, but hermitages were set aside for those worthy and capable of following a contemplative life, but they were expected to return to the monastery on Sundays and festivals in order to take part in a communal celebration of the liturgy. To be allowed to follow the life of a hesychast was an honour vouchsafed to the few. At the Lavra Athanasius made provision for only five hermitages.[2] Athanasius's intrusion of this form of the 'common life' was resented by the hermits of the Holy Mountain, who until then had been the dominant element.

Several of the monastic founders of the eleventh century were inspired by the lavriot form of monasticism: St Christodoulos, the founder of the monastery of St John the Theologian on the island of Patmos, for example. He came originally from Anatolia, but ran away from home as a boy to become a monk. He wandered from place to place until he reached Palestine. The raids of the Bedouin forced him to return to Asia Minor where he became a monk on Mount Latros. He was eventually made *protos* or head of this monastic confederation. He fled, like so many other monks, in the face of Turkish raiding. In his old age he looked back to Mount Latros as a model of the monastic life. There it was possible to follow your spiritual inclinations and capacities. He claimed to be a devotee of the eremitical life, while the majority followed the 'common life'. He was idealising the lavriot style of monasticism. He remembered with pleasure how they would all gather together on Sundays to celebrate the liturgy, while the rest

[2] Meyer, *Die Haupturkunden*, 115.16–20; Cf. D. Papachryssanthou, 'La vie monastique dans les campagnes byzantins du VIIIe au XIe siècle', *B* 43(1973), 166–80.

of the week was spent in isolation singing psalms and engaged in handicrafts.[3]

St Meletios the Younger was another Anatolian runaway; this time from the prospect of marriage, but this was in the mid-eleventh century before conditions in Asia Minor had begun to deteriorate. He came to Constantinople and was tonsured in the monastery of St John Chrysostom, but he did not care for the hubbub of the capital. He led a wandering life that took him on pilgrimage to Thessalonica, Rome, perhaps Santiago de Compostella, and Jerusalem. He spent three years in the Holy Land but the raids of the Bedouin forced him to depart. He made his way to Thebes where he had connections. He eventually settled in the hills separating Attica from Boeotia and established the monastery that still bears his name. His personal regime was brutal, but he was kinder to his disciples. He was an ascetic, who delighted in the rewards that pain brings. His feet became infested with worms. St Meletios treated them like pearls, or so his hagiographer says. In contrast to the way he wilfully neglected himself, he paid careful attention to the celebration of the liturgy.[4] At various distances from the monastery church he built a series of hermitages. It would therefore seem that he too followed the lavriot form of the monastic life.[5]

In contrast, St Cyril Phileotes was loathe to leave home and family. He came from Philea in Thrace. Derkos was the bishopric of the area. It was forty odd miles from Constantinople. Like Christodoulos and Meletios he was late in life to be the recipient of Alexius I Comnenus's favours. But his path to the monastic life was very different. He married young and had children. He tried within the bounds of marriage – not always successfully – to follow a Christian life. He then embraced a regime of contemplation and asceticism. This was still within the family home, where he built himself a cell, just large enough for him to kneel down and say his prayers. At this stage, he seems much closer to a kind of lay piety that easily spilt over into heresy.[6]

Near the village his family owned a church that was falling into ruins. His brother restored it and turned it into a monastery.[7] Cyril eventually joined him, but lived the life of a hermit in a cell he built close by. In other words, the form of life that he chose was close to the lavriot form of monasticism, but it was even closer to that of the recluse (*enkleistos*),

3 Miklosich & Müller VI, 60–1; E.L. Vranouse, *ΤΑ ΑΓΙΟΛΟΓΙΚΑ ΚΕΙΜΕΝΑ ΤΟΥ ΟΣΙΟΥ ΧΡΙΣΤΟΔΟΥΛΟΥ, ΙΔΡΥΤΟΥ ΤΗΣ ΕΝ ΠΑΤΜΩ(Ι) ΜΟΝΗΣ* (Athens, 1966), 87–127:

4 Meletios the Younger, 1–12, 41–7.

5 A. K. Orlandos, 'Ἡ μονὴ τοῦ Ὁσίου Μελετίου καὶ τὰ παραλαύρια ἀυτῆς', *ΑΡΧΕΙΟΝ ΤΩΝ ΒΥΖΑΝΤΙΝΩΝ ΜΝΗΜΕΙΩΝ ΤΗΣ ΕΛΛΑΔΟΣ* 5(1939), 45–53, 107–18.

6 Cyril Phileotes, 66–7.

7 Ibid., 104–5.

which was a characteristic of monasticism in Constantinople in the eleventh century. St Cyril Phileotes was known in the capital's monastic circles. At one stage in his life he had made a point of walking in to Constantinople to visit the church of the Blakhernai every Friday night. This was to witness the 'customary miracle', as it was known, when an icon of the Virgin was mysteriously unveiled.[8] There is nothing to suggest that he was influenced by the Constantinopolitan fashions in monasticism. He seems to have been a law unto himself: very much an exemplar of the idiosyncrasies of Byzantine monastic life.

In the provinces monastic life therefore continued much as it had always been, but this was not true of Constantinople. In the late tenth century Symeon the New Theologian resuscitated the mystical tradition of Byzantine monasticism, but he was to die in obscurity. His memory and his works were only kept alive by Nicetas Stethatos who was to become abbot of Stoudios. Symeon's relics were translated to Constantinople in 1052 and he was subsequently canonised, thanks to the support of the Patriarch Michael Cerularius. His influence on the monastic revival at Constantinople from the middle of the eleventh century remains debatable.

His theology of the divine light seems only to have been moderately influential, but his stress on the importance of confession would be echoed in the rule drawn up for the monastery of the Theotokos Euergetis.[9] This monastery was founded in 1049 on his family property outside Constantinople by an ex-civil servant called Paul. The rule was drawn up by his disciple and successor Timothy and was to have enormous influence. It paid special attention to the role of the abbot. Among his major responsibilities was hearing the confessions of the monks. He was to make himself available twice a day to hear confessions.[10] Originally, the monastery had two abbots: a recluse and a free agent (*anetos*). When the former died the latter was expected to take his place. Timothy decided that this arrangement offended against free will and therefore legislated that in future there would only be a single abbot, but he could follow the life of a recluse, if he chose.[11] This meant never venturing outside the monastic enclosure. The main function of the abbot was contemplation. This would be to the spiritual benefit of the community as a whole. It would enhance his role as father confessor.

It is not clear who or what provided the inspiration for such a conception of the function of an abbot. It is only a possibility that it derived from the example of Symeon the New Theologian, but a possibility that deserves to be considered. The Theotokos Euergetis was not the only

[8] Ibid., 83–4.
[9] P. Gautier, 'Le typikon de la Théotokos Evergétis', *REB* 40(1982), 5–101.
[10] Ibid., 28–33.
[11] Ibid., 46–51.

Constantinopolitan monastery that revolved around a recluse as abbot. A recluse of the monastery of Kyr Philotheos attended the council of Blakhernai in 1094, which is a sign of the prestige accorded to such figures.[12] Together with a eunuch called John, Kyr Philotheos founded the monastery that would be named after him about 1035 and had gone into seclusion. This may be the first example of the practice at Constantinople. The foundation of this monastery is recorded by Nicetas Stethatos in his *Life* of Symeon the New Theologian. Nicetas introduced Philotheos to Symeon's ascetical and mystical teachings. This was followed by a vision of the holy man, who gave Philotheos instruction and advised him to visit his tomb at Chrysopolis. This Philotheos did. He took away with him an icon of Symeon and more of his writings, so that, in Stethatos's words, 'he has within him the saint in his entirety'. Kyr Philotheos became a posthumous disciple of the New Theologian. He turned his monastery into a centre of his cult. He instituted an annual celebration in his honour. This example suggests that the eleventh-century monastic revival at Constantinople was inspired, at least in part, by Symeon's example and teaching.[13]

The monastery of the Theotokos Euergetis would become far more influential than that of Kyr Philotheos. This was not only on account of its rule, but also because of the popularity of the monastic florilegium, known as the *Euergetinos*, which was compiled by its founder Paul. It did not make use of a very wide range of texts. Its novelty was the inclusion of extracts from a large number of saints' lives, mostly culled from the metaphrastic versions.[14] J. C. Anderson has recently argued that Paul's florilegium was a source of the Theodore Psalter.[15] This illustrated manuscript was the work of a monk of the monastery of Stoudios and was commissioned by the Abbot Michael. It was completed in February 1066. It marks a turning point in the illustration of psalters. 'L'irruption des saints' is one way of describing its novelty.[16] It confirms Ch. Walter's dictum: 'Cult of the saints was the most powerful motive

[12] J. Darrouzès, 'Le mouvement des fondations monastiques au XIe siècle', *TM* 6(1976), 162: he considers that this points to a relaxation of standards. The rule of the Theotokos Euergetis, however, allowed its abbot to visit Constantinople, if summoned by the emperor or patriarch: Gautier, 'Le typikon de la Théotokos Evergétis', 46–51.

[13] I. Hausherr, *Un grand mystique byzantin* (Orientalia Christiana Analecta 14) (Rome 1928), 214–21. The fact that Philotheos went on pilgrimage to Symeon's tomb at Chrysopolis indicates that he founded his monastery well before 1052 when the relics were translated to Constantinople.

[14] *Dictionnaire de Spiritualité* (Paris, 1937–), v, 502–3.

[15] J.C. Anderson, 'On the nature of the Theodore psalter', *Art Bulletin* 70(1988), 550–68, at 564–7.

[16] Cf. L. Mariès, 'L'irruption des saints dans l'illustration des Psautiers grecs du moyen âge', *Analecta Bollandiana* 68(1950), 153–63.

force in iconographical development after the Triumph of Orthodoxy.'[17] In the case of the Theodore Psalter it is Constantinopolitan saints that receive the most attention. Its editor S. Der Nersessian has interpreted this as a way of proclaiming Constantinople as the New Sion on account of its sanctuaries and saints.[18] At the very least, it suggests a strong awareness of Constantinople as the preeminent centre of the monastic life.[19]

The revival of monasticism at Constantinople was reflected in the vogue for illustrating monastic classics. Barlaam and Joasaphat, the *Ladder* of St John Climax, and the metaphrastic lives were all illustrated for the first time in the eleventh century. Another monastic classic was the *Physiologus*, which provided moral instruction in the shape of a bestiary. Illustrated versions existed, including the Smyrna *Physiologus*. Kathleen Corrigan has used it to argue that an illustrated *Physiologus* was in existence by the ninth century, but it only contained illustrations of the animal stories, not of their moral significance. Interpretative illustrations were added in the eleventh century and display close parallels with the Theodore Psalter. Some provided object lessons for the monastic life. For example, the beaver's willingness to sacrifice its testicles taught the virtues of chastity and must have been of peculiar comfort to the many eunuchs that found a haven in the monastic life.[20]

The evidence of the art suggests a monastic revival at Constantinople in the eleventh century, but without any very specific features. J. C. Anderson suggests that new lessons were derived for the monastic life from the example of saints. They were expected to provide an inspiration for the conduct of life rather than a guide to individual salvation.[21] There is little to link the art to the ideas that lay behind the rule of the Theotokos Euergetis. The art is associated primarily with the monastery of Stoudios which, but for Nicetas Stethatos, would not be associated with the currents of monastic renewal. Stethatos began to promote the cult of St Symeon the New Theologian only after he had

17 Walter, *Art and Ritual*, 197.

18 S. Der Nersessian, *L'illustration des Psautiers grecs du moyen âge, II. Londres Add. 19.352* (Paris, 1970), 89–98. Cf. C. Walter, 'Christological themes in the Byzantine marginal psalters from the ninth to the eleventh century', *REB* 44(1986), 287.

19 J.R. Martin, *The Illustration of the Heavenly Ladder of John Climacus* (Studies in Manuscript Illumination 5) (Princeton, 1954), 150–63, for a general survey of the problem of monastic art in the eleventh century.

20 K. Corrigan, 'The Smyrna Physiologus and its eleventh-century model', *Seventh Annual Byzantine Studies Conference*: Abstracts of Papers (Boston, 1981), 48–9. The Smyrna Physiologus was a Palaeologan copy: see O. Demus, 'Bemerkungen zum Physiologus von Smyrna', *Jahrbuch der österreichischen byzantinischen Gesellschaft* 25(1976), 235–57.

21 Anderson, 'On the nature', 550, 561, 566.

been readmitted to the monastery of Stoudios *c.*1035.[22] There is also one possible, but very tenuous, thread linking Stoudios to the monastery of the Theotokos Euergetis, which seems to have become the main centre of monastic reform at Constantinople. Its founder Paul was the author of a collection of catechisms, which were a faithful rendering of those of St Theodore of Stoudios. Some of the readings have suggested to Père Leroy that Paul must have consulted the works of Theodore in the Stoudios library.[23]

The vigour and creativity of monastic art in the eleventh century is a reflection of the strength of the monastic revival at Constantinople in the eleventh century. It was a return to the traditions of the common life with a renewed emphasis on the liturgy and on charity. The novel element was the place given to confession. This heightened the spiritual authority of the abbot. The frontispiece of the Theodore Psalter shows the investiture of the abbot of Stoudios by Christ with the symbols of office. J.C. Anderson interprets this scene as endowing the abbot with a duty to instruct the community in orthodoxy and in monastic virtues.[24] It owes much to imperial iconography and bears witness to the enhanced spiritual authority of the abbot. In other monasteries the abbot went into seclusion to find the spiritual powers required of his office. These were all the more necessary now that his great responsibility was to act as a father confessor to his community.

The spiritual qualities of an eleventh-century abbot are illustrated by a miniature from a manuscript of the *Ladder* of St John Climax (Vatican Cod. gr. 394). It shows St John expounding the virtues of chastity and temperance to two monks and pointing to a third identified as 'the monk Nicholas of the Lophadion'. Another inscription provides the explanation: 'St John says that this is the chaste monk Nicholas who has always maintained a complete indifference to Vive la différence'.[25] The monk Nicholas is to be identified with the future Patriarch Nicholas III Grammatikos (1084–1111) who founded and became abbot of the monastery of Lophadion in Constantinople.[26] In other words, the artist is singling out a living abbot as an exemplar of monastic virtues. Nicholas may well appear in two other miniatures devoted to the theme of exile (*xeniteia*). It shows an unnamed monk leaving his parents' home and setting out for the monastery of Lophadion.[27] Nicholas indeed left his native town of Antioch in Pisidia to seek refuge at

22 Hausherr, *Un grand mystique byzantin*, 193–5.
23 J. Leroy, 'Un nouveau témoin de la grande catéchèse de St Théodore Studite', *REB* 15(1957), 73–88, at 87 n.1.
24 Anderson, 'On the nature', 564, 568.
25 Martin, *The Heavenly Ladder of John Climacus*, 69–70: fig.107.
26 J. Darrouzès in *TM* 6(1976), 163; Darrouzès, 'L'éloge de Nicolas III', 11–17.
27 Martin, *The Heavenly Ladder of John Climacus*, 56–7: figs.74–5.

Constantinople. Though they cannot be identified other monks depicted in these miniatures are also likely to have been contemporaries.[28] It was as if to proclaim that the age of saints had not passed. This was a theme of St Symeon the New Theologian. He condemned as heretics 'those who say that there is no one in our times and in our midst who is able to keep the Gospel commandments and become like the holy Fathers'.[29]

Perhaps too much attention has been paid to Symeon's theology of the divine light: his mysticism seems, in any case, to have had a muted reception. It was other features of his teaching that provided the inspiration behind the monastic revival at Constantinople; above all, the role of the abbot as a teacher, spiritual father, and father confessor.[30]

Comnenian patronage[31]

The development of new themes of monastic art is testimony to the breadth of the monastic revival at Constantinople in the eleventh century. It was not just a matter of the monastery of the Theotokos Euergetis. The monastery of Stoudios lent its venerable prestige to this monastic revival, which was, in any case, a tribute to the coenobitic traditions of the monastery. The Comneni were perhaps fortunate to have connections with Stoudios. The Emperor Isaac Comnenus was brought up there and, after his abdication in 1057, retired there. When his nephew Alexius I Comnenus ascended the throne in 1081, the monasteries of Constantinople were a force that counted. It was a two-way process: the monasteries profited from the backing of members of the ruling class, who in their turn had the kudos of association with a prestigious institution.[32] For this reason the character, scope, and fortune of a monastic revival owed much to the influence and interests of its supporters and patrons.

One of the ways in which the Byzantine ruling elite impressed itself on society was through the patronage of monasteries and nunneries. The political history of the Empire must therefore have influenced the pattern of monastic foundations and refoundations. Political upheavals left their mark. The inroads of the Turks into Asia Minor forced monastic leaders to seek refuge at Constantinople and elsewhere. As a result,

[28] E.g. the Monk Sabbas (ibid., 58: fig 77); the Monk Peter (ibid., 67: fig. 103); the Monk Luke (ibid., 67: fig.103).

[29] Symeon the New Theologian, *Catèchèses*, ed. B. Krivocheine (Paris 1963–5), 3 vols., III, 176–80. Cf. Martin, *The Heavenly Ladder of John Climacus*, 160.

[30] K. Holl, *Enthusiasmus und Bussgewalt beim griechischen Mönchtum. Eine Studie zu Symeon dem neuen Theologen* (Leipzig, 1898), 110–27.

[31] See Magdalino, *Manuel I Komnenos*, 119–20.

[32] See Galatariotou, *The Making of a Saint*, 4–5, for a discussion of the relationship between material and symbolic capital.

the centre of gravity of Byzantine monasticism shifted westwards.[33] Even more important was the triumph of the Comneni family, who with their allies came to constitute a new ruling elite. In traditional fashion they were great founders and refounders of monasteries. The initiative came in the first place from Alexius's mother Anna Dalassena. She founded the monastery of Christ Pantepoptes. It was here that she retired and died and was presumably buried.[34] After her death it was her daughter-in-law the Empress Eirene Doukaina who oversaw dynastic patronage of monasteries. Her mother was Maria of Bulgaria, another patron of monasteries. She it was who was responsible for refounding and reconstructing the ancient monastery of St Saviour in Chora.[35] The Empress Eirene Doukaina's major work was the foundation of the nunnery of the Theotokos Kekharitomene, where she retired and where she was to die and to be buried. Alongside it she founded the monastery of Christ Philanthropos, which was to serve as her husband Alexius Comnenus's last resting place.[36] Although the initiative behind this double foundation came from his empress, Alexius Comnenus gave his blessing and his support. His brother Adrian who became the monk John was with his wife Zoe Doukaina (the nun Anna) the founder or refounder of the monastery of the Theotokos Pammakaristos at Constantinople.[37]

Alexius I Comnenus's seizure of power in 1081 was followed by the transfer of considerable wealth and landed property to a fairly tight circle around the new emperor. A proportion of this was used for the foundation of monasteries that brought the imperial family prestige and spiritual solace. But it was not only the immediate members of the imperial family, who used their wealth to found new monasteries. It was also Alexius Comnenus's trusted followers. His commander-in-chief, the Grand Domestic Gregory Pakourianos founded the monastery of the Theotokos Petritziotissa near Philippopolis, which he endowed handsomely.[38]

Alexius Comnenus and his family did not restrict their generosity to what might be termed dynastic foundations. They were just as active promoting the work of 'holy men': St Meletios in the hills of Attica; St Christodoulos on the island of Patmos; St Cyril Phileotes in

33 See Darrouzès, 'Le mouvement des fondations monastiques', 171–6.

34 Janin I, 527–9.

35 Ibid., 549; P.A. Underwood, *The Kariye Djami* (London, 1967), I, 8–10.

36 Janin I, 539–41.

37 H. Belting, C. Mango, and D. Mouriki, *The Mosaics and Frescoes of St Mary Pammakaristos (Fethiye Camii) at Istanbul* (Dumbarton Oaks Studies xv) (Washington, DC, 1978), 6–10. On the identification of the founders, see Polemis, *Doukai*, 55.

38 P. Gautier, 'Le typikon du sébaste Grégoire Pakourianos', *REB* 42(1984), 5–146; P. Lemerle, *Cinq études sur le XIe siècle byzantin* (Paris, 1977), 113–91.

Thrace; Manuel, bishop of Stroumitsa in Macedonia.[39] In Constantinople Alexius Comnenus and Eirene Doukaina were patrons of John the Faster who refounded the monastery of the Prodromos of Petra. They provided the funds that turned it into one of the city's most splendid monasteries. Earlier in the century John Mauropous had entered it as a monk and he retired there *c.* 1075 after he resigned the see of Euchaita. He wrote an encomium of St Baras, the supposed fifth-century founder of the monastery. It was mostly based on oral traditions, but must have helped to popularise the cult. John Mauropous died early in Alexius I Comnenus's reign. The monastery was assigned by the Patriarch Nicholas Grammatikos to John the Faster. He came originally from Cappadocia and built up a reputation for holiness, which eventually attracted the attention of the Emperor Alexius Comnenus.[40] The support given by Alexius Comnenus and his family to a series of monastic founders at the end of the eleventh century is unprecedented in Byzantine history. The initiative came from his mother Anna Dalassena who even before her son ascended the throne of Constantinople was a great patron of holy men.

The Comneni were reacting to a surge of monastic piety, but they were also redirecting and harnessing it. Their dealings with St Christodoulos are revealing. When the saint first solicited imperial help, Alexius I Comnenus wished to use his talents to reorganise the monastic communities at Zagora on Mount Pelion. Christodoulos began to draw up a rule, but thought better of it. For reasons that he never properly explained, their style of life did not appeal to him. Thanks to the intervention of Anna Dalassena, the emperor relented and allowed Christodoulos to depart for Patmos. As we have seen, Christodoulos idealised the lavriot way of life. At Patmos, however, he instituted a coenobitic regime, one where the stress was upon the liturgy and celebrating God in song, or in Christodoulos's own words 'Man hymns the creation of God by imitating as far as humanly possible "the anthem of the angels".' It may only have been circumstances that made Christodoulos adopt the coenobitic way of life for his new foundation, but it is more likely to have been under the influence of the new enthusiasm for the 'common life' current in Constantinople. He would have become aware of this during his stay in the capital, when he was trying to win the support of Alexius Comnenus. He is known to have discussed with the emperor his plans for a monastery on Patmos. The emperor expressed doubts

39 Darrouzès, 'Le mouvement des foundations monastiques', 165–7.

40 Ibid., 161 n.2; H. Gelzer, 'Kallistos' Enkomion auf Johannes Nesteutes', *Zeitschrift für wissenschaftliche Theologie*, 29(1886), 67–77; P. Canart, 'Le dossier hagiographique des SS. Baras, Patapios et Raboulas', *Analecta Bollandiana* 87(1969), 445–59; A. Karpozilos, *ΣΥΜΒΟΛΗ ΣΤΗ ΜΕΛΕΤΗ ΤΟΥ ΒΙΟΥ ΚΑΙ ΤΟΥ ΕΡΓΟΥ ΤΟΥ ΙΩΑΝΝΗ ΜΑΥΡΟΠΟΔΟΣ* (Ioannina 1982), 46–50, 137–9.

about Christodoulos's intention to dispense with any work force to aid the monks to bring the island under cultivation. His doubts turned out to be well founded. They seem to have been founded in the practicalities of the 'common life'.[41]

The discussions between the emperor and the monastic leader must have gone further than mere practicalities. They must have touched upon the character of the new foundation. Christodoulos's decision to adopt a coenobitic regime surely owed something to Alexius's advice. This does not mean that Christodoulos was entirely guided by the monastic fashions of the capital. The rule which he drew up for the monastery of St John the Theologian on the island of Patmos has nothing to say about confession. This was central to the monastic regime instituted at the monastery of the Theotokos Euergetis just outside Constantinople.

As we know, this monastery was one of the centres, perhaps the centre, of a revival of monasticism that took place in the capital around the middle of the eleventh century. Its rule remained influential to, at least, the end of the twelfth century. Its prestige owed much to the Comneni, who adopted it for their foundations. Eirene Doukaina used its rule as the model for the *typikon* she drew up for her foundation of the Theotokos Kekharitomene; her son the Emperor John II Comnenus for the monastery of the Pantokrator and another son Isaac Comnenus for the monastery of the Kosmosoteira.[42] Eirene Doukaina's brother the Grand Duke John Doukas was a benefactor of the monastery of the Theotokos Euergetis.[43] The continuing influence of this monastery therefore owed much to support that it received from members of the imperial house, whether Doukas or Comnenus. At one level, this is a reflection of the piety of the imperial family, but at another it is sign of how the Comneni harnessed a monastic revival. If this was only in part for spiritual reasons, it enhanced their reputation for piety. The political strength of Alexius I Comnenus depended not a little on the support that he had from the monasteries and monastic leaders. In return, Alexius I Comnenus had a responsibility for the well-being of monasteries and for the eradication of abuses.

Kharistike

The abuse that attracted particular attention was a perennial feature of Byzantine society: the lay patronage of monasteries.[44] It had become

41 Miklosich & Müller VI, 64–7.

42 M.J. Angold, 'Were Byzantine monastic *typika* literature?', in *The Making of Byzantine History. Studies Dedicated to Donald M. Nicol on his 70th Birthday*, ed. R. Beaton and C. Roueché (Aldershot, 1993), 50.

43 Gautier, 'Le typikon de la Théotokos Evergétis', 92

44 Thomas, *Private Religious Foundations*, 1–4 and *passim*.

institutionalised from the turn of the tenth century in the shape of the *kharistike*.[45] We have seen how Alexius intervened to check abuses associated with *kharistike*. This was done, at least partly, in response to the criticisms of the monk John of Oxeia, later to become patriarch of Antioch. Though sometimes critical of the emperor, John of Oxeia was not one of his opponents. He remembered the emperor's kindness to him. He acted more as the emperor's conscience. Alexius's attack on *kharistike* allowed him to isolate opposition within the church. It made it all the easier for the emperor to pose as the promoter of a monastic revival.[46]

John of Oxeia's tract against *kharistike* is polemic, but nonetheless instructive for that. It purported to take the form of a history of monasticism. Pride of place was given to the victory over the iconoclasts,[47] but *kharistike* now seemed set to encompass what the great iconoclast emperor Constantine V had failed to achieve: the destruction of monasticism.[48] John of Oxeia reminded his audience that the original and laudable motive behind *kharistike* was the improvement of dilapidated monasteries, but it did not take very long before prosperous monasteries were being granted out to laymen.[49] The justification for this was that a lay patron protected a monastery from arbitrary taxation (*epereiai*), but the truth was that it was only an excuse for profit.[50]

John of Oxeia sketched the damage done by lay patrons to their monasteries which they treated as private property.[51] They creamed off the profits and treated the abbot and monks like serfs. The result was the utter ruin of monastic churches, conventual buildings, and estates. More interesting is his analysis of how monastic life suffered. The monks often ceased to celebrate the liturgy and other services, because the lay patron diverted revenues to secular ends. Even more insidious was the way the authority of the abbot was undermined and with it monastic order and discipline. The ordinary monk depended upon the *kharistikarios* for his rations, however meagre they might be.

45 Ahrweiler, 'Charisticariat'; E. Hermann, 'Ricerche sulle istituzioni monastiche bizantine. *Typika ktetorika*, caristicari e monasteri "liberi"', *OCP* 6(1940), 316–47; R. Janin, 'Le monachisme byzantin au moyen âge. Commende et typika (Xe-XIVe siècle)', *REB* 22(1964), 1–44; Lemerle, 'Un aspect du role des monastères à Byzance' (= Lemerle, *Le Monde de Byzance*, no.XIII); Thomas, *Private Religious Foundations*, 149–213; M. Kaplan, 'Les monastères et le siècle à Byzance: les investissements des laiques au XIe siècle', *Cahiers de Civilisation médiévale*, 27(1984), 71–83.

46 Gautier, 'Réquisitoire', 114–16.

47 Ibid., 102–5.

48 Ibid., 122–3. Cf. J.C. Anderson, 'The date and the purpose of the Barberini psalter', *Cahiers archéologiques* 31(1983), 35–60, at 50–60, where he argues that the psalter was commissioned by Alexius Comnenus from the Stoudios workshop to defend himself against the charge of iconoclasm.

49 Gautier, 'Réquisitoire', 106–9.

50 Ibid., 114–17.

51 Ibid., 118–19.

He therefore looked to him, rather than to the abbot, for guidance. The abbot soon found himself isolated. A lack of discipline combined with a tendency on the part of the lay patron to keep the monks on short rations produced another evil: monks started to engage in all kinds of business activities.[52] The standard of monastic life suffered in other ways. A *kharistikarios* could install whom he liked as a monk without paying any attention to the normal formalities which prescribed a probationary period of three years. He could also foist on a monastery lay brothers, who might come close to outnumbering the monks. They introduced all kinds of secular activities, until the monastery was little better than an inn.[53]

John of Oxeia's description of monastic life can hardly have been objective. He was probably generalising from one or two notorious examples. His purpose was polemical. His intention was to uphold the ideal of the 'common life' which he thought threatened by *kharistike*. John of Oxeia claimed that all monasteries were now granted to the laity with the exception 'of a few recently founded and easily enumerated coenobitic monasteries',[54] but he feared that they would go the same way as other 'ancient and great' monasteries devoted to the 'common life'. It is not difficult to recognise in these 'recently founded and easily enumerated coenobitic monasteries' foundations such as the Theotokos Euergetis. One of the features of such foundations was their independence. This was held to be a prerequisite for the proper ordering of the common life. From this standpoint lay patronage was intolerable. It undermined the fabric of the church by placing the laity above the monks.[55] In keeping with the ideals of monastic revival John of Oxeia had a very high estimate of the status of the monk. He believed that the Pseudo-Dionysius had placed the monastic estate immediately after the priesthood. Monastic consecration was in his opinion a 'second baptism which restored the first'.[56] This was not theologically sound, but John of Oxeia would have found support in the writings of Symeon the New Theologian. So too would his contention that 'confessions and disclosures of sins and the penance [prescribed] for them and the absolution [granted] have been transferred to the monks, just as is still seen happening now'.[57] The importance of John of Oxeia's tract against *kharistike* lies in its defence of the monastic ideal associated with the monastery of the Theotokos Euergetis.

52 Ibid., 122–7.
53 Ibid., 120–3.
54 Ibid., 109.271–2.
55 Ibid., 114–15.
56 Ibid., 98–101.
57 Ibid., 105.221–3.

There was one thing that perplexed John of Oxeia: the way *kharistikarioi* were prepared to destroy some monasteries, while at the same time founding others.[58] He might almost have been thinking of Michael Attaleiates, who besides being an historian of note carved out a bureaucratic career under the Emperors Romanos Diogenes, Michael VII Doukas, and Nicephorus Botaneiates.[59] In 1077 he put the finishing touches to his foundation of an almshouse at Raidestos, which was his thanksoffering for a successful life. For administrative purposes he attached it to the small monastery of Christ Panoiktirmos which he created out of part of his mansion at Constantinople. He was at pains to prevent his foundation and its endowment passing into the hands of *kharistikarioi*: a possibility that he found disturbing.[60] To avoid such an outcome his monastery had to be independent. He furnished it with a series of imperial chrysobulls guaranteeing its liberty[61] and drew up a *typikon* or rule which emphasised its independent status.[62] He was scarcely motivated by any commitment to monastic reform, still less by any spiritual objections to *kharistike*. He reveals that he held various monastic houses, including a nunnery, in *kharistike* and saw nothing wrong in passing on his rights to his son.[63] Attaleiates was a shrewd man and the first that we come across who saw how independent monastic status could be exploited for private ends. Under the cover of monastic independence he created a family trust which he placed in the hands of his eldest son Theodore, who was to pass it in his turn to his heir. He was to draw two-thirds of the foundation's surplus revenues.[64]

Nothing makes Attaleiates's real intentions quite so plain as his stipulation that the properties he bequeathed directly to his son were also to enjoy the same privileged status as the foundation's estates.[65] At a dangerous time in Byzantine political life tying up a family's fortune in this way was a prudent measure. It ruled out confiscation and had the added advantage of meeting the formal requirements of piety. The Comneni did not exploit the independent monastery for family advantage quite as blatantly as Michael Attaleiates. But a combination of aristocratic piety and self-interest best explain the virtual disappearance of *kharistike*.

58 Ibid., 129. 573–8.
59 Kazhdan/Franklin, 23–86; Lemerle, *Cinq études*, 65–112; Thomas, *Private Religious Foundations*, 179–85.
60 P. Gautier, 'La *diataxis* de Michel Attaleiate', *REB* 39(1981), 33. 248–62.
61 Miklosich & Müller v, 135–45.
62 Gautier, 'La *diataxis* de Michel Attaleiate', 41.392–4.
63 Ibid., 47.506–17.
64 Ibid., 53.608–18.
65 Ibid., 45.455–64.

Mount Athos under the Comneni

Alexius I Comnenus and his family supported the monastic revival associated with the Theotokos Euergetis. They used its rule for their own foundations. They disassociated themselves from the practice of *kharistike*. They derived some prestige from association with the most vibrant currents of monastic reform. For the emperor this renewal of the ideal of the 'common life' must have had another attraction. It offered a means of bringing order to Byzantine monasticism.

Almost as prestigious as the monasteries of Constantinople were those of Mount Athos. It therefore hardly comes as a surprise that Alexius I Comnenus was the most generous of benefactors to its leading monastery of the Lavra. Between 1081 and 1109 he issued eleven chrysobulls in its favour and one *sigillion*.[66] If he did not show the same generosity to other Athonite houses, he was concerned about the well-being of the Holy Mountain and intervened in its affairs on a number of occasions.

The turn of the eleventh century saw the monasteries of Athos deeply divided over two issues: the first revolved around the admission of eunuchs and boys; the second around the presence on Athos of Vlach shepherds with their families and flocks. The trouble seems to have begun around the beginning of Alexius's reign with the restoration of the monastery of Xenophon by the former Grand Droungarios Symeon.[67] He was a eunuch and enormously rich. He had served the Emperor Nicephorus Botaneiates, but had then begged to be released so that he could follow a monastic vocation on Mount Athos. Not long after his arrival he was expelled from the Holy Mountain by the *protos*, on the grounds that he was a eunuch and his three companions were beardless boys. They had no business on Athos. Symeon looked to the emperor for support in his capacity as the patron of Athos. In 1083 Alexius Comnenus intervened on his behalf. The *protos* of Mount Athos reluctantly reinstated Symeon as abbot of Xenophon,[68] but stipulated that nobody under the age of twenty was to enter the monastery and certainly not another eunuch.[69]

The scandal did not go away. Less than ten years later there were denunciations against the presence of boys and eunuchs in the monasteries of Athos, which were brought to Alexius Comnenus's attention. He dismissed them with the words, 'They have Moses and the

66 *Lavra*, I, nos. 43–6, 48–52, 55–6, 58.

67 See A. Kazhdan, 'A date and an identification in the Xenophon No.1', *B* 59(1989) 267–71.

68 *Actes de Xénophon*, ed. D. Papachryssanthou (Archives de l'Athos 15) (Paris, 1986), no. 1

69 Ibid., no.1, ll.255–6.

prophets.' He wanted to know if those who brought the complaints were hesychasts or abbots. Learning that they were the former, he wanted to know whether they had permission from their superiors to lay their complaints before the emperor. They were told to go back to the *protos* of the Holy Mountain, who was given strict instructions that he was to allow no monk to go to Constantinople without proper authorisation. The emperor was incensed by the presence of so many Athonite monks hanging around the squares of the capital. He had them rounded up and as a warning cut off the noses of some of them. He had the ringleaders sent to the patriarch to be disciplined. The patriarch ordered them back to Athos. He told them that they had no business agitating over the presence of eunuchs and boys. They would do better to think on the reasons why they embraced the monastic life rather than conjuring up demons. The matter should be left to the patriarch, the emperor, and the *protos*.[70]

But the *pittakion* or letter that the patriarch then despatched to the monks of Athos had little to say about the problem.[71] It was more concerned with scholars and literati and people from the palace who had settled on Athos and were now looking for an excuse to return to the capital without losing face. It sounds as though Symeon, the abbot of Xenophon, was not the only court official who retired to Athos. It looks rather that opponents of the Comnenian regime sought safety on Athos, as Michael Psellus had once done on Bithynian Olympus at a time of political embarrassment. Their presence and attitudes to the monastic life would have been a challenge to the traditions of Athos. It comes as no surprise that opposition to them was strongest among the hesychasts. The patriarch's solution to these divisions was set out in a letter to the emperor. His advice was that these monks from the capital should not be allowed to remain on the Holy Mountain.[72]

Soon after this, the Patriarch Nicholas Grammatikos ordered the expulsion of the Vlachs who wintered on Mount Athos, apparently on pain of interdict. Their women and children were deemed a distraction from the monastic life. This produced a bitter reaction from the monks, who came in great numbers to the capital to lobby their cause. It was claimed that there were only old monks left on the Holy Mountain.[73] More was at stake than at first appears. The patriarch was trying to bring Mount Athos more closely under his supervision. The monks hoped that they might find a champion in Alexius Comnenus. Though the emperor did warn the patriarch that Mount Athos came under imperial and not patriarchal jurisdiction, he did not persist

70 Meyer, *Die Haupturkunden*, (Leipzig 1894), 170–3.
71 Ibid., 174–5; Grumel, 958.
72 Meyer, *Die Haupturkunden*, 175.30–6; Grumel, 959.
73 Meyer, *Die Haupturkunden*, 163–70; Grumel, 978–91.

with this line of argument. He seems to have been as anxious as the patriarch to bring a greater degree of discipline to the hesychasts of the Holy Mountain. He provided the *protos* of the Holy Mountain with a *nomocanon* containing the canons of St Basil and the laws of Justinian which was to be read out at every assembly held at Karyes, the administrative centre of Athos.[74] He demanded from the abbots a list of their queries and grievances. These were presented to the patriarch who provided appropriate responses. These have survived as a series of instructions on spiritual matters to the monasteries of Athos.[75] They were intended to put an end to the divisions existing on the Holy Mountain and to tighten up discipline, but not to institute any measure of reform.

There was an undercurrent of criticism of Athonite monasticism among the metropolitan bishops, which surfaced after Alexius Comnenus's death. The monks of Athos were accused of mixing water with wine, receiving pirates, and continuing to admit eunuchs and boys. The question of whether the patriarch had placed the Holy Mountain under an interdict raised its head once again. The Emperor John II put the matter in the hands of the Patriarch Leo Styppes (1134–43). At the emperor's prompting synod found in favour of Athos.[76]

These details come from a narrative that was started by John Tarchaniotes, who was *protos* of Athos *c.* 1107, and finished by John Chortaitinos. Both played a direct part in the negotiations with the emperor and the patriarch. The purpose of the narrative was to vindicate the independence of the Holy Mountain from patriarchal authority.[77] Central to this was a claim that the Patriarch Nicholas had placed it under an interdict. On his deathbed Nicholas asked John Chortaitinos if he had ever seen a copy of it. He said no, but there were others that claimed to have. The patriarch dismissed them as troublemakers.[78] The explanation that later circulated was that a *protos* of Athos had forged the patriarchal interdict, as a way of restoring order on the Holy Mountain, which had been compromised by the presence of eunuchs and boys and Vlach women.[79] There is a strong suspicion that the Patriarch Nicholas connived at either the forgery or the explanation. The narrative cannot

74 Meyer, *Die Haupturkunden*, 170.5–9.

75 Grumel, 977, 982–4.

76 Meyer, *Die Haupturkunden*, 181.3–29; Grumel, 1008.

77 There are many difficulties associated with this document, not least establishing the dates of the *protoi* of Athos: see J. Darrouzès, 'Liste des prôtes de l'Athos', in *Le Millénaire du Mont Athos*, I (Chevotogne, 1963), 407–47, at 413–17. Over the dates of the *protos* Hilarion V. Grumel, 'Les prôtes de la sainte-montagne Athos sous Alexis Ier Comnène et le patriarche Nicolas Grammaticos', *REB* 5(1947), 206–17, is to be preferred.

78 Meyer, *Die Haupturkunden*, 179,ll.15–22.

79 Ibid., 181–2.

conceal that Mount Athos experienced a deep crisis at the turn of the eleventh century, which harmed its prestige. Its monasteries were not a force in the spiritual life of the Byzantine Empire under the Comneni.

After Alexius Comnenus's death not even the Lavra received imperial benefactions. The archives of the Athonite monasteries have few documents of any kind from the twelfth century. It is tempting to explain this in terms of the upheavals of the early thirteenth century, when for a short while Athos came under the control of the victorious Latin church, but why should documents from the eleventh century and even before have survived in considerably larger numbers? The lack of documentation points rather to a marked lack of interest by the imperial government in Mount Athos. This presupposes not only a decline in its material fortunes but also in its spiritual prestige. The eclipse of the monastic confederacies was bound to leave its mark on Byzantine monasticism. It weakened its ascetic and mystical component. It left the coenobitic monasteries of Constantinople as the exemplars of the Byzantine monastic ideal.

St Cyril Phileotes

All ruling elites need spiritual sustenance. The Comneni were no exception. Anna Dalassena ensured that 'holy men' and father confessors were part of their network. She sent her young son Alexius off to war with a monk to ensure his spiritual welfare. One of the 'holy men' that she patronised was Cyril Phileotes.[80] But that was long before her son became emperor. The Comneni seemed to forget about Cyril, but he grew more ancient and more venerable; more respectable, too, once he gave up living at home and settled in a monastic community. His fame once again reached Constantinople, only some thirty or forty miles away. First officers close to the emperor came to consult him. The saint sent them on their way, having lectured them on the vanity of riches and worldly success.[81] St Cyril's reputation increased. He claimed to have had a dream which predicted Alexius Comnenus's victory over Bohemond in 1108.[82] The emperor sent his brother-in-law the *protostrator* Michael Doukas to investigate and to obtain the saint's blessing for the imperial family. The saint wanted to know why he had come to seek the blessing of a sinner like him, estranged from God. The *protostrator* professed that he would be happy to exchange his high birth, rank, and power for the saint's sins. This did not surprise the saint, for high birth and worldly power were vanities when set beside

80 Cyril Phileotes XVII, i-v. 90–4.
81 Ibid. XXXIV-XXXV, 143–53.
82 Ibid. XXXVI, 154.

the struggle for eternal salvation: 'Consider well born not those born of the good and beautiful, but those who prefer what is good and beautiful.' There was no point to pride in ancestry, since we all trace our descent to clay, whether nourished in the purple or worn down by poverty. True nobility rested in contempt for riches and glory; real power belonged to those who knew how to rule themselves and to subject their body and spirit to reason; good government depended upon the application of existing laws. Innovations were to be shunned.[83]

These were old-fashioned views. They were at odds with the reality of Comnenian government, where birth was all important and all manner of innovations were introduced. The *protostrator* nevertheless brought an enthusiastic report back to the emperor. Alexius Comnenus therefore set out with his whole family to visit the 'holy man'. He received a lecture on the nature of imperial authority. He was told that the authentic emperor was the master of his passions, for only then could he administer true justice and act as the father of his people. St Cyril quoted Maximus the Confessor to the effect that 'imperial rule is government according to the law'. The saint's views were predictably traditional, but he was able to reassure Alexius Comnenus that he was fulfilling his responsibilities before God. His reorganisation of the Orphanage of St Paul displayed his care for the poor and dispossessed; his conversion of barbarians to Christianity his duty to spread the Christian message. The saint rejected the emperor's humble confession that the cares of office left him no time to think on God. If 'remembrance of God is the heartache that comes in the search for faith', then the emperor could rest easy in his mind. His support for the faith, for churches and monasteries, and his care for the people entrusted to him by God were ample testimony to his piety.[84]

This is what the emperor and his family needed from a 'holy man': endorsement and approval of their style of government; to be told that it conformed to the highest ideals of the imperial office. This was all the more important because of the criticism there had been that Alexius Comnenus was an innovator. The emperor's need for moral support is apparent from a mural of the Last Judgement which he commissioned. It showed him standing to the left of Christ among the sinners. An inscription reveals Alexius's state of mind: 'A river of fire swirls around me, a sleepless worm is within me . . . Only by fire shall I be saved'. Alexius seems to have been conscious of the moral failings of his rule.[85] Alexius visited Cyril Phileotes a second time. He was preparing a campaign against the Turks. He wanted to know if the

[83] Ibid. XLVI, 211–25.
[84] Ibid. XLVII, 225–35.
[85] P. Magdalino and R. Nelson, 'The emperor in Byzantine art of the 12th century', *BF* 8(1982), 124–26 (= P. Magdalino, *Tradition and Transformation*, no.VI).

time was propitious. The saint advised delay: counsel that the emperor heeded.[86]

Nicholas Kataskepenos, the author of the *Life* of Cyril Phileotes, included a short appreciation of Alexius Comnenus, based on personal experience. The emperor was always eager to receive monks and treated them with great consideration. Nicholas Kataskepenos had heard the emperor attribute the success of his reign to the prayers of *his* holy monks and the trust he placed in them. Alexius recounted how, as a very young man, his spiritual father had cured him through his prayers of an illness, when he was campaigning against Russell Balliol. The emperor's generosity to monasteries – and not just those in Constantinople – was duly noted. Nicholas Kataskepenos closed his account with a story he had heard from a monk who had attended the emperor during an illness. The monk arranged the imperial bedcovers to make the patient more comfortable, convinced that this was an act of lese-majesty. He could hardly believe his eyes when he saw the emperor inclining his head in gratitude. He was too frightened to return the greeting, but recognised it as a sign of the emperor's 'Christ-like humility' (*khristomimeton tapeinosin*).[87]

This was not a phrase chosen at random. It aligned the emperor with the latest trends in piety. We have already seen how these were reflected in new images, such as the 'Man of Sorrows' (*Akra Tapeinosis*). This showed Christ dead on the cross with his head inclined. It emphasised His humanity and made a deliberate appeal to human emotion. H. Belting traces the inspiration behind this new iconography to the liturgical changes associated with the Theotokos Euergetis. As we have seen in another context, these put great stress on Christ's sufferings as a man.[88] Here we have a detail which confirms Alexius Comnenus's devotion to the monastic piety of the time. His support for the currents of monastic reform associated with the Theotokos Euergetis contributed to their triumph. They came to constitute the monastic ideal that dominated the Comnenian church. There was a price to pay. Association with the ruling dynasty sapped the vitality of monastic life. The rule of the Theotokos Euergetis became synonymous with the order which the Comnenian emperors wished to impose on monastic communities. They displayed a deep suspicion of other, perhaps anarchic, forms of monastic life.

86 Cyril Phileotes LI, 243–4.
87 Ibid., XLVII, ix-xiii. 232–5.
88 Belting, 'An image and its function'. See above, pp. 69–72.

14

MANUEL I COMNENUS AND THE MONASTERIES

THE death of Alexius I Comnenus brought with it no slackening of monastic foundations by members of the house of Comnenus. John II Comnenus founded the monastery of the Pantokrator at Constantinople. It was to be his resting place, and it was to serve to commemorate his memory along with other members of the imperial family. Attached to it was a hospital, which was a practical memorial to the emperor's piety. The inspiration behind this foundation was his Empress Eirene, but she died almost before work had begun and it became a memorial to her.[1] The foundation of monasteries and nunneries was not just the work of emperors and empresses. Other members of the house of Comnenus were active in this field. About 1130 John Comnenus, a nephew of Alexius Comnenus and Theophylact's *bête noire*, converted his palace into the monastery of the Holy Trinity Euergetes. He retired there and became a monk.[2] His piety had been nurtured by long conversations with Cyril Phileotes.[3] Isaac Comnenus, a son of the Emperor Alexius, restored the church of St Stephen in Aurelian and turned it into a dependency of his main foundation of the Kosmosoteira in Thrace.[4] It was here that he was eventually buried. He had originally had a tomb prepared in the Constantinopolitan monastery of St Saviour in Chora. As we have seen, this monastery was rebuilt at the end of the eleventh century by his maternal grandmother Maria of Bulgaria. Isaac proceeded to restore it once again. He had possibly inherited founder's rights over it.[5]

[1] *Synaxarium Constantinopolitanum*, ed. Delehaye, 887–90; P. Gautier, 'L'obituaire de Pantocrator', *REB* 27(1969), 247–8; P. Gautier, 'Le typikon du Christ Sauveur Pantokrator', *REB* 32(1974), 26–31; Janin I, 529–38.

[2] Janin I, 522–4; Varzos I, 134–46.

[3] Cyril Phileotes LIII, ii. 249.

[4] Kosmosoteira, 70–1; Janin I, 488.

[5] Underwood, *The Kariye Djami*, I, 10–13; Janin I, 549.

Manuel Comnenus and monastic reform

Manuel I Comnenus was generous after a fashion to the monasteries of Constantinople. He confirmed their estates and incomes by a chrysobull of 1158.[6] Eustathius noted almost in passing in his funeral oration for Manuel Comnenus that in contrast to his predecessors he preferred to restore old churches and monasteries, rather than found new ones.[7] Manuel, in fact, became increasingly critical of the wealth of the monasteries and towards the end of his reign revived the legislation of the Emperor Nicephorus Phocas with its prohibition on the further acquisition of landed property by monasteries. He chided his father and his grandfather and his relatives for endowing their monasteries with rich estates. His views on monasticism are revealed in his plans for a monastery dedicated to the Archangel Michael. He was unhappy about the way monks of all sorts were congregating in the capital. He preferred monks to 'set up their habitation in out-of-the-way places and desolate areas, in hollow caves and on mountain tops'.[8] The site the emperor chose for his new foundation was some distance outside Constantinople at Kataskepe near the entrance to the Black Sea. He did not endow it with lands, which he considered to be a distraction from the proper performance of a monastic vocation. Instead, the monks received annual allowances from the treasury. The monastery was to serve as a model of monastic propriety. To this end Manuel Comnenus recruited for his foundation monks distinguished for their piety and asceticism.[9]

The silence surrounding Manuel Comnenus's plans has suggested that the monastery of Kataskepe was not a success.[10] There is no evidence that Manuel Comnenus founded any other monasteries. This has been taken to mean that he did not share his family's enthusiasm for monasticism.[11] Certainly not to the same extent. Manuel only gave limited support to monasteries founded or refounded during his reign. One of Manuel's ministers, the *mystikos* George Kappadokes, set about restoring the monastery of St Mamas outside Constantinople. The work was completed by 1158.[12] In 1162 another *mystikos* Nicephorus restored the Bithynian monastery of the Theotokos Elegmoi.[13] The

6 Zepos I, 381–5; Dölger, *Reg.* 1419. See Svoronos, 'Privilèges', 330–3.

7 Eustathius I, 207–8. See Magdalino, *Manuel I Komnenos*, 298. Manuel restored the refectory at the monastery of St Mokios.

8 Nicetas Choniates, transl. Magoulias, 118.

9 Ibid., 206–8; Eustathius I, 208.8–36. See Magdalino, *Manuel I Komnenos*, 298–9.

10 Janin I, 354–5.

11 Magdalino, 'The Byzantine holy man', 62–5 (= Magdalino, *Tradition and Transformation*, no.VII).

12 Eustratiades, 'Τυπικὸν', 256–311; Janin I, 327–8.

13 A.A. Dmitrievskij, *Opisanie liturgicheskikh rukopisej* (Kiev, 1895), 3 vols., I/1, 716–17; Janin II, 145–6.

mystikos had a special responsibility for the upkeep of monasteries.[14] However, the two *mystikoi* undertook their ventures in a private rather than a public capacity. The emperor did provide some backing. The *mystikos* Nicephorus was able to obtain an annual grant from the emperor of 100 *nomismata* for the Theotokos Elegmoi.[15] This was in line with Manuel Comnenus's stated intention to support monasteries with grants of revenues rather than lands. The *mystikoi* followed the emperor in not endowing these monasteries with new estates, though they recovered as much of their original property as they could.

Manuel Comnenus did not break completely with the Comnenian tradition of monastic patronage. Like other members of the imperial dynasty before him he continued to favour the rule of the Theotokos Euergetis for the foundations with which he was associated. The hagiography produced at Manuel's court celebrated his grandfather Alexius I Comnenus's work as a monastic patron. But it can also be read as a guide to Manuel's plans. Take the *Lives* of Hosios Meletios, for example. They were composed by men close to Manuel Comnenus.[16] There is one detail in particular that suggests that the life of the saint was made to conform to Manuel Comnenus's ideas about monasticism. Alexius Comnenus granted Meletios not land, but revenues. The virtue of the saint was all the greater for the way he refused the full sum offered by the emperor. He limited himself to taking an annual income of 422 *nomismata* from the revenues of Attica, which was scarcely enough to cover his expenses.[17]

In similar fashion Alexius Comnenus did not endow Cyril Phileotes's monastery with landed property, but granted it a tax concession and some ready cash.[18] Even if the *Life* of St Cyril Phileotes was not written for Manuel Comnenus's benefit, it anticipated or reflected many of his ideas about monasticism. The author was Hosios Nicholas Kataskepenos. Very little is known about him.[19] He was a disciple of Cyril Phileotes, though not a member of his community. He corresponded with the Empress Eirene Doukaina. He must have written the *Life* of Cyril Phileotes after 1121, for he records that in that year, eleven years after the saint's death, he opened up his tomb and found the head still intact and giving off an odour of sanctity.[20] The rest has to be deduced. The title Hosios suggests that he was a monastic founder. It was accorded both to Christodoulos and to Meletios the

[14] Magdalino, 'The not-so-secret functions of the *Mystikos*' (= Magdalino, *Tradition and Transformation*, no.XI).
[15] Dmitrievskij, *Opisanie liturgicheskikh rukopisej*, 717.
[16] By Nicholas, bishop of Methone, and Theodore Prodromos: Beck, *Kirche*, 639.
[17] Meletios the Younger, 49.
[18] Cyril Phileotes XLVII, viii. 231–2.
[19] Beck, *Kirche* 639; Cyril Phileotes, 13–15.
[20] Cyril Phileotes LV,iv. 262.

Younger. The surname Kataskepenos indicates a connection with the monastery of Kataskepe. There is therefore a strong possibility that he was the original founder of the monastery and that Manuel Comnenus promoted or continued his work.

The lessons to be learnt from the *Life* of Cyril Phileotes tally with Manuel Comnenus's ideas about monasticism. The saint operated in the Thracian countryside rather than in Constantinople. His piety was originally highly unconventional. His way of life was apparent from his nickname *Sesideromenos.* This was a name given to ascetics who bound themselves in chains. They were exhibitionists who attracted much attention on the streets of Constantinople under John II Comnenus and Manuel. Cyril gave up the practice after a lecture from a monk about the spiritual dangers it entailed.[21] He also played the fool for Christ's sake[22] and at times followed a life little different from other wandering monks. He followed a way of life that would later be described as idiorrhythmic, but he abandoned it and entered a coenobitic community. The author of his *Life* put into his mouth a vigorous denunciation of wandering monks as the bane of monastic life.[23] Cyril emerges from his *Life* as a reformed non-conformist and therefore an excellent example to persuade all those ascetic exhibitionists who flocked to the capital to mend their ways. The historian Nicetas Choniates describes monastic life at Constantinople under Manuel Comnenus in the following terms:

> Some monks sought the praise of men and set up their whited sepulchres in full view of those entering the churches, and, even when dead, they desired to depict themselves as crowned in victory and with cheerful and bright countenances. They built their holy monasteries in the marketplace and at the crossroads and confined themselves to these as though in caves, not choosing the path of moral virtue as characterizing the monks but rather the tonsure, the habit, and the beard.[24]

This description is corroborated by other contemporary accounts of the religious life of Constantinople under John II and Manuel I Comnenus. They leave an impression of a dynamic exhibitionism.[25] 'Holy men' flaunted their different ascetic specialities. Some found patrons among the aristocracy. John Tzetzes moaned about the fashion among the aristocracy for collecting chains and other mementoes of 'punk monks' for their private chapels.[26] He also campaigned against a monk who had established a hermitage attached to the church of the Holy Apostles,

21 Ibid., XVI, ii.88–9.
22 Ibid., XV,i. 86.
23 Ibid., XXIV. 112–17.
24 Nicetas Choniates, transl. Magoulias, 118.
25 See Magdalino, 'The Byzantine holy man', 51–66.
26 Tzetzes I, no.104, 150–2.

but had been driven out because of his doubtful reputation. Tzetzes had now learnt that he was hoping to recover it with the support of a patron, the *protosebastos*. He denounced the practice of creating hermitages in the city: 'troughs of feasting and adultery' was how he described them.[27]

These were perennial features of life in the capital, but Manuel Comnenus was as anxious as his grandfather to control the anarchic elements that always infiltrated monastic life at Byzantium. There was a very narrow dividing line between unconventional asceticism and popular heresy. There is the example of a hesychast and a saintly bishop being forced to eat cheese and meat before the patriarchal synod to scotch rumours that they had fallen into the Bogomil heresy.[28] There was a renewed Bogomil scare from the end of John II Comnenus's reign. Unconventional, what would later be dubbed idiorrhythmic, forms of monasticism came under attack from supporters of traditions of the 'common life'.[29] Interpretation of this attack is difficult. There were inconsistencies. There is therefore a temptation to conclude that there was perhaps little serious to criticise about the state of Byzantine monasticism in the mid-twelfth century; the critics having their particular axes to grind. Equally, there seems to have been a degree of disillusionment among those close to Manuel Comnenus; in which case it is likely that the sudden attention paid to the exhibitionism on the streets of Constantinople reflected a loss of direction. Theodore Balsamon bewailed the failure of the coenobitic ideal at Byzantium.[30]It would seem that Manuel Comnenus's effort to give it new life was a failure, at least in and around the capital. Manuel Comnenus's reputation in Constantinopolitan circles as a sensualist contrasted with his grandfather's reputation for piety. Manuel was not known as a great patron of monks. Consequently, he was not able to inject the necessary spiritual concern for the well-being of monasticism. His solutions were mechanical and administrative. The springs of the monastic revival associated with the Theotokos Euergetis were running dry in Constantinople, but they continued to trickle out into the provinces.

In the provinces Manuel Comnenus was remembered quite differently. Catia Galatariotou has recently drawn attention to the awe which 'our most pious emperor Manuel Comnenus' inspired in the Cypriot saint Neophytos the recluse. For him he was an ideal emperor on a par with Constantine the Great.[31] Manuel also supported the work against

[27] Ibid., no.14, 25–7. Cf. no.55, 75–7, where Anna Comnena was warned of similar disreputable elements connected with her household.

[28] Rhalles & Potles, II, 68.

[29] Magdalino, 'The Byzantine holy man', 59–62.

[30] Rhalles & Potles III, 411.

[31] Galatariotou, *The Making of a Saint*, 213–16.

heretics carried on by St Hilarion of Moglena in Macedonia.[32] The Bithynian monastery of Elegmoi restored by the *mystikos* Nicephorus prospered with Manuel's help. In 1196 it was the burial place of the archimandrite of the monasteries of Mount Olympus.[33] It was presumably now one of the major Olympian monasteries. Another of the monasteries that Manuel Comnenus supported was the Theotokos Makhairas on the island of Cyprus. The rule drawn up by Abbot Neilos owed much to that of the Theotokos Euergetis.[34]

Manuel Comnenus's reign was a time when a significant number of new monasteries were founded in the provinces. It is difficult to trace them to any imperial initiative, but there is evidence of imperial support. Manuel Comnenus's support for monasticism should therefore not be dismissed as of negligible importance. The monasteries of Constantinople continued to enjoy a golden age of sorts. They were very prosperous thanks to the emperor's generosity early on in his reign. There were even those, such as Eustathius of Thessalonica, who held them up as the ideal of monastic life, but this was a point of view informed by a good deal of nostalgia and wishful thinking.[35] The monasteries of Constantinople no longer possessed that moral authority which Alexius Comnenus had cultivated so brilliantly.

Other monastic patrons

Bishops were among the most prolific promoters of new monastic foundations in the provinces, even if they preferred to encourage founders in their work, rather than acting on their own account. They were often a channel through which Constantinopolitan ideals passed on to the provinces. We have seen how the rule of the Theotokos Euergetis formed the basis of that drawn up for the Cypriot monastery of the Theotokos Makhairas. Its first founder was a hermit fleeing from the Holy Land to the safety of Cyprus. It was then very small, not more than five or six monks, but the founder obtained from the Emperor Manuel Comnenus a rent of fifty *nomismata* and a grant of property. The second founder was Neilos who provided the monastery with its rule. He was a foreigner to Cyprus and joined the monastery in 1172. His abilities soon showed themselves when he organised food supplies from Cilicia at a time of famine. He was appointed to succeed to the

[32] E. Turdeanu, *La littérature bulgare du XIVe siècle et sa diffusion dans les pays roumains* (Paris, 1947), 82–3; D. Angelov, *Les Balkans au moyen âge. La Bulgarie des Bogomiles aux Turcs* (London, 1978), IIa, 27.

[33] C. Mango, 'The monastery of St Abercius at Kurşunlu (Elegmi in Bithynia)', *DOP* 22(1968), 169–76; Janin II, 146.

[34] Galatariotou, *The Making of a Saint*, 215–16.

[35] Eustathius I, 237.53–70. See below, pp. 353–9.

abbacy and began to build up the community and the wealth of the monastery. He made sure that the privileges granted to the monastery by Manuel Comnenus were confirmed and added to by Isaac II and Alexius III Angelus. He had some local support including that of the bishop of Tamasia. By the end of his abbacy Neilos succeeded to the episcopal throne of Tamasia, which emphasised the close ties between his monastery and the bishopric.[36]

Neilos was a monastic organiser. Quite different was his contemporary Neophytos who was a recluse, but the success of his hermitage outside Paphos depended on the support of the local bishop. For seven years Neophytos hid away in his cave. All the time the bishopric was vacant. Only when it was filled by Basil Cinnamus did Neophytos acquire a patron. The new bishop encouraged him to become a priest and to take disciples. He provided supplies and cells began to be built around the hermit's cave to house the increasing number of his followers. After Basil Cinnamus's death his successor as bishop of Paphos continued to act as patron of the Neophytos's monastery.[37]

It was not of course only in Cyprus that bishops took an active interest in monastic foundations. In 1143 Leo, bishop of Argos and Nauplion, transferred the nunnery of the Theotokos Areia to its present site at Hagia Mone just outside Nauplion. The original foundation was too close to the seacoast and exposed to pirate raids. This the bishop therefore converted into a monastery.[38] In 1080 Manuel, the bishop of Stroumitza, but formerly a monk, founded the monastery of the Theotokos Eleousa.[39] Leo, bishop of Mesembria, played a major part in the foundation of the monastery of St John Phoberos in 1112. He had originally been abbot of the monastery before becoming a bishop. He was buried in the monastery and his reputation for holiness was such that the sick would anoint themselves with oil from the candle that burnt before his shrine in the hope of effecting a cure.[40] The rule of this monastery too was based on that of the Theotokos Euergetis.

There is a danger in distinguishing too sharply between different kinds of foundation depending upon the status of the founder. Monasteries were founded and refounded. The monastery of St John Phoberos owed its existence to a monastic initiative backed by a local bishop who was once abbot of the monastery. But it was soon to attract aristocratic patronage. In 1143 Eudocia Comnena, a niece of Alexius I Comnenus, gifted a large sum of gold for the purchase of an estate. In return, her husband was to be specially commemorated along with their son, who

36 Tsiknopoulos, *ΚΥΠΡΙΑΚΑ ΤΥΠΙΚΑ*, 9–17, 64.
37 Galatariotou, *The Making of a Saint*, 168–9.
38 Miklosich & Müller v, 178–90.
39 Notre-Dame de Pitié, 6–9, 69–70.
40 *Noctes* 61; Janin II 7–8.

had become a monk of the monastery.[41] Also commemorated was Leo Hikanatos, a powerful figure at the court of John II Comnenus, together with his wife and children. He had presumably been of some service to the monastery to merit this honour.

There is another danger. The surviving evidence puts a disproportionate emphasis upon monastic foundations as an imperial, aristocratic, or episcopal preserve. Anybody could found a monastery. Its long-term survival without powerful backing was perhaps another matter. There used to stand on a hill outside Philadelphia in Asia Minor the monastery of the Theotokos Skoteine. Its origins went back to a chapel built at the end of the twelfth century by a metalworker of the town. He had gone to the hill with his journeymen to collect charcoal. He was suddenly moved to pray, as though by divine inspiration. He commemorated the moment by building a chapel dedicated to the Mother of God. It is easy to detect in this act a strong element of conversion, for the metalworker was soon to abandon his family, become a monk, and to settle permanently in the chapel. He was joined by his father and two brothers. Once the community had grown to six monks, he realised that he would have to organise it more formally. He persuaded a monk from the district of Sampson, on the coast, to become abbot of the community and entrusted him with the education of his son Maximus, who duly became a monk and succeeded as abbot of the monastery. His will is dated November 1247.

Under his guidance the community grew from twelve to eighteen and finally to twenty monks. The original chapel was now far too small. It could only take three monks at a time and Maximus decided that a new church would have to be built. He gradually built up the property of the monastery thanks to endowments from some of the most important local families, such as Phocas and Mangaphas, but there were also small gifts from local people along with purchases and exchanges. The monastery had considerable livestock. Maximus even acquired quite an impressive library, containing sixty-seven manuscripts. There were also additional manuscripts kept in the monastery's three *metochia* or dependencies.[42]

The metropolitan of Philadelphia is not singled out as a patron of the foundation, but his authority was recognised. The success of the monastery can be attributed to the way it attracted the support of local society from the highest to the lowest. Though described as plying a rude trade, Maximus's father appeared to have important contacts both locally and further afield. Over the choice of an abbot for his foundation

41 *Noctes*, 61–4; Varzos I, 172–4, 303–4.

42 S. Eustratiades, 'Η 'εν Φιλαδελφία μονὴ τῆς Υπεραγίας Θεοτόκου τῆς Κοτεινῆς' *ΕΛΛΗΝΙΚΑ* 3 (1930), 325–8.

he consulted the abbot of the monastery of Nea Mone at Latros. The isolation and independent spirit of Philadelphia and its people may in part explain the success of the Theotokos Skoteine. It became a focus of local piety and patriotism.[43]

The detailed information which has survived about the foundation of the monastery of the Theotokos Skoteine redresses the balance, for it relates to a monastery of purely local importance, where there was no recourse to the imperial court and administration, where even the local bishop scarcely had a role. Such foundations must have been numerous. One has only to think of the many churches in the Peloponnese dated in the main to the twelfth century, some of which served monasteries, but the circumstances of their foundation are unknown.[44] The motives and forces behind such foundations are likely to have been rather different from those behind more important foundations.

Because many different motives and circumstances were at work it makes it difficult to trace clear-cut patterns and rhythms in the monastic foundations in the Comnenian era. It was open to anybody to found a monastery and, if this was a step that, in practice, few took, many Byzantines aspired to make some gift to a monastery or a nunnery, in the hope of spiritual rewards. At this level, monastic life continued much as it had always done, but, as we have seen, there were periodically movements for monastic renewal. One such culminated in the work of St Athanasius the Athonite at the end of the tenth century. Another is associated with the monastery of the Theotokos Euergetis at Constantinople. It made its influence felt through the writings of its founder Paul and its *typikon* or monastic rule which became a model for a considerable number of the monasteries established in the twelfth century, both in Constantinople, but also in Cyprus. But there were other currents of monastic renewal, perhaps more traditional, associated with Christodoulos of Patmos and Hosios Meletios. The interest and support of the house of Comnenus intensified and prolonged this monastic revival. More than a modicum of piety may have inspired the imperial family to take up this stance, but there can be no disguising the political advantages that accrued to a new dynasty. At worst, monasteries might have become centres of opposition. At the very least, the variety of monastic life at Byzantium was a disturbing element in Byzantine society. Alexius Comnenus understood that his hold on power necessitated a return to good order. This most certainly applied to monastic life, given the role of monasteries in Byzantine

43 H. Ahrweiler *et al.*, *Philadelphie et autres études* (Byzantina-Sorbonensia 4) (Paris, 1984), 39–54.

44 Bon, *Le Péloponnèse byzantin*, 138–47.

society. The promotion of the rule of the Theotokos Euergetis by the Comneni was a means to this end. It upheld the primacy of the common life. Its influence continued to be felt, especially in the provinces, to the end of the twelfth century. But in the end Comnenian patronage became stifling. This is evident from Manuel Comnenus's monastic policy. He could hardly be said to be anti-monastic. He lent valuable support to provincial foundations. He wanted to preserve his grandfather's settlement which harnessed monastic revival to dynastic interests. However, his experiment at Kataskepe does not appear to have produced a renewal of 'coenobitic' order in and around the capital, which was his intention. Instead, the streets and precincts of Constantinople became an arena for monastic exhibitionism.

Nunneries

So one is tempted to conclude from the canonist Theodore Balsamon's assessment of the state of Byzantine monasticism around the end of Manuel Comnenus's reign.[45] He was convinced that the common life was in decline, certainly in comparison with the West. It was being ousted by what might be termed an idiorrhythmic form of monasticism. The result was that individual monasteries only numbered half a dozen monks at best. This was a recipe for anarchy. Balsamon exempted from his strictures nunneries, for they alone had preserved the coenobitic tradition intact. There is a strong element of polemic behind Balsamon's views, but they draw attention to a novel feature of monastic foundations under the Comneni: the disproportionately large numbers of nunneries that were founded.

The importance accorded to nuns and nunneries was something new. At the end of the eleventh century John of Oxeia painted a depressing picture of the condition of nunneries. The richest were given to archontes in their wives' name; poorer ones to people of lower social standing. They were treated as private property. Little, sometimes nothing, was left to the nuns. Lay patrons were known to build their residences within the cloister to ensure possession in perpetuity. It meant that they and their servants were living in close proximity with nuns. All discipline went by the board. The nuns took the opportunity to play off the abbess against the lay patron and to undermine her authority.[46]

The revival of nunneries owed much to the women of the house of Comnenus. Best known is that of the Theotokos Kekharitomene founded by the Empress Eirene Doukaina. There survives the rule

45 Rhalles & Potles III, 411.
46 Gautier, 'Réquisitoire', 124–7.

that she drew up for it on the basis of that of the Theotokos Euergetis. There is the same insistence upon the necessity of the common life. This, not the wealth of the nunnery or the number of nuns, was the essential.[47] Perhaps there is less stress on confession than there was in the Theotokos Euergetis. It was enough that all the nuns were to have the same father confessor, who was to be a eunuch. The seclusion of the nuns was all important. Apart from the father confessor and the steward, who was to be a respectable eunuch, men were forbidden to enter the nunnery under any circumstances lest some harm might come to the 'Brides of Christ'. Nuns might enjoy a brief encounter with male relatives in the gatehouse, but only under the supervision of the mother superior. A nun could leave the house to visit a dying parent, but she had to do so in the company of two other nuns.[48] Privacy was so prized that the empress decreed that the nunnery was not to be overlooked.[49] A building that did was pulled down on the emperor's orders. This nunnery was something of an aristocratic retreat. The empress had a residence built within the compound. She made provision for her daughters and granddaughters and other aristocratic women. The nuns were expected to devote a considerable portion of their time on commemorations of the imperial family. The prominence enjoyed by the women of the imperial family provided the initial impulse behind the new importance attached to nunneries.

But nunneries were not only founded in the twelfth century by the high aristocracy. The most interesting was a foundation for twelve nuns made about the year 1160 by the father of Gregory Antiochus. More is known about Gregory than about his father. Gregory was a littérateur and a bureaucrat. His career culminated at the end of the twelfth century with the important post of Grand Droungarios. Professor Kazhdan rejects an attempt to link him with the imperial house of Comnenus. If he was connected to the imperial house, why then, queries Professor Kazhdan, should he have so frequently referred to his lowly origins? It may well have been to emphasise the gulf that now separated him from the grander members of the Comnenian court, for the Antiochoi had been a distinguished family, but they had fallen from the highest ranks of the court aristocracy following a conspiracy against Alexius Comnenus.[50]

Significant in this respect is the stipulation made by Gregory's father

47 P. Gautier, 'Le typikon de la Theotokos Kécharitomène', *REB* 43 (1985), 30–3, 40–1

48 Ibid., 54–65.

49 Ibid., 128–9.

50 Anna Comnena XII, V, 4: III, 69.17 (ed. Leib); Darrouzès, 'Notice sur Grégoire Antiochos', 83–92; Kazhdan/Franklin, 200; M. Loukaki, 'Contribution à l'étude de la famille Antiochos', *REB* 50(1992), 185–205, at 200–2, where the eminence of Gregory Antiochos's family background is emphasised.

that his foundation was designed for girls who had no dowry, but some education. This slightly odd combination of poverty and education will best apply to families that had come down in the world. His son tells us that

> he founded the convent on the following conditions: the nuns should cultivate the holy scriptures; nobody ignorant of letters was to enter it, even if they came from the palace; a single exception being made for two out of the dozen nuns who made up the community. He decided that these could be admitted, even if they were illiterate, for it would be of benefit for the service of the house of the Lord.[51]

Why should Gregory Antiochus's father have invested virtually all the family's remaining wealth in the founding of a nunnery? The answer was that he desired to be buried in the nunnery. He protested that he was only motivated by spiritual desires and that he had no thought of material gain. Perhaps he protested too much, because he also sought from the patriarch complete freedom for his foundation. What this meant in practice was that members of his family were to have control over the administration of the nunnery. It was his experience that nuns often assumed possession of nunneries and then passed them on to their heirs. He did not want this to happen with his foundation. He hoped that members of his family would benefit from his work.

Gregory Antiochos's father reveals much about the motivation behind the foundation of a nunnery and about the problems that a founder foresaw. Founding a nunnery was almost certainly the fashionable thing to do in mid-twelfth-century Constantinople. This applied both to members of the highest ranks of court society and to families that were trying to restore their fortunes. The motivation was extremely complex. Spiritual concerns were probably uppermost. The Byzantines were 'much exercised by death' and thought hard about their place of burial and proper commemoration. Gregory Antiochos's father was also confronting a social problem that may have been especially marked among families that had fallen from power: the inability to provide a suitable dowry for all the daughters of the family. It was always difficult for a founder to ensure that his foundation would continue to provide the benefits, spiritual and otherwise, that he anticipated. The best guarantee was that its administration remained in the hands of his family. To ensure that this happened it was essential that the independence of the foundation was safeguarded. The legal status of monastic foundations was always a pressing problem, not only because of the wealth tied up in them, but also because of the bearing it had on

51 Darrouzès, 'Notice sur Grégoire Antiochos', 86.

their ability to fulfil their prime role, which was spiritual. These are the major themes illuminated by Gregory Antiochos's father and his foundation.

Underlying his desire to be buried in a nunnery may have been something else which gave nunneries a new prominence: a reevaluation of the spiritual role of women.[52] John Apokaukos, the metropolitan of Naupaktos, gave some thought to the matter. He argued that greater provision should be made in the provinces for nunneries. He cited the example of Constantinople, where before 1204 there were many nunneries. The metropolitan praised the inhabitants of the capital for the way they regarded men and women as equals, at least in spiritual terms. Women were, in his opinion, just as capable of chanting hymns as men, but he felt that in the provinces there was a lack of recognition of the essential equality between men and women. There an older view prevailed: a religious vocation was deemed to conflict with a woman's primary role as mother. As a result, there were very few nunneries, at least in the region known to Apokaukos. Such nuns as there were clustered around the precincts of churches in wretched huts. This was very different from Constantinople. John Apokaukos cites a series of examples of monasteries in the capital which were turned into nunneries in the course of the twelfth century. Even in neighbouring Thebes its renowned twelfth-century metropolitan, John Kaloktenes, had founded a number of nunneries. Apokaukos was therefore delighted to give his approval for the conversion of the monastery of the Blakhernai at Arta into a nunnery. This was done on the initiative of Theodore Angelus, the ruler of Epiros, and his consort. It was now filled with nuns of aristocratic parentage.[53]

The interest in founding nunneries at Constantinople seems connected, in the first instance, with the triumph of a court aristocracy. It was partly that, as we have seen, women wielded great influence in the bosom of aristocratic families and partly that there was a greater equality of the sexes at this level of society. This attitude filtered down through Constantinopolitan society and out into the provinces. So often it was women who preserved the solidarity of the family through commemorations. The prominence of nunneries under the Comneni and Palaeologi reflects aristocratic concerns: monastic life expressed and catered for the deepest needs of an aristocracy.

[52] Cf. J. Darrouzès, 'Un recueil épistolaire du XIIe siècle. Académie roumaine Cod. Gr. 508', *REB* 30(1972). nos.175–6, 225, where nuns ask Manuel I Comnenus for aid in rebuilding the refectory of their convent because Christ has also come for the female sex.

[53] Papadopoulos-Kerameus, 'Συνοδικὰ', no.3, 14–20.

Aristocratic patronage of monasteries

There is no point in making too strong a distinction between the imperial dynasty of Comnenus and other aristocratic houses. Both had much the same interests in monastic life. Aristocratic patronage of monasteries continued alongside dynastic patronage. If it is less well documented, this was because the accession of Alexius Comnenus to power had meant the eclipse of most other great families. The Palaeologi were an exception to this rule. George Palaeologus was one of Alexius I Comnenus's most important allies in the coup d'etat which brought the Comneni to power. His namesake, the Grand Heteriarch George Palaeologus, had a distinguished career under Manuel Comnenus as a military commander and diplomat.[54] He built the monastery of St Demetrius at Constantinople and restored the important monastery of the Theotokos Hodegoi, better known as the Hodegetria.[55]

His intentions were dynastic. St Demetrius was the patron saint of the Palaeologus family. In the narthex of the church of the Hodegetria he had a mosaic commemorating all the emperors with whom he was connected, going back to Romanos IV Diogenes and Constantine X Doukas.[56] The Palaeologi were not swallowed up by the imperial family nor were they slighted, as happened to so many other formerly great families. They retained their independence and a clear identity. They were precursors of a more general development at the top of Byzantine society. In the course of Manuel Comnenus's reign a series of aristocratic families began to emerge in their own right. This became all the clearer in the troubled years that followed the death of Manuel Comnenus in 1180: the Comneni would give way to a series of aristocratic families as the dominant element in Byzantine society. Patronage of family monasteries was one of the ways of asserting social dominance.

Although these aristocratic families concentrated their power in Constantinople, they also began to build up estates and interests in the provinces. This was reflected in their foundation of new monasteries. A good example is the monastery of St Panteleimon at Nerezi, just outside Skopia. It was founded in 1164 by Alexius Angelus.[57] He may also have been the founder of the monastery of the Prodromos

54 O. Lampsidis, 'Beitrag zur Biographie des Georgios Paläologos des Megas Hetareiarches,' *B* 40(1970), 393–407.

55 Varzos II, 862–3; Janin, I 96–7, 209. George Palaeologus was also a patron of the church of St Michael the Archangel outside Serdica/Triaditsa. He had an icon of the archangel flanked by himself and his son set up over the entrance to the church.

56 C. Mango, *The Art of the Byzantine Empire, 312–1453* (Englewood Cliffs, NJ, 1972), 227–8.

57 Varzos I, 654–5.

near Thermopylae where Michael Choniates found refuge.[58] The need felt by the aristocracy to found monasteries intensified after 1204, as different families sought to establish their rights to various territories. The most successful claimed imperial status and set up their courts in exile. In the European provinces it was the house of Angelus. At Arta Theodore Angelus and his consort renovated the church of the Blakhernai and added a chapel when they converted it into a nunnery. This church served as a burial place for the Angelus family.[59]

We have already met Theodore's brother Constantine Doukas. He was an enemy of the metropolitan of Naupaktos, John Apokaukos, but this did not prevent him founding at least one monastery – that of the Prodromos to the south of Arta – and adding an outer narthex to the monastery of the Theotokos Barnakoba, near Naupaktos.[60] Theodore Angelus would be succeeded in the rule of Epiros by his nephew Michael II Angelus. He made Arta the centre of his operations and founded there the monastery known as the Kato Panagia, while his consort Theodora founded a convent dedicated to St George, where she was buried.[61]

In Thessaly the example of the Angeli was followed by the Maliasenoi who were the most powerful family of the region. Though they refrained from assuming imperial authority they enjoyed a very large measure of autonomy. They founded two family monasteries in the first half of the thirteenth century, one at Makrinitissa and the other at Portaria.[62]

There is less information about Asia Minor, possibly because Theodore Lascaris was crowned and anointed emperor as early as 1208 and had few rivals. We hear instead of aristocrats taking monastic vows and retiring to monasteries. Andronicus Kontostephanos retired to the Bithynian monastery of Elegmoi where he died on 23 February 1209 as the monk Antony.[63] Another aristocrat John Angelus became a monk in the monastery of the Theotokos Eleousa near Nicaea.[64] He was a brother of the ex-emperor Alexius III Angelus, who was confined by his son-in-law the Emperor Theodore Lascaris in the monastery of Hyakinthos or the Koimesis at Nicaea. This monastery came to be identified with the Lascarid dynasty. Not only were Theodore Lascaris and his consort Anna buried there, but also his father-in-law Alexius III Angelus.[65] Theodore's son-in-law and successor the Emperor John III Vatatzes (1222–54) founded a nunnery

[58] Michael Choniates II, 328.18, 355.17–19.
[59] Nicol I, 197–8; Nicol II, 239–40.
[60] Varzos II, 663.
[61] Nicol I, 200–3.
[62] Polemis, *Doukai*, 142.
[63] Mango, 'The monastery of St Abercius'; Janin II, 146.
[64] Varzos II, 726. This monastery is not catalogued by Janin II.
[65] Janin II, 121.

dedicated to St Antony at Nicaea,[66] but he moved his capital from Nicaea to Nymphaion close to Smyrna. The establishment of a new capital was accompanied by the foundation of at least two monasteries in the surrounding area. One of these was at Sosandra dedicated to the Theotokos Gorgoepekoos. It was to serve as the burial place for both himself and his son and heir Theodore II Lascaris. Not far away his consort Eirene founded a monastery at Kouzenas also dedicated to the Theotokos.[67] The underlying purpose behind these foundations was dynastic. There is nothing to suggest that they reflected any strong current of monastic revival. There was during the period of exile an idealisation of Constantinopolitan monasticism, as it had existed before 1204; for instance, in the writings of John Apokaukos. The rulers of the successor states that followed the destruction of the Byzantine Empire in 1204 felt the need to provide their petty capitals with the trappings of the Queen of Cities. Monasteries were one way of doing this. They were following the example of the early Comneni.

66 Ibid., 111.
67 Ahrweiler, 'Smyrne', 94–6.

15

THE ROLE OF THE MONASTERIES UNDER THE COMNENI

A variety of motives, admitted and unadmitted, lay behind the decision to found a monastery or to support the work of a monastic founder. It was an enterprise that earned great spiritual merit, but equally enhanced standing in the community. Most founders set out their motives in the *typika* they drew up to guide their communities.[1] Bishop Manuel of Stroumitza prefaced the rule he gave the monastery of the Theotokos Eleousa with the old saying that 'Man's life is but a shadow.'[2] Reality was the 'abrupt and terrible decision of an implacable God'.[3] Like so many others, he was oppressed by the transitory nature of this world. Neophytos the recluse expresses the feeling vividly. From when he was very young he absorbed the anxieties of those around him. He was unimpressed by worldly success, since there was only death to look forward to. He kept his thoughts to himself, for they would only be dismissed as the product of youth and ignorance, but he recognised them as heaven-sent, for they pointed him in the direction of a monastic vocation.[4] The monk John who was the moving spirit behind the restoration of the monastery of St John Phoberos was equally convinced of the vanity of this world. He recognised that man has a double nature: heavenly and earthly. The greater responsibility was to cultivate the former and this could best be done within the confines of a monastery.[5] The stress was inevitably upon the community whose life approached the angelic and was dedicated to the glorification of God. Although the emphasis might differ slightly, founders perceived the chief function of a monastery as spiritual. It hovered between this

1 On the motivation of monastic founders, see R. Morris, 'Monasteries and their patrons in the tenth and eleventh centuries', *BF* 10(1985), 185–231.
2 Notre Dame de Pitié, 68.6
3 Ibid., 68.15–16.
4 Tsiknopoulos, *ΚΥΠΡΙΑΚΑ ΤΥΠΙΚΑ*, 74–5.
5 *Noctes*, 1–5.

world and the next. Monks were the living dead, capable through their prayers and way of life of intervening on behalf of both the quick and the dead.[6]

Aristocratic and monastic founders

The search for salvation was a common thread, uniting monastic founders, aristocrat and commoner alike. But in other respects, there were differences.[7] The aristocratic founder put his family's interests, material and spiritual first, while founders with a monastic background, such as Bishop Manuel, Neophytos the recluse, and the monk John, thought more in terms of the creation and of the well-being of a community. Neilos, the abbot of the Theotokos Makhairas, to take another example, wanted to be sure that his death was not followed by anarchy and the disintegration of his community. It was this that prompted him to draw up a rule for the monastery.[8]

Aristocrats looked upon a monastery as a thanksoffering for a successful or privileged life, but also, more often than not, as an insurance policy against attendant spiritual failings. The thought of the Last Judgement could weigh heavy. Michael Attaleiates presented his foundation of Christ Panoiktirmos as a thanksoffering to God for a successful career, but the immediate occasion was the death of his wife which had started him pondering on the last things.[9] The Empress Eirene Doukaina started from the opposite direction. She was struck by the wonders of creation and how the Mother of God united God, man, and creation. She felt that from early childhood she had come under Her special protection and guidance. Her foundation was undertaken out of a sense of gratitude that she had been brought safely through the trials and tribulations of public life.[10] Her son, the *sebastokrator* Isaac Comnenus, in contrast, thought of himself as a sinner. His foundation of the Theotokos Kosmosoteira was to make amends, but also to acknowledge that he had been saved from 'the deep pit of unbelief'.[11] The Grand Domestic Gregory Pakourianos admitted that he too was a sinner and a seeker after pleasure. He was terrified of the Last Judgement, but he had confidence in his orthodox faith and this had been the impulse behind his decision to found the monastery of the Theotokos Petritziotissa.[12]

6 Gautier, 'Le typikon du Christ Sauveur Pantokrator', 131.
7 See C. Galatariotou, 'Byzantine *ktetorika typika*: a comparative study', *REB* 45(1987), 77–138, at 136.
8 Tsiknopoulos, *ΚΥΠΡΙΑΚΑ ΤΥΠΙΚΑ*, 9–10.
9 Gautier, 'La *diataxis* de Michel Attaleiate', 23–4, 29–30.
10 Gautier, 'Le typikon de la Théotokos Kecharitomène', 18–29
11 Kosmosoteira, 20.18–27.
12 Gautier, 'Le typikon du sébaste Grégoire Pakourianos', 18–30.

A monastery was therefore an investment: 'an investment in eternal life' as C. Galatariotou puts it so felicitously.[13] To this end the monks were to provide a constant stream of prayer on behalf of the founder and were to perform commemoration services. In this way, the safety of his or her soul might be the better protected in the next world and his or her memory preserved in this. Aristocratic founders did not think of themselves in isolation from their families and followers. Their intention was almost always that their foundation unite them with those they cared about. This might involve arrangements for the burial of their descendants in due course. A good example is provided by the monastery of St Mary Pammakaristos at Constantinople. The children and grandchildren of the founders John Comnenus and Anna Doukaina along with their spouses were buried in tombs arranged along the north and south aisles.[14] The monastery was clearly intended to serve as a family mausoleum.

Aristocratic founders almost always ensured that their descendants would receive commemoration in their monasteries and that prayers would be offered up for their salvation. In an idealised way they were trying to maintain family and other ties in perpetuity. The grave was to be no barrier. Gregory Pakourianos reburied his beloved brother Aspasios in his own tomb at the Petritziotissa monastery. What is more, the monks for his new foundation were recruited in the main from the remnants of his warband, who had served him so faithfully.[15] When Eirene Doukaina founded the Kekharitomene nunnery, it was not quite her *gynaeconitis* in a new guise, but there were similarities. The empress clearly favoured ladies-in-waiting as candidates for entry into her foundation. She also ensured that they would have an adequate number of serving women. Then, there was the care she took for the nunnery's subsequent administration. She entrusted this to various of her daughters. But the main purpose of the foundation was the safety of her and her family's souls and the preservation of their memory. This meant that in some sense the nunnery must exist outside time or remain untouched by time. To this end she insisted that the convent's buildings must never be altered. She even went so far as to obtain an order from her husband to this effect. Though she could not always be with her community, they were to act as though she was present in spirit. She intended the Kekharitomene to be a shrine to her family.[16]

[13] Galatariotou, 'Byzantine *ktetorika typika*', 91.

[14] P. Schreiner, 'Eine unbekannte Beschreibung der Pammakaristoskirche (Fethiye Camii) und weitere Texte zur Topographie Konstantinopels', *DOP* 25(1971), 219–48, at 226–30; Belting, Mango, and Mouriki, *Mosaics and Frescoes*, 5–10.

[15] Gautier, 'Le typikon du sébaste Grégoire Pakourianos', 18–23, 44–5.

[16] Gautier, 'Le typikon de la Théotokos Kecharitomène', 36–41, 128–9, 132–7.

In the case of most aristocratic founders this was the primary purpose. The *sebastokrator* Isaac Comnenus was something of an exception.[17] The sense of family is muted. He arranged for the commemoration of his parents, but no other members of the imperial family. Instead he insisted that his trusted companion Leo Kastamonites and his secretary Michael should be remembered in the prayers of the monks. He wanted them buried in a place of honour in the *exonarthex* of the monastery church.[18] His own tomb was to be in the narthex. He had originally prepared a tomb for himself in the Constantinopolitan monastery of St Saviour in Chora. Once he had founded the Kosmosoteira he preferred that this should be his last resting place. He therefore ordered that the tomb he had constructed at St Saviour in Chora should be dismantled and transferred to his new foundation. He left behind at St Saviour in Chora a portrait done of him as a young man, but he insisted that the associated portraits of his parents should be rehung close to his new tomb, along with an iconostasis, which held a mosaic of the Mother of God. The care which Isaac took to specify the arrangements of his tomb emphasise how important a consideration this was in his decision to found the monastery. At one end of his tomb was to be placed an icon of the Mother of God Kosmosoteira 'for all time to intervene for his miserable soul'. It was very precious to him. He described it as having been sent to him from God. At the other end of the tomb was to be an icon of Christ. Every evening following vespers the abbot and the whole community were to enter the enclosure round the tomb and were to offer up prayers to the icons for his soul.[19] Isaac was aware that in time the icons would deteriorate. He therefore left instructions that they should periodically be retouched 'by some distinguished artist'.[20]

Bearing in mind the now discarded distinction between aristocratic and monastic psalters, it would be unwise to insist on too clear a division between aristocratic and monastic founders. They were as often as not working within the same framework of ideas. The *typikon* of the Theotokos Euergetis provided the model for the rules of aristocratic and monastic foundations alike. Isaac Comnenus excluded any family control of his monastery, so did Gregory Pakourianos.[21] Bishop Leo of Argos and Nauplion equally so, but he did make provision in the aristocratic fashion that his monastery should commemorate members of his family.[22] Does this mean that the structure and function of a

17 As noted by Galatariotou, 'Byzantine *ktetorika typika*', 107.
18 Kosmosoteira, 69–70.
19 Ibid., 63–4.
20 Ibid., 71.
21 Ibid., 26.8–9; Gautier, 'Le typikon du sébaste Grégoire Pakourianos', 88–95.
22 Miklosich & Müller v, 189.

monastery was independent of a founder and his motives? As with so much of the history of Byzantium it is A.P. Kazhdan who has identified the problem. He advances the idea that the monastery was a 'duplikat' or replica of the Byzantine family.[23] He sees the coenobitic houses reproducing the ordered structure and hierarchy of an aristocratic household. This contrasted with the idiorrhythmic communities which mirrored the weakness of Byzantine family life among the poorer sections of society. The close connection between monastic and family life is amply demonstrated by St Cyril Phileotes, who initially followed his calling within the bosom of his family.[24]

Contemporaries indicate the importance of idiorrhythmic monasticism. It contributed to the flux and vitality of Byzantine monastic life, but by its very character remains more or less impossible to pin down. Our evidence deals almost entirely with coenobitic houses. A.P. Kazhdan was struck by the social gradations within these monasteries. Special provision was made for servants within the community. Gregory Pakourianos allowed monks of the highest social standing to keep servants, but nobody else, not even an officer of the monastery.[25] At the Theotokos Kosmosoteira there were to be fifty monks and twenty-four servants;[26] at the Pantokrator fifty monks and thirty servants.[27] The distinction was quite clear: the former were responsible for the celebration of church services – Isaac Comnenus calls them *monachous hymnodous*;[28] the latter for the more menial occupations. The Pantokrator rule referred to them as *douleutai*. They were to serve as bakers, gardeners, cooks, and as assistants to the officers of the monastery who were to be selected from the monks who served in church. The rule even specified that four of the *douleutai* were there for the personal service of the monks, down to bathing them.[29] At the Theotokos Kekharitomene even the habits worn by the nuns contributed to a sense of hierarchy. The *mega schema* – or 'greater habit' – was reserved for those nuns who celebrated the church services. In normal circumstances they went through a probationary period of three years. The 'lesser habit' was for the other sisters. They had only to wait six months to qualify, but were assigned menial occupations.[30] The Empress Eirene Doukaina fixed the number of nuns provisionally at twenty-four with six serving women:[31] a division that was to continue

[23] Kazhdan, 'Vizantinijskij monastyr' XI-XII vv.', 48–70.
[24] See above, p. 268.
[25] Gautier, 'Le typikon du sébaste Grégoire Pakourianos', 45–51.
[26] Kosmosoteira, 21.4–6.
[27] Gautier, 'Le typikon du Christ Sauveur Pantokrator', 60–1.
[28] Kosmosoteira, 21.3.
[29] Gautier, 'Le typikon du Christ Sauveur Pantokrator', 60–1.
[30] Gautier in, 'Le typikon de la Théotokos Kecharitomène' 76–77,and n.9
[31] Ibid., 40–1.

after death. A special place was reserved in the convent's cemetery for the servants of the sisters; another for those nuns who attained to the *mega schema*; yet another for the remaining sisters together with servants who had become nuns.[32]

C. Galatariotou contends that this kind of social differentiation was typical of aristocratic foundations. In others there was a greater emphasis upon equality among the members of the community.[33] The rule of the monastery of St John Prodromos Phoberos specified that there were to be no servants,[34] as did that of the Theotokos Makhairas.[35] But the early experiences of Neophytos the recluse show that there was always some division between monks who did the menial tasks and those who served in church. Neophytos came from a peasant family. On entering the monastery of St John Chrysostom at Koutsovendis he was set to tend vines. His lack of schooling made him ill-suited for other tasks. But once he had acquired his letters, it was a different matter. He served in the monastery church and was entrusted with a minor office.[36] Promotion of this kind is hard to imagine in an aristocratic establishment.

There is a strong presumption that different monasteries would recruit from different social backgrounds. Founders with a monastic background tend to have little to say about recruitment. The exception is Christodoulos who stipulated that the abbot must examine candidates about their intentions and vocation. There was always a danger that they might be fleeing from their creditors or poverty and only looked upon the monastery as a refuge. Such people were to be turned away. If the abbot decided that a postulant had a genuine vocation, he was to instruct him for forty days.[37] Christodoulos had a very high opinion of his foundation, which, he believed, had the potential to become another Sinai.[38] He wanted to maintain the highest standards. He was interested in vocation not in social rank.

Aristocratic founders, by way of contrast, favoured the entry into their establishments of people of some social standing. Gregory Pakourianos gave preference to members of his own family, especially if they had rank and ability, when it came to recruiting monks for his foundation.[39] The Empress Eirene Doukaina made special provision for the entry of noblewomen into the Theotokos Kekharitomene. In their case, the entrance requirements could be relaxed.[40] At the Pantokrator

32 Ibid., 114–19.
33 Galatariotou, 'Byzantine *ktetorika typika*', 95–101, 116–20.
34 *Noctes*, 58.
35 Tsiknopoulos, ΚΥΠΡΙΑΚΑ ΤΥΠΙΚΑ, 40.
36 Ibid., 75–6. See Galatariotou, *The Making of a Saint*, 13–14.
37 Miklosich & Müller VI, 78.
38 Ibid., 64.
39 Gautier, 'Le typikon du sébaste Grégoire Pakourianos', 104–7.
40 Gautier, 'Le typikon de la Théotokos Kecharitomène', 36–9, 76–7.

the Emperor John II Comnenus specified that monks did not have to provide a dowry (*apotage*), because it was the quality of the new recruits that counted. This did not prevent him almost in the same breath from assigning a privileged position to those of high birth and intellectual attainments.[41]

There was also a professional dimension to recruitment to aristocratic foundations. We have seen how Gregory Pakourianos initially recruited monks for his monastery from the remnants of his warband.[42] Michael Attaleiates was a bureaucrat. He recommended for his monastery accountants, notaries, and secretaries,[43] just the kind of people he had supervised in the past. He appreciated their abilities and hoped they would be of benefit to his foundation.

The tradition of the common life gave a degree of unity, but there were differences in the structure and purpose of a monastery, which stemmed from the founder and his purposes. At its crudest, an aristocrat saw his foundation as a focus of his family's needs. Commemorations and prayers for the founder and his family tended to be at the centre of the religious life of such a foundation. A monk founder regarded a monastery more as an end in itself; as a self-sustaining community. The celebration of the liturgy was almost sufficient in itself. In the words of Christodoulos 'by imitating the "anthem of angels" as far as is humanly possible, man celebrates the creation of God'.[44] This, he believed, was the heart of monastic life. Charity counted for very little with Christodoulos. For his time he was exceptional. The rule of the Theotokos Euergetis put due stress on charity and pious works. It may be that aristocratic founders paid more attention to the exercise of charity than others. They thought in terms of a clientèle drawn from all walks of life. The sick, the halt, and the lame were a new clientèle. The Emperor John II Comnenus intended that the Pantokrator monastery should care for the old and infirm, the poor and the lepers. They in their turn would be sent as emissaries before God.[45]

Monasteries and charity

Monasteries had a responsibility for the poor and defenceless. A normal feature of monastic life was the distribution of food to the poor at the gate of a monastery, but the range of social services undertaken by different monasteries went much further than this. In the twelfth century you would have found attached to monasteries almshouses,

41 Gautier, 'Le typikon du Christ Sauveur Pantokrator', 60–1.
42 Gautier, 'Le typikon du sébaste Grégoire Pakourianos', 18–23.
43 Gautier, 'La *diataxis* de Michel Attaleiate', 58.
44 Miklosich & Müller VI, 70.
45 Gautier, 'Le typikon du Christ Sauveur Pantokrator', 26–30.

hospitals, pilgrim hostels, the upkeep of bridges, baths and bakeries. Monasteries had fulfilled charitable functions for a very long time. The question is: did monasteries in the twelfth century have a larger role to play in this respect than had previously been the case? There is not a great deal to go on.[46] If Byzantine monasteries seem in the twelfth century to have extended the scope of their charitable works, then this may only be a reflection of more plentiful evidence. However, Michael Attaleiates's arrangements for the almshouses he established at Raidestos and Constantinople are a possible pointer to a larger role for monasteries. He had originally thought of entrusting his charitable foundation to the care of priests, but then decided to attach it to a monastery. This he created out of part of his palace in Constantinople. He fails to give an explicit reason for changing his mind, but implicit in the rule he drew up were the tax advantages that accrued from the foundation of a monastery.[47]

Such a consideration may explain why it became more usual to associate charitable institutions with monasteries rather than as in the past to create charitable foundations, the so-called *euageis oikoi.*[48] T.S. Miller has argued that in one area, the provision of hospitals, monasteries had long been active. He traces this back to the seventh century and the decline of urban life in the Byzantine Empire. This may have been true outside Constantinople. St Athanasius the Athonite, for instance, had a hospital built for his foundation of the Lavra on Mount Athos. At least, to begin with, it cared for outsiders as well as the monks.[49] One of the few competent medical compendia produced in the Byzantine Empire before the eleventh century was *On the Constitution of Man.* Its author was a monk-physician called Meletios, who came from a monastery in the Bithynian town of Tiberiopolis.[50] In the provinces there may have been a tradition of hospitals attached to monasteries, but this seems not to have been the case in Constantinople. The hospitals that survived there from the time of Justinian, such as that of St Sampson, do not seem to have been attached to monasteries.[51]

The medical profession at Constantinople was in lay hands. A.P. Kazhdan has charted the high status attained by doctors by the early twelfth century and the respect accorded to them. This was in contrast

46 See J. Herrin, 'Ideals of charity, realities of welfare', in *Church and People,* ed. Morris, 151–64.

47 Gautier, 'La *diataxis* de Michel Attaleiate', 37.

48 D. J. Constantelos, *Byzantine Philanthropy and Social Welfare* (New Brunswick, 1968), 111–36.

49 T.S. Miller, *The Birth of the Hospital in the Byzantine Empire* (Baltimore, 1985), 118–40; T.S. Miller, 'Byzantine hospitals', *DOP* 38(1984), 53–63.

50 R. Renehan, 'Meletius' chapter on the eyes', *DOP* 38(1984), 159–68, at 159.

51 T.S. Miller, 'The Sampson hospital of Constantinople', *BF* 15(1990), 101–36; Constantelos, *Byzantine Philanthropy,* 191–3.

to their rather lowly standing two centuries earlier and the distrust their ministrations inspired.[52] This might be thought to provide an explanation as to why hospitals in the capital were not attached to monasteries. However, it was not a consideration that prevented John II Comnenus attaching a hospital to his monastery of the Pantokrator. This hospital was not staffed by monks, but by professional doctors. It was open to people of every social standing. The scale envisaged was impressive. There were to be fifty beds divided among five wards: surgical; eyes and intestines; then two wards reserved for men with other diseases. The fifth ward was for women only. Overall charge of medical care at the hospital was in the hands of two *primmikerioi*. In addition, there were two doctors and assistants for each ward. The administration was entrusted to the chief orderly (*nosokomos*) and a deputy. The plans for the Pantokrator hospital are the most elaborate known for a hospital at Byzantium. This is almost certainly a reflection of the high standard reached by Byzantine medicine in the twelfth century.

When Alexius I Comnenus refounded the orphanage of St Paul he established it as an independent charitable foundation. The church of St Paul's was staffed by secular clergy and not by monks.[53] John Comnenus preferred to attach his hospital to a monastery. He did so, in the first place, almost certainly out of piety. He considered the sick, just like the poor, to be the special friends of Christ and their prayers to be particularly efficacious. Whether financial considerations played a part is hard to say. Its endowment included a number of monasteries, so that it became the centre of a monastic confederation.

The foundation of the Pantokrator hospital was not exactly a break with tradition. Since the tenth century emperors had founded monasteries for charitable purposes, but they were administered along with other charitable institutions. The difference lay in the independence of the Pantokrator. John Comnenus was recognising that charity in all its forms was primarily a monastic responsibility. Charity was still an imperial duty, but it was best delegated to an independent monastery.

John Comnenus's brother the *sebastokrator* Isaac attached a hospital to his foundation of the Kosmosoteira. It was situated in the outer bailey of the monastery. There were beds for thirty-six patients, but medical care was not of the high standard envisaged at the Pantokrator. It was a hospital in the old-fashioned sense of a place that cared for the elderly.[54] Some of the patients were expected to stay until they died. Perhaps this will explain why the staff was so small: there were only eight orderlies

52 A.P. Kazhdan, 'The medical doctor in Byzantine literature of the 10th–12th centuries', *DOP* 38(1984), 43–51.

53 Included in the complex was a convent of Georgian nuns.

54 Kosmosoteira, 65–6.

with one superannuated (*klasmatikos*) doctor in charge. In contrast, there was to be a 'capable and experienced doctor' always on call for the monks.[55] But the founder ensured that there was an adequate supply of drugs and other medicaments for the hospital. He insisted on food and bedding of a decent quality for the patients who were also, if need be, to have access to the monastery baths. The founder made provision for adequate heating and lighting. Isaac's decision to add a hospital to his monastery was taken for pious reasons. The word he uses for 'patients' is brothers, meaning 'our brothers, the poor'. In the middle of the chapter devoted to the arrangements for the hospital, Isaac suddenly inserted an emotional passage, reminding the abbot and monks that, ill as he was, he had been doing all he could to hasten the building of the monastery. He enjoined them to make sure that the work was finished.[56] He felt that it was essential for his spiritual welfare.

The hospital was not the only responsibility of the monastery. Isaac Comnenus charged the monastery with the upkeep of two bridges he had had constructed across the floodplain of the river Maritsa. He did this for the benefit of travellers. He set up on one of them an icon of the Mother of God and expected passers-by to pray for his soul. Again we see the same mixture of piety and spiritual self-interest. He was struck by the analogy with the bridge that he would soon have to cross to the heavenly tents.[57]

Isaac believed that care for travellers brought spiritual rewards. They were not to be ill-treated by the monks. This meant that they were not to levy the customary tolls which Isaac had enjoyed in his lifetime. Isaac did not construct any hostel to receive them, unlike Gregory Pakourianos, who entrusted the administration of three hostels for travellers to his foundation of the Theotokos Petritziotissa. One was situated reasonably close to the monastery: below the town of Stenimachos, where two roads met. The other two were in the vicinity of Chrysopolis on the Gulf of Strymon. One of them stood by the bridge at the mouth of the river Strymon. Both were close to the Via Egnatia. They had been built by Pakourianos in memory of his brother Aspasios. Daily allowances were set aside from the produce of estates belonging to the monastery to meet the needs of travellers. Each hostel was served by one of the monastery's *paroikoi*, who had to mill the corn, and fetch wood and water. Pakourianos provided his hostel at Stenimachos with an oven and a stove so that on winter days travellers could warm and dry themselves and relax. He also had a

55 Ibid., 48.34.
56 Ibid., 53–6.
57 Ibid., 51.25–6.

tower built to protect it from brigands.[58] Michael Attaleiates wanted to add to his almshouse at Raidestos a special pavilion (*kyklion*) for the reception of foreign pilgrims on their way to the Holy Land. He set aside special weekly allowances for their sustenance.[59] The foundation of hostels was a pious act. Monastic founders felt that there was special merit in helping the disadvantaged: the poor, the sick, and the elderly or those far from home: the pilgrim and the traveller. They believed that the sufferings of these people made their prayers the more efficacious.

These were the ostensible reasons for the charitable responsibilities which they attached to their monastic foundations. They were also very often men and women of great practical ability with a strong interest in the effective functioning of their foundations. They never suggest that there was some ulterior economic motive behind their foundation of hostels of one sort and another. In practice, they ought to have made travel through the Byzantine Empire that much easier, though there is no way of telling how well any of the hostels worked. Pakourianos and Attaleiates both issued stern injunctions to those that came after them to respect their wishes about the support of their hostels. Pakourianos even suggested that, should the revenues of his foundation increase, the allowances for the hostels should go up proportionately. There is a strong suspicion that the founders' intentions were not followed to the letter; that there would not always be a welcoming fire at the inn. The maintenance of hostels or of bridges was a burden on the monasteries to which they were attached. Their expense would come to be resented as the founder's memory receded.

What was to be spent on hostels or distributed in charity on different occasions is carefully itemised in the *typika* drawn up by the founders, but how great a proportion it represented of a monastery's budget is usually a matter of guesswork. Most founders were likely to be aware of the practical consequences of their decision to load their foundations with charitable functions. In one case we know what the proportion was: Neilos specified that 2% of the revenues of his foundation of the Theotokos Makhairas should be spent on the poor and on lepers.[60] But there was no question of attaching any hostels to his monastery. He preferred to found a nunnery which was to receive 8% of the monasteries' revenues. While another 8% was to go to support the priests of the Blakhernitissa – a local church more probably than the important church at Constantinople. Neilos was a great organiser. He felt that his monastery could spend up to 18% of its revenues on good works of one sort or another. Whether or not this

58 Gautier, 'Le typikon du sébaste Grégoire Pakourianos', 110–15; Lemerle, *Cinq études*, 179.

59 Gautier, 'La *diataxis* de Michel Attaleiate', 48–9.

60 Tsiknopoulos, *ΚΥΠΡΙΑΚΑ ΤΥΠΙΚΑ*, 64.4–12.

is typical is another matter, but Neilos was a man of good sense and his was a sensible example to follow. Whatever, it underlines that in order to carry out their charitable functions monasteries had to be effective economic units.

On occasion, charity could be turned to the economic advantage of a monastery. The *sebastokrator* Isaac Comnenus provided baths for the monks of the Kosmosoteira, but he also ordered baths to be built outside the walls of the monastery. These were to be open to the public. Women were to be allowed to use them on Thursdays and Fridays only. Isaac left strict instructions that these baths were to be rented out.[61] In other words, they were regarded as a business venture. As Paul Magdalino has recently shown, there were public baths attached to a number of monasteries in Constantinople and the provinces.[62] This was still the case in the twelfth century. In a few cases they seem to have continued the work of the *diakoniai*. These were lay confraternities devoted to good works which begin to appear in Constantinople at the end of the sixth century. Their charitable functions were absorbed in the course of time by the monasteries of the capital. However, it is equally clear that monasteries might run baths as a business. In the mid-twelfth century the bathhouse of the restored monastery of St Mamas provided it with an income.[63]

The enterprise shown by some monks could be the cause of criticism. John Tzetzes complained about monks going around Constantinople selling fruit and vegetables at inflated prices and getting away with it because they were a good cause. He does make it clear that the monks he had in mind were not those belonging to the great monasteries of the capital, but the irregulars: the stylites and the hermits who had rejected the coenobitic life.[64] But this does not mean that coenobitic communities were not orientated to the market. Isaac Comnenus impressed upon the abbot of the Kosmosoteira the advisability of waiting for a favourable opportunity to buy oil on the market at neighbouring Ainos. He was not to make his purchases from pedlars, but directly from the ships that offloaded their cargoes of oil at Ainos.[65] It was advice that his mother the Empress Eirene Doukaina would have seconded, for she recommended that the nuns of the Kekharitomene were to buy their habits from the markets of Constantinople, but only when the supply was plentiful and the price correspondingly low.[66] Isaac

61 Kosmosoteira, 66.16–26.
62 P. Magdalino, 'Church, bath and *diakonia* in medieval Constantinople', in *Church and People*, ed. R. Morris, 165–88.
63 Eustratiades, 'Τυπικὸν', 306.39–40.
64 Tzetzes I, no.57, 79–84.
65 Kosmosoteira, 50.1–4.
66 Gautier, 'Le typikon de la Théotokos Kecharitomène', 101. 1480–5.

bequeathed to the Kosmosoteira the port of Sagoudaous with its ships and its fondaco (*phoundoux*). He explained that his father the Emperor Alexius I Comnenus had issued him with a chrysobull exempting him from the payment of harbour dues and customs duties for twelve ships with a total capacity of 4,000 *modioi* or bushels. This privilege he passed on to his monastery.[67]

Commercial interests

At first sight, this interest in trade and the workings of the market would seem to have been wished upon a monastery or nunnery by their aristocratic founders, but many monasteries – and not just aristocratic foundations - were anxious to obtain fiscal exemptions for their ships. In 1088 St Christodoulos obtained a chrysobull exempting a Patmos ship of 500 *modioi* from customs duties and other tolls.[68] This grant was duly confirmed by John II Comnenus in 1119.[69] By 1186 the monastery had acquired another two ships and the Emperor Isaac Angelus was induced to exempt these from the payment of customs duties.[70] But these were both lost at sea. The monks invested in a new, but larger ship with a capacity of 1,500 *modioi* and were exempted from the payment of any duties or tolls on it.[71] In 1197 Alexius III Angelus added exemption for a second ship of 500 *modioi*.[72] Both ships were lost and in 1203 a new ship of 2,000 *modioi* was handed over to the monastery. It too was to be exempt.[73] Patmos's situation will help to explain the monks' preoccupation with shipping, but their persistence suggests that something more was at stake than just provisioning the monastery. This may have been the original justification for an exemption from customs duties, but a ship with a capacity of 2,000 *modioi* points to larger ambitions.

The Athonite monasteries had had ships engaging in trade from the tenth century. Both John Tzimiskes and Basil II tried to limit their use to the immediate needs of the monks. Over the eleventh century the Lavra acquired exemptions for seven ships up to a total capacity of 16,000 *modioi*. In 1102 Alexius I Comnenus reduced this to four ships of a capacity of 1,500 *modioi* each.[74] The Lavra used the exemptions it obtained for its ships not just to obtain necessities,

67 Kosmosoteira, 52–3.
68 Patmos I, no.7.
69 Ibid., no.8.
70 Ibid., no.9.
71 Ibid., II, no.56.
72 Ibid., I, no.11.
73 Ibid., II, no.60.
74 A. Harvey, *Economic Expansion in the Byzantine Empire 900–1200* (Cambridge, 1989), 238–9.

but also to trade in the products of its estates. Wine was a major item. In 1196 the government of Alexius III Angelus claimed that the monastery had not been exempted from the payment of duties on wine. The monastery successfully challenged this claim.[75] The effort made to check the commercial privileges of monasteries by officials of Alexius III Angelus was a failure. This was apparent in the grant he made to the new monastery of Chilandar on Mount Athos. It was to receive exemption for a ship of 1,000 *modioi* plying along the northern Aegean coasts from the mouth of the Maritsa to Thessalonica.[76]

The monasteries of Mount Athos and the monastery of St John at Patmos possessed, it might be objected, exceptional influence. Did less favoured foundations show the same interest in the economic potential of their estates? Probably not, because it tended to be the exceptions that managed to survive over a period of a century or more. Byzantine monasteries were often ephemeral affairs. But it is worth remembering that the monastic organiser who showed the most intense interest in the economic well-being of his monastery was Neilos who drew up the *typikon* for the relatively modest Cypriot monastery of the Theotokos Makhairas. When it came to choosing a new abbot, Neilos made it clear that the only qualities that counted were practical ones (*tas praktikas aretas*).[77] He arranged for a distribution to be made to the poor on the feast of the Assumption (15 August), but he warned against the dangers of being overgenerous. Provision for the poor should not be on so lavish a scale that the monastery suffered shortages. It might undermine its financial position. One of Neilos's main objectives was to ensure that the monastery's income would always exceed its outgoings.[78] The coffer containing the monastery's money was to be ceremonially inspected each month by the abbot and the elders (*prokritoi*) of the monastery. Neilos modelled his *typikon* on that of the Theotokos Euergetis at Constantinople, but diverged from it on matters of personal interest. Most often, these turn out to relate to the management of the monastery's estates and financial affairs.

Finance and economic opportunities ought to have been a major concern of all monasteries. Their survival depended upon good management. That for some founders and abbots was almost an end in itself. Aristocratic foundations could afford to be more generous in their provision of charity. It was not entirely a matter of Christian duty. Largesse was an aristocratic virtue, but it was also a means

75 P. Lemerle, 'Notes sur l'administration byzantine à la veille de la IVe croisade d'après deux documents inédits des archives de Lavra', *REB* 19(1961), 258–72 (= Lemerle, *Le Monde de Byzance*, no.XXIV).

76 Harvey, *Economic Expansion*, 240–1.

77 Tsiknopoulos, *ΚΥΠΡΙΑΚΑ ΤΥΠΙΚΑ*, 58.

78 Ibid., 18.

of nursing a clientèle. Through their charitable activities monasteries and nunneries could therefore play a pivotal role in the exercise of aristocratic and dynastic influence on society. Other monasteries were more ambivalent. The material and spiritual well-being of the monastery came before the needs of the poor. Neophytos the recluse becomes almost querulous when he reviews the pressures there were on the resources of his monastery. The Latin conquest of Cyprus meant that refugees started to look to Neophytos for succour. He did his duty, but complained that it disturbed his peace and quiet. It was a distraction from the true goals of a monastic life, which were spiritual.[79]

79 Ibid., 79–81.

16

THE MONASTIC ESTATE AND SOCIETY

COLLECTIVELY and individually monasteries were great landowners. This must have had profound consequences for the shape of Byzantine society. However, it is a subject that defies any positive, let alone quantitative, approach. Evidence about agrarian society in Byzantium comes overwhelmingly from monastic sources. Information about lay landownership is scanty. The assumption is normally made that in terms of title and management there was little difference between monastic and lay estates. In some cases the landed endowment of a monastery came in the form of all or part of an aristocratic estate. A good example is the monastery of the Theotokos Petritziotissa – better known as Bachkovo – founded by Gregory Pakourianos who was Alexius I Comnenus's Grand Domestic.[1] The implication is that there was no specifically monastic contribution to the development of agrarian relations. We shall see that monastic estates were organised around *metochia* or dependent monasteries, but these were more or less identical with *proasteia* or villas - manors might be a more accurate translation. Because we know so much more about monastic estates than lay estates, our perspective on Byzantine society is paradoxically restricted. It is not possible, for example, even to estimate what proportion of land was held by monasteries. The assumption is both that it was considerable and that it was growing steadily from the tenth century. The eleventh century witnessed the creation of a number of important monasteries. Though endowments were often made out of the property of decaying monasteries, there is a good chance that this spate of foundations resulted in more land passing into the dead hand of the monasteries. The actions taken by Manuel I Comnenus towards the end of his reign to limit further acquisition of landed property by monasteries tend to corroborate this possibility. It was not only the amount of land that the monasteries acquired: it was also the terms they enjoyed and the rights they possessed over the land and the peasants settled there.

[1] Lemerle, *Cinq études*, 113–91.

There is now general agreement that Byzantine agrarian society experienced a period of decisive change that was completed in the course of the twelfth century. The peasantry increasingly lost its free status and became the dependants or *paroikoi* either of the state or of individual landowners. This meant that in addition to the taxes due to the state the peasantry were liable to pay their lord a tithe (*morte*) and might owe various services. The tithe and services varied with the wealth of each peasant household. These were now classified according to their economic potential. At the top came those households that disposed of a pair of oxen and a holding of commensurate size, followed by those with a single ox and the land to go with it. Below them came those without regular holdings. This classification is first found in a document of 1073, which recorded the transfer of land and peasants from an imperial domain to the emperor's cousin Andronicus Doukas.[2] This suggests that it was on imperial domains that the changes affecting the peasantry occurred earliest and most completely. But monasteries were among the earliest beneficiaries of these changes. In addition to imperial grants of land and rights to settle a specified number of peasants, they also received various exemptions. These normally included freedom from the payment of taxes to the state, but they might go further than this and contain the right to collect taxes from their estates. The state was much more reluctant to surrender to the holders of privileged property its rights of justice and administration. But this would come. The state retained the right to check privileged property. The main aim was to ensure that an estate had neither more land than it should have had nor more *paroikoi* settled than it was entitled to. Land and dependent peasants might on occasion be confiscated by the state, but more usually the status quo was confirmed.

To use western terminology there was a manorialisation of rural society. How complete this was is very difficult to say, since almost all the evidence relates to this very process. Equally, the role of the monasteries remains unclear. On the face of it, the surviving documentation suggests that it was decisive, since monasteries appear to have received more extensive privileges than did lay landowners and to have received them earlier. There can be no certainties, only the balance of probabilities.

The appearance of *paroikoi* seems to have been connected with the state's reaction in the tenth century to the challenge posed by the great military families of Anatolia. The institution was developed from the reign of Basil II (976–1025) on the estates of imperial foundations and extended to favoured monasteries under his successors. Then

[2] Miklosich & Müller VI, 4–15; Patmos II, no. 1, 7–20

under Alexius I Comnenus apanages were created for members of the imperial house, which were equally privileged estates and held on terms not dissimilar from the great monastic estates. By Manuel Comnenus's reign this principle had been applied fairly generally as a way of supporting the officers of the standing army, but the size of these grants or *pronoiai*, as they were called, was necessarily rather smaller than those made either to great monasteries or to members of the imperial family. Characteristic of all these grants were the rights enjoyed over *paroikoi*, so much so that they were sometimes termed attributions of *paroikoi*. By the end of his reign Manuel Comnenus was trying to maintain a clear dividing line between different kinds of privileged property. This is likely to mean that he was hoping to prevent what would happen all too frequently in the thirteenth and fourteenth centuries: *pronoiai* passing into the dead hand of the monasteries.

Continuity was a major advantage enjoyed by a growing number of monasteries. Since most of our evidence comes from the archives of monasteries that have survived a good many centuries, this is a feature of the documentation. It is not to be dismissed out of hand, for Byzantine monasticism always possessed a core of ancient monasteries. Some of these were in Constantinople, such as St Saviour in Chora with a continued existence back to the mid-sixth century or St John of Stoudios back to the mid-fifth century. They had their ups and downs, but their age gave them prestige that attracted patrons and allowed them to maintain their wealth. In the provinces, as already observed, it was not so much a question of individual monasteries, as of holy mountains, such as Bithynian Olympus, Mount Latros, and Mount Athos. They were monastic confederations under a *protos* or an archimandrite. Individual monasteries might decline, but the confederation continued with new foundations being made. The vast majority of Byzantine monasteries continued to be small and with only a short lifespan, unlikely to survive much more than a generation after the death of the founder. One still has to set beside the continuity of the few the instability of the many.

All too often there was a chronic inability to manage the landed wealth with which these monasteries were endowed. It was a problem of some concern to the imperial government. One solution was to subordinate in one way or another failing monasteries to new foundations or to more successful monasteries. The Emperor Nicephorus Phocas (963–9) thought the answer was to bring in lay patrons to manage monastic estates. Lay patronage was always a problem. However passionately, monastic founders and reformers proclaimed the need for monasteries to be entirely free of any worldly entanglements, it was an unrealistic ideal. The fact is that in order to survive they needed estates to support them. This inevitably involved them in the problems of lay society as landowners, often as landowners who relied upon the support of a lay patron.

It is more than possible that the grant of privileged status on an increasing scale to monastic estates over the eleventh and twelfth centuries did make for greater stability. There is a distinct impression that the survival rate of monasteries improved with more efficient management of resources. Such an impression receives some support from the subsequent success of many of the monastic foundations of the time. Some have survived to the present, notably Nea Mone on the island of Chios, St John the Theologian on the island of Patmos, and Hosios Meletios on the slopes of Mount Kithairon in Attica, and others, such as St John of Petra, the Theotokos Kosmosoteira, and the Pantokrator, would remain rich and prestigious monasteries, while Byzantium survived.

The structure of the monastic estate

It need hardly be said that the size and structure of monastic estates were diverse. At the beginning of Alexius I Comnenus's reign the Lavra admitted to possessing 42,705 *modioi* of land, excluding its estates in Kassandra. The government inspector thought it was rather more.[3] It has been calculated that another Athonite monastery – Iviron – possessed at around the same time estates of similar size together with rights over 246 *paroikoi* and their families.[4] However, Alexius I Comnenus set about checking the growth of monastic estates. This is clearest in the case of Iviron. By 1104 it had lost eleven of the twenty-three estates it had possessed in Macedonia at the beginning of Alexius's reign. These the monastery never recovered. The number of *paroikoi* settled on its old estates fell from 246 to 172. These losses were more than made up by the acquisition in 1103 of the estate of Radolibos gifted by Symbatios and Kale Pakourianos. It brought the monastery rights over 122 *paroikoi*. There were to be no further significant acquisitions of property by Iviron for nearly 150 years. It would seem that Alexius succeeded in halting the expansion of monastic property, which had been running out of control. The expedient he employed for the purpose was fiscal. In 1089 the rate of taxation was increased. Monasteries, and presumably other landowners too, were found to hold too much land in relation to their new tax assessment. The surplus (*perisseia*) was confiscated by

[3] *Lavra* I, no.50, and p.70.

[4] *Iviron* II, no.52; J.Lefort, 'Une grande fortune foncière aux Xe-XIIIe siècles: les biens du monastère d'Iviron', in *Structures feodales et feodalisme dans l'Occident méditerranéen (Xe-XIIIe siècles)* (Colloques internationaux du centre national de la recherche scientifique no.588) (Paris, 1980), 727–42, at 728–34.

the government. It was a general measure. Only a few favoured houses, such as the Lavra, escaped.[5]

Alexius Comnenus did make some grants of land and rights to monasteries, but on a relatively modest scale. The monastery of the Theotokos Eleousa at Stroumitsa received a grant of 500 *modioi* of land in 1085 from Alexius Comnenus and subsequently rights over twelve *paroikoi* and their families.[6] Even an important monastery, such as St John the Theologian on the island of Patmos, received relatively little in the way of endowment. It received the small islands of Patmos and Leipsoi and land on neighbouring Leros, but had to surrender to the state its possessions on the island of Cos.[7] It was forbidden to acquire further landed property. It was only after 1204 that this monastery began to build up its estates on any scale. It acquired considerable property along the facing coasts of Asia Minor, thanks very largely to the generosity of the emperors of Nicaea. In 1221 Theodore I Lascaris gifted the monastery the *metochion* of Pyrgos which became the nucleus of its concentration of property around Palatia, the ancient Miletus.[8]

Another recipient of the favours of the emperors of Nicaea was the monastery of the Theotokos Lembiotissa (or Lembo) situated in the low hills a few miles to the east of Smyrna. It was founded by the Emperor John Vatatzes in 1228. Its main endowment was the suburban estate of Bari, which before 1204 had been in the hands of the Constantinopolitan monastery of the Pantokrator. The emperor added the monastery of St George outside the fortress of Smyrna and ploughlands in the plain of Memaniomenos which had formed part of the imperial demesne lands. These were generous gifts which constituted the core of the monastery's landed wealth. The happy survival of its cartulary makes it possible to follow in detail how starting from this base the monastery of Lembo built up its estates. It depended upon a strategy of piecemeal, but not haphazard, acquisition, in which purchase featured almost as often as pious bequests.[9] At first, Lembo was able to count on much local good-will. The head of one of the major Smyrniot families granted Lembo the *metochion* of Sphournou, which lay scarcely a mile away. It had previously belonged to the ancient monastery of Rouphinianai – in Latin hands after 1204.[10] A local priest bequeathed Lembo his family monastery of St Panteleimon outside the

5 *Lavra* I, 70–1; *Iviron* II, 28–31; Svoronos, 'Privilèges', 337–45; Harvey, *Economic Expansion*, 92–6.

6 Notre Dame de Pitié, 27.2–15, 29.9–10.

7 Miklosich & Müller VI, 94–5; Patmos I, no.4; Dölger, *Reg.* 1214.

8 Miklosich & Müller VI, 180–2; Patmos I, no.13; Dölger, *Reg.* 1755. See Patmos I, *86–7.

9 Miklosich & Müller IV, nos. 1–6. See Ahrweiler, 'Smyrne', 55–74.

10 Miklosich & Müller IV, 7, 32–4.

nearby town of Mantaia. It was in a poor state of repair and the priest was having difficulty in preserving his rights over its property.[11] It was the old story of a new and prosperous foundation providing a solution for older monasteries in a state of decay.

To begin with, Lembo had two main blocks of land: in the hills around the monastery reaching down to the sea at Bari, and in the plain of Memaniomenos. They were complementary. Memaniomenos produced wheat; the hills had their olives, vineyards, and arable plots. On the plain the monastery was able to extend its estates. It received a very generous donation of arable land from the widow of a high court functionary,[12] but it also bought up land where it could. In the hills it was increasingly a matter of purchasing small plots of land or batches of olive trees from peasant families. The initial imperial endowment created a momentum of estate building that lasted to the end of the century.

Monasteries that depended on imperial grants for the nucleus of their estates were surely the exception, even if we are better informed about them. More typical, at least in the way it acquired its property, was likely to have been the monastery of the Theotokos Skoteine outside Philadelphia in Asia Minor. Its properties were built up piecemeal through purchase and exchange and through the gifts of local people. In some cases, the purchase price was a few sheep. More usually money was used, the price varying from two to thirty *hyperpera*. The size of the individual properties is sometimes given, ranging from 10 to 100 *modioi*, but there was also an individual grant from a local dignitary, amounting to no less than 2,000 *modioi*. Although not possessing estates on the same scale as some of the Athonite or Constantinopolitan monasteries, this obscure monastery was a land-owner of some consequence, at least around Philadelphia.[13]

Metochia *and* Proasteia

The influence that a monastery might have on local society depended, in the first place, upon how it organised and ran its estates. Neilos, abbot of the monastery of the Theotokos Makhairas on the island of Cyprus, gave a great deal of thought to his monastery's estates. He insisted that they should be concentrated within easy reach of the monastery. He imagined that those situated some distance away might hold in store spiritual dangers to those sent to administer them. They were to be leased out or exchanged, but the rest of the monastery's

[11] Ibid., 7–8, 56–9.
[12] Ibid., 232–6.
[13] Theotokos Skoteine, 332–8.

property was to be administered directly and was never to be alienated in any way.[14] They were to be entrusted to old and wise monks, 'dead to any passion'. The name given to them was *metochiarioi*, that is to say administrators or bailiffs of the monastery's *metochia* or dependencies.[15] They were to have no responsibility for any revenues, but were to look after the agricultural implements and the stocks kept on the estate. Money for legitimate expenses would be forwarded to them by the *oikonomos*, who would see that both the bailiffs and those monks who worked the fields received their allotted rations. The *oikonomos* oversaw the harvest and the vintage, but to help him he had brothers sent from the monastery to register the yield.[16] Some of the agricultural labour was carried out by the monks themselves. This was not unprecedented. Neilos's contemporary, Neophytos, spent his first five years in another Cypriot monastery – of Koutsovendis – tending one of its vineyards.[17] Neilos's monastery also employed wage labourers.[18] At the very end of the twelfth century it was to receive a grant of twenty-four *paroikoi* from the Emperor Alexius III Angelus.[19] Since by that time Cyprus had passed under the control of the Lusignans, the grant must have remained a dead-letter, but it was indicative of the way that monasteries were increasingly relying on dependent peasants for the exploitation of their estates. Monasteries continued to use wage labourers, but more and more their condition was assimilated to that of *paroikoi*.[20]

Monastic estates were usually organised around *metochia*. These had often originally been independent monasteries. If we take the example of the monastery of the Pantokrator at Constantinople, we find that a number of monasteries, six in all, were subordinated to it and served as its *metochia*. It was in many ways the head of a monastic confederation. These dependent monasteries were concentrated along the Asiatic shores opposite Constantinople. They were foundations of a respectable antiquity, but their regimes were, in all but one case, suspect.[21] Subordinating them to the Pantokrator was in the first instance a measure of monastic reform. They were brought under the supervision of the abbot of the Pantokrator. But they were also wealthy institutions in their own right. Their administration was placed in the hands of *oikonomoi* appointed from the Pantokrator. Any surplus income was to be forwarded to the Pantokrator. To that extent these

14 Tsiknopoulos, *ΚΥΠΡΙΑΚΑ ΤΥΠΙΚΑ*, 48.9–19.
15 Ibid., 47–8.
16 Ibid., 38–9.
17 Ibid., 75.24–5.
18 Ibid., 38.21.
19 Ibid., 17.3–4.
20 Angold, *A Byzantine Government*, 138–9.
21 Gautier, 'Le typikon du Christ Sauveur Pantokrator', 69–71.685–727.

dependent monasteries provided a basis for the management of landed wealth in the vicinity of the capital. The Pantokrator was generously endowed with property and rights by John II Comnenus and his empress. They were scattered over much of the Empire. In many ways, its organisation was closer to that of the charitable foundations of an earlier period. Its administration was in the hands of a number of *oikonomoi*, some of whom were responsible as we have seen for its dependent monasteries, but the bulk of its properties were run like any great imperial or aristocratic estate. They were placed under accountants and estate managers (*pronoetai*).[22]

The Pantokrator was an imperial creation. Its estates and organisation did not grow organically. This is in contrast with the monastery of the Theotokos Skoteine near Philadelphia. We have seen how its estates were built up piecemeal from the turn of the twelfth century. They were organised around *metochia*. The monastery's inventory shows that its property was grouped around the monastery and four *metochia*. Normally *metochia* were old monasteries that had been acquired by the monastery, but in one instance the abbot records that he had had a new *metochion* custom built around a new church dedicated to St Procopius.[23] This example shows not just that the *metochion* was essential to the organisation of monastic estates, but that on occasion it had to be created from scratch. It consisted of a complex of buildings around a church.

A similar pattern also appears in the organisation of the estates of the Athonite monastery of Iviron. An inventory (*praktikon*) of its properties – Radolibos excluded – survives from 1104.[24] The monastery possessed significant properties in and around Thessalonica. These were grouped around monasteries or churches. The most important inside the city walls was known as the *metochion* of Leontia. It consisted of a church dedicated to the Prodromos and other buildings.[25] It must have served as a centre of administration for the properties of Iviron at Thessalonica, in the same way that the *metochion* of St Andrew Peristeriai did for those of the Lavra.[26] Outside Thessalonica Iviron's properties were grouped into *proasteia*. There were eight excluding Radolibos. In the majority of cases they had at their centre a group of buildings described as a *metochion*. In one instance, a *metochion* controlled more than one *proasteion*.[27] The Iviron inventory describes the lay-out of its *metochia* in great detail. They were built

22 Ibid., 113–15.1414–45.
23 Theotokos Skoteine, 334.39–40.
24 *Iviron* II, no.52, 228–48.
25 Ibid., 237–8.327–57.
26 *Lavra* I, 61.
27 *Iviron* II, 245.571–2.

around an enclosed courtyard, sometimes defended by a tower, and consisted usually of a church, living quarters, and ancillary buildings that might serve various purposes: stables, hayloft, kitchens, bakeries. They closely resemble the complex at the *proasteion* handed over to Andronicus Doukas in 1073. It consisted of a domed church, a cross hall with four chambers, a bathhouse, and various dwellings round about.[28] It was a manorial complex and *proasteion* is accurately translated as manor. It is obvious that *metochion* and *proasteion* came to be used more or less interchangeably. It is worth considering the implications.

Village institutions

Proasteia only start to appear as a significant feature of the Byzantine rural economy from the early tenth century. They were almost certainly the lineal descendants of the late Roman villa, around which in some areas large estates had been organised. The villa suffered in the upheavals of the seventh and eighth centuries. In contrast, the village prospered, if, for no other reason, because of the way it became the foundation of provincial administration. Many essential tasks, such as the raising of taxation and soldiers for the armies of the themes, came to rest with the villages themselves. The key was the village court composed of the *oikodespotai* or heads of families. It was responsible for settling the majority of local disputes on the basis of the *Farmers' Law* – an unofficial compilation which took shape in the seventh and eighth centuries and continually modified remained in use throughout the Byzantine epoch and into the *Tourkokratia*.[29]

What effect did the growth of *proasteia* and other kinds of privileged property have upon the village community? In the tenth century the imperial government claimed that it undermined the village community and the very foundations of the state. It is a claim that has been treated with a fair amount of scepticism by modern historians, who see as the imperial government's chief concern a bid to strengthen its own hold over the peasantry by reducing them to the condition of state *paroikoi*.[30]

J. Lefort has recently reopened the question apropos Radolibos, a *proasteion* or *metochion* of the Athonite monastery of Iviron. He contends that by the middle of the eleventh century village communities

28 Miklosich & Müller VI, 5–6; Patmos II, 9.

29 G. Ostrogorsky, 'La commune rurale byzantine. Loi agraire – traité fiscal – cadastre de Thèbes', *B* 32(1962), 139–66; Harvey, *Economic Expansion*, 18–20, 75–9; J. F. Haldon, *Byzantium in the seventh century* (Cambridge, 1990), 125–72.

30 See G. Ostrogorsky, *Quelques problèmes de la paysannerie byzantine* (Brussels, 1956), *passim*.

were coming under pressure precisely because of the creation of *proasteia* on their territories.[31] For one thing, *proasteia* were separated from the village for fiscal purposes. This had implications for legal status and ownership of property which were to a large extent determined by fiscal considerations. The village community was not likely to exercise any effective authority over a *proasteion* within its territory. J. Lefort believes that the effect was to deprive the peasantry of land. In his words, 'these communities were being strangled by the large estates which surrounded and penetrated within them, until many small proprietors had no other choice but to become *paroikoi* on a great estate'.[32]

A concrete example of what was happening at this time is provided by a dispute between the community of Adrameri near Thessalonica and another Athonite monastery, the Lavra. *Paroikoi* of its *metochion* of St Andrew Peristeriai had cultivated land claimed by the peasants of Adrameri. This led to a dispute, which never finally came to court, because in 1076/7 the parties came to a compromise. The Adrameriots waived their claim to the disputed property against the payment of seventy-two *nomismata*.[33]

There are several lessons to be drawn from this case. The first is the difference of interests there was between a peasant community and dependent peasants settled on a privileged estate. Another is the utility of a lord, who could support his *paroikoi*; in this case, with cash. *Metochia* and *proasteia* were usually worked by *paroikoi*. Their dependence marked them off from other peasants and frequently new settlements were created for them close to the administrative centre. This is likely to have been to the detriment of the original settlement.

How were these *proasteia* organised? Did the heads of households or *oikodespotai* continue to control the affairs of the village? Did they form a court, which settled most of the disputes that arose within the community? This is what happened in older villages. The answers depend very much on the way the *proasteion* had been created. It was possible for a whole village to be handed over to a landowner. It might then be described as a *proasteion*, but the old village institutions continued much as before. If, however, a *proasteion* was created out of part of a village's territory, then its peasantry was unlikely to build up the rights and institutions characteristic of a village. It is striking how little material the comparatively rich Athonite archives provide on village institutions from the turn of the thirteenth century.[34]

31 Lefort, 'Une grande fortune', 728–34.
32 Ibid., 732–3.
33 *Lavra* I, no.37, 213–15.
34 A.E. Laiou-Thomadakis, *Peasant Society in the Late Byzantine Empire* (Princeton, 1977), 49–59.

This is in contrast to the cartulary of the monastery of the Theotokos Lembiotissa, near Smyrna, where there is plenty of information about the village community. The *oikodespotai* are seen to play an important role in local affairs. They heard a variety of cases, not just limited to property disputes; they were called upon to provide sworn testimony for the imperial and ecclesiastical authorities. Their local knowledge was called upon for the establishment of boundaries. Around Smyrna the village organisation was still effective to the end of the thirteenth century, despite a well-documented growth of privileged property in the area over the same period. This is best explained by the fact that grants of privileged property, whether immunities or *pronoiai*, tended to consist of villages.[35]

As we know, Lembo's main endowment was the village of Bari. It is referred to interchangeably as a *proasteion* and as a village. At its centre was the chapel of St George, 'which the monks have turned into a *metochion*'.[36] The monastery's other property, as was only to be expected, was grouped around *metochia* within the boundaries of other villages. These *metochia* will on occasion be referred to as *proasteia*. They may have had peasants settled around them, but there is no hint that they possessed any of the village institutions. One of these was the *proasteion* of Sphournou. The monastery's rights there were challenged by a *pronoia*-holder. Evidence was given by representatives from various neighbouring villages, but not from Sphournou. It was eventually taken to the imperial court where the *pronoia*-holder represented not only his own interest, but also the rights of the villagers settled on his *pronoia*. The outcome was that there was a division of the disputed property in the presence of representatives of neighbouring villages.[37] Among other things, this case suggests that villagers had something to gain from having a lord to represent them before the imperial authorities. The lord in question was a *pronoia*-holder. Did a monastery perform a similar role for its villagers?

What happened at Bari? The only recorded occasion when the heads of households took part in court proceedings was in 1228. A certain property within the bounds of the village was claimed by a neighbouring village. The dispute came before the metropolitan of Smyrna. The *oikodespotai* were called to give evidence in the traditional way.[38] But this was before the village was formally handed over to Lembo. Thereafter there may be plenty of evidence about the activities of *oikodespotai* of surrounding villages, but not from Bari. Now it is the abbot and the officers of the monastery who

35 Angold, *A Byzantine Government*, 260–4.
36 Miklosich & Müller IV, 3.7–8. Cf. ibid., 16–17.
37 Ibid., 32–43. See Ahrweiler, 'Smyrne', 60.
38 Miklosich & Müller IV, 187–9.

appear before various courts in cases involving Bari, and not the *oikodespotai*.[39]

There was nothing straightforward about what was happening around Smyrna in the early thirteenth century. There was a very complicated interplay of interests, which might align lord and peasant or might divide them. On the face of it there was no reason why the abbot and monks of Lembo should not have represented the interests of their peasantry more effectively than the *oikodespotai*. But other examples suggest that the peasantry used village courts against their lords, though not necessarily in their own interest. The village courts were quite capable of returning verdicts that went against their lords. There is the example of a village court forcing the lords of the village to return olive trees they had illegally seized from Lembo.[40] Another lord summoned his *oikodespotai* to hear a case that he was bringing against the monastery. The monks insisted that there was no case to answer, but they were advised by the *oikodespotai* to fetch their deeds or the case would go by default to their lord who had already done them much harm in the matter. The court eventually found in favour of the monastery against the lord of the village.[41] In these cases, Lembo was the beneficiary of the independent spirit that village courts continued to show.

This does not mean that the monastery would have tolerated similar independence on the part of its own peasantry. It held the advantage of continuity of possession. In contrast, there was a rapid turnover of secular landowners in the region. This may account in part for their reliance on the existing village institutions. We find that Lembo's relations with the people of Bari soon deteriorated. They abandoned their holdings and sought refuge in neighbouring towns and villages.[42]

Practically speaking, the lot of the peasantry should scarcely have changed with reduction to *paroikos* status. Labour services were not very heavy. There was a tithe to pay to the lord, but this must often have been compensated by escape from the oppressive attentions of imperial tax gatherers. Nevertheless, peasants – and especially prosperous peasants – resented being reduced to the condition of *paroikoi*. It would be rather sentimental to suggest that they mourned their loss of freedom. It is more likely that they realised that they would have less freedom to run their own affairs. We are dealing in possibilities rather than certainties. The evidence from Lembo and later from the Athonite monasteries suggests that the creation of *metochia* and *proasteia* by monasteries weakened the existing village organisation. In contrast,

39 Ibid., 278–81.
40 Ibid., 92.
41 Ibid., 128–9.
42 Ibid., 261–2.

secular landowners appear to have been content to allow the system of village courts to continue to function. When economic and political conditions turned against Byzantium from the late thirteenth century, the decay of village institutions on monastic estates left a peasant society increasingly vulnerable to monastic landlords. The impact that monasteries had on rural society through the creation of *proasteia* and *metochia* seems to have been more complicated and far-reaching than J. Lefort suggests. It does not seem as though their encroachments 'strangled' the village community. Nor do the demands made by monastic landlords seem to have impoverished the peasantry; at least, not before the early fourteenth century. It seems more a question of the creation of a manorial organisation around a *metochion*, which allowed monastic landowners to dispense with a village organisation. This had very deep roots in Byzantine rural society and had ensured the peasantry a large measure of autonomy, but on monastic estates this was less and less the case.

This is not to deny that the growth of monastic estates may at first have been to the advantage of the peasantry settled on them. As Alan Harvey has demonstrated, it is difficult to assess exactly how significant a role monasteries played in the countryside as agricultural improvers. There is good evidence for the building of mills and the introduction of irrigation schemes, as well as the planting of olive groves, and vineyards on the part of monastic landlords. But in this they were not that different from secular landowners. It may be that their most important contribution was continuity of agricultural practice.[43]

The pastoral role of monasteries

There was one important sphere where monasteries differed from their lay counterparts. Monasteries and their founders considered that they had a responsibility for the spiritual and material welfare of the peasants settled on their estates. In his *typikon* for the Theotokos Kosmosoteira the *sebastokrator* Isaac Comnenus repeatedly begged the monks not to oppress their peasants.[44] He also had a new church built for the peasants settled round about the monastery, but on certain occasions they were to be admitted to services in the main church of the monastery. The abbot was not to allow them to partake of eggs, cheese, and meat on Thursdays and Fridays nor to miss church services on Sundays and the great festivals of the year, 'for pastoral authority should lead them, whether they like it or not, to the good and should

43 Harvey, *Economic Expansion*, 120–62.

44 Kosmosoteira, 56.58–9.

not allow them to fall prey to heretics on the prowl (*noeton lykon*)'.[45] How far these instructions were carried out is of course impossible to know. But the intentions were good!

In the countryside, but not only in the countryside, monasteries played an important pastoral role. Large numbers of churches were entrusted to their care. The Iviron inventory lists eleven churches on its various estates and another nine in and around Thessalonica.[46] These were mostly attached to dependent monasteries and *metochia*. The local population would not necessarily have regular access to them. In the case of only a single church does the inventory note that a priest was in residence. He presumably had pastoral duties.[47] It is only towards the end of the twelfth century that we have good evidence that the monastery of Iviron was concerned about the spiritual needs of the peasants settled on its estates. It was part of the energetic efforts that Abbot Paul (*c.* 1170–83/4) made to restore the fortunes of Iviron. He repaired the monastery buildings that had become dilapidated and had a hospital built. Outside the Holy Mountain he restored the *metochion* of Bolbos and had a church built in the village. He also had village churches built and decorated on two other of the monastery's estates. He was clearly catering to the spiritual needs of the peasantry.[48] The care taken over the decoration of these village churches is indicative of an interest in their spiritual welfare. It was very much a case of providing the 'books of the illiterate'. Abbot Paul adopted a policy of extending the monastery's pastoral work by building village churches. The monastery was presumably responsible for supplying priests.

Certainly, supplying a priest was one of the conditions that attached to a grant made to the monastery of Lembo by the Emperor John Vatatzes. It consisted of a former imperial palace. The monastery was to see to its upkeep and to provide a priest to officiate in the church attached to it.[49] This was in addition to the churches of its various *metochia*. Monastic churches of one sort or another must have helped cater for the spiritual needs of much of the rural population. Whether this made the peasantry more amenable to the demands made upon them by monastic landowners is another moot question, but there is another dimension to the problem. Churches were not just a source of spiritual solace. They were also a source of income for their owners. This is well illustrated by a case brought by a local bishop before Demetrius Chomatianos, the archbishop of Ohrid. It concerned a village which came into the possession of a neighbouring monastery.

45 Ibid., 68.29–31.
46 *Iviron* II, 232–45.
47 Ibid., 235.267–8.
48 Ibid., 10–11 (no.165), 36–7.
49 Miklosich & Müller IV, 145; Dölger, *Reg.* 1739.

The parish priest died and the villagers were persuaded to use the monastery church instead of their parish church. The local bishop saw this as an infringement of his proper authority, but it was more than this: weddings and baptisms were now carried out by the abbot and the bishop was deprived of the fees that he would normally have enjoyed. The archbishop found in favour of the bishop against the monastery, but it was not only a matter of spiritual authority that was involved. In his summing up Chomatianos was very clear that the villagers should continue to make their customary renders at harvest time to the bishop. In the course of the hearing the local bishop reminded the archbishop of another incident in his diocese. A local dynast had deliberately founded a monastery and subordinated it to patriarchal authority in order to exclude the bishop from a village in which the former had his residence.[50] It would have been a way of tightening his control over the local population and extracting further dues.

If the evidence from Smyrna is anything to go by, then the use of monastic privilege to exclude episcopal authority would have significant implications for the village. Around Smyrna the village courts came under the supervision of the bishop's administration. Their judgements were authenticated by the *chartophylax*. It is possible that episcopal backing was a vital factor behind the independence that these courts continued to display. The estates of a privileged monastery, such as Lembo, lay outside episcopal jurisdiction. This may help to explain the apparent collapse of communal institutions in villages controlled by the monastery.[51]

The growth of monastic estates and privileges made for changes in the organisation of rural society. Just as there was a shift – it is true over a long period – from a free to a dependent peasantry, so the *metochion* or *proasteion* increasingly became the focus of rural life. Monasteries were at the forefront of this change. Associated with this was a drive for complete monastic autonomy, which was directed in the first instance against episcopal interference. However, as the example of the local dynast demonstrates, there were often secular interests lurking in the background. As monasteries acquired greater autonomy, so ironically they became an even greater temptation to the laity. *Kharistike* might cease to be a problem, but lay patronage remained as important as ever.

50 Chomatianos, no.80, 339–50.

51 Angold, *A Byzantine Government*, 270–6.

17

LAY PATRONAGE AND THE MONASTERIES[1]

THE close connection between society, aristocratic or otherwise, and the monasteries ensured that lay patronage continued.[1] The forms it took changed. We have seen how *kharistike* went out of fashion, not least because it ceased to suit aristocratic interests, but it was never condemned as such and it lingered on. It even had its defenders.[2] Founders of monasteries remained, however, suspicious of *kharistike*.[3] A monastery brought low by the rapacity of *kharistikarioi* became something of a twelfth-century commonplace.[4] In 1147 the *mystikos* George Kappadokes found the monastery of St Mamas outside Constantinople on the point of dissolution: *kharistikarioi* had descended upon it, 'like ravening wolves'. The community was reduced to two monks who were not able to reside in the monastery, but 'wandered around seeking their daily bread'.[5] The *mystikos* proposed to restore the monastery. His offer was gratefully accepted by the bureau of the patriarchal church to which it was subject. It was suggested that he should receive it in *kharistike* for two lives. This he found unsatisfactory: it would almost guarantee a repetition of the old cycle of restoration and dilapidation. He therefore requested that the monastery should be withdrawn from the authority of the patriarchal church and given to him in full possession.[6] This received patriarchal assent and was confirmed by an imperial chrysobull. George Kappadokes next appointed an abbot who was to be responsible for rebuilding the community. The *mystikos* did not live to see the completion of the work of restoration. Had he lived, he would in the normal way have drawn up a founder's *typikon* or rule to regulate the life of the monastery. This task was left to the abbot he had

[1] See in general Thomas, *Private Religious Foundations*, 214–43.
[2] See below, pp. 337, 355.
[3] E.g. Michael Attaleiates.
[4] E.g. St John Prodromos Phoberos: *Noctes*, 51.
[5] Eustratiades, 'Τυπικὸν', 306.1–2.
[6] Ibid., 257–60.

appointed.[7] St Mamas was, like so many other monastic foundations of the Comnenian era, to be an independent (*autodespoton*) monastery regulated by a founder's *typikon*.[8] What we are witnessing here is a discredited form of lay patronage, the *kharistike*, giving way to a more acceptable one.

Ephoreia *and* typika

Monasteries had always striven for total independence. This threatened anarchy. Both the imperial government and the ecclesiastical authorities felt the need to impose a degree of order over monastic life. Their solution was the subordination of monasteries to episcopal control. The obligations of monasteries to their bishop were always contentious, as much in the twelfth century as in any other Byzantine epoch; in fact, all the more so, because of the increasing numbers of independent monasteries. It was claimed on their behalf that their *typika* exempted them from episcopal jurisdiction. Theodore Balsamon considered this point carefully. He rejected the view that *typika* had no legal force and accepted that the founder of a monastery had a right to issue a *typikon*, but he added a rider: any stipulations it might contain contrary to civil or canon law were not valid.[9] He was consequently opposed to the idea that a *typikon* might have the power to exclude episcopal authority from a monastery. Balsamon's opinion will only have helped to harden what was becoming normal practice by the end of the twelfth century: independent monasteries did not entirely disavow episcopal authority, but restricted it to the formality of the *anaphora*, that is the commemoration of the bishop in the prayers of the community.

Founders' *typika* can be traced back at least to that drawn up in the sixth century by St Sabbas for his Lavra outside Jerusalem, but it is only from the turn of the tenth century that they begin to be issued in any numbers.[10] They later came to be associated with the creation of independent monasteries.[11] The most influential in this respect was the *typikon* of the Theotokos Euergetis.[12] We have seen how it became a model for several twelfth-century rules, notably of houses founded by members of the Comnenian dynasty. The *typikon* begins with a brief account of the foundation of the monastery. It details the celebration of services and the provisions for the hearing of confession, which was placed at the centre of monastic life. The duties of the various

7 Ibid., 260.
8 Ibid., 257–60.
9 Rhalles & Potles II, 236, 650–3.
10 See K.A. Manaphes, *ΜΟΝΑΣΤΗΡΙΑΚΑ ΤΥΠΙΚΑ* (Athens 1970), 60–66.
11 Thomas, *Private Religious Foundations*, 220.
12 Gautier, 'Le typikon de la Théotokos Evergétis', 5–101.

officers of the monastery were set out, as were the procedures to be followed for the appointment of a new abbot. The provisions the *typikon* contained aimed to meet most of the eventualities of life in a monastery, as well as to set out standards of behaviour. They aimed at a renewal of the ideal of the common life. It became virtually an article of faith that this could only be accomplished, if the monastery enjoyed total independence from outside interference. The *typikon* almost invariably stipulated that nobody was to exercise superior rights over the monastery, not the ordinary, nor any layman; not even the emperor and the patriarch. So it is somewhat ironic that imperial chrysobulls and increasingly patriarchal rescripts provided the guarantees of monastic independence.[13]

Founders of monasteries were interested in founder's rights (*ktetorikon dikaion*). These were a perennial feature of Byzantine monasticism. They were given legal form by Justinian's legislation.[14] They were various and included the right to burial and commemoration, occasionally the right to appoint the abbot or abbess. There might also be obligations, such as seeing to the upkeep of the monastery and supervising its administration.[15] Founder's rights, it was discovered, could best be safeguarded through inclusion in a *typikon*. It was part of the way the independent monastery was turned into an aristocratic trust, which could be passed on to one's heirs.

The first surviving example of this process of subversion was Michael Attaleiates's foundation of the monastery of Christ Panoiktirmos. His intention was not simply that the excess revenues of the monastery should go to himself and his heirs, but also that rights of lay patronage should stay with his family. Even this eventuality held dangers that did not escape Michael Attaleiates's vigilance. What if founder's rights passed into the hands of some unscrupulous descendant? If that should happen, Michael Attaleiates directed that rights of patronage over the monastery should be taken from him and given to another relative - even a woman - who was worthy of the position. However, he still had hesitations about removing an unworthy patron. He did not want him to be deprived of his livelihood without a proper hearing. He therefore sketched out a complicated procedure for the deposition of written evidence. Should it prove impossible to find another patron from Attaleiates's relatives to replace the man found wanting, then the community was to take over the direction of the monastery's affairs, but half of the surplus revenues (instead of two-thirds) was to be paid to the dismissed patron.[16] It is quite clear that Attaleiates

[13] Ibid., 44.
[14] Thomas, *Private Religious Foundations*, 53–8.
[15] Ibid.
[16] Gautier, 'La *diataxis* de Michel Attaleiate', 71.900–920.

envisaged the post of patron of the monastery as a full-time job with a commensurate salary.

The word Attaleiates used for lay patronage of his monastery was *ephoreia.* This was a practice which during the eleventh century coexisted with *kharistike.* The connection may have been even closer, for it came in for criticism from the Patriarch Nicholas Grammatikos as part of his campaign against *kharistike*: holders of *kharistike* were apparently content with the *ephoreia* of a monastery, since this did not involve the registration of its estates and other property. In other words, it might give the holder a freer hand to exploit the wealth of the monastery.[17] Lay patrons preferred grants of *ephoreia* (or supervision) of a monastery. The lay patron would now be known as the ephor or, less usually, as the *epitropos* of the monastery.[18] In theory, the ephor enjoyed rights of administration only, but these normally brought a suitable material reward. With increasing restrictions on *kharistike* recourse to *ephoreia* must have become even more attractive.

While *kharistike* was deemed incompatible with monastic independence, *ephoreia* became the acceptable face of lay patronage. Even so there were misgivings about its possible exploitation. These were most strongly felt among the Comneni and their supporters. Alexius Comnenus's commander-in- chief, Gregory Pakourianos, specified that his monastery of the Theotokos Petritziotissa was not to come under the hereditary authority of his family. Too often he had seen the consequences that such an arrangement produced. Different members of the family struggled for control, producing divisions among the community and causing damaging lawsuits.[19]

The Empress Eirene Doukaina, on the other hand, appointed her daughter the nun Eudocia as ephor of the Theotokos Kekharitomene, the nunnery she founded.[20] The empress had no intention of using it as a trust for her daughter. She has stern things to say about a patron having respect for the independence of the nunnery. However, she had constructed within the precinct of the Theotokos Kekharitomene a palace which served her as a residence. She intended it to go to her daughter Eudocia, but she died. It was therefore allotted to her most famous daughter, Anna Comnena, with the provision that on her death it passed to the latter's daughter Eirene. It was the empress's wish that it should stay in her branch of the family, in the female line. Anna Comnena was also to exercise the *ephoreia* over the nunnery. After her death it was to pass jointly to her sister Maria and her daughter Eirene with succession to this position passing down in the

17 Darrouzès, 'Dossier', no. 2, 158–9.
18 Ahrweiler, 'Charisticariat', 14; Thomas, *Private Religious Foundations*, 218–20.
19 Gautier, 'Le typikon du sébaste Grégoire Pakourianos', 88–95.
20 Varzos I, no.37, 254–9.

female line. Once again, we see the combination of an independent foundation and *ephoreia*. The provisions of Eirene Doukaina's *typikon* were designed, among other things, to ensure that the ephor carried out her responsibilities and did not use the position to exploit the wealth of the nunnery. There was always the consolation of 'the most luxurious' palace adjoining the nunnery.[21]

The Empress Eirene Doukaina's son Isaac adopted much the same arrangement at his foundation of the Theotokos Kosmosoteira. He built himself a residence just outside the monastery precinct.[22] Both mother and son wished to reside in the odour of sanctity. Isaac, however, refused to appoint any ephor to oversee his foundation, saving only the Mother of God.[23] He was convinced that 'not granting an *ephoreia* over the monastery would save it from the hands of the unjust and [prevent] the manifest destruction of this monastery'.[24] He gave instructions for the palace to be pulled down, if the people staying there started to be a nuisance.[25]

It was not only members of the house of Comnenus who expressed their reservations about the *ephoreia* of monastic establishments. Leo, bishop of Argos and Nauplion, founded a monastery and a nunnery. He appointed the abbot ephor of the nunnery, but refused to appoint any ephor for the monastery. He did not even allow his successors on the episcopal throne any rights of administration. Their agents were not to enter the monastery, but to remain at the gate. Bishop Leo's suspicions were such that he would not allow any citizen of Nauplion to become abbot, because he was bound to be overfond of his relatives.[26] John Apokaukos displayed similar misgivings, when he granted the *ephoreia* of a monastery within his diocese of Naupaktos to a godson. He lectured him on the sacred duty he was taking up and warned him that it was not an opportunity for gain. He contented himself with the thought that, though a layman, his godson was also a eunuch and therefore more likely to take his responsibilities seriously, since he would have no children to provide for.[27]

Ephoreia was therefore not so very different in its aims and results from *kharistike*. If it seems largely to have avoided the bad reputation which attached to the latter, this may well have been because it was not so obviously a financial arrangement. Perhaps its greatest attraction was that it could be regulated by a monastery's *typikon*.

[21] Gautier, 'Le typikon de la Theotokos Kecharitomène', 33–5, 136–47.
[22] Kosmosoteira, 73.29–31.
[23] Ibid., 26.21–6.
[24] Ibid., 26.14–16.
[25] Ibid., 73.31–4.
[26] Miklosich & Müller v, 182, 185.
[27] Apokaukos II, no.v, 6–7.

This allowed a measure of control over the activities and choice of an ephor. It is also a reminder that *ephoreia* came into prominence with the monastic revival of the eleventh century. Founders assigned it a spiritual dimension that *kharistike* never had. The emphasis was on moral responsibility, whence the heart-searching in which some founders indulged. This was often a fiction, as Michael Attaleiates reveals. He was as concerned with the material as the spiritual rewards that an ephor was to enjoy. It was a fiction designed to conceal a contradiction at the heart of the monastic ideal. To fulfil their spiritual function monasteries had ideally to be separated from society, but this required considerable material resources, which left them indebted to society. There was a corollary: monasteries were an expensive investment made by individuals, who wanted to ensure the efficacy of their investment, both for themselves and for their communities and their families. This required an element of lay supervision, for which some recompense might be expected. As a form of lay patronage *ephoreia* was a way of reconciling aristocratic influence over monasteries with the ideals of the monastic revival of the eleventh century. To all appearances it respected the independence of the monastery in keeping with the *typikon* of the Theotokos Euergetis.[28]

Stauropegial foundations

Lip service continued to be paid to the ideal of the 'common life', but fashions were changing. Theodore Balsamon may have anguished over the decline of the coenobitic tradition,[29] but this did not prevent him advocating the advantages of lay patronage in the shape of *kharistike*. He contemptuously dismissed John of Oxeia's criticism in the following words: 'No attention should be paid to the writings of the late John, patriarch of Antioch, who was opposed to the grant of monasteries to private individuals and termed such business impiety.'[30] From a strictly legal point of view Balsamon was quite right. *Kharistike* was never officially condemned. But there was more to it. Balsamon was disassociating himself from the distrust there had been of lay patronage of monasteries. He understood the practical benefits it offered the church. These emerge from a grant made at the end of the twelfth century by the bishop of Mitylene. Under its terms a local landowner received a monastery in his diocese in *kharistike* for two lives. In return, the recipient agreed to make an annual payment of ten *nomismata* to the bishop and another ten *nomismata* to the latter's

28 Cf. Thomas, *Private Religious Foundations*, 218–20.
29 Rhalles & Potles III, 411.
30 Ibid. II, 614–15.

brother-in-law. This was ostensibly to cover the taxes the monastery owed.[31]

Kharistike continued sporadically, but it made no sustained recovery. This was largely because *ephoreia* adapted itself to the new pressures that played on lay patronage and to the new opportunities these presented. However genuine their piety aristocrats had used *ephoreia* as a means of ensuring a modicum of control over their foundations. They tried to protect their interests by enshrining the terms of the *ephoreia* in the monastery's *typikon*. As we have seen, *typika* by themselves did not carry sufficient weight at law to ensure that their injunctions were respected. The founders and organisers of independent monasteries therefore sought in addition both imperial and patriarchal guarantees of their foundations' status. These effectively removed their monasteries from any local jurisdiction. They now exercised their *ephoreia* under imperial and patriarchal supervision. In practice, this often gave lay patrons greater freedom of action.

Such monasteries were known as imperial and patriarchal monasteries or, slightly misleadingly, as stauropegial foundations. The founding of every monastery required a *stauropegion* or 'blessing over the foundations'.[32] This took the form of the planting of a cross, whence the name *stauropegion*. It was normally performed by the local bishop and was an earnest of the rights that he would subsequently exercise over the monastery. As a special concession the *stauropegion* could be made in the name of the patriarch, in which case the monastery would depend directly on the patriarchal church.[33] The advantages of the patriarchal *stauropegion* were deemed such that monasteries sought to obtain it retrospectively. The monastery of St John of Patmos is a case in point: only being recognised by the patriarch as a stauropegial monastery in 1133, nearly fifty years after its foundation.[34]

The practice reached scandalous proportions and individual bishops began to protest,[35] but it was left to the Patriarch George II Xiphilinos (1191–8) to tackle the problem systematically. He had become aware of how serious it was while still a deacon. Once patriarch he seems to have placed it at or near the top of his agenda. His purpose was to support the rights of local bishops. He tried to put an end to the most flagrant abuses. For example, it was the practice to build churches on property belonging to stauropegial foundations and then claim that they

[31] H. Hunger and O. Kresten, *Das Register des Patriarchats von Konstantinopel*, I (Vienna, 1981), no.86, 498–500.
[32] Rhalles & Potles II, 650.
[33] Thomas, *Private Religious Foundations*, esp. 215–16, 238–43.
[34] Miklosich & Müller VI, 102–3; Grumel, 1005.
[35] E.g. the bishop of Pyrgion in 1176: Grumel, 1131.

too came directly under patriarchal authority. The patriarch stipulated that such churches were to remain under the bishop's jurisdiction. Equally, the bishop was to retain control over monasteries which claimed the patriarchal *stauropegion* retrospectively. The patriarch also recognised that bishops had the right to exact *kanonika* from such churches and monasteries.[36]

The patriarch's stance was uncharacteristically altruistic. It was at odds with Theodore Balsamon's views about stauropegial monasteries. He was distinctly unsympathetic towards metropolitans and bishops who protested against the practice of obtaining patriarchal *stauropegia* for monasteries. He saw no reason why this practice to be valid had to have the positive approval of canon law. All knew that canon law had nothing specific to say on the matter. It was rather an unwritten custom that had prevailed since time immemorial. As far as Balsamon was concerned the patriarchal *stauropegion* was a legitimate demonstration of the superior rights that the patriarchate exercised over its subject dioceses.[37] Such attitudes at the heart of the patriarchal administration must have helped promote the spread of patriarchal *stauropegia* in the course of the twelfth century. Furthermore, the revenues at stake can hardly have been negligible. This makes the Patriarch George Xiphilinos's measures against patriarchal *stauropegia* all the more mysterious. The only conclusion is that they had given rise to serious abuses, which outweighed any benefits they brought to the patriarchate.

After 1204

The growth of stauropegial monasteries from the middle of the twelfth century had implications for lay patronage, but these did not become clear until after 1204. The fall of Constantinople and the establishment of the Latin Empire of Constantinople created a hiatus. For the time being monasteries in Frankish-occupied Greece survived as best they could, often looking to the papacy for support.[38] In the areas of Byzantine resistance monasteries relied on the protection offered by local leaders and landowners. It took time for patriarchal authority to be effectively reestablished after the patriarchate moved to Nicaea. There was little to prevent monasteries in the Byzantine successor states of Nicaea and Epiros assuming stauropegial status, whether they were entitled to it or not. They did so with the express purpose of escaping

[36] Grumel, 1179–80, 1185.
[37] Rhalles & Potles II, 40–2.
[38] E.A.R. Brown, 'The Cistercians in the Latin Empire of Constantinople and Greece', *Traditio* 14(1958), 78–96; B. Bolton, 'A mission to the orthodox: the Cistercians in the Latin Empire', *Studies in Church History* 19(1976), 169–82.

from the jurisdiction of the local bishop and enhancing the control of a lay patron.

There are examples of patrons building new monastery churches next to the old and with the same dedication, but claiming patriarchal *stauropegion*. They would then set about appropriating the property of the old foundation, confident that the local bishop no longer had any authority over the monastery.[39] Lay patrons justified their position by laying claim to founder's rights (*ktetorikon dikaion*) over monasteries, whether they were entitled to them or not. If the local bishop challenged the enjoyment of such rights, the lay patron simply arranged to have the monastery placed under the patriarchal *stauropegion* and thus beyond episcopal reach.[40] It was also possible to claim that the patriarchal *stauropegion* extended to all the dependencies and dependants of a stauropegial monastery, so that a monastery that was converted into a *metochion* of a stauropegial monastery would be removed from the jurisdiction of the local bishop.[41]

Even before 1204 the growth of stauropegial monasteries presented the patriarchate with problems of organisation. They were placed under the supervision of patriarchal exarchs. Thus, the Patriarch John Kamateros (1198–1206) appointed the metropolitan of Naupaktos, John Apokaukos, patriarchal exarch with responsibility for the stauropegial monasteries of his province.[42] This was the obvious solution to the problem: leave the supervision of patriarchal monasteries to the local hierarchy. But there was always a temptation, not always resisted, to prefer patriarchal agents for the position. Around 1215 John Apokaukos found himself replaced as exarch by a patriarchal notary called Sampson – a name that suited Apokaukos's talent for invective. The metropolitan protested that he had carried out the duties of the office scrupulously and that he was better fitted for the responsibilities than an ex-public notary of no great stature. He also protested at the way a favourite of the ruler Theodore Angelus had been made exarch of the monasteries of Bagenitia, which formed part of his province.[43] His protests were ineffective.

Such incidents underlined the anomalous position of stauropegial monasteries. They might have been nominally subordinate to the patriarch, but in the conditions existing after 1204 they were effectively under lay control. The question inevitably came to the attention of Demetrius Chomatianos, autocephalous archbishop of Ohrid. He was the dominant figure of the orthodox church in the West and the prime

39 Rhalles & Potles v, 119 (= Laurent, 1314); Chomatianos, 343–4.
40 Chomatianos, 337–40.
41 Rhalles & Potles v, 120 (= Laurent, 1314).
42 Apokaukos I, nos. 51–3, 57.
43 *Noctes*, 293–4.

mover of resistance to the patriarchate at Nicaea. He did not deny that there was canonical support for the practice of the patriarchal *stauropegion*, but he insisted that this in no way diminished episcopal authority over so-called stauropegial monasteries. As far as he was concerned, patriarchal rights were a mere formality, but Chomatianos went further than this. He condemned out of hand the common belief that stauropegial rights extended to all the properties of such monasteries. He cited the decision of the Patriarch George Xiphilinos in support of his opinion.[44]

Chomatianos faced the same problem as that patriarch. Both hoped to counter the worst abuses of stauropegial rights by reinforcing the authority of the ordinary. It is doubtful whether Chomatianos would have had any more success than the patriarch. In any case, the matter was effectively taken out of his hands with the defeat and subsequent imprisonment of Theodore Angelus in 1230 by the Bulgarians. Theodore's territories disintegrated. There was no longer any purpose in continued resistance to the claims of the patriarchate at Nicaea. In 1233 the ecclesiastical schism between Nicaea and Epiros was brought to an end.[45]

The problems of the orthodox church in the West were now the responsibility of the Nicaean patriarch Germanos II. The state of the monasteries came high on his agenda. Along with the stauropegial foundations there were also the so-called imperial monasteries, which claimed complete exemption from episcopal authority. He gave his exarch in the West instructions to subordinate them to whoever held the *stauropegion*: the patriarch or the ordinary.[46] This did not put an end to the matter. In 1246 the ruler of Epiros Michael Angelus confirmed the foundation of a monastery by the head of the great Thessalian family of Maliasenos. He granted it total independence. This was done without reference to the ecclesiastical authorities. The grant was made in recognition of the man's loyalty and military prowess, but most of all for his struggles on behalf of the 'Rhomaic land'. This is a clear example of a monastery being treated as though it was real estate pure and simple.[47] Ten years later, however, it was taken for granted that the monastery came under the spiritual authority of the local bishop.[48] Presumably the principle set out by Germanos II had come to be accepted, at least where spiritual authority was concerned. Monasteries were subject either to the local bishop or to the patriarch.

44 Chomatianos, 345–50.
45 Karpozilos, *Ecclesiastical Controversy*, 87–95.
46 E. Kurtz, 'Christophoros von Ankyra als Exarch des Patriarchen Germanos II', *BZ* 16(1907), 137–9 (=Laurent, 1265).
47 Miklosich & Müller IV, 346–9.
48 Ibid., 356.

Did the success of the bishop in regaining spiritual authority over the monastery in question mean that in practice Chomatianos's opinion prevailed? That is to say, patriarchal rights over monasteries were only a formality. Not if the Patriarch Germanos II had anything to do with it! He understood the matter quite differently. His interpretation of the decision of the Patriarch George Xiphilinos about stauropegial rights diverged from that of Demetrius Chomatianos. He did not consider patriarchal authority a mere formality. Where there was a patriarchal *stauropegion* the local bishop was to have no authority and no right to exact the *kanonika*. In such cases power rested with the patriarchal exarch down to the examination of candidates for the priesthood, the authorisation of marriages, and the endorsement of confessors.[49]

In Anatolia Germanos II was confronted with the same problem of the growth of stauropegial monasteries. It was particularly acute in Paphlagonia. He decreed that where there was any doubt about jurisdiction these monasteries should come under the authority of patriarchal exarchs, and not the local bishops. This produced an outcry in synod. The patriarch was forced to revoke his decree, admitting that stauropegial rights did not extend to dependencies. This was done on the basis of a decision attributed to the Patriarch Germanos I. This was a combination of myth-making and face-saving, since there is no doubt that the act in question was the decision of the Patriarch George Xiphilinos.[50]

The Patriarch Germanos II concluded that stauropegial monasteries along with imperial monasteries were a scandal. Though there were exceptions, they were too often a guise, not just for lay patronage, but for private ownership, far more blatant than had been the case with *kharistike*. The patriarch's solution was to place these monasteries under the supervision of patriarchal exarchs. Both in Anatolia and in the West this produced complaints from the local hierarchy, which he was forced to heed.

In 1238 Germanos travelled to the West to review the state of the church there for himself. Such an undertaking was unprecedented, but curiously this episode is ignored by the biographical and narrative sources. It is only known because an inscription records that he went in person to affix his *stauropegion* to a monastery being founded near Arta. A note to a *nomocanon* records the same for a chapel in the theme of Nikopolis.[51]

It has become clear that around the patronage of monasteries there was a complicated interplay of different interests. Germanos

49 Rhalles & Potles v, 110–12 (= Laurent, 1259).
50 Rhalles & Potles v, 112–13 (= Laurent 1260).
51 V. Laurent, 'Charisticariat et commende à Byzance' *REB* 12 (1954), 100–13 (= Laurent, 1288).

II and his successors did their best to maintain the principle that stauropegial monasteries came under the authority of the patriarchal administration. On the island of Mitylene there was a long-running dispute between the metropolitan bishop and patriarchal exarchs for control of a number of monasteries on the island. The most important was the monastery of St George. The problem was that the monks had abandoned their original foundation and had settled in *metochia* and churches subject to the metropolitan bishop, but the patriarchal exarchs still claimed authority over them on the grounds that their monastery was originally a patriarchal foundation. The Patriarch Arsenius ordered the monks to produce their documents which they did. It transpired that the monastery was entirely independent (*autodespoton*), subordinate neither to the patriarch nor to the metropolitan bishop - a state of affairs to which the latter took exception. The patriarch's solution was to bar his exarchs from the *metochia*, but retain for himself the *anaphora* of the monastery.

The patriarchal exarchs also took advantage of a lengthy stay by the previous metropolitan bishop at Nicaea to appropriate the administration of a number of the island's other monasteries. The metropolitan naturally protested and obtained some partial satisfaction in the sense that the patriarch ordered an inquest. It certainly did not put an end to the dispute because it was brought yet again to synod as late as 1324. There were many interests involved, not least those of the monasteries themselves. These might be best served by playing off patriarch against metropolitan. In one case the abbot came to the Patriarch Arsenius, claiming quite speciously that his monastery was patriarchal. The patriarch provided him with a diploma of office. This had then to be declared null and void, when the true state of affairs emerged.[52]

How different interests were accommodated emerges from the case of the Thessalian monastery of the Theotokos Makrinitissa. It was founded by Constantine Maliasenos, the head of one of the great families of the region. He entrusted supervision of the construction of the new monastery to the bishop of Demetrias, who was honoured to be associated in the project. Despite this, the monastery came under the patriarchal *ephoreia*. Maliasenos feared that otherwise the bishop's successors might seek to appropriate the monastery for their church. In 1245 he persuaded the bishop to issue a deed confirming the monastery's patriarchal status and warning off his successors.[53] In 1256 his son Nicholas obtained patriarchal approval of its status. As his father had suspected the bishop of Demetrias had attempted to bring the

52 Hunger and Kresten, *Register des Patriarchats von Konstantinopel*, I, nos. 79–84, 456–96; (= Laurent, 1326, 1331, 1358–60).
53 Miklosich & Müller, IV 382–3.

monastery under episcopal authority. He had disputed Nicholas's right to appoint a new abbot, which, if successful, would have undermined the family's control over the monastery. Nicholas turned to the Patriarch Arsenius at Nicaea. The patriarch agreed that no election of an abbot would in future be conducted without the knowledge, participation, and approval of Nicholas Maliasenos. This was an acknowledgement of the founder's rights that the latter had inherited over the monastery from his father. The patriarch, in his turn, found a simple but dramatic way of ensuring recognition of his spiritual authority. He insisted that only a patriarchal exarch had the right to induct the new abbot into his office, even if this meant some delay. These arrangements suggest an alliance of aristocrat and patriarch against the local bishop. But it was not quite that. The ordinary had to be placated. The patriarch recognised that one of the monastery's *metochia* came under the local bishop's *stauropegion*. Consequently, for that one *metochion* the bishop was to enjoy both *anaphora* and *kanonikon*.[54] All parties should have gone away satisfied! The case of Makrinitissa is instructive for the way it reveals the interplay of a variety of interests around a monastery. Patronage could be shared. This surely reflects a return to some order in the affairs of the monasteries of Thessaly and the West.

It also points to acceptance of lay patronage as a normal state of affairs. This is a long way away from the wave of criticism that had been directed from the turn of the eleventh century against lay patronage of monasteries. It undermined *kharistike*, which was deemed incompatible with monastic independence. It was replaced by *ephoreia*. Though something of a pious fraud, this allowed a founder and his family to share in the spiritual benefits associated with the monastic revival of the time. Once this faltered, *ephoreia* became a form of lay patronage identified with founder's rights. These varied, but were normally set out in the *typikon* of a monastery. They usually included representation of the monastery's interests before the secular authorities. Sometimes the ephor had a say in the appointment of a new abbot. The benefits he was to receive in return were not usually specified. Though there were doubts in some quarters about the exact value of *ephoreia* to a monastery, it became a cover that allowed founder's rights to acquire the respectability of long usage. They were often associated with a claim that the monastery enjoyed a complete immunity. The precise legal status of founder's rights was unclear. This often worked to the advantage of the patron, who was not above using the pretext of a monastery's independent status to buttress his own position.

Independent status was often enshrined in a monastery's *typikon*. But patrons found it useful to reinforce this with imperial and patriarchal

[54] Ibid., 353–7 (= Laurent, 1333).

guarantees. This meant that the imperial government and increasingly the patriarchal administration began to acquire a vested interest in lay patronage, because it provided a base for extending their authority into the provinces. The patriarchal administration had strong material incentives in the shape of the right to collect *kanonika* from stauropegial foundations. In this Theodore Balsamon acted as a spokesman for the patriarchal interest. He reveals a changed attitude to lay patronage. He rejected the notion that even in the shape of *kharistike* it was necessarily harmful to the well-being of a monastery. But this was an old debate, resuscitated to counter lingering prejudices against lay patronage.

J. P. Thomas comes to the careful conclusion that the 'demise of the *charistike* [*sic*] itself left the church divided on what role, if any, laymen should continue to play in the foundation and direction of religious institutions'.[55] But this is to miss the point. It was surely that the agitation against *kharistike* helped to justify the role that the Comnenian dynasty assumed as protectors of monastic reform. At another level, it worked in favour of monastic founders and those that enjoyed or usurped founders' rights. The institution of *ephoreia* gave a new respectability to lay patronage. As long as it was not blatantly abused the church accepted it as a natural part of monastic life. Lay patrons may have benefited materially from their monasteries, but far more valuable was the influence they derived from their association with institutions that were central to Byzantine society.

55 Thomas, *Private Religious Institutions*, 237.

18

THE CONDITION OF THE MONASTERIES UNDER THE COMNENI

IN the end, the state of the monasteries depends upon a subjective judgement. Objective criteria, such as numbers of monks and wealth of monasteries, are not satisfactory, because they tell us nothing about the quality of monastic life. Monasticism appears to best advantage, at least in retrospect, in times of adversity. People looked back on the struggle of the monks against the iconoclast emperors in the eighth and ninth centuries as the heroic age of Byzantine monasticism. Its spirit was enshrined in the writings of Theodore of Stoudios. In material terms, the iconoclast period was probably not a great age of monasticism. It was also the case that monks were not unanimously opposed to iconoclasm.[1] The work of monastic reformers also gave greater emphasis to particular periods and places, but one of the great figures of Byzantine monasticism, Symeon the New Theologian, operated in a rather quiet period and died in comparative obscurity in 1022. His life and writings only came into prominence some thirty years after his death thanks to the efforts of Nicetas Stethatos.[2]

Symeon's influence remains problematical. There was a posthumous connection with the monastery of Kyr Philotheos. The founder of the monastery was guided by a vision he had of the New Theologian and devoted himself to the study of his teachings.[3] Founded at around the same time was the monastery of the Theotokos Euergetis. This house was to have a great influence on the monastic revival at Constantinople. However, its founder Paul does not appear to have been directly inspired by Symeon's writings. He was the compiler of a famous guide to monastic spirituality. This took the shape of a florilegium known as the *Synagoge*, or *Euergetinos*. Paul failed to include any extracts from the

[1] See I. Ševčenko, 'Hagiography of the iconoclast period', in *Iconoclasm*, ed. A. Bryer and J. Herrin (Birmingham, 1977), 113–31.

[2] Hausherr, *Un grand mystique byzantin*, 189–95.

[3] Ibid., 214–20. See above, pp. 269–70.

works of Symeon the New Theologian.[4] This may be because Symeon had yet to be rehabilitated by the Patriarch Michael Cerularius. The *typikon* of the Theotokos Euergetis was drawn up after Symeon's canonisation in 1052. It shows a marked sympathy with two elements of Symeon's teaching: his stress on the importance of confession and on the mysticism of light.[5]

Symeon the New Theologian is therefore likely to have provided some of the impulse behind the monastic revival at Constantinople, but the impact of his teachings was muted. They were transformed and mediated in various ways: for example, through the Theotokos Euergetis' *typikon*, which stressed the importance of the 'common life', more than the mystical path to the Godhead. Its emphasis on the ideal of the independent coenobitic monastery had, as we have seen, a special appeal for the Comneni.[6] It offered them a way of imposing order on monastic life. This may in the end have been stifling, but the Comneni ensured the continuing preeminence and prosperity of the monasteries of the capital. The Theotokos Euergetis retained some, perhaps much, of its prestige. In the late twelfth century it was there that the Serbian St Sava went to study monasticism.[7] There were, however, few new foundations from the mid-twelfth century. Manuel Comnenus's efforts to raise the standards of spiritual life may not have met with much success, but there were monks at Constantinople, whose spiritual advice was much sought.[8] There were also exhibitionists seeking patrons. It was less a matter of decline, more a loss of clear direction, which is also apparent outside the capital.

The lavriot form of monasticism continued to have its appeal for some founders, but its inspiration was waning with the decline of the holy mountains, such as Olympus and Latros, which had been the main exponents of this form of monasticism. They suffered at the hands of Turkish marauders in the later eleventh century and never fully recovered their standing. Even more serious was the eclipse of Mount Athos. Its prestige benefited enormously from St Athanasius's foundation of the Lavra. It brought imperial approval and support. We have already seen how generous Alexius I Comnenus was to the Lavra at the beginning of his reign. Imperial favour waned, however, in the wake of a series of scandals. These revealed the reality of Athonite monasticism. Alexius and his patriarch were horrified by the hesychasts who poured on to the streets of Constantinople to

4 I. Hausherr, 'Paul Evergétinos a-t-il connu Syméon le Nouveau Théologien?', *OCP* 23(1957), 158–79.
5 Gautier, 'Le typikon de la Théotokos Evergétis', 6–11, 18–23, 28–33.
6 See above, pp. 273–6.
7 Obolensky, *Six Byzantine Portraits*, 132, 137.
8 E.g. Michael Glykas, see below, pp. 380–1.

lobby their cause. Their appearance offended the conventional tastes of the house of Comnenus, who preferred to promote monasticism in Constantinople, where they could keep an eye on it. Mount Athos seems to have dropped out of the mainstream of Byzantine monasticism. Its rise to prominence depended so much on imperial favour that its withdrawal was bound to have an adverse effect. The eclipse of Athos emphasised the capital's role as the centre of Byzantine monasticism.

Eustathius on the state of monasticism

This is the impression left by Eustathius of Thessalonica's tract calling for a reform of monasticism.[9] It was written after the death of Manuel Comnenus.[10] Eustathius was by then archbishop of Thessalonica. The tract was addressed to the monks of his province. Relations between a bishop and monks were always likely to be difficult. Eustathius was soon at odds with the monks of Thessalonica.

Eustathius's criticisms of monasticism in his time fall under three main headings: monasteries were too much of the world; monks despised learning; and monks were no respecters of bishops.[11] Monastic reluctance to accept the authority of the local bishop was a perennial theme, but Eustathius develops it into a struggle for control of the church. His intention is polemical and he introduces a large element of exaggeration, but he has some justification. Churches did pass into the hands of monasteries, which played an important pastoral role locally.

Eustathius had also to scotch a monastic view of episcopal authority. He argued that a bishop was failing in his duties, if he withdrew into monastic seclusion, but this was the general expectation. An energetic bishop left himself open to the popular jibe, 'What is he doing, behaving like a bishop and not curling up in a corner like a monk?'[12] What alarmed Eustathius was not so much the prospect that the episcopal bench would be flooded by monks. It appealed to his mordant temperament that monks could expect to be treated badly by former colleagues who had become bishops. Eustathius records a typical exchange: 'Why do you come down so heavily on your fellow

[9] *Episkepsis Biou monakhikou epi diorthosei ton peri auton*, in Eustathius I, 214–67.

[10] Ibid., 230.61–2. It is not possible to give a more precise dating. His sarcastic reference to monks organising for a 'holy war' (ibid., 255.9–10) may be an allusion to that other 'holy war' he mentions: the defence of St Sophia by the Patriarch Theodosius Boradiotes in April 1181 (ibid., 273.45). But who is the emperor he apostrophises as 'the most holy equal of the Apostles' (ibid., 241.61)?

[11] Ibid., 262.12–15: 'They reckon that if there were no bishops, they would be everything in the world and that there would be no church that was not subject to those dressed all over in black.'

[12] Ibid., 247.47–50.

monks? Because I am a bishop.'[13] Much worse to Eustathius's way of thinking was the right claimed by monks to subject a bishop's conduct of his office to scrutiny.[14] If a bishop ever bowed to such a demand, he would find his authority much reduced. Monks sought to undermine episcopal authority in many ways. They begrudged the bishop his right of *anaphora*; they refused to accept ordination from their bishop, when they entered the priesthood, preferring to dupe some other bishop to perform the ceremony.[15]

These charges are easily corroborated. As we have seen, the withdrawal of monasteries from episcopal authority was a feature of the twelfth century. The argument was that without complete independence a monastery could not fulfil its spiritual responsibilities. This elicited no sympathy from Eustathius. He argued that without the discipline of episcopal authority monastic life lost any meaning or direction. Its objectives became increasingly secular.

Eustathius presents the monasteries of his province as agrarian units. Estate management and maximising profit were becoming their chief concern. Eustathius was saddened by their 'unabashed search for more property'.[16] A favourite stratagem was to induce a rich landowner to enter a monastery. The monks would 'promise holiness without pain, salvation without sweat, immediate access to God, and entrance to a paradise, from which the flaming sword was missing'.[17] In return, the landowner was expected to bequeath his property to the monastery. Eustathius reckoned that one of two things was likely to happen, if the landowner fell in with the monks' plans. The reality of monastic life might turn out to be rather different from that painted by the monks. The landowner would not be treated with the deference he expected. His protests would be countered by the relevant portions of the monastery's *typikon*, which enjoined poverty upon all the members of the community. The other possibility was quite different: the monks would be so anxious to retain the properties he had brought with him that they would do all they could to accommodate him. The life of the landowner-turned-monk would hardly change at all. He would continue to administer his estates. Such laxity added to the secular complexion of the monastery, for he would also keep his servants and, as Eustathius observed, a disproportionate number of maidservants.[18]

Eustathius complained that monks received no instruction in a pious and contemplative life. Instead, they learnt about storing corn and wine

[13] Ibid., 247.86–9.
[14] Ibid., 247.51–70.
[15] Ibid., 261.42–87.
[16] Ibid., 222.31–2.
[17] Ibid., 243.19–22.
[18] Ibid., 243.45–87.

and the best time to sell; how to tax the peasantry and administer the monastery's estates. However, the receipts did not go to the community as a whole, but to the management represented by the abbot and the officers of the monastery.[19] Eustathius paints a picture of a typical abbot. He was most impressive, his face dominated by a full beard. He would call the community together and begin to talk, but there was nothing of any spiritual value. He concentrated instead on the efficient management of the monastery's estates. He discoursed on their various products, such as olive oil and figs, but he was only concerned about their quality. Their spiritual associations were of no interest to him.[20] A perusal of twelfth-century *typika* suggests that Eustathius was not that wide of the mark. They pay particular attention to estate management. The *typikon* of the Theotokos Makheiras, it will be remembered, stressed that when it came to the choice of a new abbot the only qualities that counted were practical ones.[21]

An abbot's concern about the well-being of his monastery's estates was often reflected in his last will and testament. Sometimes he regarded this as his major achievement. For example, Abbot Neophytos restored the fortunes of the Athonite monastery of Dokheiariou. He recorded in his will that he had acquired much wealth for the monastery and he warned his successor against squandering it. He recommended the planting of vineyards and orchards.[22] Much the same spirit pervades the will drawn up in 1157 of Theoktistos, abbot of Patmos. In it he recorded with pride the pains he had taken to build up the wealth of the monastery.[23] Both abbots were convinced of the spiritual worth of their concern for the material needs of their communities: it was a way of safeguarding the independence of their monasteries. Eustathius judged this preoccupation with material advantage unhealthy for the spiritual life of the monastery. The abbot and monks were bound to be sucked into all manner of quarrels and litigation. To defend and extend the interests of their monasteries the monks would band together in gangs and terrorise local people.[24] The surviving archives and cartularies of Byzantine monasteries are monuments to their litigiousness and their monks' readiness to brawl in defence of their interests.

Eustathius was convinced that the emphasis on practical abilities diminished true commitment to the monastic ideal.[25] When they prayed, monks no longer knelt down. They just dipped at the knees,

19 Ibid., 242.21–48.
20 Ibid., 258–9.
21 Tsiknopoulos, *ΚΥΠΡΙΑΚΑ ΤΥΠΙΚΑ*, 58.
22 *Docheiariou*, no.6, 95–6.
23 Miklosich & Müller VI, 106–8.
24 Eustathius I, 255.59–73; 261.18–38.
25 Ibid., 241–2.

in the way a brigand would.[26] He disapproved of the surly way monks wandered around the streets, using their staves like rods of iron. They poked their noses into people's doorways in the hope of hospitality; they checked out the *agora* for business; they went to the bathhouses.[27] They had no interest in listening to the scriptures. Passages might be read out in the refectory, but the words were drowned by the sound of monks' masticating, blaspheming, and gossiping.[28] It was like a farmyard and that was about their intellectual level. Eustathius was horrified by the disregard for learning that prevailed in the monasteries of his province. Refusing to study the classics of Byzantine spirituality meant that monks were wilfully ignorant of the monastic ideal and tradition.[29] How, Eustathius wondered, could an illiterate or semi-literate monk be expected to teach the message of the gospels?[30] What use were practical abilities, when it came to debating theological propositions?[31] Eustathius hoped to remedy this deficiency by putting together a florilegium of spirituality. In the course of his work, he found he needed to consult one of Gregory of Nazianzus's works. He heard that it was in the library of a nearby monastery, but on closer enquiry learnt that it had been sold. For all that he was a worthy and educated man, the abbot justified the sale with the words, 'What need have we of such books!' Eustathius's anger turned to laughter: 'What need did such monks have of anything, if they were unable to appreciate such books!'[32]

Monks were unable to understand the value of a library.[33] They were not comfortable in the presence of the educated. They drove learned men out of their communities and positively preferred to recruit the illiterate.[34] This line of criticism echoes the fears of the founder of St John Prodromos Phoberos. He wanted it to be a community of twelve literate monks. He was convinced that literate monks were more likely to observe the vow of poverty than illiterate monks who did not fear the Lord and were slaves to their bellies.[35]

In his condemnation of monks as anti-intellectual Eustathius was taking up a position in a longstanding debate. The tone of his tract on the reformation of the monasteries is polemical. It would be unwise to take all he has to say at face value. If his commentaries

26 Ibid., 252.2–5.
27 Ibid., 245.14–30.
28 Ibid., 251–2.
29 Ibid., 249.85–94.
30 Ibid., 245.7–12.
31 Ibid., 250.3–8.
32 Ibid., 249.45–84.
33 Ibid., 245.40–63.
34 Ibid., 244.69–95.
35 *Noctes*, 57–8.

on Homer are excepted, this tract is the longest work that survives from Eustathius's pen, substantially longer than his account of the capture of Thessalonica by the Normans. Yet the amount of specific incident is minimal, just three anecdotes. There are reasons to doubt that at this time Byzantine monasteries, even those in the depths of the provinces, were as hostile to learning as Eustathius insisted. The colophons of manuscripts reveal that much copying went on even in provincial monasteries. This evidence is corroborated by the lists of manuscripts that survive for different monasteries. These are often included along with monastic *typika* which display an awareness of how important manuscripts are for the monastic life.

Take the monastery of the Theotokos Skoteine outside Philadelphia. It was almost as remote from Constantinople as it was possible to get in the Byzantine Empire of the twelfth century. It was founded by an iron worker, exactly the kind of person that Eustathius blamed for the anti-intellectualism of the monasteries. But he made sure that his son, who succeeded him as abbot, received a good education. When the son drew up a *typikon* for the monastery, it then held seventy manuscripts, and there were further manuscripts in the monastery's three *metochia.* To be sure, a large proportion of these manuscripts were service books of one sort or another. There were no secular manuscripts, but there was an interesting selection of theology, commentary, edification, and hagiography: Theophylact of Bulgaria's commentaries on the gospels; the *Catacheses* of Theodore of Stoudios; the *Margaritai*; an *Hexaemeron* attributed to Chrysostom; Barlaam and Joasaphat; the *Ladder* of St John Climax; many of the metaphrastic lives and others.[36] This was perhaps richer and more various than many monastic libraries, but it was the kind of selection that could be expected. Anything more would be unreasonable.

One suspects that Eustathius was unreasonable in his expectations, while his condemnation of the recruitment of illiterates is given the lie by the career of St Neophytos. He was an illiterate Cypriot peasant who entered a monastery and was sent to tend its vineyards, a task for which his background suited him. This, but not the sequel, conformed to Eustathius's prejudices.[37] Neophytos taught himself how to read, which led to his promotion to a monastic office. He subsequently founded a monastery, which had a small collection of manuscripts, including a version of the *Physiologus.* In his *typikon* he laid particular stress on their value.[38] He became a great teacher and has left behind a truly

36 Theotokos Skoteine, 331.5–39.
37 Eustathius I, 242.6–7.
38 Tsiknopoulos, *ΚΥΠΡΙΑΚΑ ΤΥΠΙΚΑ*, 75–6, 82–3.

impressive body of sermons and meditations.[39] The experience of a saint provides dangerous material for generalisation, but it is sufficient to make us think twice about accepting Eustathius's blanket charges against the monks of his province.

Byzantine monasteries did not exert the same intellectual influence as their counterparts in the West, nor did they have the same educational role.[40] Schooling at Byzantium was always predominantly secular, but schools were occasionally attached to monasteries. Their purpose, though, was to prepare boys for a monastic vocation. At the Cypriot monastery of the Theotokos Makhairas there was a rather confusing situation. In normal circumstances, boys were not to be admitted for the sake of learning sacred letters. They were to wait until they began to grow a beard, but boys with a vocation were given a special dormitory and received instruction in the psalter and the order of service.[41] Gregory Pakourianos was equally reluctant to have boy monks residing in his monastery. He lodged them outside and provided a priest to teach them the scriptures. His intention was that they would in due course provide his monastery with priests.[42] This was not an attitude to education that would have met with Eustathius's approval, but it was surely being unrealistic to expect more than this. Book learning played only a small part in Byzantine monastic life. Routine and attitude were far more important.

Eustathius's criticisms were levelled specifically at the monks and monasteries of his province. They did not apply to those of Constantinople, the islands of the Propontis, and along the Bosphorus. He believed that these maintained the highest standards. While he doubted the possibility of finding a single pious monk around Thessalonica, it was quite the reverse in Constantinople. There no dissolute monks were to be found![43] They were as far removed from those of Thessalonica as heaven is from earth![44] Eustathius's paean in praise of the monks of Constantinople arouses suspicion, because it is so lacking in concrete detail.[45] Earlier in his tract he retails an anecdote about the Constantinopolitan monastery of St John of Petra. It only goes to strengthen these suspicions. One night on the spur of the moment the Emperor Manuel Comnenus decided to organise a wedding feast in the palace of the Blakhernai. It was 'Cheese week' and the necessary delicacies were hard to come by. The emperor sent his messengers to the

39 Galatariotou, *The Making of a Saint*, 19–39.

40 H.-G. Beck, 'Bildung und Theologie im frühmittelalterlichen Byzanz', in *Polychronion*, ed. Wirth, 69–81.

41 Tsiknopoulos, *ΚΥΠΡΙΑΚΑ ΤΥΠΙΚΑ*, 50.

42 Gautier, 'Le typikon du sébaste Grégoire Pakourianos', 114–17.

43 Eustathius I, 262.70–86.

44 Ibid., 241.60–70.

45 Ibid., 234–5.

nearby St John of Petra on the off-chance that it might have something to offer. It turned out that the monastery could supply everything, down to red and black caviare. Though others might think differently, Eustathius saw this as an example of good monastic management. It was his contention that such generous use of their resources justified the wealth that the monks had at their disposal. 'Otherwise it were better that they should die the most miserable death from famine than to possess disproportionate property.'[46]

Eustathius admitted that in this instance it was not the poor who were benefiting, but claimed that this was something of an exception. It was more often the case that the wealth of Constantinople's monasteries was employed to relieve hunger and famine and to ransom prisoners of war.[47] Such generosity contrasted with the parsimony of the monks of Thessalonica, who in times of famine would only give the poor their vinegar and bran! Once again Eustathius's prejudices show through.

Eustathius recommended the monks of Constantinople as guides to those tormented by the darkness of the spirit and the encircling gloom.

> The monks of Constantinople will teach you moreover that assimilation into the cloud of darkness is not something obscure, difficult to see and understand, dependent upon what lurks hidden, brooding, and festering in the recesses of the soul. Instead, it depends upon the virtue in you; uncelebrated and so unrevealed. You ought at once to become light and the cloak of concealment about you will be in imitation of God, round Whom are clouds and darkness. You will not simply be the dark, but the gloom will encircle you, concealing the light of virtue, which, being hidden, is bound to burst forth in a new guise, resembling, whether you like it or not, a bright lamp. God, the Father of lights, loves such lights: or in other words, good deeds. Knowledge of them resounds like the echoing thunder. They burst like lightening across the oecumene, shining before men. Their odour is not like the divine, but its sweet smell wafts upwards to heaven itself.[48]

All would then rush to the monk to whom the light was vouchsafed to partake of his experience.[49] The mysticism of the divine light was associated with the teaching of Symeon the New Theologian. It would seem from Eustathius's description that the tradition was maintained in the monasteries of Constantinople, but, more than that, he believed that it contributed to the superiority of Constantinopolitan monasticism. He

[46] Ibid., 230–1.
[47] Ibid., 222.84–96.
[48] Ibid., 237.53–70.
[49] Ibid., 237.71–3.

maintained that the elite of Byzantine monasticism was concentrated, like a pillar of light, in the capital.[50]

Eustathius's stance on monasticism is easy to discern. He was clearly an advocate of Manuel Comnenus's effort to raise the standard of monasticism through the foundation of the monastery of St Michael Kataskepenos. This features with extravagant praise in Eustathius's funeral speech for the emperor.[51] This monastery was situated at some distance from the capital near the mouth of the Bosphorus, but it was usual to include the monasteries of the 'Straits' along with those of Constantinople.[52] Manuel refused to endow his foundation with landed property. He believed that it was the cause of unnecessary cares. One of his aims was to restrict the amount of landed property in the hands of monasteries.

Eustathius, for his part, was especially critical of the damaging effects that concern with landed property had on the monastic vocation. Such cares were better taken out of the hands of the monks and handed over to lay patrons. He regretted that the system of *kharistike* had fallen into disfavour and advocated its revival.[53] Though no *kharistikarios*, Eustathius was a guardian of the Constantinopolitan monastery of Christ Philanthropos and is found intervening on its behalf.[54] Through the support of lay patrons – and in the case of St Michael Kataskepenos the emperor – monks would be better able to concentrate on the contemplative life. They would be able to keep the cares of the world at a distance and would have no excuse for venturing out of the monastic precincts. Eustathius was scathing about holy men of various kinds – stylites, dendrites, holy fools - who were happy to make a public exhibition of themselves.[55] This too was in line with Manuel Comnenus's efforts to drive such people off the streets of Constantinople.

The Ptochoprodromos's satire against abbots

Eustathius was identified with Manuel Comnenus's monastic measures which concentrated on Constantinople. Isolated in Thessalonica the metropolitan assumed that they had succeeded. He could hold up the monasteries of Constantinople as an example to the monks of his province. There may have been an element of self-deception. Others levelled against the monks of the capital the same criticisms that Eustathius directed against those of Salonica. Best known is a satire about conditions in the Constantinopolitan monastery of Kyr

50 Ibid., 234.69–70.
51 Ibid., 208.8–68.
52 See Zepos I, 381.
53 Eustathius I, 244.20–41.
54 Ibid., 320.67–81. The word used for guardian is *antileptor*, the equivalent of ephor.
55 Ibid., 94–7.

Philotheos.[56] This was the work of the 'Ptochoprodromos', who may or may not be identical with the littérateur Theodore Prodromos. It is written from the standpoint of a novice of humble background. He is much put upon and badly fed. In contrast the abbot and his cronies live a life of luxury. The monastery of Kyr Philotheos was notorious. At the beginning of Manuel Comnenus's reign this monastery had been reduced to a state of near anarchy because of the frequent changes of abbot. The *typika* and the precepts of the founder were ignored; monastic virtues were neglected.[57]

It is possible that Prodromos was commenting on this state of affairs. His poem contains a plea to the abbot to reform his ways:

> The monastery was not founded for you; it isn't your patrimony
> So that you and your relatives can consume its wealth
> While you drive us away as though we were strangers.

The poem also includes a threat to take matters to the emperor and patriarch if nothing was done.[58] The 'Ptochoprodromos' addressed the poem to the Emperor Manuel. It was meant more than half seriously as an invitation to the emperor to intervene and to put an end to a scandal.[59] The poet was using humour to alert the emperor to irregularities in the monastic life of the capital. The poem is full of humorous exaggeration designed to appeal to the emperor and his favourites. Even so its great value lies in the different perspective it provides. The poet is looking at monastic life from the bottom up: what it meant to be a poor novice in a great Constantinopolitan monastery. Social standing continued to count for a great deal within the monastic portals. Wealth made a difference. The novice is told:

> He has ten pounds of gold in his account
> You don't have a follis to bless yourself
> Or to buy a candle for your tonsure
> Look at him, he gave the monastery an icon
> Silks shot through with silver and two candlesticks
> You came barefooted and bare-arsed
> You aren't the son of *sebastos* or a *kouropalates*
> You are a costermonger's son.[60]

The novice, for his part, did not bring the monastery estates to administer. He was just a humble little monk from off the Milion.[61] In other

[56] Prodromos, no. III, pp. 48–71; E. Jeanselme and L. Oeconomos, 'Le satire contre les higoumènes. Poème attribué à Théodore Prodrome', *B* 1(1924), 317–39.
[57] P. Gautier, 'Les lettres de Grégoire, higoumène d' Oxia', *REB* 31 (1973), 214–18.
[58] Eustathius I, 237.53–70.
[59] Prodromos, no. III, lines 440–3.
[60] Ibid., lines 84–93.
[61] Ibid., lines 352–4.

words, all he was good for was to fetch and carry and perform menial tasks. The monastic *typika* provide many examples of the preferment enjoyed by monks of aristocratic descent. They could expect either to have their own servants or to make use of the services of monks of humbler background. Eustathius was also aware of the social divisions that existed within monasteries. Power was concentrated in the hands of the abbot and the officers of the monastery. They made sure that they controlled its incomes for their own benefit.[62] In the case of the monastery of Kyr Philotheos this was all the more blatant for the way the monastery boasted two abbots, a father and a son.[63] When challenged they cited the monastery's *typikon* to thwart the novice. Otherwise its stipulations were ignored, as were imperial orders and judgements of synod.[64] There is no doubt a great deal of truth about the realities of monastic life contained in the Ptochoprodromos's satire. More often than not, they were accepted as part of a necessary discipline and order.

Among so many other things the novice also complained about the way he was confined to the monastery precincts, while the abbot and favoured monks rode around the city with their escorts and visited the imperial palace.[65] Characteristically, we find John Tzetzes boasting to a monk that he too now has a mule to take him about the city.[66] Tzetzes's dearest wish was to retire to the comfort of a corrody in one of the capital's many prosperous monasteries. This was another – and relatively blameless – feature of Byzantine monasticism. Tzetzes found himself constantly thwarted. He vented his frustrations by cataloguing the deficiencies of monastic life at Constantinople. Just as in Eustathius's Salonica, so at Constantinople monks went around the streets and houses selling their wares. Tzetzes professed to be horrified by the way the rules of the common life were flouted and disregarded. It gave too much scope for the hermit, the stylite, and the wandering monk.[67] He deplored the exhibitionism of holy men and still more the vogue among the aristocracy for collecting their mementoes in the shape of the chains and fetters they had worn. These were destined for their private chapels, where they would be displayed as prize exhibits.[68]

Theodore Balsamon was also uneasy about the licence enjoyed by holy men in Constantinople. He connected it with what he judged to be

62 Eustathius I, 242.45–8.
63 Prodromos, no. III, lines 33–5.
64 Ibid., lines 240–4.
65 Ibid., lines 266–70.
66 Tzetzes I, no.49, 70.15–24.
67 Ibid., no.57, 79–84.
68 Ibid., no.104, 151–2, translated by Magdalino in 'The Byzantine holy man', 54–5.

the near collapse of coenobitic monasticism at Byzantium. This charge comes as a surprise given the way the *typika* of the time enjoined strict observance of the common life.[69] But he was not the only one to make this observation. John of Oxeia, patriarch of Antioch, at the turn of the eleventh century had his difficulties with the monks of his monastery of the Hodegoi. He claimed that they abandoned the common life because it interfered with their social life, which included singing in a choir with women. John tried to stop them leaving the monastery for the pleasures of the capital by appointing a doorkeeper, but the monastery's eight doors thwarted him.[70] John of Oxeia's experiences reflect the rather loose organisation of monastic life. Compared with the West coenobitic monasticism at Byzantium was weak. It had something to do with the size of Byzantine monasteries, which were usually rather small, a community of perhaps six to ten being normal.

Because it was informal and loosely organised Byzantine monasticism was an easy target for criticism, for it fell short of a great ideal that was almost impossible to realise. Monasticism was entangled in secular society and never escaped its imprint. Even its critics took this for granted. John Tzetzes derived great satisfaction from his acquaintance with Joseph, abbot of the Pantokrator. There were letters of lavish thanks for a visit or for a gift of perfume from the abbot.[71] But best of all the abbot eventually granted him the corrody he so desired.[72] We also find Tzetzes drafting a letter to the abbot of another great Constantinopolitan monastery,[73] but on behalf of a client. The man had forfeited the emperor's favour and sought refuge from life's trials in the monastery. There was no suggestion that he wished to become a monk. There was only the assumption that in times of difficulty there was always a monastery to turn to.[74] Few had much difficulty in reconciling such an assumption with the ideal of the monastery as separate from the world.

The reality of Byzantine monastic life under Manuel I Comnenus is not obscured by any overriding personality or great impulse for monastic revival. The eclipse of the holy mountains meant that there were no great independent upholders of the monastic ideal. That is why Eustathius had to place such emphasis upon the monasteries of Constantinople. Dissecting monastic life in his province Eustathius had before him an 'ideal' of the great coenobitic monasteries of the capital and the Byzantine 'home counties'. Manuel Comnenus's efforts

69 Rhalles & Potles III, 411.
70 Gautier, 'Jean V l'Oxite', 148.29–36.
71 Tzetzes I, nos.51–3, 72–4.
72 Ibid., no.79, 117.14–20.
73 Of Christ Pantepoptes: see Janin I, 527–9.
74 Tzetzes I, no.9, 17–18.

to revitalise these monasteries through the inspiration of his foundation of St Michael Kataskepenos may have produced few concrete results, but they fuelled Eustathius's criticism of the standard of monastic life that he found at Thessalonica. His conclusions were unfair, but, as long as allowance is made for his bias, he has left us with a portrait of the everyday face of Byzantine monasticism. It was hopelessly muddled with the world. How could it be otherwise when administration of estates and husbanding of resources were among the most pressing concerns of any monastery? At stake was the continuity of the community. They were loosely organised and ill-disciplined, but they could respond to the needs of local society. They gave shelter; they gave a modicum of spiritual sustenance. Their role was modest but essential. They were scarcely the stairway to heaven. The more extravagant forms of spirituality were to be seen on the streets of the capital and other towns too. Thessalonica had its stylite. Eustathius felt obliged to remind him of the spiritual responsibilities and of the dangers of his way of life.[75] Byzantine asceticism retained all its old variety of expression into the twelfth century. It could be taken as a sign of its continuing vigour, even if the authorities disapproved.

The monastery of St John the theologian at Patmos[76]

Proof comes in the shape of the life of St Leontios of Jerusalem. His career may have culminated in the patriarchal throne of Jerusalem, but it began on the streets of Constantinople, for Leontios was one of those exhibitionists frowned upon by right-thinking clerics. He ran away from home when he was very young. He can only have been in his early teens. He made his way to Constantinople and adopted the life of a fool for Christ's sake. The people of Constantinople regarded him as a seven-day wonder (*teras*)! His speciality was to run around the streets of the city with burning coals in his hands; every so often stopping to cense the icons that stood at crossroads and street corners. That was not his only trick. He would frequent the baths, where he would take off his cloak and put it in the furnace to see if it would catch light. It never did. Having taken this precaution he would throw himself into the furnace without apparently suffering any harm. This was all part of an apprenticeship that would fit him for his monastic vocation. His next step was to attach himself to the bishop of Tiberias, who was living as a hermit on a hillside overlooking the Bosphorus. The bishop decided to return to his see in Palestine. He took Leontios with him. They stopped briefly at Patmos and then spent the winter on

75 Eustathius I, 186.19–53.
76 Patmos I, *3–*91.

the island of Cyprus. The bishop refused to allow Leontios to continue any further and abandoned him. Leontios made his way back to Patmos where Abbot Theoktistos received him as a probationer. He was not allowed to join the community there and then because he was still an adolescent. He was therefore assigned to the abbot's quarters for study and meditation. Abbot Theoktistos discerned his exceptional qualities and groomed him as his successor.[77]

Leontios found a flourishing community. When he succeeded to the abbacy in 1157 it numbered some 75 monks.[78] By the end of the century this figure had risen to nearly 150, making it one of the largest monasteries within the Byzantine Empire.[79] Some of the credit for the success of the monastery of St John the Theologian on the island of Patmos must go to the founder St Christodoulos. He provided solid foundations. He obtained the island of Patmos and grants of property from the Emperor Alexius Comnenus on neighbouring islands. Almost as vital was exemption from tolls and customs duties for the monastery's boat. He provided his community with a rule or *typikon* which would guide its life and preserve his memory.[80]

The island of Patmos was deserted when Christodoulos took possession in 1088. There was no running water, just a few wells that were running dry. The island was more or less treeless. Patmos is a small island. The government inspector reckoned that about a sixth of the island was cultivatable, mostly with difficulty. Only a quarter of this was potential ploughland – a mere 160 *modioi*. There were no buildings except for a miserable chapel, where tradition had it St John wrote his Apocalypse.[81] It was built within the ruins of an ancient temple that stood on the highest spot on the island. There was soon a story that Christodoulos had taken ceremonial possession of the island by destroying a statue of Artemis.[82]

Christodoulos brought in settlers, some of whom were originally from the island but had abandoned it in the face of Turkish raids. By 1089 there were twelve peasant households with a recorded population of forty-one established on Patmos.[83] They were assigned the northern part of the island.[84] Work went ahead on building the monastery. In the midst of this Christodoulos was called away to Constantinople. He exhorted the monks not to quarrel among themselves and to carry out their allotted duties. He left the monastery in charge of the *oikonomos*

77 Leontios of Jerusalem, 381–9; ed Tsoungarakis, 36–55.
78 Miklosich & Müller VI, 108–10; Patmos I, *44–*45.
79 Miklosich & Müller VI, 131.4–5.
80 Ibid., 19–80; Patmos I, *21–*49.
81 Miklosich & Müller VI, 56–7.
82 Vranouse, *ΧΡΙΣΤΟΔΟΥΛΟΣ*, 52; Patmos I, *10 and n.1.
83 Miklosich & Müller VI, 58.
84 Ibid., 67; Patmos I, *41.

Sabbas and the monk Joseph Iasites. The monastery then numbered some thirty monks. Its organisation was taking shape. Monks were appointed to supervise the monastery's estates on neighbouring islands. Other monks were deputed to take the monastery's boat to the 'Straits', where they were to sell its cheese and buy provisions for the monastery. Christodoulos then arranged for them to proceed to the capital where they were to pick him up. There was one detail, however, that underlined how precarious the monastery's position was. Christodoulos advised the monks to garrison the monastery from the beginning of May, to reinforce the bastions with stones, and to prepare for a siege.[85]

The beginning of May was the start of the raiding season. By 1092 the Turkish raids had become so bad that Christodoulos evacuated his monks to the safety of Euboea. This was a real test. From the start Christodoulos had difficulty with a group of his monks. They were dismayed by the harsh conditions that they had found on the island of Patmos. Their contribution to the building works was minimal. They refused to obey Christodoulos. For a time there was a schism within the community. Christodoulos's opponents eventually came and sought his forgiveness.[86] This fissure opened up again during the exile in Euboea. Christodoulos names three monks who simply deserted him. About a dozen stayed with him, while the rest of the community was scattered. Christodoulos's final plea was that his corpse should be taken back to his monastery.[87] He died on 16 March 1093.

He made arrangements for the administration of the monastery of Patmos. He appointed as his successor a godson, who was a patriarchal notary and had already invested heavily in the monastery. But Christodoulos attached conditions that made the post less attractive: his godson was to become a monk and his relations were to have no part in the monastery. The godson had no desire to be tonsured, nor did he wish to leave the safety of Constantinople and brave the fury of the elements and of the Turks. He duly relinquished his rights over the monastery and handed its administration to the community,[88] which chose Joseph Iasites as the new abbot. By now the Byzantine fleet was beginning to dominate the waters of the Aegean. It was feasible to think of returning to Patmos. This was done under the guidance of Iasites

85 Miklosich & Müller VI, 144–8. For the attribution of this document to the founder of Patmos, Christodoulos, see Patmos I, *34–*5.

86 Miklosich & Müller VI, 66.16–32.

87 Ibid., 81–90, esp. 89.22–4.

88 Ibid., 90–4. The man's name was Theodosius Kastreisiou. Christodoulos describes him as his *kharistikarios*. His investment of 200 *nomismata* in the monastery was returned.

and with the help of two of the founder's trusted companions, Sabbas and Neophytos, both of whom would succeed in turn to the abbacy.[89]

It is difficult to recover details of their restoration of the monastery. They continued to enjoy the favour of Alexius I Comnenus. In 1099 he granted tax-free status to twelve of the monastery's dependent peasants.[90] Potentially more valuable was the annual grant to the monastery from the receipts of the duke of Crete of 24 *nomismata* and 300 *modioi* of wheat. The emperor was acceding to a request made by Abbot Joseph Iasites, who pleaded his monks' lack of necessities.[91] This suggests that numbers were increasing once again. The estates of the monastery could not support a growing community.

A new chapter in the monastery's history began with the appointment *c.* 1118 of Theoktistos as abbot. He was not one of Christodoulos's companions. He had come to Patmos as a comparatively young man after a spell in Palestine and Cyprus. Joseph Iasites was then abbot of Patmos and took him on as a disciple. Iasites's death seems to have produced a series of disputed elections. Neophytos and Sabbas were, in turn, made abbot and, in turn, resigned. This left the way open for Theoktistos's election as abbot.[92] He died in 1157 after a reign of perhaps forty years.[93] His will reveals the success he had in maintaining and extending the privileges of the monastery. This involved a number of visits to the imperial court at Constantinople. He does not, however, conceal the difficulties the monastery experienced during his abbacy. It endured pirate raids, which had to be bought off. Just as unwelcome were the attentions of the tax collector of Samos. Theoktistos appointed Leontios, the future patriarch of Jerusalem, to succeed him.[94] Leontios was Theoktistos's favourite disciple. He had made him *oikonomos* of the monastery. Leontios greatly respected his master for his spiritual qualities, but would describe him soon after his death as 'simple and unbusinesslike'.[95] Specifically, Theoktistos had been willing to recognise that the monastery came under the spiritual authority of the bishop of Ikaria. He was therefore colluding in the diminution of his monastery's independent status. Leontios immediately set about rectifying this state of affairs. He persuaded the

89 Patmos I, *17, *59. There is a later tradition that Sabbas returned to Patmos with Christodoulos's library before the founder's death.

90 Miklosich & Müller VI, 94–5; Patmos I, 186; Dolger, *Reg.* 1214.

91 Miklosich & Müller VI, 100.19–30 (cf.106–7); Patmos I, 82.14–19.

92 Miklosich & Müller VI, 107.2–6.

93 Theoktistos specifically says in his will that he reigned for about thirty years (Miklosich & Müller VI 107.22–3). However, he equally states that he obtained confirmation of privileges from John II Comnenus. This is dated July 1119 (Patmos I, 85).

94 Miklosich & Müller VI, 106–8.

95 Ibid., 115.5–6.

patriarch to restore Patmos's to its full independence as a stauropegial monastery.[96] At the same time he obtained imperial protection against the activities of the tax collectors of Samos.[97] Leontios made another visit to Constantinople in 1176 in order to obtain satisfaction over the payments owed to the monastery by the duke of Crete. He had the support of the Grand Droungarios. Thanks to his good offices the Emperor Manuel Comnenus chose him as the new patriarch of Jerusalem.[98]

Leontios may not have immediately appointed a successor as abbot of Patmos. He made his favourite disciple Arsenius *oikonomos* of the monastery and may have left him in charge of the monastery. Arsenius duly became abbot some seven years later and remained in office until his death which occurred around the fall of Constantinople in 1204. He had great success in defending and extending the monastery's estates and privileges.[99] He was a great builder and a promoter of Patmos's reputation for holiness and spiritual renown.

The monastery of St John the Theologian on the island of Patmos possesses the fullest records of any monastery from the Comnenian period. It is the only monastery for which it is possible to write anything like a continuous history for this period. At first sight, it seems to bear out many of Eustathius's strictures on the monastic life. The abbots seem preoccupied with the material well-being of the monastery. They made frequent trips to Constantinople to further its interests. They even offered places in the monastery to landowners able to provide a sufficient endowment. One donor specified in a deed of covenant that he should be allowed to eat with the monks if he wanted or in his cell. He also insisted on keeping a servant at the expense of the monastery.[100] But documents of this sort provide a one-sided impression. They say little about the spiritual and intellectual life of the monastery.

A catalogue of the monastery's library survives from the year 1200.[101] It gives the lie to Eustathius's blanket condemnation of monasteries as sinks of wilful ignorance. The catalogue reveals the care and pride that the monks of Patmos took in their library. The most precious

96 Ibid., 113–17; Grumel 1049. Cf. Patmos I, *64–*6.

97 Miklosich & Müller VI, 110–13; Patmos I, 197–200; Dolger, *Reg.* 1423.

98 Miklosich & Müller VI, 117–19; Patmos I, 219–21; Dolger, *Reg.* 1439. Cf. Leontios of Jerusalem, 412–13; ed.Tsougarakis, 104–9.

99 Leontios of Jerusalem, 414; ed. Tsougrakis, 108–11. See Patmos I, *77–*84; D. Mouriki, ''Όι τοιχογραφίες τοῦ παρεκκλησίου τοῦ ῾αγίου Ἰωάννου τοῦ Θεολόγου στὴν Πάτμο', *ΔΕΛΤΙΟΝ ΤΗΣ ΧΡΙΣΤΙΑΝΙΚΗΣ ΑΡΧΑΙΟΛΟΓΙΚΗΣ ΕΤΑΙΡΕΙΑΣ*, ser.4, 14(1987–88), esp. 257–60.

100 Miklosich & Müller VI, 133–6.

101 Ch. Diehl, 'Le trésor et la bibliothèque de Patmos au commencement du 13e siècle', *BZ* 1(1892), 488–525 (Text 511–25); Ch. Astruc, 'L' inventaire dressé en septembre 1200 du trésor et de la bibliothèque de Patmos: édition diplomatique', *TM* 8(1981), 15–30 (Text 20–30).

manuscripts are carefully described. The main illustrations are itemised together with the bindings and fastenings. In some instances, the names of donors or copyists are given. The cataloguer made a real effort to indicate the contents of some manuscripts or to identify them by providing an accurate title. For the convenience of the monks he might also give the name by which a manuscript was known at Patmos. For example, that most popular of florilegia – the *Melissa* – was called St Nikon.[102] There was also a collection of *encomia* known to the monks as the *Alexandrinos*.[103] As a final refinement the cataloguer divided the manuscripts into parchment and oriental paper. Presumably they were stored separately. The cataloguer even notes one manuscript which was a mixture of parchment and paper.[104]

In 1200 the library's holdings consisted of 330 manuscripts. By Byzantine standards it was a most impressive collection. It contained more or less everything that a pious Byzantine might want to read or consult. It was not, however, the library of a classical scholar. Classical authors are poorly represented: just two manuscripts of Aristotle, of which one contained the *Categories*,[105] but Aristotle had his uses, even in a monastic setting! It was a monastic library. There was a preponderance of service books of all kinds. Of the 330 manuscripts no less than 127 were for liturgical purposes: Gospels, Acts of the Apostles, Psalters, Euchologia, Synaxaria, Sticharia, Panegyrika, Kontakia, Menaia, and so on. There were many saints' lives, mostly metaphrastic. The Fathers of the church were well represented; in particular, their commentaries on the different books of the Bible, Old Testament and New Testament. The spiritual classics of Byzantium were available: the *Rules* of Pachomius, the Lausiac history, the *Philokalia*, the *Ladder* of St John Climax, works of Ephraem the Syrian and Isaac the Syrian, the *Catecheses* of Theodore the Studite, the *Pandektes* of Antiochos, a monk of the Lavra of St Sabba, the *Ascetica* of St Basil, by which must be meant his instructions for the monastic life.

This was a working library. Its purpose was instruction in the monastic way of life. The nature of that instruction was anchored in the classics of Byzantine spirituality. This does not mean, however, that it was unchanging. The selection of works in the Patmos library is revealing. It shows the influence of the eleventh-century monastic revival at Constantinople. The library possessed the *Chapters* of St Symeon the New Theologian. The cataloguer paid particular attention to this manuscript, placing a cross beside it in the left-hand margin. He was also at pains to emphasise the importance of the author by giving

[102] Diehl, 'Le trésor', 518, 522; Astruc, 'L'inventaire', 25.118–19, 28.192.
[103] Diehl, 'Le trésor', 517; Astruc, 'L'inventaire', 24.87.
[104] Diehl, 'Le trésor', 516, 522; Astruc, 'L'inventaire', 24.84, 29.203.
[105] Diehl, 'Le trésor', 518, 523; Astruc, 'L'inventaire', 25.112, 30.223.

him his fullest nomenclature, in a way he does for no other author. The entry runs as follows: 'Another book having the *Chapters* of *our* [my italics] holy father Symeon, priest and abbot of the monastery of St Mamas of Xylokerkos, called the Second Theologian.'[106] This almost amounts to a manifesto, or at least to a profession of loyalty to his mystical approach. The library also boasted two copies of the *Euergetinos*. Again the cataloguer felt the need to describe it in some detail: 'Another book of the Sayings of the Fathers compiled by the founder of the all holy Theotokos Euergetis, whence it has acquired the title of *Euergetinos*.'[107] There is one more entry in the catalogue that reveals the way the monastery kept abreast of the latest developments of Byzantine spirituality. It refers to the *Chapters* of Abbot Isaiah the Hesychast. He is to be identified with the influential mystic of that name who was operating in the last decades of the twelfth century.[108]

What was the nature of instruction at Patmos? Was there a school attached to the monastery? We know how ambivalent the attitude was in Byzantine monasteries to monastic schools. St Christodoulos made no provision for a school in his *typikon*. But the quality of recruits to the monastic life was a question that concerned him. It was the duty of the abbot to cross-examine postulants as to their intentions and the sincerity of their vocation. Christodoulos did not want those who were just fleeing from life's misadventures. The abbot must satisfy himself that the recruit had a genuine vocation. If he did, he was to receive instruction from the abbot over a period of forty days.[109] This is what happened when Leontios applied to join the monastery. Abbot Theoktistos discerned his aptitude for the monastic life. However, he was still too young to enter the monastery, even as a probationer. He was therefore assigned to the abbot's quarters for study and contemplation.[110] In practice, they must have served as a kind of school. This may also have been the case in Christodoulos's day. He refers to 'the boys I have brought up for God since infancy' as a distinct group within the monastic community.[111] They must have provided future recruits for the monastery.

The bond of abbot and disciple was one of the strongest within the community. It determined the succession to the abbacy. Theoktistos

106 Diehl, 'Le trésor', 517; Astruc, 'L'inventaire', 24.91–92.

107 Diehl, 'Le trésor', 516, 523; Astruc, 'L'inventaire', 24.83, 29.209–10.

108 Diehl, 'Le trésor', 521; Astruc, 'L'inventaire', 27.165–6. On Isaiah, see below pp. 380–1. Another entry just before this may be of interest: 'Another small book having the letters of Michael, monk and deacon, to his spiritual father' (Diehl, 'Le trésor', 521; Astruc, 'L'inventaire', 27.164–5). It is tempting to identify the author with Michael Glykas.

109 Miklosich & Müller VI, 78.5–28.

110 Leontios of Jerusalem, 389; ed. Tsougarakis, 52–5.

111 Miklosich & Müller VI, 83.10–11.

was the favourite disciple of the second abbot Joseph Iasites and eventually succeeded to the abbacy. Leontios was equally Theoktistos's favourite disciple and successor. Leontios, in his turn, had a favourite disciple in Arsenius, who would also become abbot. Such favouritism was also a cause of division within the monastery. This is apparent from the will of Abbot Sabbas. He stresses that his injunctions were directed to the whole community and not 'as some allege . . . just to his disciples and true children'.[112] In other words, there was a suspicion that an abbot favoured his disciples over other members of the community.

Abbot Sabbas left a substantial number - at least, thirty-four – of manuscripts in his will to the monastery. Most of these can be identified with manuscripts catalogued in 1200. The cataloguer chose not to record these gifts, while itemising those made by Sabbas's predecessor Joseph Iasites. No matter, the point is this: Christodoulos's immediate successors took care to build up the monastery's library. They were almost certainly guided by Christodoulos's example. Books feature prominently in the codicil that he added to his will, as he lay dying. He recounted how he rescued the library of the monastery of Stylos on Mount Latros. The Turks were plundering the region. So, Christodoulos hired a ship and sent the manuscripts to Constantinople, where they passed into the safekeeping of the patriarchate. Synod subsequently judged that a fourth part of the library should go to Christodoulos and his new foundation.[113] This formed the nucleus of the monastery's library.[114]

Christodoulos also emphasised the importance of spiritual instruction. When on one occasion he was absent on business at Constantinople, he deputed this task to one of the older monks.[115] A monastic education had different ends in view from a secular education. Booklearning was only a start, but the Patmos library contained some basic textbooks: two on grammar, a lexicon, and a medical textbook. At a more advanced level there were two manuscripts of Aristotle.[116] One included the *Categories*, which was the basis of the study of logic. A monastic education consisted of instruction by the abbot or by a senior monk supplemented by private study and meditation. This impression receives support from the *Life* of St Leontios, but he can hardly have been typical of the monks of Patmos. He was much addicted to flagellation. He would creep out at night to the cemetery and lie in the coffins of the newly dead. This was to keep death always before him.

112 Ibid., 243.17–20.
113 Ibid., 87.12–13.
114 Leontios returned one volume to the monastery of Stylos: ibid., 431.1–10.
115 Ibid., 145.1–4.
116 Diehl, 'Le trésor', 499.

He wept copiously over the corpses whose coffins he shared. According to his biographer his tears wiped away the sins of the dead. This was taking the intercessory role of a monk to extremes.

However excessive, however morbid, this was part of Leontios's monastic education. In his case, it was a prelude to study. By this time he had been admitted to the congregation and had been given a minor post in the monastery church. He was vouchsafed a miraculous vision in which a hand gave him bread to eat. He took it as a sign that the time had come to devote himself to study. This consisted very largely in memorising saints' lives and a range of theological works. Leontios's biographer specifies that in addition he learnt off by heart the *Dogmatike Panoplia* of Zigabenos.[117] Sure enough a copy of this work is entered in the catalogue of 1200.[118]

The achievements of St Christodoulos's successors at Patmos were by any standards impressive. It was a beacon of monastic culture. It possessed a fine library and boasted copyists and calligraphers. It also produced patriarchs and bishops which must have enhanced its prestige.[119] They in turn remembered Patmos with gratitude and affection. The earliest life of St Christodoulos was written by an ex-monk of Patmos who became metropolitan bishop of Rhodes. Athanasius, patriarch of Antioch (1156–70), was another product of Patmos.[120] He has left this description of Patmos:

> [Can you not] see the monastery girdled around by strong walls; with its interior dignified by much artistic effort? There is the inexplicable beauty of the church, gleaming in the brilliance of the marble cladding, illuminated by the gold-glinting effervescence of the holy icons. See the choir of dignified fathers and the holy tomb, which, like some bubbling spring, pours forth streams of miracles. But step a little way outside. You will see the beauty of the meadows, both broad and shady, brimming with fine fruit trees. Look at the abundant foliage of the trees, heavy with blossom, bearing beautiful and luxuriant fruit; all the more astounding because they grow out of the dry rock. In due season you will see the meadows covered in smiling crops, waving gently in the light sea breezes; inviting the harvester's sickle, in tune with the rhythms of the land which abounds in flocks about to bring forth their young. Then there are the vineyards weighed down with clusters of grapes. Who can enumerate the variety and quality of vegetables, not to mention the innumerable flocks of sheep and goats which provide a copious source of milk?[121]

117 Leontios of Jerusalem, 391–2; ed. Tsougarakis, 60–1.
118 Diehl, 'Le trésor', 518; Astruc, 'L'inventaire', 25.122.
119 Patmos I, *44–7, 78*-84.
120 A. Failler, 'Le patriarche d'Antioche Athanase 1er Manassès', *REB* 51 (1993), 64–6.
121 Patmos I, *78.

This is an idealised description. It was written around the time that Leontios succeeded to the office of abbot. The monastery still faced dangers. It continued to be the target of pirate raids. But we can believe that the monastery prospered; that it was dignified with fine buildings and that the island was carefully cultivated.

The description comes from an *encomium* in honour of the translation of the relics of St Christodoulos. It was designed to enhance the mystique of the monastery, which centred on the cult of the founder.[122] The monks celebrated the anniversaries of his death and of the translation of his relics with special services. His tomb was an object of veneration. The first *Life* of St Christodoulos was written around 1143. By this time all, or nearly all, his original companions must have been dead. There was a need for a *Life* to preserve his memory. This was followed by a second *Life* written towards the end of the twelfth century. It was more succinct and corresponded to the need to popularise the cult. These lives were supplemented by *encomia* and narratives of miracles. The cult of St Christodoulos was given new impetus by Arsenius, abbot of Patmos, at the end of the twelfth century. He seems to have been responsible for refurbishing the funerary chapel of St Christodoulos. Such a possibility receives corroboration from his decision to commission a new *encomium* on the translation of the relics of the saint from Theodosius Goudeles, a monk of the monastery.

Arsenius did not, however, only promote the cult of the founder. He was still more devoted to the memory of his master, Leontios, patriarch of Jerusalem. He encouraged Goudeles to write his *Life* and supplied him with much of the information. The *Life* was completed in 1203 or shortly thereafter. Leontios's achievements and devotion to Patmos added lustre to the monastery. Arsenius's efforts to promote the cult of his master may have been still more elaborate. He had the side chapel now dedicated to the Virgin Mary added to the southern side of the monastery church. Doula Mouriki argues that its original dedication was to none other than Leontios, patriarch of Jerusalem. Its purpose was to serve as a cenotaph for Leontios who had been laid to rest in the church of St Michael at Steirou in Constantinople.

There is no indication in the *Life* of Leontios that there were any plans to translate his relics to Patmos. Mouriki's argument relies on the iconography of the side chapel. It is clearly inappropriate for a chapel dedicated to the Virgin Mary. It has instead a strong bias towards the patriarchate of Jerusalem. There are a series of portraits of patriarchs of Jerusalem. Alas, none can be identified as Leontios, so the clinching piece of evidence is missing. All we have is the circumstantial evidence brilliantly marshalled by Mouriki, which

[122] Vranouse, *ΧΡΙΣΤΟΔΟΥΛΟΣ*, 58–66.

allows the possibility that the chapel was dedicated to St Leontios. Whether it was or not is less important than the way the iconography of the chapel points to the connection with the church of Jerusalem exemplified in the career of Leontios. Arsenius was using the renown of his spiritual father for the benefit of the monastery. He may even have been going further: trying to turn Patmos into a nursery of saints.[123] The cult of St Leontios continued to be cultivated at Patmos. His feast was celebrated on 14 May, the anniversary of his death. The monastery still possesses an icon of the saint dating from the Palaeologan period.

Were the cults fostered by the abbots and monks of Patmos for internal consumption and satisfaction or did they have a wider appeal? It might seem at first sight that Patmos's isolation ensured that the monastic ideal was cultivated there with a minimum of reference to or interference from the outside world. The majority of the miracles performed by St Christodoulos were for the benefit of the monastery. He was credited with rescuing the monastery from a series of piratical attacks. As bad as any pirate was a tax collector from Samos called Pegonites. But after one visit to Patmos his ship nearly sunk. He returned to beg forgiveness from the saint and promised to respect the monastery's immunity.[124]

Consciously or unconsciously the abbots and monks of Patmos used the cult of their founder to promote the fame of the monastery which spread far and wide. So, Latins came not only to plunder, but also to venerate St Christodoulos. In 1187 while operating in Byzantine waters the Sicilian admiral Margarites stopped at Patmos. He wanted to take the relics of the saint back to Sicily. He offered the monks in exchange revenues from either Euboea or Crete. The monks refused. Margarites therefore seized the relics and put them aboard his galley, but it ran aground near the harbour mouth and the monks rescued St Christodoulos. Four years later Patmos was to receive a still more distinguished visitor from the West: Philip Augustus, king of France, who was on his way home from the third crusade. He presented the monastery with a gift of thirty bezants and asked to be allowed to take away some relic of the saint, but his request was refused. A member of his retinue accordingly bit off the tip of one of the saint's fingers and departed with this memento, but a storm soon got up. It was thought safer to turn back and return the relic to Patmos. Another triumph for St Christodoulos![125]

123 See Mouriki, 'Οι τοιχογραφίες', 205–66. On 254–7 Mouriki notes the prominent position accorded in the decoration of the chapel to St James the Less, first bishop of Jerusalem. Could he be the dedicatee?.

124 Vranouse, *ΧΡΙΣΤΟΔΟΥΛΟΣ*, 53, 56 .

125 Ibid., 71–5.

The miracles of the saint contain a marked anti-Latin element. The saint uses his powers to protect his monastery from Latin attacks and to prevent all or part of his person and the power this represented falling into the hands of the Latins. There is equally an anti-Latin tinge to the *Life* of St Leontios. This is most pronounced in the sections relating to his stay as patriarch at Jerusalem, where he encountered the hostility of the Latins. Previously, as abbot of Patmos, Leontios had to face Latin seafarers. They came initially asking for supplies. When Leontios refused to comply with their demands, they burnt the monastery's ship. Leontios went out to meet them, holding aloft an icon of St John the Theologian. The Latins immediately departed for Ikaria, where a freak wave sent them to the bottom.[126]

The *Life* of St Leontios contains much that was only of interest to a monastic congregation. He had, for example, to discipline by miraculous means a contrary monk who had been refused a new pair of sandals. This was a detail that would have aroused any monk's interest. But the *Life* also reveals something of the network of supporters that a monastery had to cultivate. Patmos depended heavily on the incomes it received from Crete. While still *oikonomos* of the monastery Leontios was sent to supervise their collection. The officer responsible for the taxes of Crete came from the Straboromanos family. He had a servant called George who had become a spiritual son of Leontios. He not only smoothed Leontios's path, but also gave him lodgings in the monastery of St George which he had founded.[127] The collection of these revenues did not only require the support of local officials. It also needed the continuing favour of the emperor. It was vital to have good connections at court. Leontios was lucky enough, as we know, to have the support of the Grand Droungarios, a member of the powerful Kamateros family.[128]

Thanks to the efforts of successive abbots Patmos became an important centre in the Aegean. It became a port of call on a route which became increasingly popular with the establishment of the crusader states. Patmos was able to profit thereby. It acquired a series of exemptions from customs and port dues for its ships. An episode from the *Life* of St Leontios suggests that there may have been an affinity between Patmos and the seafarers and sea captains (*naukleroi*) of the Aegean. On a journey to Constantinople through the islands along the Anatolian coast Leontios was invited into the home of Mauro, a merchant who originally came from Amalfi. He had long been settled in the Byzantine Empire. He was prosperous, but he and his wife were childless. He

[126] Leontios of Jerusalem, 402–3; ed. Tsougarakis, 82–3.
[127] Ibid., 395–6; ed. Tsougarakis, 66–7.
[128] Ibid., 412; ed. Tsougarakis, 104–5.

asked Leontios to bless them, which he did. In due course, they had a daughter.[129]

This is not to suggest that Patmos was bidding to become a new Delos.[130] But it was able to tap some of the wealth flowing through the Aegean. It provided a new religious focus for the region. It was becoming a pilgrimage centre. If the miracles of St Christodoulos emphasise the attentions of the Latins, this was because they were a new and increasingly important element in the life of the Aegean. The material success of Patmos has to be explained first in terms of how the monastery exploited local opportunities, but it went far deeper than this. It depended on Patmos's deserved reputation as a guardian of the monastic ideal. Its history in the twelfth century is a testimony to the enduring vigour of Byzantine monasticism. If any Byzantine monastery of the twelfth century realised the ideal set out by Eustathius, it was Patmos. There is some force to his criticism of the condition of the monasteries in his own time. The monasteries of Constantinople were respectable enough, but they had become comfortable havens rather than the spiritual workshops that some of them had been in the eleventh century. Mount Athos had ceased to inspire, but the monastic tradition at Byzantium was deeply enough rooted to produce a monastery, such as Patmos, which for a time maintained the highest standards of the monastic life.

Conclusion: the monastic saint

The monastery of St John the Theologian on the island of Patmos provides a corrective to Eustathius of Thessalonica's strictures about Byzantine monastic life in the twelfth century. This should not be taken to mean that Patmos was somehow a typical Byzantine monastery of the period. It was quite exceptional. This was highlighted by its ability to produce not one but two saints at a time when hagiography and the creation of new cults are reckoned to be in decline.[131]

The lack of new hagiography and cults of new saints is not entirely a Comnenian phenomenon. It should be traced back to the turn of the tenth century, when Symeon Metaphrastes was completing his official cycle of the *Lives* of the saints. With the contemporary *menologium* of Basil II Metaphrastes's work brought a new sense of order and purpose to hagiography and the cult of the saints. His *Lives* were held in the highest regard. There was little purpose now in rewriting ancient hagiography. They set a daunting standard for the production

129 Ibid., 408–9; ed. Tsougarakis, 94–7.

130 Cf. E. Malamut, *Les îles de l'Empire byzantin VIIIe-XIIe siècles* (Byzantina Sorbonensia 8) (Paris, 1988), 2 vols., II, 446–53.

131 Magdalino, 'The Byzantine holy man', 52–4.

of new hagiography and contributed to a more exacting appraisal of the criteria for sanctity. This Symeon the New Theologian knew to his cost. At exactly the time that Metaphrastes was writing official disapproval put paid to Symeon's efforts to promote the cult of his spiritual father Symeon Eulabes.[132] The canonisation of Symeon himself was a long-drawn-out and mysterious affair which owed much to the support of the Patriarch Michael Cerularius. There was as yet no official process of canonisation at Byzantium. It remained a haphazard process at Byzantium until the fourteenth century. Saints continued to 'emerge' at Byzantium. It depended on the creation of a cult which required some, if not all, of the following elements: festival of commemoration, a special order of service, or *akolouthia*, an icon of the saint, and a saint's *Life*, which provided proof of his sanctity. This normally included evidence of miraculous powers or divine intervention.[133] This should have been a recipe for a riotous bloom of cults, but this was not the case in the eleventh and twelfth centuries.

To blossom the cults of saints needed the continuing support of a community or an institution, which was more often than not a monastery. This may explain why there are so few saintly bishops. The incipient cults of Eustathius of Thessalonica and Michael Choniates soon withered away. The only twelfth-century bishop to acquire the status of saint was the obscure Hilarion, bishop of Moglena, but his background was monastic. In any case, his cult only emerges into the light of history in late fourteenth-century Bulgaria.[134] Another Comnenian saint was Eirene, empress of John II Comnenus. She was the moving spirit behind the foundation of the monastery of the Pantokrator, which preserved her memory.[135] Her example bears out the importance of monastic support for the creation of saints. This is equally evident in the cases of Cyril Phileotes and Meletios the Younger, who along with Christodoulos and Leontios, were the major new saints of the Comnenian epoch.

Cyril died in 1110 and Meletios a year or two earlier. Like Christodoulos who died in 1093 they might seem scarcely to count as figures of the Comnenian era. Their cults were, however, products of the age. They did not assume a clear shape until the mid-twelfth century, when the *Lives* of these saints were all first written. We know that the *Life* of Christodoulos was written by John, metropolitan of Rhodes, a former

132 Hausherr, *Un grand mystique byzantin*, 99–129.

133 Macrides, 'Saints and sainthood in the early Palaiologan period', in *The Byzantine Saint*, ed. Hackel, 83–7.

134 Turdeanu, *La littérature bulgare.*, 82–3.

135 Cinnamus (Bonn), 10.2–8; *Synaxarium Ecclesiae*, ed. Delehaye, 887–90; P. Gautier, 'L'obituaire de Pantocrator', *REB* 27 (1969), 247–8; Gautier, 'Le typikon du Christ Sauveur Pantokrator', 26–31.

monk of Patmos. The *Lives* of Cyril and Meletios were composed by far more distinguished authors with impressive court connections. That of Cyril was the work of Hosios Nicholas Kataskepenos, who must have been a monastic leader of some standing. He was a correspondent of the Empress Eirene Doukaina.[136] Meletios the Younger is blessed with not one but two *Lives*, that were produced either simultaneously or within a very few years of each other. The first was by Nicholas, later bishop of Methone, who was a prominent figure in the ecclesiastical politics of the early part of Manuel I Comnenus's reign. He was writing thirty-six years after the saint's death, which gives a date in the 1140s.[137] The second *Life* is by an even better known writer, Theodore Prodromos. The two *Lives* complement one another in the sense that Nicholas writes from the point of view of the community which Meletios created, while Prodromos is more interested in the saint's Constantinopolitan connections. But it is not possible to go further than this. The circumstances in which the *Lives* were produced are obscure. We do not, for instance, know who commissioned them. It is exactly this kind of detail which would have illuminated the development of these cults.

There is one other twelfth-century saint. This is the Cypriot Neophytos the recluse. He was very much a product of the Comnenian era. He was born in 1134 and died in 1214 or very soon afterwards. Thanks to Catia Galatariotou's brilliant study[138] we are probably better informed about his life and sanctification than almost any other Byzantine saint. She is able to provide a new perspective. She is able to present the process of sanctification through Neophytos's own writings. This produces an immediacy that is lacking for those cults – and they are the vast majority - where we are largely dependent on hagiography, for the hagiographer will seek to objectify the process of sanctification. It is a topos of hagiography that a saint does not consciously seek to promote his cult. In contrast, Neophytos at times seems to be doing this quite blatantly. The decoration he commissioned for his cave church not only has him as a supplicant, but also shows him between the Archangels Michael and Gabriel being borne aloft to heaven. By way of contrast, St Leontios refused to have an icon painted of him during his lifetime. After his death artists were consistently unable to make a likeness of him. This was taken as miraculous confirmation of his wishes.[139] Neophytos was not so self-effacing. He was his own publicist. He was convinced that he had been singled out by God. He wrote a tract significantly called the *Sign of God*. It gave an account of what

[136] Cyril Phileotes, 13–15.
[137] Angelou, *Nicholas of Methone*, xiii-xiv, xxx-xxxi.
[138] Galatariotou, *The Making of a Saint*, esp.95–147.
[139] Leontios of Jerusalem, 432–3; ed. Tsougarakis, 152–5.

he took to be his miraculous deliverance. He had been hollowing out new quarters above his rock church when he was trapped by a rock fall, but managed to wriggle free. The importance of his escape to his search for sanctification is underlined by the way he commemorated it as a special feast day for which he composed an *akolouthia*.[140] Neophytos did not wait for death or others for the creation of his cult. It scarcely comes as a surprise that no *Life* of Neophytos was ever written. It would almost have been superfluous, since he had prefaced the *typikon* for his monastery with an autobiographical account of his life.[141]

There was much that was highly irregular about Neophytos's search for sanctification. At least, he never claimed to be a miracle-worker. He was content to point to those signs that showed that God had chosen him for His work. This was to minister to the people of Christ. His concept of his role was close to that of the Old Testament prophet. He believed that God spoke through him. It was for this reason that he put such emphasis on his lack of schooling and the apparently miraculous way in which he acquired an education. A series of sermons, meditations, and other writings poured from his pen. Their importance to Neophytos is evident from the way he catalogues them in the *typikon* he drew up for his monastery.[142] They won a wide audience throughout Cyprus. After Neophytos's death the autographs of his works were treated as his relics.[143]

But why did the people of Cyprus listen? Galatariotou explores with great finesse the need that a society had for a saint. Twelfth-century Cyprus was in an exposed position on the frontiers of the Byzantine Empire. It was subjected, as we have seen, to ruthless exploitation by the Byzantine government. Neophytos criticised the rapacity of the imperial administration and of the local ascendancy alike. This was a traditional function of the holy man in Byzantine society: to offer a degree of hope by using his moral authority to intervene with the powers that be.[144] After Manuel I Comnenus's death in 1180 the situation in Cyprus deteriorated still further. It was first seized in 1184 by the Byzantine usurper Isaac Comnenus and then fell into the hands of the crusader king Richard Coeur de Lion in 1191. The next year a Cypriot rising was put down with peculiar ferocity by the Templars. Neophytos's role changed. He had to convince the Cypriots that despite all these disasters, which would be capped by the fall of Constantinople in 1204, orthodoxy and Empire still retained their validity. God's wrath

140 Galatariotou, *The Making of a Saint*, 109–15.
141 Tsiknopoulos, ΚΥΠΡΙΑΚΑ ΤΥΠΙΚΑ, 69–104.
142 Ibid., 83.16–31; Galatariotou, *The Making of a Saint*, 261.
143 Galatariotou, *The Making of a Saint*, 123.
144 See P. Brown, 'The rise and function of the holy man in late antiquity', *Journal of Roman Studies*, 61(1971), 80–101.

on his people would be stayed. Neophytos was able to provide some consolation by looking back to the rule of Manuel I Comnenus, whom he presented as an ideal emperor.[145]

The people of Cyprus required the virtue of a saint to sustain them through a crisis. Neophytos provided more than just hope. His monastery became a haven for those fleeing from the oppression of Frankish domination. But moral authority by itself was not sufficient, as Galatariotou rightly emphasises. To be effective it needed a network of close supporters. Neophytos was fortunate enough to have a brother who was abbot of one of Cyprus's great monasteries, Koutsovendis. He also had the support of Basil Cinnamus, the bishop of Paphos. Neophytos acknowledged in his *typikon* how vital this was. It was Basil who induced him to become a priest and to lay the foundations of a monastic community around his hermitage in the hills above Paphos. Basil benefited from the relationship. He was an outsider, an aristocratic bishop from Constantinople. His support of Neophytos provided him with local credibility.[146] Neophytos's network of supporters was not exclusively ecclesiastical. He also numbered members of the local ascendancy among his patrons, some of whom became his spiritual sons. This, as we know, was one of the more powerful bonds of Byzantine society.

Catia Galatariotou has provided a convincing paradigm of the place of a Comnenian saint in local society. He is no longer a wonderworker so much as an inspired teacher who builds up a network of supporters. How well do Cyril Phileotes and Meletios the Younger fit this pattern? It is a difficult comparison to make. Their lives were not so dramatic and none of their writings have survived. Meletios is known to have drawn up a *typikon* for his community, which enjoyed some local influence.[147] It may well have contained autobiographical material in the way of *typika*.[148] We have to rely on the testimony of their *Lives* written some time after their deaths. The result is a much more conventional presentation of a saint and his quest for sanctification than is the case with Neophytos. It is also done with an eye to exploiting the saint's reputation and contacts for the benefit of his community.

Much of Cyril Phileotes's *Life* is devoted to describing his apprenticeship as a holy man. It was vital to establish a saint's credentials. Normally, a holy man withdrew from the world. Cyril contrived to remain part of his family and community. His life and ministry were mainly passed in or close to his home town of Philea in Thrace. It was a region that suffered for most of the later eleventh century from the raiding of

145 Galatariotou, *The Making of a Saint*, 168–84.
146 Ibid., 168–9.
147 Miklosich & Müller v, 180.
148 Angold, 'Were Byzantine monastic *typika* literature?', 53.

the Petcheneks and the Cumans. Cyril shared the trials and tribulations of the local community. He had to flee because of a Petchenek raid. He made arrangements to ransom some of those carried off.[149] On another occasion his daughter lost an eye in an accident.[150] A neighbour's child had thrown a stone at her. This was a banal enough incident, but of a kind that could have disturbed the peace of a peasant community for generations. The saint's forbearance diffused the bitterness. It was easy for local people to identify with Cyril. His miracles, such as they were, were performed for their benefit. After his death his cult began to develop with local support. The most important step was taken eleven years after his death by his hagiographer Nicholas Kataskepenos who opened up his tomb and put his head on display. It served in lieu of an icon! Local people were overjoyed to be reunited with him, but only three miracles are recorded as performed at his tomb. Two of them relate to a local shipowner who was one of Cyril's patrons.[151] Cyril scarcely comes into the category of a wonderworker.

He was instead a spiritual counsellor to the emperor and the imperial elite. He was able to instruct the Emperor Alexius I Comnenus in his moral duties and to assure him of God's satisfaction. Cyril claimed to have foreseen in a dream Alexius's triumph over Bohemond.[152] Such was Alexius's trust in him that he postponed an expedition against the Turks on his advice.[153] With members of the imperial administration, such as Eumathios Philokales, Cyril was far more critical. Eumathios departed with the saint's blessing, determined to repent of his past conduct.[154] These contacts were all important to his posthumous reputation. They almost certainly made the difference between the success and failure of his cult which local connections alone could not sustain. They highlight one facet of a saint's role: the power to validate political power through inspired advice and criticism. The saint provided a bridge between a local community and the centre of the Empire. It could take quite tangible forms. Alexius's gratitude to Cyril was shown in imperial largesse. Most of this Cyril would later distribute to local people in a time of famine.[155]

Again Cyril was fulfilling a traditional function of the holy man. New was his insistence on his right to teach. This he shared with Neophytos. He objected to a local priest who began to minister to the local community. He saw the priest as a competitor. Since, as a priest,

149 Cyril Phileotes, 123–36.
150 Ibid., 80–3.
151 Ibid., 262–4.
152 Ibid., 154.
153 Ibid., 243–4.
154 Ibid., 153.
155 Ibid., 231–2, 235–7.

the latter had a right and a duty to preach to his congregation, he first contested the orthodoxy of the priest's sermons. He then cast doubt on the validity of his holy orders. He wanted proof. He compared the priest with Judas Iscariot, because he had betrayed Christ through his sins. Cyril remained to be convinced that he had truly repented. Again, he needed proof. The purpose of this exchange is clear: it stressed the pastoral responsibilities of the saint. He had a duty to teach. It was also designed to emphasise the superiority of the virtuous ascetic over the priest.[156]

This was also a theme taken up in Nicholas of Methone's *Life* of Meletios the Younger, but far more brutally. Meletios expelled one of his monks from the community. The monk went to Thebes and was ordained a priest. He would later take part in a procession to Meletios's monastery organised by the people of Thebes, who were suffering a drought. They duly received the saint's blessing and were rewarded with a shower of rain. However, Meletios wanted his revenge on the presumptuous monk. He insisted that he remove his sacerdotal vestments and hide himself in a ditch. The people were horrified by Meletios's behaviour: they pulled the man out of the ditch and made him put on his vestments again. The procession resumed its way back to Thebes. Just as it was entering the city, the priest was struck by lightning and died. It was an incident that confirmed Meletios's power.[157]

Both the *Lives* of Meletios the Younger focus on the acquisition of virtue, or spiritual power, and its exercise. The saint uses it to dominate his community. Monks who gainsay him tended to die or go mad.[158] Monks from other monasteries, for instance, neighbouring Daphni, find the regime at Meletios's monastery too demanding.[159] This was intended to underline Meletios's superiority as a religious leader, as was the account of the visit paid to him by the abbot of the Constantinopolitan monastery of Psychosostis. Meletios was able to see into men's hearts. He understood that the abbot was troubled by religious doubts. He was able to set him at his ease and advise him about the spiritual counsellors he should consult when he returned to the capital.[160] The saint is using his spiritual powers as a father confessor. Meletios was less clearly a teacher than either Neophytos or Cyril. Instead his hagiographers emphasise his role as a confessor. He was careful to obtain from the Patriarch Nicholas Grammatikos

156 Ibid., 154–63.
157 Meletios the Younger, 13–14.
158 Ibid., 15–16.
159 Ibid., 55–6.
160 Ibid., 24–6.

authorisation to hear confessions.[161] He was able to perform acts of healing through inducing confessions.[162] This aligns Meletios with the Euergetine tradition which placed confession at the centre of the monastic life.

There is a greater emphasis on the monastic community in the *Lives* of Meletios the Younger than in the *Life* of Cyril Phileotes. Meletios was an outsider from Cappadocia. There is less identification with the local community and its troubles. Meletios's energies are mainly directed towards establishing and dominating monastic communities first outside Thebes and then on the slopes of Mount Kithairon, where his monastic church still stands. But a saint could not completely isolate himself within his monastery. At one point Nicholas of Methone stops his narrative of the saint's activities and reflects: 'It was not only monastic and private concerns that absorbed the saint's care and attention, but also public and secular affairs.'[163] A saint's spiritual powers were to be deployed for the benefit of society at large. In the first instance, this would take the form of offering the Emperor Alexius Comnenus advice about the conduct of a campaign against the Cumans.[164] This won him the support of the emperor, who rewarded the saint with a modest subvention from the revenues of Attica.[165]

The imperial connection was far less important to Meletios than it was to Cyril Phileotes. Instead he built up close ties with the imperial governors of the theme of Hellas, who had their residence in neighbouring Thebes. A succession of governors and members of their retinue consulted Meletios and benefited from his wisdom, his foreknowledge, and his healing powers.[166] They must have played some part in spreading the saint's fame.

One of them, Bardas Hikanatos, was governor of Hellas on three separate occasions. At the end of his second tour of duty he came to pay his respects to the saint, who predicted that he would return once more. Which he did, just in time to assist at the saint's funeral.[167] Imperial governors were outsiders. It was worth courting the good-will of a holy man with local contacts and prestige. Equally, Meletios

161 Ibid., 48.
162 Ibid., 34–5, 53–4.
163 Ibid., 26.14–15.
164 Ibid., 26–7.
165 Ibid., 44.
166 I.e. the Grand Duke, John Doukas; Michael Kastamonites; Bryennius, 'duke of Thebes'; Constantine Khoirosphaktes, *praitor* of Hellas and the Peloponnese; Epiphanios Kamateros, *anthypatos* of Hellas and the Peloponnese; Bardas Hikanatos, *praitor* of Hellas and the Peloponnese; Leon Nikerites, *praitor* of Hellas and the Peloponnese.
167 Meletios the Younger, 59.

benefited from their attentions. The material advantages were perhaps less important than the confirmation he thus received of his spiritual powers and dominance. It enhanced his standing among local people, who were equally anxious to enjoy his blessing. Meletios performed the traditional role of the holy man as an intermediary between local society and the representatives of imperial authority.

It is inevitable that in its broad outlines the figure of a Comnenian saint will bear a distinct resemblance to that of his forerunners from late antiquity onwards. There are, however, telling differences of emphasis. More is made of the didactic role of the saint. This may take the form of preaching and teaching and/or that of acting as confessor. It had as its corollary the superiority of the ascetic, be he a priest or not, over the secular clergy. Here we touch on one of the major concerns of the Comnenian church: who had the right to hear confessions? It was a question that the canon lawyer Theodore Balsamon kept returning to. He was vexed by the way simple monks acted as confessors. Nor was it sufficient for monks to be ordained priests for them to hear confessions. They had to obtain the express permission of the ordinary. Balsamon wished to vindicate episcopal control over confession. He went to lengths to refute the prevailing view that priest monks (*hieromonachoi*) alone were worthy to hear confession. This, in his opinion, was a usurpation of episcopal authority.[168] Balsamon was going against the tide. The twelfth-century Latin theologian Hugh Eteriano who knew Byzantium inside out was convinced that confession had passed out of the hands of the bishops and into those of the monks.[169] This had already started to happen at the turn of the eleventh century. The then *chartophylax* of St Sophia observed that 'nowadays confession is heard in secret or in a corner by monks and not publicly in the cathedral by a bishop, as was the case in the past'. He was not quite sure why this had happened. He thought that it might have been the bishops' fault, in the sense that they recoiled from the task 'because of the hubbub of the crowd'. They preferred instead to delegate the task to monks.[170] Monks who acted as confessors should also have been priests, but that was by no means always the case.[171]

It was vouchsafed to the few to become saints. It is difficult to suppress the thought that it was often a matter of luck. There were others who seem equally well qualified to be revered as saints, but, for whatever reason, were not. The Comnenian saints were exemplary

168 Rhalles & Potles II, 616–19; III, 310–12, 314–15.

169 Migne, *PG*, 140, 548D.

170 P. Gautier, 'Le chartophylax Nicéphore. Oeuvre canonique et notice biographique', *REB* 27(1969), 182.3–8.

171 E.g. at the monastery of the Theotokos Euergetis: Rhalles & Potles III, 311–12 = Grumel, 1159.

figures. They not only conformed to traditional assumptions about the nature of sanctity; they also met new requirements. In a sense, they reflect the growing importance in the twelfth century of monks or, more often, abbots as teachers and confessors. They wielded enormous influence. Take, for instance, Cyril Phileotes's spiritual father, who resided in the monastery of St Philip on the Bosphorus. This is how he was described: 'He not only came from an aristocratic family, but was endowed with every virtue and possessed outstanding powers of discernment. For which reason many came to visit him for their spiritual benefit, not only members of the laity, but also the most pious among the abbots.'[172] Much the same could have been said about Gregory, abbot of Oxeia, in the early part of Manuel Comnenus's reign. He acted as father confessor and spiritual guide to members of the imperial family and of the Comnenian aristocracy. He specialised in writing letters of consolation at times of personal crisis.[173]

A more unorthodox figure was Michael Glykas. If he is to be identified with Michael Sikidites, as seems probable, then he had a reputation as a magician.[174] He served at court. He was rash enough to reprove Manuel Comnenus for his obsession with astrology. He was disgraced in 1159 and blinded. The remainder of his life was spent as a monk. His views on theological problems were eagerly sought and his spiritual counsels valued. They were collected under the title *Chapters on the Uncertainties of Holy Scripture.*[175] The majority of them are addressed to monks, some from important families of the capital. But his circle also included members of the laity, the majority of them prominent at court.[176] He also ministered to Theodora Comnena, Manuel Comnenus's niece and mistress.[177] She had tried to murder a rival. Michael Glykas consoled her with the thought that salvation was not out of the question, as long as she was truly penitent.

Spiritual instruction was mostly a matter of seeing into men and women's hearts, but it could occasionally embrace a mystical approach. About 1200 Abbot Isaiah compiled a spiritual guide for the nun Theodora, daughter of the Emperor Isaac II Angelus. It contained a pronounced mystical element. Isaiah put a particular emphasis on

[172] Cyril Phileotes, 99.

[173] Gautier, 'Les lettres de Grégoire'.

[174] Nicetas Choniates, 147–50. This is J. Darrouzès's view (*Dictionnaire de Spiritualité*, VI 505–7), as against that of K. Krumbacher, *Michael Glykas. Eine Skizze seiner Biographie und seiner litterarischen Thätigkeit nebst einigen unedierten Gedichte und Briefe desselben* (Munich, 1895).

[175] Michael Glykas.

[176] John Doukas [Kamateros], Grand Heteriarch (ibid., nos.23, 53); Constantine Palaeologus (ibid., nos. 36–7, 42, 76); Andronicus Palaeologus (ibid., no.44); Alexius Kontostephanos (ibid., no.63).

[177] Ibid., no. 57. See Varzos II, no.150.

the Jesus prayer: 'Lord Jesus have pity on me, Son of God help me.' He maintained that 'anyone who turned over this prayer in his heart day and night until his or her death, far from the world, can go before Christ with assurance'. The essence of his mystical instruction was concentration on Jesus Christ.[178] As we know, this trend was reflected in the art of the time. New iconographies, such as the *threnos*, the *epitaphios*, and the 'Man of Sorrows' concentrate on Christ's humanity and sufferings and emphasise human emotion.[179]

Far from being moribund and materialistic, as some twelfth-century critics suggested, Byzantine monasticism was capable of innovation. Most striking perhaps was the emphasis contemporaries placed on the importance of nunneries and the spiritual needs of nuns. Abbot Isaiah was not content only to provide his spiritual daughter, the nun Theodora, with a book of instruction. He also compiled a *Meterikon* for her; that is to say a selection of the wise sayings of women ascetics. It provided a pendant to the *Paterikon*, which till then was all that was available to nuns. Isaiah was aware that his compilation was a new departure. He expected criticism, but he was determined to ignore it. The spiritual needs of Theodora were more important. He hoped that his work would teach her 'that it was not only men who because of their strength of character were capable of the severe demands of the ascetic life'.[180]

Admittedly, this interest in nuns and nunneries did not provide the basis for a monastic renewal of the kind that occurred in the eleventh century. This was artificially prolonged by the attentions of Alexius Comnenus and his family, who wished to benefit from association with it. It petered out after Alexius's death. Manuel Comnenus's efforts to raise the standard of monasticism do not seem to have borne fruit. This only threw into sharper relief the ascetic exhibitionism on the streets of Constantinople. It was denounced by leading churchmen as indecent. In many ways, it was relatively harmless. It was a stage that many respectable figures of the monastic world went through, including Cyril Phileotes and Leontios.

Manuel Comnenus's failure also underlined the materialism of many monasteries, which seemed far too absorbed with estate management and the acquisition of property. It might be argued that this was only a process of consolidation. Perhaps it was a necessary facet of monastic life. Patmos maintained the highest standards and it was ruled over by abbots of great spiritual understanding. They did not see any contradiction between care for their estates and the material prosperity of their

178 J. Gouillard, 'Une compilation spirituelle du XIIIe siècle: "Le livre II de l'abbé Isaie"', *EO*, 38(1939), 72–90.

179 Belting, 'An image and its function', 1–16.

180 I. Hausherr, 'Le Mètèrikon de l'abbé Isaie', *OCP* 12(1946), 286–301.

monastery and their spiritual responsibilities. They were deemed complementary. The judgement of critics of twelfth-century monasticism was clouded by the ideal espoused by the Comnenian dynasty. This revolved around the independent coenobitic monastery. But the focus was moving to the abbot or monk who served as the spiritual adviser or father confessor to a circle which consisted not only of the monks of the community but also of outsiders. These might be other monks or abbots; they might also be members of the laity. This change is reflected in the attention that abbots paid to their pastoral role. This might take the form of preaching, teaching, and spiritual counselling. Perhaps its most graphic manifestation was church-building. Monasteries were probably the major force behind the extensive construction of new churches in the twelfth century. However imperceptibly, monastic life changed, but there is no sign of monasteries losing their grip on Byzantine society.

PART V

RELIGION AND SOCIETY

19

LAY PIETY: FRAMEWORK AND ASSUMPTIONS

THE arrival of the Comneni saw the completion of a process of change in the organisation of Byzantine society. The Byzantines had traditionally divided society into two groups: the powerful and the poor. As we know, the powerful were those who had access to political power through membership of the elite, which included the higher clergy; the poor consisted of the general run of tax payers. Though crude, this division reflected an underlying reality: the redistribution of much of Byzantium's surplus wealth from the peasant producer to the hierarchies of church and state. By the eleventh century, however, writers were finding this two-fold division of society increasingly unsatisfactory. A middle class – the *mesoi* – was beginning to make its presence felt. Its members were predominantly in business and trade. They were most visible in Constantinople, where commerce and manufactures were still concentrated. In the capital the gilds provided them with an organisation of their own. Kekavmenos – that guide to Byzantine political life in the eleventh century – recognised their influence. He advised that you placed informants in all the gilds, so that you knew what they were planning.[1]

On the face of it, it might seem that the gilds and other associations would have provided an aspiring middle class with a vehicle to articulate and promote its ambitions. Such a possibility was blunted by a distinct preference on the part of the middle class for traditional status. They sought to turn their wealth and influence into office and rank. We have already seen how Christopher of Mitylene mocked the pretensions of successful tradesmen who sought positions within the church.[2] They were just as eager to obtain for themselves and their sons rank at the imperial court or a place in the administration. Michael Psellus considered that this was undermining the fabric of the state.[3] Psellus was

1 Kekavmenos (ed. Wassiliewsky/Jernstedt), 5.1–8; (ed. Litavrin), 124. 20–4.
2 Christopher of Mitylene (ed. Kurtz), no.63, 37–9.
3 Psellus, *Chronographie*, ed. Renauld, I, 132.15–21.

himself a *parvenu*, who came from a gild background. He had chosen another – and more hallowed – avenue of social promotion: education.

This was equally true of his fellow bureaucrat and historian Michael Attaleiates who came from even more obscure origins, but thanks to his education rose to senatorial honours. A.P. Kazhdan has singled out his social views for special scrutiny.[4] He was not an aristocrat nor a military man, but looked to them for protection. He was sympathetic to middle-class aspirations, but his religious and cultural orientation derived from his 'betters'. To quote Kazhdan, he 'adopts the ideals of his protector and sings the praises of nobility, valour and generosity'.[5] He was the paradigm of that group which has come to be called 'bourgeois gentry'. They were rentiers residing in Constantinople or some provincial city. They owned both urban and rural properties. They tended to distance themselves from trade, even if, like Psellus, that was the family background. They retained, however, a lively interest in the market. They had an even stronger interest in education, because it opened up the path to a career in the imperial government and the church.

Their role was brought into sharper focus by the triumph of the Comneni. To quote Kazhdan once again, they 'provided the main constituency for the Comnenian dynasty'.[6] That is to say, they served the dynasty's needs. As administrators and publicists they came to form a *noblesse de robe*. Their ranks were swelled by those old aristocratic families which failed to gain entry to the charmed Comnenian circle.[7] Under the Comneni the 'bourgeois gentry' became synonymous with an educated elite, but subordinate to a ruling family with a near monopoly of power. Never was this more evident than in the rhetorical and literary productions of the time. These were intended to flatter or entertain the Comnenian ascendancy.

The 'bourgeois gentry' also supplied increasing numbers of recruits to the patriarchal church. For a time, it provided them with a stage which allowed them a degree of independence. Theological debate was an outlet for their intellectual abilities and ambitions, but even this was stifled from the middle years of Manuel Comnenus's reign. Thereafter the patriarchal church was dutifully subservient to imperial wishes with the consequences we have seen for the state of the Empire on the eve of the fourth crusade. If the patriarchal church failed to give leadership, in other respects – legal and institutional – it grew stronger thanks to the work of men, such as Theodore Balsamon. To that extent, the growing strength of the patriarchal church was founded on the

4 Gautier, 'Le *diataxis* de Michel Attaleiate', 21.44–8; Kazhdan/Franklin, 23–86.

5 Kazhdan/Franklin, 86.

6 Kazhdan/Epstein, 107.

7 See Magdalino, *Manuel I Komnenos*, 180–201.

talents and energies of the 'bourgeois gentry'. The corollary of this was its domination of the patriarchal church.

Did the emergence of a 'bourgeois gentry' make itself felt in other ways? It certainly underlay the cultural ferment of the eleventh century. Its products were responsible for the new emphasis on the Hellenic element of Byzantine culture and on a humanist ethos. They seem to have been equally responsible for the changing patterns of piety. The monastic revival of the eleventh century originated among them. The founders of the Theotokos Euergetis and of the Kyr Philotheos came from an affluent middle-class background, as did some of the supporters of Symeon the New Theologian.[8] The new stress on the religious vocation and equality of women can be traced back to none other than Psellus's mother – a true bourgeoise.[9] However, these new features would be progressively taken over by the aristocracy. The Comneni completed the process. We have seen how they absorbed the monastic revival for their own purposes. They were equally adepts of a humanist culture and education. Anna Comnena singles out Michael Psellus for high praise in her history for his intellectual attainments.[10] The adoption by the aristocracy of the innovations pioneered in the eleventh century was central to the culture and religious life of the Comnenian period. It stifled new developments, but it meant that Byzantine culture retained its cohesion.

Confraternities and families

Culturally education constituted a social divide within Byzantium. It was a major factor defining membership of the elite. Even a Kekavmenos was sensitive to the criticisms there might be of his literary style.[11] It drove a wedge between the 'bourgeois gentry' and the traders and business men who made up the new middle class. In a sense, this cut them off from their roots. A commonplace of twelfth-century literature was the resentment of struggling schoolteachers and literati against successful, but uneducated tradesmen. Their education had not brought them the material rewards anticipated.[12] Such rivalries hampered the development among the middle class of any clear cultural identity. Entry into the elite was the ideal. Where this proved to be impossible the new middle class was happy to defer to the tastes of the elite. With the appearance of a middle class gilds and confraternities might have been expected to play a more significant part in religious life at Byzantium than they did. The signs there were in the eleventh

8 Hausherr, *Un grand mystique byzantin*, 173.
9 See below, pp. 436–7.
10 Anna Comnena v, viii, 3: II, 34.5–13 (ed.Leib).
11 Kekavmenos (ed. Wassiliewsky/Jernstedt), 75–6.
12 Theodore Prodromos, no.IV, 72–83.

century that this was happening soon peter out. One or two of the gilds of Constantinople are known to have staged processions on the feast day of their patron saint. The Patriarch Luke Chrysoberges suppressed the festivities associated with the gild of notaries.[13] There is also a tantalising description of the festival of Agatha which we owe to Michael Psellus. It was staged each year at Constantinople by women working in the textile industry. It was not part of the Christian calendar, but there were religious overtones.[14] It does not appear to have survived into the twelfth century. Quite by chance there have also survived the rules of the confraternity of Our Lady of Naupaktos, which flourished in the eleventh century in the city of Thebes. Its purpose was religious: to venerate an image of the Theotokos and to provide a proper burial and commemoration services for its members.[15] Other provincial Byzantine cities are likely to have boasted one or more confraternities associated with a major church or shrine. There was a confraternity of the Hodegetria at Thessalonica which revolved around an icon of the Theotokos. There was another attached to the church of St Demetrius.[16] However, the sparsity of even incidental information about gilds and confraternities suggests that they were not a significant feature of religious life.[17]

This contrasts with the West, which was rich in corporate institutions. These provided the individual with protection, mutual solidarity, and sociability. They helped to compensate for a weak apparatus of state which was characteristic of western Europe until the later middle ages. At Byzantium the state was correspondingly strong. Deliberately or not, it discouraged the growth of corporate institutions. Ideally, the state provided the individual with the protection deemed necessary. In practice, the individual was often ranged against the power of the state. The most obvious protection was that provided by the family.

The family constitutes the core of most societies, but it has been usual in recent years (in the wake of A.P. Kazhdan) to attribute a nigh exclusive role to the family at Byzantium, as if it alone constituted the fabric of lay society.[18] In fact, Byzantine society was a good deal

[13] Christopher of Mitylene (ed. Kurtz), no.136, 91–8; Rhalles & Potles II, 451–2; Grumel, 1093.

[14] Sathas V, 527–31. See A.E. Laiou, 'The festival of 'Agathe'. Comments on the life of Constantinopolitan women', in *Byzantium: Tribute to Andreas N. Stratos*, I (Athens 1986), 111–22 (=A. E. Laiou, *Gender, Society and Economic Life in Byzantium* (Aldershot, 1992), no. III).

[15] J. Nesbitt and J. Wiitta, 'A confraternity of the Comnenian era', *BZ* 68 (1975), 360–84.

[16] Eustathius II, 94.24–5; 142.3–10.

[17] *Pace* P. Hordern, 'The confraternities of Byzantium', in *Studies in Church History* 23(1986), 25–45.

[18] See A. Kazhdan and G. Constable, *People and Power in Byzantium* (Washington, DC, 1982), 32–3.

more complicated than this. In the first place, the structure and size of families varied. The nuclear family may have been the norm among the peasantry, but even here it was not uncommon for households to consist of three generations.[19] The tendency was for households to get larger as families got richer. At the top of society aristocratic families revolved around the *oikos*.[20] This can literally be translated as 'House'. The Latin *familia* is perhaps a more accurate rendering. It was the family in the sense of an extended household. Beyond the immediate members of the family it would contain servants and retainers. Ideally, it was a self-contained unit, but there would also be numbers of clients and hangers-on.

There were also alliances or friendships. There were many nuances to these friendships.[21] They were not always very close. There was a thin dividing line between friendship, patronage, or just mutual advantage, but a great deal of emotion might occasionally be invested in friends. 'I carry your image in my soul and the folds of my soul absorb it intellectually. You are always with me in my memory, but I want to see you with my eyes and to hear your sweet voice in my ears.'[22] So Michael Psellus wrote to one of his friends. Some of the strongest ties of friendship were among former pupils of a teacher or among the followers of a spiritual father. Veneration of the teacher or the spiritual father created bonds akin to those generated through the family. How sexually charged these relationships were never transpires. If one ignores certain aspects of monastic life, Byzantium never boasted a homosexual culture, but these networks of friends performed something of the same function. They were essential for those engaged in public life. These ties might be solemnised by the act of *adelphopoiesis*, which created a blood brotherhood. This is a well-attested custom among the Byzantines. It was used by, among others, a number of emperors. It may never have had any backing in law and officially the church frowned on it. However, an order of service was elaborated to celebrate it. When the emperor Michael III adopted the future emperor Basil I as his brother, there was a church ceremony.[23]

Complementing these networks were others forged at the font. Baptism was an institution that only existed because of the church. The

19 The most detailed discussion of the structure of the peasant household is in Laiou-Thomadakis, *Peasant Society*, 223–42.

20 See P. Magdalino, 'The Byzantine aristocratic *oikos*', in *The Byzantine Aristocracy*, ed. Angold, 92–111 (= Magdalino, *Tradition and Transformation*, no.II).

21 Mullett, 'Byzantium', 15.

22 Michael Psellus (ed. Kurtz/Drexl) II, no.138.

23 Zhishman, *Eherecht*, 285–9; E. Patlagean, 'Christianisation et parentés rituelles: le domaine de Byzance', *Annales ESC* 33(1978), 625–36, at 628–30 (= E. Patlagean, *Structure sociale, famille, chrétienté à Byzance* (London, 1981), no.XII).

spiritual relationships created through it were essential to the functioning of Byzantine society. The church was determined to retain control over baptism and to ensure that the spiritual relationships created counted for as much as the ties of blood and marriage; and possibly more. For example, the church insisted that the prohibited degrees applied to spiritual relations in the same way as to family ties. The godchildren of the same sponsor were not supposed to marry. Neither could they marry their sponsor's natural children. This notably increased the impediments to marriage. There were strategies that could be adopted to circumvent the inconveniences created. Ruth Macrides observes that it was usual for the children of a marriage to have the same godparents and concludes: 'this practice would appear to have been the unofficial response of the people to the problem posed by marriage prohibitions'.[24]

Baptism is a good place to end this survey of Byzantine social relations. Baptism was *the* requirement for membership of the orthodox church. Though it might on occasion be delayed, it was almost unheard of for it to be forgone. It gave the church a responsibility for the spiritual welfare of each individual. The church was involved almost from the beginning in the destiny of the individual. The turning points and intimate relationships of any life were likely to be marked or cemented by a church service. This was one way in which the church maintained a measure of control over family life. It also fixed the age of consent and established impediments to marriage. It laid down the prohibited degrees. The church might offer dispensation, as long as an appropriate penance was performed. This was part of an accommodation that the church reached with lay society, but it ensured recognition of the moral and spiritual supervision it exercised over family life. It meant that the status and condition of marriage would be the force field where church, family, and society interacted with the greatest intensity.

This suggests a rather formal, even legalistic relationship between the official church and lay society. Faith scarcely enters into it. At this level, the official church had few attractions for lay society. Public worship was all too often a matter of form. We have already noted the complaints there were that parish churches were being neglected and that confession was becoming a monastic monopoly. The new middle class appears to have followed the lead of the aristocracy and to

[24] R.J. Macrides, 'The Byzantine godfather', *BMGS* 11(1987), 139–62, at 146. Much less important was adoption. Leo VI stipulated that this should receive the blessing of the church, but it seems to have remained optional. The canon lawyer Theodore Balsamon argued that the same marriage prohibitions applied to an adopted child as to a natural one, but few seem to have followed him. As Ruth Macrides observes, the function of adoption was largely charitable. It was a way of supporting orphans and providing dowries for poverty-stricken brides: R.J. Macrides, 'Kinship by arrangement: the case of adoption', *DOP* 44(1990), 109–18.

have focused their piety on family monasteries, churches, and chapels. Fashions of lay piety seeped out from the monasteries. Worship became an increasingly private affair. Lay piety largely escaped the supervision of the official church, or so it would seem from Theodore Balsamon's criticism of various manifestations of lay piety, such as the use of private chapels. Any investigation of lay piety is hampered by a lack of texts that provide a lay perspective. *Faute de mieux* we have to turn to the poem of *Digenes Akrites* and Kekavmenos's *Advice and Counsels.* Neither text deals primarily with the church and lay society. The poem presents a portrait of a Byzantine aristocrat in the guise of an adventure story. Kekavmenos aimed to provide his sons with a guide to political and social life, but underlying both texts are assumptions about the place of religion in the life of the laity. These may be the more valuable for not being spelled out.[25]

Kekavmenos

Kekavmenos remains an elusive figure. He was a soldier who began his career under Michael IV (1034–41). He saw service in many parts of the Byzantine Empire. He became governor of the theme of Hellas with his residence at Larissa in Thessaly. It was a place with which his family had longstanding connections. One branch had estates in the vicinity. Kekavmenos's own properties cannot have been far away. It was probably there that he composed soon after 1075 a 'Book of Counsels' for his sons. It was designed to equip them for various careers in Byzantine public life. It contains a fund of wisdom and experience culled not only from Kekavmenos's own life, but also from that of other members of his family. There are difficulties in the way of using this text as a guide to conditions and currents of opinion in late eleventh-century Byzantium. Contemporaries rarely understand their own times, but they do experience them. Nobody should pretend that Kekavmenos's experience was somehow typically Byzantine, but he is likely to have confronted many of the same dilemmas as his contemporaries. His reactions and his solutions were his own, but they provide a starting point. We have to be grateful for small mercies: at least, we gain access to the experiences of a career that covered much of the eleventh century. Kekavmenos wanted his sons to have the benefit of this experience when they came to choose a career. He also sought to inculcate his own high standards of behaviour. Kekavmenos may have

25 See P. Magdalino, 'Honour among Romaioi: the framework of social values in the world of Digenes Akrites and Kekaumenos', *BMGS* 13(1989), 183–218 (= Magdalino, *Tradition and Transformation*, no.III).

been given to moralising, but this means that he felt a need to relate conduct to Christian teachings.[26]

We may only be dealing with the experiences of a single individual, but their value is increased because we can place Kekavmenos fairly exactly in his social setting. He was a soldier who had held high command and had been a military governor in northern Greece. He came from that officer class that had suffered as a result of the administrative changes brought in by Constantine Monomachos. These favoured civilian administrators. Monomachos does not emerge well from Kekavmenos's book.[27] There are cautionary tales of relatives who tried to take advantage of the opportunities opened up by Monomachos's reforms and suffered as a result.[28] Kekavmenos shows his contempt for the administrators in the capital. To his way of thinking they were little better than 'mimes'.[29] But Kekavmenos had a high opinion of the eunuch Nikephoritzes, who is often taken to epitomise all that was worst about the civilian government of Michael VII Doukas (1071–8).[30] This apparent aberration is easily explained. Nikephoritzes had previously held high office in the Peloponnese and Hellas and had made himself useful to Kekavmenos's family.

At a time of rapid change Kekavmenos recommended in the first instance remaining true to the old military virtues of service and loyalty. But the support of the family was vital. Kekavmenos put it in his own pithy way: 'Do not forget your relatives and God will not forget you!'[31] He reminded his sons of the paramount importance of the *oikos*. Without sound household and estate management it was impossible to live of one's own. Autarky was one of the ideals of Byzantine society at all levels. The *oikos* was a defence against an uncertain world and its dangerous alliances and temptations. It should never be breached, even innocently. Friends should *not* be invited to stay. They should be lodged elsewhere. Kekavmenos draws an alarming picture of the dangers of allowing a friend to stay. He will note down every detail about your domestic arrangements and will then use these to slander or make fun of you. Worse he will have access to your womenfolk. He will watch their every movement and make fun of them or worse he may try to seduce your wife. If he succeeds he will boast about it.[32] But danger lurked even closer. Kekavmenos includes a cautionary tale

[26] See P. Lemerle, *Prolégomènes à une édition critique et commentée des 'Conseils et Récits' de Kékauménos* (Brussels, 1960), 18–40; G.G. Litavrin, ed., *Sovjety i rasskazy Kekavmjena* (Moscow, 1972), 49–61.

[27] Kekavmenos (ed. Wassiliewsky/Jernstedt), 18.18–24, 99.21–2; (ed. Litavrin), 152.30–4.

[28] Ibid. (ed. Wassiliewsky/Jernstedt), 39–40; (ed. Litavrin), 194–6.

[29] Ibid. (ed. Wassiliewsky/Jernstedt), 8.31, 94.12–13; (ed. Litavrin), 132.26.

[30] Ibid. (ed. Wassiliewsky/Jernstedt), 73.11–15; (ed. Litavrin), 266.22–7.

[31] Ibid. (ed. Wassiliewsky/Jernstedt), 52.25; (ed. Litavrin), 222.32.

[32] Ibid. (ed. Wassiliewsky/Jernstedt), 42–3; (ed. Litavrin), 202.12–24.

about an exemplary wife – 'versed in the holy scriptures'. The emperor wanted her for his mistress. She resisted the temptation, but allowed herself to be seduced by a young man who had been welcomed into the household as a relative.[33]

Kekavmenos advised that you lock up your daughters, because 'a shameless daughter dishonours not only herself, but her parents and the whole family'.[34] He also warned his sons against the wiles of women:

> Be on your guard when you are with a woman, even if she seems modest, and do not become familiar with her. You will not escape her snares, for your eyes will swivel in their sockets and your heart will pound and you will have no control over yourself. The devil has provided her with three weapons: her appearance, her words, and her sex.[35]

Women were best avoided in Kekavmenos's opinion. He thought it a mistake to quarrel with them and an even bigger mistake to be friendly with them.[36]

This is an extreme reaction to women, suggesting not only their danger but also their power. Kekavmenos was expressing the fears of a patriarchal society: women must not be allowed to get out of control. Their sexuality ensnared men and distorted their sense of judgement. Women could so easily become a disruptive element. To prevent this, they were to be cherished, monopolised, bartered, and protected, as the most valuable of possessions. In a sense, they were. A significant proportion of a family's wealth was tied up in their dowries. However, Kekavmenos did subscribe to the idea that a good wife was beyond the price of pearls, or, as he put it, 'Whoever buries his wife has lost half of his livelihood, more if she was a good woman.'[37] A good wife ensured well-brought-up children, a household which was at peace with itself, in a word a husband without a care in the world. The danger was that a widower might be tempted to marry again. He would fall into the snares of the matchmakers. The second marriage would never be as happy as the first. Supposing it was with a widow, she would remember her first husband, while he would still pine for his wife. There were bound to be difficulties with his children. His new wife might turn him against them.[38]

Success in the world was founded on the security of the family and the household. Its day to day management was in the hands of

33 Ibid. (ed. Wassiliewsky/Jernstedt), 43–4; (ed. Litavrin), 204.7–30.
34 Ibid. (ed. Wassiliewsky/Jernstedt), 51.8–9; (ed. Litavrin), 220.9–11.
35 Ibid. (ed. Wassiliewsky/Jernstedt), 54.21–6; (ed. Litavrin), 226–8.
36 Ibid. (ed. Wassiliewsky/Jernstedt), 61.20–23; (ed. Litavrin), 242.9–10.
37 Ibid. (ed. Wassiliewsky/Jernstedt), 55.30–1; (ed. Litavrin), 230.8–9.
38 Ibid. (ed. Wassiliewsky/Jernstedt), 56.1–30; (ed. Litavrin), 230–2.

the wife. The enterprise succeeded or foundered on her competence. Marriage was a vital element for the success or failure of a family. Kekavmenos chooses to dwell on the dangers of a second marriage, but his forebodings apply to any marriage. The importance of marriage would mean that family life, if not necessarily society, revolved around women. No wonder there was such distrust, even a fear of women. They could make or mar a man. This has always been the paradox of a patriarchal society.

Kekavmenos stressed that the life of the household was not just a matter of organisation, but required religious and spiritual values: 'I do not disparage wealth, but I prefer a pious disposition (*phronesis*)' sums up Kekavmenos's attitude.[39] At first sight, his piety appears conventional enough. He counselled against overwork because it would entail missing church services. It was by attending church services that you showed yourself to be a loyal servant of God. He also recommended reciting a psalm at midnight. The privacy of the hour allowed a man to concentrate his thoughts on God.[40] Each night he should reckon up the deeds of the day. If they were good, he should give thanks to God; if not, take heed for the morrow.[41] He advised study of the scriptures, but this was best done when alone. If you sat reading a sacred text and somebody came and disturbed you, it was best to close the book and talk. If you continued reading, you would be considered one of the following: a hypocrite, an incompetent, or a poseur.[42]

Kekavmenos's piety owed much to a bishop of Larissa that he had got to know while serving as governor in Hellas. He quotes the bishop's opinion about reading. To benefit from a text it was necessary to read it from cover to cover. Dipping into it was the mark of a babbler.[43] How well he followed this advice is difficult to know. He garbles a passage from the *Collationes* of John Cassian.[44] He may have had it at second hand. This may equally have been true of his acquaintance with secular texts. He recommended the value of studying military tactics and ancient history. He refers on two occasions to the *Roman History* of Dio Cassius, but neither suggests a direct acquaintance with the text. He probably knew it through some *florilegium*.[45] He certainly knew his Bible which is the text he most frequently quotes and alludes to. Ecclesiasticus appealed to him in particular. Kekavmenos litters his text with Biblical commonplaces: the impossibility of 'serving God and

39 Ibid. (ed. Wassiliewsky/Jernstedt), 50.30; (ed. Litavrin), 220–2.

40 Ibid. (ed. Wassiliewsky/Jernstedt), 38.11–21; (ed. Litavrin), 192–4.

41 Ibid. (ed. Wassiliewsky/Jernstedt), 61.4–7; (ed. Litavrin), 240.21–4.

42 Ibid. (ed. Wassiliewsky/Jernstedt), 64.10–14; (ed. Litavrin), 248.8–12.

43 Ibid. (ed. Wassiliewsky/Jernstedt), 60.21–7; (ed. Litavrin) 240.8–14.

44 Ibid. (ed. Wassiliewsky/Jernstedt), 52.15–17; (ed. Litavrin) 222.22–4. See Lemerle, *Prolégomènes*, 103–4.

45 G. Buckler, 'Writings familiar to Cecaumenus', *B* 15(1940–1), 133–43.

Mammon';[46] 'Fear God rather than men.'[47] He adds some of his own: 'Without God it is not even possible to catch sparrows.'[48]

He counselled against the sins of omission. The example of Pilate should be a lesson to any judge. His fault was not that he condemned Christ, but that he had given in to the demands of the mob and had surrendered Him to the Jews.[49] Kekavmenos also takes the story of Dives and Lazarus. The rich man did no harm to Lazarus. He had simply failed to help him, when he was in a position to do so. This was almost worse. It was the duty of the rich to support the poor through benefactions.[50] The importance of charity as a social duty is continually stressed.[51] Though he warned against the dangers of having any contact with holy fools,[52] he advised the cultivation of monks. Do not turn them away because they appear simple. The apostles were simple men and they illuminated the world.[53] Kekavmenos expected his sons to go to church. He warned that you did not go to church to eye the women. You should keep your gaze firmly fixed on the sanctuary.[54] There were other dangers about attending church. It was assumed that this would be on a feast day. Your creditors might take the opportunity to embarrass you in front of people.[55]

Kekavmenos had no time for superstitions. Do not pay attention to dreams or any kind of divination was his advice.[56] Satyrs and dragons also exercised the popular imagination. St Antony was supposed by some to have been guided by a satyr through the desert. Kekavmenos refused to believe this. God made two kinds of rational beings: angels and men. There were no others. No prophets or apostles were sent to enlighten satyrs. Christ did not come to save them. There were, Kekavmenos admitted, similarities with the myth of the centaurs, but John of Damascus, or so he believed, had shown this belief to be false. Kekavmenos disposed of dragons with much the same line of argument. He was willing to accept that they might be numbered with the animals, but not that they were capable of taking on human form and seducing women.[57]

46 Kekavmenos (ed. Wassiliewsky/Jernstedt), 19.6; (ed. Litavrin), 154.16.
47 Ibid. (ed. Wassiliewsky/Jernstedt), 2.31–2; (ed. Litavrin), 120.20–1.
48 Ibid. (ed. Wassiliewsky/Jernstedt), 12.30–1; (ed. Litavrin), 142.8–9.
49 Ibid. (ed. Wassiliewsky/Jernstedt), 2.15–25; (ed. Litavrin), 120.4–15.
50 Ibid. (ed. Wassiliewsky/Jernstedt), 2.5–15; (ed. Litavrin), 120.1–4.
51 Ibid. (ed. Wassiliewsky/Jernstedt), 3.14–15, 39.3–8, 49.31–3; (ed. Litavrin), 120.24–6, 194.21–6, 216–18.
52 Ibid. (ed. Wassiliewsky/Jernstedt), 63.21–8; (ed. Litavrin), 246.17–23.
53 Ibid. (ed. Wassiliewsky/Jernstedt), 49.28–31; (ed. Litavrin), 216.26–9.
54 Ibid. (ed. Wassiliewsky/Jernstedt), 47.12–13; (ed. Litavrin), 212.7–8.
55 Ibid. (ed. Wassiliewsky/Jernstedt), 37.13–23; (ed. Litavrin), 190.26–30.
56 Ibid. (ed. Wassiliewsky/Jernstedt), 50.1–14, 60.1–9; (ed. Litavrin) 218.2–16, 238.16–24.
57 Ibid. (ed. Wassiliewsky/Jernstedt), 80–3. See Lemerle, *Prolégomènes*, 109–13.

Kekavmenos envisaged the possibility that one of his sons might go into the church. In due course he might be offered a bishopric or even the patriarchal throne, but he should not accept the honour unless he was vouchsafed a vision from God. Here Kekavmenos seems to have absorbed some of the mystical teaching fashionable in the eleventh century,[58] but he was quick to point out the dangers of false apparitions. He stressed the importance of a bishop or a patriarch's charitable activities. He should see to orphans and widows; he should ransom captives. He should not be dazzled by the pomp of the office. He should not devote himself to building up the wealth and estates of the church and find comfort in the thought that he was doing it not for his children, but for God. Kekavmenos had seen several bishops acting in exactly this way. He attributed it to the cunning of the devil, who deceives us into believing that we act with the best of intentions. Kekavmenos contrasted the greed of bishops with the charity of St Nicholas and St Basil.[59]

This is but the voice of one layman. It is valuable because it is a voice that is not often heard. Orthodoxy was central to Kekavmenos's life. His piety was sincere, if conventional. He refused to tolerate insults to the holy icons and the Godhead. A man should be willing to lay down his life in defence of orthodoxy.[60] Attending church services was a duty, but it was to be complemented by private study and devotion. Superstitious customs and beliefs were dismissed. There was a distaste for the more extreme forms of asceticism, but monks were welcomed. Kekavmenos had mixed feelings about the church itself. He was critical of the accumulation of wealth by the church. One can almost detect in his writings the germs of that local hostility which plagued sophisticated Comnenian bishops. The pious bishop of Larissa with his grim spiritual wisdom was Kekavmenos's model bishop. Bishops should be men of God. Their function was to care for the spiritual well-being of both rich and poor. They should devote themselves to prayer and charitable works, not to more material concerns.

Digenes Akrites

A different, if complementary, perspective emerges from the poem of *Digenes Akrites.* This poem is not strictly comparable with Kekavmenos's 'Book of Advice'. It is a work of imaginative literature. The experience it reflected has a different – less concrete – quality from that of Kekavmenos. However, the poem would have been aimed at

58 J. Darrouzès, 'Kékauménos et la mystique', *REB* 22(1964), 282–5.
59 Kekavmenos (ed. Wassiliewsky/Jernstedt), 51–2; (ed. Litavrin), 220–2.
60 Ibid. (ed. Wassiliewsky/Jernstedt), 45.24–5; (ed. Litavrin), 208.15–16.

an audience that might well have contained the likes of Kekavmenos and his sons, for there is a consensus that the earliest surviving version of the poem – that contained in the Grottaferrata manuscript – is very close to the original which received literary form at the turn of the eleventh century.[61] This derived from oral traditions circulating round the borderlands of Byzantine Anatolia from the late ninth century. The literary form chosen was the verse romance. This reflects a court milieu and was designed to appeal to a court aristocracy which had been cut off from its roots in Anatolia by the Turkish conquest that followed the battle of Mantzikert in 1071. The poem contains a nostalgic distillation of life along the Anatolian frontiers, as it had existed at the height of Byzantine power. It celebrates the way its hero 'put down the arrogance of all the Hagarenes / And plundered [their] cities and annexed them to the Empire.'[62] There is no attempt at chronological precision. But details of geography and administration are accurate, or nearly so. The deeds of Digenes Akrites are not set in some never-never land, but one that is identifiably Byzantine and orthodox.

The poem is just as suffused with a trust in the power of the Christian God as Kekavmenos's 'Book of Advice'. Hagiography provides some of the diverse elements out of which the poem was shaped.[63] Christ and his saints are regularly invoked. Digenes and his wife prided themselves on their Christian virtues, especially almsgiving.[64] They prayed every day to God that they would be vouchsafed a child. When their prayers were not answered, they still gave thanks to God and ascribed their childlessness to their own faults. In some ways, orthodoxy is even more in evidence in the poem than it is in the pages of Kekavmenos. This is perhaps natural enough, given that the poem is set on the frontiers with Islam. Religion is the defining factor. Digenes's father, a Muslim emir, came over to the Byzantine side; 'forgot his kin, his parents, and his native land / Even denied his faith for a girl's love.'[65]

The girl in question was the daughter of a Byzantine general, whom he had carried off in the course of a raid on Byzantine territory. For love of her he was willing to abandon his faith and leave his mother and

61 For dating see G. Huxley, 'Antecedents and context of Digenes Akrites', *Greek, Roman, and Byzantine Studies* 15(1974), 317–38; N. Oikonomidès, 'L'épopée de Digénis et la frontière orientale de Byzance aux Xe et XIe siècles', *TM* 7(1979), 375–97; H.-G. Beck, *Geschichte der byzantinischen Volksliteratur* (Munich, 1971), 63–97; R. Beaton, *The Medieval Greek Romance* (Cambridge, 1989), 27–48. The texts used are *Digenes Akrites*, ed. and transl. J. Mavrogordato (Oxford, 1956) and *Digenes Akrites. Synoptische Ausgabe der altesten Versionen*, ed. E. Trapp (Vienna, 1971). The Grottaferrata version will be cited Gro.

62 Gro. VII, lines 203–4: ed. Mavrogordato, 228–9; ed. Trapp, 346.

63 E. Trapp, 'Hagiographische Elemente im Digenes-Epos', *AB* 94(1976), 275–87.

64 Gro. VII, lines 184–5: ed. Mavrogordato, 227; ed. Trapp, 342.

65 Gro. III, lines 11–12: ed. Mavrogordato, 44–5; ed. Trapp, 130.

other dependants behind in Syria. Later he was able to persuade them to join him on Byzantine soil and convert to Christianity. The episode is presented in terms of the superiority of orthodoxy over Islam. As governor of Hellas, Kekavmenos also had to come to terms with a foreign presence: this time, the Vlach shepherds who then dominated the mountains of northern Greece and came down to the plains of Thessaly in the winter. Kekavmenos warned his sons against them. They were 'a totally untrustworthy and crooked people, who had no correct belief in God'.[66] For Kekavmenos their lack of orthodoxy was their defining characteristic, from which their other faults stemmed.

Within Byzantine society Kekavmenos assimilated evil-doers who prospered to 'Jews, heretics, and Saracens'.[67] They were the kind of people who posed a threat to the centre of his existence – his *oikos*. The same fears are present in the poem of *Digenes Akrites*. As we shall see, these will concentrate on the threats to Digenes's wife. As with Kekavmenos, so in the poem there is a degree of identification of wife and *oikos*. Kekavmenos has very little concrete detail about the physical arrangements of his *oikos*. He prefers to dwell on a well-run household and efficiently managed estates. In the poem of *Digenes Akrites* the emphasis is different. The poet instead describes in detail the glories of the palace which the hero had built for himself and his wife. The poet, in other words, prefers to dwell on the physical aspect of the *oikos*.[68] He also includes a telling detail that Kekavmenos overlooks. In the courtyard of his palace Digenes Akrites built a church dedicated to St Theodore, where he buried his father and later his mother.[69] It served as a family shrine. Private churches and chapels were an important feature of aristocratic life.

Kekavmenos's main purpose was to provide his sons with good advice about their careers. Everything else was incidental. The reverse is true of the poem of *Digenes Akrites*. The hero's career may have culminated in his personal appointment by the emperor as 'warden of the marches', but it is subordinated to the details of his personal life. The poem is organised around the stages of his life: his birth and upbringing; his marriage; his death. Of these it is marriage which provides the poem with its central episode. The poem presents some of the choices and possibilities facing a young Byzantine aristocrat. Digenes and Eudocia, the daughter of a Byzantine military governor, fall in love. Digenes wants his father to ask for her hand in marriage. His father tells him that he has already done so and has been refused. Digenes therefore decides to abduct the girl, who goes with him all

66 Kekavmenos (ed. Wassiliewsky/Jernstedt), 74.5–7; (ed. Litavrin), 268.14–16.
67 Ibid. (ed. Wassiliewsky/Jernstedt), 38.29; (ed. Litavrin), 194.16–17.
68 Gro. VII, lines 42–108: ed. Mavrogordato, 218–23; ed. Trapp, 326–34.
69 Gro. VII, lines 109–51: ed. Mavrogordato, 222–5; ed. Trapp, 334–6.

too willingly. The runaways are pursued by the girl's brothers at the head of a posse of retainers. Digenes wheels round and routs them. The girl's father is impressed and now offers her in marriage to Digenes. He rolls off the rich dowry that comes with her hand, but links this with residence in his household. The General assures Digenes that he would be given precedence in the household over the girl's brothers. Digenes resists the temptation. He insists that he is marrying Eudocia for love, not for her dowry. Instead he takes her to his parents' house where the marriage is celebrated. The dowry he finally accepts is less impressive than the one that he was originally offered.

From a detailed, if fictional, account of a wedding the church is conspicuously absent. There is no mention of the marriage taking place in a church or of a priest officiating; only an isolated reference to the church's blessing (*hierologia*). This probably means that the church's role is taken for granted. The emphasis is on the marriage contracts, on the exchange of gifts between the families, and on the wedding festivities as the essential features of a marriage; not on any part played by the church. There was a good chance that bride and groom were related within the prohibited degrees and would have been under the age of consent. Such possibilities raise not a flicker of concern, though the orthodox church had been seeking for some time to tighten up on these aspects of marriage. The moral dilemma explored in the poem was quite different. It focused on the struggle between the needs of lovers and the interests of the girl's family. The hero and heroine were so overcome by the power of love that convention meant nothing. The family, for its part, feared the loss of a valuable asset, for the girl was a symbol of its wealth and prestige. Her elopement might leave it open to ridicule. The honour of the family was at the mercy of a girl.[70] It was a dilemma that Kekavmenos understood well.

The role and teaching of the church was incidental, but not negligible. The ideal of marriage espoused by the poem was compatible with the church's views, but it was not wholly Christian. Being faithful, for instance, was not so much a matter of following the precepts of the church. It had more to do with the dictates of love. This was the most powerful force shaping the destiny of the hero and heroine, though in conformity with God's purpose. The reciprocal ties forged by love are the foundation of the strong spiritual and moral quality of the marriage of Digenes and Eudocia. Its strength will be tested in various ways. There are the temptations of the flesh which Digenes fails to resist. He is guilty of adultery, first, with the girl of Meferke and then with

70 M.J. Angold, 'The wedding of Digenes Akrites: love and marriage in Byzantium in the 11th and 12th centuries', in *Η ΚΑΘΗΜΕΡΙΝΗ ΖΩΗ ΣΤΟ ΒΥΖΑΝΤΙΟ*, ed. Maltezou, 201–15.

the Amazon Maximo. On both occasions he was conscious that he was committing a sin and was prey to contrition. He was aware that it was not just God that he was offending by his adultery, but also his wife. 'Being ashamed as having greatly wronged her'[71] he went back to murder Maximo in order to ease his conscience! His lapses into adultery betrayed the vows he had freely made to his wife before their marriage. In a way, his wife was his conscience.

Digenes atoned in part for his adulteries by protecting his wife from the many dangers that assailed her. Dragons metamorphosing into handsome young men tried to seduce her; brigands threatened to carry her off, and lions to devour her.[72] But her role was not entirely passive. In order to conquer the brigands Digenes needed her encouragement, which she gave with the words, 'Be a man.'[73] Digenes recalled these words as he lay dying.[74] He confessed that his heroic deeds were done out of an excess of love for her: 'And many other things too, for your love, my soul, I did, to win you utterly.'[75] His wife was something more than Digenes's conscience. She was the moral centre of his life.

Their separation by death was unbearable. Digenes found the thought of his Eudocia being left behind as a widow hard to contemplate. As he lay dying he urged her to find another husband. She replied with an impassioned prayer to God and the Theotokos for her husband's recovery. If that was not possible, she prayed that she too might be allowed to die. This was vouchsafed to her. She expired with the expiring Digenes, who gave thanks to God 'That my soul bears not pain unbearable that she should be alone here and a stranger.'[76] This death scene provides the final expression of a romantic view of marriage which suffuses the poem. It is quite compatible with Christian teaching, but the inspiration is not wholly Christian. The romantic ideal of married love is one that can be traced back to secular roots at the beginning of the Christian era. It gave the married couple a degree of autonomy, since it was an expression of their free will; or, more precisely, love was the force that made this possible.[77]

How very different this all was from Kekavmenos's practical, not to say, matter of fact, attitude to marriage! Do we therefore have in the poem of *Digenes Akrites* an idealisation of marriage which was far removed from reality? An idealisation of marriage, certainly, but

71 Gro. v, line 286: ed. Mavrogordato, 158–9; ed. Trapp, 256.
72 Gro. vi, lines 45–80.
73 Gro. vi, lines 248: ed. Mavrogordato, 176–7; ed. Trapp, 278.
74 Gro. viii, line 112: ed. Mavrogordato, 238–9; ed. Trapp, 360.
75 Gro. viii, lines 121–2: ed. Mavrogordato, 238–9; ed. Trapp, 360. K. Galatariotou, 'Structural oppositions in the Grottaferrata *Digenes Akrites*', *BMGS* 11(1987), 29–68, at 65–6 was the first to stress this important point.
76 Gro. viii, lines 193–4; ed. Mavrogordato, 242–3; ed. Trapp, 368.
77 M. Foucault, *Le souci de soi* (Paris, 1984), 90–100.

not too far removed from reality. Something not so very different can be discerned behind Kekavmenos's grudging remarks about the value of a good wife. Both Kekavmenos and the poet agree upon the importance of the *oikos* and the central role played by the wife. The poem concentrates on marriage. It was critical to any family's fortunes. Kekavmenos betrays his concern, when he advises that daughters of a marriageable age should be kept under lock and key. Otherwise, they might easily disgrace their families. Kekavmenos receives corroboration from the poem. Eudocia was indeed confined in a separate chamber.[78] Only her closest relatives and maidservants had ever seen her countenance.[79] In this instance though the power of love rendered these precautions futile.

Marriage is a family concern. The church is not much in evidence. It is the same with piety. The poem of *Digenes Akrites* and the counsels of Kekavmenos are impregnated with conventional orthodox piety, but a priest or a monk hardly ever appears. Kekavmenos recommends attending church services, but this was part of the routine of life. He also insists upon private devotions. These might be guided or inspired by a man of spiritual wisdom. In Kekavmenos's case he was a bishop that he had come to know. Otherwise the hierarchical and the monastic church scarcely impinge on the world of Kekavmenos. The palace of Digenes Akrites houses a church, where Digenes and his mother gave his father an honourable burial. Nothing is said about the presence of a priest, but a Christian funeral was important. The most solemn undertaking that Digenes could make to his wife was to forswear a Christian burial, should he ever offend her.[80] It reveals the power of sanction that inhered in church ceremony.

There is a paradox: both the poem of *Digenes Akrites* and the 'Counsels' of Kekavmenos assume that orthodoxy and its rituals were an integral part of everyday life and thought, but pay scant attention to the church and priesthood. It may be that this was a matter of the church being taken for granted or it may be that both texts looked back to a time when the church could be taken for granted, in the sense that it fitted in with the requirements of society. It solemnised the key moments of any life: birth, marriage, and death. It conspired to dignify and justify the interests of the family and the *oikos*, which were the main concern of both Kekavmenos and the poem of *Digenes Akrites*. What both texts make plain is the central importance of women and marriage to the survival, let alone the prosperity, of the family and the *oikos*.

78 Gro. IV, line 269; ed. Mavrogordato, 90–1; ed. Trapp, 180.
79 Gro. IV, lines 497–9; ed. Mavrogordato, 104–5; ed. Trapp, 196.
80 Gro. IV, line 560; ed. Mavrogordato, 108–9; ed. Trapp, 200.

Conclusion

There may be objections to using Kekavmenos's 'Counsels' and the poem of *Digenes Akrites* as a way of probing the Byzantine *psyche.* Their preoccupations and assumptions may not have been that typical. Both texts were the products of an aristocratic milieu. But where religion was concerned Byzantine society was surprisingly homogeneous. We have seen how a rising middle class took its lead from the aristocracy. Nobody could have been less aristocratic than the iron worker who founded the monastery of the Theotokos Skoteine in the hills around Philadelphia on the Anatolian frontiers of the Empire.[81] His motives would have struck a chord with any aristocrat. He wanted to create a setting which would express his piety – his need to give thanks to God – and would provide a memorial for himself and the members of his family. It allowed him to harness the power of the church and orthodoxy for private, or at least family, ends. What both texts catch is the extent to which religion had become privatised by the turn of the eleventh century. It was a danger that the official church was beginning to wake up to.

Another danger was heresy. It was always feared that the weaker spirits might be prey to the guile of heretics or that popular superstition would spill over into heresy. Kekavmenos rejected superstitious ideas, but they suffuse the poem of *Digenes Akrites.* Kekavmenos may have had no truck with dragons metamorphosing into handsome young men ready to seduce women, but it is a motif worked up in the poem.[82] A way of thought deeply rooted in the classical past keeps bubbling through the surface of the poem. The sun is frequently invoked as an avenger of crimes or as a reminder of sins for which no atonement has been made.[83] The poem of *Digenes Akrites* again points to the homogeneity of religious experience at Byzantium. The aristocracy were not above indulging in superstition and magic.[84] It was not some kind of popular preserve. Equally they participated in those festivals and pilgrimages that might easily be dismissed as manifestations of 'popular religion'. They were the patrons of holy men whose bizarre behaviour might easily give rise to suspicions of heresy. It all sounds innocent enough but the official church began to see a challenge to its authority.

It began to clamp down on what it deemed to be irregular aspects of worship. It might only be that a hagiographical text was too naive or crude for official taste. Perhaps the church had its reasons for believing

[81] S. Eustratiades, 'Τυπικὸν', 3(1930), 325–6.
[82] Gro. VI, lines 45–80; ed. Mavrogordato, 164–7; ed. Trapp, 260–4.
[83] H. Gregoire, *Autour de l'épopée byzantine* (London, 1975), no.XVI.
[84] Rhalles & Potles IV, 251.

that out in the country diabolical rituals were conducted in out of the way chapels, but it is likely to have been more innocent than this. It is easy to dismiss it all as official paranoia. It was in fact more serious. The measures taken by twelfth-century patriarchs against manifestations of popular religion were symptomatic of a determined effort on the part of the church to exercise more effective control over lay society. Previously an easy going relationship between the church and society had tolerated much in the way of custom and had failed to check the increasingly private character of Byzantine worship. It had given the monasteries greater independence and scope. A series of patriarchs beginning with Alexius the Studite (1025–43) determined to reassert the authority of the church. They paid particular attention to the question of marriage. It was not difficult to see that this was the central institution of any society. The Byzantine church strove to exercise ever closer supervision over marriage and sought to regulate it ever more strictly.

20

LAW AND MARRIAGE

IN their different ways Kekavmenos and the poet of *Digenes Akrites* emphasise the central importance to Byzantine society of marriage. At the same time they ignore the church's role. Scarcely a word is said about the celebration of a wedding in church, still less that this had become an essential legal requirement. There is not a hint of the efforts made by successive patriarchs to bring marriage law under the effective control of the church. This was partly because at the turn of the eleventh century older habits of thought still persisted. It can also be attributed to the anomalous status of marriage in a Christian society, in that it was both a contract and a sacrament. Supervision of marriage was therefore uncomfortably divided between the church and the civil authorities. From the time of Constantine the Great onwards the civil law was shaped by the need to take into account the church's view of marriage. This culminated in a series of novels issued by Leo the Wise (886–912). His main concern was to bring the law up to date. That meant harmonising the Roman tradition of law with the needs of a Christian society. Marriage was one field where it was felt that there were major discrepancies between the 'old law', as Roman law in its Justinianic form was called, and the canons of the church. Special attention had been given to marriage at the council *In Troullo* (691/2). Its rulings remained to be assimilated by the civil law.

The importance of marriage is evident from the amount of space it occupied in Leo VI's legislation. By his time celebrating a wedding in church was an ancient practice, but it was not yet a legal requirement. Leo VI would put an end to any uncertainties by legislating that an ecclesiastical ceremony was essential for the validity of any marriage.[1] This emphasised the role of the church and the essentially sacramental character of marriage. Leo VI looked into other aspects of marriage. Somewhat ironically in view of his own marital difficulties he endorsed

[1] P. Noailles and A. Dain, eds., *Les nouvelles de Léon VI le Sage* (Paris, 1944), Nov. 89, 295–7.

the church's teaching about remarriage: a second marriage was acceptable if appropriate penance was done. Under certain circumstances even a third marriage might be condoned, but a fourth marriage was prohibited.[2] The institution of concubinage inherited from Roman law was outlawed.[3] Leo VI devoted special attention to betrothal. It was originally a contract pure and simple, but from the late eighth century it became more usual for betrothal to receive the blessing of the church, thus emphasising differences between civil and canon law. The Emperor Leo VI legislated that before the age of consent no betrothal should receive the blessing of the church.[4]

By his Novel 109 Leo VI established two forms of betrothal: there was the simple betrothal which took place in the old way from the age of seven upwards, but there was also betrothal with the blessing of the church which could only be celebrated once the age of consent was reached. This was an important step in the assimilation of betrothal to marriage, so that the same norms applied to betrothal as they did to marriage. In his legislation over marriage Leo VI sought to bring the civil law into line with the church's teaching. Novel 109, however, ends with an important qualification. The emperor was not bound by its provisions. Using his discretionary powers (*oikonomia*) he could permit the consecration of betrothal before the age of consent, 'for it is permitted to those entrusted by God with the administration of secular affairs to disregard the laws that bind subjects'.[5] Leo VI intended to maintain control over the legislative and legal processes, as was apparent from his actions over his fourth marriage. Ironically, this was the start of a reappraisal by the church of its role in marriage. It became less and less content to leave the initiative in the hands of the emperor and more determined to supervise and shape marriage law on its own account.

The first clear sign of this came in 997 when the Patriarch Sisinnios issued his tome on the prohibited degrees.[6] Leo VI's legislation had passed over the prohibited degrees and there were discrepancies on the matter between the civil and canon law. They demanded an authoritative statement. The Tome of Sisinnios prohibited the marriage of two brothers or two sisters to two first cousins or the marriage of an uncle and a nephew to two sisters or of an aunt and niece to two brothers. The implications of this ban were that affinity to the sixth degree now came

2 Ibid., Nov. 90, 297–9.

3 Ibid., Nov. 91, 299–301.

4 C. Schwarzenberg, 'Intorno alla benedizione degli sponsali in diritto bizantino', *BZ* 59(1966), 94–109, at 100–1; J. Dauvillier and C. de Clerq, *Le mariage en droit canonique oriental* (Paris, 1936), 32–4; Zhishman, *Eherecht*, 142–44.

5 Noailles and Dain, eds., *Nouvelles de Leon VI*, 357.4–6.

6 Rhalles & Potles v, 11–19; Grumel, 804; Zhishman, *Eherecht*, 319–22; J. Dauvillier and de Clerq, *Le mariage en droit canonique oriental*, 136–7.

within the prohibited degrees. The patriarch himself admitted that this was an innovation, which did not accord with the prevailing civil law. In the past, it had always been the emperor who had intervened to harmonise the norms of civil and canon law in this field. Why Basil II condoned the initiative of the patriarch on this occasion is a matter of guesswork. Later commentators assumed that the Tome of Sisinnios must have had the emperor's formal approval, but there is no sign that this was the case.

The patriarch made no reference to the emperor. He justified his measure by a comparison with the children of Israel, who had used circumcision as a way of separating themselves from other races. Such considerations no longer applied: 'Now we have become the New Israel and all have been made one.'[7] Under the new dispensation the exclusivity of Israel had become redundant. The gentiles were now included in God's covenant. Accordingly, marriage should be from as wide a circle as possible. To this end God had closed the inner gates of marriage. 'Wherefore the whole oecumene has been opened to those wishing to enter the state of matrimony, whereas the way to kinship has been yoked to the holy laws and made more difficult of access.'[8] The need for the New Israel to ensure that it was not disfigured by the spirit and practices of the Old reflects a distinctively Byzantine outlook. The New Israel must cast off the restrictive inward-looking attitudes of the Old.

This line of argument was reinforced by invoking the dictum of St Basil which condemned any marriage, 'where the names of the family (*genos*) are confused'. St Basil was apparently pointing to the ambiguous relationships that some marriages produced. If, for example, two brothers married two first cousins of a different family, the brothers would now also become *syngambroi*, that is relations by marriage, while their brides would have become sisters-in-law, as well as cousins. Their children would be first cousins on their fathers' side and second cousins on their mothers' side.

K.G. Pitsakes has pointed to the casuistry of the arguments that the Patriarch Sisinnios used in support of his measure: he did not cite the canons of church councils, but relied principally on the opinion of a Father of the church. What is more, it was an opinion that was framed with quite another matter in mind.[9] It opened up the possibility for endless innovation on the part of the patriarch, if opinions delivered by the Fathers of the church on specific matters were to be given general validity and were then to supersede the provisions of civil law.

7 Rhalles & Potles v, 13.
8 Ibid.
9 Pitsakes, '"Παίζοντες"', 223–6.

The effects of such an extension of the prohibited degrees were easy to envisage: lineages would be kept distinct and cousin marriages to a minimum. In other words, the Tome of Sisinnios must have had serious implications for the marriage strategies of the great families.[10] This would have been useful to Basil II in his struggle against the aristocracy and may explain his surprising complacency over the matter.

Sisinnios's initiative produced a wave of criticism which gathered strength after Basil II's death. It was headed by the foremost jurist of the time Eustathius Romaios. His legal opinions and decisions underlie much of the *Peira*, that legal handbook which was compiled around 1040 in the court of the Hippodrome. It shows that older patterns of marriage continued despite Leo VI's legislation: concubinage was still common as was divorce by consent. In other words, marriage could still be treated as though it was largely a matter of contract. The *Peira* also reveals that much, perhaps most, marriage litigation then went before the civil courts.[11] This is in contrast with the situation later on in the eleventh century. The failure of jurists to get the Tome of Sisinnios repealed or modified seems to have been the signal for an increasing proportion of marriage litigation going before the church courts. The tome emphasised the moral and spiritual dimension to marriage. It pointed to the ecclesiastical courts as the proper place for deciding matrimonial causes.

Among the critics of the Tome of Sisinnios was Demetrius, metropolitan of Cyzicus in the mid-eleventh century. This might seem a strange stance for a metropolitan bishop to take, but he based his arguments on the seventeen years that he spent in the Quaestor's office before entering the church. There he was accustomed to deal with cases involving the prohibited degrees both those that were directly referred to the bureau of the Quaestor and those that were submitted by provincial judges. It would therefore seem that along with other responsibilities, such as supervision of the rights of minors, the Quaestor's office dealt with matrimonial cases. Nicholas Skribas, another member of this office, would also produce a tract critical of the Tome of Sisinnios along very similar lines to that of Demetrius of Cyzicus. Apart from any qualms about the legal foundations of the Tome of Sisinnios, this criticism will have been prompted by fears that the Quaestor's office was losing control over different aspects of matrimonial litigation to the patriarchal synod. This is borne out by the gradual eclipse of the Quaestor and his office from the middle of the eleventh century.[12] Cases involving the prohibited

10 E.g. Grumel, 933 – June 1023.

11 D. Simon, 'Das Ehegüterrecht der Peira. Ein systematischer Versuch', *FM* 7(1986), 193–238.

12 By 1166 the Quaestor was no longer at the head of one of the four major tribunals at Constantinople: Magdalino, *Manuel I Komnenos*, 262.

degrees started coming more often than not before the patriarchal tribunal.[13]

The church's victory went further than this: it also obtained approval for a broad interpretation of the Tome of Sisinnios. The tome did not just apply to the specific relationships it regulated. These happened to be of the sixth degree of affinity. Henceforward all relationships of this kind were a bar to marriage. There was a further refinement. The prohibited degrees would be extended to the seventh degree of consanguinity; the argument being that blood relationships were a more serious bar to marriage than relationships by marriage. K.G. Pitsakes has singled out the Tome of Sisinnios as the great divide in the development of the prohibited degrees, not so much because it entailed a radical extension of the prohibited degrees, but because of 'the new line of reasoning and the new perspective on things that it introduces'.[14] In practical terms, it would leave the initiative for further innovation in the field of marriage law with the patriarchs of Constantinople, while the patriarchal synod was increasingly recognised as the final court of appeal for marriage litigation.

The Patriarch John Xiphilinos (1064–75) set about extending the provisions of the Tome of Sisinnios to betrothal. The patriarch noted that the civil law treated betrothal as more or less equivalent to marriage. To clear up any confusion he enacted that legal betrothal – that is with the blessing of the church – was to have the rank and status of marriage. In other words, the provisions of the Tome of Sisinnios would apply to betrothal. In addition, should anybody break off an engagement and marry another this should be treated as bigamy.[15] In this the patriarch was acting entirely on his own initiative. His tome did not receive immediate imperial approval. This may have been a studied rebuke for the way the patriarch took matters into his own hands. It would have been a way of denying the patriarch's measure validity under civil law. Nicephorus Botaneiates (1078–81), however, gave it his approval once he had ascended the throne. He had need of the church's support.[16] This was the state of affairs on the eve of Alexius Comnenus's accession to power in 1081. The church had assumed the initiative over marriage law.

Should we be surprised that Kekavmenos and the poet of *Digenes Akrites* were apparently unaware of the hard line that the church was taking over marriage or thought it unworthy of comment? Probably not! Its importance was far from clear and it is unlikely that as yet

[13] Schminck, 'Kritik am Tomos des Sisinnios', 219–30; H. Hunger, *Byzantinische Grundlagenforschung* (London, 1973), XI.

[14] Pitsakes, '"Παίζοντες"', 222–3.

[15] Rhalles & Potles v, 51–2; Grumel, 896 – 26 iv 1066.

[16] Schminck, 'Zur Entwicklung', 557.

very many people were affected. By and large it was still a problem for lawyers, civil and ecclesiastical. Kekavmenos's outlook was deeply conservative, while the poem of *Digenes Akrites* is informed by a nostalgia for the old life along the Anatolian frontiers. Both clung to the values of an earlier age. Kekavmenos had misgivings about many things, but modifications to the law of marriage would scarcely have seemed a threat to his way of life.

Church and marriage under Alexius I Comnenus[17]

The Patriarch John Xiphilinos's tome on betrothal produced a serious problem. His pronouncement that the Tome of Sisinnios now applied to betrothal as well as to marriage was all very well,[18] but it was not clear whether this meant that betrothal under the civil law had lost its validity. Did betrothal now have to receive the blessing of the church in order to be valid? A gap had opened up between the civil and the ecclesiastical law. It was left to Alexius I Comnenus to propose a solution. He stipulated that only betrothal which had been solemnised by the church was fully valid and on a par with marriage. Alexius set out the formalities of a proper betrothal. It had to be solemnised by the church and the parties had to have reached the age of consent. Though it should not occur on the same day or even, as sometimes happened, at the same hour, marriage was expected to follow hard on the heels of betrothal. Finally, the emperor laid down the penalties that might be inflicted on those disregarding the provisions of his law: the notary responsible for drawing up the offending agreement was to lose his stall and the fisc might levy an appropriate fine on both parties.[19]

Alexius had apparently capitulated to the wishes of the church, but this was deceptive. It was a way of asserting the imperial prerogative to legislate over marriage. In any case, he left a loophole. In line with the legislation of Leo VI he maintained that other forms of betrothal remained subject to the norms of the civil law. The uncertainties about the legal status of betrothal remained. By March 1092 it was the subject of a memorandum submitted by one of the top civil judges.[20] It drew attention to the sharp difference of opinion there was among the judges of the Hippodrome about the dissolution of betrothal. It was becoming increasingly common for parties to dispute the old procedure under the civil law whereby betrothal could be dissolved through the payment of a fine. They cited the emperor's novel to the effect that the only valid betrothal was that solemnised after the age of consent by the church.

17 Rhalles & Potles v, 277–9.
18 Ibid., 53–4; Grumel, 897.
19 Zepos I, 305–9; Dölger, *Reg.* 1116.
20 I.e. the Grand Droungarios of the Watch, John Thrakesios.

One party on the judicial bench favoured the old procedure, because otherwise, there really was no distinction between betrothal and marriage. The other party thought that, where betrothal conformed to the ecclesiastical model, it should not be dissolved. Only old-style betrothal from the age of seven should be dissolved. The judge added his own misgivings about insisting that the age of betrothal had to be identical with the age of marriage, that is at the age of consent. He considered that it would be beneficial for society,[21] if the age of betrothal returned to what it had been originally. Parents liked to arrange for their children's futures, as soon as they could. To do this they were now very likely to perjure themselves about their children's ages.[22]

In his rescript Alexius remained adamant that only a betrothal blessed by the church and contracted at the age of consent could be considered fully valid. He also stipulated that it was not possible to break off a betrothal by the payment of a fine. The causes for the dissolution of a betrothal were exactly the same as those applying to marriage. But he reiterated the rider introduced by Leo VI in his Novel 109: the emperor had the right to issue dispensations over the age of betrothal as he saw fit. He specified that this applied to both kinds of betrothal. Equally, he insisted that consummation should not occur until the age of consent. Nor should betrothal before the age of consent be used as a way of evading the prohibited degrees. Alexius entrusted the judge with the task of publicising the measure: he was to inform all law courts, provinces, and bishops too.[23]

Behind this was a specific case for which Alexius Comnenus had issued an imperial *prostagma* in March 1092. He used his powers of dispensation to allow a marriage where the parties were related in the sixth degree of affinity.[24] This ruling was presented to the patriarch and synod who accepted it and duly registered it,[25] but it was not to the liking of a section of the episcopal bench. In May 1092 the metropolitan of Philippopolis demanded an authoritative ruling from the patriarch and synod as to whether an uncle and nephew could marry an aunt and niece, which was the relationship in question. It was important, he maintained, for his pastoral responsibilities. The bishop was reminded of the emperor's ruling. Three other bishops then insisted that they needed time to consider it in detail before they could express an opinion.[26] The metropolitan of Philippopolis claimed that he still did not know how this all affected the Tome of Sisinnios. This is not the only

[21] Zepos I, 320.40. *Politeuma* is the word used for society.
[22] Ibid., 319–21.
[23] Ibid., 321–5; Dölger, *Reg.* 1167.
[24] Rhalles & Potles I, 283–4; IV 559; Dölger, *Reg.* 1168.
[25] Rhalles & Potles I, 284; V 58–9.
[26] Rhalles & Potles V, 58–9; Grumel, 963.

time that a bishop would display a profound attachment to the Tome of Sisinnios. It was as though it represented a peculiarly ecclesiastical view of marriage. The synod was reconvened on 14 June 1092 and the three bishops expressed their satisfaction with the emperor's ruling.[27] This was a success for the emperor. He had reestablished the important principle that the emperor had the right to make dispensations over the prohibited degrees. He had also regained the initiative over marriage litigation and legislation.

In the aftermath of Alexius's rulings over marriage and betrothal the question that exercised the church concerned marriages of slaves. It seems that masters were reluctant to allow their slaves to marry with the blessing of the church. They supposed that this would be taken as a sign that they were free. In 1095 Alexius would pronounce that this was not the case, but all masters had a responsibility to see that their slaves' unions received the official blessing of the church.[28] He made this ruling in answer to two petitions, one came from the patriarch who was worried by the numbers of slaves flocking to St Sophia and claiming that they came of free stock. One of the arguments used by their masters against their claims for liberty was that the unions of slaves were never blessed by the church at Byzantium. In other words, masters prevented their slaves from marrying with the blessing of the church, lest this was used as a pretext for claiming freedom.

The other petition came from the metropolitan of Thessalonica, who was faced with exactly the same problem. This is an interesting episode on several counts. It shows how the disadvantaged turned for protection and justice to the church, which at this point does not seem to have had the confidence to act independently, but turned to the emperor for a proper ruling. This is quite understandable, given that the main issue concerned the rights of a master over a slave which was a matter for civil rather than canon law. We also learn that it was commonly assumed that marriage in church was taken as proof of free status. In the event, Alexius declined to give this assumption the support of law, but this may have been out of a sense of humanity. He did not wish to deny slaves the benefits of a Christian marriage. Nevertheless, this assumption underlines the importance that attached to the church's blessing of a marriage. It is almost as though it represented some kind of enfranchisement; in the sense that through it the newly wedded couple took their full place in society.

This does not mean that marriage legislation took social convenience into account. One has only to look at the Patriarch John Xiphilinos's

[27] Rhalles & Potles v, 59–60; Grumel, 965.

[28] Zepos I, 341–6; Dölger, *Reg.* 1177.

effort to assimilate betrothal to marriage. Betrothal was now only to be contracted at the age of consent and was to be duly solemnised in church. It was realised at the time that this was not socially beneficial. A return to the original age of seven and upwards would have had its advantages. Though disapproving, Alexius I Comnenus explained the attractions of early betrothal for the vast mass of people. Ease of intercourse between those betrothed from an early age 'kindled the flame of love' is how he put it.[29] To justify his measures on betrothal John Xiphilinos cited moral and legal considerations. These Alexius could not disregard. Underlying Xiphilinos's measures was a desire to demonstrate the church's control over marriage and its moral supervision of society. This was a challenge both to the emperor and to the civil law. At first, Alexius was inclined to temporise. But he was not only able to maintain imperial rights over marriage law; he also succeeded in preserving the jurisdiction of the civil courts over matrimonial causes. Alexius recognised the claims of the civil courts to jurisdiction over matrimonial causes. J. Zhishman argued that as a result 'in the exercise of its jurisdiction over marriage the church was to be guided in the relevant decisions by civil law'.[30] It seems rather to have been the other way around: over marriage the emperor imposed on the civil courts the norms of canon law, as a means of validating their jurisdiction over marriage. This was of a piece with Alexius's church settlement. He wished to present himself as the upholder of orthodoxy and the protector of the interests of the church. At the same time, he was determined to retain the initiative in legislative matters.

In the sphere of marriage law, as in so many others, Alexius succeeded in reasserting imperial authority. He did not directly challenge the innovations made in this field by patriarchs from Sisinnios onwards. He preferred to give them his qualified approval, while retaining imperial rights of dispensation. It provided the basis for an understanding with the church. The emperor accepted the principle that marriage law should in future be shaped in accordance with ecclesiastical norms. It was a price that had to be paid, if he was to check the drift of marriage litigation from the civil to the ecclesiastical courts.

The application of marriage law under Manuel I Comnenus

Such an uneasy compromise could not last. Marriage law was to become an issue once again under his grandson Manuel Comnenus. In general he cooperated with the church. He confirmed the Patriarch Luke Chrysoberges's refusal to allow any relaxation of the prohibition

29 Zepos I, 308.2–4.
30 Zhishman, *Eherecht*, 152.

of marriages between those related by blood in the seventh degree.[31] However, his effort to repeal the Tome of Sisinnios brought him into conflict with a section of the episcopal bench and was only partly successful. Only tact on both sides prevented an open breach.[32]

Over the Tome of Sisinnios Manuel was on the defensive and had to express contrition for his intervention. His interest seems connected with the role that marriage played in his foreign and dynastic policies. Manuel Comnenus was careful to control the marriages of the aristocracy. A commoner who took an aristocratic bride without his consent might find himself minus both his bride and his nose.[33] It would seem that Manuel used the imperial tribunal to supervise aristocratic marriages. One case that came up before it concerned the wife of an aristocrat who wished to separate from her husband and become a nun. In such cases it was normal for the wife to spend three months in a nunnery before receiving the tonsure. This was to make sure that her motives were genuine. The emperor decided that not only should this custom apply in this particular case, but that henceforth it was to have the force of law.[34] In this instance, Manuel acted to clarify a minor point of marriage law. Where important principles were involved, he sought the support and agreement of the church. Where he expected resistance, he preferred not to meet it head on but to work through his allies on the episcopal bench. There were still resentments. After Manuel's death the canonist Theodore Balsamon would express his disapproval of the way the emperor had tried to set aside the Tome of Sisinnios. He insisted that the imperial order no longer applied, adding 'I pray that it will never be enforced, knowing that the reason why it was enacted was arbitrary and therefore will not effect anything good.'[35] These are very strong words coming from such a partisan of imperial authority. It shows how much the Tome of Sisinnios meant to a canon lawyer. It stood for a view of marriage that emphasised its moral and spiritual dimension. It was a view that saw marriage as the church's peculiar responsibility.

As *chartophylax* of St Sophia Theodore Balsamon had a special responsibility for matrimonial affairs and litigation. Among other things he supplied authorisation to priests for the celebration of marriages and betrothals after ascertaining whether or not there was

31 Rhalles & Potles v, 95–8 (Grumel, 1068); Zepos I, 408–10 (Dölger, *Reg.* 1468).

32 Rhalles & Potles I, 291; Zepos I, 425 (Dölger, *Reg.* 1341); Darrouzès, 'Questions de droit matrimonial'; Schminck, 'Zur Entwickling', 566–7.

33 Rhalles & Potles IV, 189.

34 Zepos I, 426; Dölger, *Reg.* 1572. The woman in question was the wife of Pyrrogeorgios, who came from a distinguished military background. He must be descended from the famous archer George Pyrros: Anna Comnena v vi, 2, VII ix, 6: II, 28. 5, 119.9–10 (ed. Leib).

35 Rhalles & Potles I, 291.

just cause or impediment.[36] However, the Tome of Sisinnios apart, Balsamon devotes surprisingly little space in his commentaries to marriage law. This seems to reflect a large degree of accommodation which had been reached over marriage between the church and the civil authorities. Balsamon considered it largely favourable to the church. Changes in marriage law required the consent of the patriarch and synod. The church, for its part, retreated from the extreme positions it had increasingly taken from the end of the tenth century. Balsamon cited a complicated case involving betrothal and the prohibited degrees that came before the Patriarch Nicholas Mouzalon (1147–51). The parties came from the highest ranks of the court aristocracy.[37] Synod decided that their marriage was not impeded by the betrothal of the bride's sister to the groom's first cousin, because betrothal was not fully marriage.[38] This would not have pleased the Patriarch John Xiphilinos, but it suggests that cases involving the prohibited degrees had to be submitted to synod, even if they related to members of the imperial family.[39]

Balsamon paid particular attention to one aspect of marriage: the question of consent. He noted that under the 'old law' all that was necessary for the validity of a marriage was the consent of the parents, but nowadays a church service was essential.[40] Balsamon was at great pains to underline the importance to marriage not only of the church's blessing, but also of the consent of the parties, and not just their parents. The discussion turned to abduction. This raised another aspect of consent. Frequently, abduction was carried out with the connivance of the victim. Was the full force of the civil law to apply? Civil law more or less ignored the question of consent. The church was more lenient. Where consent was given, even where the girl made only a half-hearted token of resistance, the church was not willing to condemn the abductor.[41] Balsamon added the rider that should the parents or guardians then give their assent it was not enough. The blessing of the church was necessary. It might be withheld until an appropriate penance had been performed.[42] The thrust of Balsamon's discussion is clear. The church had its own prescriptions for infringements of marriage law which were more humane than those that applied under civil law. It recognised the overriding importance of the consent of the

36 Zhishman, *Eherecht*, 672–3.

37 They were the Grand Droungarios Stephen Comnenus, a great nephew of the Emperor Alexius I Comnenus, and a daughter of the Grand Domestic John Axouch.

38 Rhalles & Potles IV, 276.

39 Rhalles & Potles I, 291; IV, 223; Zepos I, 429; Dölger, *Reg.* 1568; Grumel, 1167.

40 Rhalles & Potles IV, 183, 187.

41 Ibid., 171–2.

42 Ibid., 183.

parties to a marriage, but in such a way that control over marriage rested with the church rather than the parents.

It so happens that from the end of the twelfth century have survived the details of a case of alleged abduction. They provide an insight into how matrimonial litigation was conducted. The case concerns the second marriage of Alexius Capandrites, a landowner from Epiros. His version of events was that he was a widower and had married a widow (divorcee?), the sister of another landowner. Seven months after the celebration of the marriage his new brother-in-law seized him and married off his bride to somebody else. Capandrites eventually brought his case to the Patriarch George Xiphilinos (1191–8). In support he produced the sworn evidence of his fellow archontes of Coloneia in Epiros to the effect that no force had been used to win his bride. It could not therefore be a case of abduction. He also took the precaution of procuring an imperial *prostagma* confirming the validity of his marriage. Capandrites obtained a favourable decision from the patriarchal synod. However, his second wife then presented evidence before the synod to the effect that Capandrites had abducted her with the help of an armed retinue and forced her to marry him. She knew this was wrong because his first wife was her second cousin, which meant that they were related within the prohibited degrees. In the face of this evidence the synod agreed that there was a case for the annulment of the marriage. It handed over further investigation to the bishop of Coloneia and the metropolitan bishop of Dyrrakhion.[43] In the meantime Capandrites had obtained from the judges of the velum an opinion which deemed his second marriage to be valid and not within the prohibited degrees.[44]

The ecclesiastical courts seem to have been largely responsible for this case. If most of the litigation came before the patriarchal synod, the final decision was left to the local bishop and his metropolitan. They may also have had a part in initiating it. Capandrites, it will be remembered, presented synod with an affidavit of his fellow archontes. This came in the form of an episcopal submission (*semeioma*). This can only mean that the bishop of Coloneia had already been collecting evidence on the case. It is also clear that litigants in marriage suits did not make exclusive use of ecclesiastical courts. They were happy to take any steps that might further their cause, whether this was obtaining an imperial *prostagma* or the opinion of a civil court. It could work the other way around. A case was brought before the patriarchal synod in 1167 by a private citizen. In his absence one of his neighbours had brought a priest to his house, who proceeded to bless the betrothal of

43 Ibid. v, 103–5; Grumel, 1192–3.

44 Rhalles & Potles v, 395–6.

his son and the neighbour's daughter. The man wanted to know if the betrothal was solemn and binding. The synod was unanimous that it had no validity. This was not a legal decision, simply an opinion, which could then be cited in whatever court eventually considered the case.[45] A similar case came before the Patriarch George Xiphilinos at the end of the century. A secretary of the metropolitan bishop of Corinth was duped into signing a marriage contract. His family was worried because it might spoil his chances of ecclesiastical preferment. They took the case to the patriarch, who ordered the bishop to annul the marriage and to throw those responsible into prison. They also took the precaution of having the patriarchal decision confirmed by a civil court.[46] It would therefore probably be wrong to see ecclesiastical and civil courts in open competition for control over marriage litigation, if only because so much depended on the litigants. What is clear is that they perceived the necessity of involving the ecclesiastical courts. On balance, ecclesiastical courts were becoming more important for settling matrimonial causes.

Sex, marriage and the church

From the middle of the twelfth century the patriarchs saw the moral supervision of marriage as an important element in their pastoral duties. Luke Chrysoberges (1156–69) pronounced in synod that married couples were to abstain from sex for three days before taking communion. The laity took communion rather seldom in Byzantium, but it was normal for newly weds to take communion after the marriage ceremony. If they then indulged in sex the patriarch insisted that they were liable to penance.[47] The linking of abstinence from sex with the taking of communion vested both sex and communion with greater significance and emphasised that marriage was a sacrament as well as a contract. It helped to counter the popular view that consummation rather than anything else validated a marriage. The church wanted it clearly recognised that it was the ceremony of blessing that gave a marriage its full validity. It was put this way apropos of betrothal: 'It is not sexual intercourse but the ceremony of blessing which causes betrothal to be considered as marriage.'[48] But a judgement of the Patriarch Michael Ankhialos' (1169–76) shows the confusion that existed on exactly this point. A member of the clergy was refused permission to marry a relative of his dead fiancée – even though the betrothal had not received the blessing of the church; but there was a rider: if it so

45 A. Schminck, 'Ein Synodalakt vom 10. November 1167', *FM* 3(1979), 316–22.

46 Apokaukos I, no.13, 72–5.

47 Rhalles & Potles III, 302–5; Grumel, 1083.

48 Rhalles & Potles I, 291–2.

happened that the betrothal had taken place, before his dead fiancée had reached the age of seven, then the new marriage would receive the blessing of the church. The reasoning behind this was that the age of seven was reckoned to be the time when a girl developed sexual instincts, or, as it was quaintly put, 'a desire to be deflowered intervenes'. However, the patriarch doubted whether even this degree of restraint normally applied among the laity. The patriarch thought that it was only the wives of the clergy who were virgins when they married![49]

This was not simply clerical prejudice and prurience. John Apokaukos was appalled by what he called the Naupaktos disease: loss of virginity before the age of consent. The people of Naupaktos apparently deemed it shameful if their daughters had not lost their virginity before the age of consent.[50] This attitude was not confined to Naupaktos but spread throughout Byzantine society.[51] Early consummation was a custom that testified to a need to get daughters settled as soon as possible and a presumption that consummation rather than the church's blessing gave the union binding force. The importance of consummation was underlined by the appearance in the mid-tenth century of the *theoretron*. This was the equivalent of the western 'Morning-gift', a reward for virginity. This the bride or would-be bride now received in addition to the prenuptial gift (often called the *hypobolon*), which under Justinianic law was supposed to match the dowry brought by the bride. In the *Peira* the *hypobolon* was fixed at half the value of the dowry and the *theoretron* at one twelfth. While the bride only had conditional rights in the *hypobolon*, the *theoretron* was hers entirely. The *Peira* presents the *theoretron* as an innovation. 'Its appearance is more recent than the law' (i.e. the Basilics) was the way the compiler referred to it.[52] In fact, it can be traced back to the marriage customs of ancient Greece. The unveiling ceremony which preceded the marriage was known as the *anakalypteria* or *theoretra*.[53] But it was not part of Roman law and therefore unknown to the Justinianic tradition. It would seem that the custom continued and surfaced in the mid-tenth century as a bride-gift. It underlines the importance of custom in the shaping of marriage.

Despite centuries of Christian influence upon marriage law at Byzantium older patterns showed remarkable powers of survival.

49 Ibid., 292; Grumel, 1142.

50 Apokaukos I, no. 9, 67.18–22; M.J. Angold, 'Ἡ Βυζαντινὴ ᾽εκκλησία καὶ τὰ προβλήματα τοῦ γάμου', *ΔΩΔΩΝΗ* 17(1988), 186.

51 E. Patlagean, 'L'enfant et son avenir dans la famille byzantine (IVe–XIIe siècles)', *Annales de démographie historique* (1973), 85–93 (= Patlagean, *Structure*, no. XI).

52 Zepos IV, 103–4; see Simon, 'Das Ehegüterrecht der Peira', esp. 223–30.

53 Eustathius, *Commentarii ad Homeri Iliadem pertinentes*, III, ed. M. Van der Valk (Leiden, 1979), p. 315 [=881, 31]: 'ή πρὸ τῶν γάμων θέα, ἴσως τὰ λεγόμενα θεώρετρα'.

Concubines were deprived of any legal rights by Leo VI, but the institution still continued and in practice concubines and their children enjoyed some protection for their rights from the courts.[54] Divorce by consent had been abrogated by Justinian and this had been confirmed by the Eclogues, but it continued into the twelfth century.[55] Early marriage and betrothal before the age of consent also persisted. It was not just the convenience of the family that counted. Early betrothal was held to make for compatibility. Though neither canon nor civil law recognised incompatibility as grounds for divorce, in practice, it was, even if other reasons had to be cited.[56] Around Ohrid, admittedly in a Slav rather than a Greek part of the world, families appear to have made their own arrangements for separation with the minimal participation of the authorities, civil or ecclesiastical.[57]

The persistence of such customs reflected the desire of any family to shape the conventions of marriage to suit its needs. After all, its very future depended on the marriages it contracted for its members. A tidy part of its property was likely to be tied up in different marriages. It could not be exclusively guided by the church in such matters, since quite different criteria were operating. The family interest wanted stability and demanded progeny. In case of mishap – a failure to produce children, for example – it wanted easy dissolution of the marriage. Equally, the institution of concubinage provided a safety valve. It was a way of restricting the number of legitimate descendants and avoiding the complications associated with remarriage. Too often the children of one marriage would be at loggerheads with those of another.

The church, for its part, had to respond to the needs of society. It had to come to terms with the customary side of marriage. It had to demonstrate the utility of its supervision of marriage. Paradoxically, the church's strongest weapon was the emphasis it put on the moral and spiritual dimension to marriage. It gave the state of matrimony meaning, which was not without its attractions to lay society. The church could also offer dispensation to those who had transgressed its moral code. This may have been a factor, as we shall see, which encouraged the laity to take marriage suits to the ecclesiastical courts.

54 A. Laiou, 'Contribution à l'étude de l'institution familiale en Epire au XIIIème siècle', *FM* 6(1984), 284–300.

55 D.Simon, 'Zur Ehegesetzgebung der Isaurier', *FM* 1(1976), 16–43, at 33–7.

56 Angold, 'Η Βυζαντινή', 189–91.

57 Chomatianos, no.103. Cf A.E. Laiou, 'The role of women in Byzantine society', *JÖB* 31/1 (1981), 233–60.

The dossiers of Chomatianos and Apokaukos: divorce and the marital state

We know that the writings of Demetrius Chomatianos and John Apokaukos constitute a unique source for Byzantine history. They are far and away the most detailed episcopal records that survive from Byzantium.[58] Their field of action was Epiros and Macedonia during the period of exile after 1204. Their writings reflect the conditions of that time and place. It is likely that after initial disruption produced by the fall of Constantinople in 1204 and its aftermath conditions in these provinces were not altogether different from what they had been before 1204. A surprising proportion of the litigation that came before their courts involved marriage in one way or another. The writings of Chomatianos and Apokaukos are the richest source surviving from Byzantium for marriage litigation. They leave the impression that marriage provided much of the business of episcopal courts. Such indications as there are suggest that this was already the case in the twelfth century.

The details of a surprising number of divorce petitions have been preserved by Apokaukos and Chomatianos. Divorce is by definition a marriage in the process of disintegration. Very few marriages in the middle ages ended in divorce and those that did were hardly likely to be typical, but it would be unrealistic to suppose that those marriages that did not end in divorce were without their problems. Divorce petitions are therefore likely to illuminate the state of marriage, or, at least, the pressures of marriage. Divorce was made all the more difficult because the law, canon and civil, only recognised two legitimate grounds for divorce: a wife's adultery and a husband's impotence. In fact, incompatibility was a more usual reason for an unhappy marriage. John Apokaukos knew that the law did not recognise this as sufficient grounds for divorce. He considered this an unfortunate oversight.[59] Both he and Chomatianos found a remedy. They treated threats of suicide made by wives at loggerheads with their husbands as grounds for divorce, thus finding a way round the problem of incompatibility. They considered suicide as the 'greater evil'. They argued that an unhappy marriage produced such despair that it subverted the church's obligation to bring salvation.[60] There may have been an element of casuistry, but it met society's need in certain circumstances for the easy dissolution of marriage.

Unhappy marriages also brought their fair share of domestic violence. The arrival of a young bride among her husband's family could

[58] See above, pp. 156–7.

[59] Apokaukos I, no.7, 64–5.

[60] See P. Karlin-Hayter, 'Indissolubility and the "greater evil". Three thirteenth-century divorce cases', in *Church and People*, ed. Morris, 87–105.

produce problems. There was the tragedy of a father killing his son who had been trying to protect his new wife from his mother's bullying.[61] Equally, there were marriages where the wives resolutely refused to have anything to do with their husbands because they had been foisted on them by their parents, when they would have much preferred another. There were wives who strayed because their husbands for whatever reason – often because they were soldiers – were too long absent. There were wives deserted by feckless husbands. Though the details are often vivid, thanks to Apokaukos's literary skills, these cases are banal enough. What is striking is the resolution shown by many women determined both to put an end to a worthless marriage and to ensure that their interests and property were secured. A high proportion of divorce proceedings were instituted by women, which confirms the impression of the relative freedom of action enjoyed by women.[62]

One can only admire the finesse and humanity which Demetrius Chomatianos and John Apokaukos brought to their treatment of divorce cases.[63] They paid special attention to the needs of women. They subscribed to the notion of a degree of equality of the sexes and recognised that women had special needs.[64] They observed that wives came to dislike husbands who denied them sex. Husbands also had an obligation to provide their wives with an appropriate standard of living. A case came before Demetrius Chomatianos, where the wife would have nothing to do with her husband. Her hatred for him stemmed from her parents' insistence that she marry him, when she loved another. She had deserted her husband and had stayed with other people for months at a time. Chomatianos decided that she must have been guilty of adultery and was therefore liable to the penance prescribed by canon law. However, because of the poverty she had suffered she was spared the penalties laid down by the civil law.[65] Women could also be young and foolish. In another case Chomatianos recognised that a young wife – she was only twelve – had been led into adultery by the wiles of a servant. He therefore granted the husband a divorce, if he so wished, but reminded him that the law allowed a period of two years during which he could take back his erring wife.[66]

[61] Apokaukos I, no.14.

[62] Laiou, 'Contribution'; Angold, ''Η Βυζαντινὴ', 179–94; Laiou, 'The role of women', 233– 41; G. Prinzing, 'Sozialgeschichte der Frau im Spiegel der Chomatenos-Akten', *JÖB* 32/2 (1983), 453–62; H.N. Angelomatis-Tsoungarakis, 'Women in the society of the despotate of Epirus', *JÖB* 32/2(1983), 473–80.

[63] Angold, ''Η Βυζαντινὴ', 188; Karlin-Hayter, 'Indissolubility', 104.

[64] Papadopoulos-Kerameus, 'Συνοδικὰ', 15.1–2.

[65] Chomatianos, no.141.

[66] Ibid., no.139. Cf. no.137.

The leniency displayed by Apokaukos and Chomatianos did not mean that they turned a blind eye to the teachings of the church. They were careful, for example, that where the wife's adultery was grounds for divorce she should not be allowed to marry her lover, however much her behaviour had been provoked by her husband's conduct. This was in accord with St Basil's dictum that the church's blessing did not lessen the adultery. In any case, to condone adultery would be to encourage it and that would never do.[67] Nor did Apokaukos and Chomatianos condone under-age marriages. This was a scandal, especially where there was a large discrepancy in age between husband and wife. Apokaukos mocks the sight of a grown man accompanied by a wife who skips along at his knees and the peculiar temptation of such unions – an affair with the mother-in-law.[68] Apart from their sexual incongruity they were opposed on the ground that under-age parties were not able to give their consent to the union. The church held that the consent of the parties was an essential element for the validity of marriage.[69] Chomatianos and Apokaukos were unanimous in condemning marriages where coercion was used. This applied just as much where it involved the husband as it did the wife. For instance, John Apokaukos released a young cleric from a marriage forced on him by the 'lady of the manor' with one of her aging Vlach servants.[70]

Not all divorce cases in the provinces went immediately before the ecclesiastical courts,[71] but it is safe to assume that the vast bulk did. In many respects, the church courts provided a more satisfactory service than the civil courts. The civil law prescribed in several instances rather harsher penalties than did canon law. Chomatianos was well aware of this. In one case, where magic and poison were involved, he recommended the use of penance and contrasted this with execution by the sword or, at the very least, blinding and mutilation prescribed by the civil law.[72] In cases of manslaughter Apokaukos invariably imposed penance and forbad the civil authorities to intervene in the case, which he saw more as a sin than a crime: 'for confiscation of the murderer's property cannot absolve him of such a sin, only the fulfilment of ecclesiastical injunctions.'[73]

It would seem that for a series of offences the church was deliberately substituting penance for more obviously severe punishments

67 Angold, 'Ἡ Βυζαντινή', 190–1; Karlin-Hayter, 'Indissolubility', 90–4.

68 Angold, 'Ἡ Βυζαντινή', 188.

69 The canonist Zonaras insisted that a daughter could not oppose her father's wishes except where the intended groom was in some way unworthy. This gave plenty of scope for friction within the family: Karlin-Hayter, 'Indissolubility', 102–3.

70 John Apokaukos I, no.19, 79–81.

71 E.g. Chomatianos, no.127.

72 Ibid., no.27.

73 See Angold, 'Ἡ Βυζαντινή', 192.

prescribed by civil law. Professor Simon considers this a rather superficial conclusion.[74] In his opinion, it was never a question of substituting the norms of canon law for those of the civil law; of replacing one system of law by another. On the contrary, they complemented one another and cooperation between the ecclesiastical and civil courts was the rule.[75] This line of argument receives support from a case of seduction that was brought before Chomatianos. He began by outlining the differences there were in the punishments prescribed by civil and canon law. The former insisted on a heavy fine: a litre of gold or half the seducer's property to the – in this case, willing – victim; the latter imposed stringent penance. Perfectly evenhandedly, Chomatianos imposed both penalties on the seducer.[76] Nobody will deny the force of Professor Simon's argument. Civil and ecclesiastical courts were not openly in competition with one another. However, the dossiers of Chomatianos and Apokaukos reveal a shift towards the church courts and ecclesiastical punishments. This was largely because litigants preferred to use the ecclesiastical courts where they could.

As Professor Simon himself indicates, the settlement of disputes was very much in the hands of the parties themselves.[77] Judgement was therefore very often more a matter of arbitration rather than imposing a decision. In such a situation moral authority was what counted. The emphasis placed by the church courts on penance as an appropriate punishment only underlined this. It is clear that litigants were sometimes moved by their consciences, especially where marriage was concerned. They worried that they had fallen into that 'concealed sin': contracting in all good faith a marriage within the prohibited degrees. These were not regarded as an unnecessary inconvenience, more as a trap for the unwary. One man confessed that before he got married he had had sex with the second cousin of his father-in-law's mother! He was anxious to know whether this escapade might constitute an impediment to marriage. Under-age marriage was very common. It too produced pangs of conscience, as did breaking the church's stipulations about remarriage. The church was the obvious place to go to have such doubts resolved, sometimes with very satisfactory results. One woman had to confess that she had been married not three but four times, something that the church refused to countenance. She was relieved to learn that her first two marriages did not count in the eyes of the church, since she had been under the age of consent at the time. Consequently, she was not guilty of the sin she thought she

74 Simon, 'Byzantinische Provinzialjustiz', 315–24.
75 Cf. Karlin-Hayter, 'Indissolubility', 90.
76 Chomatianos, no.74.
77 Simon, 'Byzantinische Provinzialjustiz', 317–21.

was committing. Instead, she had to do penance for a lesser offence: her under-age marriages.[78]

The church was the obvious place to go on marital matters because so much of the paper work involved in a marriage was the responsibility of the church. The *chartophylax* of the local bishopric issued marriage licences and it was his duty to see that there was no just impediment to a marriage. The marriage contracts were nearly always drawn up by a local notary. By the thirteenth century the notarial organisation was usually annexed to the episcopal administration. Although not invariably the case, such deeds and contracts could be registered in the episcopal archives.[79] The church building was the place where much legal business was transacted. It was here that oaths were administered, judgements given, and documents drawn up.[80] It was to the church that a man went to denounce a run-away wife, as a first step in obtaining a divorce from her.[81] It was outside the church that those under the ban of the church would fall at the feet of their neighbours and beg forgiveness for their sins.[82] The penitent thus exposed himself to the mercy of public opinion. It cannot have been a pleasant experience. But it was a reasonably satisfactory way of resolving disputes that were petty. If they seldom ended in murder, they invariably disrupted the local community. The church provided a screen that allowed the parties to settle their differences and eased acceptance back into the community.

The parties to marriage litigation were normally most concerned about the fate of the property tied up in a marriage. Chomatianos and Apokaukos invariably restored the dowry and the profits of marriage, as they were called, to the woman, while the prenuptial gifts went back to the husband. Even where there was no question of divorce the division of property provided Chomatianos's court with a considerable volume of business. A large proportion of it concerned rights to dowries, but there were other property disputes, especially where there had been remarriage or a man had taken a mistress or a concubine. Rights of inheritance became extremely complicated. It was in this area, to judge from the dossiers of Apokaukos and Chomatianos, that the business brought to the church courts increased markedly. On balance, this seems to have been a natural progression from the church's responsibilities in the field of marriage rather than the consequence of special circumstances existing in Epiros after 1204.

78 Angold, 'Ἡ Βυζαντινὴ', 192–3.
79 Ibid., 193. Cf. Notre Dame de Pitié, 114.17–18.
80 E.g. Chomatianos, nos.106, 452, 454 = D.Simon, 'Witwe Sachlikina gegen Witwe Horaia', *FM* 6(1984), 325–75, at 332.88–95, 334.127–38.
81 Apokaukos II, no.16.
82 Ibid. I, no.14.

The fall of Constantinople clearly affected government in the provinces, but the effects at best can only have been temporary, for the structure of provincial government continued much as it had done before 1204. It may even have been that bit more effective for the presence of a ruler in the provinces rather than in distant Constantinople. Against this, the traditions and practice of civil law had always been at their strongest in Constantinople and its loss must have strengthened the ecclesiastical courts at the expense of the civil. The disappearance of the courts of appeal housed in the capital must have worked to the benefit of Chomatianos's court, for one of the attractions of taking a case before Chomatianos was that he was just as expert in the civil law as he was in canon law. Apokaukos's legal skills have rather unfairly been called into question, but he too showed a good knowledge of the civil law.[83]

Both Chomatianos and Apokaukos began their careers before 1204. They owed their legal knowledge and training to that upsurge in the study of canon law associated with John Zonaras, Alexius Aristenos, and above all Theodore Balsamon. These eminent canonists founded the study of canon law on a thorough knowledge of civil law and its sources. The fact that bishops and their officers – Chomatianos had been *chartophylax* of Ohrid before being made its archbishop – were well versed in both laws may be the most important factor behind the growing prestige of ecclesiastical courts, but this started before 1204. The proof is provided by Eustathius of Thessalonica. He complained that not a day went by without men and women coming to him and presenting their marriage suits. The variety of marital tragedies depressed him. What could he do for a husband whose wife had deserted him for a brothel? The archbishop concluded that he would have to provide not just spiritual remedies, but contrive more sophisticated ones as well.[84]

The greater use being made of the ecclesiastical courts must have made for a wider understanding, if not a readier acceptance, of the church's view of marriage. It is not as though this had radically altered since the fourth century. St Basil was far and away the greatest influence on the church's teachings about marriage. By and large these had been absorbed into the mainstream of Byzantine life through their adoption by the civil law. Change had been gradual, if not imperceptible. It had not noticeably enhanced the church's influence over marriage. The quarrel over Leo VI's fourth marriage in the opening years of the tenth century announced the church's intention of taking a stronger line over the enforcement of marriage law. From the turn

[83] Fogen, '*Horror iuris*', 47–71, at 58–63.
[84] Eustathius I, 64.8–30.

of the tenth century a series of patriarchs set about introducing more stringent regulations of marriage and betrothal. There was resistance to these which continued into the twelfth century. But by the turn of the century this appears to have disappeared and the church's views seem to have prevailed. This does not mean that they were always complied with. Under-age marriage continued, as did unions within the prohibited degrees and third or even fourth marriages, but there was no general inclination to ignore the church. The very opposite. The church could offer remedies in the form of appropriate penance. *Pari passu* matrimonial litigation increasingly went to the church courts and in its wake a very large proportion of quarrels over property.

This was not only because the church courts offered a more effective service; it was also because the church's teaching on marriage was seen to be advantageous to the family: in particular, to women. It was not just that the church courts respected a woman's property rights and provided special protection for the dowry. The civil courts would have done the same. It was more that they paid regard to the status of women. Their consent was necessary to a marriage. This was one of the major objections to early marriage. An under-age bride was in no position to give her consent. This often made marrying off daughters as young as possible an attractive proposition: parents did not have to consider their wishes, which might not coincide with their own. It is not as though the church deliberately set out to court women, but marriage was part of its pastoral responsibilities. The rights of women and especially widows had to be protected along with other disadvantaged groups – orphans, for example. Women therefore enjoyed greater consideration than they might have expected from the civil courts. But women litigants were not just concerned with their own interests. They were responsible for the well-being of their households and families. The church stressed the primacy of marriage. It attacked irregular unions; its insistence on the church's blessing as a prerequisite of marriage gave the institution greater dignity. Its objections to remarriage gave the family greater solidarity because it lessened the likelihood of damaging quarrels over inheritance between the children of different marriages. The family coalesced around the wife and mother. The church favoured a family structure that in practice gave the wife and mother a great deal of power, to the extent of sometimes appearing in person before the law courts. The family remained the decisive element in Byzantine society, but now in alliance with the church. This was the major shift that occurred over the twelfth century. The proof is provided by the dossiers of Apokaukos and Chomatianos.

21

BYZANTINE WOMEN

AT Byzantium there were always exceptional women to be found wielding exceptional power. This is in the nature of a patriarchal society. Such societies may exploit and oppress women, but women are indispensable to their proper functioning. This creates possibilities that allow women to work the system to their advantage. In ruling circles these were increased by the covert character of Byzantine politics. There were many opportunities for the informal exercise of power. This contrasted with the restricted status of women. It was this discrepancy that made women seem so dangerous and lay at the bottom of much of the prejudice against women. The status of Byzantine women was no better than it was in many other patriarchal societies. They were expected to be dependants, first on their fathers, then on their husbands. Marriage was their natural state and the family and household their setting. Among the aristocracy they were segregated in the women's quarters – the *gynaeconitis* – where they were tended by eunuchs. They wore veils, were kept in seclusion, and were denied access to public life and, more often than not, to education. In most respects the law discriminated against women. There were also the usual prejudices against women nurtured by Christianity. They were the daughters of Eve. Their sexuality was dangerous and a constant temptation. It was to be channelled and controlled through marriage or the veil.

A woman's position was precarious. Her influence fluctuated according to circumstances: from family to family; from generation to generation, even within a lifetime. It depended very largely on identifying herself with her family, her husband, and her children. She scarcely counted in her own right, but as the embodiment of family interest she might be a very powerful figure. There is good reason to suppose that as the power of aristocratic families increased from the tenth century, so did the influence of their women. They had considerable responsibilities for the running of their households, which by the standards of the time were significant enterprises. Rather more than in the past a few aristocratic women found their roles spilling out into the public domain. They seem by and large to have been better educated than they had been in the past. This was by force of necessity, for more than basic literacy was needed for the conduct of affairs at Byzantium.[1] It went further than this. There was more interest in intellectual pursuits. Women from the imperial house of Comnenus were patrons of men of letters and of literary circles. There may be some uncertainties about the exact relationship between patron and writer at the Comnenian court, but it gave these women a higher profile, even if their main purpose was to publicise the good name of their family.[2] Even Kekavmenos's apprehension about the dangers to family honour presented by a wayward daughter can be taken as back-handed recognition of the growing importance within the family of wives and daughters.[3]

Women before the law

It is always easier to register the changes that occur in the upper rungs of society than elsewhere. Did the greater prominence of women at court and in the capital reflect a general improvement in the position of women? The dossiers of John Apokaukos and Demetrius Chomatianos suggest that it did. They have to be used with caution, when used as evidence for the state of society. By definition lawsuits reflect the exceptional rather than the norm. To differing degrees they show individuals under stress, but they may reveal what is happening under the surface of normality, which is so hard to penetrate. If the business coming before law courts is any guide to the realities of public life, then in thirteenth-century Epiros women had quite a prominent part to play in it. It has been calculated that they appeared or were represented in approximately 70% of the cases considered by Demetrius Chomatianos.[4] This is an impressive figure. It reflects the high proportion of cases involving either marriage or dowry in the Chomatianos dossier. But these provided some of the staples of Byzantine litigation because they were central to disputes over inheritance. One way and

1 Laiou, 'The role of women', 249–53.

2 M.E. Mullett, 'Aristocracy and patronage in the literary circles of Comnenian Constantinople', in *The Byzantine Aristocracy*, ed. Angold, 173–201.

3 Good general treatments of the position of women at Byzantium are J. Herrin, 'In search of Byzantine women: three avenues of approach', in *Images of Women in Antiquity*, ed A. Cameron and A. Kuhrt (London, 1983), 167–89; L. Garland, 'The life and ideology of Byzantine women', *B* 58(1988), 361–93; J. Beaucamp, 'La situation juridique de la femme à Byzance', *Cahiers de civilisation médiévale*, 20(1977), 145–76; G. Buckler, 'Women in Byzantine law about 1100 AD', *B* 11(1936), 391–416; Laiou, 'The role of women'; A.E. Laiou, 'Observations on the life and ideology of Byzantine women', *BF* 9(1985), 59–102.

4 Laiou, 'The role of women', 233–41. Cf. Prinzing, 'Sozialgeschichte der Frau im Spiegel der Chomatenos-Akten', 450–62.

another women had an interest in such matters. It emphasises the pivotal role of women in a patriarchal society.

It is true that women often relied upon male members of the family to represent them before a court.[5] There are, however, other instances where women were quite capable of conducting their own cases. A Maria from the island of Corfu went all the way to Ohrid to lay before Demetrius Chomatianos her husband's misuse of her dowry. Her family originally came from Constantinople and had fled to Corfu after 1204. She was married into the Makrembolites family: one that had been prominent in the capital from the early eleventh century.[6] This is not the only example of a woman of aristocratic lineage conducting her own case.[7] This was only to be expected: aristocratic women would have had more opportunity to assert themselves; they would also possess presence and the habit of command. Less expected is that women of quite ordinary backgrounds were also to be found presenting their cases.[8] They were almost all widows, which was significant. It meant that they were temporarily at the head of the family. With this proviso, it would seem that what was true of aristocratic women was at least partly true of other women. They were identified with the interests of their families and were therefore involved in the crises of family life. But it was more than this: women had the strongest possible interest in defending their rights to their dowries.

The law gave the dowry special protection. Under all circumstances it remained the wife's property, even if administered by her husband. If she died first, then the property entailed in her dowry would go to her children if she had any. If she outlived her husband, then she recovered full possession of her dowry. She already had control over the *theoretron* or wedding gift, which was always her full property. She also received a dower from her husband's property. She administered family property on behalf of her children. In the usual way of things, widowhood brought women greater independence and wider legal powers. But, as Dr H. Sarudi- Mendelovici has recently pointed out, the privileges women enjoyed before the law 'were not the result of a recognition of the higher legal capacity of women. They were instead social measures based on the assumption that women being inferior to

[5] Chomatianos, nos.19, 47, 52, 53, 55. Cf. Apokaukos I, no.4. Prinzing, 'Socialgeschichte der Frau im Spiegel der Chomatenos-Akten', gives the following figures: nine cases where women represented themselves; eight where their husband acted for them and nineteen where other male members of the family acted for them.

[6] Chomatianos, no.50 = Papadopoulos-Kerameus, 'Συμβολὴ', no.1. Kazhdan ranked the Makrembolitai seventeenth in his list of Byzantine families: *Sotsial'nyj sostav*, 116.

[7] Chomatianos I, no.20.

[8] Ibid., nos. 45, 58. Cf. Apokaukos I, nos.13, 28, 68.

men, were unable to protect their property.'[9] One of the ironies of a patriarchal society is the way that women will often control substantial property. This was seen as a weak point in the transmission of property and with it the continuity of the family. Women were to be prevented by law from squandering the family's wealth!

This was the law at its least prejudiced! It recognised and protected women's rights within the family. Otherwise, it sought to deny women a legal role. For example, Novel 48 of the Emperor Leo VI (886–912) deprived women of the right to act as witnesses to legal transactions. The reasons given for this measure are instructive. In the first place, women had been trespassing on affairs that properly belonged to men. This was to insult men. In the second, in court women came under the gaze of men. This was an impropriety. In a word, allowing women to testify confused the boundaries between the sexes. Women had, in consequence, very restricted rights of participation in public and legal life.[10] Respectable women were expected to stay at home. They could not go to entertainments or to the hippodrome without the express approval of their husband. If they did, it was grounds for divorce.[11] For respectable women to come out on the streets of Constantinople in any numbers signalled something quite out of the ordinary. Michael Psellus was struck by the presence of large numbers of women in the rioting that led to the overthrow of the Emperor Michael V.[12]

The church and women

The church could be just as dismissive of women as the civil law. In the twelfth century there were churchmen who continued to refine the old stereotypes about women. The controversial theologian Michael Glykas set out the theological position. He was wrestling with the question of whether after the resurrection there would still be sexual differences. His view was that the female of the species had only been created on sufferance.[13] He believed that

> it was patently obvious that before the creation of woman the life of man was on a higher plane. If male and female existed from the beginning, why should Eve have been produced afterwards, that is to say after the creation of Adam, after God had appointed him lord [of creation], after He had led

9 H. Sarudi-Mendelovici, 'A contribution to the study of the Byzantine notarial formulas: the *Infirmitas Sexus* of women and the *Sc. Velleianum*', *BZ* 83(1990), 72–90, at 74.

10 Buckler, 'Women in Byzantine law'; Beaucamp, 'La situation juridique'.

11 Zepos IV, 98.

12 Michael Psellus, *Chronographie*, ed. Renauld, I, 102.4–15.

13 Michael Glykas I, 102.3–4.

all the animals before him and subordinated them to him, after he had given each its name?[14]

It was not necessary to cite Eve's part in the fall. The inferiority of the female sex was embedded in the process of creation. The resurrection would restore man to *his* original perfection.

Similar attitudes to women would be expressed in more concrete form by another twelfth-century churchman. The canon lawyer Theodore Balsamon was moved to indignation by the thought that some women might aspire to holy orders. He conceded that an order of deaconesses might have existed in the early church, but it no longer existed. Some women ascetics might be referred to as deaconesses, but this was misleading. It was impossible for a woman to fulfil the duties of a deacon because she was barred from the sanctuary.[15] On two occasions Balsamon cites as proof of the depravity of the Latin church its admission of women into the sanctuary.[16] He reiterates that there is no such thing as a recognised order of women elders. Abbesses were the only women with the right to discipline other women. Balsamon closes his discussion with the following observation: 'For a woman to preach in a parish church where a crowd of men are assembled and women of different opinions is most unbecoming and harmful.'[17] Balsamon saw women as a real or a potential threat to the good order of the church. Their pretensions easily slid over into heterodoxy, if only out of ignorance. Churchmen such as Balsamon constantly suspected women of being ready to dress up in men's clothing and act the Python. They dabbled in fortune telling and magic. Balsamon even recorded a famous case of magic involving a Comnenian princess.[18]

At this point Balsamon's concern about the dangers presented by women merges with a distinctively monastic voice. This has recently been explored for the twelfth century by C. Galatariotou in the writings of St Neophytos the Recluse. His attitudes bear some similarity to the opinions expressed in Leo VI's legislation. Women are dangerous and evil when they trespass on male territory and lay claim to the exercise of power. As daughters of Eve women are only potentially evil. Power makes them truly the instruments of the devil. Like so many ascetics Neophytos became a monk in order to escape marriage. He was horrified by the idea of female sexuality, which constituted power

[14] Ibid., 100.12–18.

[15] Rhalles & Potles II, 254–6.

[16] Ibid., 466; III, 212.

[17] Ibid. III, 181.

[18] Ibid. II, 444; III, 109; IV, 251. See R. Greenfield, 'Sorcery and politics at the Byzantine court in the twelfth century: interpretations of history', in *The Making of Byzantine History*, ed. Beaton and Roueché, 73–85.

over men. He saw this as a continuing battle between sins which he presents as female and virtues which he has as male. Only when a woman was a dependant of a man – as daughter or wife – was she safe. This dependence deprived her of access to power and made her respectable; harmless might be a better word.[19]

At least, Neophytos recognised that women had a role within the family and their nature could be fulfilled in marriage. The entry on women in the early thirteenth-century *Thesaurus* of Theognostos is an outpouring of spite. The most the author will allow is that woman is a necessary evil. The venom is such that it still comes as a shock. The editor of the text, Father Munitiz, has suggested that it was in some way a commentary on a *cause célèbre* at the Nicaean court.[20] One day the Emperor John Vatatzes's mistress forced her way into the monastery to which the great scholar Nicephorus Blemmydes had retired. She was popularly known as the Marchesina and was an Italian lady-in-waiting of the Emperor's second wife, Costanza Lancia. Blemmydes had a reputation for being difficult. He was something of a misogynist. The wife of a dear friend had once tried to seduce him. He still bore the psychological scars of the encounter. It was entirely in character that he should have barred entry to the Marchesina. One of her retinue was so incensed that he went for his sword. He might well have killed Blemmydes had it not stuck in the scabbard. The Marchesina and her party were driven from the monastery by the force of Blemmydes's personality. Blemmydes treated the incident as a miracle and regarded it as a victory over the devil. It was one of the central episodes of his life. He included it in both his autobiographies and he wrote an *Open Letter*, in which he publicised his version of events.[21] He denounces the Marchesina in much the same words that Theognostos uses for women generally. This incident has to be seen as a hysterical monastic reaction against the prominence of women in court circles.

Blemmydes's mentor, the Patriarch Germanos II, took a more humane, if still condescending, view of women. It is set out in a sermon he preached on the feast of Orthodoxy.[22] The heroine was the Empress Theodora. She was venerated as a saint for her part in the triumph of orthodoxy in 843. There was an old saying, the patriarch remembered, to the effect that the husband is the wife's head. It was therefore appropriate that Theodora was able to cure the headache that her husband, the Emperor Theophilos, was suffering . This was a prelude to the empress's greater success in clearing her husband's memory of

19 C. Galatariotou, 'Holy women and witches: aspects of Byzantine conceptions of gender', *BMGS* 9(1984/5), 55–94.

20 J.A. Munitiz, 'A "wicked woman" in the 13th century', *JÖB* 32/2 (1983), 529–37.

21 Blemmydes I, 35–6; II, 67, 91–4.

22 Germanos II, no.14, 321–31.

the taint of iconoclasm. 'While Eve was the cause of Adam's death, Theodora revived a husband who had become a corpse. She turned death into a new life, for through her prayers she procured for him immortal life, even though he had suffered spiritual death.'[23] The patriarch's message to women was clear: they might be the less sound part of nature, but they were expected to bear the weight of men's failings and to stop them 'being swept into the pit of perdition'.[24] Women should be guided by the forbearance that Theodora showed. He quoted 1 Corinthians 7.16 to underline the responsibilities of a wife: 'For what knowest thou, o wife, whether thou shalt save *thy* husband?' What, the patriarch asked, should a wife do, if her husband came home drunk or beat her for no better reason than getting the worse of a bargain? Wives should be patient and realise that it was only the devil that made their husbands behave in such a fashion. Calm him down and pray that an angel of peace enter the house. If her husband was absent from home on business, it was a wife's duty to think about him constantly, while she carded wool, and prayed for his well-being. The patriarch was convinced that 'there was nothing sweeter than the concord of husband and wife', when they become not just one flesh but one soul. A wife should love and help her husband in both body and spirit. She should seek his salvation through prayers, tears, alms, and worship, 'for you are able, women', the patriarch maintained, 'by these means to save your husband even after death'.[25] The spiritual energies of women were to be channelled towards their husbands' salvation.

The stereotypes created for women were taken for granted, as part of a natural order. The Patriarch Germanos II assumed that the loss of a husband would leave a good wife with no other thought than to be buried with him. He expected her to use what strength she had to grieve for him.[26] This is part of a sentimental stereotype, but it corresponded to reality. Hearing that his mother was ill Nicholas Mesarites hastened to Constantinople only to find that he was too late. His mother was already dead. He learnt that her last wish was to be buried with her husband, a request which he duly carried out.[27] It was also common for widows to take the veil out of a sense of grief. One who did describes the depths of despair the death of her husband produced: 'I did not know how I could remain in the world nor how I could live according to its ways nor how I could possibly heed its dreams nor vainly fight against its shades and fantasies.'[28]

[23] Ibid., 322.27–30.
[24] Ibid., 322.19–21.
[25] Migne, *PG*, 140.661.
[26] Germanos II, 325.8–12.
[27] Mesarites III, 26–7.
[28] H. Delehaye, *Deux typika byzantins de l'époque des Paléologues* (Brussels, 1921), 24.23–5.

It is not surprising that women almost always accepted their stereotyping. From childhood they were conditioned to know their place: subservient to a father and then to a husband; confined to the domestic sphere. This stereotyping was often reinforced by very early marriage. With this went a very heavy burden of guilt. Women were always having to atone for Eve's sin. It fitted well with a male need for scapegoats. But women embraced their stereotyping just as eagerly as men. The veil was an object of reverence. It merited a special attention when it came to the interpretation of dreams. It was believed to represent not the woman who wore it, but the well-being of her husband and children, in other words, a mother's role.

The power of women

But there is another side. Guilt, subservience, self-sacrifice, and humility may also be a source of power. Society imposed upon women a responsibility to make amends. This took the concrete form of caring for the spiritual and material welfare of husband and family. It was difficult to separate the well-being of a family from its honour. The outlook and deportment of the women of a family contributed signally to its honour and standing. This placed women in a position of some power because they could so easily disgrace a family. Kekavmenos's remarks about the dangers of a wayward daughter immediately come to mind, but a runaway or adulterous wife was still more shaming. Chomatianos has a case where a wife ran away out of hatred of her husband. The court proceedings were almost more than he could bear. He could scarcely testify such was his shame. He could no longer stand his wife's hatred. He had searched for her everywhere, but this had only disrupted his livelihood. Worse it had earned him the contempt of his neighbours.[29] Apokaukos has a similar story. There was a soldier with an adulterous wife. He had to suffer not only injury from his wife and her lovers but also the contempt of the town, when the news got around. 'He had grinned and borne what she was doing to him, because of its shameful nature and because of local gloating', but now no longer![30] Women could so easily expose the weaknesses of men and undermine the foundations of a patriarchal society. This was their strength. They could not easily be discounted.

There was a discrepancy between stereotype and reality.[31] It was recognised and was explained away. The most convenient expedient was to turn the occasional woman into an honorary man. A woman

[29] Chomatianos, no.143.
[30] Apokaukos II, no.16.
[31] The problem has been well explored by Garland, 'The life and ideology'.

who had control of her own property was treated in the lawyer's phrase, 'as if property rights made her a man'.[32] Chomatianos described a woman who had brought her case to his court all the way from Corfu as 'having a ready and able and manly disposition'.[33] This device – and its limitations – are well caught in Nicetas Choniates's story about Anna Comnena. Her husband Nicephorus Bryennius failed to go through with the coup she was organising against her brother, the Emperor John II. She was so angry that she is supposed to have turned on him with the words, loosely translated: 'Why was I not the one with the balls?'[34]

Another explanation for the ascendancy that wives often exercised over their husbands was to ascribe it to the irrational force of love. The power of love is one of the themes of the poem of *Digenes Akrites*, but it was a general assumption. It was not just limited to literature.

Women might not have been essential to the apparatus of the hierarchical church and state, but they were to the functioning of a patriarchal society. Its continuity and well-being were in the end founded on women. Occasionally this might be recognised. For all their supposed gullibility they often showed more presence of mind in a crisis than men did. Men had reluctantly to give them credit for their practical virtues. It was conceded that 'women are an ingenious race (*genos*) and extremely competent in an emergency'.[35]

The ideal was that of the long-suffering, compassionate wife who manages the fortunes of the family. It began to take shape at Byzantium in the late ninth century and can be traced back to a handful of the lives of female saints, such as Anastasia of Aigina, Mary the Younger, and Thomais of Lesbos. They suffer at the hands of their husbands, but this is accounted a kind of martyrdom. Despite everything they uphold the ideal of Christian marriage.[36] Their example gave a spiritual value to a woman's role in marriage, which, if not lacking, was underplayed. E. Patlagean has shown how this model of the good wife replaced that of the female ascetic as the ideal of female sanctity. It must be taken as some indication of the growing importance of the wife within the

[32] *Peira sive Practica ex actis Eustathii Romani*, xxiv, 15 = Zepos iv, 92: 'οἱονεὶ ἀρρηνοθεῖσα τῇ κυριοτήτι.

[33] Chomatianos, no.50.

[34] Nicetas Choniates, 10.55–6. A literal translation would go as follows: 'Being not a little vexed that she had female pudenda – slit-shaped and hollowed out, while Bryennius had the male appendage – pendulous and globular.' Magoulias's translation (p.8) of this passage betrays a comic imagination worthy of a Tom Sharpe novel.

[35] P. Gautier, 'Le *De Daemonibus* du Pseudo-Psellos', *REB* 38(1980), 163.440–1.

[36] See E. Patlagean, 'L'histoire de la femme déguisée en moine et l'évolution de la sainteté féminine à Byzance', *Studi medievali*, ser.iii. 17(1976), 597–623, at 619–22 (= Patlagean, *Structure*, no.xi); A.E. Laiou, 'Η ἱστορία ἑνὸς γάμου: ὁ βίος τῆς Ἁγίας Θομαίδος τῆς Λεσβίας', in *Η ΚΑΘΗΜΕΡΙΝΗ ΖΩΗ ΣΤΟ ΒΥΖΑΝΤΙΟ*, ed. Maltezou, 237–51.

family. The new model was at least founded on the assumption of the spiritual equality between men and women.

The battered wife as a spiritual role model for women was only a short-lived theme of Byzantine hagiography. It disappears in the course of the tenth century along, it has to be said, with new women saints. There is a dearth of women saints in the twelfth and thirteenth centuries. Only two are recorded. Both were the wives of rulers: Eirene, who became the nun Xene, the consort of John II Comnenus, and Theodora, the consort of Michael II Angelus, of Epiros. There was a strong dynastic element. Eirene's life and works were conventional enough. She fitted the stereotype of the ideal wife and mother to perfection. She devoted herself to charitable works. She was the protector of widows and orphans and a patroness of monks. She was the inspiration behind the foundation of the Pantokrator monastery at Constantinople. She died happy in the knowledge that her husband would complete her work. She was buried in the Pantokrator, where John II eventually joined her.[37] She was the epitome of Comnenian piety.

The *Life* of Theodora is altogether different. It revived the theme of the wife mistreated by her husband. Theodora was a devout young woman. Despite her station she retained a proper humility, which may explain why her husband took a mistress. This woman was contemptuously known – with that Byzantine talent for nicknames – as Gangrene. She used magic to turn Michael Angelus against his wife, who despite being pregnant was exiled from court. Nobody was to receive her or even mention her name. With her new-born child she lived a life of great misery, wandering from place to place. Not once did she utter a word of reproach against her husband. Five years passed and there was a coup at court. Gangrene was seized by some of the chief men and Michael Angelus was forced to take back Theodora. This ushered in a period of calm and prosperity. Theodora devoted herself to charitable works. She founded monasteries and a convent, to which she retired on her husband's death and became a nun. She died in her turn and was buried in the nunnery now known as St Theodora's. Miracles began to be worked at her tomb, which still survives. It became a place of pilgrimage.[38]

We are dealing with a work of hagiography. We know that political considerations explain Michael Angelus's mistreatment of his wife, but these were of no concern to a hagiographer.[39] Instead he concentrated on the theme of the virtuous wife and the wicked mistress, but underlining the succour the former received from the church. It

37 *Synaxarium Ecclesiae*, ed. Delehaye, 887–90; Varzos I, 219–22.
38 Migne, *PG*, 127. 903–8.
39 See Nicol I, 128–31, 149–50, 159–60.

was a priest who finally had the courage to take her in and give her sanctuary. It pointed to the solidarity of church and women.

The mother of Michael Psellus

The virtuous wife was also the theme of the *encomium* delivered by Michael Psellus at the funeral of his mother.[40] There are elements of hagiography. Psellus claimed that there were those 'who would number her among the saints and martyrs'.[41] It is an idealised portrait, but there are concrete features. For example, we learn that it annoyed Psellus's mother to think that because she was female she was denied an education. Without her mother knowing she was able to pick up the rudiments of an education: this, Psellus noted, was without the aid of an elementary teacher.[42] Her passionate interest in her son's studies allowed her to continue her education vicariously.[43] She was a formidable mother. She did not get her son off to sleep by telling him fairy stories, but preferred stories from the Old Testament, such as the sacrifice of Isaac. She lectured him on virginity and hellfire.[44] It is easy to believe that 'there was nothing feminine about her, apart from her sex. For the rest her soul gained in strength and became more like a man's.'[45] Psellus meant these words as the highest compliment. She overshadowed her husband. Psellus had to insist that there was nothing feminine about his father, but he does so defensively. He recognised that his mother was the dominant force within the household: 'the moving spirit and discoverer of all that was best'.[46]

Like many women she found an outlet for her energies in her devotions and in charitable work. Once a year she went to tend the poor. She would have done it more frequently, but she did not wish to alarm her husband.[47] Her desire was always to embrace a monastic way of life.[48] The opportunity came when her elder daughter died. She had first to convince her husband that he wanted to become a monk. Psellus's father seems almost as reluctant to enrol in the monastic ranks as Psellus himself was later to be, but he allowed himself to be persuaded. His wife retired to a hermitage (*asketerion*), which she erected near her daughter's grave. She became an ascetic and followed a life of contemplation. This was done quite independently. She did

40 Sathas, *MB* v, 3–61.
41 Ibid., 51.
42 Ibid., 7.
43 Ibid., 21.
44 Ibid., 17.
45 Ibid., 16.
46 Ibid., 19. Noted by Garland, 'The life and ideology', 377.
47 Sathas, *MB* v, 23–4.
48 Ibid., 22–3.

not receive the tonsure from a spiritual father.[49] There seems to have been something slightly irregular about her manner of life. She calls to mind those women ascetics who claimed to be deaconesses and aroused the suspicions of Theodore Balsamon. Some of her opinions were extremely radical: Psellus tells us that 'she judged male and female impartially, not favouring the one sex above the other, on the grounds that to do so was [the opinion] of an unreflecting observer and a [sign] of an unsound judgement. Instead she assigned to each equality, for, if the physique of the sexes differs, their intelligence is equal and identical.'[50] No wonder she attracted devotees among women. They flocked to her deathbed: to touch her and to obtain some memento of her. Her habit was torn up into 1,000 keepsakes.[51] Psellus's mother sounds, in her way, just as remarkable as her son. Her views on the essential equality of men and women were quite novel. They must have been part of that ferment of ideas that occurred in Constantinople in the eleventh century. Initially, there were few who would subscribe to such a belief, but it was one that gained ground. It lay behind the spate of new nunneries founded under the Comneni.

Ptochoprodromos's virago

Psellus's portrait of his mother is an exercise in filial piety. He does not disguise how she dominated her family who went in awe of her. Prodromos provides a pendant, or perhaps the other side of the coin. He sketches the misadventures of a hen-pecked husband. He hopes that his complaints will not get back to his wife or he might as well be buried alive. He went in terror of his wife. She made his life a misery. There were constant complaints about his incompetence and his failure to provide for her adequately. She liked to contrast her high birth with his lowly Constantinopolitan origins. She listed her many responsibilities about the house. She was doorkeeper, sacristan, choirmaster, and village notary all rolled into one. This appropriation of ecclesiastical offices gives an interesting twist to how a wife saw her duties. It somehow sanctified them. Prodromos ends his sketch with the latest incident in the domestic saga. His wife had driven him out of the bedroom with a broomstick. He went to get himself something to eat, but she kept the cupboard locked, so he went hungry. In despair he dressed up as a foreign pilgrim and asked for alms. His children did not recognise him and started to drive him away from the house, but his wife stopped them. She did not recognise him either. She took it as

49 Ibid., 32–3.
50 Ibid., 51.
51 Ibid., 50.

an opportunity to fulfil a wife's charitable obligations. She invited him in and treated him to an excellent meal.[52] This sketch was meant only to amuse. It should not be taken too seriously. At least, it shows that in the twelfth century women were seen as a force to be reckoned with. In its humorous way it bears out some of the impressions implicit in Psellus's eulogy of his mother.

Spiritual consolations

Ultimately, the growing influence of women worked to the advantage of the church. At one level, it was a matter of psychology. Only the church could offer spiritual protection against the special dangers that surrounded women and alleviate the extra burden of guilt that it imposed upon women. It could persuade them that they were unclean because they menstruated and yet forgive them. But it was childbirth that reveals better than anything the power exercised by the church over women. It was an ordeal made more frightening by the superstitions that surrounded it. These crystallised around the figure of Gello and her agents the *geloudes* and *strigae*. Gello was 'a force opposed to births and existence itself'. Her agents sucked the life blood from new-born babies. The church offered protection in the shape of exorcism, but emphasised the impurity of the mother, which had left her prey to such demons. She could only be cleansed through 'churching'. This occurred forty days after the birth, which was also the normal time for the baptism of the child. The church dramatised childbirth, temporarily expelled the mother from its midst, and then used its sacramental power to welcome her back into the community of the faithful together with the new-born child. Childbirth or its prospect taught women from an early age to look to the church for solace and support.[53]

This manifested itself in the need felt by women for spiritual guidance. This meant in the upper reaches of society consulting fashionable spiritual fathers. A niece of the Emperor Manuel I Comnenus turned for consolation to Michael Glykas,[54] who had won for himself a high reputation for spiritual wisdom. She despaired of salvation after trying to murder a rival in a fit of jealousy. Michael Glykas offered soothing words, citing examples from the scriptures and from history of the truly contrite. Some of the women who brought their cases to Demetrius Chomatianos showed the same need for spiritual consolation. One threw herself on the ground before the archbishop and confessed her sins 'with many tears and groans'. In some ways her story reveals

52 Prodromos, no. I, 30–7.

53 See I. Sorlin, 'Striges et géloudes. Histoire d'une croyance et d'une tradition', *TM* 11(1991), 411–36.

54 Michael Glykas II, 118–27.

the power of women within the household as vividly as anything. One of her servants was a persistent thief. To chasten him she had his hands cut off. As a result, he had died. To mutilate a dishonest servant was in the nature of things; to bring about his death was cause of contrition. She turned to the archbishop for absolution.[55] This is an extreme case, but there were others that equally suggest that an attraction of ecclesiastical justice to women, but not only to women, was its spiritual dimension. Chomatianos and Apokaukos also showed, as we have seen, a surprising consideration for the needs and condition of women. Chomatianos urged a husband to have his adulterous wife back, for she was young and foolish and easily led astray. In other words, she conformed to the stereotypical woman.[56] More surprising is his judgement in another divorce case. The wife was found guilty of adultery. She would have to perform the penance laid down by canon law, but Chomatianos forbad the application of the penalties prescribed by civil law, because her unhappy marriage had brought her much misery. His words are worth quoting: 'Instead of punishment, hunger and the resulting misery and degradation suffice for the female sex.'[57] It was a view bound up with a belief that husbands had a duty to support their wives.

The growing reliance of women on ecclesiastical courts was part of a complicated evolution. It was not deliberately sought by the church. The starting point was the interest taken by the church in marriage law. The intentions were in the first place pastoral: to raise the standards of a Christian society. Marriage was the key institution. It had a decisive influence on the legal rights of women, given that these were very largely tied up with the property brought by both partners to a marriage. This interest in marriage law coincided with a slight, but significant, increase in the influence of women within the family. But more than this was needed. The twelfth century saw concerted work done on canon law. It provided what the Byzantine church had been lacking: an effective foundation for ecclesiastical justice. It may not have been the intention, but in the process canon law assimilated much of the civil law. To judge by the detailed records left by Chomatianos and Apokaukos the ecclesiastical courts offered more effective justice than did the civil courts. This was especially the case with family property. For obvious reasons this was of particular concern to the women of any family. Since so much family property was tied up in dowries and other nuptial gifts, it made sense to use the ecclesiastical courts.

55 Chomatianos, no.124.
56 Ibid., no.139.
57 Ibid., no.141.

Women occupy an ambivalent role in a patriarchal society. They are its strength and its weakness. 'A wife represents the power and the authority of her husband' was a commonplace, when it came to interpreting dreams.[58] The interpretations put upon dreams reveal many of the everyday assumptions of Byzantine life. A wife could make or mar her husband. This is what made marriage so dangerous an enterprise and daughters so volatile a commodity. A woman's role might appear to be secondary, but within the family it was pivotal. There was a discrepancy between her status and her responsibilities. No wonder women were expected to show practical ability.

The old stereotypes of women persisted. However, in one respect, the twelfth century saw a significant adjustment of the stereotype. There was more general recognition that women were the equals of men in moral worth. This reflected the growing influence of women which came, at least at the top of society, with the increasing power of the family in relation to the state. A major concern was family property in which women had a direct interest. They came to see in the ecclesiastical courts their best protection. This contributed to a significant shift of certain areas of legal business from the civil to the ecclesiastical courts. The most important related to marriage. In the mid-eleventh century most marriage suits came before the civil courts, even the prohibited degrees. By the early thirteenth century this had ceased to be the case. It goes without saying that marriage was the cornerstone of secular society. It was through the supervision of marriage that the church would have the most immediate impact on the laity. Much of the wealth of society was tied up in marriage. So was its moral health. The church was at last in a position to inculcate its ideal of marriage. An older view had hung on stubbornly, in which the moral and spiritual dimension of marriage was subordinated to the contractual element. The church's emphasis on the moral and spiritual side of marriage conformed with the new stress on a wife's moral qualities.

58 *Achmetis Oneirocriticon*, ed. F. Drexl (Leipzig, 1925), p.74.8; see M. Oberhelman, 'The interpretation of dream symbols in Byzantine oneirocritic literature', *BS* 47(1986), 8–24, at 22–3, who rightly stresses that women are never considered in their own right, but only in the context of the family.

22

LAY PIETY AT BYZANTIUM: BELIEFS AND CUSTOMS

THE argument is that over the twelfth century Byzantine society made far greater use of the ecclesiastical courts than had been the case in the past. It was felt that they catered more effectively than the civil courts for the specific needs of the family. These were largely dictated by the women of the family, whether actively or passively. In some cases, it was because a woman was the head of a family, but more often it was a matter of family property going with the hand of a woman. This increase of the flow of litigation to the ecclesiastical courts was only indirectly the result of action by the church. Successive patriarchs had sought to establish the church's control over marriage legislation. A compromise was reached under Alexius I Comnenus, which was largely favourable to the church. More important than this were the advantages that accrued to litigants who took their cases to the ecclesiastical courts. These included more sympathetic treatment of women and their rights. The net result was that the church exercised a greater hold over lay society.

Was this also the case where belief and religious observance were concerned? Byzantines sometimes seem to have been more reluctant to go to church than to make use of the ecclesiastical courts! They partook of communion infrequently, normally at Easter and perhaps at the other great festivals of the year, but this is less a sign of irreligion and more an indication of the awe invested in the eucharist. There seems to have been a drift away from the public churches to private places of worship. This the ecclesiastical authorities only began to find worrying in the twelfth century. They also tried to clamp down on popular festivals and customs; for the first time since the council *In Troullo* (691–2). Then pagan survivals were a serious problem, but not in the twelfth century. It was much more an effort to bring popular piety under the control of the church. It raises very difficult questions about the hold that the church had over people's deepest beliefs. Were there not areas nearly impervious to the influence of the orthodox church?

There is one thing that the 'Counsels' of Kekavmenos and the poem of *Digenes Akrites* – at least the Grottaferrata version – leave little doubt about: Byzantine society was thoroughly impregnated with conventional orthodox piety. However, this coexisted with a whole range of popular beliefs which were scarcely Christian. Digenes Akrites could be mistaken by his opponents for the spirit of a place.[1] How else were they to explain his superhuman prowess? A dragon makes its appearance in the poem and so does an Amazon. Ancient practices resurface. The sun was invoked as an avenger.[2] But death is the acid test, for it is here that the teaching of the church comes face to face with a deep stratum of popular beliefs and practices.[3] The church's hold on society will depend to a degree on the guidance and the consolation it is able to offer in the face of death.

Death

Digenes's death is the climax of the poem, even if there is an element of bathos. However painful, death from backache is not heroic. This contrasts with the folksong tradition which has Digenes wrestling with Charos – the personification of Death – on the marble threshing floor. Hans-Georg Beck has examined the death of Digenes in great detail.[4] He uses it to support his argument that the teaching of the Byzantine church about death and resurrection was too imprecise to carry conviction at a popular level. Popular beliefs about death continued to concentrate on the shadowlands of Hades. These were contrasted with the beauties of nature and the pleasures of this world. Beck argues that this reflects the failure of the orthodox church to fashion an approach to the hereafter that caught the imagination of the ordinary people. He argues further that this can be taken as a sign of how little influence the official teaching of the church had outside the educated few.

Beck is able to discover in the poem of *Digenes Akrites* attitudes to death that seem little different from those that circulated in Greece in the Heroic Age and continue in the tradition of *moirologia*.[5] The Escorial version of the poem reveals a vision of the afterlife that is as bleak as that of the *moirologia*. Digenes tells his wife, 'Today we must be parted for I am setting off for another world, black and doubly dark. I am going down to Hades.'[6] Central to Beck's argument is the proposition that the Escorial version better reflects popular views about

[1] Gro. VI, lines 320, 324: ed. Mavrogordato, 182–3; ed. Trapp, 282, 284.
[2] Grégoire, *Autour de l'epopée byzantine*, no.XVI.
[3] See L.M. Danforth, *The Death Rituals of Rural Greece* (Princeton, 1982), 25–69.
[4] H.-G. Beck, *Die Byzantiner und ihr Jenseits. Zur Entstehungsgeschichte einer Mentalität* (Munich, 1979).
[5] Cf. E. Vermeule, *Aspects of Death in Early Greek Art and Poetry* (Berkeley, Los Angeles, and London, 1979).
[6] Esc. lines 1774–5: ed. Trapp, 360.

death than does the Grottaferrata. It does not display the same signs of a learned literary treatment as the latter and is therefore less likely to reproduce the clerical attitudes of the highly educated.

The differences on this score should not, however, be exaggerated. There is much that is common to both. For instance, Digenes's wife Eudocia offers a prayer to God that her husband might be spared. Beck notes that it is modelled on the church's prayers for the commendation of the souls of the dead to God. But Eudocia is using the words not to protect the soul of her husband from everlasting death, but to preserve his life in this world. Beck sees in this a lack of interest in any afterlife and a preoccupation with this world. This may be so, but Eudocia's prayer is found in both the Escorial and the Grottaferrata versions. Its inclusion in both displays a deep familiarity with Christianity, even if the emphasis is on life rather than death. It seems to point to that familiar interpenetration of Christian and secular values. This is as characteristic of the Escorial version as it is of the Grottaferrata. In other words, both versions testify to the coexistence of a popular stratum of belief about death along with the teachings of the church.

Digenes observed the formalities of a Christian burial for his father and his mother. He interred them in the chapel of St Theodore that he erected in the courtyard of his palace. He regretted that he had not been present at his father's death. He had therefore not been able to close his eyes and wash his body.[7] These were part of the customary rites, but he had no thoughts to spare about the fate of either his father or his mother's soul. The death of his mother was an opportunity to celebrate her life: how she had helped to bring peace to the borderlands through her marriage and through giving birth to Digenes.[8] Digenes and Eudocia were not, as it happened, buried in a church but a funeral was celebrated with hymns and all the goods in the house were given to the poor. This was a custom associated with the deaths of bishops. But there were other rites that had little to do with Christianity. The mourners garlanded Digenes's tomb and circled round it.[9] The speech that Digenes made as he realised that death was inevitable was not about repentance of his sins nor about the state of his soul. It was about the bitterness of separation from 'all this world's delights' and above all from his wife. He then rehearsed the glories of his life.[10] The threnody of the mourners at Digenes's funeral centres on death's power and spite. How it brings down the bravest of men. Death, Charos, and Hades form a sinister trinity: 'these three man-killers, the three unpitying, and every age, all beauty withering, wasting all glory.

7 Gro. VII, lines 139–40: ed. Mavrogordato, 224–5; ed. Trapp, 336.

8 Gro. VII, lines 193–202: ed. Mavrogordato, 228–9; ed. Trapp, 344, 346.

9 Gro. VIII, line 247: ed. Mavrogordato, 246–7; ed. Trapp, 372.

10 Gro. VIII, lines 65–141: ed. Mavrogordato, 236–41; ed. Trapp, 356–62.

The young they spare not, nor respect the old, nor fear the strong, nor honour the wealthy, beauties they pity not, but turn to dust, and all things work to mud and stinking ash'.[11] Above all, it is Charos who is the personification of death. As with his counterpart, Love, his power appears to be independent, but it has sanction in 'Adam's transgression and God's decree'.[12] In this way the power of Charos is reconciled with Christian teaching. The threnody can then close in true Christian spirit with a lament for the vain pleasures of 'the deceiving world'.[13] 'Woe to those that sin and repent not, to those that trust in youth and vaunt their strength!'[14] The poet concludes with the conventionally Christian hope that at the Last Judgement Christ will have mercy on Digenes and his wife, together with 'all who delight and live in orthodoxy'.[15]

The Grottaferrata version of *Digenes Akrites* presents a point of view about death, which combines Christian and secular elements. Beck disputes how representative this was of popular attitudes to death. On the basis of the Escorial version of the poem he posits a nearly complete separation of popular views on death from those held by the clergy and the educated elite. His case, however, is somewhat weakened by the dramatic appearance in the Escorial version of the angel of death:

> He imagined an angel of fire coming from out of heaven and when Digenes saw him, he was sore afraid and he called for his good wife, so that she could witness the apparition. 'Do you see, good woman, the angel who comes to take me? My hands tremble at the thought of the angel and my shoulders shiver at the thought of angel.' He entreats the angel.[16]

It is a vision of horror which Digenes then implicitly identifies with Charos.[17] This suggests the same intermingling of Christian and secular beliefs that is apparent in the Grottaferrata version. At this point it is more matter of fact than the Escorial version, but it concurs that Digenes 'gave up his soul to the angels of the Lord'.[18]

Death is described in the Escorial version as dramatically as it is sometimes depicted in Byzantine art.[19] The refectory of the Athonite monastery of Dionysiou has a death scene. Behind the deathbed there is an angel. With his right hand he thrusts a sword into the chest of the

[11] Gro. VIII, lines 270–6: ed. Mavrogordato, 248–9; ed. Trapp, 374.
[12] Gro. VIII, line 282: ed. Mavrogordato, 248–9; ed. Trapp, 374.
[13] Gro. VIII, line 294: ed. Mavrogordato, 248–9; ed. Trapp, 374.
[14] Gro. VIII, lines 296–7: ed. Mavrogordato, 248–9; ed. Trapp, 374.
[15] Gro. VIII, line 304: ed. Mavrogordato, 250–1; ed. Trapp, 376.
[16] Esc. lines 1755–61; ed. Trapp, 356.
[17] Esc. lines 1769–72; ed. Trapp, 360.
[18] Gro. VIII, line 196; ed. Mavrogordato, 242–3; ed. Trapp, 368.
[19] R. Stichel, *Studien zum Verhältnis von Text und Bild spät- und nachbyzantinischer Verganlichkeitsdarstellung* (Byzantina Vindobonensia 5) (Vienna, 1971), *passim*; C. Walter, 'Death in Byzantine iconography', *Eastern Churches Review*, 8(1976), 113–27.

deceased; with his left he empties the contents of a cup over him. To the left of the angel there is a black demon who is identified as Death. The inscription explaining the scene confuses the angel and death: 'Lo suddenly and unseen Death came to me, like a robber.With his fearful sword he snatched my soul from out of my heart and made me drink the cup of bitter death'.[20]

This reflects a general confusion between Death and the Archangel Michael, which is also present in the poem of *Digenes Akrites*. The scene itself is a monastic reworking of a less ambivalent artistic treatment of death. This was the subject of a twelfth-century *ekphrasis*, entitled *Verses to Charos*. It goes as follows:

> This swarthy man you see
> represents, stranger, ferocious death
> The chalice he holds in his palm
> is the cup of common death
> overflowing with murderous death.
> In the fullness of time
> he cuts the affection that binds true lovers
> with his long curved sword

Though it may be a Christian funerary monument that is being described, there is very little that is Christian here. The image of Charos derives directly from classical representations of Thanatos and Lethe.[21] This scene bears out much of what Beck is saying, but it is important to remember that Byzantine art had the capacity to take over classical themes and infuse them with a Christian meaning.

Beck's treatment of the Byzantine view of death is important. He has been able to bring out aspects that have largely been ignored. Charos – the personification of death – is scarcely Christian, despite occasionally being identified with the Archangel Michael. But Beck only provides a partial view and ignores much that is inconvenient to his line of argument. If Christian teaching about the afterlife meant so little to the Byzantine, would he or she have spent so much care and money on providing prayers for the dead? Monastic foundations were often made by men and women who felt that death was approaching. They wanted a monument to themselves and their families, but even more than this they desired intercession for their souls and the hope of salvation.[22] As C. Galatariotou has perceptively remarked, 'but even though this was never officially endorsed by

20 Stichel, *Studien zum Verhaltnis*, 17–19, 25.

21 Moravcsik, 'Il Caronte bizantino', *Studi bizantini e neoellenici*, 3(1931), 47–68, at 50–2; Stichel, *Studien zum Verhaltnis*, 19–20.

22 Morris, 'Monasteries', 215–20.

the Orthodox church, the Byzantines believed in the possibility of changing or at least alleviating the verdict on one's soul after death, while it was passing through the *telonia* – the heavenly toll houses – and later'.[23]

Mention of the heavenly toll houses brings us to a popular belief about the fate of the soul after death conveniently ignored by Beck. This belief goes back to at least the fourth century AD. It is set out very fully in the vision of St Basil the Younger, dating from the tenth century. The soul had to go through a series of tollgates, twenty-two in all. At each information about the deceased's life was collected by a good and a bad angel. The good and the bad deeds were weighed in the balance before a decision was reached as to whether his or her soul went to heaven or Hades. St Basil's vision involved Amma Theodora, one of his spiritual daughters. He provided her with two guardian angels and a purse full of gold pieces to redeem her as she passed through the tollgates of the air. He was spiritually rich enough to help her on her way.[24]

Beck is dismissive of such beliefs because they seem to him to be a product of hagiography and therefore impregnated with a monastic outlook, which, he asserts, did not command the allegiance of the people as a whole. A better balanced assessment would emphasise that these beliefs were part of the way a Christian mythology was created out of the metaphor of the imperial administration. The journey of the soul after death was likened to the difficulties the ordinary citizen faced in his dealings with 'the customs officers, logothetes, and tax-collectors'.[25] As we shall see, it was not only over death that this metaphor was used to create a Christian mythology.

Death was the special preserve of the monastic life. The funerary chapels attached to monasteries were the preferred place of entombment for the rich and powerful. Embracing the monastic life was seen as a preparation for death. Though there were those who had a monastic vocation from childhood, it was more usual to enter a monastery, when a person reached mature years; when the time had come to contemplate the well-being of one's soul. It is impossible to create an accurate age profile of the Byzantine monk and nun, but it was a common practice to retire to a monastery. Hovering between this world and the next, the monastery was an appropriate place to prepare for death.

Speculation about the hereafter may well have been largely left in the hands of monks. They were acknowledged to be the eschatological

[23] Galatariotou, 'Byzantine *ktetorika typika*', 95.
[24] G. Every, '"Toll gates on the air way"', *Eastern Churches Review* 8(1976), 139–51.
[25] H. Hunger, 'Die Herrschaft des "Buchstabens"', *ΔΕΛΤΙΟΝ ΤΗΣ ΧΡΙΣΤΙΑΝΙΚΗΣ ΑΡΧΑΙΟΛΟΓΙΚΗΣ ΕΤΑΙΡΕΙΑΣ* ser.4.12(1984), 17–38, at 34–6.

experts. A commonplace of hagiography has monks gathered round a dying brother and, as he lay on its threshhold, interrogating him about the world to come. The hierarchical church was wary of eschatology. Apocalypses might claim to provide an authentic guide to the next world, but they were almost all tainted by heretical origins. Eschatological lore therefore tended to creep into the orthodox tradition through hagiography. This became more marked from the tenth century. The *Lives* of St Andrew the Fool for Christ's Sake and of St Basil the Younger are both products of the mid-tenth century.[26] Both contain visions of the world to come. Though slightly different in conception the Apocalypses of the Mother of God and of St Anastasia also date from approximately the same time. Both purport to bring back report of visits to the next world undertaken with the Archangel Michael as guide. Though the four accounts have different emphases – we have noted the place given in Vision of St Basil the Young to the tollgates of the air – they are all true to ancient traditions about the world to come. They concentrate on the immediate fate of individuals, who are consigned soon after death either to paradise or to the abyss. This will be followed in due course by the Last Judgement.[27]

There was a deep conviction that after death there would be a struggle for the soul between the forces of good and evil. The death scene in the refectory at the monastery of Dionysiou has in its upper register two demons trying to snatch away the soul borne aloft by the angel of the Lord. The fears engendered are eloquently expressed in a prayer penned by a monk of the monastery of St Saviour in Chora at Constantinople. It is contained in the colophon he added to a manuscript he had copied in the year 1088–9:

> Remember me in Your kingdom, when You distribute rewards amid the splendour of Your saints to those that loved Your holy and divinising commands; when those eager to accomplish good works are received into the eternal life, while those that held their own lives in contempt are led away by the demons whom they obeyed to destruction and perdition, to the inheritance of that fire of Gehenna, and to fellowship with them and eternal sodality; from which save me, Lord, instil in me the prick of remorse and repentance through Your great mercy.[28]

26 L. Ryden, 'The life of St Basil the Younger and the date of the life of St Andreas Salos', in *Okeanos, Essays Presented to Ihor Ševčenko on his 60th Birthday*, ed. C. Mango and O. Pritsak (Cambridge, Mass., 1983) (= *Harvard Ukrainian Studies*, 7(1983), 568–77).

27 E. Patlagean, 'Byzance et son autre monde. Observations sur quelques récits', in *Faire Croire. Modalités de la diffusion de la reception des messages religieux du XIIe-XVe siècle* (Collection de l'Ecole française de Rome, 51) (Rome 1981),201–21.

28 K. Lake and S. Lake, *Dated Greek Manuscripts to the Year 1200* (Monumenta Palaeographica Vetera, ser. i) (Boston, 1934), x, p.18.

This might be described as the monastic view of death, but it was widely disseminated. The Patriarch Germanos II assured his audience that 'his hair stood on end every-time he contemplated the moment that his soul would be divorced from his body and he would be consigned to evil spirits with their wild and pitiless gaze'. 'Bitter death – the Ferryman – will come', he told the congregation,

> hurrying relentlessly, severing the threads of life . . . that bind us to the earth and earthly things; the rulers of the air, merciless executioners, the pirates who infest the wastes of the upper air sally forth in their mad rage. They do and say all they can to grieve the soul. They reproach us for all we have done with their help and push us into Hades because we have sinned with their connivance, for the Devil is both the enemy and the avenger.[29]

Faced with so terrible a prospect it was possible to derive consolation of a kind from the parable of Dives and Lazarus (Luke 16:19–31). This provided the main scriptural guide to the fate of the soul after death: the righteous gathered into the bosom of Abraham and the rich man amid the torments of hell were powerful images. They gave hope to the poor and threatened the complacency of the rich and powerful. The lessons of the parable provided the church with some of its best ammunition against the indifference of lay society. The parable also constituted the strongest evidence for supposing that soon after death a decision was made about the soul's fate. The bosom of Abraham was the immediate reward in the next world for good works done in this.

It was a commonplace that prelates might joke about. For instance, John Apokaukos told his younger contemporary George Bardanes about a dream that he had had. In it he had seen the two of them walking together in the precincts of St Sophia. Bardanes had then invited Apokaukos to see the cell that had been set aside for him. Apokaukos interpreted the dream as follows:

> The Patriarch Abraham, whose patriarchal bosom is the repose of the saved, as we have been told, has offered you repose in his bosom, which you have merited because of your good works, and you will find these things in due season. You will be the conductor of my soul, now that you have learnt these things about yourself![30]

Apokaukos's tone is jocular, but it is clear that there was a belief that those vouchsafed a place in Abraham's bosom were able to intercede for others.

Such ideas may have had the support of the hierarchy of the church, but they were not developed as part of a strict eschatology. Much was left unclear. Was the bosom of Abraham identical with paradise and

[29] Germanos II, 270.14–22.
[30] Papadopoulos-Kerameus, 'ΚΕΡΚΥΡΑΪΚΑ', no.4, p.341.

how did it relate to the kingdom of heaven? Was it only an intermediate stage in the onward journey of the soul? Orthodox teaching was content to stress Christ as the type of the risen man. Through His descent into hell Christ had destroyed the dominion of death. He had released the righteous from the confines of hell. Henceforth they might go straight to paradise. He had broken down the barriers between eternity and the world. Communion with God and a foretaste of the life to come were all now possible, but it was necessary to await the Last Judgement for a final resolution. Orthodox theology very largely aimed to explain death away.[31] It was almost as though the posthumous fate of the soul was too serious a matter for theologians. As J. Pelikan observes, 'the East maintained that whatever the "intermediate state" [of the soul] might or might not be, the church on earth did not have the right to claim jurisdiction over it'.[32]

This was in contrast to the western church, which from the mid-eleventh century elaborated the doctrine of purgatory. This sought to provide a very exact account of the soul's posthumous fate and the role that the church continued to play in its destiny. The reluctance of the orthodox church to grapple with this theological problem does not mean that it never raised its head. Michael Glykas kept coming back to it, even if he did so reluctantly. He did not think that it was proper to examine the question because it lay outside 'ecclesiastical tradition'.[33] He told one correspondent that

> there are many things that holy scripture passes over in silence. This teaches us the importance of humility and not to become puffed up with theories and develop an overweening sense of our importance. Do not be disappointed by ignorance, for the day will come, when Christ himself will teach you those mysteries which are now beyond your comprehension.[34]

It was with reluctance that he provided one or two of his correspondents with a guide to the eschatological lore of the orthodox church. They all came from monastic circles. Their interest cannot be dismissed as being of only personal importance. The chances are that they were responding to the demands of their spiritual charges who needed guidance on these matters.

Michael Glykas sought to provide conventional answers, founded as far as possible on scriptural authority. Christ was the model for the redeemed man.[35] Great weight was placed on His words to the penitent thief: 'Today shalt thou be with me in paradise' (Luke 23.43).

31 J. Meyendorff, *Byzantine Theology* (Oxford, 1975), 218–22.
32 J. Pelikan, *The Spirit of Eastern Christendom (600–1700)* (Chicago, 1974), 280.
33 Michael Glykas I, 71.15–16; 82.12; 89.13–14; 257.7–8; II, 215.12–15.
34 Ibid., II, 424.8–13.
35 Ibid., I.71–2.

This was taken to mean that thenceforward it was possible for the righteous to enter paradise.[36] But Glykas had also to turn to the hagiographical tradition. He quotes St John Climax to support the view that after death the righteous go to heaven and sinners to hell;[37] St Barsanuphius to illustrate the reality of the Toll Gates of the Air.[38] He cites the experience of Daniel the Stylite, St Sabbas, and St Sisoes, who at the moment of their death had a vision of the world to come.[39] He found that the hagiographical tradition opened up questions that would not go away. He did his best to answer them with the help of scriptural authority. The most urgent revolved around the relationship of the quick and the dead. On the basis of the parable of Dives and Lazarus Glykas concluded that the dead retained a concern for the well-being of the living. Had the rich man not begged Abraham to send Lazarus to the house of his father, so that his five brothers might be saved?[40]

Glykas was asked whether good works done on behalf of the dead could wipe away their sins entirely. The key text was a prayer of St Basil of Caesarea: 'The Dead do not praise You, O Lord, nor have they the freedom to make confession to You from Hades, but we, the living, make supplication for their souls.' Glykas gave his qualified approval. Commemorations for the dead on the third, ninth, and fortieth day after death, as well as a year later, had the authority of the Apostles, but he followed Dionysius the Areopagite in believing that such intercession worked for venial, but not mortal sins.[41] Was it possible for sinners in hell to repent? Glykas gave his approval to the notion elaborated in the sixth century by St Dorotheos of Gaza that after death sinners remain conscious of their sins.[42] He also cited Symeon the New Theologian, the only time that he does, to the effect that it is a sinner's conscience that burns in hell. This is the cause of the unendurable pain.[43] Theophylact of Bulgaria developed this line of thought still further in his commentaries on the Gospel of St Mark. Glykas quotes the passage with approval.[44]

It is notable that Glykas should have made use of such recent authorities for the elucidation of this question. He must have realised that he was on dangerous ground, because he begins with a disclaimer: to investigate scripture too critically was a fault. In typical Byzantine

36 Ibid., 136–49.
37 Ibid., 244.14–19.
38 Ibid., 244.19–24. Cf. 243.12–18.
39 Ibid., 252–3.
40 Ibid., 250–1.
41 Ibid., II, 55–6.
42 Ibid., I, 242.8–13.
43 Ibid., II, 225.5–11.
44 Ibid., 222.1–5.

fashion he preferred to follow the Fathers of the church in their interpretations, but on this question they did not provide clear guidance. It was a sign of the novelty of the problem. It was not dissimilar to that faced in the West over purgatory. The description of hellfire as the pangs of conscience is reminiscent of purgatorial fire.[45] Equally, the stress on intercession for the dead is part of the same complex of ideas. For the development of their ideas about purgatory western theologians relied heavily on the authority of Pope Gregory I.[46]

Gregory was well known to the Byzantines as Gregory Dialogus. His Dialogues had been translated into Greek. Glykas made use of them. He quoted the pope's letter to the deacon Peter in support of the view that the just go to heaven and the wicked to hell.[47] But when asked whether after death the soul was consigned to corporeal fire, he took issue with Gregory who appeared to support such a view. Glykas did not think that it conformed to scriptural authority. He found this disturbing; so much so that he suggested that there might have been a scribal error. Orthodox tradition was clear that hellfire had no material substance.[48] In twelfth-century Byzantium, therefore, death was an area where traditional answers were being queried, much to the discomfort of a man such as Michael Glykas. He preferred to speculate as little as possible. The orthodox church can hardly be said to have provided the guidance needed in face of the uncertainties of death.

It is impossible to say how far Glykas was trying to protect orthodox positions against Latin teachings. Byzantine theologians did not directly encounter the western doctrine of purgatory until after 1204. It then came as something of a shock. The first specific reference to it comes in the account that George Bardanes drew up of his debate with a Franciscan in 1235. It centred on the fate of the souls of sinners . The friar set out his church's teaching on purgatory. Bardanes found the concept so alien that he could only gloss it, as 'a place of cleansing'. The Greeks, as yet, had no word for it. Bardanes found the idea of purgatory disturbing. It had affinities with Origenist notions that hell was not eternal and that even demons might eventually be released from their torments. The orthodox church has never accepted the doctrine of purgatory. It was wary of venturing into areas where there were no guides, where the church had no right to make specific pronouncements.

At first, the western church maintained that the orthodox church's views about the fate of the soul after death were close to their own. Pope Innocent IV (1243–54) was of the opinion that they were more

45 J. Le Goff, *The Birth of Purgatory* (Chicago, 1984), 42–4.

46 Ibid., 88–95, 206–7.

47 Michael Glykas I, 241.9–11, 244.8–11.

48 Ibid., II, 380–2.

or less identical. It was merely that the Greeks had failed to devise the appropriate terminology.[49] The Dominican compiler of the *Contra Errores Graecorum* of 1252 was equally convinced that the Greeks entertained notions close to the western teaching on purgatory. He cited the Byzantine wall-paintings and mosaics that he had seen. These showed 'angels of light escorting the souls of saints to heaven and the angels of Satan separating with a fair degree of force the souls of the sinners from their bodies and bearing them away with them to hell'.[50] The Dominican was correct. One has only to think of the painting of Neophytos the recluse in his cave church, which shows him being borne aloft to heaven between the angels Michael and Gabriel;[51] or of the death of the sinner in the refectories of the monasteries of St John at Patmos or of Dionysiou.[52] Furthermore, Michael Glykas uses words that are almost identical with those of the Dominican to describe the death of sinners: 'At the hour of their death these [the souls of the wicked] are dragged down by force into Hades by the demons.'[53] They might almost be describing the same scene.

One of the key texts in the debate over purgatory is 1 Corinthians 3.15: 'But he himself shall be saved, yet so as by fire.' The Dominican claimed that a Byzantine theologian had glossed the passage as follows: 'We believe that fire *cathartic*, that is to say cleansing, in which the souls of the dead are assayed like gold in a furnace.'[54] Unusually, he does not identify his source. He may be referring to a passage from a sermon of the Patriarch Germanos II dealing with the sufferings of the sick. The patriarch praised the way God 'assayed them like gold in a furnace and purified their souls'.[55] But he was referring not to the next world, but to this; to the way misery in this life tried the metal of the poor and unfortunate and fitted them better than the rich and powerful for a seat in heaven. The patriarch urged all 'to purify their souls here below through this the best of furnaces. Otherwise the work of each, whatever it might be, would be tested by fire.'[56]

It is easy to sympathise with the Dominican. The Greeks were so evasive. There were elements in the orthodox tradition which pointed in the direction of the doctrine of purgatory. However, the challenge of the Latin church left orthodox theologians increasingly reluctant to commit themselves on the matter. Was it not sufficient

49 Le Goff, *The Birth of Purgatory*, 283–4.
50 Migne, *PG*, 140. 513B; Angold, 'Greeks and Latins after 1204', 77–8.
51 Galatariotou, *The Making of a Saint*, 131.
52 Stichel, *Studien zum Verhältnis*, 18–19. Cf.132–8; Walter, 'Death in Byzantine iconography', 118.
53 Michael Glykas I, 242.13–14.
54 Migne, *PG*, 140.514.
55 Germanos II, 285.9–10.
56 Ibid., 285.26–8. Cf. Michael Choniates II, 133.27.

that there was a final resolution in the shape of the Last Judgement? Byzantine agnosticism is all too evident in the debates over purgatory at the council of Florence–Ferrara (1438–9). The best the orthodox representatives could do was to state that the souls of the just 'attain to and do not attain to' the joys of heaven. 'The souls possess them perfectly as souls, but they will possess them more perfectly at the Last Judgement with their bodies.'[57] This agnostic point of view was highly enlightened, but it left plenty of latitude for a whole range of beliefs and superstitions to develop about the fate of the soul after death. Most of these had Christian credentials, whether in the form of an elaboration of the Dives and Lazarus story or in the mythology of the tollgates of the air. These provided the foundations for a monastic explanation of death, which became deeply engrained in the popular consciousness. Beck is wrong to be so dismissive. Official agnosticism, on the other hand, left room for the bleak shadowlands of Hades that contrasted with the joys of this world. To that extent Beck is right.

The commemoration of the dead

The nihilism of this view must have matched the initial grief and emptiness that death brings, but the pain will be eased through familiar ritual. Through funeral rites the church offered the bereaved a measure of consolation. Funerals attract very little attention in the sources for the Byzantine period.[58] This is in contrast with late antiquity. At the turn of the fourth century St John Chrysostom inveighed against funerary practices that smacked of paganism or offended public decency. He criticised women for the exhibitionism of their grief during funeral processions. They were behaving like Bacchae. He equally objected to the custom of making offerings at the tomb. He promoted the ideal of dignified and restrained mourning. As M. Alexiou notes, Chrysostom believed that tolerating pagan customs would be 'fatal to the Church'.[59] He was seeking to set the stamp of the church on funeral rites. Thereafter the shape of the funeral service did not change very noticeably, nor the extravagance of funeral processions. Psellus has left a vignette of his sister's funeral. Her golden hair could be seen hanging over the bier. It made such an impression that people dismounted from their horses and came down from their tenements to join in the funeral procession and add to the lamentation.[60] Eustathius of Thessalonica would not have approved. He objected to funeral processions that

57 J. Gill, *The Council of Florence* (Cambridge, 1959), 120.
58 M. Alexiou, *The Ritual Lament in Greek Tradition* (Cambridge, 1974), 24–35.
59 Ibid., 28.
60 Sathas, *MB* v, 32–3.

were more like triumphs than funerals. They were supposed to be an opportunity to pay respect, but very often they were used to insult the memory of the dead.[61]

Whether the funeral customs of Modern Greece can be read back into the middle ages is another matter.[62] In Modern Greece death is the preserve of women or, as L.M. Danforth puts it so well, 'men are out of place in a women's world of death'.[63] Was this also the case at Byzantium? As we have seen, one of the tasks expected of a Byzantine widow was to mourn her husband. This was taken very seriously. The law laid down a year of mourning. There were consequences for any widow who remarried within that period or got herself pregnant.[64] But this was a matter of convention rather than feeling. It scarcely allows us to conclude that death was the exclusive concern of women. Men did not always have a passive role at Byzantine funerals. At the funeral of Psellus's sister a relative remarked: 'A father performs the funeral lament for his daughter, while her mother stands beside him, inconsolable in the face of such calamity'.[65] In this case, at least, it was the father who was responsible for the ritual lament, but Psellus's mother would then retire to a hermitage close to her daughter's grave. It was presumably sited in or close to one of the city cemeteries. It would have allowed her to tend her daughter's grave. Tending graves remains in modern Greece the almost exclusive duty of women.

In the early church it was usual to bury Christians in cemeteries situated outside the city walls. Looking back on this period the canonist Theodore Balsamon was under the impression that the dead were laid to rest in some corner or other, just as happened in his own day with Christians living under Muslim rule. It had been usual in Byzantine cities to bury the dead within the walls from at least the seventh century.[66] This meant pressure to bury the dead within churches. Balsamon argued against this practice, but had no objection to interment in unconsecrated chapels attached to churches.[67] For those of sufficient wealth and influence this became increasingly desirable. Balsamon thought that funerals should be dignified occasions and tombs should be conspicuous, 'for today we celebrate funerals as an

[61] Eustathius I, no.XIV, 51–2, pp.110–11.

[62] See R.M. Dawkins, 'Soul and body in the folklore of modern Greece', *Folklore* 53(1942), 131–47; J. Du Boulay, 'The Greek vampire: a study of cyclic symbolism in marriage and in death', *Man* n.s.17(1982), 219–38; Danforth, *Death Rituals*, 35–69. Exhumation is an important part of these rituals, but it is more or less ignored in the medieval sources. This may be because it is very largely a family matter.

[63] Danforth, *Death Rituals*, 19.

[64] Zepos IV, 91–2, 96.

[65] Satha, *MB* V, 29.29–30.1.

[66] G. Dagron, 'Le christianisme dans la ville byzantine', *DOP* 31(1977), 9.

[67] Rhalles & Potles, IV, 479 .

occasion not of sorrow, but of rejoicing and triumph'. The departed should be greeted 'with incense and lamps and an impressive throng'. Not all approved. Balsamon reveals that many bishops had come under the ban of the church for the way they had officiated at memorial services for nobles and magnates. They were guilty of pronouncing eulogistic prayers, in iambics or some other metre. Similarly treated were church readers who delivered funeral orations as if they were at a wedding and added a musical accompaniment.[68] Among the nobility funerals and memorial services were being celebrated more magnificently than in the past. At first, this occasioned disquiet within the church, since it seemed to go counter to the Fathers of the church. In contrast, Balsamon by and large approved of the development.

Among the aristocracy death was being invested with greater pomp. The church provided an arena where its members could make a play of their social ascendancy. It was the same with baptism. The Patriarch Germanos II noted that in his day bishops rarely conducted baptisms 'except as a special favour to emperors and magnates'.[69] The church had to make these concessions to social demands, but it was also a way of making itself indispensable. This was true across society. It provided the necessary rituals. This does not exclude the continued existence or the development of ideas about death that have little that is Christian about them. One has to think in stages of mourning: the initial bitterness followed by reflection on the meaning of death. The care taken over the commemoration of the dead would have been almost meaningless without some adherence to a Christian view of the fate of the soul after death. It was usual to commemorate the deceased on the third, ninth, and fortieth days, as well as on the anniversary of the death. These dates were more or less the same as those for pagan commemorations of the dead, but they were now justified by their association with Christ. On the third day He rose again; on the ninth day He appeared to His disciples again and on the fortieth He ascended into heaven.[70] A Christian myth was also elaborated. It was attributed to the Egyptian ascetic Makarios the Great and explained the purpose of the requiem services. The soul was at first loath to leave the familiar places of this life, but then with the help of the prayers of the faithful on the third day it was brought by angels to the kingdom of heaven, 'to do reverence to the God of all'. For six days it lingered in paradise, but on the ninth day it was taken to Hades. On the fortieth it was led back into the presence of God and a decision was made as to

68 Ibid., III, 551. See Macrides, '*Nomos* and *kanon*', 79.
69 Germanos II, 292.8–10.
70 Migne, *PG*, 127.877.

its 'place of incarceration'.[71] Many popular variants of this myth have survived. Some say that the soul hovers around the earth for forty days until presented by Charos to the Archangel Michael. The archangel then conveys the soul to heaven for judgement.[72]

This is the mixture of Christian and pagan beliefs that we have seen before. Pagan practices associated with the dead lingered on into the twelfth century. Nicetas, metropolitan of Thessalonica, in the mid-twelfth century, was faced with a query about the custom of priests slaughtering doves on the graves of the departed. The metropolitan was willing to tolerate the custom as long as it was purged of any suspicions of paganism. It was to be understood that no hint of sacrifice was intended; that the slaughter of doves was part of the preparations for a meal in honour of the departed.[73] The metropolitan was clearly intent on ensuring that a popular custom remained under the auspices of the church.

The interpretation put upon it by the participants was surely different. There was a belief that the souls of the dead were freed on the Sunday before Lent by the sacrifice on their graves of hens or doves and that they remained at liberty until Whitsun and the feast of Rosalia.[74] This went back to the pagan festival of Rosalia which commemorated the dead. It continued to be celebrated in the early thirteenth century, as one learns from the details of a case that came before Demetrius Chomatianos, the archbishop of Ohrid. A shepherd had been killed in the course of the festivities of Rosalia. The archbishop fails, however, to connect the festival with commemoration of the dead. He talks only of young men going the round of villages 'and with certain games and musical instruments and bacchic jumping up and down and lewd play-acting request gifts from the local inhabitants to their profit'. But it was forbidden by canon law, 'as inspired by Hellenic error and inebriation', just like the banned festivals of the Bota and Broumalia. The archbishop condemned it as 'alien to the Christian way of life.'[75] His failure to link it to the commemoration of the dead must have been deliberate. It seems impossible that under the Roman Empire this festival had had such a purpose and continued to have it into modern times, and that this was not the case during the middle ages. The archbishop preferred to see it as mindless hooliganism. By definition a prelate would have found any continuation of pagan rites devoid of serious purpose. These festivals

71 I. F. Hapgood, *Service Book of the Holy Orthodox–Catholic Apostolic Church* (New York, 1922), 612–13; P.J. Fedwick, 'Death and dying in Byzantine liturgical traditions', *Eastern Churches Review* 8(1976), 152–61.

72 Danforth, *Death Rituals*, 45.

73 Rhalles & Potles v, 387–8.

74 Alexiou, *Ritual Lament*, 47.

75 Chomatianos, no.120.

would have been an occasion for merrymaking, but then so were the great feasts of the Christian year. But underlying the Rosalia was a stratum of belief that was not Christian. The souls of the dead went to the shadowlands of Hades, but were released for a brief interlude each year. It is difficult to avoid the conclusion that the Byzantines maintained two different sets of beliefs about the fate of the soul after death. This was possible because of the reluctance of the orthodox church to clarify its eschatological beliefs beyond subscribing to the notion of the Last Judgement.

Popular festivals

There were other secular festivals. The council *In Troullo* (691–2) (canon 62) had outlawed celebration of the Calends, Bota, Broumalia, and the festival of Spring on 1 March. It also outlawed women dancing in public and secret ceremonies where the names of pagan gods were invoked; Dionysius was singled out for special condemnation. Commenting on this canon Theodore Balsamon admitted that the Calends were still celebrated, as was the Rosalia out in the provinces, but the Bota and Broumalia are described as though they had ceased to exist.[76] The Broumalia may have had its origins in Rome, but in Constantinople it came to be associated with Dionysius. It lasted from 24 November until 1 January and became a season of jollification. Leo VI tried to bring it under Christian auspices by dedicating it to the Mother of God.[77] It was outlawed by Romanos Lecapenus, but revived by Constantine Porphyrogenitus. It was still in existence in the eleventh and twelfth centuries, but in a slightly different form. It was no longer a season of festivities, but a single day given over to the meeting of friends.[78] It was also kept by the emperor, for Theodore Prodromos describes as 'a day of cosmic joy, the day of Broumalion, when an imperial banquet is organised and relatives make merry and servants rejoice'.[79] Theodore anticipated that this would at last be the occasion when the emperor bestowed upon him the much-sought corrody at St George in the Mangana. It would therefore seem that the connection between the distribution of imperial largesse and the Broumalion continued. It was clearly a social occasion without any religious significance. It underlined the way that Byzantine social life retained an independence of the Christian calendar.

This is also the lesson of the feast of Agatha. This was the subject

76 Browning, 'Theodore Balsamon's commentary', 423–4.

77 J.R. Crawford, 'De Bruma et Brumalibus festis', *BZ* 23(1914/19), 365–96.

78 Christopher of Mitylene (ed. Kurtz), no.115, 81.

79 Theodore Prodromos, *De Manganis*, ed. S. Bernardinello (Padua, 1972), no.III, lines 78–80.

of perhaps the most interesting of Psellus's investigations into popular culture. It was a festival that was restricted to women. It was for female loom workers, weavers, and carders. There were processions and singing and dancing. There were also competitions in which different weaving skills were displayed and judgement made by the old women, who were the masters of the craft and were responsible for the organisation of the festivities. 'It is not in vain that they turn the spindle or wind the distaff or regulate the shuttle, but with a definite purpose and for the sake of what is good, which they celebrate with hymns and annual processions.' But it did not come under the auspices of the church. Priests were excluded, but this did not mean that the women lacked respect for the symbols of religion. They set up images, as though in the precincts of a church, and decked them with trinkets. They approached their rituals and danced and sang, with a seriousness associated with the Christian faith.[80] Psellus does his best to give an entirely secular affair some semblance of a Christian meaning. Agatha is interpreted to mean a search after what is good, in other words the Christian God. As we shall see, there was a need - felt not only by the church - to give popular manifestations of this sort a Christian meaning. Psellus's description makes it clear that for the celebration of their festival the women of Constantinople had borrowed some of the trappings of a Christian festival. It goes almost without saying that these popular celebrations were tinged with much that was Christian. But the feast of Agatha, like other popular festivals, such as the Calends or the Rosalia, demonstrates the extent to which social life in Byzantium remained independent of the church.

The information about the feast of Agatha is tantalising. It suggests among other things another dimension to the position of women. It makes one wonder whether other groups of workers celebrated in this fashion. It is known, for example, that the notaries celebrated as their special holiday the feast of the Holy Notaries, Marcian and Martyrius, on 25 November. Christopher of Mitylene has left a description of their procession through the Forum of Constantine to the church of the Holy Notaries. They were dressed up in a motley of costumes, some wearing crowns or actors' masks, others women's garments. The atmosphere was that of a carnival.[81] This time it was a Christian festival that borrowed popular elements, but that was a normal occurrence. Christopher of Mitylene remembered one celebration of St Thomas's day which got so out of hand that it turned into a brawl and many were injured.[82]

80 Sathas, *MB* v 527–31; Laiou, 'The festival of "Agathe"'.
81 Christopher of Mitylene (ed. E. Kurtz), no.136, 91–8.
82 Ibid., no.1, 1–2.

The most important event in the Byzantine social round was the Calends which celebrated the new year beginning on 1 January. Theodore Balsamon rightly traced it back to Roman custom. He is dismissive of the way peasants celebrate it in a more pagan fashion and connect it with the moon. His contemporary Eustathius of Thessalonica provided an altogether more positive evaluation of the festival. His correspondent disapproved of the merriments. To Eustathius's mind this only added to the general enjoyment. He told his correspondent: 'Everybody who values Roman [traditions] is celebrating the Calends and reckons among the happiest days those given over to joy.' Eustathius approved of the custom of exchanging presents. It was a way of cleansing society of its enmities and renewing good fellowship.[83] It was also a time of rowdy festivities. Groups would go around seeking gifts at this time of the year, singing songs and improvising praises.[84] It was also the practice for one of the company to dress up as a king and direct 'the customary lewd and disorderly games',

> for on the day of the calends of January worthless men calling themselves Christians, [but] continuing pagan customs parade with great pomp. They alter their appearance and dress up in the shape and form of the devil. They girt themselves with goatskins and altering their facial expression they put off the good in which they were reborn and repossess the evil in which they were born. They claim to have renounced the devil and his works through baptism, but to have been enrolled once again by him in evil and disgusting activities.[85]

Stripped of its hagiographical excess, you have a description of a carnival.

The church was suspicious of all social activity outwith its auspices. One thinks of St John Chrysostom's denunciation of the evils of the hippodrome and the theatre. It is difficult to see that the festivities associated with the Calends constituted any real threat to the church, but they favoured the survival of non-Christian beliefs. One such was the superstition about the *baboutzikarioi*. These were hobgoblins who were active between Christmas and Epiphany.[86] Michael Psellus derived them from a nocturnal demon called Babo who is mentioned in the Orphic songs. He claimed to know somebody who saw these apparitions in the daytime as well as at night. But he dismisses this

83 Eustathius I, letter 7, 315–17.

84 John Tzetzes, *Chiliades*, ed. Th. Kiessling (Leipzig, 182b). XIII, Hist. 475.239–50; Tzetzes II, p.523.

85 F. Cumont, 'Les actes de S. Dasius', *Analecta Bollandiana* 16(1897), 11–12.

86 These survive in modern Greek folklore as the Kallikantzaroi, see Ph. Koukoules, 'Καλλικάντζαροι', *ΛΑΟΓΡΑΦΙΑ*, 7(1923), 315–28; K. Romaios, 'Οι Καλλικάντζαροι', *BNJ* 18(1945–9), 49–87. W. Puchner, 'Die "Rogatsiengesellschaften"', *Südostforschungen*, 36(1977), 109–58

as the vain imaginings of a man, who was not only timid but also short-sighted. During the festivities he bumped into revellers and mistook them for the dreaded *baboutzikarioi*.[87] This is an interesting piece of rationalisation. It is perhaps too simplistic to seek the origins of the *baboutzikarioi* in the mummery associated with the celebration of the Calends. It is more likely that the mummery was designed to celebrate and appease the mischievous spite of chthonic spirits.

Popular sayings

Michael Psellus was fascinated by popular customs, riddles, and sayings. Psellus was intrigued by the popular greeting exchanged at Ascension: 'Today the holy post-horses and tomorrow the Ascension (σήμερον τὰ ἁγία κοντούρα καὶ αὔριο ἡ 'Ανάληψις).' The horses used by the imperial post in Roman times were distinguished by their cropped tails, whence the name *kontoura*.[88] They were renowned for their strength and speed. So, when people started to think about the power necessary for Christ's ascent into heaven, the horses of the imperial post came to mind. It is one of the more amusing examples of the way a Christian mythology was shaped out of the parallels perceived between the kingdom of heaven and the Roman imperial establishment. Psellus tries not very successfully to give a more uplifting tone to the saying. The lack of a tail somehow eased ascent.[89] It was explained rather more elegantly in a contemporary collection of popular sayings: 'And just as an earthly ruler sends his messages and gives his answers through an emissary, the so-called *kountouriaris* [i.e. somebody mounted on a *kontouron*], so the same thing happens with the heavenly king, with the angels ascending.'[90]

This interest in popular sayings and customs was continued in the twelfth century by Eustathius of Thessalonica in his commentaries on Homer and by Michael Glykas. They felt compelled to give popular sayings a good Christian meaning. In this they were following Psellus's lead. So Psellus interprets the saying 'Sit and watch the backyard and not the sea' in the following way: the sea reflects the inconstancy of human life. Reason makes us seek the shelter of our back yard which represents the original paradise.[91] Some of the sayings collected are the

87 Sathas, *MB* v, 571–2.
88 Ibid., 533.
89 Ibid., 532–6.
90 K. Krumbacher, *Mittelgriechische Sprichworter* (Munich, 1894; repr. Hildesheim and New York, 1969), 98–9.
91 Sathas, *MB* v, 541–2.

wisdom of many generations: 'Look after your belongings, so that you do not turn your neighbour into a thief';[92] 'When your neighbour gets the scab, buy oil of cedar';[93] or 'one swallow does not make a spring' which goes back to classical times. They are all given a Christian interpretation, however contrived it may be. Most of the sayings do reflect a Christian milieu and mentality, but only a very few of them have any direct connection with the church. No sayings about priests and monks survive in these collections, but there is: 'An evil bishopric nurtures the bishop', which must have given food for thought.[94] There is also: 'A large church and little grace' or alternatively 'a small church and much grace',[95] which may explain the Byzantine preference for small churches. 'I departed from matins and found the liturgy waiting for me'[96] was no doubt meant ironically: 'Out of the frying pan into the fire!' From the legends associated with the building of St Sophia comes the saying 'St Sophia managed with a ha'porth of oil',[97] but this is the only one connected with a specific Byzantine church. Some sayings derive from the Bible and one came from an apocryphal gospel: 'We kept her unmarried and she turned out to be pregnant'.[98] This was said of the Virgin Mary, but it must have been used ironically.

The popular sayings reveal a society that had little time for the church as an institution, but one that had an easy familiarity with aspects of Christian teaching. There was a marked emphasis on the expulsion from paradise, the wiles of the devil, and the saving grace of Christ. The harrowing of hell and Christ's triumph over Hades were the inspiration for a number of sayings, such as 'there where we have lingered so long, and John and all [the others] were dancing'. John the Baptist was supposed to have welcomed Christ to Hades with the words, 'This is he of whom I spake' (John 1.15) and then all started dancing for joy.[99] The interpretations, rather than the sayings themselves, stress the imminence of death and the various prospects it holds. 'Before we drown, pay the fare'[100] is explained as follows: death creeps up on us while we are immersed in everyday cares. Best you pay the Lord his fare, 'so that you pass unpunished through . . . the tollgates of the air'.[101] Even more emphasis is placed on the Last Judgement. The

[92] Krumbacher, *Mittelgriechische*, 92–3.
[93] Ibid., 100.
[94] Ibid., 106.
[95] Ibid., 101.
[96] Ibid., 101.
[97] Ibid., 97.
[98] Ibid.
[99] Ibid., 101, cf. 94, 102.
[100] Ibid., 86.
[101] Cf. ibid., 97.

parable of Dives and Lazarus is also brought into play.[102] It fitted with Christian teaching about the poor. 'The poor man drank the wine and forgot his debts' could be interpreted as the spiritual rewards awaiting the poor.[103] 'Consume your wealth and God will open a way for you' was taken to mean that if you shared your wealth with the poor, God would open up a way for your soul through the tollgates of the air.[104] These sayings could be used to reinforce basic Christian teaching. 'Cut your debts, cut your sorrow' was about repentance.[105] Your debts were your schedule of sins, which you could atone for through the sorrow of penitence. The intemperancy of youth could be dismissed with the words, 'a callow young man who ravages his own land'.[106]

The fact that a Christian interpretation might be found for popular sayings does not necessarily mean that this was the only possible interpretation. Some seem scarcely amenable to a Christian explanation. There was the chilling 'a dead man has no friends',[107] but these turn out to be words attributed to Christ as he chided his disciples from the cross. The popular sayings collected in the eleventh and twelfth centuries reveal a thorough acquaintance with Christianity. By dint of repetition the interpretations put upon them must have become common currency, but it is a Christianity of a basic kind. It focuses on the wages of sin, constant vigilance against the devil and his agents, and the hope of salvation. It emphasises the victory of the New Testament over the Old and the blind ingratitude of the Jews.[108] There is in contrast rather little in the way of animus against the Saracens,[109] beyond being identified as agents of the devil. Little attention is paid to the sacraments. 'I wish I knew who was making dough; he has to bake his bread on Thursday' was taken to refer to the Last Supper and was directed against the Latin practice of using wafers instead of bread in the communion,[110] but this comes from a later collection and may not have been current in the eleventh and twelfth centuries.

A slightly different angle emerges from the Dreambook (*Oneirocriticon*) of Achmet ben Sirin.[111] This was the pseudonym adopted by a Byzantine author, anxious to give his compilation cosmopolitan allure. He was probably writing around the early eleventh century. His

102 Ibid., 89.
103 Ibid., 90.
104 Ibid., 109.
105 Ibid., 80.
106 Ibid., 99.
107 Ibid., 113.
108 Ibid., 75, 79, 85, 98, 102, 104, 111.
109 Ibid., 91, 99.
110 Ibid., 114.
111 *Achmetis Oneirocriticon*, ed. Drexl. See F. Berriot, *Exposions et significacions des songes* (Geneva, 1989), 31–5; M. Oberhelman, 'Prolegomena to the Byzantine *Oneirokritika*', *B* 50 (1980), 487–504; Oberhelman, 'The interpretation of dream symbols', 8–24.

Dreambook was a great favourite at the court of Manuel I Comnenus, who encouraged its translation into Latin. Much of the material was of Oriental origin, but it was designed to meet Byzantine needs. For example, there was one chapter devoted to priests and another to icons.[112] The interpretation of dreams is not very sophisticated. Personification and analogy are the normal means employed. The naivety of approach allowed many everyday assumptions to surface. The *Oneirocriticon* can provide a rough and ready guide to some of the prejudices of the laity.

The priest emerges as a figure of authority, but with his proper station and responsibilities. If you saw yourself in a dream with the rank of priest and you were praying on behalf of your flock, then you could expect to lead the people and to be beloved of all.[113] But suppose you had a dream, in which a priest was wearing his vestments and entering a place where he had no business to be. This would mean that the people of that place were going to suffer at the hands of the authorities.[114] What if you saw a priest in your dreams enter your house and go to sleep on your mattress? The interpretation was double-edged: you would be on good terms with the priest, but he would seduce your wife![115]

Then there were dreams in which you saw different parts of a priest's body growing larger or smaller. These meant that his power over the local people would either increase or decrease.[116] If a layman dreamt that he was ordained a priest or a deacon, it pointed to success and prosperity. But if in the dream he then abandoned holy orders, it meant that his success would turn to ashes.[117] But the power of the priest derived from his faith. If you learnt in a dream that the local priest was dead, you should conclude that the priest had lost his faith, or, if the priest had fallen ill, that his faith was suspect.[118] A priest seen in a dream abandoning his order was deemed to be on the point of committing a sin for which he would repent.[119] If a priest had a dream in which he lost part of his vestments, it meant that his priesthood was coveted by another.[120] Finally, the following meaning was put on a dream where a priest was on good terms with the ordinary people: the priest was humbling himself before God and was strong in his faith.[121] This was perhaps an ideal state of affairs, for the image of

[112] *Achmetis Oneirocriticon*, ed. Drexl, 103–7.
[113] Ibid., 9.12–15.
[114] Ibid., 103–7.
[115] Ibid., 104.2–5.
[116] Ibid., 104.10–21.
[117] Ibid., 104–5.
[118] Ibid., 104.5–9.
[119] Ibid., 104.22–3.
[120] Ibid., 105.8–10.
[121] Ibid., 104.23–6.

the priest that emerges otherwise is of a remote and powerful figure separate from lay society.

The attitude to monks that emerges from Achmet's Dreambook is ambivalent. If anybody dreamt that they received the monastic tonsure, it meant grave troubles ahead.[122] If a monk had a dream in which he was dispensing water to the people, as long as it was clear, he could console himself with the thought that he was preaching salvation. If, however, it came out cloudy, he was spreading heresy.[123]

A whole chapter is devoted to icons. A dream about icons was nearly always propitious, as long as they were not encrusted with gold, because gold so often brought sorrow. The most interesting dream was about commissioning an icon. Success in any venture would be proportionate to the accuracy with which the icon was executed.[124] Priests and icons, even monks form part, but only a small part, of everyday consciousness. The treatment of icons and priests in the Dreambook reveals that they were both sources of power. To be efficacious icons had to conform as closely as possible to an ideal type. Priests were distant figures, but fallible, because liable to loss of faith. Monks might be the agents of salvation or of heresy.

Christianity is ingrained in the text. The resurrection of the dead seen in a dream foretold justice, for at the resurrection God was the supreme judge.[125] To dream that you were entering paradise was a propitious sign. It was a dream that came from God and meant that you were saved, or, if you were a sinner, that you would repent and be saved. At all events, it promised wealth in this world. If you saw yourself condemned to the fire of Gehenna, you were certainly an evil-liver and this gave you an opportunity to repent.[126] A visit in a dream from an angel, even if it only turned out to be a eunuch, was a token of good tidings. A visit from Christ Himself was still better. If He spoke, all His words must be committed to memory. The person seeing such a vision was blessed. The chances were that he would soon die, but he could be confident that salvation was his.[127]

Conclusion: the Comnenian church and popular festivities

Orthodoxy was central to Byzantine life, but this coexisted with a rich amalgam of beliefs and festivities that was scarcely orthodox. This gave lay society a degree of independence from the official church, which

122 Ibid., 20.21–3.
123 Ibid., 145.1–3.
124 Ibid., 106–7.
125 Ibid., 3–4.
126 Ibid., 4–5.
127 Ibid., 6–7.

was for long surprisingly tolerant. Despite prohibitions by Justinian repeated in the Basilics people still made fun of the monks and clergy, by putting on masks or dressing up as monks or nuns. The clergy too participated. They might put on military uniform and wave a sword around or they would pretend to be monks or some kind of animal. Members of clerical households would flick their fingers like charioteers, drape their jaws with seaweed (pretending to be seagods?), or make out that they were doing women's work, all to make the onlookers laugh. These activities were associated with Christmas and Candlemas. They might even be encouraged by the church. The Patriarch Theophylact (933–56) is supposed on good authority to have introduced them into the church of St Sophia.[128] Candlemas was the season of the year when in the West the feasts of fools were held. There seems to be a good chance that the Patriarch Theophylact was trying to institute something similar, so that the festivities associated with the Calends would be drawn within the orbit of the church, but this demanded some response from the clergy. They were expected to enter into the spirit of the occasion.

This tolerance on the part of the church was at odds with the more exalted concept of patriarchal authority that increasingly prevailed from the mid-eleventh century. The Patriarch Nicholas Grammatikos was the first to act. He was horrified by the revels that took place in St Sophia at Christmas and Candlemas. 'They transformed houses of prayer into places of business and the haunt of robbers (Matthew 21.13) and holy festivals into outrageous gatherings.' The patriarch denounced those that took part as 'devotees of Dionysius'. They corrupted themselves and others 'by confounding the sacred and the profane'.[129] The patriarch drove them from St Sophia.

In doing so Nicholas Grammatikos made the separation of the sacred and the profane part of the agenda for the Comnenian church. From the middle of the twelfth century the church clamped down on all manifestations of popular religion down to the most insignificant. Patriarch Luke Chrysoberges (1157–69) outlawed the festivities accompanying the feast of the Holy Notaries.[130] They were corrupting a Christian occasion! The Patriarch Nicholas Mouzalon (1147–51) learnt that one village gave special honour to the cult of St Paraskeue, but that their cult was based on a *Life* written by one of the villagers. It did less

[128] Rhalles & Potles II, 451–2; Grumel, 1093. F. Tinnefeld, 'Zum profanen Mimos in Byzanz nach dem Verdikt des Trullanums', *BYZANTINA*, 6(1974), 321–43, at 334 n. 59, sees no reason to use this passage from Balsamon as evidence that clerical games were instituted by the Patriarch Theophylact. He contends that this is just an inference made by Balsamon on the basis of Skylitzes's *History*. It seems to me a reasonable inference to make. Tinnefeld is being overscrupulous.

[129] Darrouzès, 'L'éloge de Nicolas III', 50.652–71.

[130] Rhalles & Potles II, 451–2; Grumel, 1093.

than justice to the saint's angelic conduct. The patriarch ordered that it should be burnt and commissioned an officially approved *Life* to take its place.[131] At the end of the century the traditional reading of the Life of St Xenophon and the accompanying procession which was a popular occasion was curtailed to accommodate a sermon on St Gregory the Theologian by the metropolitan of Chalcedon. A deacon of St Sophia thought this more edifying, ignoring the popular resentment it caused.[132]

The Patriarch Michael Ankhialos' (1170–8) outlawed the celebrations that traditionally took place at Constantinople on the evening of 23 June. Vases were filled with sea water, and people would throw in various objects. Then a young girl, who had to be an eldest daughter, would be dressed as a bride. She would take out an object at random and predict the fate of its owner. There would be merrymaking. People built bonfires and jumped over them for luck. They went down to the sea shore and collected water which they threw over their houses which they had previously garlanded. This was done in the opinion of the patriarch in honour of the Satan that dwelt therein. Balsamon claimed that these rites had now ended through the vigilance of priests and leading figures in the neighbourhoods.[133] The church treated this custom as devil worship, but it was clearly not limited to the capital alone. Jumping over bonfires on 23 June continues in Greece and the southern Balkans to this very day.

Priests and monks who in any way connived at popular practices were condemned by synod. Balsamon lists those that suffered. There was the *protos* of a monastic confederation who kept the membrane of a new-born child in a medallion. It had been given to him by a woman as protection against his detractors.[134] The abbot of the monastery of St Saviour in Chora was dismissed for taking meat and cheese into the sanctuary. He believed that these would then provide a cure for various ailments.[135] Many monks and some abbots were condemned for consulting women fortune tellers who frequented churches or hovered round icons.[136]

Byzantine popular piety was deeply Christian. It was nevertheless marked by a wariness and independence of the church. It found its outlet in its own customs and festivals. Alongside a Christian mythology there were also pagan survivals that were normally given some Christian meaning. Once paganism had ceased to count as a serious

[131] Rhalles & Potles II, 453.
[132] Papadopoulos-Kerameus, 'Ἐπιγράμματα', no.8, p.470.
[133] Rhalles & Potles II, 458–9; Grumel, 1140. Kazhdan & Epstein, Ex.9, 239–40.
[134] Rhalles & Potles II, 446.
[135] Ibid., 5.
[136] Ibid., 446.

threat the church had been happy to tolerate popular customs and had even given its tacit approval. This changed in the twelfth century. The church became suspicious of popular customs and festivals. They smacked of devil worship. There was an element of official paranoia which was connected with the renewed attack on heresy. The orthodox church was determined to assert its control over belief. It was difficult to tell where popular custom ended and heresy began.

The act of the Patriarch Michael Ankhialos' outlawing the celebrations on 23 June was reenacted in the early thirteenth century in the *synodikon* of the Bulgarian Tsar Boril (1207–18).[137] It was isolated among a series of condemnations of Bogomil teachings. A link between the Bogomil heresy and popular rites and superstitions was largely a figment of official paranoia. The orthodox church may have found a charge of heresy a convenient way of attacking popular practices. Theodore Balsamon was deeply suspicious of what went on in rural churches built by the local peasantry: women were supposed to foretell the future in a state of trance; men pretended to be possessed and did unspeakable things which Balsamon fails to specify.[138] These activities could easily spill over into devil worship or heresy. Balsamon was convinced that out there in the provinces there were settlements entirely dominated by the Bogomils.[139]

137 J. Gouillard, 'Une source grecque du *Sinodik* de Boril: la lettre inédite du patriarche Cosmas', *TM* 4(1970), 361–74.

138 Rhalles & Potles III, 509–10.

139 Ibid. I, 246.

By the fourteenth century the festivities associated with the Calends were being transferred to Apokreo, the carnival held before Lent. The first clear reference comes in a letter dating from the early fourteenth century (J. F. Boissonade, *Anecdota nova* (Paris, 1844), 215–18). But it was already a social occasion in the eleventh century, if not so hectic as it was to become (Christopher of Mitylene (ed. Kurtz), no.102, 63–4). Some verses dated 1273 suggest that for those of a pious disposition Apokreo was still a period of preparation for the rigours of Lent (Sp. P. Lampros, ''Επιγράμματα Θωμᾶ Γοριανίτου', *ΝΕΟΣ ΕΛΛΗΝΟΜΝΗΜΩΝ* 12(1915), 435–6). It may be that the transfer of festivities to Apokreo was an indirect result of the measures taken by the Comnenian church against popular festivities, in the sense that Apokreo may have received the church's grudging approval: it could at least be given a clear Christian context.

23

THE BOGOMILS

THE Bogomil heresy was the last of the dualist heresies to plague the orthodox church, which it did down to the end of the middle ages. It fed on popular piety, customs and superstitions. It had almost nothing in common with the 'philosophical' heresies of the eleventh and twelfth centuries. These belong to the intellectual history of the Byzantine Empire and were part of the squabbling, often of a political character, that went on in the struggle for preferment within the precincts of the patriarchal church. The only thing that unites a John Italos and a Basil the Bogomil was that they would both be arraigned by the Emperor Alexius I Comnenus on charges of heresy. There was on both occasions a high political content in the charges of heresy. It was a useful way of cowing political opponents and asserting authority in the streets and squares of Constantinople. Heresy could also be a figment of official paranoia. Any hint of nonconformity might be taken as political subversion. But one should resist the temptation to explain heresy away in this fashion. The Byzantine authorities were dealing with a real phenomenon, even if they misunderstood it and had every reason to misrepresent it and exaggerate it.

From its earliest days the Christian church had singled out dualism as a major threat. Among other things it offered an attractive solution to Christianity's Achilles' heel – the problem of evil. It proposed that mankind was caught between the opposing forces of good and evil. There could be different views on the nature of this conflict. Absolute dualism insisted that evil derived its power from a quite independent source and was therefore on an equal footing with good. There were other dualist sects who adopted a modified position. They saw evil as ultimately beholden to good. All, however, were agreed that the material world was dominated by evil and that man had within him some spark of the good. Only initiation into a special knowledge (*gnosis*) allowed man to release the good within him. This in turn made possible escape from the consequences of evil and opened up the path to salvation. It was part of a system of belief that pointed to the creation of gathered communities fired with missionary zeal.

For a number of reasons Byzantine society was susceptible to such a message. In the first place, it was a hierarchical society. As with any hierarchical society, there was a degree of alienation. But it was felt the more strongly at Byzantium because of the contrast between the hierarchical organisation of church and state and the ideal of the Apostolic church. The equality and sense of community of the early church provided an alternative inspiration. This was largely absorbed by the monastic ideal which tolerated a fair degree of nonconformism, but a dualist solution always beckoned. This is what happened with the Paulicians in the eighth and ninth centuries. There is unlikely to have been any institutional continuity between the different dualist movements, but they had access to the same apocryphal and apocalyptical texts. They were important because of the arcane knowledge they imparted. This gave a sense of mission and election. These texts provided a thread of continuity.

This kind of literature circulated and merged with tracts on demonology. Demons were an essential part of the Byzantine thought-world. N.H. Baynes graphically describes the hold they had on the mentality of the time. He concludes: 'And they are even more terrifying than the bacilli of our modern world, for they are inspired by a maleficent will and that will is directed against man.'[1] The Byzantines inherited their lore of demons from the Hellenistic world, Jews and Egyptians included. Christian theologians had to collate it with and subordinate it to their own systems of thought. It could be used as part of an explanation of the existence of evil. This was done very largely in terms of the Fall. Adam succumbed through Eve to the temptation of the devil. Thereafter human beings were susceptible to the power of evil wielded by demons who were the devil's agents. But this was tolerated by the Christian God as punishment for Adam's transgression and as a way of testing man's free will. In this way the notion of God's absolute control over creation is preserved. Evil did not derive its power from some alternative source, but was an act of disobedience that God saw fit to suffer until he sent Christ to the world. Christians were expected to take comfort from the thought that evil did not have an existence independent from God. As a result, they were encouraged to believe that the power of demons was illusory.

This was the official line, but doubts remained. Why, despite Christ's incarnation, ministry, passion, and resurrection, was evil still so dominant? Such difficulties were met, at least, in part, by what R.P.H. Greenfield has identified as an alternative tradition of demonology at Byzantium. It accorded real power to demons which 'were *not*

[1] N.H. Baynes, *Byzantine Studies and Other Essays* (London, 1960), 7.

seen as delusions, nor were they generally thought to be allowed only by God's permission'.[2] Many, perhaps most, Byzantines would have subscribed to such beliefs. This alternative tradition had an important implication. It pointed in the direction of dualism. To quote R.P.H. Greenfield again,

> once the demons were thought to possess real, independent power of their own the world was no longer a place in which all forces, all powers, both good and evil, were immediately or ultimately subject to and 'managed' by the one good God. Instead the world of men was filled with spiritual forces which, though still of course opposed, were now independent of each other and to some extent equal in power.[3]

Bogomilism offered 'a particularly well structured and clearly thought out version' of this alternative tradition of demonology.[4] In other words, the Bogomils were presenting a structure of belief, parts of which were familiar and acceptable to a very large section of Byzantine society. The Bogomils put particular emphasis upon the power and pervasiveness of demons. They claimed to be able to offer their initiates protection. This may have been part of their attraction.[5]

If often dormant, dualism was endemic in Byzantine society. Monasticism provided a complacent host, for taken to extremes many monastic ideals and practices verged on the heretical. Monks and ascetics had a vested interest in exaggerating the power of demons. They advocated the suppression of bodily needs and urges. This often came suspiciously close to the dualist condemnation of this world as evil. It was sometimes difficult, as we shall see, to distinguish a 'holy man' from a heretic. The threat from dualism was all the more insidious for the way it was ingrained in society and its beliefs. Bogomilism may never have been a threat to the Byzantine state, as such. It never became a mass movement, although the example of Bosnia in the late middle ages suggests that it had this potential.[6] The Byzantine authorities could not ignore it because it called in question the ideal order that the Byzantine hierarchy represented. Its criticism was the more powerful for being founded in the teachings of the New Testament.

Because it was embedded in Byzantine society and because monastic life in all its varieties provided camouflage, Bogomils have always been hard to locate on the ground. Even their origins in Bulgaria are obscure.

[2] R.P.H. Greenfield, *Traditions of Belief in Late Byzantine Demonology* (Amsterdam, 1988), 166.
[3] Ibid., 166.
[4] Ibid., 175.
[5] Ibid., 169 n. 520.
[6] *Pace* J.V.A. Fine Jr, *The Bosnian Church: A New Interpretation* (New York, 1975).

One can sympathise with J.V.A. Fine Jr.'s despairing efforts to pin them down.[7] He concludes:

> Bogomilism's importance has been tremendously exaggerated in all historical works. In fact – other than nuisance value to alarmist Orthodox churchmen and the curiosity value of its interesting world view – one would be justified in writing a history of medieval Bulgaria without mentioning the Bogomils at all, just as one could write a history of the United States without mentioning the Mennonites and Shakers.[8]

The trouble with this conclusion is that only a history of the United States written from a rather narrow perspective would exclude the Mennonites and Shakers. They may not be that important in themselves but they took to extremes a much wider experience of nonconformity that was characteristically American. The Bogomils fit a similar pattern in Byzantium.

The origins of the Bogomil heresy can be traced back to Bulgaria and the reign of Tsar Peter I (927–69). It was a dualist heresy which pitted the God of the Old Testament against the God of the New. The material world created by the God of the Old Testament was evil. Characteristic was the dismissal of all authority, ecclesiastical and political. The orthodox church had no validity. There was a very strong emphasis upon the moral teaching of the New Testament contained in the Sermon on the Mount. The question of where Pop Bogomil, the originator of the heresy, found his teachings does not really concern us. There may have been contact with Paulician ideas, though Paulicians were not moved in large numbers into the Balkans – they were settled around Philippopolis – until *c.* 975, which was after the appearance of the Bogomil heresy. More powerful forces were the monastic ideal, which was revived in Bulgaria by St John of Rila (died 946), and the social teaching of the New Testament, which seemed to contradict the pomp and power of the orthodox church.

What does concern us is the connection, if any, between this stage of the Bogomil heresy and the next, which emerged in Constantinople in the mid- to late eleventh century. There is comparatively plentiful evidence about the Constantinopolitan stage of the Bogomil heresy, but there is no attempt to link it directly to a Bulgarian forerunner. It therefore seems reasonable to conclude that they had little more than the name in common. It was a usual practice to identify new heresies with more ancient ones. In a Byzantine context the epithet Bogomil would add insult to injury because of its Bulgarian associations, rather

7 J.V.A. Fine, Jr, 'The Bulgarian Bogomil movement', *East European Quarterly*, 11 (1977), 385–412.

8 John V.A. Fine, Jr, *The Early Medieval Balkans* (Ann Arbor, 1983), 179.

like Whig and Tory in late seventeenth-century England with their Scottish and Irish connotations. We have, at the very least, to start from the assumption that there was not necessarily any direct connection between Byzantine Bogomilism and the original Bogomil heresy in Bulgaria.

Heresy in the eleventh century[9]

The turn of the tenth century seems to have been a time of religious ferment in the Byzantine Empire. It was met with a corresponding determination on the part of the hierarchy of the orthodox church to clamp down on dissent and nonconformity. The career of Symeon the New Theologian is a case in point. His promotion of the cult of his spiritual father Symeon Eulabes aroused the suspicion of the patriarchate because it was becoming so popular. He was condemned for inscribing on the icon of his spiritual father the designation St Symeon. His mystical teachings attracted at that time less scrutiny, but propositions can easily be extracted from his works that spill over into heresy. His attack upon the hierarchy of the church and his devaluation of baptism were both in line with Bogomil teaching. St Symeon the New Theologian is unlikely to have been the inspiration for Byzantine Bogomilism, but his mysticism with its stress on the primacy of spiritual experience was one of the currents circulating in the eleventh century, which the authorities at different times strove to combat as dangerously subversive. The threat from Symeon seemed all the greater because of his metropolitan connections. He was the abbot of the important suburban monastery of St Mamas. But in some ways this made it easier for the authorities to counter his activities than those of Eleutherios of Paphlagonia and his followers in Asia Minor.

There are parallels between the cult of Symeon Eulabes promoted by Symeon the New Theologian and that of Eleutherios of Paphlagonia (died *c.* 950), who founded a monastery in Lycaonia. This became the centre of a local monastic network. After his death his followers buried him in the monastery church and he was honoured as a saint. His icon was on display. His community developed some peculiar practices. Each of the monks was allowed two wives and there were charges of sexual licence, even if the practice was justified as proof of the monks' indifference to worldly and sexual pleasure. It was part of the mystic's struggle for perfection and salvation. Eleutherios taught that this struggle was between the Holy Spirit and the devil who sought control over man's

9 I have been guided by J. Gouillard, 'L'hérésie dans l'Empire byzantin dès origines au XII siècle', *TM* 1(1965), 299–324, at 312–22; J. Gouillard, 'Quatre procès de mystiques à Byzance (vers 960–1143). Inspiration et autorité', *REB* 36(1978), 5–81, at 8–19; M. Jugie, 'Phoundagiagites et Bogomiles', *EO* 12(1909), 257–62.

soul. The mystic's role was limited to constant prayer. Neither baptism nor communion helped in this struggle for perfection, while veneration of the cross and honour to the Mother of God were irrelevant.

Like Symeon the New Theologian or his spiritual father, Eleutherios was first and foremost a mystic, but he failed, even more than Symeon, to guard against the dangers of heresy that were inherent in the mystical tradition at Byzantium. His teachings were alarmingly similar to the tenets of the Massalian heresy with its stress on the power of prayer. His community proved very tenacious, surviving him by nearly a hundred years. It was condemned under the Patriarch Alexius the Studite (1025–43). Its members were ordered to remove the body of Eleutherios from its place in their monastic church and to burn his books and the icons of him. They had to sign a statement abjuring his beliefs. They were given the option of either having an orthodox abbot appointed over them or being dispersed to monasteries with a good reputation. That is the last we hear of Eleutherios's followers, but they may well have lingered on, for they had already survived measures taken against them by the Patriarch Polyeuktos (956–70), more than half a century earlier.[10] With both Eleutherios and Symeon it is easy to see how the mystical tradition could produce heretical teachings, but their ideas seem to have been confined to a monastic milieu.

Monasticism was very flexible. It could be used by heretics as a cover for their activities, but it went further than this. It also provided a model for the organisation of a community or a movement. This becomes apparent from Euthymios of the Peribleptos's account of a heretical group known as the Phoundagiagitai who operated mainly in north-western Anatolia in the theme of Opsikion during the first half of the eleventh century. Euthymios fails to give a derivation for their name. He does mention Phounda as a disciple of Mani, but leaves the reader to draw his own conclusions. Such finesse – quite out of keeping with the rest of the tract – leaves open the possibility of a different explanation. The name may derive from *phounda* – a purse - and refer to their pilgrim-like character. Euthymios claims to have encountered the Phoundagiagitai on three separate occasions. The first was when he was young. He went back with his mother on family business to his native theme of Opsikion. This was in the reign of Basil II (975–1025), when the future emperor Romanos Argyros was civil governor of the theme - the date must be close to the year 1000. They took their business to the governor's tribunal. There they found one John Tzourillas arraigned before the court on a charge of rape.[11] Euthymios describes him as the originator of the heresy. Even then he

[10] Grumel, 850.
[11] G. Ficker, *Die Phundagiagiten* (Leipzig, 1908), 66–7.

was recognised by local people as a heretic. For three years he had been preaching in the neighbouring theme of Thrakesion and around Smyrna with some success. He had already converted his native village, which was large and populous. Euthymios learnt that there were no more than ten Christians left there and they went in terror of their lives.[12] This suggests that at the time of writing which was after the death of the emperor Romanos Argyros (1028–34) the Phoundagiagitai were still a powerful force.

The local people referred to Tzourillas as a priest or as an abbot,[13] but there is no reason to believe that he had been ordained. They dated the start of his career to the moment when he separated from his wife. Their intention must have been, like many another couple, to enter the monastic life, for she became known as the 'abbess' and he as the 'abbot'. This presumably means that they organised their followers into a semblance of a monastic community. Euthymios has nothing to say about the organisation of the community. He concentrates on Tzourillas's teaching. The main tenets were these: wives had to be put away; baptism and communion were without validity; no reverence was to be paid to the cross; the priesthood was to be rejected; God alone was holy.[14] Euthymios accused Tzourillas's followers of dissimulation. They would attend church services, but would claim, as the Bogomils were later supposed to do, that any mention of the righteous referred specifically to them and not to the orthodox Christian.[15] Euthymios also accuses them of breaking up church services on the grounds that they offended against Christ's injunction: 'But thou, when thou prayest, enter into thy closet, and when thou hast shut thy door, pray to thy Father which is in secret' (Matthew 6.6).[16] This was a favourite text of the Bogomils.

Euthymios also claimed to have witnessed the service which the heretics celebrated in secret. The leader would stand and say, 'Let us worship the father, son and Holy Ghost.' The congregation replied, '[As is] meet and right.' They then started to recite the Lord's prayer, but showing contrition by bobbing their heads up and down. Euthymios noted that they did not turn to the East to pray, but that any direction would do.[17] Though he would recount other encounters with heretics, he has no more to say about Tzourillas and his followers. His description suggests a group which had rejected the priesthood and the official church, but which was striving to revive the teaching

[12] Ibid., 67–8.
[13] Ibid., 66.17.
[14] Ibid., 69–76.
[15] Ibid., 77–8.
[16] Ibid., 79–80.
[17] Ibid., 77.19–25.

of the New Testament. It was also inspired by a desire to spread the word of God, whence the devotion to Peter and to Paul.[18] Euthymios claimed that they travelled the length and breadth of the Byzantine Empire trying to make converts.[19]

He had come across them elsewhere – he does not specify the location, but perhaps in Constantinople where he was a monk. They succeeded in seducing his pupil, who then divulged their teachings to Euthymios.[20] He was flattered by Euthymios's apparently sincere interest and arranged a meeting with his new masters. Euthymios was impressed by the way the leader of the group knew by heart the Gospels and the letters of St Paul together with the Psalms, the Lives of the Fathers, and even some of St John Chrysostom. He was told that this feat of memory was made possible through the action of the devil.[21] On the strength of this encounter it seems – the details are vague – that Euthymios obtained a commission to investigate these heretics, for the next thing we know is that he has four of them chained up and is threatening them with death.[22] He extracted a confession, containing a more detailed account of the heretical teachings than the one he provided in his account of Tzourillas, but his first concern was with their initiation into the sect. This was done by reciting the apocryphal Apocalypse of St Peter over the head of the neophyte, who was, however, under the impression that the words were from the Gospels.

These heretics rejected all orthodox sacraments and institutions, even monasticism, but they were happy to dissimulate their beliefs. They even built churches. Euthymios had heard from a trustworthy source that one had been built on the banks of the Bosphorus by a false monk and priest, who had desecrated it by installing his latrine behind the altar; thus revealing himself for the heretic he was.[23] Euthymios insisted that they worshipped the devil, who had been expelled by God the Father for stealing the sun and the soul. They believed that there were seven heavens created by God, but the eighth, which is the visible world, was the creation of the devil.[24] One has to take so much on trust; Euthymios could be making it all up, but the existence of an Apocalypse of St Peter rings true. The various dualist sects, whether in the Balkans or in the West, relied heavily on apocrypha. The version of the expulsion of the devil and his creation of the world is a variant on other dualist accounts. Euthymios has them subscribing to absolute dualism:

[18] Ibid., 56–8; cf. 41. 21–2.
[19] Ibid., 63. 25–6.
[20] Ibid., 21–2.
[21] Ibid., 22–3.
[22] Ibid., 23.15–20.
[23] Ibid., 26–7.
[24] Ibid., 33–4.

> They teach not to expect the resurrection of the dead, nor the second coming nor the Last Judgement, but that all power over earthly things with hell and paradise belongs to the lord of this world, that is to say the devil, and that he puts his friends in paradise and his enemies in hell, and that he has nothing in common with God, but that God reigns in the heavens and the lord of the world on earth.[25]

This is very much a gloss put on their teaching by Euthymios who like other orthodox wished to present them as devil worshippers. However, he relates their belief that the devil stole the sun and the soul from God. This is at variance with absolute dualism. Euthymios also has the heretics proclaiming: 'It is given to us and not to others to know the mysteries of God, as has been written in the Gospel.'[26] This points to the New Testament as their source of inspiration.

The confession that Euthymios extracted from the four heretics provides strong reason for believing that dualists were operating in Constantinople around the middle of the eleventh century. Euthymios labels them Phoundagiagitai. He asserts that they were friends and allies of Tzourillas and were thinking of spending the winter with him,[27] which is as may be. People in the Opsikion theme might label these heretics Phoundagiagitai, but Euthymios thought they were identical with the Bogomils who were to be found not only in the West, but also in the theme of Kibyrraiotai.[28] Included within the boundaries of this theme was the ecclesiastical province of Pamphylia, where the followers of Eleutherios of Paphlagonia were still active. It seems too much of a coincidence for Euthymios to be alluding to a different group.

Euthymios's long account of the Phoundagiagitai reveals that by the time of the Patriarch Alexius the Studite (1025–43) the orthodox church was well aware of the activities of various dissident groups operating in Anatolia. Their inspiration came from a literal understanding of the message of the New Testament, but they found in dualist lore a justification for their attack upon the established church. There is no real need to insist upon any direct connection with the Bulgarian Bogomils.[29] This was a connection that Euthymios and no doubt others made on the basis of certain similarities of outlook and teaching. It is also clear that these dissidents were beginning to penetrate Constantinople, if only in twos and threes.

[25] Ibid., 38.15–22.
[26] Ibid., 37.15–16.
[27] Ibid., 37.7–11.
[28] Ibid., 62.10–13.
[29] It is true that Tzourillas has a Slav ring to the name, but not very much can be made of that.

Heresy in Constantinople[30]

Before the eleventh century heresy had been largely a provincial phenomenon which left the capital untouched. But it was becoming more vulnerable. It was partly that the authorities had less control over the people of the capital, who were a significant political factor from the uprising against Michael V in 1042 until Alexius I Comnenus's coup in 1081. Over that period of some forty years they were hard to discipline. It was a time of ferment intensified by the influx into Constantinople of people of all sorts and conditions, foreigners as well as provincials. The streets of the capital were alive with religious charlatans and exhibitionists, each striving for the attention of an audience and with luck of a patron. The Chiot monks Nicetas and John provide a good example. They came to Constantinople with their Python Dosithea and attracted the support and patronage of the Patriarch Michael Cerularius (1043–58).

The great patrons of holy men were the aristocratic families who were establishing a base for operations in the capital. Alexius Comnenus's mother Anna Dalassena had a string of holy men in her pocket. One of them was Cyril Phileotes. He came to Constantinople to consult a famous monk called Hilarion, who approved of his way of life, though he thought excessive the chains that Cyril sported. Hilarion used him as a go between with Anna Dalassena, who was impressed by him and asked for his blessing. This he gave, predicting a great future for her children. In return, he received money.[31] He hung around the capital, but failed to establish himself. There were others that did.

There was, for example, Neilos who came from Calabria. He was not well educated and his interpretation of the scriptures was simple minded, but, as Anna Comnena remarked, 'having gathered around him a not undistinguished band of followers, he was taken up by great families as a self-appointed teacher, partly because of his apparent virtue and ascetic way of life, partly because of the secret knowledge he was supposed to possess.'[32] His 'secret knowledge' concerned the mystery of *theiosis* or divinisation. He taught that Christ became divine only after his resurrection as a reward for his virtuous life, but just as all humanity was present in the humanity of Christ, so the virtuous Christian could expect divinisation after death. It was an extreme Nestorian position. Neilos refused to accord to the Virgin Mary the title of Mother of God.

This led to debates with representatives of the Armenians of the

[30] In general, D. Gress-Wright, 'Bogomilism in Constantinople', *B* 47(1977), 163–85.
[31] Cyril Phileotes, §16–17, 88–94.
[32] Anna Comnena x, i, 2: II, 187.14–18 (ed.Leib).

capital, who would have found such ideas diametrically opposed to their monophysite creed. Once Neilos's ideas were being openly debated, Alexius had to act and he had him condemned by the patriarchal synod.[33] Neilos was one of many ill-educated holy men peddling half-baked ideas for which there was an eager market in Constantinople; particularly, it would seem, among the great houses of the capital. Not all holy men were poorly educated. Anna Comnena devotes a few lines to Theodore Blakhernites.[34] Despite being an ordained priest he was supposed to have spread Messalian teachings and to have 'undermined some of the great houses in the capital'. He was examined by the emperor and informed of the error of his ways. Since he too refused to reform, he was sent for condemnation by the patriarchal synod. J. Gouillard has been able to show that Blakhernites was more important than the few lines devoted to him by Anna Comnena suggest. He almost certainly belonged to the clergy of the church of the Blakhernai, whence the personal interest that the emperor took in his case. If he was condemned as a Messalian, his ideas were derived directly from the writings of Symeon the New Theologian. There was the same stress on absorption into the Godhead through a trance or vision. Like Symeon, Blakhernites believed this gave the mystic a spiritual authority which set him on a par with the priestly hierarchy.[35] Once again, it shows how thin was the dividing line separating the mystical tradition from heresy.

This is not to say that mysticism gave birth to dualist heresy. It was more that it created a climate which made it an attractive solution to the anxieties of the time. The penultimate decade of the eleventh century was critical for Byzantium. The meaning of Mantzikert was becoming apparent. Constantinople was surrounded on all sides by enemies. Men were beginning to say that God had abandoned Byzantium to its fate.[36] These uncertainties gave greater prominence to mystics and ascetics and fed a thirst for arcane learning. Dualism provided a radical solution. It gave shape and purpose to vague and contradictory ideas. It put a new and heretical gloss on mystical teaching and ascetic behaviour, which previously had seemed harmless enough.

33 I have followed Gouillard, 'Le synodikon de l'orthodoxie', 202–6 rather than N.G. Garsoian, 'L'abjuration du moine Nil de Calabre', *BS* 35(1974), 12–27 who would like Neilos to be a neo-Paulician. His south Italian origin militates against this. She cites the condemnation in the *synodikon* of Orthodoxy of the Bogomils of Panormos, in order to prove the existence of dualism in southern Italy. It has been normal to assume that Panormos refers to Palermo in Sicily, but it is far more likely that it refers to the island of Panormos which was one of the islands in the Propontis, particularly because these islands still had a reputation as a lair of heretics in the mid-twelfth century.

34 Anna Comnena x, i, 6: II, 189.7–18 (ed. Leib).

35 Gouillard, 'Quatre procès de mystiques à Byzance', 19–28.

36 Gautier, 'Diatribes', 23.1–3.

Basil the Bogomil[37]

The man responsible for taking this step at Byzantium was a certain Basil. At the time of his condemnation it was alleged that he had been spreading his heretical teachings for fifty-two years, which would take the beginning of his ministry back to the middle of the eleventh century.[38] Both Anna Comnena and John Zonaras present him as the teacher, instigator, and inspiration behind the Bogomils of Constantinople.[39] He may have been building on dualist ideas that, as we have seen, were already seeping into Constantinople. He is supposed to have studied heretical teachings for fifteen years before he started his ministry.[40] Under cross-examination Basil divulged a single revealing incident from this time of his life. It concerned his acquisition of his copy of the Gospels. He told his inquisitor: 'When I bought this copy of the Gospels I met with an old man in a deserted place. Calling me by name, he told me that I had bought a great treasure, for this book alone escaped the hands of John Phrysostom (for thus do the filthy-mouthed called Chrysostom).'[41] It was widely believed in heretical circles that Chrysostom had doctored the Gospels, thus cutting off Christians from the true faith of the early church. Much of Basil's teaching took the form, ostensibly, of an effort to recover the tenets of the early church through careful study of the New Testament. This was certainly aided by familiarity with various apocryphal texts. These were believed to have escaped falsification by the Fathers of the church. They would have added a dualist dimension to Basil's thought.

Basil was not some uneducated holy man. Anna Comnena may have described him as a monk and he certainly affected a monastic habit, but he was by profession a doctor.[42] We may just catch a glimpse of him at an earlier stage of his life in an anecdote of Michael Psellus. An antique relief roused the curiosity of the court of Constantine X Doukas (1059–67). Somebody called Basil was asked for his opinion. He emphasised the esoteric meaning, which attached to the relief. Psellus countered this with a display of true erudition.[43] He dismissed Basil

37 See D. Obolensky, *The Bogomils* (Cambridge, 1948), 168–229; S. Runciman, *The Medieval Manichee* (Cambridge, 1947), 63–93; M. Loos, *Dualist Heresy in the Middle Ages* (Prague, 1974), 84–95.

38 Ficker, *Phundagiagiten*, 111.1–2; Zonaras, XVIII 23, 21: III, 743.11–13 (ed. Bonn).

39 Anna Comnena XV, viii, 3: III, 219–20 (ed. Leib); Zonaras XVIII 23, 19–22: III, 743.5–13 (ed. Bonn).

40 As n. 38.

41 Migne, *PG*, 130, 1317A–B.

42 Anna Comnena XV, viii, 3: III, 219.20–1 (ed. Leib); Zonaras XVIII, 23, 20: III, 743.9 (ed. Bonn).

43 Psellus (ed. Kurtz/Drexl) II, no.clxxxviii. See G. Dagron, 'Psellos, épigraphiste', in *Okeanos*, ed. Mango and Pritsak (= *Harvard Ukrainian Studies* 7(1983), 117–24).

as a magician. Was he hinting at his opponent's heretical leanings? Bogomils were supposed to refer to themselves as *magi*.[44] If Basil had frequented court circles, it would help to explain an episode that otherwise seems quite bizarre: his interview in private with Alexius I Comnenus and his brother Isaac, when they persuaded him to divulge his beliefs by pretending that they were ready to become his disciples.[45] This suggests that Alexius and his brother were personally acquainted with Basil. The impression of a man who moved in the highest circles is reinforced by Anna Comnena's remark that his teaching 'had penetrated even the greatest houses'.[46]

Basil is presented as having a very large following drawn from all sides, but the hardcore was provided by twelve Apostles and a number of female disciples.[47] This all suggests that, like other holy men, he built up a body of adherents over a period of years. His success must have depended on his willingness to offer still more extreme views, which whatever his original intentions soon developed a distinct dualism. His originality lay in his willingness to create an organisation to propagate his teachings. He presumably took as his model some notion of the early church.

Euthymios Zigabenos provides the most detailed account of Basil's teachings. He first set them out in a tract commissioned by the Emperor Alexius I Comnenus.[48] This provided the basis for the section he devoted to the Bogomils in his *Dogmatike Panoplia*. This too was commissioned by the emperor and contained a general refutation of heresy.[49] Zigabenos's account was based upon a cross-examination of Basil. It reveals three distinct elements to Basil's teachings: a dualist myth; a demonology, and a New Testament ethic. His dualism rested on a version of the fall of Lucifer. He believed that the devil was the elder son of God, but was expelled from heaven for inciting the angels to rebellion. The devil managed, however, to retain possession of the divine power of creation. He was thus able to create first the earth and then Adam, into whom he tried to breathe life, but without success. He therefore turned to God for help, the bargain being that, if God provided his creature with a soul, they would have joint dominion over him. So that he could multiply they created Eve, but the devil became envious, seduced Eve in the shape of a serpent. From that moment he lost his divine powers, but God stayed his anger and allowed him continued rule over whatever he had created since his fall.

44 Migne, *PG* 130.1321C.
45 Anna Comnena xv, viii, 4–5: III, 220–1 (ed. Leib).
46 Ibid. xv, ix, 2: III 224.6–7 (ed. Leib).
47 Ibid. xv, viii, 3: II, 219.22–5 (ed. Leib).
48 Ficker, *Phundagiagiten*, 89–111. See 90.19–22.
49 Migne, *PG* 130.1289–332.

In due course God came to realise the injustice thus done to man. He took pity on the human soul which was His creation. To which end He brought into being another son, whom the Bogomils identified with the Archangel Michael. He came down to earth and entered the Virgin Mary through her right ear. She knew nothing of this, nor of the birth, but just found Christ wrapped in swaddling clothes in the cave beside her. The Bogomils accepted Christ's ministry and his crucifixion, death, and resurrection, but maintained that he only appeared to suffer as a man. He descended into hell, overcame the devil, clapped him in irons and confined him to hell. His mission accomplished he returned to his Father and took the throne on His right side previously occupied by the devil.[50] This presentation of the dualist myth is somewhat inconsequential.[51] It seems a rather lame rationalisation designed to provide a theoretical justification for the ethical teaching of the Bogomils, which emphasised that they were the pure in spirit, while the established church and society were imbued with evil.

The Bogomils saw the forces of evil everywhere at work. Only they had been able to liberate themselves from the demons that infested all other men. Zigabenos questioned Basil very closely on the question of relics of saints and the miracles they produced. Basil replied that 'the demons who taught the saints while living inherit them and remain in their tombs, retain possession of their souls, and perform wonders on their behalf, in order to deceive the foolish and to persuade them to honour the impure as holy'.[52] Zigabenos then asked him why it was that those possessed by demons sought help from the cross. His answer was that the cross was much loved by demons because it had encompassed our Saviour's death.[53] The Bogomils also claimed that churches were infested by demons, each according to rank, so that the devil originally had the church of the Holy Sepulchre at Jerusalem, but then moved to St Sophia in Constantinople.[54]

Zigabenos's treatment of Bogomil beliefs about demons has an immediacy which contrasts with his conventional, if inconsistent, presentation of their myth of the fall. He had cross-examined Basil on his beliefs about demons. His answers were reported in direct speech. As we know, the Byzantines were obsessed by demons and developed a whole lore about them, on which the Bogomils built. Basil told Zigabenos that 'it is written in our Gospels the word of the Lord saying: "Honour the demons, not so that you will benefit from them, but so that they do you no harm."' He then interpreted this to mean

50 Ficker, *Phundagiagiten*, 91–4.
51 Cf. Loos, *Dualist Heresy*, 84–95.
52 Migne, *PG*, 130. 1309B; Ficker, *Phundagiagiten*, 99–100.
53 Migne, *PG* 130. 1312B; Ficker, *Phundagiagiten*, 99.24–27.
54 Migne, *PG* 130. 1313D; Ficker, *Phundagiagiten*, 96.19–28.

that it was necessary to honour the demons who inhabited churches, for neither Christ nor the Holy Ghost could prevail against them because God tolerates their dominion over the whole world until its ending – which does not quite square with Zigabenos's exposition of the Bogomil myth![55] The inconsistency is likely to be an accurate reflection of Basil's ideas and of a failure to weld the different strands of his thought into a coherent whole.

To avoid the harm the demons could do, people had to show them due reverence, 'flattering them by partaking of the sacrifices ministered by them and by worship of the material icons, which things are raised up in their honour'.[56] Basil was referring to communion and the veneration of the icons, both of which the Bogomils rejected, as belonging to the material world and therefore the work of the devil. Also rejected were all the sacraments of the orthodox church, along with the liturgy and the veneration of the cross and relics.

Their alienation from orthodox society is apparent from their rejection of marriage, in support of which they cited Matthew 22.30: 'For in the resurrection they neither marry nor are given in marriage.'[57] Their attack on the orthodox church was firmly anchored in the New Testament: 'Beware of false prophets' was taken to refer to the Cappadocian Fathers and John Chrysostom, who provided the foundations of orthodox teaching.[58] In contrast, it was like 'Casting pearls before swine' for a Bogomil to reveal his beliefs to an orthodox Christian,[59] to which was added a further gloss: those that came for instruction were treated as if they were dogs or swine. They had first to be purged by fasting and prayer as a preliminary to their initiation into the sect.

The Bogomils kept their ceremonies and institutions to a minimum. They took the text: 'But thou, when thou prayest, enter into thy closet' (Matthew 6.6), as a prohibition against entering a church to pray.[60] Their only prayer was the Lord's prayer, which they repeated seven times a day and five times at night with constant genuflexions.[61] They likened themselves to the wise man who built his house upon a rock which they identified with the Lord's prayer.[62] They fasted every Monday, Thursday, and Friday until the ninth hour.[63] They wore monks' robes, which, to Zigabenos's mind, was designed to deceive the

55 Migne, *PG* 130. 1316C; Ficker, *Phundagiagiten*, 97.21–34.
56 Ficker, *Phundagiagiten*, 97.24–7.
57 Migne, *PG* 130. 1325D; Ficker, *Phundagiagiten*, 106–7.
58 Migne, *PG* 130. 1328D; Ficker, *Phundagiagiten*, 108.8–14.
59 Migne, *PG* 130. 1328B; Ficker, *Phundagiagiten*, 107–8.
60 Migne, *PG* 130. 1328B; Ficker, *Phundagiagiten*, 107.14–18.
61 Migne, *PG* 130. 1313–16; Ficker, *Phundagiagiten*, 100.21–7.
62 Migne, *PG* 130. 1329A-B; Ficker, *Phundagiagiten*, 108.27–32.
63 Migne, *PG* 130. 1320C-D; Ficker, *Phundagiagiten*, 101.30–4.

unwary,[64] but may only have been emblematic of their piety. Initiation into the sect began with a period of confession, continence, and prayer, then the Gospel of St John was placed on the neophyte's head, the Holy Ghost was invoked and the Lord's prayer intoned. He or she then went into retreat, after which there was an examination. If the members of the community, male and female, were satisfied as to the candidate's fitness, they would complete the initiation by once again placing the Gospel on his or her head and chanting a hymn of thanksgiving.[65]

Anna Comnena suggests that Basil surrounded himself with twelve 'Apostles' who were responsible for spreading his teachings.[66] Zigabenos does not specifically mention them. Instead he indicates the existence of an elite among the Bogomils known as Theotokoi who were equally teachers. They must be identical with Anna Comnena's 'Apostles'. They were the most godly members of the community. The Holy Spirit was held to dwell in them. They were called Theotokoi – bringers forth of God – because having the word of God within them they gave birth to it through their teaching. These people were supposed not to die, but to be transported in their sleep to the kingdom of heaven – after the manner of the Mother of God, the Theotokos. Their discarded bodies dissolved into dust and ashes.[67]

The Bogomils claimed to be the true Christians. They believed that the Sermon on the Mount was directed to them: they were the poor in spirit; the Beatitudes applied exclusively to them.[68] The orthodox were by contrast like the Scribes and Pharisees and would not enter the kingdom of heaven. This comparison rested on the assumption that the orthodox had received an education (*grammatike paideusis*) and took an overweening pride in the fact.[69] This identification of education and orthodoxy reflected a view that the orthodox church was the preserve of a small, highly educated elite, which denied the word of God to society at large. Bogomils were reluctant to accept into their number anybody with an education. They cited in justification the example of Christ who had turned away the Scribe.[70]

The Bogomils' sense of community was founded on a passionate devotion to the New Testament. They revered the New Testament, but rejected the Old Testament, with the exception of the Psalms and Prophets, which foretold the coming of Christ.[71] Basil was capable of deploying a deep knowledge of the New Testament very skilfully.

64 Migne, *PG* 130. 1320C; Ficker, *Phundagiagiten*, 101.8–12.
65 Migne, *PG* 130. 1312C-D; Ficker, *Phundagiagiten*, 100–1.
66 Anna Comnena XV, viii, 3; ix, 2: III, 219.22, 224.4 (ed. Leib).
67 Migne, *PG* 130, 1317C-D; Ficker, *Phundagiagiten*, 100–1.
68 Migne, *PG* 130, 1325A; Ficker, *Phundagiagiten*, 105.27–33.
69 Migne, *PG* 130, 1325C; Ficker, *Phundagiagiten*, 106.11–18.
70 Migne, *PG* 130, 1329B.
71 Migne, *PG* 130, 1292B; Ficker, *Phundagiagiten*, 98.10–20.

Zigabenos confronted him with the usual charge that he hid his true beliefs under the guise of orthodox piety. Basil cited in defence of this hypocrisy the words of Christ himself: 'All therefore whatsoever they bid you observe, *that* observe and do; but do not ye after their works.' (Matthew 23.3). It was his contention that Christ too had been forced to dissemble.[72] Once again he was able to justify his behaviour by the example set by Christ himself. Zigabenos was not quite able to hide his discomfiture.

We are forced to rely almost entirely for our knowledge of the Bogomils of Constantinople on the account provided by Euthymios Zigabenos. We have to take his information on trust. This is perhaps the easier to do because Zigabenos's treatment is based upon his cross-examination of the Bogomil leader, which at different points comes to the surface. Basil emerges as a formidable opponent. He had created a community and an ethic which looked back to the Apostolic church. He believed that he had recovered the true faith which had been distorted by the Fathers of the church. Orthodoxy as an institution was rejected as evil. Churches were the haunt of demons. There were various strands to Bogomil belief. This produced inconsistencies. Basil was not able to create an entirely coherent body of thought. This can produce difficulties for the modern historian. Milan Loos first subscribed to the proposition that Bogomil beliefs were controlled by a dualist theology and were not a mere rationalisation of confused and basic ideas.[73] He later preferred to see them as representing a broad popular strand of ideas, but failed to make clear whether these were dualist or something else.[74]

It is quite impossible to retrieve the stages of Basil's religious development, beyond noting, as we have already done, that there were three distinct strands to his thought: a dualist myth; a demonology, and a New Testament ethic. Dualism was scarcely an integrating, let alone a controlling, force. At best, it provided a weak rationalisation for a world in which a community of the pure in heart struggled against an evil and unjust society. But dualism followed the grain of Byzantine dissent, which stemmed from the obvious contrast between a hierarchical church and society and the ideal of the early church. The one, unlike the other, offered almost no sense of community.

This conflict at the very heart of Christianity was eased by monasticism, which in its way maintained the ideal of the early church and provided its members with a strong sense of community. There was, as we have seen, much that was dualist about the monastic and

72 Migne, *PG* 130, 1317A.

73 M. Loos, 'Certains aspects du bogomilisme byzantin des 11e et 12e siècles', *BS* 28(1967), 39–53 at 47.

74 Loos, *Dualist Heresy*, 87–9.

ascetic ideal. There was a struggle between good and evil; there was a contrast of body and soul. Monasticism at Byzantium was impressively flexible and furnished almost any group with an ideal and a pattern of organisation. It also provided camouflage. The Bogomils just like other groups before them adopted some of the outward features of monasticism, but they remained lay communities. They were giving expression to a lay piety that found its inspiration in the New Testament and equated orthodox society with the Scribes and the Pharisees. Dualism was the obvious theological concomitant to such a stance. Recourse to dualism must have been all the easier for the recollections there were of dualist traditions. Various apocrypha and perhaps other writings continued to circulate. They constituted a corpus of arcane knowledge, mastery of which contributed to the charisma of a dissident religious leader. This body of heterogeneous beliefs was often labelled Euchite by orthodox theologians, but increasingly the term Bogomil was preferred. This does not mean that Basil's followers referred to themselves as Bogomils, which was a slur word. It is quite conceivable – in the light both of their devotion to the Sermon on the Mount and of later developments in the West[75] - that they liked to think of themselves as the pure in spirit (*katharoi te(i) kardia(i)*). Basil is perhaps a more important figure than is usually allowed. Sir Dimitri Obolensky observed long ago that he altered the quality of dualist belief by applying a more rational and allegorical approach.[76] But his contribution went further than this. Before him dualist heresy had been a provincial phenomenon. He refashioned it to suit metropolitan expectations and revived its evangelical ambitions. At a time of great uncertainty his teachings must have had their attractions; and not only to the capital's poor and uneducated. There is no way of telling the size of Basil's following. But it was sufficient to worry Alexius I Comnenus.

The trial of Basil the Bogomil

Exactly when Alexius I Comnenus proceeded against Basil is never made clear by Anna Comnena. She conveniently leaves a lacuna where the date of the affair should have been. She includes the episode at the very end of her history as a prelude to her father's last illness and death. However, Basil's condemnation has to be before 1111 because the Patriarch Nicholas Grammatikos (1084–1111) was party to it. Basil's initial examination can be dated even earlier. It must be before 1104, the last possible date for the death of Alexius Comnenus's brother, the

[75] See below, pp. 491–3.
[76] Obolensky, *Bogomils*, 218–19.

sebastokrator Isaac, who played a major part in the examination.[77] The historian Zonaras places the event after the passage of the first crusade.[78] There was an interval, the length of which is never indicated, between Basil's initial examination and his final condemnation to the pyre. After his original confession he was confined in a house close to the imperial palace,[79] while his supporters were being rounded up. They were condemned to be burnt by an assembly presided over by the emperor. Pyres were lit, but the sentence was not carried out because of the hostility of the crowd. This must be a sign that Basil and his followers enjoyed popular support. The majority were then released, on the surely spurious grounds that they had shown themselves to be orthodox by going to the pyre with a cross. Others were put in prison, but Basil's Apostles were kept apart. Efforts were then made by church leaders, and even by the emperor himself, to instruct them and show them the error of their ways. Throughout this Basil stood firm. It seems to have been the Patriarch Nicholas at the head of the synod who finally took the decision to have him burnt. The emperor gave his assent. Basil was burnt in the Hippodrome. His close supporters were incarcerated and duly died.[80] The whole episode could easily have been drawn out over several years.

The authorities sought to discredit Basil's claims that he would not die, but, as a Theotokos, would ascend to heaven in a trance. Zigabenos provides the official account. After his condemnation Basil was subjected to torture. He realised that he had been deceived. His followers were suffering in prison despite the promises made to him by the emperor. They accused him of betrayal. It was this that broke Basil. Hardly able to stand, he was taken out into the Hippodrome and bundled on to the waiting pyre.[81] Zigabenos is all the more plausible for the way he tells a story discreditable to Alexius Comnenus so ingenuously. Anna Comnena's account written forty years or more after the event is more fanciful. Basil was defiant to the end. The public executioners were worried that some kind of miracle would take place. They threw his cloak on to the fire. Basil is supposed to have said, 'Look! My cloak flies up to the sky!' Just as his soul would, that was the unspoken assumption. The executioners threw him on the pyre and he was entirely consumed. There was just one thin line of smoke in the middle of the flame.[82] Comparing the two accounts, it is difficult not to conclude that Basil's death by burning was soon embroidered

77 Varzos I, 78.
78 Zonaras XVIII 23, 19; III, 743.5–6 (ed. Bonn).
79 Anna Comnena XV, viii, 6–7: III, 221–3 (ed. Leib).
80 Anna Comnena XV, 10, 3–4: III, 227–8 (ed. Leib).
81 Ficker, *Phundagiagiten*, 110–11.
82 Anna Comnena XV, 10, 4: III, 228, 3–4 (ed. Leib).

into legend. The details preserved by Anna Comnena also suggest that it might easily have become the subject of a Bogomil myth. Presented slightly differently there are all the elements needed for the ascent of a Theotokos.

The execution of Basil is unlikely to have ended the Bogomil threat. In 1107 Alexius I Comnenus promulgated his edict for the reform of the clergy. There are hints that it was issued in the aftermath of Basil's execution. The edict contained measures clearly directed against a continuing problem of heresy in the capital. It created an order of preachers attached to the patriarchal church. Their main purpose was to supervise the moral and religious life of the different neighbourhoods of Constantinople. They were to ensure that the people recognised them as their spiritual fathers, 'so that instead of wolves there were shepherds receiving the inner thoughts of men'.[83] 'Wolves' was a conventional way of referring to heretics and at this time to Bogomils, in particular. The emperor was also concerned at the spiritual dangers there were from vagrant monks frequenting the alleys and meeting points of the capital.[84]

The Chrysomallos affair

The Bogomils were constantly being accused of disguising themselves as monks the more easily to deceive the unwary. Alexius Comnenus presents the creation of an order of preachers as designed to meet an insidious but unspecified threat to Christian order and belief.[85] This is most likely to have been the continuing menace of the Bogomils. Alexius was only building on the work of the Patriarch Nicholas Grammatikos. Soon after his accession in 1084 the patriarch began to recruit a body of preachers who had the specific task of protecting the people of Constantinople from heresy. This was in his eulogist's opinion the patriarch's major achievement. It is difficult to imagine that there would have been two separate orders of preachers, both attached to the patriarchal church. It is therefore more than likely that the creation of an order of preachers was essentially the work of the patriarch, though later receiving imperial approval.[86] It indicates how seriously the threat from heresy was taken. Emperor and patriarch both perceived a continuing threat to orthodoxy on the streets of Constantinople still existing in the years following the condemnation of Basil the Bogomil.

The order of preachers leaves almost no trace in the later sources.

83 Gautier, 'L'édit d'Alexis Ier Comnène', 193.235–6.
84 Meyer, *Die Haupturkunden*, 172.20–4.
85 Gautier, 'L'édit d'Alexis Ier Comnène', 179–83.
86 Darrouzès, 'L'éloge de Nicholas III', 53.689–95.

Once the perceived threat had disappeared, it was presumably diverted to other ends; teaching most obviously. It was not until towards the end of the Emperor John II Comnenus's reign that there was another Bogomil scare. In May 1140 one Constantine Chrysomallos was condemned posthumously. He had died sometime before in the monastery of Kyr Nicholas. Some monks of the monastery went through his papers and found scandalous material which, they claimed, had circulated among his followers. Further enquiries revealed the existence of other copies. There was one in the possession of the abbot of the monastery of St Athenogenes; another belonged to a George Pamphilos, who held the rank of *proedros* and was therefore a man of some consequence. The monks who made the original denunciation produced another copy which they said had come from a monk of the Gerokomeion.

Chrysomallos's writings took the form of 'Centuries' – that is a series of short chapters; in this case, some 250 all told. They were deemed to contain Bogomil and Messalian tenets. The synod concentrated on their rejection of baptism. Chrysomallos contended that nobody became a true Christian, however high they might rise in the ecclesiastical hierarchy, through baptism alone, for it could not deliver anybody from the power of Satan. This could only be achieved by initiation 'through the intervention and the laying on hands of the overseers of this great mystery and of the experts in sacred knowledge'. These 'overseers' and 'experts' were spiritual adepts. All was in vain – repentance and confession, unless you had thus been filled with the gifts of the Holy Ghost. The synod judged this stress on spiritual illumination to be Messalian, while the initiation ceremony was Bogomil. The manuscripts containing Chrysomallos's writings were to be burnt and all those adhering to his teachings were to be anathematised. Nobody was to preach without the authorisation of the church and new works had first to be approved by the church. The abbot and the *proedros* Pamphilos were cleared of adhering to Chrysomallos's teachings and showed themselves truly penitent, claiming that they had been victims of their ignorance and their tender regard for Chrysomallos. Even so, the abbot was removed from his monastery and sent to another to receive instruction.[87]

And there we might have been content to leave it – an enigmatic episode without any clear significance – were it not for Theodore Balsamon's commentary on canon 60 of the 'Apostolic Canons'. There he labelled Pamphilos a heretic and accused him of circulating Chrysomallos's heretical works as orthodox under the title of 'Golden Maxims of Theology'.[88] J. Gouillard noticed that a tract attributed to

[87] Rhalles & Potles v, 76–82; Grumel, 1007; Gouillard, 'Quatre procès de mystiques à Byzance', 56–67.

[88] Rhalles & Potles II, 78.

Chrysomallos, entitled, 'Nobody can be saved, unless he has first acquired humility' was almost identical with Discourse VIII of Symeon the New Theologian. Gouillard therefore proposed that after the trial Pamphilos circulated Chrysomallos's works along with the Discourses of Symeon the New Theologian, but the better to disguise them he altered their literary form from centuries to homilies. Against this argument is the wording of the title given to Chrysomallos's works: Maxims (ἔπη). This applies much better to the centuries or short chapters that we know Chrysomallos composed than it does to homilies, but there is no reason why Chrysomallos should not also have been the author of homilies. In favour of this is the doubtful authenticity of many of Symeon's Discourses. Gouillard notes that his Discourse XIII starts with the statement that the devil has been at work for 6,600 years or more. This would give a date after 1091/2 and could not be the work of Symeon.

In any case, the Discourses appear to represent more a tradition of mystical thought inspired by Symeon, rather than necessarily works by him. A large number of the Discourses has been attributed to Symeon's spiritual heir Nicetas Stethatos. This strengthens the possibility that Chrysomallos also contributed to the corpus, but how many of the Discourses should be attributed to Chrysomallos remains problematical; only Discourse VIII can be with any confidence. Gouillard nevertheless demonstrates the striking similarities – sometimes word for word – between the propositions extracted from Chrysomallos's writings by the synod and passages from the Discourses attributed to Symeon. This does not mean that these Discourses must therefore have been the work of Chrysomallos. It is more likely that Chrysomallos was drawing on a tradition inspired by Symeon. This emerges most clearly in their agreement on the necessity of the baptism of the spirit at the hands of a spiritual father. Gouillard notes another point in common: a stress on the baptism of the spirit did not mean that either Chrysomallos or Symeon rejected baptism, as such. A spiritual baptism was a way of restoring the validity of the original baptism. Gouillard would like Chrysomallos to be a follower of St Symeon and not tainted by heretical teachings.[89]

There is certainly nothing to connect him with Basil and the Bogomils. Chrysomallos is never accused, for example, of subscribing to the dualist myth. There were, however, elements of incipient dualism in his thought. He claimed that the true Christian possessed two souls: one sinful and the other without sin. Anyone possessing but a single

89 J. Gouillard, 'Constantin Chrysomallos sous le masque de Syméon le Nouveau Théologien', *TM* 5(1973) 313–27; Gouillard, 'Quatre procès de mystiques à Byzance', 29–39.

soul, could not lay claim to the name of a true Christian. This is so inconvenient for Gouillard's argument that he is reluctant to accept that this could be part of his thought, but Chrysomallos also subscribed to another typically Bogomil view. He maintained that respect for the authorities was tantamount to adoring Satan. Gouillard is willing to accept that such a view might have its roots in Symeon's thought. As has already been suggested, Symeon's mysticism taken to extremes easily spilled over into dualism and was one of the strands contributing to a heterogeneous body of belief which came to be labelled Bogomil.

There is something sinister about Chrysomallos, that is reminiscent of Basil the Bogomil. He was clearly a teacher who had built up a group of devoted followers both in the monasteries of Constantinople and outside. They included men of high rank. He seems to have been neither a monk nor a priest, though he ended his days in a monastery. Other religious leaders of the time were normally drawn from the ranks of the monks and clergy, while he was a layman. His activity, like that of Basil, lay outside the established church and was for that reason alone suspect. He was critical of orthodoxy and authority. His teachings almost inevitably acquired a dualist tinge.

His starting point seems to have been the mystical tradition associated with Symeon the New Theologian, which sets him apart from Basil the Bogomil, for the latter showed no interest in the possibilities of mysticism as a vehicle for the criticism of the contemporary order. Basil's disquiet was founded on the ethic of the New Testament. Whatever its origins and inspiration dualism continued to have an appeal in Constantinople. Among its attractions was the outlet it provided for lay piety and the basis it supplied for criticism of the established church, at a time when the latter was becoming increasingly hierarchical in its attitudes and institutions. It may not just be a coincidence, as Paul Magdalino had recently observed, that the patriarchal synod seems to have been the moving force behind Chrysomallos's posthumous condemnation. Its main aim was 'to deter others from writing and teaching on their own authority'.[90]

The Cathar mission

The posthumous condemnation of Constantine Chrysomallos was not the end of this Bogomil scare. Under the Patriarch Michael the Oxite (1143–6) synod condemned various Bogomils to be burnt because of their obduracy.[91] A famous holy man and a pious bishop of Elaia

90 Magdalino, *Manuel I Komnenos*, 276 .
91 Rhalles & Potles I, 191; Grumel, 1020.

came under suspicion of being Bogomils, because of their extreme asceticism and addiction to fasting. They had to clear themselves by eating eggs and cheese before synod.[92] In 1143 two Cappadocian bishops were condemned by synod on charges of Bogomilism, of which they were almost certainly innocent. At best, they were guilty of irregularities, such as ordaining deaconesses and allowing them to take over the functions of deacons, and of entertaining notions, such as the conviction that the monastic state had a monopoly of salvation, but this may in part be explained by their remoteness from Constantinople. Religious observances on the fringes of the Byzantine Empire were often erratic,[93] but the prevailing fear of heresy meant that they might easily be construed as Bogomil practices. The bishops were condemned to solitary confinement to allow them to meditate on the error of their ways, but more immediately to isolate them from their supporters.[94] These included the monk Niphon who had already acquired a considerable reputation for holiness. He was confined in the Constantinopolitan monastery of the Peribleptos, but continued to insist that the Cappadocian bishops were orthodox. His obduracy led to condemnation in 1144 as a Bogomil.[95] The next Patriarch Cosmas Atticus (1146–7) was one of Niphon's supporters and had him released. This incidentally gave the patriarch's opponents a case against him: for consorting with a convicted heretic. Cosmas insisted that Niphon was orthodox. There were strong political undercurrents to the episode.[96] This might suggest that the charges of Bogomilism were political in origin and that the Bogomil scare had no substance to it. This would be a tempting solution, were it not for clear evidence from a completely different quarter that at this juncture Bogomils were still active.

Thanks to recent work, above all, that of Bernard Hamilton, there seems to be no doubt not only that the Cathar heresy of western Europe was an offshoot of Bogomilism, but also that close contacts continued to exist between the Bogomils and the Cathars. The first intimations of the penetration of Bogomil ideas into the West come in a letter of 1143 of the prior of Steinfeld in the Rhineland to St Bernard of Clairvaux. He wanted guidance about new heretics who had recently made their appearance at Cologne. At their head were a bishop and his companion claiming to be the heirs of a secret tradition going back to the time of the martyrs, 'which had been preserved in Greece and certain other lands'.

92 Rhalles & Potles II, 68.

93 Ibid., 370, 463.

94 Ibid. V, 85–7; Grumel, 1012; Gouillard, 'Quatre procès de mystiques à Byzance', 39–43, 68–81.

95 Rhalles & Potles V, 88–91; Grumel, 1013, 1015.

96 See above, pp. 78–9, and Magdalino, *Manuel I Komnenos*, 277–80.

They called themselves Apostles and had their own pope.[97] From the Rhineland the heresy spread to Languedoc.

It was around Toulouse that it put down its deepest roots. The prelates of the region soon awoke to the dangers, but found themselves openly defied by the heretics at an assembly that met at Lombers in 1165.[98] This was followed by the mission to the Cathars by the Bogomil Papa Niquinta or Nicetas, either in 1167 or a few years later.[99] He presided over an assembly of the leading Cathars of Languedoc and further afield held at Saint-Felix de Caraman.[100] Representatives of the following Cathar communities were present: France, Lombardy, Albi, Carcassone, and Aran. Nicetas acted on behalf of the Cathar community of Toulouse. He consecrated new bishops for Toulouse, Carcasonne, and Aran and confirmed in office those for France, Lombardy, and Albi. He renewed their initiation into the 'church' through the ministration of the *consolamentum* or laying on of hands. This was necessary because these communities had previously followed the rituals of the Bogomil 'church' of Bulgaria, while Nicetas was the head of the 'church' of Drugunthia. His church subscribed to an absolute dualism of 'two Gods or Lords without beginning and without end, the one good and the other bad', while the 'church' of Bulgaria believed in 'a single omnipotent "good" God without beginning, who created the angels and the four elements'. It was the visible world alone that Satan created and dominated, but only through divine forbearance.[101]

Like any good Christians these heretics wanted to ensure that they were following the correct teaching. There was also the more practical question of the organisation of the different 'churches' or communities. Nicetas was asked about the practice of the primitive church as to the boundaries of the different communities. He assured his audience 'that the seven churches of Asia were distinct and separate and that they did nothing in any way contradictory to another'. They should be guided by the example of the Bogomil 'churches' in the East, namely Romania, Drugunthia, Melenguia, Bulgaria, and Dalmatia. They each had distinct boundaries, but acted in harmony, thus preserving the ideal of the early

97 R.I. Moore, *The Origins of European Dissent* (Oxford, 1977), 168–96; H.-C. Puech, *Sur le Manichéisme* (Paris, 1979), 395–427; Loos, *Dualist Heresy*, 103–61.

98 W.L. Wakefield and A.P. Evans, *Heresies of the High Middle Ages* (Records of Civilization LXXXI) (New York, 1969), no. 28, 189–94.

99 D. Obolensky, 'Papa Nicetas: a Byzantine dualist in the land of the Cathars', in *Okeanos* ed. Mango and Pritsak (= *Harvard Ukrainian Studies*, 7(1983), 489–500).

100 B. Hamilton, *Monastic Reform, Catharism, and the Crusades 900–1300* (London, 1979), no. IX, where he demonstrates the authenticity of the documents relating to this Cathar council.

101 Wakefield and Evans, *Heresies*, 159–67.

church. The representatives of the Cathar communities in Languedoc then proceeded to establish clear diocesan boundaries.[102]

This evidence for the active participation of Bogomils from Byzantium in the affairs of the Cathar communities of southern France can be supplemented with information about those of Lombardy. The original community was headed by a certain Mark and followed the rituals and teaching of the 'church' of Bulgaria. These were challenged by Papa Nicetas who was visiting Lombardy and Mark and his followers accepted those of Nicetas's church of Drugunthia. Some years later a representative of the Bulgarian Bogomils came to Lombardy and cast doubts on the validity of Nicetas's consecration. He had a story that the 'bishop' of Drugunthia, from whom Nicetas's consecration had stemmed, had once been found with a woman in his room. This caused the Cathars of Lombardy to split up into a series of communities, each seeking consecration from the various Bogomil 'churches' of the East.[103]

The image that emerges of the Bogomils from western sources is at variance with the impressions left by the Byzantine sources. They appear to be well organised, divided up into a series of 'churches' which took as their model the seven churches of Asia. At their head were 'bishops', each with a helper who would in the normal course of events succeed. Although harmony was supposed to prevail among the different 'churches', one of them, the church of Drugunthia had developed a more rigorous dualist theology, which was a source of tension, certainly among the Cathar communities in the West, and presumably in the East too.

The list of Bogomil churches given by Papa Nicetas has aroused great interest and efforts have been made to identify them. The 'churches' of Romania, Bulgaria, and Dalmatia present few problems. Romania is clearly Constantinople; Bulgaria is slightly more difficult, but it is more likely to refer to modern Macedonia than modern Bulgaria, because Ohrid was the centre of the Bulgarian church.[104] Dalmatia is usually referred to in western sources as Sclavonia. Melenguia has always been a problem. Modern scholars have been rather enthusiastic about identifying it with the Slav tribe of the Melings who continued to occupy the Taygetos range in the Peloponnese. However, there is no evidence to connect this tribe with heresy. This identification therefore

[102] E. Peters, *Heresy and Authority in Medieval Europe* (Philadelphia, 1980), no.19, 121–3.

[103] Wakefield and Evans, *Heresies*, 159–67.

[104] It may not just be a coincidence that Adrian Comnenus, the archbishop of Bulgaria, had a prominent part to play in the condemnation of the two Cappadocian bishops as Bogomils.

seems less plausible than the old one with the town of Melnik, which was one of the more important centres of the southern Balkans in this period.[105]

That leaves Drugunthia.[106] It is usual to derive it from the name of a Slav tribe called the Drougoubitai and to place the 'church' either in Macedonia where they are first attested or in Thrace, where they are supposed to have later settled.[107] Speculation runs riot, but there is another possibility worth considering, which at least has the merit of dealing in facts. The Salonican historian John Cameniates places the Drougoubitai to the west of Thessalonica, in what would become by the twelfth century the theme of Moglena.[108] Bishop of Moglena from *c.* 1134 until his death in 1164 was St Hilarion. He was remembered for his work among the Bogomils of the region. They stoned him unconscious on one occasion, but he refused to let the people of Moglena take their revenge on them. He visited Constantinople. He had heard a rumour that the Emperor Manuel I Comnenus might convert to the Bogomil faith. It proved unfounded. The emperor encouraged him in his efforts against heresy in his diocese. These were capped by his foundation of a church dedicated to the Holy Apostles on the spot where the heretics used to hold their prayer meetings.[109]

The activities of St Hilarion therefore make it very tempting to locate the 'church' of Drugunthia in the region of Moglena. One of the reasons that has deterred scholars from making this identification is that, although Nicetas was 'bishop' of Drugunthia, he was based in Constantinople. This has persuaded scholars that Drugunthia must have been located within easy distance of the capital. A possible explanation for Nicetas's presence in Constantinople was that he was forced to seek refuge there to evade the attentions of St Hilarion. And who would have been in a better position to undertake a mission to the West or who would have been more eager to recoup his losses than a Bogomil 'bishop' who had been driven from his 'see'?

A peculiarity of the 'church' of Drugunthia was its rigorist dualist theology. The Bogomils, whether in Bulgaria in the tenth century or at Constantinople at the turn of the eleventh, had never subscribed to absolute dualism. It has been argued above that their dualism was at

105 Acropolites I, 77–8.

106 It also appears in the western sources as Drogometia and Dugunthia.

107 Obolensky, 'Papa Nicetas', 491–2.

108 John Cameniates, *De Expugnatione Thessalonicae*, ed. G. Böhlig (Berlin and New York, 1973), 7–8. See A. Kazhdan, 'Some questions addressed to the scholars who believe in the authenticity of Kameniates' "Capture of Thessalonica"', *BZ* 71(1978), 301–14; P. Gautier, 'Clement d'Ohrid, évêque de Dragvista', REB 22(1964), 199–214.

109 Turdeanu, *La littérature bulgare*, 82–3; Angelov, *Les Balkans au moyen âge*. IIa, 27.

best superficial and by all accounts continued to be so. The temptation has been to trace the dualism of the 'church' of Drugunthia back to the Paulicians of Philippopolis; even to identify the two. This was an additional reason for wishing to locate the 'church' of Drugunthia in Thrace, where the Paulicians were settled.[110] The Paulicians certainly espoused absolute dualism, but their military ethos set them apart from the Bogomils. Though a Paulician community continued to exist at Philippopolis down to the eighteenth century, it seems to have kept itself very much to itself. Its loss of dynamism can perhaps be traced back to its treatment at the hands of Alexius I Comnenus.[111]

There is no evidence of absolute dualism among the Bogomils until Nicetas's mission to the West. Bernard Hamilton therefore suggests very reasonably that the adoption of this teaching by the 'church' of Drugunthia must have been very recent,[112] but the circumstances elude us. There may have been some kind of Paulician influence; it may just have been a natural development; it might have been a reaction to the challenge of the mission field, which had been a preserve of the 'church' of Bulgaria until Nicetas's visit to the West. Bernard Hamilton also proposes a Paulician background to Nicetas's understanding of the seven churches of Asia, for they too provided the inspiration for the organisation of the Paulician communities.[113] As long as this is not taken to mean that the Bogomils borrowed their organisation directly from the Paulicians, there is much to be said in favour of this view. Both the Paulicians and the Bogomils looked back to the early church as a model and an ideal. Nicetas only includes five Bogomil 'churches' in his list, all in the European provinces of the Byzantine Empire. In addition, there is good evidence for a Bogomil 'church' centred on Philadelphia in western Asia Minor.[114]

The Bogomil scare

Taking the western evidence into account, the Bogomil scare at Constantinople in the early 1140s appears justified. The authorities may have tried some of the wrong men, but the Bogomils would appear to have organised themselves into distinct communities in the preceding years, continuing the work begun by Basil the Bogomil and his Apostles. There is good evidence of the Bogomils spreading out into the European provinces. The *Life* of St Hilarion provides evidence for Bogomil activity

110 Sir Dimitri Obolensky was once inclined to accept this identification, but now rejects it: Obolensky, 'Papas Nicetas', 496–7.
111 Anna Comnena XIV, viii, 1–9: III, 177–82 (ed. Leib).
112 Hamilton, *Monastic Reform*, no. VII.
113 Hamilton, 'The Cathars and the seven churches of Asia', *BF* 13 (1989), 269–95.
114 Wakefield and Evans, *Heresies*, 337.

in the area to the west of Thessalonica in the mid-twelfth century. There is no sign of the Bogomils operating in that region in the eleventh century. John Tzetzes introduces us to a defrocked priest from Adrianople who was condemned as a heretic under the Patriarch Michael the Oxite and narrowly escaped being consigned to the flames, which was the fate of others at this time.[115] Michael Italikos complained that his see of Philippopolis was infested with heretics. Theodore Prodromos sympathised with him but was sure that he would be able to deal with them.[116] The fight against heresy continued under the Patriarch Michael Ankhialos' (1170–8). Eustathius of Thessalonica congratulated the patriarch on his success and graphically sketched a scene he had witnessed of heretics recanting.[117] Bogomils were still present in Macedonia in the mid-thirteenth century. We have the testimony of one of the officers of the Patriarch Arsenius (1254–60), who had been sent to discipline them.[118]

There is therefore reasonably good evidence both for the spread of the Bogomil heresy in the southern Balkans over the early twelfth century and for the efforts made by patriarchs and prelates to eradicate it from the 1140s onwards. This makes it less easy to dismiss as fantastical the information about heresy contained in the dialogue entitled *Timotheos or about Demons.* This has traditionally been ascribed to Michael Psellus, but its most recent editor, the late Paul Gautier, is unwilling to accept this attribution, in part because the oldest manuscript tradition has no such attribution. There is another consideration: this dialogue forms an integral part of a series of dialogues involving a character called the Thracian. The last of the dialogues has him being cross-questioned by a bishop of Methone. This bishop is in all probability to be identified with Nicholas of Methone, a major theologian of the mid-twelfth century. Apart from St Athanasius, who was bishop of Methone in the mid-ninth century, Nicholas was the only holder of the see of any distinction. In the dialogue the bishop of Methone complains of the sad state of his see. Nicholas of Methone did exactly the same at a council held at Constantinople in 1157. There is therefore a distinct possibility that *Timotheos* was his work. The choice of the dialogue form also points to the mid years of the twelfth century, since it was especially popular at that time among writers associated with the imperial court.[119]

115 Tzetzes I, 75–7.

116 Browning, *Studies on Byzantine History*, no. VI.

117 A.P. Kazhdan, 'Novye materialy o bogomilakh (?) v Vizantii XII v.', *Byzantino-Bulgarica* 2(1966), 275–6.

118 J. Darrouzès, 'Des notes marginales du Vindobonensis Historicus Graecus 70', *REB* 45(1987), 59–75, at 71.

119 Gautier, 'Le *De Daemonibus* du Pseudo-Psellos', 105–94: text 134–94.

The Thracian begins by explaining that he has been away from Constantinople for two years and more on an assignment against heretics, who he calls Euchites and Enthusiasts.[120] This was a polite way of referring to the Bogomils. Timotheos was agog to know all about them. The Thracian was at first coy about giving details, but, paraphrasing Euthymios Zigabenos, Timotheos remarked that just as doctors found it useful to be able to recognise harmful drugs, so knowledge of noxious beliefs might have advantages.[121] The Thracian saw the force of this argument and began by tracing the heresy back to Mani. But its adherents were not strict dualists. They believed instead in a trinity of powers. They assigned transcendental authority to God the Father; dominion over the heavens to God's younger son and power over this world to His elder son.[122] This is incidentally a very fair statement of the moderate dualism that was professed by Basil the Bogomil. It must also have accorded with a very general belief about the continuing struggle between Christ and the devil. According to the Thracian some of the heretics worshipped both of God's sons indiscriminately; others the younger son Christ; yet others the elder son Satanael. Though he has nothing to say on the matter, this presumably means that they all acknowledged God the Father.

The Bogomils believed themselves to be the true followers of Christ. A charge that they worshipped both Christ and Satanael might be founded in their recognition of the latter as the lord of creation, but they were never devil-worshippers, as the Thracian suggests in the *Dialogue*. There are the usual slanders against heretics. The Thracian has them eating excrement, raping young girls in a sordid initiation ceremony, and nine months later sacrificing and eating the fruit of their labours. These are conventional charges made against heretics, which go back at least to Epiphanius of Salamis at the turn of the fourth century. They are, for example, nearly identical with the description left by Guibert of Nogent of the activities of a group of heretics in northern France at the turn of the eleventh century. Both accounts are likely to go back to a common literary source.[123]

The Thracian claimed to be relying on an informant whom he had rescued from heresy.[124] Given the divisions of belief that were appearing among the Bogomils in the mid-twelfth century, the Thracian might have only been relating the slanders being exchanged between different groups of heretics. The informant might also have been

[120] Ibid., 133.5–9.
[121] Ibid., 133.21–5.
[122] Ibid., 135.29–39.
[123] Guibert de Nogent, *Histoire de sa vie 1053–1124*, ed. G. Bourgin (Paris, 1907), 212–15.
[124] Gautier, 'Le *de Daemonibus* du Pseudo-Psellos', 149–50.

hoping to please his interrogator by supplying him with all the most lurid details. But this is to assume that there is a historical basis to the dialogue. This depends very largely on whether the Thracian's informant was a real person. He is described as a monk called Mark from the Mesopotamites family.[125] The Thracian is supposed to have met him during his travels 'near the peninsula bordering Hellas'. This has been variously identified as the Thracian Chersonnese or the Khalkidike. But the former is too distant from Hellas to qualify, so really is the Khalkidike. The Peloponnese, or Mount Pelion,[126] seem better choices, in which case the form of words points to somewhere near Athens or Thebes as the place of meeting. This receives support from a marginal note which adds: 'This Mark was a native of Thebes. At first, he was a *didaskalos* of the Bogomils, but later became an orthodox [Christian], whom the Thracian came across, when sent against the Bogomils.'[127]

This note indicates that a near contemporary believed he had good grounds for identifying the Thracian's informant with a historical person. For what it is worth, in the early twelfth century there was a Michael Mesopotamites who was a functionary of the theme of Hellas and therefore operating from Thebes, which was the capital of the theme.[128] This provides a tenuous connection between the Mesopotamites family and Thebes. This marginal note therefore provides reasonable grounds for believing that the dialogue was founded on historical information and was not pure fiction.

This is reinforced by one incident recounted by the Thracian. Timotheos had challenged him to explain why he should have put any trust in the strange things that he had learnt from this Mark. The Thracian believed that they were corroborated by an incident at the obscure Thessalian town of Elasson. There was a 'holy man' there whose prophesying had won him a following. He predicted to them that a man was coming who would persecute them for their faith. He would seize the 'holy man' and many others, who would be put on trial, but he would not succeed in taking the 'holy man' back in chains to Constantinople. The description he gave his followers of the persecutor exactly matched the Thracian, though at the time he had scarcely set off from Constantinople on his mission. The Thracian was informed of this by various people coming from those parts. On arrival he had the 'holy man' brought before him. He wanted to know how he could predict the future. The 'holy man' told him that he had been

[125] Cf. M. Wellnhofer, 'Die thrakischen Euchiten und ihr Satanskult im Dialoge des Psellos *ΤΙΜΟΘΕΟΣ Η ΤΩΝ ΔΑΙΜΟΝΩΝ*', *BZ* 30(1929/30), 477–84.

[126] I owe the suggestion of Mount Pelion to Paul Magdalino.

[127] Gautier, 'Le *de Daemonibus* du Pseudo-Psellos', 149 apparatus.

[128] Katsaros, *ΙΩΑΝΝΗΣ ΚΑΣΤΑΜΟΝΙΤΗΣ*, 126–7.

initiated by a wandering Libyan. He also told him that he was about to suffer various ailments for his attack on heresy. The Thracian assured Timotheos that things turned out exactly as the heretic predicted, for he had come close to death and would most surely have died were it not for Christ's saving grace.[129]

Underlying the dialogue there therefore seems to have been a mission to Hellas to root out the heretics there. To judge by its *synodikon* the church in Hellas took the threat from the Bogomils very seriously.[130] The general information provided by the Dialogue about the heretics conforms to what is known about Bogomil teachings. The extreme charges of devil worship are a reflection of the line of defence developed by the orthodox against the Bogomils. It was based on a travesty of Bogomil beliefs. The orthodox could not accept that following their initiation into the sect Bogomils were filled with the power of the Holy Ghost. They therefore claimed that the initiation ceremony drove out the gift of baptism and the grace of the Holy Ghost and introduced an evil spirit that made the heretic a dwelling place of Satan.[131] But this is sheer calumny.

There can also be little doubt that the Bogomils attracted delinquents of all kinds. The incident recounted by the Thracian of the 'holy man's' initiation by a wandering Libyan, bizarre as it sounds, rings true. The 'holy man' would, though, almost certainly have claimed that the inspiration behind his prophecies came from the Holy Ghost and not from demons. This would have been the same whether he was a Bogomil or not. The dividing line between heresy and eccentricity was very narrow. But this provided heretics with the camouflage they needed. It vexed Theodore Balsamon. He claimed to have seen many such 'holy men' wandering around the cities of the Empire. They pretended to be possessed and exploited this for gain. Balsamon was disturbed to learn that far from being punished they were often revered for their holiness. He made his objections known and secured several convictions, but he admitted that in at least one case he was wrong and had acted out of ignorance. But his decision had not been arbitrary. He had consulted good men who had earlier in their careers followed this way of life. They assured him that it was spiritually harmful and conducive to satanic practices.[132]

The number of Bogomils can never have been very large in absolute terms. An Italian inquisitor of the mid-thirteenth century thought that the five Bogomil churches of the East had less than 500 members.[133]

[129] Gautier, 'Le *de Daemonibus* du Pseudo-Psellos', 159–63.
[130] Gouillard, 'Le synodikon de l'orthodoxie', 232–7.
[131] Darrouzès, 'Des notes marginales', 71.
[132] Rhalles & Potles II, 441–2.
[133] Wakefield & Evans, *Heresies*, 337.

If he was thinking only of those fully initiated into the sect, then he might well be right, but there were many hangers-on and sympathisers. The Bogomils were a serious challenge, even if their numbers were comparatively small. Their claim to form the true church and to have preserved the ideals and organisation of the early church could be dismissed as arrant nonsense, but it contained a serious criticism of the hierarchical church: that it was indifferent to the communal ideal of the Apostolic church. The Bogomils in many ways were better attuned to the rhythms of popular piety. They provided explanations of the actions of demons and offered protection against them. They exploited the continuing devotion in all sections of society for 'holy men' whose life was devoted to a ceaseless struggle against demons. So much of popular piety revolved around a 'holy man' or a spiritual father and this was the shape that Bogomil communities took. There was a strongly nonconformist strand to Byzantine society, perhaps as a reaction to its public life which was highly regimented and conventional. Monasticism in all its strange variety was the normal mode of expression for Byzantine nonconformism. Bogomilism built on this. It was feared because it was so difficult to distinguish from monasticism and was the more dangerous because it was so difficult to separate from lay society. Its characteristic feature was not, at least to begin with, its dualist theology. It was much more a revival of lay piety and its origins are difficult to disentangle from other aspects of religious revival in the eleventh century. It provided a vehicle for lay piety which, when not hostile to the established order, was indifferent to it.

From the mid-eleventh century the orthodox church found it more difficult to tolerate dissent than it had in the past. It was a way of asserting itself. Dissent was driven underground and acquired a dualist colouring. The fight against heresy was symptomatic both of alienation from the official church and of the latter's growing power. However, on the surface, Byzantium continued to show its old assurance. Very little appeared to change. It retained a rather secular outlook. The elite entertained a genuine understanding of and enthusiasm for a classical past. At all levels of society a wide range of beliefs and celebrations were tolerated that had very little to do with Christianity. There was a surprising lack of regard for the institutional church. It was chiefly appreciated for providing the rituals that regulated the most important rites of passage. Church was a place to gather and to display yourself, particularly on the occasion of the great festivals of the Christian year. Worship was, in contrast, more of a private affair. This ensured that religion was always taken seriously. Conversion was always a possibility. Almost always this meant embracing the monastic life. The coexistence of a secular outlook that sometimes seemed almost pagan with extreme religiosity was typical of Byzantium. It suggests the great range of experience open to the Byzantines which gave their civilisation its strength, vitality, and balance.

This facade was torn away in the decades that followed Manuel Comnenus's death in September 1180. The fissures in Byzantine political and social life were there for all to see before the launching of the fourth crusade. The fall of Constantinople to the Latins in 1204 was not a foregone conclusion. It was a close run thing, but Byzantium had shown itself to be increasingly vulnerable to Latin pressure and intervention. The Latins not only challenged Byzantium's imperial pretensions, but also called in question its orthodoxy. Byzantium found itself on the defensive. Its citizens were resentful of Latin success and presumption. In the face of the Latin challenge Byzantium appeared brittle. The fall of Constantinople was the result of a loss of morale. The Latin question divided Byzantine society and diminished its capacity for decisive action. It magnified internal divisions that had seemed of little consequence.

The Latin question tested Byzantine society. It was so divisive in the twelfth century because the problem was framed but no clear answers emerged. These were forced upon the Byzantines in response to the fall of Constantinople in 1204. The loss of the city threatened the disintegration of the Byzantine polity, but the identification of the Latin church as the true enemy of orthodoxy helped in the process of reconstituting the Byzantine Empire in exile. Restored Byzantium was rather different from the Empire of the Comneni, however much it took it as its model. The importance of the period of exile from 1204 to 1261 is that it revealed some of the enduring strengths of Byzantium. It also crystallised those processes of change that can be glimpsed going on below the surface under the Comneni. In a sense the period of exile provides a judgement for good and ill on Byzantine society under the Comneni and elucidates the relationship of church and society.

PART VI

EXILE 1204–1261

24

BYZANTIUM AND THE LATINS

THE fall of Constantinople to the Venetians and the soldiers of the fourth crusade on 13 April 1204 meant the temporary destruction of the Byzantine Empire. It has been usual to explain this event in political terms or just as a matter of bad or good luck, depending upon the viewpoint. There is no denying that chance had an important role to play, but events turned out the way they did, largely because of the deepening malaise that had been afflicting Byzantium from the time of Manuel Comnenus's death in 1180. Its most obvious signs were political: dissensions among the ruling dynasty and all kinds of provincial unrest, which undermined effective government. The moral authority of the rulers declined. Michael Choniates, the archbishop of Athens, denounced the Constantinopolitan ruling class for their indifference to the fate of provincial cities.[1] How far was the church implicated in this failure of morale? It would be unfair to accuse a Michael Choniates, even a Eustathius of Thessalonica, of contributing to the demoralisation of the time. They strove to maintain a degree of order; they remained loyal to Constantinople; they had the well-being of their communities at heart. Perhaps there were other bishops who tried to do the same.

But at Constantinople there was little sense of urgency on the part of the patriarchal church. It was paralysed by internal bickerings. It provided little in the way of moral guidance. At a time of impending crisis it was unable to give a clear lead. It was a failure that was in character. The patriarchal church was not inclined to stand up to imperial pressure. This was evident in 1183 when the Patriarch Theodosius found that his opposition to the usurpation of Andronicus I lacked support, even within the church. There was nothing for it, but to resign under humiliating circumstances. Later generations found Isaac Angelus's treatment of his patriarchs scandalous: 'Isaac appointed five patriarchs of Constantinople in the nine years that he reigned;

[1] Michael Choniates II, 83.

dismissing one and appointing another, not for any good reason or on any canonical grounds, but for entirely arbitrary reasons'.[2]

Most demoralising was his dismissal of the Patriarch Dositheos. This patriarch was at the heart of Byzantine resistance to the passage in 1189 of Frederick Barbarossa and the German crusaders. His removal from office did much to discredit the anti-Latin stance of the church. Anti-Latin sentiment became less of a force on the streets of Constantinople. There were no signs of popular resistance, when the crusaders stormed the city in April 1204. The patriarch of the day, John X Kamateros, failed to provide any leadership. In his correspondence with Pope Innocent III he limited himself to a polite rebuttal of papal claims to primacy. There was no sense of urgency. Typically, he ended one letter with lavish praise of the Byzantine Emperor Alexius III Angelus.[3]

Of all Byzantine emperors Alexius was perhaps the least deserving of praise. But recent humiliations had shown how dangerous it was for a patriarch to take issue with an emperor. It was safest to accept that the emperor knew best. He was the arbiter, the *epistemonarkhes*, of the church. The history of the Comnenian church underlined how dependent the patriarch had become upon imperial authority. Divisions within the church in Constantinople played their part in this. They forced the patriarch to look for imperial support. The Latin issue was one obvious cause of division. Prudence suggested that the patriarchs of Constantinople should follow the imperial lead. If foreign policy so dictated, they would pursue polite negotiations with the papacy over the possibility of a reunion of the churches. They left the initiative over this matter in the hands of the emperor.

The reshaping of the Byzantine sense of identity

The late twelfth-century patriarchs of Constantinople, Dositheos excepted, cannot be accused of stoking up anti-Latin sentiment. There is no denying its existence at Constantinople at that time, but it lacked shape and direction. Its leaders are hard to identify. The orthodox patriarchs of Jerusalem and Antioch were a possible focus of anti-Latin feelings at Constantinople. They were normally resident in the capital because Frankish rule prevented them taking up residence in their sees. Leontios, orthodox patriarch of Jerusalem, was an exception. He succeeded in visiting his see, apparently in secret, in the mid-1170s. This was at a time of cooperation between the Byzantine emperor and the Franks. But it did not prevent him being imprisoned by the

[2] Migne, *PG*, 140. 800–1.

[3] A. Papadakis and A.-M. Talbot, 'John X Camaterus confronts Innocent III', *BS* 33(1972), 35.22–9; Spiteris, *La critica bizantina*, 261–81.

Frankish authorities. He escaped but then returned to Constantinople. He thought that his escape was miraculous. It contributed to his reputation for sanctity. His *Life* was written shortly before the fall of Constantinople in 1204 by a monk of Patmos. It dwells on his animus against the Latins. He dismissed the catholic faith as mumbo-jumbo. After his return to Constantinople in the late 1170s he was a figure of some importance in the ecclesiastical circles of the capital. He was the Patriarch Theodosius's stoutest ally.[4]

Another orthodox patriarch in exile did much to shape anti-Latin sentiment in the late twelfth century. This was the canonist Theodore Balsamon. He was promoted to the patriarchal throne of Antioch soon after the death of Manuel I Comnenus.[5] His hostile stance towards the Latins predates his promotion, but it seems to have become more virulent thereafter. Some of his more intolerant opinions about the Latins are to be found in the answers he gave around 1195 to a series of enquiries made by Mark, orthodox patriarch of Alexandria. Balsamon did not merely reject the notion of papal primacy. He also claimed for the church of Constantinople all the privileges granted to the papacy by the Donation of Constantine. He did this on the grounds that Canon 28 of the council of Chalcedon had given the church of Constantinople equal status with the church of Rome.

Rome had since forfeited its rights to these privileges. It had not only fallen into the hands of the barbarians, it had also fallen into heresy. It had separated itself from the church universal. So when the patriarch of Alexandria wanted to know if it was permissible to give communion to Latin prisoners of war, Balsamon told him that they had to renounce the errors of their church first.[6]

This exclusion of the Roman Church from communion with other orthodox churches was an extreme position. Byzantine theologians of the time were almost always willing to concede a primacy of honour to the pope. This at least provided a basis for negotiation and the hope – vain, we know – of compromise. In Balsamon's scheme there was no place for the papacy and the Latin church. Papal primacy with its monarchical assumptions was a challenge to the position of the Byzantine emperor who was the arbiter of a Christian society. It challenged too Constantinople's claim to be the preeminent centre of Christianity by virtue of its imperial status. Balsamon was redefining

4 Leontios of Jerusalem, 420–6; ed. Tsougarakis, 128–41. See Rose, 'The *Vita* of St Leontios'.

5 See V. Tiftixoglu, 'Zur Genese der Kommentare des Theodoros Balsamon', in *TO BYZANTIO*, ed. Oikonomidès, 489.

6 Katsaros, *ΙΩΑΝΝΗΣ ΚΑΣΤΑΜΟΝΙΤΗΣ*, 307–57, would like the Replies to Mark of Alexandria to be entirely the work of John Kastamonites, rather than merely his draft which was then worked up by Balsamon. Kastamonites's lack of reputation as a canon lawyer tells against Katsaros's view.

the bases of a Byzantine identity – emperor, capital, church, and people – but now in opposition to the Latin West. It was a radical step and it attracted criticism at the time. Not for nothing has Sir Steven Runciman singled out Balsamon as the 'villain on the Orthodox side for the development of the schism'.[7]

Theodore Balsamon was the first Byzantine lawyer to make a serious study of the Donation of Constantine. Its implications for the nature of papal primacy were alarming. He was, however, able - with a casuistry that was typically Byzantine - to turn the Donation of Constantine to the advantage of the church of Constantinople. To do so, he excluded Rome from membership of the Christian commonwealth. He was not so much reflecting public opinion as giving it a new dimension, which would be important for the future. Even if there were the occasional disagreements his legal commentaries would be the authority to which later generations of orthodox prelates and canon lawyers would turn. In other words, Balsamon was responsible for working an anti-Latin bias into Byzantine canon law.

His work had the influence it did because it coincided with a steady growth of anti-Latin feeling in Constantinople over the twelfth century. Sir Steven Runciman has pointed to 'the growth of popular animosity' as the single most important factor in the estrangement of Byzantium from the West.[8] Its importance goes far beyond the question of the schism of the Greek and Roman churches. It touched the very being of Byzantium. It reflected the way that the Byzantine identity was being reshaped in an anti-Latin sense. This would have a decisive bearing on the relations between church and society. The late twelfth century was an important stage in the emergence of a new sense of identity. The new ingredients and themes can be identified, but they had yet to crystallise into a new amalgam capable of absorbing older beliefs and assumptions.

The Byzantine identity was complex. The Byzantines were both the new Romans and the new Israelites. They were the chosen people of the New Testament. They saw the Jews as their chief rivals and competitors. This meant that a Byzantine identity would be constructed in opposition to the Jews. As we have seen, prejudice against the Jews was deeply ingrained in the Byzantine mentality at all levels of society.[9] They would never be forgiven for their treatment of Christ. At Byzantium discrimination against the Jews often merged into persecution. In a sense, it confirmed the Byzantine belief in themselves as the new chosen people. Persecution and prejudice against the Jews

7 S. Runciman, *The Eastern Schism* (Oxford, 1955), 157. Cf. Spiteris, *La critica bizantina*, 224–47.

8 Runciman, *The Eastern Schism*, ch.6.

9 See above, pp.183–4, 398, 462, and Magdalino, *Manuel I Komnenos*, 386.

were always features of Byzantine life. We have seen the difficulties Eustathius of Thessalonica had when Jews started moving into Christian areas of the city and occupied house property belonging to his church.[10] He foresaw popular resentment building up against the Jews and turned to the patriarch for advice in his predicament. At about the same time another archbishop, Nicetas of Chonai in western Anatolia, had no such compunctions. He did not hesitate to drive the Jews out of his diocese. For this he was much honoured by that most attractive of Byzantine bishops, Michael Choniates.[11] The great traveller Benjamin of Tudela visited many of the Jewish communities in the Byzantine Empire in the course of Manuel Comnenus's reign. Most were large and prosperous. They were engaged in the silk industry and other manufactures. But they suffered discrimination. At Constantinople they had moved out of the city, across the Golden Horn to Pera. Benjamin noted that the 'Greeks hate the Jews and . . . strike them in the streets.' We learn that at this time Greeks used to address Jews they met in the streets in the following contemptuous terms: 'Oh sheepish bleater from Bethphage, oh honourable Beelzebub, oh Hebrew with a heart of stone, the Lord has come and hurled lightnings at your head.'[12] The hostility of the Byzantines to the Jews can be explained in part by their influx into the Empire in considerable numbers from the turn of the tenth century. It was also inseparable from their conviction that they were the chosen people of the new dispensation. Persecution of the Jews continued after 1204. The Nicaean Emperor John III Vatatzes proved his orthodox credentials by ordering the conversion of all Jews within his dominions.[13]

Under the Comneni Byzantine xenophobia was directed as much against the Armenians as it was against the Jews. This hostility is harder to explain. It was not just that the Armenians had settled in large numbers throughout the Byzantine Empire from the early eleventh century. It probably had more to do with their loyalty to their Monophysite Christianity. They formed distinct communities. The Byzantine church soon identified them as a problem. In the mid-eleventh century there was a concerted effort to force the Armenian church into union with the orthodox church and thereafter there were recurrent, but vain attempts to achieve this end. At best, there were occasional local successes. Theophylact of Ohrid reports the

[10] Eustathius I, 339–40.
[11] Michael Choniates I, 53.11–25.
[12] Sharf, *Byzantine Jewry*, 132–57.
[13] P. Charanis, 'The Jews in the Byzantine Empire under the first Palaeologi', *Speculum* 22(1947), 75–7; S.B. Bowman, *The Jews of Byzantium 1204–1453* (Alabama, 1985), 13–17.

conversion of an Armenian community.[14] From the late twelfth century Byzantine attitudes towards the Armenians became increasingly intolerant. In his account of the Norman sack of Thessalonica in 1185 Eustathius of Thessalonica bitterly reproves the Armenians. They actively cooperated with the Latins during the siege of the city. They then shared in the Latin triumph. They threatened and abused the Byzantines and exploited Latin protection to demand exorbitant prices for bread. They oppressed the Byzantines in a thoroughly Latin way (*latinikos*).[15] The fall of Constantinople would see Armenians once again supporting the Latins. The Armenians settled in north-western Asia Minor welcomed the crusader armies in 1204. They would be massacred by the local Greek inhabitants when the Latins withdrew the next year.[16]

The Byzantines came to look upon the Armenians as a Latin third column. Their hatred for the Armenians had become entwined with hostility to the Latins from early on. The Byzantines recognised an affinity between the two peoples. They felt that both were tainted with Jewish practices. There was something to Byzantine intuition. Latins and Armenians might differ over christology, but they had customs in common. Both, for instance, used azymes and unmixed wine in the communion service. The Patriarch Michael Cerularius's attack on the use of azymes was originally directed, not against the Latins, but against the Armenians.[17] To a limited degree, the Latins inherited the Byzantines' longstanding animus against the Armenians.

To the mid-eleventh century the Byzantines had shown surprisingly little prejudice against the Latins, doubtless because contacts were restricted. Thereafter Jonathan Shepard detects a marked shift of attitudes on the part of the Byzantines. It underlay a series of pamphlets that denounced the Latins for their unclean eating habits and their Jewish tendencies.[18] These tracts were a product of the schism of 1054. They may have originated with the patriarch and the clergy of St Sophia, but their crudity suggests that they were intended for popular consumption. They would seem to have done their work, for Michael Cerularius was able to mobilise the mob against the papal legates. They were temporarily forgotten once the immediate fuss died down, but they contained charges against the Latins that would later be resuscitated over and over again. They helped to fix an image of the

[14] Theophylact II, 336–41.

[15] Eustathius II, 124–6.

[16] Nicetas Choniates, 601–2; Villehardouin, *Conquête de Constantinople*, ed. Faral II, 194–5.

[17] E. Petrucci, 'Rapporti di Leone IX con Costantinopoli', *Studi Medievali* ser.iii. 14/2(1973), 769–71.

[18] J. Shepard, 'Aspects of Byzantine attitudes and policy towards the West in the tenth and eleventh centuries', *BF* 13 (1989), 67–118, at 94–6.

Latins which had a wide and crude appeal across Byzantine society. It did not deal in the niceties of theology or the courtesies of diplomacy.

The question is how and when was this image fixed? The crusades were not alone to blame. They intensified a love–hate relationship between Byzantium and the West and produced a lengthy period of reassessment. In many ways, mutual esteem increased. The Comnenian court enjoyed a reputation in the West as a school of chivalry, while Latin prowess appealed to its warrior ethos.[19] Westerners adopted the cults of Byzantine warrior saints. Westerners on their way to or from the Holy Land were willing to make a detour in order to visit a shrine, such as Patmos, or to pay their respects to a holy man, such as Hosios Meletios.[20]

Equally, fraternisation between crusaders and local Greeks could be the cause of alarm in ecclesiastical circles. In 1099 a Byzantine theologian was staying at Rhodes where the Pisan and Venetian fleets were wintering en route for the Holy Land. He noted with horror that the local people were beginning to adopt the Latin custom of using azymes in the communion service.[21] The orthodox hierarchy remained deeply suspicious of the Latin church. There was substance to the complaints made by Latins that the orthodox purified altars after use by Latins and were reluctant to allow mixed marriages unless the Latin partner accepted orthodox practice.[22] Orthodox theologians also began to be aware of the true nature of papal primacy. It first becomes an issue in the debates of 1112 between Byzantine and Latin theologians.[23] The importance of the issue became clearer from the middle of the twelfth century. The Roman church insisted that in essence it was the church universal. It was the fount of all authority and the guardian of the Christian faith. The implications for orthodoxy were worrying. As we have seen, the Byzantines soon contrived a defence against papal claims. Anna Comnena was able to incorporate it in the *Alexiad*,[24] which she completed in the aftermath of the second crusade. She reveals how deep distrust of westerners already went.

By the middle of the twelfth century there were Byzantines – and not only in ecclesiastical circles - who were coming to see papal primacy as a challenge to orthodoxy, even as an affront, but it was hardly a threat to its existence. By themselves these theological and ecclesiological issues were insufficient to force the Byzantines to refashion their sense of

19 See Migne, *PL*, 182. 672–3; Angold, *The Byzantine Empire*, 205–6.
20 Meletios the Younger, 32–3.
21 Darrouzès, 'Nicolas d'Andida', 208.17–33.
22 Odo of Deuil, *De profectione Ludovici VII in orientem*, ed. V.G. Berry (New York, 1948), 54–6.
23 Darrouzès, 'Les documents byzantins', 51–9; Spiteris, *La critica bizantina*, 70–84.
24 Anna Comnena I, xiii, 4:1, 48.12–23 (ed. Leib).

identity. More mundane considerations came into play. There were mutterings in the bureaucracy under Manuel I Comnenus about the advantages enjoyed in imperial service by foreigners. These resentments are expressed with some force in a letter written by George Tornikes, the metropolitan bishop of Ephesus, who was trying to obtain a post at court for an uncle:

> I cannot believe that a Philhellene and a lover of freedom would docket a Hellene with barbarians nor a free man with people who are slaves by nature. I cannot abide the sort of people who use the barbarian tongue, nor, if I may speak my mind, those apparent servants of Mars. They are the kind of people who are on such good terms with barbarians that they prefer the barbarian to the Hellene, alleging against the Hellene, though a hero and a lover of the Muses and Hermes, that of the two he is the inferior.[25]

This is the first unequivocal use of 'Hellene' to mean Byzantine. The normal usage was 'Romaios' or Roman. It was a way of stressing that what set the Byzantine above and apart from the foreigner was 'Hellenic' culture. There was always something slightly precious about this identification of Byzantine and 'Hellene'. It was belletrist and confined to the highly educated, but it should not be discounted. It was an expression of an increasingly important cultural orientation. It reflected disenchantment with foreign - and especially Latin – infiltration of the Byzantine court on the part of a group with influence at court and in the church.[26] But it was also associated with a sincere attachment to Constantinople itself. The intelligentsia were becoming disturbed by the state of Constantinople. It was, to their way of thinking, assuming an unpleasantly cosmopolitan character. John Tzetzes reels off the list of the greetings in a variety of foreign languages now needed for everyday life in the capital.[27] It was probably intended as a bitter jest. The people of Constantinople were increasingly the products of sin and miscegenation, if one believes a contemporary. He described them as 'the sordid droppings of prostitutes and adulterous connections, the offspring of servant girls bought for cash, sprung – from who knows where ? – from the Ros or the descendants of Hagar or the rest of the racial stew'.[28] The historian Nicetas Choniates ascribed the moral decline of the people of Constantinople to the presence of so many foreign elements in their midst.[29] There was disquiet at the

[25] Tornikès, 129.2–7.
[26] See Magdalino, *Tradition and Transformation*, no. XIV; P. Magdalino, ed., *The Perception of the Past in Twelfth-Century Europe* (London, 1992), 155–6.
[27] Moravscsik, *Studia Byzantina*, 283–92.
[28] Germanos II, 288.
[29] Nicetas Choniates, 233–4.

readiness displayed by some Byzantines to abandon traditional garb for Latin dress, 'which did not even cover your hands and knees'! It made a mockery of ancestral values.[30] But it was not all sour criticism. Theodore Balsamon made this ringing declaration: 'I am, however, the purest-blooded (*akraiphnestatos*) Constantinopolitan and by the grace of God have played a most vital role [in the affairs] of the most holy throne of Constantinople.' The occasion was, however, unexpected. He was defending the church of Constantinople's right to the privileges accorded to Rome under the Donation of Constantine. He concluded: 'I therefore desire and pray that the bishop of Constantinople have, without prejudice, all the privileges granted to it by the holy canons.'[31] Balsamon unites a devotion to Constantinople with a defence of its church against Latin pretensions. Here you have the elements necessary for the reworking of the Byzantine identity.

This has little to do with 'the growth of popular animosity'. It reflects rather the misgivings and the idealism of the educated elite. But one can well believe Nicetas Choniates when he describes the resentments occasioned among the people of Constantinople by the presence of foreigners. They fanned out from the docks along the Golden Horn into the rest of the city and took local girls to wife.[32] But such exasperation by itself was unlikely to reshape the Byzantine sense of identity. At a local level hostility towards foreigners seems to have been directed by the imperial authorities rather than to have been an expression of popular feelings.[33]

'Popular animosity' against the Latins may well have existed before the middle of Manuel Comnenus's reign, but is hard to find. This changes in 1166 with the theological controversy over the meaning of the words 'My Father is greater than I.' This took on an anti-Latin twist, once the emperor supported what was seen to be a Latin interpretation of this text. Manuel Comnenus relied on the guidance of a Latin theologian, the Pisan Hugh Eteriano, who describes the atmosphere of the time. 'Latins', he tells us, 'were pointed out on the streets of the capital as objects of hatred and detestation.'[34] The controversy over 'My Father is greater than I' was a major crisis. We have seen how almost all the church was ranged against the emperor. There was also dissent within the imperial court led by Alexius Kontostephanos and Nicephorus

30 Darrouzès, 'Un recueil épistolaire du XIIe siècle', 225 (no.174).

31 Rhalles & Potles II, 285–6. See P. Magdalino 'Constantinople and the 'εξω χώραι in the time of Balsamon', in *TO BYZANTIO*, ed. Oikonomidès, 179–97, esp. p.183.

32 Cinnamus, 281–2.

33 E.g. G.L.F. Tafel and G.M. Thomas, *Urkunden zur älteren Handels – und Staatsgeschichte der Republik Venedig* (Fontes Rerum Austriacarum, Abt. 2, XII–XIV) (Vienna, 1856–7), I, 129, 3–4: Dec. 1150; Meletios the Younger, 32–3.

34 Dondaine, 'Hugues Ethérien', 481.

Bryennius.[35] Manuel was able to cow opposition, but discontent at the emperor's measures lingered on to the end of his reign.[36]

The importance of the episode is that it pointed to a fusion of the anti-Latin sentiments of the higher clergy and a section of the court with the resentments of the populace of Constantinople. Their latent xenophobia was directed specifically against the Latins. Involved in the agitation against the emperor were not only members of the clergy, but also monks.[37] This was a pointer to the future, for the monks would later be among the most active promoters of anti-Latin propaganda and sentiment.

Manuel Comnenus only damped down anti-Latin feelings in the capital. They would flare up again in a far more violent form. In 1182 the people of Constantinople massacred the Latins resident in their midst. This was precipitated by the political upheavals that followed the death of Manuel Comnenus in 1180. But there was also a religious dimension. Greek priests and monks seem to have been responsible for whipping up the mob against the Latins. They singled out a Roman cardinal for a peculiarly revolting death and slew western pilgrims who were lodged in the Hospitaler house at Constantinople.[38] There was popular enthusiasm too for the decision to oppose the passage of Frederick Barbarossa's crusade through the Byzantine Empire in 1189.[39] These incidents show not only that there was popular hostility to the Latins on religious grounds, but also that it could be stoked up and might be tapped for political purposes. It could also evaporate. It was not quite yet a permanent factor of Byzantine life. The Byzantine identity was still in the process of being refashioned, even if all the new ingredients were now present.

Events in the immediate aftermath of the crusader conquest of Constantinople suggest that cooperation with the Latins rather than hostility to them was uppermost in the minds of many Byzantines. In some cases, hatred of the Byzantine elite took precedence over any objections to the Latins. It is usual to single out an episode recounted by Nicetas Choniates. After the sack of Constantinople by the Latins he, along with other members of the Byzantine elite including the patriarch, was allowed to leave the city. They moved off out into the Thracian countryside and immediately became objects of derision for the local people. Provincials and peasants took real pleasure in their

35 Varzos II, 294. n. 4.

36 P. Magdalino, 'Enlightenment and repression in twelfth-century Byzantium. The evidence of the Canonists', in *TO BYZANTIO*, ed. Oikonomidès, 362; Magdalino, *Manuel I Komnenos*, 289.

37 Rhalles & Potles II, 455–6.

38 William of Tyre: Guillaume de Tyr, *Chronique*, ed. R.B.C. Huygens (Corpus Christianorum. Continuatio Mediaevalis, 63 and 63A) (Turnhout, 1986), 1022–4.

39 See C.M. Brand, *Byzantium Confronts the West 1180–1204* (Cambridge, Mass., 1968), 176–88

discomfiture. They could at long last vent their resentment against a ruling class that had for so long taken them for granted.[40] Included in that ruling class was a high proportion of churchmen. In both the capital and the provinces surviving members of the ruling class were hurrying to come to terms with the Latins, to shore up some fragments against their ruin.

It was not long before it became clear that the conquest of Constantinople threatened not only the Empire, but the very existence of orthodoxy. The crusaders created not only a Latin Empire, but also a Latin patriarchate of Constantinople. The orthodox Patriarch John Kamateros abandoned the city and took up residence in the provincial town of Didymoteichos. His inaction was demoralising.[41] The leadership of the orthodox church in Constantinople passed into the hands of monks. Their representatives took the leading role in the debates there were with Latin theologians. They saw the Latin conquest as a test of their faith. They could so easily have fled from the city, like so many others, but they preferred to stay. They rejoiced in the opportunity to atone for their sins. The Latins might have deprived them of all their material possessions, but not of their 'revered and orthodox faith'.[42] They were to find that the Latins sought to deprive them of this too.

However well-intentioned Pope Innocent III may have been,[43] he never had effective control over the organisation of a Latin church on Byzantine soil. The pope may have intended that in those sees where there was a predominantly Greek population – which was almost everywhere – there should be Greek bishops. In practice, Greek bishops were driven out and Latins installed in their place. Latin abbots were placed over some of the richest Greek monasteries.[44] There was wholesale expropriation by the conquerors, lay and ecclesiastic alike, of the wealth of the Greek church. Initially, this onslaught on orthodoxy only added to the demoralisation and disorientation of the Greeks. They had no effective leaders. Centres of opposition to the conquerors in Epiros and Asia Minor were still in the process of being organised. In Constantinople it was monks, as we have seen, who came forward as representatives of the orthodox community.

They were not, at first, inclined to challenge the validity of the Latin conquest. They accepted it as a punishment for their sins. They

40 Nicetas Choniates, 594–5.

41 *Pace* P. Wirth, 'Zur Frage eines politischen Engagements Patriarch Johannes' X Kamateros nach dem vierten Kreuzzug', *BF* 4(1972), 239–52.

42 Mesarites I, 62.27–9.

43 D. Baker, ed., *Relations between East and West in the Middle Ages* (Edinburgh, 1973), 95–108.

44 See J. Richard, 'The establishment of the Latin church in the empire of Constantinople (1204–1227)', in *Latins and Greeks*, ed Arbel *et al.*, 45–62; Brown, 'Cistercians'.

may have hoped for support from Pope Innocent III, who posed as a champion of the rights of orthodox communities. When in 1206 the orthodox patriarch died in exile, the Greeks of Constantinople petitioned Innocent III: they sought his permission to proceed to the election of a new orthodox patriarch of Constantinople. For all his posturing it was not possible for the pope to accede to such a request, for it would mean sanctioning the existence of two patriarchates of Constantinople: that would be schism indeed. His refusal signalled the end of the search for a religious settlement that might have allowed the Greeks to accept the Latin Empire.

Disabused of the hopes they had placed in Innocent III the Greeks of Constantinople turned instead to Theodore Lascaris. Under him Nicaea had become a centre of resistance to the Latin advance into Asia Minor. By 1208 Theodore had extended his authority over much of western Anatolia. He had gathered around him many of the Constantinopolitan elite, including bishops and members of the clergy of St Sophia. In March 1208 in response to the pleas of the Greeks of Constantinople he took the decisive step of authorising the election of a new orthodox patriarch at Nicaea. The man selected, Michael Autoreianos, had before 1204 been the patriarchal *sakellarios*. Almost his first action was to crown and anoint Theodore Lascaris emperor. The Byzantine Empire was reborn in exile.

Resignation before the fact of the Latin conquest was replaced by indignation: the sack of Constantinople was a crime and an affront to orthodoxy. The change of mood is apparent in Constantine/Cyril Stilbes's charges (*aitiamata*) against the Latins.[45] Stilbes was appointed metropolitan of Cyzicus shortly before the fall of Constantinople. He soon found himself dispossessed and sought refuge with Theodore Lascaris. His tract against the Latins was compiled soon after the mission of the papal legate Cardinal Pelagius to Constantinople in 1213. This mission was the cause of apprehension at Nicaea and demanded a categorical statement of orthodox charges against the Latins. Some of the old points of difference between the Greek and Latin churches were raised: the Latin addition of the *filioque* to the Nicene creed and the use of azymes by the Latins in the communion service. Over the twelfth century Byzantine theologians had begun to pay more attention to the question of papal primacy. Their criticism was always within the bounds of reason. This could not be said of Stilbes's treatment of the question. He claimed that the Latins did not consider the pope merely to be the successor of St Peter, but to be the Apostle in person, or

45 J. Darrouzès, 'Le mémoire de Constantin Stilbès contre les Latins', *REB* 21(1963), 50–100: text 61–91. See Angold, 'Greeks and Latins after 1204', in *Latins and Greeks*, ed. Arbel *et al.*, 67–9.

perhaps something more, for they came close, he asserted, to deifying the pope and proclaiming him lord of all Christendom. They insisted that the church universal recognise their deification of the pope. This was pure polemic. Whereas in the past Byzantine theologians were normally content to tolerate differences of practice between the two churches, Constantine Stilbes was not. The Latins did not venerate images. They sat through church services. The sanctuary in Latin churches was open for all to see and the laity, including sometimes women, congregated around the altar during services, chiming in as though they were in a law court. Stilbes was the first Byzantine on record to denounce the Latin practice of granting indulgences. As far as he was concerned, these made possible the forgiveness of not only past sins and crimes, but also those still to be committed. He doubted whether the Latins could justify their use of indulgences even in terms of their own suspect ecclesiastical traditions. Oaths, he claimed, had little meaning for the Latins because the pope was capable of releasing them not just from those that they had already sworn, but also from those that they might take in the future. Stilbes objected to the way the Latins made fun of the Greeks for eating before communion. He had heard that they considered the Bogomils the most pious of the Greeks and disparaged them as worse than Jews or Saracens. These were scarcely tolerable insults.

Constantine Stilbes developed a theme which has already made an appearance in the *Alexiad*: the devotion of the Latin clergy to war. Stilbes has Latin prelates escorted to mass by naked youths. These were then sprinkled with holy water: a ceremony which was supposed to turn them into invincible warriors. There seems to be an echo here of the role of the Latin church in the making of a knight. In the same way, Stilbes distorted the crusading ideal when he suggested that the Latins taught that those dying in battle went to paradise. The Latin church never subscribed to any such belief, but it was widely believed by those participating in the first crusade that, if they died fighting the infidel, their reward was a martyr's crown.[46] The crusaders' sack of Constantinople confirmed Stilbes in his conviction that the Latin faith had been perverted by its espousal and promotion of war. The crusaders had desecrated the churches of Constantinople. Knights had ridden their horses into the cathedral of St Sophia and had profaned its altar. They had slaughtered the orthodox who had sought sanctuary in the churches. They had burnt or trampled under foot the holy images. Their priests and bishops were supposed to have desecrated icons while they were celebrating the liturgy. The worst of it was that the

[46] See H.E.J. Cowdrey, 'Martyrdom and the first crusade', in *Crusade and Settlement*, ed. P.W. Edbury (Cardiff, 1985), 46–56.

Latin clergy did nothing to check the excesses of their soldiers. It was more that they condoned them, where they did not actively promote them. A bishop holding a cross aloft had been seen leading the assault on Constantinople.

There was a hardening of hearts among the Greeks in exile. The war against the Latins received religious sanction from the new patriarch Michael Autoreianos. He remitted all the sins committed in this life by soldiers dying in battle for the defence of their country and for the safety of God's people.[47] The Byzantines always saw themselves as the new chosen people. The fall of Constantinople only reinforced the parallels between them and the people of Israel. Like them the Byzantines were now experiencing exile. For Nicetas Choniates the waters of Lake Ascania were his waters of Babylon.[48] Nicetas Choniates found a place for himself at Nicaea as a propagandist for the Emperor Theodore I Lascaris. In a series of speeches, some delivered by the emperor himself, he elaborated an ideology of exile. Like a new Moses or Zorobabel the emperor would return the seat of Empire to its rightful place, the New Jerusalem, Constantinople.[49] Byzantine ideology and sense of identity were given a decisively anti-Latin twist. The events of 1204 crystallised in exile a new sense of identity. The Latins were barbarians who had descended on the Byzantines from the West,[50] and had put Constantinople to the sack. Nicetas has the city beseeching the emperor to revenge the wrongs inflicted by these barbarians: 'With your arrows exact vengeance on the Italians for my tears.'[51]

Nicaea as the centre of orthodoxy[52]

There were hopes that Theodore Lascaris would be able to drive the Latins from Constantinople. They ran high after his victory over the Seljuq sultan in 1211,[53] but this was followed by his defeat at the hands of the Latin Emperor Henry of Hainault. It was no longer realistic to think in terms of the imminent recovery of Constantinople. The immediate aim now became the gathering in of orthodox communities

47 N.Oikonomidès, 'Cinq actes inédits du patriarche Michel Autôreianos', *REB* 25(1967), 117–19; Laurent, 1205.

48 Nicetas Choniates, *Orationes et Epistulae*, ed. I.A. van Dieten (Berlin and New York, 1972), 205.27–30. Cf. ibid. 147.4–6, 168.26–9. See M.J. Angold, 'Byzantine "Nationalism" and the Nicaean Empire', *BMGS* 1(1975), 49–70.

49 Nicetas Choniates, *Orationes*, 128. 24–7, 147.1–7, 160.19–20, 175.32–4.

50 Ibid. 178.2–3, 208.32–3.

51 Ibid. 147.3–4. See now M. Loukaki, 'Première didascalie de Serge le Diacre: éloge du patriarche Michel Autôreianos', *REB* 52 (1994), 167–9.

52 See H. Ahrweiler, 'L'expérience nicéenne', *DOP* 29(1975), 21–40; Angold, 'Greeks and Latins after 1204'.

53 Nicetas Choniates, *Orationes*, 175, 31–5.

under the authority and protection of the emperor and patriarch, even if in exile at Nicaea. This might take various forms. Bishops from Latin-held territories sought refuge at Nicaea. Those who stayed on with their flocks, such as Michael Choniates, hailed Nicaea as a new centre of orthodoxy. Theodore Lascaris wanted to send ships to bring Michael Choniates from his place of exile on the island of Keos to Nicaea, but the prelate declined. His first duty was to the people of his see, but he urged his favourite pupil, George Bardanes, to depart and make a name for himself at Nicaea – advice that was not in the end taken. In 1209 the bishop of Paphos in Cyprus came to Nicaea to obtain confirmation of the election of the new orthodox archbishop of Cyprus, Esaias, from the patriarch and his synod. The church of Cyprus was autocephalous and therefore did not come under the direct authority of the patriarch. The approach made to Nicaea by its representative was a sign of troubled times, but it gave hope that Nicaea would be recognised as the new centre of the orthodox world. The link with the Cypriot church was maintained. Its next archbishop journeyed to Nicaea to receive the traditional investiture from the emperor.[54]

Of more immediate concern to the emperor and patriarch at Nicaea was the orthodox community in Constantinople. As the recovery of the capital became an increasingly remote possibility, so they could best keep their claims alive by offering hope and guidance to the Greeks of Constantinople. But it was more than that. The patriarchal church established in exile at Nicaea was the church of the Constantinopolitans.[55] The patriarch Michael Autoreianos and his officers were drawn from the clergy of St Sophia. Nicholas Mesarites found himself acting as a go-between for the people of Constantinople in their dealings with Nicaea. He came from an old Constantinopolitan family and before 1204 had been a deacon of St Sophia. He was the messenger who brought the letters from the Greeks of Constantinople requesting that Theodore Lascaris proceed with the election of a new patriarch of Constantinople. Once elected patriarch Michael Autoreianos appointed him his *referendarius* or liaison officer with the palace.

In 1214 Nicholas Mesarites was hastily despatched by the emperor to Constantinople. This was in response to the pleas of the monks of Constantinople.[56] The new papal legate Cardinal Pelagius was threatening them with persecution if they did not submit to the papacy. Mesarites was able to arrange an audience with the cardinal to plead on behalf of the monks. He wondered if the Catholic church approved of the breaking up of monastic communities: of monks being forced to

54 See M.J. Angold, 'The problem of the unity of the Byzantine world after 1204: the Empire of Nicaea and Cyprus (1204–1261)', in *ΠΡΑΚΤΙΚΑ ΤΟΥ ΠΡΩΤΟΥ ΔΙΕΘΝΟΥΣ ΚΥΠΡΟΛΟΓΙΚΟΥ ΣΥΝΕΔΡΙΟΥ* (Levkosia, 1972), II, 1–6.

55 Mesarites III, 11.18–19.

56 Ibid., 19.26–9.

wander from place to place. The cardinal's persecution of the monks showed that he was no better than a tomb-robber.[57] The cardinal was not impressed. He told Mesarites that he would have dealt with the monks even more harshly, but for a plea made to him by the Emperor Theodore Lascaris. He hoped that the emperor would become a loyal son of Rome, in which case not only would no harm come to the monks of Constantinople but the orthodox clergy would be able to officiate in their churches once again.[58] The emperor's efforts to protect the Greeks of Constantinople were complemented by those of the patriarch: he exhorted the orthodox community at Constantinople to remain true to their faith in the face of Latin persecution.[59]

The patriarchs may now have had their residence at Nicaea but they remained deeply attached to the people of Constantinople. They expressed their concern for their fate in the encyclicals that they addressed to them on the occasion of their elevation to the patriarchal throne. In 1223 the new patriarch Germanos II wrote congratulating the orthodox community in Constantinople: in the face of Latin oppression its members had remained steadfast in their orthodox faith. He wrote to the abbot and monks of the Constantinopolitan monastery of St John of Petra applauding their opposition to the Latins, but warning them to be on their guard against Latin heresy, which was insidious. Germanos II did not limit himself to moral and spiritual encouragement. On one occasion he intervened directly with the Latin patriarch of Constantinople on behalf of some Greek priests who had been imprisoned on account of their faith.[60]

It was the example of the Greeks of Constantinople that the patriarch would finally recommend in 1223 to the Greeks of Cyprus. The archbishop of Cyprus was then in exile; nobody knew where. The Latin authorities were demanding that the Greek bishops submit to the Latin archbishop of the island. The Greek community accordingly despatched one of their bishops accompanied by an abbot to seek guidance from the patriarch at Nicaea. The matter came before the patriarchal synod. The spirit of the meeting was that discretion was the better part of valour and that the bishops should submit. The patriarch was then brought face to face with a Constantinopolitan delegation, consisting of clergy, monks, and laity, indignant at a possible surrender to Latin pressure. The Greeks of Constantinople had equally been

57 Ibid., 24.25.

58 Ibid., 26.11–28.

59 A.I. Papadopoulos-Kerameus, 'Θεόδωρος Εἰρηνικὸς Πατριάρχης οἰκομενικός', *BZ* 10 (1901), 187–92; Laurent, 1219.

60 J.Gill, 'An unpublished letter of Germanus, patriarch of Constantinople', *B* 44(1974), 142–51 (= J.Gill, *Church Union: Rome and Byzantium (1204–1453)* (London, 1979), no.III); Laurent, 1233, 1277.

confronted with a demand for submission to the church of Rome and they had stood firm. Anything else would have been 'a betrayal of the faith handed down from their fathers'.[61] They hoped that the Cypriots were aware of the meaning attached to the form of submission demanded by the Latins. They warned that the Latins 'are all – laity and priests alike – imbued with the spirit and customs of war. So they consider the giving of hands a sign of defeat and complete subjugation, for this is how the defeated are accustomed to act in battle.'[62] Closer acquaintance with the Latins confirmed the Byzantine prejudice that the Latin faith had been distorted by their addiction to war. The stand of the Constantinopolitans convinced the patriarch that the exercise of economy was not appropriate. He therefore counselled the Cypriots to follow the example of their compatriots in Constantinople and stand firm in the face of Latin demands.[63]

Neophytos, the archbishop of Cyprus, considered the patriarch's advice to the church in Cyprus an unwarranted infringement of its autocephalous status. In 1229 Germanos II again addressed the Greeks of Cyprus, criticising those bishops and priests who were willing to submit to Rome. He emphasised the spiritual dangers attendant on acceptance of Latin teachings. The pope had undermined the unity of the church universal by arbitrarily setting himself above the other patriarchs. He had set at nought the authority of the general council by adding the *filioque* to the creed. Latin teaching on the procession of the Holy Spirit was entirely without proper foundation in the teachings of the Fathers and the councils. The patriarch appealed to the laity to shun any priests or bishops who had submitted to Rome. It was better that they prayed alone in their houses than associate with collaborators.[64] On the island resistance to Latin demands was led by the monks. It culminated in 1231 with the martyrdom of thirteen monks from the Kantariotissa monastery. Germanos accused the archbishop of Cyprus, Neophytos, of having connived at their martyrdom. The archbishop rejected the accusation, but he was in a false position: he wished to safeguard the autocephalous status of the Cypriot church. To protect it against the interference of the patriarch at Nicaea, he was willing to come to terms with the Latin authorities. It was left to the monks and people of Cyprus to continue the struggle against the Latins. In 1232 the Patriarch Germanos II interceded on their behalf with Pope Gregory IX and protested about the martyrdom of the thirteen monks.[65]

[61] Migne, *PG*, 140. 609D.
[62] Migne, *PG*, 140. 609C.
[63] Sathas, *MB* II, 5–14; Laurent, 1234.
[64] Migne, *PG*, 140. 616–20.
[65] J. Gill, 'The tribulations of the Greek church in Cyprus 1196–c.1280', *BF* 5(1977), 73–93 (=Gill, *Church Union*, no.IV).

In Cyprus and at Constantinople anti-Latin sentiment persisted and may even have intensified. It would seem that it was felt most strongly among the monks and laity. The hierarchy was disposed to temporise. Germanos himself was constrained by the display of indignation on the part of the delegation from Constantinople to adopt a sterner position over the submission of the clergy in Cyprus to the church of Rome. The fall of Constantinople did not just give an anti-Latin twist to the Byzantine sense of identity. It also restored the centrality of orthodoxy which had been masked by the remoteness of the patriarchal church from popular concerns. The struggle against the Latins gave the orthodox church renewed popular approval and support.

The coming of the friars[66]

The patriarchs in exile at Nicaea led the struggle against Latin domination. They did their best to confirm Greek communities under Latin rule in their orthodox faith. Their stand was to be complicated by a new factor in the Latin challenge to the orthodox: the friars. They early on found in the Latin Empire of Constantinople an outlet for their talents. By 1220 the Franciscans were established at Constantinople and the Dominicans arrived soon afterwards. It was a Dominican who initiated the debate over the azymes that would eventually lead to the martyrdom of the Kantariotissa thirteen.[67] At Constantinople Dominicans induced the Greek abbot of the monastery of St Mamas to put his signature to a document approving the Latin teaching on azymes.[68] In many ways, the friars were a more formidable threat to orthodoxy than the crusaders ever were. It was not only their skill in debate: they also displayed a side of Latin Christianity that was more acceptable to the orthodox church. They repudiated the martial trappings that gave the Latin church such a bad reputation among the Greeks and preferred to follow the path of reason and persuasion. They made efforts not only to steep themselves in Greek patristics, but also to acquire a working knowledge of the Greek language.

The patriarchal church in exile made its first direct contacts with the friars in 1231 or 1232. The Emperor John Vatatzes passed into the care of the Patriarch Germanos II a party of five Franciscans, who had sought his protection after their misadventures while crossing Anatolia. The patriarch was impressed by their sincerity, their attachment to the ideal of apostolic poverty, and their humility; so unlike the usual run of Latins. They came, they assured him, to mend the

66 R.L. Wolff, 'The Latin empire and the Franciscans', *Traditio* 2(1944), 213–37 (= R.L. Wolff, *Studies in the Latin Empire of Constantinople* (London, 1976), no.VII).

67 Sathas, *MB* II, 25.20.

68 Laurent, 1287.

seamless robe of Christ torn apart by schism. The terms in which they presented their mission were bound to appeal to the patriarch: they wished to restore unity and concord among the five patriarchates. They seemed to be subscribing to the Byzantine ideal of the pentarchy. It was possible to imagine that there was a new spirit working in the Latin church which might allow a reunification of the churches on terms acceptable to the orthodox church.[69]

Germanos II used the Franciscans as intermediaries with the papal curia to propose preliminary negotiations to that end. Two years later in January 1234 a mission made up of two Franciscans and two Dominicans reached Nicaea from Rome. They came not as legates, but as papal envoys. They were empowered to participate in an exchange of views with the patriarch, but not to take part in the proceedings of a church council. Over the next few days preliminary discussions took place over the *filioque*. They did not go well. The Emperor John Vatatzes rebuked the papal envoys for using syllogisms, which, he thought, only clouded the issues.[70] Two days later the friars were able to confound their Greek opponents. One of their number read out in Greek the *anathema* pronounced by St Cyril of Alexandria: against those denying that the Spirit through which Christ performed his miracles was his own Spirit.[71] The friars argued that this supported the Latin doctrine that the Holy Spirit proceeded from God the Son as well as from God the Father. As far as they were concerned, there was no more that could be usefully said for the moment on the topic.

The patriarch wound up the debate on the grounds that no further progress would be made until the orthodox patriarchs of Jerusalem, Antioch, and Alexandria arrived to take part in a council. Having no authority to participate in such a council, the envoys departed for Constantinople, but requested to be kept informed.[72] Just before they left the emperor asked them, 'If the Lord Patriarch is willing to obey the Roman church, will the Lord Pope restore his jurisdiction?' The envoys replied, 'If the patriarch renders obedience and what is due to his Mother, we believe that he will enjoy in the eyes of the Lord Pope and the whole Roman church greater consideration than

69 Sathas, *MB* II, 41–2. See J.Gill, *Byzantium and the Papacy 1198–1400* (New Brunswick, 1976), 64–72.

70 H. Golubovich, 'Disputatio Latinorum et Graecorum seu Relatio apocrisariorum Gregorii IX de gestis Nicaeae in Bithynia et Nymphaeae in Lydia 1234', *Archivum franciscanum historicum* 12(1919), 436.

71 Ibid., 443. On the debate over the procession of the Holy Spirit, see J. Munitiz, 'A reappraisal of Blemmydes' first discussion with the Latins', *BS* 51 (1990), 20–6, who insists that Blemmydes's position was correct. He accepted the Spirit's indwelling in the Son, but did not see this as implying that the Spirit proceeded from the Son.

72 Golubovich, 'Disputatio', 444.

he might expect.'[73] This reply gave the Greeks higher hopes than the careful phrasing perhaps warranted.

In the middle of March they received an invitation from Germanos II to attend a council that was assembling at Nymphaion, the imperial residence near Smyrna, to discuss the union of churches. They sounded opinion in Latin Constantinople. It was agreed that they should go, even though it exceeded their instructions. The Latin Empire was on the brink of collapse and they might be able to negotiate a welcome truce with the Nicaean emperor.[74] They were in something of a false position. Once debate was joined they stalled. They insisted on first considering the question of the azymes, but asked about Pope Gregory IX's position on the matter they replied that it would be necessary to consult him. The Greeks did manage to extract from the papal envoys one significant admission. The Greeks pointed to the sack of Constantinople by the crusaders as justification for their hostility to the Roman church and for their refusal to inscribe the pope's name in their diptychs. The envoys protested that what occurred at Constantinople was not done with the approval of the Roman church. It was the work of laymen, sinners and excommunicates, presuming on their own authority.[75] But otherwise, they insisted, their charges against the Greeks were well founded. The friars accused the Greeks of washing altars after they had been used by Latins; of forcing Latins who attended their churches to renounce the Latin sacraments. Still worse, the Greeks were guilty of removing the pope's name from the diptychs as though he were a heretic.[76] The envoys then demanded to be allowed to depart.

The emperor did his best to soothe them. He would arrange their return to Apulia. It so happened that there were galleys ready and waiting to take his emissaries to the papal curia. The emperor was hoping to negotiate a reconciliation with the pope. The papal envoys told him bluntly that without a union of churches there could be no reconciliation, for which reason they were unwilling to introduce his emissaries at the papal curia. That being the case, the emperor decided that there was no point in despatching an embassy to Rome.[77] A few days later the emperor tried a final ploy. He could see that an impasse had been reached on the questions of the azymes and the *filioque*. Why should the Greeks not accept the Latin azymes and the Latins the Greek position on the *filioque*? Whether the emperor was serious or not is not easy to say, but the papal envoys took him seriously. They replied, 'Know this that the Lord Pope and the Roman church will not abandon

[73] Ibid., 445.
[74] Ibid., 445–6.
[75] Ibid., 452.
[76] Ibid., 451.
[77] Ibid., 452–3.

a single iota of their faith.'[78] The council broke up soon afterwards, with the Greek delegates, yelling after the departing friars, 'It is you who are the heretics.'[79]

This incident suggested that there were irreconcilable differences between the two churches, which not even the friars could break down. Relations between Nicaea and the papacy remained frigid for years to come, but contact was not entirely lost with the Franciscans. Elias of Cortona, master general of the order, was sent on a mission by the Emperor Frederick II to the East. He was responsible for arranging a truce between Nicaea and the Latin Empire and was probably involved in the negotiations that led to the marriage of the Nicaean Emperor John Vatatzes and Frederick II's bastard daughter Costanza Lancia. The marriage was celebrated in 1241/2 and cemented the alliance between the two emperors. Their common enemy was the papacy.[80]

This did not prevent John Vatatzes making overtures in 1248 to Pope Innocent IV over the possibility of a reunion of churches. The Greek emperor had heard that John of Parma had been appointed minister general of the Franciscans. He was apparently impressed by his reputation for sanctity and this gave him hope for a successful end to any negotiations with the papacy. It may be that the initial impression made by the sincerity and sanctity of the Franciscan friars at the court of Nicaea outlasted the bad impression made by the departure of the papal delegation from the first council of Nymphaion. Whatever its outcome the council gave some cause for optimism. It was not just the disavowal by the Latin delegates of the conquest of Constantinople by the fourth crusade. It was also their very willingness to discuss the issues separating the two churches at a church council organised by the Greeks.[81]

John Vatatzes's diplomatic offensive was impressive. He not only employed two Franciscans from Constantinople as his intermediaries with the papal curia; he also used the good offices of his sister-in-law who was queen of Hungary. Innocent IV duly despatched a delegation under John of Parma to Nicaea. A council assembled at Nymphaion towards the end of 1249. The proceedings were effectively under the control of the Emperor John Vatatzes. He offered recognition of papal *plenitudo potestatis* in return for assurances that the papacy would no longer send aid to Latin Constantinople. The question of the procession

78 Ibid., 462.

79 Ibid., 464.

80 E. Lempp, *Frère Elie de Cortone* (Paris, 1901), 146–7.

81 Gill, *Byzantium and the Papacy*, 88–95; L. Stiernon, 'Le problème de l' union gréco-latine vue de Byzance. De Germain II à Joseph 1er (1232–73)', in *1274. Année charnière: mutations et continuités* (Paris, 1977), 148–52; A. Franchi, *La svolta politico-ecclesiastica tra Roma e Bisanzio (1249–1254)* (Rome, 1981).

of the Holy Ghost was more difficult. The Latin position was challenged at the council by the Greek spokesman, Nicephorus Blemmydes.[82] But this was not sufficient to remove the basis for further negotiations.

A Byzantine delegation was despatched to the papal curia, bearing a deferential letter from the Patriarch Manuel II. In it he applauded the pope's efforts to bring unity to the church. He singled out the following topics for discussion: the oecumenical council, the honour due to the papacy, and the claims that the pope had over against the patriarch. Nothing was said specifically about any theological differences. The Byzantine delegation was invested with plenary powers and the patriarch bound himself to accept whatever was decided between his delegates and the pope.[83] The Byzantine delegates were to have various adventures on their way, but, when they finally arrived at Perugia, they found Innocent IV in a conciliatory mood. He acclaimed the sincerity of the Greek church's desire for union and willingness to accept papal primacy. He temporised on the question of the procession of the Holy Ghost. The Greeks refused to accept the addition of the *filioque* to the creed, unless its validity could be adduced from scripture or through some *divinum oraculum*. Innocent IV accepted that broadly speaking Greek and Latin teaching coincided, while hoping that the Greeks might some day be persuaded to adhere to the Latin position on the procession of the Holy Ghost. Even more hopeful was the pope's offer of formal recognition of the Greek patriarchate.[84] Negotiations continued, but in 1254 the architects of *entente*, Pope Innocent IV, the Emperor John Vatatzes, and the Patriarch Manuel II, all died within a few months of each other. The impetus was lost.

John Vatatzes was succeeded by his son Theodore II Lascaris, who tried to revive negotiations with the papacy in 1256 over the reunion of churches. The new Pope Alexander IV despatched an envoy who met the Nicaean emperor and his new Patriarch Arsenius Autoreianos at Thessalonica. The papal delegation was received with due honour, but it was soon clear that it was in no position to make any concessions. The papal envoy was tied by his very detailed instructions. He returned to the pope, but in the company of a Byzantine embassy bearing a letter from the patriarch. Its tone was suitably irenic. The Patriarch Arsenius seems even to have dropped for the moment from his titulature the epithet 'oecumenical', which gave such offence to the papacy. But it could not disguise the impasse that had been reached. The pope was unwilling to deliver Constantinople to the Greeks and the Greeks could

[82] Blemmydes, 67–73.

[83] Franchi, *La svolta*, 167–79, where he argues convincingly that the patriarch's letter should be dated to the summer of 1250, as against Laurent 1319, who would prefer summer 1253.

[84] Ibid., 193–215.

not otherwise accept reunion on the terms demanded by the papacy. Alexander IV saw no point in despatching another delegation for talks that were bound to be fruitless.[85]

Perhaps the most striking feature of the Patriarch Arsenius's letter to the pope is its insistence on the role of the emperor in any negotiations over the reunion of churches. The pope was urged to collaborate directly with the emperor. It was only the emperor who possessed the qualities needed, if the gaping chasm separating the two churches was to be bridged.[86] It was a return to the deference to imperial authority that had characterised the patriarchs of the late twelfth century. Negotiations over the union of churches allowed the emperors to recover the initiative in ecclesiastical affairs. John Vatatzes took charge of the proceedings of the two councils where the union of churches was discussed. He even put forward his own suggestions on ways of resolving the theological differences separating the two churches.

There seems to have been no protest on the part of the orthodox church. But a dangerous gap was opening up. John Vatatzes returned to the ploys of his twelfth-century predecessors, but the Latins were now identified as the enemy of the orthodox faith. The issue was complicated by the activities of the friars, but they would come to be seen – quite rightly – as a threat to orthodoxy. The question of the union of churches was almost bound to drive a wedge between the emperor and the orthodox church. So it proved. Michael VIII Palaeologus would use John Vatatzes's negotiations with the papacy as a precedent for his own. These culminated in 1274 in the union of churches at Lyons, but his actions, unlike those of his predecessor, polarised Byzantine society. It was in some ways his misfortune to bring negotiations to a successful conclusion. The lesson of Michael Palaeologus's unionist endeavours was this: despite appearances the potential for the polarisation of Byzantine society over the issue of the union of churches was notably increased by the fall of Constantinople in 1204. It could hardly be otherwise, given the way that the Byzantine identity was now constructed in opposition to the Latins.

Scholars at the Nicaean court generalised the use of 'Hellene' to mean Byzantine. It was a way of asserting their cultural superiority over the Latins.[87] The leader of anti-Latin opinion at the Nicaean court was the future emperor Theodore II Lascaris. A noted scholar and theologian he saw the Latin challenge very much in cultural terms. He presided over a debate that took place at the Nicaean court between Greek scholars

[85] Laurent, 1332; Stiernon, 'Le problème', 151–2; Gill, *Byzantium and the Papacy*, 98–100.

[86] Whether the letter reflects Arsenius's true position is open to doubt, since it was drafted for him by the metropolitan of Thessalonica, Manuel Disypatos.

[87] See Angold, 'Byzantine "Nationalism"', 64–6.

and members of a Hohenstaufen delegation. He awarded victory to the Greeks. He claimed that it reflected great credit on the 'Hellenes'. Theodore was the self-appointed leader of a fight against cultural barbarism at the Nicaean court. He took exception to the enthusiasm there was among the young men of the court for popular literature.[88] He saw this as evidence of pernicious Latin influence on popular Byzantine romances. His task was to foster the study of philosophy, for there was a danger that 'Philosophy' might abandon the Greeks and seek refuge among the Latins. Such a danger had already been underlined by the performance of the papal envoys in the debates at Nicaea and Nymphaion. 'Hellene' did not have an exclusively cultural connotation. It might on occasion merge with an ideology of Empire. In a letter to Pope Gregory IX the Emperor John Vatatzes not only claimed to have received the gift of royalty from Constantine the Great, but also emphasised his 'Hellenic' descent and exalted the wisdom of the Greek people.[89] He was presenting 'Hellenic' culture as an integral part of the Byzantine polity in defiance of Latin claims. The events of 1204 brought into sharp focus an image of the Latins that had been taking shape since the time of the first crusade. The sack of Constantinople convinced the Byzantines that the Latins were a brutish people. Their devotion to war had perverted their Christian faith. Far from restraining their natural tendencies the Latin church had encouraged them for its own ends: the papacy was exploiting the militant Christianity of the crusade to provide a violent solution to the religious differences which existed between Rome and Constantinople. This view appeared to receive confirmation from the occasional bouts of persecution to which the Latins resorted in their dealings with the orthodox communities of Cyprus and Constantinople. The Latins became the major enemy of orthodoxy and a threat to its existence. Their demands for submission were to be resisted at all costs. The great task was to drive them from Constantinople. There was a strong populist flavour to these anti-Latin feelings. They took root among the monks and laity and were never eradicated. There was almost invariably a hostile reaction to any deal with the Latins that might compromise orthodoxy.

However, the old traditions of Byzantine *realpolitik* soon reasserted themselves at the Nicaean court. It was recognised that an agreement with the papacy might well be the key to the recovery of Constantinople. Such a possibility was enhanced by the appearance of the friars. They revealed a face of Latin Christianity which was quite different from the warlike image associated with the crusades. They gave hope that

[88] Beaton, *Medieval Greek Romance*, 151–9.

[89] V. Grumel, 'L'authenticité de la lettre de Jean Vatatzès, empereur de Nicée au pape Grégoire IX', *EO* 29(1930), 452–4.

reason and Christian charity would prevail in negotiations with Rome. This was a possibility which might be used to counter the likely opposition to any such negotiations. There are no signs of opposition to the negotiations carried on by the Emperor John III Vatatzes at the two meetings with friars in papal service which were held at the palace of Nymphaion in 1234 and 1250. The emperor had the support of his patriarchs and was able to enlist the help of Nicephorus Blemmydes, the leading orthodox theologian of his time. There can be no disguising that the emperor was in total control of these negotiations. The patriarch had only a subordinate role. The dominating stance of the emperor could be justified on the grounds that it was a matter of diplomacy, as much as of religion. It might also have been construed as an unwarrantable extension of imperial authority that was liable to endanger orthodoxy.

This was the pitfall that awaited Michael VIII Palaeologus. The difficulties he faced over the union of churches stemmed in part from the bitter sense of betrayal felt by the bulk of his subjects, but this was sharpened by the conviction that he was exceeding the bounds of imperial authority. The fall of Constantinople almost inevitably produced a reappraisal of imperial authority and its relationship with the church.

25

IMPERIAL AUTHORITY AND THE ORTHODOX CHURCH

In exile the emperors of Nicaea laid claim to the authority of their Byzantine predecessors, pending the recovery of Constantinople. This was an attraction of negotiations with the papacy. These appeared to give credence to their universalist pretensions. Such claims had begun to have a hollow ring to them even before 1204. The fall of Constantinople tested, in a way that nothing else could have, the enduring strengths of the Byzantine imperial institution. The emperors of Nicaea were 'ridiculed as men without a state forced by necessity to sojourn far from the imperial throne'.[1] They were able to take some comfort from the presence of an orthodox patriarch at Nicaea: it allowed them to pose as the guardians of orthodoxy. The notion of the emperor as the *epistemonarkhes* or arbiter of the orthodox church was quickly revived.[2]

We have seen how the emperors of Nicaea cooperated with their patriarchs in efforts to protect the orthodox under Latin rule. They also strove to preserve the unity of the orthodox world as it existed before 1204. This gave the emperors of Nicaea a degree of influence that went way beyond the narrow territories that they at first controlled in western Asia Minor. But the destruction of the Byzantine Empire in 1204 was bound to underline the discrepancies there always were between the boundaries of empire and church. It also emphasised how heavily the emperor would have to rely upon his patriarch in the conduct of relations with other orthodox countries. The patriarchs of Constantinople would come to have responsibilities that went far beyond the political interests of their emperors.

Concessions had to be made to preserve a semblance of unity. It was a major achievement of the patriarchs at Nicaea that the orthodox church survived the period of exile more or less intact. The major

[1] Georges Pachymérès. *Relations historiques*, ed. A. Faillier, transl. V. Laurent (Paris, 1984), 2 vols., I, 211.5–6. Cf. Loukaki, 'Première didascalie', 166.99–111.

[2] Mesarites II, 31.7–9; E. Kurtz, 'Tri sinodal'nykh gramoty mitropolita Efesskago Nikolaja Mesarita', *VV* 12(1906), 104.25–8.

challenge came from the papacy. There was always a danger that local churches would turn to the papacy in the face of Nicaean claims. This is what happened in Cyprus. Nicaean efforts to intervene on behalf of the Cypriots aroused the resentment of the orthodox archbishop of Cyprus. His was after all an autocephalous church. In the end, the Cypriot church preferred to come to an accommodation with the papacy.[3] There was a real danger that Serbia and Bulgaria too would pass into the papal orbit.

The orthodox church in Epiros deliberately exploited the Roman issue in order to counter Nicaean claims. In 1220 the Nicaean patriarch was planning to hold a council that Easter at Nicaea as a preliminary to negotiations with the papacy over the reunion of the two churches. The leading prelate of Epiros, John Apokaukos, metropolitan of Naupaktos, protested to the patriarch. He thought that this was a sign of weakness and would only encourage the Latins 'to close our churches, where they rule, and to commit a thousand and one mischiefs against the [orthodox] Christians subject to them'. He could see no prospect of a successful conclusion. The negotiations were all too obviously directed to diplomatic ends and were linked to the marriage alliance which the Nicaean Emperor had recently concluded with the Latin emperors of Constantinople. This Apokaukos roundly condemned. He warned that concessions to the Latins on the part of the Nicaeans were threatening schism within the orthodox church.[4] Apokaukos remained resolutely anti-Latin. 'None of the Holy Fathers accepts the religion or sacrifice of the Latins' was his opinion when consulted by the orthodox bishop of Venetian-held Corone.[5]

His colleague Demetrius Chomatianos, the archbishop of Ohrid, was just as capable of condemning the Latins as the enemies of orthodoxy. It therefore comes as a surprise that not once, but twice, he voiced opinions on the Latins of a startling liberality. On the first occasion he was consulted on the propriety of an orthodox bishop entering a Latin church and partaking of the sacraments. He saw no objections to this and gave it as his opinion that apart from the question of the *filioque* there were no serious differences of custom and teaching between the Greeks and the Latins. On the second occasion the question of the azymes was raised. He refused to condemn the Latins for this practice. Equally, he refused to consider the possibility of its introduction into orthodox usage. Different churches

3 Hussey, *The Orthodox Church*', 203–4.

4 Vasilievskij, 'Epirotica saeculi XIII.', no. 15, 265–7.

5 Apokaukos I, no.55, 111–12. Cf. A. Basilikopoulou, ''Ανέκδοτη γραφὴ τοῦ 'Απόκαυκου στὸν 'επίσκοπο Κορώνης', in *ΠΡΑΚΤΙΚΑ ΤΟΥ Β' ΔΙΕΘΝΟΥΣ ΣΥΝΕΔΡΙΟΥ ΠΕΛΟ-ΠΟΝΝΗΣΙΑΚΩΝ ΣΠΟΥΔΩΝ*, II (Athens, 1981–2), 241–8. See Apokaukos I, 132.66–8 (= *Noctes*, 278.13–15), for further views on the Latins.

had different practices was his tolerant conclusion. In his discussions of these problems Chomatianos was critical of Theodore Balsamon who insisted that Latins were only worthy to receive communion from an orthodox priest, if they first renounced their errors. This pronouncement had been made when the future archbishop of Ohrid was still a student at Constantinople. He remembered that at the time there were those who considered Balsamon's views on the Latins unnecessarily harsh.

What were the circumstances that induced Chomatianos to revive a more liberal attitude to the Latins, which 1204 and its aftermath had seemed to extinguish? He refers to an Italy teeming with famous churches dedicated to Apostles and martyrs, supreme among them being St Peter's at Rome. It is therefore conceivable that his answer was designed for some emissary on a mission to Italy. The metropolitan of Corfu George Bardanes was sent on just such a mission in 1231, at a time when the Greek ruler in the West Manuel Angelus was considering submission to the papacy.

This remains the likely background to Demetrius Chomatianos's opinion on contacts with the Latins. However, he chose to justify his favourable attitude to the Latins rather differently. He was persuaded by Theophylact of Bulgaria's conciliatory views on the schism with the Latins, which he quotes at length.[6] Theophylact was his most distinguished predecessor within living memory.[7] He had struggled hard and not without success to defend the privileges of the see of Ohrid. The fame of his commentaries on the Bible added their own prestige. Chomatianos was himself engaged in a struggle with the patriarchs at Nicaea. He was the champion of an autonomous Epirot church with his see of Ohrid as its obvious centre. In this struggle it was natural to invoke his great predecessor and to be guided by his views, even if it did mean proposing a liberal line on the Latins.

Chomatianos's opinions scarcely tally with the harsh view of the Latins that was fixed in the aftermath of the fall of Constantinople. They are best explained by political considerations. The Latin issue became part of the politicking among the various Byzantine successor states that arose after the conquest of Constantinople in 1204. In 1225 the Epirot bishops warned the patriarch at Nicaea of the likely consequences of any failure on his part to respect the autonomy of the church in Epiros. Their ruler Theodore Angelus might be forced to place it under the supervision of the pope.[8]

[6] Chomatianos, 625–30, 727–30,

[7] See above, pp. 158–72.

[8] Vasilievskij, 'Epirotica saeculi XIII', 291.16–19.

The Nicaean patriarchate and the orthodox world

For much of the period of exile the patriarchs of Nicaea were therefore on the defensive in their dealings with the papacy. In a letter to the papal curia the Patriarch Germanos II claimed that Ethiopians, Syrians, Iberians, Abasgians, Alans, Alastoi, Goths, Khazars, Russians, and Bulgarians were all obedient to the Greek church and steadfast in their orthodoxy.[9] The patriarch was guilty of exaggeration. It was an act of defiance. It was a way of emphasising that he had an oecumenical role to play that placed him on an equal footing with the pope. He was more restrained in a letter he wrote to the Epirot bishops. He claimed that his pastoral authority was recognised by the inhabitants of the Crimea, the Armenians and the Iberians, the Russians, the Melkites of Jerusalem, the Albanians of the Caucasus, and by the people of Monemvasia.[10] There seems no reason to dispute this. The Albanians are almost certainly to be identified with the Alans. Their metropolitan bishop Theodore was appointed from Nicaea. In 1223 he sent an account of his experiences among them to the patriarchal synod at Nicaea.[11]

More significant evidence of the patriarch's continuing authority in the wider orthodox community is provided by the letter Germanos II sent in 1228 to the metropolitan bishop of Russia. Its purpose was the regulation of various matters which had arisen within the Russian church. It is proof that the church in Russia still acknowledged the overriding authority of the patriarch, even if he was now in exile at Nicaea. The metropolitan bishop of Russia needed the patriarch's support against pressure from the Russian princes. The patriarch inveighed against their usurpation of ecclesiastical property and warned them that they had no business hearing cases involving divorce, abduction, and rape. These belonged to the episcopal courts.[12] The Russian church had always come under the direct control of the patriarch of Constantinople who appointed its metropolitan bishop. Before 1204 the metropolitan bishops of Russia were almost invariably Greeks, but by the middle of the fourteenth century the alternate appointment of a Russian and a Greek had become the rule. It has been suggested that this started with the appointment in 1242 of the Russian Cyril (1242–81) as metropolitan of Russia.[13] This is mostly assumption, but it has been advanced in the light of the concessions made by the

[9] Laurent, 1257.

[10] R.-J. Loenertz, 'Lettre de Georges Bardanès, métropolite de Corcyre, au patriarche oecuménique Germain II 1226–1227c.', *EEBΣ* 33(1964), 107–8.

[11] Migne, *PG*, 140. 388–413.

[12] Laurent, 1247.

[13] D. Obolensky, 'Byzantium, Kiev and Moscow: a study of ecclesiastical relations', *DOP* 11(1957), 34; J. Meyendorff, *Byzantium and the Rise of Russia* (Cambridge, 1981), 39–41.

patriarchs in exile to other Slav churches. The most telling piece of evidence is a seal belonging to the metropolitan bishop of Russia Cyril. He entitles himself not 'bishop of the metropolis of Russia', as had been proper, but 'archbishop of the metropolis of Russia'. This seal was published by Père V. Laurent. His conclusion was that this use of the title archbishop indicated that Cyril had been granted autocephalous authority. It pointed to an agreement similar to that concluded earlier between the Nicaean patriarch and St Sava, archbishop of Serbia.[14]

In 1219 the Nicaean patriarch had appointed St Sava archbishop of Serbia and his church was accorded autocephalous status.[15] It was as much as anything a recognition of the political independence of Serbia. It was a concession that was easy to make because the patriarch was surrendering very little. Traditionally, for ecclesiastical purposes Serbia came under the jurisdiction of the archbishopric of Ohrid. The incumbent Demetrius Chomatianos was understandably far from happy with the patriarch's action. He protested to St Sava about this infringement of the rights of his see.[16] It still rankled years later when he raised the matter with the new patriarch Germanos II. He complained bitterly about this unwarranted intrusion on the part of the Nicaean patriarch into the affairs of his church. It was on a par with the recent ordination at Nicaea of a Bulgarian archbishop, who also properly came under the jurisdiction of the church of Ohrid.[17]

Relations with the Bulgarian church were a pressing issue for Chomatianos. Were ordinations of the Bulgarian church valid? He sent the problem before his synod, which began by reviewing the recent history of the church. It was agreed that the Bulgarian church had submitted to Rome. A cardinal was sent out and granted the head of the church the title of patriarch – more correctly primate. Nothing is said about a break with Rome and a return to the orthodox allegiance. It was nevertheless decided that circumstances were so confused after 1204 that the ordinations of the Bulgarian church should be accepted. This decision was arrived at after the intervention of Theodore Angelus who made a plea for moderation. Theodore is not given the imperial title, which means that the incident should be dated before 1224.[18]

[14] Laurent, *Corpus* v, no.792.

[15] See Obolensky, *Six Byzantine Portraits*, 146–52.

[16] Chomatianos, 381–90.

[17] Ibid., 495–6. Referring to the ordination of the archbishops of both Serbia and Bulgaria Chomatianos uses 'αὐτόθεν', which must point to Nicaea as the place where the ordinations took place. This letter of Chomatianos to the patriarch cannot be dated precisely. Since its main purpose was to defend his coronation of Theodore Angelus in 1226/7, it is likely to date to before the latter fell into the hands of the Bulgarians in 1230. It is therefore very likely that a Bulgarian archbishop was ordained at Nicaea *c.*1230.

[18] Chomatianos, 563–70.

The events of 1228–9 provide the likely occasion for a rapprochement between Bulgaria and Nicaea. The Latin emperor of Constantinople, Robert of Courtenay, died in disgrace early in 1228, leaving the eleven year old Baldwin II to succeed him. The Bulgarian Tsar John II Asen (1218–41) proposed a marriage alliance: his daughter would marry the young emperor and he would act as regent. The Latin barons reacted to this proposal, more decisively than the Byzantines had reacted to a similar proposal made three centuries earlier by another Bulgarian tsar – Symeon. They rejected it out of hand and turned instead to John of Brienne, the former king of Jerusalem. In April 1229 the papacy approved his appointment as Latin emperor of Constantinople. Rebuffed Asen explored the possibility of an alliance with Nicaea.

It seems very possible that a Bulgarian archbishop was ordained at Nicaea around the year 1230.[19] The Bulgarian tsar certainly recognised the authority of the patriarch at Nicaea over the Bulgarian church before 1233, for Germanos II's exarch of the West took up his appointment in that year and his commission covered Bulgarian as well as Epirot territories. The exarch arranged a meeting with the head of the Bulgarian church, the archbishop of Trnovo, who had taken refuge on Mount Athos. He ordered the archbishop to return to his see. Such peremptory treatment reinforces the possibility that the archbishop had received his ordination at Nicaea. When he demurred, the exarch informed the Bulgarian tsar and requested that he have another archbishop elected. He recognised that ordination would be a problem. He suggested two possibilities: the tsar was to send the new archbishop for ordination either to the patriarch at Nicaea, or, if circumstances did not permit this, to the exarch at Thessalonica. But on no account was he to receive his ordination in Bulgaria.[20]

This rider suggests that Asen was beginning to have reservations about the subordination of his church to the patriarch at Nicaea. He was angling for a more equitable arrangement, which he achieved over the following year. He concluded a formal alliance with the Nicaean emperor John Vatatzes. This was to be cemented not only by the marriage of his young daughter to the heir to the Nicaean throne, but also by the recognition of the Bulgarian church's patriarchal status. The only restriction imposed was an obligation to commemorate the orthodox patriarch in the liturgy of the Bulgarian church, as a recognition of the patriarch's spiritual authority.[21]

In their dealings with the orthodox churches in Serbia, Bulgaria, and

[19] See above n. 17

[20] Kurtz, 'Christophoros von Ankyra', 141–2.

[21] Laurent, 1282, 1285.

very probably in Russia too, the Nicaean patriarchs can be credited with a high degree of realism. It was better to preserve a primacy of honour, rather than lose complete control. In the background was the threat from the papacy. The Bulgarian church was nominally under papal authority from 1204 to *c.* 1230, while the influence of the papacy in Serbia was underlined when in 1217 the Serbian ruler obtained a crown from Rome. If the example of Bulgaria was any guide, the next step should have been the submission of the Serbian church to the pope. The concessions made by the Nicaean patriarchs were the price to be paid for saving the Serbians and the Bulgarians from Rome. They were that much easier to make because before 1204 they had formed part of the autocephalous archbishopric of Ohrid and were therefore not directly under the control of the patriarchate of Constantinople.

Nicaea and Epiros[22]

The archbishop of Ohrid, Demetrius Chomatianos, did not take kindly to these infringements of the rights of his church. He had an elevated notion of the dignity of his see. He would assume the leadership of the orthodox church in the territories of Theodore Angelus, who became an increasingly formidable opponent of the Nicaean Empire. He was able to extend his rule from its original nucleus in Epiros until it covered most of continental Greece and the southern Balkans. With the conquest of Thessalonica in the autumn of 1224 he acquired a fitting capital. He had himself proclaimed emperor and was then duly crowned and anointed in 1226/7 by Demetrius Chomatianos. This was a direct challenge not only to the imperial pretensions of the emperors of Nicaea, but also to the rights of the patriarch. Germanos II protested bitterly: by what right did an archbishop of Ohrid crown and anoint an emperor?[23] The patriarch was apprehensive about Chomatianos's ambitions. He was claiming quasi-patriarchal status for his see. The church of Ohrid only included in its jurisdiction the churches in the northern parts of Theodore Angelus's territories. But there was a good chance that Chomatianos would extend his authority to all the churches under Theodore's rule. He had already taken it upon himself to ordain a bishop of Servia, even though this see was under the church of Thessalonica. He had written to Germanos II, claiming that this had been done because of pressure of circumstances.[24] In addition, Chomatianos's tribunal attracted litigants, from both laity and clergy, from all over Theodore Angelus's territories. It was, in

[22] See Nicol, I, 76–102; Karpozilos, *The Ecclesiastical Controversy.*
[23] Chomatianos, 483–6; Laurent, 1244.
[24] Chomatianos, 577–88.

practice, beginning to act as a court of appeal and was assuming some of the functions of a patriarchal synod. Germanos II was thus brought face to face with the spectre of two Byzantine Empires and the orthodox church of Constantinople divided into an eastern and a western church. A letter from the Epirot bishops might assure the patriarch that they intended to preserve the unity of the church by recognising his spiritual authority, but for how much would this count, if the patriarch was to be excluded from any say in the organisation of the church in the West?[25]

There was also a practical consideration that the patriarch had to take into account. The assumption of the imperial title, whether at Nicaea or at Thessalonica, could only be justified retrospectively by the recovery of Constantinople.[26] This intensified the sense of rivalry between the two Byzantine successor states. The patriarch's obligations to the Nicaean emperor ruled out any concessions to Theodore Angelus and his bishops and archbishop. The patriarch despatched an emissary to Thessalonica to see if there was a genuine desire among the western bishops for continued unity.[27] The mission failed. Canonical relations were broken off and the patriarch's name was removed from the diptychs of the churches of Theodore Angelus's territories. George Bardanes had the task of notifying the patriarch that a state of schism now existed.[28]

Fortuitously, it was not to last very long. In 1230 Theodore Angelus was defeated and captured by the Bulgarian Tsar John Asen. His power was broken. His brother Manuel secured Thessalonica and proclaimed himself emperor, but it was a sham. He had little effective authority. He tried to shore up his position by overtures to the papacy.[29] All he could do, when these failed, was to come to terms with Nicaea. He begged the patriarch to intercede on his behalf with John Vatatzes. Germanos insisted that the western bishops should be assembled and should solemnly proclaim the reunion of churches and their submission to the patriarch at Nicaea. This was duly done in the spring of 1232.[30] Germanos assumed that those western bishops appointed without patriarchal approval would now make their way to Nicaea to receive ordination at his hands, but Manuel Angelus objected to this, because of the dangers of the journey. He suggested that the patriarch would do better to despatch one of his bishops to the West in order to carry

25 Vasilievskij, 'Epirotica saeculi XIII', no.26, 288–92.
26 Ibid., 288.10–14.
27 Laurent, 1248.
28 Loenertz, 'Lettre de Georges Bardanès', 92–3.
29 Hoeck and Loenertz, *Nikolaos-Nektarios von Otranto*, 154–5.
30 Ibid., 156–8.

this out on his behalf.[31] This had been anticipated: the patriarch had already appointed the metropolitan bishop of Ankyra as exarch of all the West with responsibility for supervising the reunion of the churches. Germanos also promised in due course to visit the West, which he did in 1238.[32]

The trouble with the church in the territories of Theodore Angelus was that its organisation was divided between Ohrid and Constantinople. The patriarchs at Nicaea were determined to retain control over those sees that before 1204 were directly dependent on Constantinople. They could not therefore countenance the creation of a separate ecclesiastical organisation for the church of the western territories. This does not mean that they saw a complete identity of interests between the patriarchate and the Nicaean Empire; nor that they pursued a diplomacy that was entirely in the political interests of the emperors of Nicaea. They continued to think in terms of a larger orthodox community of which the patriarch remained the focus, wherever his residence may have been and whatever concessions may have been made to local particularism.

The debate over Byzantine unity

Theodore Angelus's assumption of the imperial title at Thessalonica challenged the prior claims of the emperors at Nicaea and cast a shadow over the continuing unity of the orthodox church. To justify his action the churchmen of his territories were forced to subject the old notion of one church one empire to scrutiny. Their views, as might be expected, contain a large measure of special pleading. They were well aware that they were challenging the dearest tenet of Byzantine political philosophy and that their actions might well put an end to any hope of restoring the old political unity of the Byzantine Empire. There was, however, something far worse: they were condoning actions which threatened to fissure the orthodox community at a time when it was striving under the leadership of the patriarch at Nicaea to recover from the loss of Constantinople to the Latins. In retrospect, their views seem far more realistic than does the die-hard espousal of traditional ideas about the integrity of the Empire that by and large characterise the last phase of Byzantine history.

George Bardanes was deputed to justify to the Patriarch Germanos II the defection of the church in Epiros. He made a plea for tolerating

31 Miklosich & Müller III, 61–2.

32 Ibid., 64–5; Laurent, 1263; Loenertz, 'Lettre de Georges Bardanès', 94–5; Hoeck and Loenertz, *Nikolaos-Nektarios von Otranto*, 158–9.

political division. He did not believe that it was inconsistent with ecclesiastical unity. In his scheme this would be guaranteed by the spiritual authority of the patriarch at Nicaea, who would continue to preside over the orthodox community. 'Let each come to an understanding on these terms, enjoying his own Sparta and being content with his lot, not casting covetous eyes to the other extremities of the earth, but living in contentment and brotherly love, fearing God and paying respect each to his own king.'[33]

In the letter that Demetrius Chomatianos wrote to the patriarch on the same matter he justified political division slightly differently. After the fall of Constantinople the Empire was in a sense divided with an equal proportion of bishops and members of the senate fleeing to the East and West, where successor states were created. The ancient customs of Constantinople for the making of an emperor or the promotion of a patriarch no longer had their old force. It was necessary to adapt to new circumstances; to accept that there was now a division of imperial authority. The East was 'sufficient unto itself' but was in no position to bring aid to the West. The hard fact, as Chomatianos saw it, was that imperial authority had been shattered by the loss of Constantinople and had to be rebuilt on a different basis, which necessitated political but not ecclesiastical division.[34]

Chomatianos's remarks should have touched a chord at Nicaea. Self-sufficiency or autarky was the aim of the Emperor John Vatatzes's economic policies. He sought to make his dominions self-supporting. Complementing this was the cultural exclusivity claimed by intellectuals at the Nicaean court. They appropriated Byzantium's Hellenic heritage. George Acropolites, the historian of the Nicaean Empire, fixed the Pindos mountains as the boundary between Epiros and 'our Hellenic land'. His master the Emperor Theodore II Lascaris identified Hellas squarely with Nicaean Asia Minor, which he also referred to as 'Our Holy Mother Anatolia'. Greeks from Nicaea were inclined to treat other Greeks as foreigners. Though stated in rather different terms the Nicaean court subscribed to the division of the old Byzantine world that had come about after the loss of Constantinople. It was a way of reconciling traditional political philosophy with the realities of the time.[35]

It would not have been politic to suggest at the Nicaean court that perhaps the church no longer required the political unity of a single empire. Nicephorus Blemmydes was anything but politic. He was

33 Loenertz, 'Lettre de Georges Bardanès', 116–17: transl by Nicol, *Epiros* I, 96–7.
34 Chomatianos, 489–90. See R.J. Macrides, 'Bad historian or good lawyer? Demetrios Chomatenos and Novel 131', *DOP* 46(1992), 187–96.
35 Angold, 'Byzantine "nationalism"', 64–6.

recognised as the greatest scholar of his time. John Vatatzes entrusted him with the education of his son Theodore Lascaris. He was the confidant of the Patriarch Germanos II who recommended him to John Vatatzes as his successor. The emperor turned down this advice. He was willing to retain him as a special adviser to the patriarch, but this Blemmydes was not willing to be. Theodore II Lascaris offered him the patriarchal office at the beginning of his reign. He turned the offer down after much heart searching. Some would say that it was done out of vanity and pique, but Blemmydes had no wish to become the emperor's tool, which was so often the patriarch's lot. The emperor was insisting that the patriarch put the territories of the ruler of Epiros under an interdict in the hope of hastening his political subjugation. Blemmydes saw this as the subordination of the church to the imperial will for quite unwarranted ends.[36]

His views were close to those of Bardanes and Chomatianos. He rejected the notion that the emperor of Nicaea possessed any authority by virtue of his imperial claims over other Greek rulers, not even over the dynast of the island of Rhodes, Leo Gabalas. Blemmydes happened to be staying on the island in 1233 when it was attacked by a Nicaean expeditionary force. He considered that Gabalas had hereditary rights to the island and these took precedence over the imperial claims of the Lascarids of Nicaea.[37] He expressed much the same opinion apropos the Greek rulers of the western lands, which he visited in 1239 when collecting manuscripts.[38] He spent time at the court of the despot Michael II Angelus, the ruler of Epiros, and sent him and his consort a letter of thanks for their kindness. It contains some charming conceits. He uses the geometry of the parallelogram to emphasise the despot's authority and the parallel role of his consort. Thanks to the harmony there was between them their land was a place 'where hearts were moved by the hand of God'. Blemmydes concludes: 'that being so let all the people of God have confidence in the godlike despots, whose renown for religious knowledge and their acceptability [in God's sight] has reached the whole *oikoumene*'.[39] This went beyond the dictates of good manners. Blemmydes was giving his approval to the notion of a panorthodox community divided into a series of political units. Harmony and cooperation would be guaranteed by the orthodox piety of the individual rulers. In many ways, this was a highly realistic assessment of the condition of the Byzantine world after 1204.

[36] Blemmydes I, 74–82: ed. Munitiz, 37–41; transl. Munitiz, 85–90.
[37] Blemmydes II, 23: ed. Munitiz, 56; transl. Munitiz, 105–6.
[38] Blemmydes I, 63: ed. Munitiz, 32–3; transl. Munitiz 79–80.
[39] Nicephorus Blemmydes, *Epistolae* apud *Theodore Ducas Lascaris, Epistolae CCXVII*, ed. N. Festa (Florence, 1898), 322.71–3.

Blemmydes was the author of the *Basilikos Andrias*.[40] This was a 'Mirror of Princes' composed for his pupil Theodore II Lascaris. Like most of the genre it is a disappointing work of the utmost conventionality. Blemmydes drops scarcely a hint about contemporary affairs, beyond blaming the fall of Constantinople on the degenerate life style of the ruling class.[41] He expands a little on this line of thought in a letter to the Patriarch Manuel II. It was critical of intellectuals. He shuddered to think how many 'dialecticians, mathematicians, and physiologists' there were in Constantinople before the fall. 'What good was their learning!'[42] Blemmydes was contemptuous of the regime that had guided Byzantium's fortunes before 1204. He was expressing the common view that the fall of Constantinople was a fall from grace. It called in question the old certainties. Blemmydes appears more hopeful of the state of affairs that had come into existence in the orthodox world in his lifetime, where there was no single central authority or capital; where unity and a sense of identity was supplied by the church. Though expressed in very different terms his views seem close to those embraced in the West by Demetrius Chomatianos.

The defence of a belief in one church one empire was left to the Patriarch Germanos II. But he too was forced to confront the meaning of the fall of Constantinople. He was critical of its people. They were racially mixed; they were *mixobarbaroi*. They were the offspring of prostitutes and adulteresses; of Russian and Saracen concubines. He had hoped that the capital would be like some Noah's ark, but sheltering a racial mishmash it had not escaped the burden of its iniquities.[43] Exile would provide an opportunity for atonement and a chance 'to purify the dialect of the tribe'. Germanos II had nevertheless to admit that for some - he dismisses them as secularly minded - exile from Constantinople had diminished the prestige of the patriarchal office.[44] He looked for support to the emperor: his labours, he trusted, would one day restore the patriarchate to St Sophia.[45] He is lavish in his praise of John Vatatzes and his success against the Latins.[46] One of the main duties the patriarch had was to offer prayers of intercession on his behalf.[47] These sentiments are conventional, as befitted a patriarch who was striving to restore the traditional order, but there is something

40 H. Hunger and I. Ševčenko (ed.), *Des Nikephoros Blemmydes* ΒΑΣΙΛΙΚΟΣ ΑΝΔΡΙΑΣ *und dessen Metaphrase von Georgios Galesiotes und Georgios Oinaiotes* (Wiener Byzantinische Studien 18) (Vienna, 1986).

41 Ibid., 52.

42 Blemmydes apud Lascaris, *Epistolae*, ed. Festa, 326.

43 Germanos II, 282–3.

44 Ibid., 288–9.

45 Ibid., 275.23–5.

46 Blemmydes I, 74–82: ed. Munitiz, 37–41; transl. Munitiz, 85–90.

47 Germanos II, 265.4–7.

new: his emphasis upon the anointing of the emperor.[48] In his words 'the chrism of Empire validates the chosen of God'. He tells the emperor to go forth boldy, 'having on your head the sign of the chrism, for God in the hour of battle will protect your head'.[49] Anointing ensured God's favour and emphasised the sacral character of the imperial office.

Unction[50]

Anointing with chrism (*myrrhon*) seems only to have become a regular part of the Byzantine coronation order during the period of exile. Its introduction was a move of some significance and would seem at first sight to be connected with the loss of Constantinople. This was the view advanced by G. Ostrogorsky.[51] He thought that it was introduced in imitation of western practice as exemplified by the Latin emperors of Constantinople. There are references to emperors being anointed at Byzantium before 1204, but Ostrogorsky thought that these should be understood metaphorically. D.M. Nicol has reopened the whole question.[52] He disputes the notion that Latin practice underlay the introduction of the rite of anointing into the Byzantine coronation order. There was a major discrepancy between Latin and Byzantine practice. In the West a king was anointed with both oil and chrism, the former was used for the head and the latter for the body. The late Byzantine ritual was quite different: the patriarch would anoint the emperor's head with chrism, tracing the sign of the cross. Oil was not used and the body was not anointed. Most revealing was a remark dropped by Demetrius Chomatianos in a letter to Germanos II. The patriarch had rebuked him for anointing Theodore Angelus as part of his coronation, accusing him of usurping a patriarchal prerogative. Chomatianos defended his action. He pointed out among other things that before 1204 it had not been the prevailing custom to anoint an emperor with chrism, but only with specially sanctified oil. That being the case, the patriarch scarcely had grounds for his accusation against him.[53] Chomatianos did concede, however, that he had anointed Theodore Angelus with chrism in imitation of Nicaean practice.[54]

48 Ibid., 275.13–16.

49 Ibid., 347.35–40.

50 For a new interpretation see Dagron, 'Caractère sacerdotal', 173–8. Cf. Macrides, 'Bad historian or good lawyer?', 194–6. The subtlety impresses, but does not quite convince.

51 G. Ostrogorsky, 'Zur Kaisersalbung und Schilderhebung im spätbyzantinischen Krönungszeremoniell', *Historia* 4(1955), 246–56.

52 D.M. Nicol, 'Kaisersalbung. The unction of emperors in late Byzantine coronation ritual', *BMGS* 2(1976) 37–52.

53 Chomatianos, 493.

54 Ibid., 489.

This gives strong support to the assumption that Theodore I Lascaris was anointed with chrism at his coronation at Nicaea on Easter Day – so V. Laurent suggests[55] - 1208. He would possibly have been the first Byzantine emperor so to be. There is no direct evidence to support this supposition. There is, however, a letter written by Theodore Lascaris early in 1208 to the orthodox clergy of Constantinople. He requested their presence at Nicaea in the third week of Lent for the election of a new patriarch. He counselled against delay, for, should a patriarch be elected any later in the year, he would not be able to carry out the traditional ritual of concocting chrism which took place each year in Holy Week.[56] However, the emperor fails to make clear why he was placing such emphasis on this ceremony. Chrism was needed in the first place for the rite of confirmation (*teleiosis*). It may simply have been the coincidence of an emperor's coronation at Easter that led to the introduction into the ceremony of anointing with chrism. It is easy to see how it would confer greater solemnity on the occasion.

As we have seen, Chomatianos assumed that previous emperors had been anointed with oil, and not with chrism. His apparent certainty on this point means that we should be wary of interpreting all earlier references to the anointing of emperors at Byzantium as merely metaphorical. Michael Italikos, the future metropolitan bishop of Philippopolis, has left a detailed description of Manuel I Comnenus's coronation in 1143, where great play was made with anointing: 'If in those days the horn and the chrism and Samuel adorned the head of David, so too with us were none of the old customs neglected, for the horn represents influence and power from above and Samuel the holy patriarch . . . while the imperial chrism is none other than the oil of good tidings.'[57] Should this be taken metaphorically? Perhaps not, for there were misgivings in some quarters about Manuel Comnenus's accession: he was John II Comnenus's youngest son and had an elder brother still living. He was not a usurper, but his right to succeed was disputed. These were circumstances that may have demanded some extra sanction for imperial authority, of the sort that anointing might supply.

This is the sense of Theodore Balsamon's discussion of the usurper John Tzimiskes's accession in 969. He claimed that anointing with oil had been included in the ceremonial of Tzimiskes's coronation. This was done with the specific aim of wiping away the stain of his usurpation of the throne. Balsamon is inferring that anointing with oil was sometimes introduced in exceptional circumstances into the

55 V. Laurent, 'La chronologie des patriarches de Constantinople au 13e siècle', *REB* 27(1969), 132–3.

56 Mesarites II, 34–5.

57 Michael Italikos, 292.

coronation service, but it did not constitute a regular part of the ritual.[58] However, the canonist was soon being accused by a younger contemporary of being less than scrupulous in his interpretation of why anointing was included in Tzimiskes's coronation. There must have been some purpose behind his dishonesty. Viktor Tiftixoglu has put forward the very reasonable suggestion that Balsamon was acting to justify the usurpation of Andronicus I Comnenus, who initially had powerful supporters among the patriarchal clergy led by the Patriarch Basil Kamateros. If this was indeed the case, then it is more than likely that Andronicus was anointed at his coronation.[59]

Andronicus's usurpation was only one of several that occurred after the death of Manuel I Comnenus in 1180. It is likely that it was at this time that anointing with oil was introduced on a more regular basis into the Byzantine coronation ritual. This is implicit in Nicetas Choniates's description of Alexius III Angelus's accession in 1195, following the overthrow of his brother Isaac: he entered the church of St Sophia and 'was anointed emperor according to custom and was invested with the symbols of Empire'.[60] Nicetas is making a very clear distinction between anointing and investiture, as though they were different ceremonies.

But why change to anointing with chrism after 1204? Contemporaries offer almost no clues. Exile reinforced the parallels between the Byzantines and the children of Israel. This emphasised David as a model of kingship. Theodore Lascaris claimed that he had been anointed after the fashion of David,[61] but the earlier association of anointing with oil and usurpation may have been embarrassing. Chrism had the advantage of being associated with the rite of confirmation (*teleiosis*). If anointing was thought to provide an outward sign of divine confirmation of an emperor's assumption of office, then the use of chrism would be the more appropriate. At a time of upheaval and uncertainty anointing with chrism gave a spiritual dimension to imperial claims to legitimacy.[62] This seems to be the force of the correspondence between Germanos II and Demetrius Chomatianos which centred on the use of chrism in the coronation rite. The two prelates were not otherwise much interested in the meaning of the

58 Rhalles & Potles III, 44.

59 Tiftixoglu, 'Zur Genese der Kommentare des Theodoros Balsamon', 506–12, 530–2.

60 Nicetas Choniates, 457.14–16.

61 Nicetas Choniates, *Orationes*, 127.21–31.

62 Cf. Michael Italikos, 77.1–3, where the Patriarch Michael Kourkouas is congratulated on being chosen as patriarch by Manuel I Comnenus, who 'has anointed him with the myrrh of *teleiosis*.' The usage is obviously metaphorical, but its application to the investiture of a patriarch by an emperor emphasises the spiritual authority of both.

ceremony of anointing with chrism; they were much more concerned with mutual recrimination and with the defence of the rights of their respective churches.[63]

Did contemporaries attach a more specific meaning to the rite of anointing? Michael Choniates, the exiled archbishop of Athens, was relieved that Theodore Lascaris had been anointed by the patriarch. It meant that 'the imperial priesthood would enjoy the fragrance of the double myrrh'.[64] Choniates seems to be linking anointing with the sacral character of the imperial office. Still more enigmatic are some lines penned by Nicephorus Blemmydes in honour of the birth of Theodore II Lascaris's only son John: 'The father of the anointed is emperor and autocrat by right of inheritance / For he is the anointed of the anointed, and you are anointed of him.'[65] These lines seem to link the ceremony of anointing to hereditary right, but the play on words also implies that the emperor was the anointed of Christ.

By the end of the thirteenth century there was open acknowledgement of the connection between anointing with chrism and the sacred character of the imperial office. At the very end of his reign Michael VIII Palaeologus took exception to the will of the ex-Patriarch Joseph I. He noticed that the epithet *Hagios* or Holy was missing from the imperial titles. This was normally accorded to emperors anointed with chrism. Michael VIII protested about this failure on the ex-patriarch's part: 'Is it because he judges me unworthy of the sanctity of my office (*hagisteia*)?' It transpired that in the original draft of the will the epithet was included, but monks in Joseph's entourage were so scandalised by the thought of it being applied to a persecutor such as Michael Palaeologus that they forced its excision. Compliant by nature the ex-patriarch was happy to placate the emperor and to restore the epithet. The emperor preferred to let the matter drop rather than confirm the charge made against him by his enemies that he acted out of derision and not with an eye to the truth.[66] This reveals how anointing with chrism was connected with the emperor's moral and spiritual conduct. Many felt that Michael Palaeologus had failed to meet the obligations imposed upon an emperor through the rite of anointing. For the emperor to be holy he had to have been anointed with chrism, but it also meant that he might be called to account for his conduct in office.

The rite of anointing with chrism thus became an avowal of the spiritual responsibilities of a Byzantine emperor. These received particular

[63] Chomatianos, 481–98; Laurent, 1244; Macrides, 'Bad historian or good lawyer?', 187–94.

[64] Michael Choniates II, 258.20–4.

[65] Nichephorus *Curriculum Vitae et Carmina*, ed. A. Heisenberg (Leipzig, 1896), Blemmydes, 110 vv. 8–9.

[66] Pachymeres I (ed. Bonn), 507; George Pachymérès, *Relations historiques*, II, 638–9.

emphasis from the time of Alexius I Comnenus's accession. The title of *epistemonarkhes* was coined for Manuel I Comnenus and accentuated the imperial role in the affairs of the church. In a sense, the rite of anointing provided ceremonial expression of this new emphasis within the spectrum of imperial authority. After 1204 orthodox churchmen at Nicaea and elsewhere continued to subscribe to the Comnenian view that the emperor was the *epistemonarkhes* of the church. In 1216 Nicholas Mesarites, now metropolitan bishop of Ephesus, talked of the emperor being deputed to this position by God.[67] Demetrius Chomatianos was equally an exponent of this view. As befitted a good lawyer he provided a succinct definition of the powers an emperor exercised in his capacity as *epistemonarkhes* of the church: he had the right to review and validate the decisions of ecclesiastical synods; to regulate the organisation of the church and to issue legislation for the benefit of the clergy.[68]

Chomatianos's defence of imperial authority over the church seems at odds with a more critical evaluation of imperial authority that sometimes appears in his writings. Professor Simon has seized upon a short passage from a legal opinion given by Demetrius Chomatianos to suggest that he was proposing a radical solution to the problem of the relationship of imperial authority to the law.[69] The question was this: was the emperor above the law or was he bound by the law? It was usually assumed that the emperor was indeed above the law, but was morally bound to abide by it. As Chomatianos saw it there were two sides to civil law: normative or equitable, on the one hand, and executive, on the other. This division roughly corresponds to the difference between *auctoritas* and *potestas*. The emperor had complete control of the executive side of the law, but it was subject to the requirements of equity. This meant that imperial power was ultimately subordinate to the normative side of the law. In other words, the emperor was not only morally, but also legally obliged to conform to the authority of the law. Implicit in Chomatianos's formulation is the notion that Byzantine society was no longer held together by the exercise of imperial power, but by the looser ties provided by the authority of the law. It was a point of view that conformed well enough to the political realities of the Byzantine world after 1204.

Chomatianos was a good enough lawyer to defend himself against any charge of inconsistency. He would have been able to point out that in his definition the powers accorded to the emperor as *epistemonarkhes* of the church were of an executive nature. Not to labour the point

67 Kurtz, 'Tri sinodal'jnikh gramoty mitropolita Efesskago Nikolaja Mesarita', 104. 25–8.

68 Chomatianos, 631.

69 Ibid., 458–9; Simon, '*Princeps legibus solutus*'.

further: there were bound to be inconsistencies in the treatment of imperial authority in the aftermath of the fall of Constantinople. It is easy to understand why writers and lawyers had such difficulties in providing adequate formulations of imperial authority. They were trying to retrieve and preserve Byzantium's heritage and yet do justice to a world where the old certainties had been lost. Anointing with chrism underlined a shift in the nature of imperial authority at Byzantium that was already apparent under the Comneni. Emperors involved themselves more deeply in ecclesiastical affairs. Equally, they relied ever more heavily upon the church for moral support. It has been noted that, as the effective power of the emperor waned, so imperial claims on the church, far from diminishing, grew ever more extravagant. They culminated in the concordat concluded about 1380 between John V Palaeologus – that most pitiful of Byzantine emperors – and the patriarchate of Constantinople.[70] Under its terms the emperor was still 'the defender of the church and its canons' and was still claiming to exercise a supervisory role over the church, but claims were all the dignity he could aspire to. By that time in what else could imperial authority be founded but the church? It marked the bitter end of a development beginning with the emperors of the house of Comnenus. They understood that imperial power to be effective required the harnessing of the authority of the church. This became even more necessary during the period of exile, when the imperial office divorced from Constantinople needed ecclesiastical approval more than ever. Anointing with chrism was the ceremonial expression of the church's support for the imperial office, or to put it another way, of the emperor's need for the church's approval.[71]

Patriarch Germanos II

The introduction of unction into the Byzantine order of coronation underlined the alliance that bound emperor and patriarch in their struggle to preserve the heritage of orthodoxy. They were faced with the twin perils of subordination to the Latin West and of the fragmentation of the orthodox world. There was a danger that the orthodox church would break up into a series of local churches. This was largely averted thanks to the efforts of the patriarchs at Nicaea. They were rather more effective than their imperial counterparts in maintaining the cohesion of the old Byzantine Empire.

This does not mean that the relationship of patriarch and emperor

[70] V. Laurent, 'Les droits de l'empereur en matière ecclésiastique', *REB* 13(1955) 1–20.

[71] Dagron, 'Caractère sacerdotal', 177.

was radically altered. Old patterns persisted. In many ways, imperial reliance on the church pointed to even closer supervision of the patriarchal office. The emperors of Nicaea wanted patriarchs who were happy to do their bidding. A good proportion of their patriarchs were nonentities. One of them, Maximos, the former abbot of the Akoimetoi, was supposed only to have been appointed because of his connections in the womens' quarters of the imperial palace.[72] On another occasion the Emperor John Vatatzes kept the patriarchal throne vacant for two years. This was done because he could find no candidate that suited him. His final choice was a man of little ability and less learning. He even had a wife. His chief qualification seems to have been that he was the head (*protopappas*) of the imperial clergy and met the emperor's main requirement: compliance with his wishes.[73]

No such reservations apply to Germanos II (1223–40). He was quite exceptional and deserves to take his place among the great orthodox patriarchs of Constantinople. His origins were humble, but he obtained an education and before 1204 was a deacon of St Sophia. At the time of his elevation to the patriarchate (4 January 1223) he belonged to a monastic community near the city of Akhyraous in north-western Asia Minor and he must have been comparatively old. His achievement was to restore the prestige of the patriarchate. He was, as has become apparent, a traditionalist. He never wavered in his support for the Emperor John Vatatzes. It was with his help that Vatatzes overcame a serious conspiracy at the beginning of his reign hatched among the great families of the court. He considered such an attack on the Lord's anointed sacrilege.[74]

Germanos set out a programme for his patriarchate in a sermon he preached at the very beginning of his reign. Running through it was a comparison with Gideon. Just as Gideon was the fifth of the Judges of Israel, so Germanos was the fifth patriarch since the fall of Constantinople, sent 'to judge the new Israel'. He saw himself as the appointed leader of this new people. Casting himself in the role of a Judge of his people reveals his assessment of his task as patriarch. He came to lead them against their enemies, but this required a change of heart on their part. Germanos sought to reform society, as a precondition of the recovery of Constantinople. He singled out as his qualification for the tasks he set himself his time at Akhyraous, when he laboured among the local people to strengthen them in the faith passed

[72] Acropolites I, 19–22.

[73] Ibid., 72, 1–7; 100, 21–3; Blemmydes I, 69; ed. Munitiz, 35.11–15; transl. Munitiz 83.

[74] Germanos II, 261–2; Acropolites I, 36–7.

down from their fathers.[75] The necessity of preaching to the people was to be one of the themes of Germanos's patriarchate.

He identified with the people, perhaps because of his own origins. He poured out his scorn on those who did not think that he was fit to occupy the office of patriarch because he did not come from the nobility and his parents were not even from Constantinople. They forgot how humble Christ's life had been. And St Peter, was he not a poor fisherman? Yet *he* had been entrusted with the keys of heaven. The patriarch wished to share the life of the poor. This would entitle him 'to call himself a brother of Christ'.[76] He was not impressed by the vanity of power, citing the example of members of the imperial family and the heirs to imperial authority:

> They are exhausted by a myriad cares, worn out by misfortunes of every kind. Not even their property is spared, to pass over what is far worse: the way they drench the face of the earth with the blood of tens of thousands, all lest they are denied their proper inheritance. Yet it will not be long before death comes and drags them unwillingly away, sending them naked to their tombs.[77]

His responsibility was to the people, but he needed their support so that he could bear the burdens of his office, but among the heaviest burdens he had to bear were the sins of his people.[78] Germanos held up the celebration of communion as an expression of these mutual responsibilities: 'Many times every year we enter the sanctuary of the church, offering the bloodless sacrifice for our own and the people's ignorance and oversights.'[79] In this way, patriarch and people were joined in the celebration of the divine liturgy. Germanos tried to impress upon his congregation that communion was not to be taken lightly. It should be approached only by those with a clear conscience. Those unworthy to receive communion were the objects of divine indignation.[80] The celebration of the divine liturgy required a proper decorum. The patriarch had a duty to ensure this. The church must be respected. It was the house of the Lord and no place for unseemly behaviour. He turned to his congregation and asked what they would do if an imperial order came enjoining silence on the inhabitants of the city on pain of imprisonment. Would they not obey? In which case, how much rather should they respect God and keep silent during church services![81]

75 Germanos II, 216.10–19.
76 Ibid., 284.16–17, 286.15–16.
77 Ibid., 230.27–35.
78 Ibid., 223.2–8, 245.15–26.
79 Ibid., 245.18–20.
80 Ibid., 248–9.
81 Ibid., 231.7–17.

How could the church best fulfil its responsibilities to His people? This was the question that he directed in one sermon to the bishops. He proceeded to lecture them about the paramount importance of preaching. In the task of bringing salvation it was more important than baptism, for what good was baptism without the word of God? He quoted 1 Corinthians 1.17, 'For Christ sent me not to baptise, but to preach the gospel.' Priests had a duty to baptise, but bishops were better engaged preaching the word of God.[82] He disliked the idea held by some that the Apostles were mere distributors of charity. He held that it was 'better to serve the needy and to make oneself useful tending them with one's own hands than simply to abdicate responsibility by tossing them a coin'.[83] Like most reformers Germanos sought to return to the evangelical ideal of the Apostolic church.

Few patriarchs put such emphasis upon the pastoral duties of the hierarchy. It is reflected in his sermons. It is not just the themes he chose but his style of preaching which was designed to appeal to a popular audience. He usually takes as a starting point some incident in his own life, often trivial, and develops from it themes that illuminated the concerns of his time. Sometimes they were of immediate relevance, such as the prospect of the recovery of Constantinople, but more often he touched on matters of general interest. He began one of his sermons by sketching a notorious quarrel between members of his clergy about precedence during the Christmas service. To make matters worse, the patriarch went on, he had then found himself abandoned by his concelebrants in the middle of distributing holy communion. The smell of the roast lamb that awaited them after the service had proved too much for them![84] The patriarch was not amused by either incident, but it was a way of catching and holding the attention of his audience. They provided him with a starting point for the theme of his sermon: the proper upbringing of a child. God the Father would be outraged by such conduct in His church, but the patriarch would act like a good tutor, who would endeavour to stay a father's anger against his children. But fathers had a responsibility to bring their children up in pious ways: to teach them the difference between good and evil 'while the child still had a soul unmarked by the letters of evil'. Their reward was to see them married in church, but an even better outcome was to dedicate them to God and enrol them in the clergy.[85] Germanos II was drawing attention to the Christian responsibilities that fathers had for their children. Equally, as we have seen, he had his views about the role of a wife. She was in a sense her husband's conscience: understanding,

[82] Ibid., 292.12–19.
[83] Ibid., 293.12–14.
[84] Ibid., 257.1–8.
[85] Ibid., 257–9.

but ultimately responsible for ensuring his salvation.[86] It does not matter that the patriarch's views were conventional. It is much more important that he considered relationships within the family to be worthy of his attention. Family life was the concern of the church.

Again his insistence on the threat to Christian society from heresy was quite conventional, but the passion with which he addressed the problem was not.[87] He claimed to have encountered heretics before he became patriarch during the time he was at Akhyraous.[88] Soon after his elevation to the patriarchal office he travelled to Lydia in order to deal with a heretic called Leontios.[89] He does not specify the nature of these heresies, but he has left three sermons directed against the Bogomils.[90] Their sheer force lends conviction to a belief that he was dealing with a living heresy. He claimed that 'he had often confronted them face to face and had shamed their foul countenances, with the help of Christ whom they insult'.[91] He took the criticisms of the Bogomils against the orthodox church seriously, because they were superficially attractive. They claimed to be closer to the spirit of the New Testament than the orthodox. They quoted one of their favourite texts, Matthew 6.6: 'Enter into thy closet, and when thou has shut thy door, pray to thy Father which is in secret.' Yet the orthodox gathered in great churches and stood around crying out loud and indulging in vain repetition. Did Christ think that 'they shall be heard for their much speaking?' (Matthew 6.7).

Germanos reduced the charges of the Bogomils against the orthodox to three items: the first was the building of churches, when a chamber would do as well; the second their habit of congregating openly, thus defying the injunction to pray in secret; and third the wordiness of their form of worship, when the Lord's prayer sufficed.[92] He set out to rebut these charges from the New Testament because he knew that the Bogomils refused to accept the Old Testament. Germanos used Christ's driving of the money changers from the Temple as proof that he approved of the use of churches, as long as they were devoted to their proper purposes. In any case, it did not matter whether one prayed in secret or not, because God could divine the sincerity of the prayer offered. It was this that mattered.[93] The Bogomils countered

86 Ibid., 322–4; Migne, *PG*, 140. 661.

87 See A. Rigo, 'Il patriarca Germano II (1223–1240) e i Bogomili', *REB* 51(1993), 91–110.

88 Germanos II, 216.15–17.

89 Ibid., 260–1.

90 Migne, *PG*, 140. 621–44, 659–76; Germanos II, 234–43; Ficker, *Phundagiagiten*, 115–25.

91 Migne, *PG*, 140. 664.

92 Germanos II, 238–9.

93 Ibid., 239–40.

by quoting the scriptures to the effect that 'the most High dwelleth not in temples made by hand' (Acts 7.48; 17.24). The patriarch was clear that it was only pagan temples and not Christian churches that were meant.[94] There were two further considerations that occurred to him: that God was everywhere and that He preferred to dwell in mankind. But he clinched his argument by quoting 1 Corinthians 11.18, where St Paul urges that all should gather in church to put an end to the divisions among the congregation. These were a breeding ground for heresies. Germanos closed with the commonsense suggestion that one reason for gathering together under a single roof was for protection against the elements. As for the orthodox form of worship, had they not been enjoined by St Paul to celebrate 'Speaking to yourselves in psalms and hymns and spiritual songs, singing and making melody in your heart to the Lord' (Ephesians 5.19)?[95]

Germanos II was continuing the attack on Bogomilism which had been a feature of the eleventh and twelfth centuries. Then there was a high political content and the emperors were deeply involved. Now it was the responsibility of the patriarch. The continued existence of the Bogomils was a reproach to his keen sense of his pastoral duties and proof of the ineffectiveness of pastoral care. The Bogomils were able to capitalise on the remoteness and elitism of the orthodox hierarchy. They were able to claim that they were the 'good Christians' because their way of life and worship was close to that of the early church. Germanos II understood the popular appeal of the Bogomil heresy, in a way his predecessors had not. They had tended to intellectualise it. Germanos II realised that he had to defend orthodox worship and practice rather than orthodox theology. We have seen the care he took to justify church services against the charges of the heretics. He also passionately defended the use of icons. The Bogomils were quite wrong to accuse the orthodox of worshipping the materials out of which icons were fashioned. The patriarch wanted to know if the Bogomils regarded the Gospels as holy. Of course, they did! But were they not made out of materials? The Bogomils were not worshipping the materials, but the words contained in the Gospels. Icons were an exact analogy. It was a clever defence, but one that rested on an appreciation of the importance of the word of God to the heretics.[96]

Germanos II was aware that the Bogomils understood Christ to have meant by bread not his body but his word. Germanos II immediately saw how dangerous this was. It not only gave added force to their rejection of the eucharist, but it also justified spreading their heresy, which

94 Ibid., 240–1.
95 Ibid., 241–2.
96 Migne, *PG*, 140. 664–5.

was none other than the word of God. Germanos II had little difficulty in refuting their interpretation.[97] He was the last Byzantine patriarch to mount a sustained attack on the Bogomils. Thereafter they ceased to be a serious problem within the Byzantine church. This is a measure of Germanos II's success. This should be attributed to the concrete character of his repudiation of Bogomil teachings and practices. But his stress on apostolic poverty and his pastoral responsibilities must have done much to undermine the attractions of Bogomilism.

With great skill Germanos II used his demolition of the Bogomil charges against the orthodox to emphasise the need for the highest standards of Christian worship. He took his patriarchal duty to ensure good order in a Christian society very seriously. Sermons were a means to this end, a way of making the church the true focus of society. Germanos was not only an effective preacher. He was also a man of action. Uniquely, he travelled extensively, not just within western Asia Minor, but also in the western territories of Epiros, which he visited in 1238. As we have seen, he took a real interest in the fate of the orthodox under Latin rule, but he was equally concerned with those in Seljuq territories.[98] He was an effective administrator who was able to bring some order to monasteries and their estates by bringing them under the supervision of patriarchal exarchs. He did not just inveigh against the dangers of heresy. He took practical steps to deal with it. He despatched a letter to the orthodox of Constantinople warning of the danger of Bogomils in their midst. Its main purpose was to detail the steps to be taken by those wishing to abjure the heresy. They had to pronounce in public eight anathemas, of which the last was directed against those who only abjured the heresy with their lips, but not in their hearts. The patriarch closed by insisting that abjuration must take place in church and in the hearing of the orthodox congregation. He gave instructions that his letter be read out aloud every Sunday and on other festivals in all the orthodox churches of Constantinople.[99]

Germanos II had a great following among the people of Nicaea. He had to protest at the warmth of his welcome as he made his way into the cathedral. He found it unseemly because it was in such contrast to the way that Peter and the Apostles were treated in their lifetimes. The patriarch insisted that he was not a bronze statue, but mortal like everybody else.[100] Once again he was at pains to emphasise the reality of apostolic poverty as the example that he sought to follow. After his death miracles were reported at his tomb, which is an indication of

97 Ficker, *Phundagiagiten*, 121–2.

98 Laurent, 1235, 1240, 1241, 1242, 1300.

99 Ficker, *Phundagiagiten*, 124–5; Laurent, 1291.

100 Germanos II, 268–71.

his high popular reputation. 'His life was saintly and he was a good shepherd of his flock' was the verdict of a contemporary.[101]

Germanos II's life and work was reminiscent of that of the Patriarch Nicholas Grammatikos. Both came from relatively obscure origins; both received a good education and embarked upon a clerical career before embracing the monastic state. Both believed in the cooperation and interdependence of the patriarchal and imperial offices. Nicholas's patriarchate ushered in a period where the church was heavily, some might say slavishly, dependent upon the emperor. In contrast, for half a century after Germanos's death there was more often than not a state of unease, if not outright hostility, between the emperor and successive patriarchs. Germanos was scarcely to blame, but he had given the patriarchate new strength, purpose, and popularity. This allowed his successors to challenge those actions on the part of the emperors, which they deemed to offend against morality and the integrity of orthodoxy.

Nicephorus Blemmydes

Germanos II's own choice of successor was Nicephorus Blemmydes. He recommended him to the Emperor John Vatatzes, but wondered whether Blemmydes would be willing to abandon his monastic life. The emperor passed him over. As a sop, the emperor suggested that Blemmydes might like to act as the new patriarch's adviser. This Blemmydes turned down. He considered that such an arrangement was an innovation. It was bound to bring him grief.[102] The next emperor, Theodore II Lascaris, eventually offered Blemmydes the patriarchate and put pressure on him to accept. He refused to be coerced. He had no desire to become the emperor's 'minister of religion'.[103]

Nicephorus Blemmydes's life and career suggest some of the troubled depths beneath the impression of serenity that the writings of Germanos II convey. We ought to know Blemmydes as well as any Byzantine, for besides his scholarly and theological works he has left letters and two autobiographies. It was somehow typical of the man that at a time when autobiography of any description was rare he should have felt the need to compile two autobiographies. They allow us to chart the psychological and social pressures which helped to mould his personality and career. He presents his life as one shaped by instinct and intuition, in which he discerned, not egotism, but the hand of God.

[101] Acropolites I, 71.23.
[102] Blemmydes I, 69; ed. Munitiz, 35.1–18; transl. Munitiz, 82–3.
[103] Blemmydes I, 74–82; ed. Munitiz, 37–41; transl. Munitiz, 85–90.

Blemmydes was born in Constantinople in 1197. His father was a doctor. The family fled to Asia Minor after the fall of the city in 1204 and it was there that he was educated. He was an apt pupil. At Byzantium education and learning opened up to men of ability but of modest origins the path to a successful career. This would be the case with Blemmydes, but his career was far from smooth. He started in the usual way by seeking service in the imperial palace. First the Emperor John Vatatzes made him undergo an oral examination at the hands of the consul of the philosophers, who still seems to have supervised higher education. Blemmydes used this opportunity to impress the emperor with his dialectical skill, demolishing the propositions of the consul of the philosophers in the process. Blemmydes cherished the memory of the calculated humiliation he inflicted on the man. Perhaps he was unwise, since it earned him a bitter enemy at court.[104] Blemmydes claimed to have won the emperor's favour, but he was quick to turn down the chance of preferment at court in favour of a clerical career. He explained this by reference to his difficult character: 'I have never been a pleasant person for the majority of people and I have never been accustomed to say and do what is agreeable, not even to those in high position!'[105] Blemmydes went instead to Nicaea and was invited by the Patriarch Germanos II to enter the patriarchal clergy.

Germanos II's reputation for sanctity may have had some bearing on his decision to enter the church. He claimed to have been a long-time friend of the patriarch.[106] They may have met when he was studying at Skamandros not far from Akhyraous where Germanos was then a monk.[107] But there is another possibility. During his first year as patriarch Germanos visited Lydia to deal with the heretic Leontios. He could hardly have failed to stop at Nymphaion, the imperial residence, where Blemmydes happened to be at the time. For whatever reason he is likely to have realised that a clerical career under Germanos II had more to offer him than imperial service. It was a choice that able and ambitious young men often had to make, but there was a new dimension which emphasised the importance of the choice. The Nicaean Empire now had two capitals. The imperial apparatus of government was centred at Nymphaion, while the patriarch continued to reside at Nicaea. This must have given the patriarch much greater freedom from imperial supervision. If one is to believe Blemmydes he soon became the patriarch's right hand man, sharing his lodgings and table. The patriarch trusted him enough to hand over the administration of the patriarchal church while he was absent on a tour in western Asia

104 Blemmydes II, 8–16; ed. Munitiz, 50–4; transl. Munitiz, 98–103.
105 Blemmydes II, 18; ed. Munitiz, 54.1–3; transl. Munitiz, 103.
106 Blemmydes I, 12; ed. Munitiz, 8.20–2; transl. Munitiz, 49.
107 Blemmydes I, 6; ed. Munitiz, 5–6; transl. Munitiz, 45–6.

Minor. Later he gave Blemmydes responsibility for the vacant church of Nymphaion.[108]

Such consideration on the part of the patriarch earned Blemmydes the envy of other members of the clergy, but he himself was quite capable of a vindictive attack upon an elderly deacon of the patriarchal church. This was done, it would seem, as a means of getting his own back on his enemy the consul of the philosophers, who was a very close friend of the deacon. Blemmydes had forbidden them to continue in a relationship, as he put it, 'that was not recognised by the laws'. They may have been blood brothers. *Adelphopoiesis* was a very common tie at Byzantium, but was not officially recognised by the church. Blemmydes certainly meant it as a charge of homosexuality.[109] Such accusations were much bandied about among members of the clergy eager to discredit their rivals. Blemmydes's enemies were able to dredge up a charge of that sort from his past. Blemmydes found himself isolated relying on the patriarch's support to escape condemnation. Though Germanos tried to dissuade him Blemmydes was determined to abandon his career in the patriarchal administration and embrace the monastic life.[110]

Blemmydes's life continued to be stormy, but his decision to become a monk opened up to him, whether this was his intention or not, a degree of power and influence that he had not previously enjoyed. It also provided a freedom of movement and action that would have been impossible for somebody engaged in imperial service or the patriarchal administration.

We have to accept that Blemmydes had a genuine monastic calling.[111] We can also believe that he chose Manasses, the metropolitan bishop of Ephesus, as his spiritual director out of a profound respect for the man's qualities. But it was a shrewd choice on other counts. It brought him into the mainstream of monastic life, because Ephesus was within easy reach of Mounts Galesion and Latros which were the major monastic centres of Asia Minor and enjoying a new lease of life. Blemmydes intended to make his mark on the monastic life. Eight days after he had professed his monastic vows he was ordained a priest in the cathedral of St John at Ephesus by Bishop Manasses. Ordination so soon after becoming a monk betrays his ambition to become an abbot or founder of a monastery. Manasses duly appointed him abbot of the monastery of St Gregory the Wonderworker at Ephesus. Monastic life

[108] Blemmydes I, 31; ed. Munitiz, 18.1–4; transl. Munitiz, 61.

[109] Blemmydes I, 19–21; ed. Munitiz, 12–13; transl. Munitiz, 54–5.

[110] Blemmydes I, 35–6; ed. Munitiz, 20–1; transl. Munitiz, 63–4.

[111] This is J.A. Munitiz's opinion: Nicephoros Blemmydes, *A Partial Account*, transl. J.A. Munitiz (Spicilegium Sacrum Lavaniense, Etudes et Documents 46) (Louvain, 1988), 37–42.

allowed Blemmydes to return to his studies. One reason he gives for abandoning his clerical career was that his 'official work impeded the continuation of his academic activities'.[112] His reputation as the foremost scholar and theologian of his time brought him once more to the attention of the emperor.

It is scarcely an exaggeration to say that John Vatatzes employed him as a special agent. He was called upon to defend the orthodox position on the *filioque* at the two meetings with papal representatives that took place at Nymphaion in 1234 and 1249/50.[113] In the absence of a court school John Vatatzes sent young men from the court to the monastery of St Gregory the Wonderworker to receive a higher education, not always with happy results. It did not prevent John Vatatzes from entrusting him with the education of his son and heir Theodore Lascaris.[114] In the meantime, Blemmydes had made a tour of the western territories in search of manuscripts. He visited Mount Athos, Thessalonica, Larissa, and Ohrid. This undertaking had the backing of the emperor, who was well aware of the potential value of contacts with the great monastic and ecclesiastical centres of the West.

There was a danger that Blemmydes might have been tempted to stay permanently in the West. Demetrius Chomatianos had just died and Blemmydes was offered the throne of Ohrid. The loss of a scholar and theologian of Blemmydes's renown would have been a blow to John Vatatzes's prestige. He wrote insisting that Blemmydes return immediately.[115] It was a sign of the great authority that Blemmydes was beginning to exercise.

This was confirmed by the Marchesina incident. The Marchesina was, as we know, John Vatatzes's Italian mistress. She took it into her head to enter Blemmydes's monastery of St Gregory in the company of her entourage. The divine liturgy was being celebrated. Blemmydes stopped the service and forced her departure. It was a studied insult and the commander of her retinue tried to kill Blemmydes. Only a miracle saved him. Blemmydes's effrontery was bitterly criticised in court circles. In response, Blemmydes issued an *Open Letter*, giving his version of the incident and denouncing the Marchesina as an adulteress. Its moral force seems to have won the day. The emperor accepted the implied rebuke. Blemmydes may well have been articulating opinion

112 Blemmydes I, 37; ed. Munitiz, 21.1–17; transl. Munitiz, 64–5.

113 Blemmydes II, 23–40, 50–60; ed. Munitiz, 56–63, 67–73; transl. Munitiz, 106–14, 119–24.

114 Blemmydes I, 49–54; ed. Munitiz, 26–9; transl. Munitiz, 71–5. Blemmydes never says specifically that he was Theodore II Lascaris's tutor.

115 Blemmydes I, 63–4; ed. Munitiz, 74; transl. Munitiz, 79–80.

that was opposed to the influence enjoyed at the Nicaean court by the Marchesina and her hangers-on.[116]

Blemmydes's monastery was exposed to the attentions of the provincial administration. The episodes were petty in themselves. They illustrate the fiscal pressures which we have seen the provincial authorities applying over and over again to churches and monasteries. Thanks to his ties with the emperor Blemmydes was able to defend his monastery from a series of provincial governors, most of whom came to unpleasant or bizarre ends.[117] Report of their deaths must have contributed to his reputation as a man of God or at least somebody who was not to be crossed. His opinion counted. Under Theodore II Lascaris there was a trial for high treason. The court agreed that the accused should be condemned to death. The emperor then consulted Blemmydes who counselled clemency. The emperor acted upon this advice though it went contrary to the opinion of the court.[118]

Theodore II Lascaris died soon afterwards, leaving a child to succeed. He appointed a regent, but he was assassinated almost at once. An assembly was convened at Magnesia to choose a new regent. The favourite was the future emperor Michael Palaeologus, who had the support of the Patriarch Arsenius.[119] Nicephorus Blemmydes was invited to attend. That was evidence enough of his standing. But still more impressive was the effort made to prevent his attendance and then to discredit him. Blemmydes claims that his enemies intended to assassinate him, but he was able to evade them. He does not indicate who exactly his enemies were, but noted the annoyance of Michael Palaeologus and the Patriarch Arsenius that he had been able to slip into the city of Magnesia undetected. Presumably, they feared that Blemmydes would be able to articulate opinion opposed to Michael Palaeologus. Blemmydes had already made remarks about the new ruler that were less than complimentary. These were collected by his enemies and forwarded to Palaeologus who wisely let the matter rest.[120]

Blemmydes's energies were now concentrated more than ever on the monastery he had founded at Emathia, not far from Ephesus, some years previously. It was dedicated to the Lord Christ Who Is.[121] This particular dedication apparently reflects a continuing interest in the

[116] Blemmydes I, 70–2, II, 49; ed. Munitiz, 35–7, 67, 91–4; transl. Munitiz, 83–5,118–19, 139–43. That this was no minor incident is evident from the attention it received in the histories of the time.

[117] Blemmydes I, 52–3, 60–2, II, 81–5; ed. Munitiz, 28–9, 31–2, 81–3; transl. Munitiz, 73–4, 78, 136–8.

[118] Blemmydes I 87–8; ed. Munitiz, 43–4; transl. Munitiz, 92–3.

[119] See Angold, *A Byzantine Government*, 80–93.

[120] Blemmydes II, 79–81; ed. Munitiz, 80–1; transl. Munitiz, 135–6.

[121] Blemmydes II, 45–8; ed. Munitiz, 65–7; transl. Munitiz, 116–18.

problem of the relationship of God the Father and God the Son which had been opened up by the debates of the mid-twelfth century. They were still going on at Nicaea when Blemmydes was a young man.[122] Around the time that he moved from the monastery of St Gregory the Wonderworker to Emathia he came under censure for reopening the question by suggesting that God the Son derived His being and creativity from God the Father.[123] This laid him open to an accusation of Arianism, since it implied the subordination of the former to the latter. The dedication was quite possibly a way of defending himself against this charge.

It may also indicate that his religious focus was changing. He ceased to take students, as he had done when at his previous monastery. The future patriarch Gregory of Cyprus came all the way from his native island, hoping to study under him. He was told that Blemmydes would not receive him. He was surrounded by a band of disciples who kept strangers at an arm's length.[124] His interest now lay in creating a religious community devoted to contemplation. It was for its benefit that Blemmydes composed his two autobiographies. They or something similar might have been used as an introduction to the *typikon* or rule which he drew up for his foundation. Unfortunately, only fragments remain.[125] It is not possible to decide where exactly the novelty of his conception of the monastic life lay. But his influence on contemporaries was considerable. In 1268 the patriarch of Constantinople Joseph I made a personal visit to Blemmydes at Emathia. He needed the old man's endorsement in his struggle with the supporters of the deposed Patriarch Arsenius. Blemmydes refused to come out of his cell to greet the patriarch and showed him no sign of respect. He made an enormous impression on his visitors. He was pure intelligence: 'his mind seemed divorced from his body'. He had no interest in human affairs which were always in a state of flux and devoted himself to the contemplation of the power of God. The patriarch received no endorsement, only a demand that he confirm his foundation charter and his will and pass them on for confirmation by the emperor. He was close to death and his main concern in this world was for the continued existence of his monastery. Vain hopes as it turned out.[126]

Blemmydes sheds a different light on church life during the period of

122 Laurent, 1212–13.

123 Blemmydes II, 67; ed. Munitiz, 76; transl. Munitiz, 128–9. Cf. Blemmydes, *A Partial Account*, 40–1.

124 W. Lameere, *La tradition manuscrite de la correspondance de Grégoire de Chypre, patriarche de Constantinople (1283–1289)* (Brussels and Rome, 1937), 181.12–22.

125 Blemmydes, *Curriculum Vitae et Carmina*, ed. Heisenberg, 93–9; J. A. Munitiz.'A missing chapter from the *typikon* of Nikephoros Blemmydes', *REB* 44(1986), 199–207.

126 Pachymérès, *Relations historiques*, II, 437–41.

exile, but he was a maverick. It is difficult to think of another Byzantine with a comparable career and profile. Not even Neophytos the recluse sought sanctification quite so blatantly.[127] Blemmydes presents his life as one in which almost from the cradle he had been singled out by God for special favour.[128] He displayed many of the traits of the Byzantine holy man, but he was also a scholar and a theologian; a courtier and a politician. He would have had all the credentials to be a great patriarch, had he not been conscious of the changes wrought by the fall of Constantinople. The emperor was no longer the guarantor of the integrity of orthodoxy. Blemmydes refused the patriarchate because Theodore II Lascaris insisted that he accept. An emperor was no longer in a position to insist. He defied the emperor when he wanted to place the lands of his Epirot rival under an interdict.[129] Others tried to pretend that exile had not changed anything. The emperor was still the *epistemonarkhes* of the church. The recovery of Constantinople in 1261 reinforced the notion that nothing had changed, but the difficulties that Michael Palaeologus encountered in his dealings with the church suggest this was not so.

Conclusion

Blemmydes lived to see the return of the capital to Constantinople. It did not seem to be a matter of great importance to him. He was not as pessimistic as some, but he did not share the general optimism expressed by Michael Palaeologus. The emperor welcomed the recovery of Constantinople as a sign that God's grace had been restored and hoped that 'just as it had fallen to us without our demanding it, so, in similar fashion, will the rest of the Empire'.[130] It was not to be. Too much had changed during the period of exile. Michael Palaeologus would have endless trouble with the church. The Patriarch Arsenius Autoreianos was his most formidable opponent. This comes as a surprise because he had clearly been selected as a compliant tool of the emperor. His letter to the papacy drafted in the autumn of 1256 shows him deferring to imperial authority over the union of churches.[131] Arsenius had a distinguished family background. On his mother's side he descended from the great family of Kamateros. He became abbot of the monastery of Oxeia. He was far from being a complete nonentity. John Vatatzes selected him as a member of a delegation to Rome.[132]

[127] See Galatariotou, *The Making of a Saint*, 71.
[128] Blemmydes II, 3–6; ed. Munitiz, 48–9; transl. Munitiz, 96–7.
[129] Blemmydes I, 74–83; ed. Munitiz, 37–41; transl. Munitiz, 85–90.
[130] Pachymérès, *Relations historiques*, I, 211.20–1.
[131] Laurent, 1332.
[132] Acropolites I, 290.113.

At first, he seemed more inclined to favour than to oppose Michael Palaeologus's rise to power. But he wanted safeguards for the rights of the legitimate emperor John Lascaris. At the joint coronation of Michael Palaeologus and John Lascaris the patriarch administered oaths whereby the two emperors swore not to conspire against each other. Should this happen the people were called upon to rise up against the usurper and the senate were to select a new emperor from their midst. Even before the recovery of Constantinople it was clear that Michael Palaeologus was determined to oust the young John Lascaris. Arsenius resigned in protest. He had the support of two influential metropolitan bishops, Andronicus of Sardis and Manuel of Thessalonica. After the return to Constantinople Michael Palaeologus was persuaded to reinstate Arsenius. The reconciliation did not last for long. Michael Palaeologus had his rival John Lascaris blinded on Christmas Day 1261 and sent into exile. Arsenius became the centre of opposition to the emperor. He had support not only within the church, but also among the people of Asia Minor. There was a serious revolt near Nicaea and open disaffection elsewhere.[133]

This episode is well enough known, but it was almost inconceivable before 1204. The church had rarely been able to count on popular support and the emperor was normally able to cow religious dissent. Arsenius does not at first sight seem as impressive a personality as the Patriarch Theodosius who had to confront Andronicus I Comnenus's usurpation and failed miserably. It was the support which Arsenius had that made the difference. He was the heir to the work of Germanos II, who had succeeded in creating popular support at Nicaea and in the surrounding region for the patriarchate. Although Nicephorus Blemmydes was supposed to have been indifferent to the struggles of Arsenius's supporters, there was no doubt about the moral authority that he and other monastic leaders wielded in western Asia Minor. It was a force that Michael Palaeologus was going to experience more and more as his reign wore on. For the first time since the iconoclast controversy monks began to shape public opinion.

Outwardly the period of exile was a time when a conscious effort was made to recover the Byzantine inheritance and to restore credibility to the old institutions and political ideas. But there was a loss of equilibrium. The balance within the Byzantine polity shifted. The moral authority of the church increased at the emperor's expense. Patriarchs and prelates might hail emperors as their saviours after Christ and praise them for delivering them from the Latin yoke, but

[133] See D.M. Nicol, *The Last Centuries of Byzantium 1261–1453* (2nd edn, Cambridge, 1993), 44–6.

it was obvious how much the authority of an emperor depended upon the church. To take one example: in order to discipline the young Michael Palaeologus the Emperor John Vatatzes first had recourse to the ordeal by hot iron. To administer this he required the support of the church. He accordingly put the metropolitan bishop of Philadelphia in charge of proceedings. But the case against Michael Palaeologus had to be dropped because of the bishop's qualms about administering the ordeal. It was an innovation unknown to the Byzantine tradition. Foiled by the bishop's reluctance to do his bidding the emperor next turned to the patriarch. He sought two things from the patriarch: the imposition of an appropriate penance on Michael Palaeologus and the administration of oaths that would bind the young man in loyalty to the emperor.[134] This incident seems symptomatic of how much the emperor had come to rely on the moral authority of the church in his dealings with members of the aristocracy.

It is indicative of the way the church was coming to exercise greater influence on society at all levels. The declining incidence of dissent suggests that the church's authority produced less resentment. The Bogomil heresy faded away. The defence of orthodoxy against the Latins aroused enthusiastic popular support. The dossiers of John Apokaukos and Demetrius Chomatianos reveal the central role that the bishop and his court played in local society. The sermons of Patriarch Germanos II reveal a patriarch who was once again able to give moral leadership. The Byzantine church emerged strengthened from the test of exile. It was able to resist the pressures brought to bear by the Emperor Michael VIII Palaeologus in his effort to impose union with Rome. This contrasts with its supine showing in the face of Andronicus I Comnenus's usurpation, which deprived it of much of its moral authority. Its subsequent passivity was symptomatic of the malaise that prevailed at Constantinople on the eve of the fourth crusade.

It was a state of affairs that was an unwelcome consequence of the Comnenian settlement, which had worked well enough for nearly a hundred years. It strengthened the institutional fabric of the church and enhanced the role of the patriarchal administration. But central to the Comnenian settlement was the emperor as the *epistemonarkhes* of the church; as the guarantor of orthodoxy and the regulator of the church. This restricted its initiative and the possibility of spiritual renewal. It distanced the ecclesiastical establishment from the community at large and contributed to a feeling of dissatisfaction, if not disaffection and dissent. It left the church hierarchy uncomfortably subservient to

[134] See Angold, 'The interaction of Latins and Byzantines'.

the reigning emperor. It masked, but also endangered the practical advances made by the church in extending its authority over society. Exile provided the conditions that allowed the church to recover its prestige. It emphasised how precious and fragile orthodoxy was. It emphasised too that imperial power could best be reconstituted with the aid of the church and operated most effectively with its support.

In ecclesiastical circles the superiority of the church was almost taken for granted. Listen to a supporter of the Patriarch Arsenius: 'Given that the lesser must obey the greater, then the church is the greater, for it has Christ as its head and the patriarch as His image. The latter sanctifies and anoints the emperor who stands in need of such grace. He should therefore in gratitude serve the church and its leader who spiritually bears the image of Christ.'[135] Michael VIII Paleologus's failure to show the necessary gratitude and subservience united church and society against him.

135 P.G. Nikolopoulos, ''Ανέκδοτος λόγος εἰς 'Αρσένιον Αὐτωρειανὸν πατρίαρχην Κωνσταντινουπόλεως', *ΕΕΒΣ* 45 (1981–2), 461.338–43.

BIBLIOGRAPHY

Collections of sources and series

Acta Sanctorum Bollandiana (Brussels, 1643–1779; Paris and Rome, 1866, 1887; Brussels, 1894–)

Archives de l'Athos (Paris, 1937–)

Dmetrievskij, A.A., *Opisanie liturgicheskikh rukopisej, khranjashchikhija v bibliotekakh pravoslavnago vostoka* (Kiev, 1895–1901; St Petersburg, 1917), 3 vols.

Dictionnaire de Spiritualité (Paris, 1937–)

Dölger, F., *Regesten der Kaiserurkunden des oströmischen Reiches* (Corpus der griechischen Urkunden des Mittelalters und der neueren Zeit. Reihe A, Abt. 1) (Munich and Berlin, 1924–65), 5 vols.

Grabler, F., *Kaisertaten und Menschenschichsale* (Byzantinische Geschichtesschreiber XI) (Graz, 1966)

Grumel, V., *Les regestes des actes du patriarcat de Constantinople, I: Les actes des patriarches, fasc. ii et iii: Les regestes de 715 à 1206* (Paris, 1947; revised edn, 1989)

Hunger, H., and Kresten, O., *Das Register des Patriarchats von Konstantinopel*, I (Vienna, 1981)

Janin, R., *La géographie ecclésiastique de l'Empire byzantin, I: Le siège de Constantinople et le patriarcat oecuménique, III: Les églises et les monastères* (Paris, 1969)

Les églises et les monastères des grands centres byzantins (Paris, 1975)

Laurent, V., *Le corpus des sceaux de l'Empire byzantin*, V, 1–2: *L'église* (Paris, 1963–5)

Les regestes des actes du patriarcat de Constantinople, I, fasc. 4: Les regestes de 1208 à 1309 (Paris, 1971)

Migne, J.P., *Patrologiae cursus completus. Series latina* (Paris, 1844–55)

Patrologiae cursus completus. Series graeco-latina (Paris, 1857–66)

Miklosich, F. and Müller, J., *Acta et diplomata graeca medii aevi sacra et profana* (Vienna, 1860–90), 6 vols.

Noailles, P. and Dain, A., eds., *Les nouvelles de Léon VI le sage* (Paris, 1944)

Papadopoulos-Kerameus, A.I., ΑΝΑΛΕΚΤΑ ΙΕΡΟΣΟΛΥΜΙΤΙΚΗΣ ΣΤΑΧΥΛΟΓΙΑΣ (St Petersburg, 1891–8; repr. Brussels, 1963), 5 vols.

Noctes Petropolitanae (St Petersburg, 1913: repr. Leipzig, 1976)

Peters, E., *Heresy and Authority in Medieval Europe* (Philadelphia, 1980)
Pitra, J.B., *Analecta sacra et classica spicilegio Solesmensi parata* (Paris, 1876–91; repr. Farnborough, 1967), 8 vols.
Regel, W., *Fontes rerum byzantinarum* (St Petersburg, 1892–1917; repr. Leipzig, 1982), 2 vols.
Rhalles. G.A., and Potles, M., *ΣΥΝΤΑΓΜΑ ΤΩΝ ΘΕΙΩΝ ΚΑΙ ΙΕΡΩΝ ΚΑΝΟΝΩΝ* (Athens, 1852–9), 6 vols.
Sathas, K.N., *ΜΕΣΑΙΩΝΙΚΗ ΒΙΒΛΙΟΘΗΚΗ* (Bibliotheca graeca medii aevi) (Venice and Paris, 1872–94), 7 vols.
Wakefield, W.L., and Evans, A.P., *Heresies of the High Middle Ages* (Records of Civilization LXXXI) (New York, 1969)
Zepos, I. amd P., *Ius graecoromanum* (Athens, 1931; repr. Aalen, 1962), 6 vols.

Primary sources

Achmetis Oneirocriticon, ed. F. Drexl (Leipzig, 1925)
Acropolites, George, *Opera*, ed. A.Heisenberg and P. Wirth (Stuttgart, 1978), 2 vols.
Actes de Docheiariou, ed. N. Oikonomidès (Archives de l'Athos, 13) (Paris, 1984)
Actes de Lavra, I–II, ed. P. Lemerle *et al.* (Archives de l'Athos 6, 8) (Paris, 1970, 1977)
Actes d'Iviron, II, ed. J. Lefort *et al.* (Archives de l'Athos 16) (Paris, 1990)
Actes de Xénophon, ed. D. Papachrysanthou (Archives de l'Athos 15) (Paris, 1986
Alberic de Tre Fontane, *Chronicon*, ed. G.H. Pertz (Monumenta Germaniae historica: SS 23) (Hanover, 1874), 631–950
Angelou, A.D., *Nicholas of Methone: Refutation of Proclus'* Elements of Theology (Corpus Philosophorum Medii Aevi - Philosophi Byzantini 1) (Athens and Leiden, 1984)
Astruc, C., 'Un document inédit de 1163 sur l'évêche théssalien de Stagi. Paris Suppl. gr.1371', *BCH* 83(1959), 206–46
'L'inventaire dressé en septembre 1200 du trésor et de la bibliothèque de Patmos: édition diplomatique', *TM* 8(1981), 15–30
Basilakes, Nicephorus, *Encomio di Adriano Comneno*, ed. A. Garzya (Naples, 1965)
Gli encomi per l'imperatore et per il patriarcha, ed. R. Maisano (Naples, 1977)
Orationes et epistolae, ed. A. Garzya (Leipzig, 1984)
Bees, N.A., and Bee-Seferle, E., 'Unedierte Schriftstücke aus der Kanzlei des Johannes Apokaukos des Metropoliten von Naupaktos (in Aetolien)', *Byzantinisch-neugriechische Jahrbücher*, 21(1976), 57–160
Berriot, F., *Exposions et significacions des songes* (Geneva, 1989)
Blemmydes, Nicephorus, *Curriculum Vitae et Carmina*, ed. A. Heisenberg (Leipzig, 1896)
Autobiographia sive curriculum vitae necnon Epistula Universalior, ed. J.A. Munitiz (Corpus Christianorum, *Series Graeca* 13) (Louvain, 1984)

A Partial Account, trans. J.A. Munitiz (Spicilegium Sacrum Lovaniense, Etudes et documents 46) (Louvain, 1988)

Boissonade, J.F., *Psellos De Operatione Daemonum* (Nuremburg, 1838)

Anecdota nova (Paris, 1844)

Browning, R., 'An unpublished address of Nicephorus Chrysoberges to Patriarch John X Kamateros of 1202', *Byzantine Studies/Etudes Byzantines* 5(1978), 37–68

Bryennios, Nicephorus, *Histoire*, ed. P. Gautier (Brussels, 1975)

ΒΥΖΑΝΤΙΝΑ ΕΓΓΡΑΦΑ ΤΗΣ ΜΟΝΗΣ ΠΑΤΜΟΥ, 2 vols. (Athens, 1980), I: ΑΥΤΟΚΡΑΤΟΡΙΚΑ, ed. E. Vranouse; II: ΔΗΜΟΣΙΩΝ ΛΕΙΤΟΥΡΓΩΝ, ed. M. Nystazopoulou-Pelekidou.

Cameniates, John, *De Expugnatione Thessalonicae*, ed. G. Böhlig (Berlin and New York, 1973)

Canart, P., 'Le dossier hagiographique des SS. Baras, Patapios et Raboulas', *Analecta Bollandiana* 87(1969), 445–59

Cedrenus, George, *Historiarum Compendium*, ed. I. Bekker (Bonn, 1838–9), 2 vols.

Chabot, J.B., *La Chronique de Michel le Syrien* (Paris, 1899–1910), 4 vols.

Choniates, Michael, ΤΑ ΣΩΖΟΜΕΝΑ, ed. Sp. P. Lampros (Athens, 1879–80; repr. Groningen, 1968), 2 vols.

Choniates, Nicetas, *Orationes et Epistulae*, ed. I.A. van Dieten (Berlin and New York, 1972)

Χρονικὴ διήγησις, ed. J.-L. van Dieten (Berlin and New York, 1975), 2 vols. English translation by H. Magoulias, *O City of Byzantium: annals of Niketas Choniates* (Detroit, 1984)

Chrysokephalos, Makarios, ΛΟΓΟΙ ΠΑΝΗΓΥΡΙΚΟΙ (Vienna, 1793)

Cinnamus, John, *Epitome rerum ab Ioanne et Manuele Comnenis gestarum*, ed. A. Meineke (Bonn, 1836). English translation by C.M. Brand, *Deeds of John and Manuel Comnenus* (New York, 1976)

Comnena, Anna, *Alexiad*, ed. B. Leib (Paris, 1937–45; repr. 1967), 3 vols. English translation by E.R.A. Sewter, *The Alexiad of Anna Comnena* (London, 1969)

Criscuolo, U., *Michele Psello, Epistola a Michele Cerulario* (Naples, 1973)

Cumont, F., 'Les actes de S. Dasius', *Analecta Bollandiana* 16(1897), 5–16

Darrouzès, J., 'Notice sur Grégoire Antiochos', *REB* 20(1962), 61–92.

'Le mémoire de Constantin Stilbès contre les Latins', *REB* 21(1963), 50–100

Documents inédits d'ecclésiologie byzantine (Archives de l'Orient chretien 10) (Paris, 1966)

'Dossier sur le charisticariat', in *Polychronion*, ed. P. Wirth (Heidelberg, 1966), 150–65

'Un recueil épistolaire du XIIe siècle. Académie roumaine Cod. Gr. 508', *REB* 30(1972), 199–229

'Questions de droit matrimonial', *REB* 35(1977), 107–57

Notitiae episcopatuum Ecclesiae constantinopolitanae. Texte critique, introduction et notes (Geographie ecclesiastique de l'Empire byzantin 1) (Paris, 1981)

'Un décret d'Isaac II Angelos', *REB* 40(1982), 135–55

'Notes inédites de transferts épiscopaux', *REB* 40(1982), 157–70

'Des notes marginales du Vindobonensis Historicus Graecus 70', *REB* 45(1987), 59–75

'L'éloge de Nicolas III par Nicolas Mouzalon', *REB* 46(1988), 5–53

Delehaye, H., *Deux typika byzantins de l'epoque des Paléologues* (Brussels, 1921)

Der Nersessian, S., *L'illustration des Psautiers grecs du moyen âge, II. Londres Add.* 19.352 (Paris, 1970)

Diehl, Ch., 'Le trésor et la bibliothèque de Patmos au commencement du 13e siècle', *BZ* 1(1892), 488–525

Digenes Akrites, ed. and transl. J. Mavrogordato (Oxford, 1956); *Digenes Akrites. Synoptische Ausgabe der altesten Versionen* ed. E. Trapp (Vienna, 1971)

Doanidou, S., 'Ἡ παραίτησις Νικόλαου τοῦ Μουζάλωνος 'από τῆς 'Αρχιεπισκοπῆς Κύπρου. 'Ανέκδοτον 'απολογήτικον ποίημα', ΕΛΛΗΝΙΚΑ 7(1934), 109–50

Downey, G., 'The church of All Saints (church of St. Theophano) near the church of the Holy Apostles at Constantinople', *DOP* 9–10(1955–6), 301–5.

Eustathius of Thessalonica, *La espugnazione di Tessalonica*, ed. St. Kyriakidis (Palermo, 1961)

Opuscula, ed. T.L.F. Tafel (Frankfurt am Main, 1832; repr. Amsterdam, 1964)

Commentarii ad Homeri Iliadem pertinentes, III, ed. M. Van der Valk (Leiden, 1979)

The Capture of Thessaloniki, transl. J.R. Melville Jones (Byzantina Australiensia 8) (Canberra, 1988); *Die Normannen in Thessalonike*, transl. H. Hunger (Graz, 1955)

Eustratiades, S., 'Τυπικὸν τῆς ἐν Κωνσταντινοπόλει μονῆς τοὺ Ἁγίου Μεγαλομάρτυρος Μάμαντος', ΕΛΛΗΝΙΚΑ, 1(1928), 245–314

'Ἡ 'εν Φιλαδελφία μονὴ τῆς Ὑπεραγίας Θεοτόκου τῆς Κοτεινῆς', ΕΛΛΗΝΙΚΑ 3(1930), 317–39

Ficker, G., *Die Phundagiagiten* (Leipzig, 1908)

Gautier, P., 'Le chartophylax Nicéphore. Oeuvre canonique et notice biographique', *REB* 27(1969), 159–95

'Diatribes de Jean l'Oxite contre Alexis Ier Comnène', *REB* 28(1970), 1–55

'Le synode des Blachèrnes (fin 1094)', *REB* 29(1971), 213–84

'L'édit d'Alexis Ier Comnène sur la reforme du clergè', *REB* 31(1973), 169–202

'Les lettres de Grégoire, higoumène d'Oxia', *REB* 31(1973), 203–27

'Le typikon du Christ Sauveur Pantokrator', *REB* 32(1974), 1–145

'Réquisitoire du patriarche Jean d'Antioche contre le charisticariat', *REB* 33(1975), 77–132

'Le *De Daemonibus* du Pseudo-Psellos', *REB* 38(1980), 105–94

'La *diataxis* de Michel Attaleiate', *REB* 39(1981), 5–143

'Le typikon de la Theotokos Evergétis', *REB* 40(1982), 5–101

'Le typikon du sébaste Grégoire Pakourianos', *REB* 42(1984), 5–146

'Le typikon de la Theotokos Kecharitomène', *REB* 43(1985), 5–165

'Quelques lettres de Psellos inédites ou déjà editées', *REB* 44(1986), 111–97.

Gelzer, H., 'Kallistos' Enkomion auf Johannes Nesteutes', *Zeitschrift für wissenschaftliche Theologie* 29(1886), 67–77

'Ungedruckte und wenig bekannte Bistumerverzeichnisse der orientalischen Kirche. II', *BZ* 2(1893), 22–72

Gill, J., 'An unpublished letter of Germanus, patriarch of Constantinople', *B* 44(1974), 142–51

Glykas, Michael, *ΕΙΣ ΤΑΣ ΑΠΟΡΙΑΣ ΤΗΣ ΘΕΙΑΣ ΓΡΑΦΗΣ ΚΕΦΑΛΑΙΑ*, ed. S. Eustratiades (Athens, 1906; Alexandria, 1912), 2 vols.

Golubovich, H., 'Disputatio Latinorum et Graecorum seu Relatio apocrisariorum Gregorii IX de gestis Nicaeae in Bithynia et Nymphaeae in Lydia 1234', *Archivum franciscanum historicum* 12(1919), 418–70

Gouillard, J., 'Une compilation spirituelle du XIIIe siècle: "Le livre II de l'abbé Isaie"', *EO* 38(1939), 72–90

'Le synodikon de l'orthodoxie: édition et commentaire', *TM* 2(1967), 1–298

'Une source grecque du *Sinodik* de Boril: la lettre inédite du patriarche Cosmas', *TM* 4(1970), 361–74

'Le procès officiel de Jean l'Italien. Les actes et leurs sous-entendus', *TM* 9(1985), 133–74

'Une lettre de (Jean) l'Italien au patriarche de Constantinople', *TM* 9(1985), 175–9

Grumel, V., 'Le *Peri metatheseon* et le patriarche de Constantinople Dosithée', *EB* 1(1943), 239–49

'L'affaire de Léon de Chalcédoine. Le chrysobulle d'Alexis Ier sur les objets sacrés', *EB* 2(1944), 126–33

'Les documents athonites concernant l'affaire de Léon de Chalcedoine', *Studi e Testi* 123(1946) 116–35

Guibert de Nogent, *Histoire de sa vie 1053–1124*, ed. G. Bourgin (Paris, 1907)

Hapgood, I.F., *Service Book of the Holy Orthodox-Catholic Apostolic Church* (New York, 1922)

Hausherr, I., *Un grand mystique byzantin. Vie de Syméon le Nouveau Théologien (949–1022) par Nicétas Stéthatos* (Orientalia Christiana Analecta 14) (Rome, 1928)

Heisenberg, A., *Nikolaos Mesarites. Die Palästrevolution des Johannes Komnenos* (Würzburg, 1907)

'Neue Quellen zur Geschichte des lateinischen Kaisertums und der Kirchenunion. I. Der Epitaphios des Nikolaos Mesarites auf seinen Bruder Johannes; II. Die Unionsverhandlungen vom 30. August 1206; III. Der Bericht des Nikolaos Mesarites über die politischen und kirchlichen Ereignisse des Jahres 1214', *Sitzungsberichte der bayerischen Akademie der Wissenschaften*, philos.-philol. und hist. Klasse, 1922, Abh.5; 1923, Abh.2–3 (Munich, 1923) (= A. Heisenberg, *Quellen und Studien zur spatbyzantinischen Geschichte* (London, 1973), no.II)

Hesseling, D.C., and Pernot, H., *Poèmes prodromiques en grec vulgaire* (Amsterdam, 1910; repr. Wiesbaden, 1968)

Hoeck, J.M., and Loenertz, R.-J., *Nikolaos-Nektarios von Otranto, Abt von Casole. Beitrage zur Geschichte der ost-westlichen Beziehungen unter Innozenz III. und Friederich II.* (Studia Patristica et Byzantina 11) (Ettal, 1965)

Hofmann, G., 'Papst und Patriarch unter Kaiser Manuel I. Komnenos. Ein Briefwechsel', *EEBS* 23(1953), 74–82

Hunger, H., and Ševčenko, I., *Des Nikephoros Blemmydes* ΒΑΣΙΛΙΚΟΣ ΑΝΔΡΙΑΣ *und dessen Metaphrase von Georgios Galesiotes und Georgios Oinaiotes* (Wiener Byzantinische Studien 18) (Vienna, 1986)

Italikos, Michael, *Lettres et discours*, ed. P. Gautier (Archives de l'Orient chrétien 14) (Paris, 1972)

Jeanselme, E. and Oeconomos, L., 'Le satire contre les higoumènes. Poème attribué à Théodore Prodrome', *B* 1(1924), 317–39

Joannou, P.P., 'Eustrate de Nicée. Trois pièces inédites de son procès (1117)', *REB* 10(1952), 24–34

'Der Nominalismus und die menschliche Psychologie Christi. Das *Semeioma* gegen Eustratios von Nikaia (1117)', *BZ* 47(1954), 368–78

'Le sort des évêques hérétiques réconciliés. Un discours inédit de Nicétas de Serres contre Eustrate de Nicée', *B* 28(1958), 1–30

Démonologie populaire – démonologie critique au XIe siècle. La vie inédite de S. Auxence par M. Psellos (Wiesbaden, 1971)

Kataskepenos, Nicholas, *La vie de saint Cyrille le Philéote, moine byzantin (+1110)*, ed. E. Sargologos (Subsidia Hagiographica 39) (Brussels, 1964)

Kekavmenos, *Cecaumeni Strategicon et incerti Scriptoris De Officiis regiis Libellus*, ed. B. Wassiliewsky and V. Jernstedt (St Petersburg, 1896; repr. Amsterdam, 1965); *Sovety i rasskazy Kekavmena*, ed. G.G. Litavrin (Moscow, 1972)

Krumbacher, K., *Mittelgriechische Sprichwörter* (Munich, 1894; repr. Hildesheim and New York 1969)

Michael Glykas. Eine Skizze seiner Biographie und seiner litterarischen Thätigkeit nebst einigen unedierten Gedichte und Briefe desselben (Munich, 1895)

Kurtz, E., 'Tri sinodal'nykh gramoty mitropolita Efesskago Nikolaja Mesarita', *VV* 12(1906), 99–111

'Christophoros von Ankyra als Exarch des Patriarchen Germanos II', *BZ* 16(1907), 120–42

Kurtz, E., ed., *Die Gedichte de Christophoros Mitylenaios* (Leipzig, 1903)

Lagopates, S.N., *ΓΕΡΜΑΝΟΣ Ο Β', ΠΑΤΡΙΑΡΧΗΣ ΚΩΝΣΤΑΝΤΙΝΟΥΠΟΛΕΩΣ-ΝΙΚΑΙΑΣ, 1222–1240, ΒΙΟΣ, ΣΥΓΓΡΑΜΜΑΤΑ, ΟΜΙΛΙΑΙ ΚΑΙ ΕΠΙΣΤΟΛΑΙ ΤΟ ΠΡΩΤΟΝ ΕΚΔΙΔΟΜΕΝΑΙ* (Tripolis, 1913)

Lake, K., and Lake, S., *Dated Greek Manuscripts to the Year* 1200 (Monumenta palaeographika vetera, ser. i) (Boston, 1934)

Lameere, W., *La tradition manuscrite de la correspondance de Grégoire de Chypre, patriarche de Constantinople (1283–1289)* (Brussels/Rome, 1937)

Lampros, Sp.P., ΚΕΡΚΥΡΑΙΚΑ ΑΝΕΚΔΟΤΑ (Athens, 1882)

'Ἐπιγράμματα Θωμᾶ Γοριανίτου', ΝΕΟΣ ΕΛΛΗΝΟΜΝΗΜΩΝ 12 (1915), 435–8

Lascaris, Theodore Ducas, *Epistolae CCXVII*, ed. N. Festa (Florence, 1898)

Laurent, V., 'Résponses canoniques inédites du patriarcat byzantin', *EO* 33(1934), 289–315

Laurent, V. and Darrouzès, J., *Dossier grec de l'union de Lyon (1273–1277)* (Archives de l'Orient chrétien 16) (Paris, 1976)

Lefort, J., 'Prooimion de Michel neveu de l'archevêque de Thessalonique, didascale de l'evangile', *TM* 4(1970), 375–93

Lemerle, P., 'Trois actes du despote d'Epire Michel II concernant Corfou connus en traduction latine', *ΠΡΟΣΦΟΡΑ ΕΙΣ ΣΤ.Π. ΚΥΡΙΑΚΙΔΗΝ* (Thessalonica, 1953), 405–26

Leontios of Jerusalem, *The life of Leontios Patriarch of Jerusalem*, in Makarios Chrysokephalos, *ΛΟΓΟΙ ΠΑΝΗΓΥΡΙΚΟΙ ΑΔ'* (Vienna, 1794), 380–434; ed. and transl. D. Tsougarakis (Leiden, 1993)

Leroy-Molinghen, A., 'Prolégomènes à une édition critique des lettres de Théophylacte de Bulgarie', *B* 13(1938), 253–62

Loenertz, R.-J., 'Lettre de Georges Bardanès, métropolite de Corcyre, au patriarche oecuménique Germain II 1226–1227 c.', *EEBS* 33(1964), 87–118

Loukaki, M., 'Première didascalie de Serge le diacre: Eloge du patriarche Michel Autôreianos', *REB* 52 (1994), 151–73

Maas, P., 'Die Musen des Alexios I.', *BZ* 22(1913), 348–69

Malakes, Euthymios, *ΤΑ ΣΩΖΟΜΕΝΑ*, ed. K.G. Bonis (Athens, 1937), 2 vols.

Manaphes, K.A., 'Θεόδωρου τοῦ Προδρόμου λόγος εἰς τὸν πατριάρχην Κωνσταντινουπόλεως Ἰωάννην XI τόν Ἀγαπητὸν', *EEBS* 41(1974), 223–42

Martin, A., 'Inscription grecque de Corcyre de 1228', *Mélanges d'archéologie et d'histoire* 2(1882), 379–89

Martin, J.R., *The Illustration of the Heavenly Ladder of John Climacus* (Studies in Manuscript Illumination 5) (Princeton, 1954)

Mesarites, Nicholas, 'Description of the church of the Holy Apostles at Constantinople', ed. G. Downey, in *Transactions of the American Philosophical Society* 47(1957), 855–924

Meyer, Ph., *Die Haupturkunden für die Geschichte der Athosklöster* (Leipzig, 1894)

Michel, A., *Humbert und Kerullarios. Quellen und Studien zum Schisma des XI. Jahrhunderts* (Paderborn, 1930), 2 vols.

Nicole, J., 'Une ordonnance inédite de l'empereur Alexis Comnène I sur les privilèges du χαρτοφύλαξ', *BZ* 3(1894), 17–20

Nikolopoulos, P.G., ''Ανέκδοτος λόγος εἰς Ἀρσένιον Αὐτωρειανὸν πατριάρχην Κωνσταντινουπόλεως', ΕΕΒΣ 45 (1981–2), 406–61

Odo of Deuil, *De profectione Ludovici VII in orientem*, ed. V.G. Berry (New York, 1948)

Oikonomidès, N., 'Cinq actes inédits du patriarche Michel Autôreianos', *REB* 25(1967), 113–45

Pachymérès, George, *Relations historiques*, ed. A. Faillier; transl. V. Laurent (Paris, 1984), 2 vols.

Papadakis, A., and Talbot, A.-M., 'John X Camaterus confronts Innocent III', *BS* 33(1972), 26–41

Papadopoulos-Kerameus, A.I., 'Θεόδωρος Εἰρηνικὸς πατριάρχης οἰκουμενικός', *BZ* 10(1901), 187–92

''Αθηναικὰ ἐκ τοῦ ιβ' καὶ ιγ' αἰῶνος', ΑΡΜΟΝΙΑ, 3(1902), 285–90

''Επιγράμματα Ἰωάννου τοῦ Ἀπόκαυκου', ΑΘΗΝΑ, 15(1903), 463–78

'ΔΥΡΡΑΧΗΝΑ', *BZ* 14(1905), 568–74

'ΚΕΡΚΥΡΑΙΚΑ', *VV* 13(1906), 334–51

'Συμβολὴ εἰς τὴν ἱστορίαν τῆς ἀρχιεπισκοπῆς Ἀχρίδος', in *Sbornik statej posvjashchemykh pochitateljami V.I. Lemanskomu*, 1 (St Petersburg, 1907), 227–50

'Συνοδικὰ γράμματα Ἰωάννου τοὺ Ἀπόκαυκου', ΒΥΖΑΝΤΙΣ, 1(1909), 3–30

Papagianne, E., and Troianos, Sp., 'Die kanonischen Antworten des Nikolaos III. Grammatikos an den Bischof von Zeitunion', *BZ* 82(1989), 234–50

Pavlov, A., 'Sinodal'nyj akt' Konstantinopol'skago patriarkha Mikhaila Ankhiala 1171 goda', *VV* 2(1895), 383–93

Peira sive Practica ex actis Eustathii Romani, in I. and P. Zepos, *Ius graecoromanum* (Athens, 1931; repr. Aalen, 1962), 6 vols., IV, 1–260

Petit, L., 'Le monastère de Notre-Dame de Pitié en Macédoine', *IRAIK* 6(1900), 1–153

'Typikon du monastère de la Kosmosotira près d'Aenos (1152)', *IRAIK* 13(1908), 17–77

Petridès, S., 'Jean Apokaukos, lettres et autres documents inédits', *IRAIK* 14 (1909), 69–100

Prodromos, Theodore, *De Manganis*, ed. S. Bernardinello (Padua, 1972)

Psellus, Michael, *Scripta minora*, ed. E. Kurtz and F. Drexl (Milan, 1936–41), 2 vols.

Chronographie ou histoire d'un siècle de Byzance (976–1077), ed. E. Renauld (Paris, 1926–8; repr. 1967), 2 vols.

Fourteen Byzantine Rulers, transl. E.R.A. Sewter (Harmondsworth, 1966)

[Pseudo-] Lucian, *Timarion*, ed. R. Romano (Naples, 1974)

Sakellion, I., 'Documents inédits tirés de la bibliothèque de Patmos. 1 Décret d'Alexis Comnène portant déposition de Léon, métropolitain de Chalcédoine', *BCH* 2(1878), 102–28

Schreiner, P., 'Eine unbekannte Beschreibung der Pammakaristoskirche (Fethiye Camii) und weitere Texte zur Topographie Konstantinopels', *DOP* 25(1971), 219–48

Die byzantinischen Kleinchroniken (Chronika Byzantina breviora) (Vienna, 1976–8), 3 vols.

Simon, D., 'Witwe Sachlikina gegen Witwe Horaia', *FM* 6(1984), 325–75

Stéthatos, Nicétas, *Opuscules et lettres*, ed. J. Darrouzès (Paris, 1961)

Symeon the New Theologian, *Catéchèses*, ed. B. Krivocheine (Paris, 1963–5), 3 vols.

Synaxarium Ecclesiae Constantinopolitanae, ed. H. Delehaye (Propylaeum ad Acta Sanctorum Novembris) (Brussels, 1902)

Tafel, G.L.F., and Thomas, G.M., *Urkunden zur älteren Handels- und Staatsgeschichte der Republik Venedig* (Fontes Rerum Austriacarum, Abt. 2, XII–XIV) (Vienna, 1856–7, 3 vols.

Theophylact of Ohrid, *Discours, traités, poésies*, ed. P. Gautier (Thessalonica, 1980)

Lettres. Introduction, Texte, Traduction et Notes, ed. P. Gautier (Thessalonica, 1986)

Tornikès, Georges et Dèmètrios, *Lettres et discours*, ed. J. Darrouzès (Paris, 1970)

Troianos, Sp., 'Ein Synodalakt des Sisinios zu den bischoflichen Einkünften', *FM* 3(1979), 211–20

Tsiknopoulos, I.P., ΚΥΠΡΙΑΚΑ ΤΥΠΙΚΑ (Nicosia, 1969)

Tsougarakis, D., *The Life of Leontios Patriarch of Jerusalem. Text, Translation, Commentary* (Leiden, 1993)

Tzetzes, John, *Chiliades*, ed. Th. Kiessling (Leipzig, 1826)

Historiae, ed. P.A.M. Leone (Naples, 1968)
Epistulae, ed. P.A.M. Leone (Leipzig, 1972)

Uspenskij, Th., 'Deloproizvodstvo po Ioanna Itala v eresi', *IRAIK* 2(1897), 1–66

'Mnemija i postanovlenija Konstantinopol'skikh pomestnykh soborov', *IRAIK* 5(1900), 1–48

Van Dieten, J.L., *Zur Uberlieferung und Veröffentlichung der* Panoplia Dogmatike *des Niketas Choniates* (Amsterdam, 1970)

Vasilievskij, V., 'Nikolaja episkopa Mefonskogo i Feodora Prodroma pisatelej XII stoletija zhitija Meletija Novogo', *Pravoslavnij Palestinskij Sbornik* 6(1886), 1–69

'Epirotica saeculi XIII. iz perepiski Ioanna Navpaktskago', *VV* 3(1896), 233–99

Villehardouin, Geoffroi de, *La conquête de Constantinople*, ed E. Faral (Paris, 1961), 2 vols.

Vinson, M.P., *The Correspondence of Leo, Metropolitan of Synada, and Syncellus* (Dumbarton Oaks Texts 8) (Washington DC, 1985)

Vranouse, E., ΤΑ ΑΓΙΟΛΟΓΙΚΑ ΚΕΙΜΕΝΑ ΤΟΥ ΟΣΙΟΥ ΧΡΙΣΤΟΔΟΥΛΟΥ, *ΙΔΡΥΤΟΥ ΤΗΣ ΕΝ ΠΑΤΜΩ(Ι) ΜΟΝΗΣ* (Athens, 1966)

'Τὸ ἀρχαιότερο σωζόμενο 'έγγραφο γιὰ τὴ Θεσσαλικὴ ἐπισκοπὴ Σταγῶν', ΣΥΜΜΕΙΚΤΑ 7(1987), 19–32

William of Tyre: Guillaume de Tyr, *Chronique*, ed. R.B.C. Huygens (Corpus Christianorum. Continuatio Mediaevalis, 63 and 63A) (Turnhout, 1986), 2 vols.

Zonaras, John, *Epitome historiarum*, ed. M. Pinder and Th.Buttner-Wobst (Bonn, 1841–97), 3 vols.

Secondary sources

Ahrweiler, H., 'L'histoire et la géographie de la région de Smyrne entre les deux occupations turques (1081–1317) particulièrement au XIIIe siècle', *TM* 1(1965), 1–204

'Charisticariat et autres formes d'attribution de fondations pieuses aux Xe-XIe siècles', *Zbornik radova vizantinoloshkog Instituta* 10(1967), 1–27

'L'expérience nicéenne', *DOP* 29(1975), 21–40

Ahrweiler, H. *et al.*, *Philadelphie et autres études* (Byzantina-Sorbonensia 4) (Paris, 1984)

Alexiou, M., *The Ritual Lament in Greek Tradition* (Cambridge, 1974)

Anderson, J.C., 'The date and the purpose of the Barberini psalter', *Cahiers archéologiques* 31(1983), 35–60

'On the nature of the Theodore psalter', *Art Bulletin* 70(1988), 550–68

Angelomatis-Tsoungarakis, H.N., 'Women in the society of the despotate of Epirus', *JÖB* 32/2(1983), 473–80

Angelou, A., 'Nicholas of Methone: the life and works of a twelfth-century bishop', in *Byzantium and the Classical Tradition*, ed. M. Mullett and R. Scott (Birmingham, 1981), 143–8

Angelov, D., *Les Balkans au moyen âge. La Bulgarie des Bogomiles aux Turcs* (London, 1978)

Angold, M.J., 'The problem of the unity of the Byzantine world after 1204: the Empire of Nicaea and Cyprus (1204–1261)', *ΠΡΑΚΤΙΚΑ ΤΟΥ ΠΡΩΤΟΥ ΔΙΕΘΝΟΥΣ ΚΥΠΡΟΛΟΓΙΚΟΥ ΣΥΝΕΔΡΙΟΥ* (Levkosia, 1972), II, 1–6

A Byzantine Government in Exile. Government and Society under the Laskarids of Nicaea 1204–1261 (Oxford, 1975)

'Byzantine "nationalism" and the Nicaean Empire', *BMGS* 1(1975), 49–70

'The interaction of Latins and Byzantines during the period of the Latin Empire. The case of the ordeal', *Actes du XVe Congrès international des études byzantines*, IV (Athens 1980), 1–10

The Byzantine Empire 1025–1204. A Political History (London, 1984)

'The shaping of the medieval Byzantine "city"', *BF* 10(1985), 1–37

'Ἡ βυζαντινὴ 'εκκλησία καὶ τὰ προβλήματα τοῦ γάμου', ΔΩΔΩΝΗ 17(1988), 179–95

'Greeks and Latins after 1204: the perspective of exile', in *Latins and Greeks in the Eastern Mediterranean after 1204*, ed. B. Arbel, B. Hamilton, and D. Jacoby (London, 1989), 63–86

'The wedding of Digenes Akrites: love and marriage in Byzantium in the 11th and 12th centuries', in *Η ΚΑΘΗΜΕΡΙΝΗ ΖΩΗ ΣΤΟ ΒΥΖΑΝΤΙΟ*, ed. Ch. Maltezou (Athens, 1989), 201–15

'Were Byzantine monastic *typika* literature?', in *The Making of Byzantine History. Studies Dedicated to Donald M. Nicol on his 70th Birthday*, ed. R. Beaton and Ch. Roueché (Aldershot, 1993), 46–70

'Imperial renewal and orthodox reaction: Byzantium in the eleventh century', in *New Constantines. The Rhythm of Imperial Renewal in Byzantium, 4th–13th centuries*, ed. P. Magdalino (Aldershot, 1994), 231–46

'Monastic satire and the Evergetine monastic tradition in the twelfth century', in *The Theotokos Evergetis and Eleventh-Century Monasticism*, ed. M. Mullett and A. Kirby (Belfast, 1994), 86–102

Angold, M.J., ed. *The Byzantine Aristocracy IX to XIII Centuries* (Oxford, BAR, 1984)

Arbel, B., Hamilton, B., and Jacoby, D. (ed.), *Latins and Greeks in the Eastern Mediterranean after 1204* (London, 1989)

Babić, G., 'Les discussions christologiques et le décor des églises byzantines au XIIe siècle. Les évêques officiant devant l'Hétimasie et devant l'Amnos', *Frühmittelalterliche Studien* 2(1968), 368–86

Baker, D., ed., *Relations between East and West in the Middle Ages* (Edinburgh, 1973)

Basilikopoulou, A., ''Ανέκδοτη γραφὴ τού 'Απόκαυκου στὸν 'επίσκοπο Κορώνης', ΠΡΑΚΤΙΚΑ ΤΟΥ Β′ ΔΙΕΘΝΟΥΣ ΣΥΝΕΔΡΙΟΥ ΠΕΛΟΠΟΝΝΗΣΙΑΚΩΝ ΣΠΟΥΔΩΝ, II (Athens, 1982), 241–8

Baynes, N.H., *Byzantine Studies and Other Essays* (London, 1960)

Beaton, R., *The Medieval Greek Romance* (Cambridge, 1989)

Beaton, R., and Roueché, C., ed., *The Making of Byzantine History. Studies Dedicated to Donald M. Nicol on his 70th Birthday* (Aldershot, 1993)

J. Beaucamp, 'La situation juridique de la femme à Byzance', *Cahiers de civilisation médiévale*, 20(1977), 145–76

Beck, H.-G., *Kirche und theologische Literatur im byzantinischen Reich* (Munich, 1959)

'Konstantinopel. Zur Sozialgeschichte einer frühmittelalterlichen Hauptstadt', *BZ* 58(1965), 11–45
'Bildung und Theologie im frühmittelalterlichen Byzanz', in *Polychronion*, ed. P. Wirth (Heidelberg, 1966), 69–81
'Kirche und Klerus im staatlichen Leben von Byzanz', *REB* 24 (1966), 1–24
Geschichte der byzantinischen Volksliteratur (Munich, 1971)
Das byzantinische Jahrtausend (Munich, 1978)
Die Byzantiner und ihr Jenseits. Zur Entstehungsgeschichte einer Mentalität (Munich, 1979)
Nomos, Kanon und Staatsraison in Byzanz (Vienna 1981)
Belting, H., 'An image and its function in the liturgy: the Man of Sorrows in Byzantium', *DOP* 34/5(1980–1), 1–16
Belting, H., Mango, C., and Mouriki, D., *The Mosaics and Frescoes of St Mary Pammakaristos (Fethiye Camii) at Istanbul* (Dumbarton Oaks Studies xv) (Washington DC 1978)
Bolton, B.M., 'A mission to the orthodox: the Cistercians in the Latin Empire', *Studies in Church History* 19(1976), 169–82
Bon, A., *Le Péloponnèse byzantin jusqu'en 1204* (Paris, 1951)
Bonis, C.G., 'Worship and dogma. John Mauropous, metropolitan of Euchaita (11th century): his canon on the three hierarchs and its dogmatic significance', *BF* 1(1966), 1–23
Bowman, S.B., *The Jews of Byzantium 1204–1453* (Alabama, 1985)
Brand, C.M., 'The Byzantines and Saladin, 1185–1192: opponents of the third crusade', *Speculum* 37(1962), 167–81
Byzantium Confronts the West 1180–1204 (Cambridge, Mass., 1968)
Brown, E.A.R., 'The Cistercians in the Latin Empire of Constantinople and Greece', *Traditio* 14(1958), 78–96
Brown, P., 'The rise and function of the holy man in late antiquity', *Journal of Roman Studies*, 61(1971) 80–101
Browning, R., 'The patriarchal school at Constantinople in the twelfth century', *B* 32(1962), 167–202; 33(1963), 11–40
'Unpublished correspondence between Michael Italicus, archbishop of Philippopolis, and Theodore Prodromos', *BB* 1(1962), 279–97
Studies on Byzantine History, Literature and Education (London, 1977)
'An unpublished address of Nicephorus Chrysoberges to Patriarch John X Kamateros of 1202', *Byzantine Studies/Etudes Byzantines* 5(1978), 37–68
History, Language and Literacy in the Byzantine World (Northampton, 1989)
'Theodore Balsamon's commentary on the canons of the council in Troullo as a source on everyday life in twelfth-century Byzantium', in *Η ΚΑΘΗΜΕΡΙΝΗ ΖΩΗ ΣΤΟ ΒΥΖΑΝΤΙΟ*, ed. Ch. Maltezou (Athens, 1989), 421–8
Bryer, A.M., 'A Byzantine family: the Gabrades, c.979–c.1653', *University of Birmingham Historical Journal* 12(1970), 164–87
Bryer, A.M., and Herrin, J., *Iconoclasm* (Birmingham, 1977)
Buckler, G., 'Women in Byzantine law about 1100 A.D', *B* 11(1936), 391–416
'Writings familiar to Cecaumenus', *B* 15(1940–1), 133–43
Cahen, C., 'Une famille byzantine au service des Seldjouqides d'Asie Mineure', in *Polychronion*, ed. P. Wirth (Heidelberg, 1966), 145–9
Cameron, A., and Kuhrt, A., eds., *Images of Women in Antiquity* (London, 1983)

Canart, P., 'Le dossier hagiographique des SS Baras, Patapos et Raboulas', *Analecta Bollandiana* 87(1969), 445–59

Charanis, P., 'The Jews in the Byzantine Empire under the first Palaeologi', *Speculum* 22(1947), 75–7

Chrysostomides, J., ed., ΚΑΘΗΓΗΤΡΙΑ. *Essays presented to Joan Hussey* (Camberley, 1988)

Classen, P., 'Das Konzil von Konstantinopel 1166 und die Lateiner', *BZ* 48(1955), 339–68

Clucas, L., *The Trial of John Italos and the Crisis of Intellectual Values in the Eleventh Century* (Munich, 1981)

Constantelos, D.J., *Byzantine Philanthropy and Social Welfare* (New Brunswick, 1968)

Constantinides, C.N., *Higher Education in Byzantium in 13th-Early 14th Century* (Levkosia, 1982)

Corrigan, K., 'The Smyrna Physiologus and its eleventh-century model', *Seventh Annual Byzantine Studies Conference*: Abstracts of Papers (Boston, 1981)

Cowdrey, H.E.J., 'Martyrdom and the first crusade', in *Crusade and Settlement*, ed. P.W. Edbury (Cardiff, 1985), 46–56

Crawford, J.R., 'De Bruma et Brumalibus festis', *BZ* 23(1914/19), 365–96

Criscuolo, U., 'Chiesa ed insegnamento a Bisanzio nel XII secolo: sul problema della cosidetta Accademia Patriarcale', *Siculorum Gymnasium* n.s. 28 (1975), 373–90

Culerrier, P., 'Les évêches suffragants d'Ephèse aux 5e-13e siècles', *REB* 45(1987), 139–64

Dagron, G., 'Le christianisme dans la ville byzantine', *DOP* 31(1977), 1–25

'Psellos, épigraphiste', in *Okeanos. Essays presented to Ihor Ševčenko on his 60th Birthday*, ed. C. Mango and O. Pritsak (Cambridge, Mass., 1983) (= *Harvard Ukranian Studies* 7 (1983), 117–24)

'Le caractère sacerdotal de la royauté d'après les commentaires canoniques du XIIe siècle', in *TO BYZANTIO KATA TON 12o* ΑΙΩΝΑ, ed. N. Oikonomidès (Athens, 1991), 165–78

Danforth, L.M., *The Death Rituals of Rural Greece* (Princeton, 1982)

Darrouzès, J., 'Liste des prôtes de l'Athos', in *Le Millénaire du Mont Athos*, I (Chevotogne, 1963), 407–47

'Kékauménos et la mystique', *REB* 22(1964), 282–5

'Les documents byzantins sur la primauté romaine', *REB* 23(1965), 42–88

'Notes sur Euthyme Tornikès, Euthyme Malakès, et Georges Tornikès', *REB* 23(1965), 148–67

Recherches sur les 'ΟΦΦΙΚΙΑ de l'église byzantine (Archives de l'Orient chrétien 11) (Paris, 1970)

'Nicolas d'Andida et les azymes', *REB* 32(1974), 199–210

'Le mouvement des fondations monastiques au XIe siècle', *TM* 6(1976), 159–76

'Les responses de Nicolas III à l'évêque de Zeitounion', in ΚΑΘΗΓΗΤΡΙΑ, ed. J. Chrystomides (Camberley, 1988), 327–43

Dauvillier, J., and de Clerq, C., *Le mariage en droit canonique oriental* (Paris, 1936)

Dawkins, R.M., 'Soul and body in the folklore of modern Greece', *Folklore* 53(1942), 131–47

Demus, O., 'Bemerkungen zum Physiologus von Smyrna', *Jahrbuch der österreichischen byzantinischen Gesellschaft* 25(1976), 235–57

Dondaine, A., 'Hugues Ethérien et le concile de Constantinople de 1166', *Historisches Jahrbuch* 77(1958), 473–83

Dostal, A., 'Les relations entre Byzance et les Slaves (en particulier les Bulgares) aux XIe et XIIe siècles du point de vue culturel', *Thirteenth International Congress of Byzantine Studies. Oxford 1966 – Supplementary Papers* (Oxford, 1966), 39–42

Du Boulay, J., 'The Greek vampire: a study of cyclic symbolism in marriage and in death', *Man* n.s. 17(1982), 219–38

Edbury, P.W., ed., *Crusade and Settlement* (Cardiff, 1985)

Epstein, A.W., 'The political content of the paintings of St Sophia at Ohrid', *JÖB* 29(1980), 315–29

Every, G., 'Toll gates on the air way', *Eastern Churches Review* 8(1976), 139–51

Failler, A., 'Le patriarche d'Antioche Athanase 1er Manassès', *REB* 51(1993), 63–75

Fedwick, P.J., 'Death and dying in Byzantine liturgical traditions', *Eastern Churches Review* 8(1976), 152–61

Fine, J.V.A., Jr, *The Bosnian Church: A New Interpretation* (New York, 1975)

The Early Medieval Balkans (Ann Arbor, 1983)

'The Bulgarian Bogomil movement', *East European Quarterly* 11(1977), 385–412

Fögen, M.T., '*Horror iuris.* Byzantinische Rechtsgelehrte disziplinieren ihren Metropoliten', in *Cupido Legum*, ed. L. Burgmann, M.T. Fögen, and A. Schminck (Frankfurt am Main, 1985), 47–71

Foss, C., *Ephesus after Antiquity: A Late Antique, Byzantine and Turkish City* (Cambridge, 1979)

Foucault, M., *Le souci de soi* (Paris, 1984)

Franchi, A., *La svolta politico-ecclesiastica tra Roma e Bisanzio (1249–1254)* (Rome, 1981)

Galatariotou, C., 'Holy women and witches: aspects of Byzantine conceptions of gender', *BMGS* 9(1984/5), 55–94

'Byzantine *ktetorika typika*: a comparative study', *REB* 45(1987), 77–138

'Structural oppositions in the Grottaferrata *Digenes Akrites*', *BMGS* 11(1987), 29–68

The Making of a Saint. The Life, Times and Sanctification of Neophytos the Recluse (Cambridge, 1991)

Garland, L., 'The life and ideology of Byzantine women', *B* 58(1988), 361–93

Garsoian, N.G., 'L'abjuration du moine Nil de Calabre', *BS* 35(1974), 12–27

Garzya, A., 'On Michael Psellos' admission of faith', *EEBS* 35(1966), 41–6

Storia e interpretazione di testi bizantini (London, 1974)

Gautier, P., 'L'épiscopat de Théophylacte Héphaistos archevêque de Bulgarie', *REB* 21(1963), 159–78

'Jean V l'Oxite, patriarche d'Antioche. Notice biographique', *REB* 22(1964), 146–57

'Clement d'Ohrid, évêque de Dragvista', *REB* 22(1964), 199–214
'L'obituaire de Pantocrator', *REB* 27(1969), 235–62
'Précisions historiques sur le monastère de Ta Narsou', *REB* 34(1976), 101–10
Gelzer, H., *Der Patriarchat von Achrida. Geschichte und Urkunden* (Leipzig, 1902)
Gill, J., *The Council of Florence* (Cambridge, 1959)
Byzantium and the Papacy 1198–1400 (New Brunswick, 1976)
'The tribulations of the Greek church in Cyprus 1196–c.1280', *BF* 5(1977), 73–93
Church Union: Rome and Byzantium (1204–1453) (London, 1979)
Glavinas, A.A., *Η ΕΠΙ ΑΛΕΞΙΟΥ ΚΟΜΝΗΝΟΥ (1081–1118) ΠΕΡΙ ΙΕΡΩΝ ΣΚΕΥΩΝ, ΚΕΙΜΗΛΙΩΝ ΚΑΙ ΑΓΙΩΝ ΕΙΚΟΝΩΝ ΕΡΙΣ (1081–95)* (Thessalonica, 1972)
Gouillard, J., 'Un chrysobulle de Nicéphore Botaneiatès à souscription synodale', *B* 29/30(1959–60), 29–41
'L'hérésie dans l'Empire byzantin dès origines au XII siècle', *TM* 1(1965), 299–324
'Constantin Chrysomallos sous le masque de Syméon le Nouveau Théologien', *TM* 5(1973), 313–27
'Quatre procès de mystiques à Byzance (vers 960–1143). Inspiration et autorité', *REB* 36(1978), 5–81
Greenfield, R.P.H., *Traditions of Belief in Late Byzantine Demonology* (Amsterdam, 1988)
'Sorcery and politics at the Byzantine court in the twelfth century: interpretations of history', in *The Making of Byzantine History*, ed. R. Beaton and C. Roueché (Aldershot, 1993), 73–85
Grégoire, H., *Autour de l'epopée byzantine* (London, 1975)
Gress-Wright, D., 'Bogomilism in Constantinople', *B* 47(1977), 163–85
Grumel, V., 'L'authenticité de la lettre de Jean Vatatzès, empereur de Nicée au pape Grégoire IX', *EO* 29(1930), 450–8
'Le miracle "habituel" de Notre-Dame des Blachèrnes à Constantinople', *EO* 30(1931), 129–46
'Les métropolites syncelles', *REB* 3(1945), 92–114
'Les prôtes de la sainte-montagne Athos sous Alexis 1er Comnène et le patriarche Nicolas Grammaticos', *REB* 5(1947), 206–17
'Sur la fuite et le retour de l'archevêque Eustathe de Thessalonique', *REB* 20 (1962), 221–4
Guillou, A., 'Production and profits in the Byzantine province of Italy (10th-11th centuries): an expanding economy', *DOP* 28(1974), 89–109
Hackel, S., ed., *The Byzantine Saint* (London, 1981)
Hajjar, P.J., *Le synode permanent* (synodos endemousa) *dans l'eglise byzantine des origines au XIe siècle* (Orientalia christiana analecta 164) (Rome, 1962)
Haldon, J.F., *Byzantium in the seventh century* (Cambridge, 1990)
Hamilton, B., *Monastic Reform, Catharism, and the Crusades 900–1300* (London, 1979)
'The Cathars and the seven churches of Asia', *BF* 13(1989), 269–95

Harvey, A., *Economic Expansion in the Byzantine Empire 900–1200* (Cambridge, 1989)
Hasluck, F.W., *Christianity and Islam under the Sultans* (Oxford, 1929), 2 vols.
Hausherr, I., 'Le Mētèrikon de l'abbé Isaie', *OCP* 12(1946), 286–301
'Paul Evergétinos a-t-il connu Syméon le Nouveau Théologien?', *OCP* 23(1957), 158–79
Hecht, W., 'Der *Bios* des Patriarchen Leontius von Jerusalem als Quelle zur Geschichte Andronikos' I. Kommenos', *BZ* 61(1968), 40–3
Hendy, M., *Studies in the Byzantine Monetary Economy, c.300–1450* (Cambridge, 1985)
Hermann, E., 'Das bischofliche Abgabenwesen im Patriarchat von Konstantinopel vom XI. bis zur Mitte des XIX. Jahrhunderts', *OCP* 5(1939), 434–513
'Ricerche sulle istituzioni monastiche bizantine. *Typika ktetorika*, caristicari e monasteri "liberi"', *OCP* 6(1940), 316–47
Herrin, J., 'In search of Byzantine women: three avenues of approach', in *Images of Women in Antiquity*, ed. A. Cameron and A. Kuhrt (London, 1983), 167–89
'Ideals of charity, realities of welfare', in *Church and People in Byzantium*, ed. R. Morris (Birmingham, 1990), 151–64
Holl, K., *Enthusiasmus und Bussgewalt beim griechischen Mönchtum. Eine Studie zu Symeon dem neuen Theologen* (Leipzig, 1898)
Hordern, P., 'The confraternities of Byzantium', *Studies in Church History*, 23 (1986), 25–45
Hunger, H., *Byzantinische Grundlagenforschung* (London, 1973)
'Die Herrschaft des "Buchstabens"', ΔΕΛΤΙΟΝ ΤΗΣ ΧΡΙΣΤΙΑΝΙΚΗΣ ΑΡΧΑΙΟΛΟΓΙΚΗΣ ΕΤΑΙΡΕΙΑΣ ser. 4, 12(1984), 17–38
Hussey, J.M., *Church and Learning in the Byzantine Empire 867–1185* (London, 1937)
The Orthodox Church in the Byzantine Empire (Oxford, 1986)
Huxley, G., 'Antecedents and context of Digenes Akrites', *Greek, Roman, and Byzantine Studies* 15(1974), 317–38
Iliev, I.G., 'The manuscript tradition and the authorship of the Long Life of St Clement of Ohrid', *BS* 52(1992), 68–73
Janin, R., 'Le monachisme byzantin au moyen âge. Commende et *typika* (Xe-XIVe siècle)', *REB* 22(1964), 1–44
Jenkins, R.J.H., 'A cross of the Patriarch Michael Cerularius', *DOP* 21(1967), 233–49
Joannou, P., 'Psellos et le monastère Ta Narsou', *BZ* 44(1951), 283–90
'Le sort des évêques hérétiques réconciliés', *B* 28(1958), 1–30
Jugie, M., 'Phoundagiagites et Bogomiles', *EO*, 12(1909), 257–62
Kalligas, H.A., *Byzantine Monemvasia* (Monemvasia, 1990)
Kaplan, M., 'Les monastères et le siècle à Byzance: les investissements des laiques au XIe siècle', *Cahiers de Civilisation Médiévale* 27(1984), 71–83
Karlin-Hayter, P., '99. Jean Doukas', *B* 42(1972), 259–65
'Indissolubility and the "greater evil". Three thirteenth-century divorce cases', in *Church and People in Byzantium*, ed. R. Morris (Birmingham, 1990), 87–105

Karpozilos, A., *The Ecclesiastical Controversy between the Kingdom of Nicaea and the Principality of Epiros (1217–1233)* (Thessalonica, 1973)
ΣΥΜΒΟΛΗ ΣΤΗ ΜΕΛΕΤΗ ΤΟΥ ΒΙΟΥ ΚΑΙ ΤΟΥ ΕΡΓΟΥ ΤΟΥ ΙΩΑΝΝΗ ΜΑΥΡΟΠΟΔΟΣ (Ioannina, 1982)
Katsaros, B., 'Μία 'ακόμα μαρτυρία διὰ τὴ βυζαντινὴ μονὴ τοῦ Κρεμαστοῦ', ΚΛΗΡΟΝΟΜΙΑ 12(1980), 367–88
ΙΩΑΝΝΗΣ ΚΑΣΤΑΜΟΝΙΤΗΣ (ΒΥΖΑΝΤΙΝΑ ΚΕΙΜΕΝΑ ΚΑΙ ΜΕΛΕΤΑΙ, 22) (Thessalonica, 1988)
Kazhdan, A.P., 'Novye materialy o bogomilakh(?) v Vizantii XII v.', *Byzantino-Bulgarica* 2(1966), 275–6
'John Doukas: an attempt at de-identification', *Le parole e le idee* 11(1969), 242–7
'Vizantijskij monastyr' XI-XII vv. kak sotsial'naja gruppa', *VV* 31(1971), 48–70
Sotsial'nyj sostav gospodstvujushchego klassa Vizantii XI-XII vv. (Moscow, 1974)
'Some questions addressed to the scholars who believe in the authenticity of Kameniates' "Capture of Thessalonica"', *BZ* 71(1978), 301–14
'The medical doctor in Byzantine literature of the 10th-12th centuries', *DOP* 38(1984), 43–51
'A date and an identification in the Xenophon No. 1', *B* 59(1989), 267–71
Kazhdan, A., and Constable, G., *People and Power in Byzantium* (Washington, DC, 1982)
Kazhdan, A.P., and Epstein, A.W., *Change in Byzantine Culture in the Eleventh and twelfth centuries* (Berkeley, 1985)
Kazhdan, A.P., and Franklin, S., *Studies on Byzantine Literature of the Eleventh and Twelfth Centuries* (Cambridge, 1984)
Koukoules, Ph., 'Καλλικάντζαροι', ΛΑΟΓΡΑΦΙΑ 7(1923), 315–28
Laiou, A.E., 'The role of women in Byzantine society', *JÖB* 31/1 (1981), 233–60
'Contribution à l'étude de l'institution familiale en Epire au xiiième siècle', *FM* 6(1984), 284–300
'Observations on the life and ideology of Byzantine women', *BF* 9(1985), 59–102
'The festival of "Agathe". Comments on the life of Constantinopolitan women', in *Byzantium: Tribute to Andreas N. Stratos*, I (Athens, 1986), 111–22
'Η ἱστορία 'ενὸς γάμου: 'ο βίος τῆς ἁγίας Θωμαίδος τῆς Λεσβίας', in *Η ΚΑΘΗΜΕΡΙΝΗ ΖΩΗ ΣΤΟ ΒΥΖΑΝΤΙΟ* (Athens, 1989), 237–52
Gender, Society and Economic Life in Byzantium (Aldershot, 1992)
Laiou-Thomadakis, A.E., *Peasant Society in the Late Byzantine Empire* (Princeton, 1977)
Lampropoulos, K., ΙΩΑΝΝΗΣ ΑΠΟΚΑΥΚΟΣ (Athens, 1988)
Lampsidis, O., 'Beitrag zur Biographe des Georgios Paläologos des Megas Hetareiarches', *B* 40(1970), 393–407
'Zur Biographie von Konstantinos Manasses und zu seiner *Chronike Synopsis*', *B* 58(1988), 97–111
Laurent, V., 'Charisticariat et commende à Byzance', *REB* 12(1954), 100–13
'Les droits de l'empéreur en matière ecclésiastique', *REB* 13(1955), 1–20

'Etienne Chrysobergès, archevêque de Corinthe', *REB* 20(1962), 214–18

'La succession épiscopale de la métropole de Thessalonique dans la première moitié du 13e siècle', *BZ* 56(1963), 284–92

'La chronologie des patriarches de Constantinople au 13e siècle', *REB* 27(1969), 129–50

Lefort, J., 'Une grande fortune foncière aux Xe-XIIIe siècles: les biens du monastère d'Iviron', in *Structures feodales et feodalisme dans l'Occident mediterranéen (Xe-XIIIe siècles)* (Colloques internationaux du centre national de la recherche scientifique no.588) (Paris, 1980)

Le Goff, J., *The Birth of Purgatory* (Chicago, 1984)

Lemerle, P., *Prolégomènes à une édition critique et commentée des 'Conseils et Récits' de Kékauménos* (Brussels, 1960)

'Notes sur l'administration byzantine à la veille de la IVe croisade d'après deux documents inédits des archives de Lavra', *REB* 19(1961), 258–72

'Un aspect du rôle des monastères à Byzance: les monastères donnés à des laics, les charisticaires', *Académie des inscriptions et belles-lettres*, Comptes Rendus 1967, 9–28

Cinq études sur le XIe siècle byzantin (Paris, 1977)

Le Monde de Byzance: histoire et institutions (London, 1978)

Lempp, E., *Frère Elie de Cortone* (Paris, 1901)

Leroy, J., 'Un nouveau témoin de la grande catéchèse de St Théodore Studite', *REB* 15(1957), 73–88

Loos, M., 'Certains aspects du bogomilisme byzantin des 11e et 12e siècles', *BS* 28(1967), 39–53

Dualist Heresy in the Middle Ages (Prague, 1974)

Loukaki, M., 'Contribution à l'étude de la famille Antiochos', *REB* 50(1992), 185–205

Macrides, R.J., 'Saints and sainthood in the early Palaiologan period', in *The Byzantine Saint*, ed. S. Hackel (London, 1981), 67–87

'Justice under Manuel I Komnenos: four novels on court business and murder', *FM* 6(1984), 156–204

'The Byzantine godfather', *BMGS* 11(1987), 139–62

'Killing, asylum, and the law in Byzantium', *Speculum* 63(1988), 509–14

'*Nomos* and *kanon* on paper and in court', in *Church and People in Byzantium*, ed. R. Morris (Birmingham, 1990), 61–85

'Kinship by arrangement: the case of adoption', *DOP* 44(1990), 109–18

'Bad historian or good lawyer? Demetrios Chomatenos and Novel 131', *DOP* 46(1992), 187–96

Macrides, R.J., and Magdalino, P., 'The fourth kingdom and the rhetoric of Hellenism', in *The Perception of the Past in Twelfth-Century Europe*, ed. P. Magdalino (London, 1992), 117–56

Magdalino, P., 'The Byzantine holy man in the twelfth century', in *The Byzantine Saint*, ed. S. Hackel (London, 1981), 51–66

'The Byzantine aristocratic *oikos*', in *The Byzantine Aristocracy IX to XIII Centuries*, ed. M. Angold (Oxford, BAR: 1984), 92–111

'The not-so-secret functions of the *mystikos*', *REB* 42(1984), 229–40

'Isaac *sebastokrator* (III), John Axouch and a case of mistaken identity', *BMGS* 11(1987), 207–14

'The literary perception of everyday life in Byzantium', *BS* 47(1987), 28–38
'Honour among Romaioi: the framework of social values in the world of Digenes Akrites and Kekaumenos', *BMGS* 13(1989), 183–218
'Church, bath and *diakonia* in medieval Constantinople', in *Church and People in Byzantium*, ed. R. Morris (Birmingham, 1990), 165–88
'Constantinople and the ἔξω χώραι in the time of Balsamon', in *TO BYZANTIO KATA TON 12o AIΩNA*, ed. N. Okonomidès (Athens, 1991), 179–97
'Enlightenment and repression in 12th-century Byzantium: the evidence of the canonists', in *TO BYZANTIO KATA TON 12o AIΩNA*, ed. N. Okonomidès (Athens, 1991), 357–74
Tradition and Transformation in Medieval Byzantium (Aldershot, 1991)
'Eros the king and the king of *Amours*: some observations on *Hysmine and Hysminias*', *DOP* 46(1992), 197–204
'The *Bagoas* of Nikephoros Basilakes: a normal reaction?', in *Of Strangers and Foreigners (Late Antiquity – Middle Ages)*, ed. L. Mayali and M.M. Mart (Berkeley, 1993), 47–63
The Empire of Manuel I Komnenos 1143–1180 (Cambridge, 1993)
Magdalino, P., ed., *The Perception of the Past in Twelfth-Century Europe* (London, 1992)
New Constantines. The Rhythm of Imperial Renewal in Byzantium, 4th–13th Centuries (Aldershot, 1994)
Magdalino, P., and Nelson, R., 'The emperor in Byzantine art of the 12th century', *BF* 8(1982), 123–83
Makk, F., *The Arpads and the Comneni* (Budapest, 1989)
Malamut, E., *Les îles de l'Empire byzantin VIIIe-XIIe siècles* (Byzantina Sorbonensia 8) (Paris, 1988), 2 vols.
Maltezou, Chr., ed., *H KAΘHMEPINH ZΩH ΣTO BYZANTIO* (Athens, 1989)
Manaphes, K.A., *MONAΣTHPIAKA TYΠIKA - ΔIAΘHKAI* (Athens, 1970)
Mango, C., 'The monastery of St Abercius at Kurşunlu (Elegmi in Bithynia)', *DOP* 22(1968), 169–76
'Notes on Byzantine monuments', *DOP* 23/4(1969–70), 272–5
The Art of the Byzantine Empire, 312–1453 (Englewood Cliffs, NJ, 1972)
'Chypre. Carrefour du monde byzantin', *XVe Congrès International d'études byzantines. Rapports et co-rapports*, v,5 (Athens, 1976)
Byzantium. The Empire of New Rome (London, 1980)
Mango, C., and Hawkins, E.J.W., 'Report on fieldwork in Istanbul and Cyprus, 1962–1963', *DOP* 18(1964), 333–9
Mango, C., and Parker, J., 'A twelfth-century description of St Sophia', *DOP* 14(1960), 233–45
Mango, C., and Pritsak, O., eds., *Okeanos. Essays Presented to Ihor Ševčenko on his 60th Birthday* (Cambridge, Mass., 1983)
Mariès, L., 'L'irruption des saints dans l'illustration des Psautiers grecs du moyen âge', *Analecta Bollandiana* 68(1950), 153–63
Matthews, T., '"Private" liturgy in Byzantine architecture: toward a re-appraisal', *Cahiers archéologiques* 30(1982), 125–38
Mayali, L., and Mart, M.M., eds., *Of Strangers and Foreigners (Late Antiquity – Middle Ages)* (Berkeley, 1993)

Meyendorff, J., *Byzantine Theology* (Oxford, 1975)
Byzantium and the Rise of Russia. A Study of Byzantino-Russian Relations in the Fourteenth Century (Cambridge, 1981)
Michel, A., *Humbert und Kerullarios. Quellen und Studien zum Schisma des XI. Jahrhunderts* (Paderborn, 1930)
Miller, T.S., 'Byzantine Hospitals', *DOP* 38(1984), 53–63
The Birth of the Hospital in the Byzantine Empire (Baltimore, 1985)
'The Sampson Hospital of Constantinople', *BF* 15(1990), 101–36
Moore, R.I., *The Origins of European Dissent* (Oxford, 1977)
Moravcsik, G., 'Il Caronte bizantino', *Studi bizantini e neoellenici* 3(1931), 47–68
'Pour une alliance byzantino-hongroise', *B* 8(1933), 555–68
Studia Byzantina (Amsterdam, 1967)
Morris, R., 'Monasteries and their patrons in the tenth and eleventh centuries', *BF* 10(1985), 185–231
Morris, R., ed., *Church and People in Byzantium* (Birmingham, 1990)
Mouriki, D., 'Οἱ τοιχογραφίες τοῦ παρεκκλησίου τῆς μονῆς ἁγίου Ἰωάννου τοῦ Θεολόγου στὴν Πάτμο', *ΔΕΛΤΙΟΝ ΤΗΣ ΧΡΙΣΤΙΑΝΙΚΗΣ ΑΡΧΑΙΟΛΟΓΙΚΗΣ ΕΤΑΙΡΕΙΑΣ* ser. 4, 14(1987–8), 205–66
Mullett, M., 'Aristocracy and patronage in the literary circles of Comnenian Constantinople', in *The Byzantine Aristocracy*, ed. M. Angold (Oxford, BAR, 1984), 173–201
'Byzantium. A friendly society?', *Past & Present* 118(Feb.1988), 3–24
'Patronage in action: the problems of an 11th-century bishop', in *Church and People in Byzantium*, ed. R. Morris (Birmingham, 1990), 125–47
Mullett, M., and Kirby, A., ed., *The Theotokos Evergetis and Eleventh-Century Monasticism* (Belfast Byzantine Texts and Translations, 6.1) (Belfast, 1994)
Mullett, M., and Scott R., eds., *Byzantium and the Classical Tradition* (Birmingham, 1981)
Mumford, L., *The City in History* (London, 1961)
Munitiz, J.A., 'Self-canonisation: the "Partial Account" of Nikephoros Blemmydes', in *The Byzantine Saint*, ed. S. Hackel (London, 1981), 164–8
'A wicked woman in the 13th century', *JÖB* 32/2(1983), 529–37
'A missing chapter from the *typikon* of Nikephoros Blemmydes', *REB* 44(1986), 199–207
'A reappraisal of Blemmydes' first discussion with the Latins', *BS* 51(1990), 20–6
Nesbitt, J., and Wiitta, J., 'A confraternity of the Comnenian era', *BZ* 68(1975), 360–84
Nicol, D.M., *The Despotate of Epiros* (Oxford, 1957)
'Kaisersalbung. The unction of emperors in late Byzantine coronation ritual', *BMGS* 2(1976), 37–52
'The papal scandal', *Studies in Church History* 13(1976), 141–68
Church and Society in the Last Centuries of Byzantium (Cambridge, 1979)
The Despotate of Epiros 1267–1479. A Contribution to the History of Greece in the Middle Ages (Cambridge, 1984)
Studies in Late Byzantine History and Prosopography (London, 1986)
The Last Centuries of Byzantium 1261–1453 (2nd edn., Cambridge, 1993)

Norr, D., and Simon, D., ed., *Gedachtnisschrift für Wolfgang Kunkel* (Frankfurt am Main, 1984)

Oberhelman, M., 'Prolegomena to the Byzantine *Oneirokritika*', *B* 50(1980), 487–504

'The interpretation of dream symbols in Byzantine oneirocritic Literature', *BS* 47(1986), 8–24

Obolensky, D., *The Bogomils* (Cambridge, 1948)

'Byzantium, Kiev and Moscow: a study of ecclesiastical relations', *DOP* 11(1957), 21–78

'Papa Nicetas: a Byzantine dualist in the land of the Cathars', in *Okeanos. Essays Presented to Ihor Ševčenko on his 60th Birthday*, ed. C. Mango and O. Pritsak (Cambridge, Mass., 1983) (= *Harvard Ukrainian Studies* 7(1983), 489–500)

Six Byzantine Portraits (Oxford, 1988)

Oeconomos, L., *La vie réligieuse dans l'Empire byzantin au temps des Comnènes et des Anges* (Paris, 1918)

Oikonomidès, N., 'Le serment de l'impératrice Eudocie (1067). Un épisode de l'histoire dynastique de Byzance', *REB* 21(1963), 101–28

'The mosaic panel of Constantine IX and Zoe in St Sophia', *REB* 36(1978), 219–32

'L' "épopée" de Digénis et la frontière orientale de Byzance aux Xe et XIe siècles', *TM* 7(1979), 375–97

'The Peira of Eustathios Romaios: an abortive attempt to innovate in Byzantine law', *FM* 7(1986), 169–92

'Tax exemptions for the secular clergy under Basil II', in ΚΑΘΗΓΗΤΡΙΑ. *Essays Presented to Joan Hussey*, ed. J. Chrysostomides (Camberley, 1988), 317–26

Oikonomidès, N., ed., *ΤΟ ΒΥΖΑΝΤΙΟ ΚΑΤΑ ΤΟΝ 12ο ΑΙΩΝΑ* (Athens, 1991)

Orlandos, A.K., 'Η μονὴ τοῦ Ὁσίου Μελετίου καὶ τὰ παραλαύρια αὐτῆς', *ΑΡΧΕΙΟΝ ΤΩΝ ΒΥΖΑΝΤΙΝΩΝ ΜΝΗΜΕΙΩΝ ΤΗΣ ΕΛΛΑΔΟΣ* 5(1939), 34–118

Ostrogorsky, G., 'Zur Kaisersalbung und Schilderhebung im spätbyzantinischen Kronungszeremoniell', *Historia* 4(1955), 246–56

Quelques problèmes de la paysannerie byzantine (Brussels, 1956)

'La commune rurale byzantine. Loi agraire – traité fiscal – cadastre de Thèbes', *B* 32(1962), 139–66

Paliouras, A.D., *Byzantine Aitoloakarnania* (Athens, 1985)

Papachryssanthou, D., 'Le date de la mort du *sebastokrator* Isaac Comnène', *REB* 21(1963), 250–5

'La vie monastique dans les campagnes byzantins du VIIIe au XIe siècle', *B* 43(1973), 166–80

Papagianne, E., *ΤΑ ΟΙΚΟΝΟΜΙΚΑ ΤΟΥ ΕΓΓΑΜΟΥ ΚΛΗΡΟΥ ΣΤΟ ΒΥΖΑΝΤΙΟ* (Athens, 1986)

Papagianne, E., and Troianos, Sp., 'Die Besetzung der Ämter im Grossskeuophylakeion der Grossen Kirche im 12. Jahrhundert. Ein Synodalakt vom 19. November 1145', *FM* 6(1984), 87–97

'Die kanonischen Antworten des Nikolaos III. Grammatikos an den Bischof von Zeitunion', *BZ* 82(1989), 234–50

Parker, J.S.F., 'The attempted Byzantine alliance with the Sicilian Norman Kingdom, 1166–67', *Papers of the British School at Rome* 24(1955), 86–93

Patlagean, E., 'L'enfant et son avenir dans la famille byzantine (IVe–XIIe siècles)', *Annales de démographie historique* (1973), 85–93

'L'histoire de la femme déguisée en moine et l'évolution de la saintété féminine à Byzance', *Studi medievali* ser.iii. 17(1976), 597–623

'Christianisation et parentés rituelles: le domaine de Byzance', *Annales ESC* 33(1978), 625–36

'Byzance et son autre monde. Observations sur quelques récits', in *Faire Croire. Modalités de la diffusion de la reception des messages religieux du XIIe-XVe siècle* (Collection de l'Ecole française de Rome 51) (Rome, 1981), 201–21

Structure sociale, famille, chrétieneté à Byzance (London, 1981)

Pelikan, J., *The Spirit of Eastern Christendom (600–1700)* (Chicago, 1974)

Petrucci, E., 'Rapporti di Leone IX con Costantinopoli', *Studi Medievali* ser. iii. 14/2(1973), 733–831

Pitsakes, K.G., '"Παίζοντες εἰς 'αλλότριους βίους"', in *Η ΚΑΘΗΜΕΡΙΝΗ ΖΩΗ ΣΤΟ ΒΥΖΑΝΤΙΟ*, ed. Ch. Maltezou (Athens, 1989), 217–36

Podalsky, G., 'Nikolaos von Methone und die Proklosrenaissance in Byzanz 11/12. Jahrhundert', *OCP* 42(1976), 509–23

Theologie und Philosophie in Byzanz. Der Streit um die theologische Methodik in der spätbyzantinischen Geistengeschichte (14./15.Jh.), seine systematischen Grundlagen und seine historische Entwicklung (Byzantinisches Archiv 15) (Munich, 1977)

Polemis, D.I., *The Doukai. A Contribution to Byzantine Prosopography* (London, 1968)

Prinzing, G., 'Entstehung und Rezeption der Justiniana-Prima-Theorie im Mittelalter', *Byzantinobulgarica* 5(1978), 269–87

'Sozialgeschichte der Frau im Spiegel der Chomatenos-Akten', *JÖB* 32/2 (1983), 453–62

Puchner, W., 'Die "Rogatsiengesellschaften"', *Südostforschungen* 36(1977), 109–58

Puech, H.-C., *Sur le Manichéisme* (Paris, 1979)

Renehan, R., 'Meletius' chapter on the eyes', *DOP* 38(1984), 159–68

Richard, J., 'The establishment of the Latin church in the Empire of Constantinople (1204–1227)', in *Latins and Greeks in the Eastern Mediterranean after 1204*, ed. B. Arbel, B. Hamilton, and D. Jacoby (London, 1989), 45–62

Rigo, A., 'Il patriarca Germano II (1223–1240) e i Bogomili', *REB* 51(1993), 91–110

Robert, L., 'Sur Didymes à l'époque byzantine', *Hellenica* 11/12(1960), 490–505

Romaios, K., 'Οι Καλλικάντζαροι', *BNJ* 18(1945–49), 49–87

Rose, R., 'The *Vita* of St Leontius and its account of his visit to Palestine during the crusader period', *Proche-Orient Chrétien* 35 (1985), 238–57

Runciman, S., *The Medieval Manichee* (Cambridge, 1947)

The Eastern Schism (Oxford, 1955)

Ryden, L., 'The life of St Basil the Younger and the date of the life of St Andreas Salos', in *Okeanos. Essays Presented to Ihor Ševčenko on his 60th*

Birthday, ed. C. Mango and O. Pritsak (Cambridge, Mass., 1983) (= *Harvard Ukrainian Studies*, 7(1983), 568–77)

Saradi, H., 'Imperial jurisdiction over ecclesiastical provinces: the ranking of new cities as seats of bishops or metropolitans', in *TO BYZANTIO KATA TON 12o AIΩNA*, ed. N. Oikonomidès (Athens, 1991), 149–63

Sarudi-Mendelovici, H., 'A contribution to the study of the Byzantine notarial formulas: the *Infirmitas Sexus* of women and the *Sc. Velleianum*', *BZ* 83(1990), 72–90

Schminck, A., 'Kritik am Tomos des Sisinnios', *FM* 2(1977), 215–54

'Ein Synodalakt vom 10. November 1167', *FM* 3(1979), 316–22

'Zur Entwicklung des Eherechts in der Komnenenepoche', in *TO BYZANTIO KATA TON 12o AIΩNA*, ed. N. Oikonomidès (Athens, 1991), 555–88

Schwarzenberg, C., 'Intorno alla benedizione degli sponsali in diritto bizantino', *BZ* 59(1966), 94–109

Ševčenko, I., 'Hagiography of the iconoclast period', in *Iconoclasm*, ed. A. Bryer and J. Herrin (Birmingham, 1977), 113–31

Sharf, A., *Byzantine Jewry from Justinian to the Fourth Crusade* (London, 1972)

Shepard, J., 'Tzetzes's letters to Leo at Dristra', *BF* 6(1979), 191–239

'Aspects of Byzantine attitudes and policy towards the West in the tenth and eleventh centuries', *BF* 13 (1989), 67–118

Simon, D., 'Zur Ehegesetzgebung der Isaurier', *FM* 1(1976), 16–43

'Ein Synodalakt aus dem Jahre 1166', *FM* 1(1976), 123–25

'*Princeps legibus solutus.* Die Stellung des byzantinischen Kaisers zum Gesetz', in *Gedachtnisschrift für Wolfgang Kunkel*, ed. D. Norr and D. Simon (Frankfurt, 1984), 449–92

'Byzantinische Provinzialjustiz', *BZ* 79(1986), 310–43

'Das Eheguterrecht der Peira. Ein systematischer Versuch', *FM* 7(1986), 193–238

Smith, M.H., III, *And Taking Bread . . .* (Paris, 1978)

Sorlin, I., 'Striges et géloudes. Histoire d'une croyance et d'une tradition', *TM* 11(1991), 411–36

Spiteris, J., *La critica bizantina del primato romano nel secol XII* (Orientalia Christiana Analecta 208) (Rome, 1979)

Stadtmüller, G., *Michael Choniates, Metropolit von Athen* (Orientalia Christiana analecta 33/2) (Rome, 1934)

Stephanou, P.E., *Jean Italos. Philosophe et humaniste* (Orientalia Christiana analecta 134) (Rome, 1949)

Stevens, G.P., *De Theodoro Balsamone* (Rome, 1969)

Stichel, R., *Studien zum Verhältnis von Text und Bild spät- und nachbyzantinischer Verganglichkeitsdarstellung* (Byzantina Vindobonensia 5) (Vienna, 1971)

Stiernon, L., 'Notes de titulature et de prosopographie byzantines. Adrien (Jean) et Constantin Comnène, sébastes', *REB* 21(1963), 179–98

'Le problème de l'union gréco-latine vue de Byzance. De Germain II à Joseph 1er (1232–1273)', in 1274. *Annee charniere: mutations et continuites* (Paris, 1977), 139–66

Stolte, B., 'Civil law in canon law', in *TO BYZANTIO KATA TON 12o AIΩNA*, ed. N. Oikonomidès (Athens, 1991), 543–54

Stylianou, A. and J., *The Painted Churches of Cyprus. Treasure of Byzantine Art* (London, 1985)

Svoronos, N., 'Les privilèges de l'église à l'époque des Comnènes: un rescrit inédit de Manuel 1er Comnène', *TM* 1(1965), 325–91

Talbot, A.-M., 'The Byzantine family and the monastery', *DOP* 44(1990), 119–29

Thomas, J.P., 'A Byzantine ecclesiastical reform movement', *Mediaevalia et Humanistica* n.s. 12(1984), 1–16

Private Religious Foundations in the Byzantine Empire (Dumbarton Oaks Studies 24) (Washington DC, 1987)

Tiftixoglu, V., 'Gruppenbildungen innerhalb der Konstantinopolitanischen Klerus während der Komnenenzeit', *BZ* 62(1969), 25–72

'Zur Genese der Kommentare des Theodoros Balsamon', in *TO BYZANTIO KATA TON 12o AIΩNA*, ed. N. Oikonomidès (Athens, 1991), 483–532

Tinnefeld, F., 'Zum profanen Mimos in Byzanz nach dem Verdikt des Trullanums', *BYZANTINA* 6(1974), 321–43

'Michael I. Kerullarios. Patriarch von Konstantinopel (1043–1058)', *JÖB* 39(1989), 95–127

Trapp, E., 'Hagiographische Elemente im Digenes-Epos', *Analecta Bollandiana* 94(1976), 275–87

Turdeanu, E., *La littérature bulgare du XIVe siècle et sa diffusion dans les pays roumains* (Paris, 1947)

Underwood, P.A., *The Kariye Djami*, I (London, 1967)

Varzos, K., *Η ΓΕΝΕΑΛΟΓΙΑ ΤΩΝ ΚΟΜΝΗΝΩΝ* (Thessalonica, 1984), 2 vols.

Vermeule, E., *Aspects of Death in Early Greek Art and Poetry* (Berkely, Los Angeles, and London, 1979)

Vernadsky, G., *Kievan Russia* (New Haven, 1948)

Walter, C., 'Death in Byzantine iconography', *Eastern Churches Review* 8(1976), 113–27

Art and Ritual of the Byzantine Church (London, 1982)

'Christological themes in the Byzantine marginal psalters from the ninth to the eleventh century', *REB* 44(1986), 269–87

Wellnhofer, M., 'Die thrakischen Euchiten und ihr Satanskult im Dialoge des Psellos *ΤΙΜΟΘΕΟΣ Η ΤΩΝ ΔΑΙΜΟΝΩΝ*', *BZ* 30(1929/30), 477–84

Wilson, N.G., *Scholars of Byzantium* (London, 1983)

Winfield, D., 'Hagios Chrysostomos, Trikomo, Asinou. Byzantine painters at work', in *ΠΡΑΚΤΙΚΑ ΤΟΥ ΠΡΩΤΟΥ ΔΙΕΘΝΟΥΣ ΚΥΠΡΟΛΟΓΙΚΟΥ ΣΥΝΕΔΡΙΟΥ*, II (Levkosia, 1972), 285–91

Wirth, P., 'Die Flucht des Erzbischofs Eustathios aus Thessalonike', *BZ* 53(1960), 82–5

'Das religiose Leben in Thessalonike unter dem Episkopat des Eustathios im Urteil von Zeitgenossen', *Ostkirkliche Studien* 9(1960), 293–4

'Ein neuer *Terminus ante quem non* fur das Ableben des Erzbischofs Eustathios von Thessalonike', *BZ* 54(1961), 86–7

'Zur Frage eines politischen Engagements Patriarch Johannes' X Kamateros nach dem vierten Kreuzzug', *BF* 4(1972), 239–52

Eustathiana (Amsterdam, 1980)

Wirth, P., ed., *Polychronion. Festschrift Franz Dölger zum 75. Geburtstag* (Heidelberg, 1966)
Wittek, P., *Das Fürstentum Mentesche* (Istanbul, 1934)
Wolff, R.L., 'The Latin Empire and the Franciscans', *Traditio* 2(1944), 213–37
Studies in the Latin Empire of Constantinople (London, 1976)
Zhishman, H., *Das Eherecht der orientalischen Kirche* (Vienna, 1864)

Additional bibliography

Angold, M. J., 'The Autobiographical Impulse in Byzantium', *DOP* 52 (1998), 225–57
'Autobiography and Identity: the case of the Later Byzantine Empire', *BS* 60 (1999), 36–59
Cataldi Palau, A., 'Una "Lettera al papa" di Irenico, cartofilace della Grande Chiesa (Teodoro Irenico, patriarca di Constantinopoli, 1214–1216)', *Bollettino della Badia Greca di Grottaferrata*, n.s. 48 (1994), 23–87.
Christodoulou, G.K., 'Un canon inédit sur la Théosémie de Néophyte le reclus composé par son frère, Jean le Chrysostomite', *REB* 55 (1997), 247–59
Flusin, B., 'Didaskalie de Constantin Stilbès sur le Mandylion et la sainte tuile (BHG 796m)', *REB* 55 (1997), 53–79
Hamilton, J., and Hamilton, B., *Christian Dualist Heresies in the Byzantine World, c.650–c.1405* (Manchester Medieval Sources) (Manchester, 1998)
Kirby, A., 'Hosios Christodoulos: an eleventh-century Byzantine saint and his monastaries', *BS 57* (1996), 293–309
Loukaki, M., *Grégoire Antichos. Eloge du patriarche Basile Kematèros* (Byzantina Sorbonensia, 13) (Paris, 1996)
Morris, R., *Monks and Laymen in the Byzantine Empire, 843–1118* (Cambridge, 1995)
Mullett, M., *Theophylact of Ochrid: Reading the Letters of a Byzantine Archbishop* (Birmingham Byzantine and Ottoman Monographs, 2) (Aldershot, 1997)
Mullett, M., and Kirby A., ed., *Work and Worship at the Theotokos Evergetis* (Belfast Byzantine Texts and Translations, 6.2) (Belfast 1997)
Mullett, M., and Smythe, D., ed., *Alexios I Komnenos: 1 – Papers* (Belfast Byzantine Text and Translations, 4.1) (Belfast, 1996)
Patlagean, E., 'Une sainte souveraine grecque Théodora impératrice d'Epire XIII siècle', *BS* 56 (1995), 453–60
Rigo, A., 'Il processo del Bogomilo Basilio (1099 ca.): una riconsiderazione', *OCP* 58 (1992), 185–211
Talbot, A.-M., *Holy Women of Byzantium. Ten Saints' Lives in English Translation* (Byzantine Saints' Lives in Translation, 1) (Washington, D.C., 1996)

INDEX

Main entries are printed in bold. For emperors and empresses see under Christian names.